third edition

GLOBAL POLITICS
Origins, Currents, Directions

Allen Sens
University of British Columbia

Peter Stoett
Concordia University

THOMSON

NELSON

Australia   Canada   Mexico   Singapore   Spain   United Kingdom   United States

THOMSON

NELSON

Global Politics: Origins, Currents, Directions, Third Edition

by Allen Sens and Peter Stoett

Associate Vice-President and Editorial Director:
Evelyn Veitch

Publisher, Social Sciences and Humanities:
Chris Carson

Senior Marketing Manager:
Murray Moman

Senior Developmental Editor:
Rebecca Rea

Permissions Coordinator:
Kristiina Bowering

Senior Production Editor:
Bob Kohlmeier

Copy-Editor:
Karen Rolfe

Proofreaders:
Vivien Leong, Sandra Braun

Indexer:
Chris Blackburn

Production Coordinator:
Helen Locsin

Creative Director:
Angela Cluer

Interior-Design Modifications:
Peter Papayanakis

Cover Design:
Peter Papayanakis

Cover Image:
Photodisc Collection/Photodisc Blue/Getty Images

Compositor:
Carol Magee

Printer:
Transcontinental

Library and Archives Canada Cataloguing in Publication

Main entry under title:

Sens, Allen G. (Allen Gregory) 1964– Global politics : origins, currents, directions / Allen Sens, Peter Stoett. — 3rd ed.

Order of authors reversed on 1st ed.
Includes bibliographical references and index.
ISBN 0-17-641677-3

1. World politics—1989– I. Stoett, Peter John, 1965– . Global politics. II. Title.

D860.S45 2004   909.82'9
C2004-902969-X

Brief Contents

Detailed Contents

PART TWO: CURRENTS

PART THREE: DIRECTIONS

Preface

Teaching global politics is a challenging occupation. Few subjects are so interdisciplinary, requiring the level of command over history, geography, science, psychology, and politics that college and university courses demand. Many continuities and enduring concepts require elaboration, while political and social developments and theoretical innovations must be explained and put into context. To make matters even more challenging, global politics is anything but a static subject. The last decade of the 20th century was a particularly tumultuous one. The collapse of the Communist regimes in Eastern Europe and the disintegration of the Soviet Union brought a remarkably swift and dramatic end to an ideological, geopolitical, and military struggle that defined the post–World War II era. The word *globalization* captures a sense of momentous change and uncertainty, even as this generation of students grapples with the reality that their lives are increasingly affected by world events and global trends. The technological changes that characterized the 20th century have altered established patterns of economic activity, global communication, and military strategy. Students have a heightened awareness of the threats to human security presented by pandemics, and this concern over their environment and the human condition continues to break down disciplinary barriers between the study of global politics and the study of science and culture. The terrorist attacks of September 11, 2001, and the Iraq War of 2003 challenge teacher and student alike as they attempt to grasp the complexities of a subject that displays features of continuity as well as change, and trends of convergence as well as divergence.

An additional challenge facing Canadian teachers and students of global politics is the lack of textbooks that are Canadian in orientation. Most international relations textbooks are American, and their examples focus almost exclusively on American foreign policy issues. One crucial function of the first and second editions of this text was to relate the academic study of global politics with its themes of continuity, change, convergence, and divergence more directly to the lives of students who reside outside the United States. The third edition of the text retains this basic philosophy. Like the rationale behind the second edition, the rationale for this new edition is practical: things change. In fact, the second edition of *Global Politics* was printed and distributed in the summer of 2001; a few days after it hit the book stores, the terrorist attacks in the United States shook the world. Since the publication of the second edition, the world has witnessed not only those large-scale terrorist attacks and the subsequent wars in Afghanistan and Iraq, but also the launching of the troubled Doha Round of world trade talks. We saw the establishment of an International Criminal Court; the intensification of violence between Israelis and Palestinians; the emergence of SARS, BSE, and avian flu and the continued spread of HIV/AIDS; the enlargement of NATO and the EU; debates over genetically modified organisms; a new commitment to the world's poor in the UN

Millennium Development Goals; and an explosive growth in global wireless networks. It was necessary to update significant portions of the book, and although it is impossible to cover everything, our intent was to make the book as contemporary as possible, while retaining our appreciation of the necessity for a solid grounding in distant and recent history.

The Cold War between East and West dominated international politics and the attention of policy makers for more than 45 years. Scholars and their students focused on issues such as strategic nuclear and military balance, nuclear arms control, the shifting tides of superpower diplomacy, the politics of alliances such as NATO and the Warsaw Pact, and the extension of the Cold War rivalry into regional conflicts. The politics of the bipolar world have also engaged many members of the public, as the superpower arms race sparked the development of a large peace and disarmament movement. However, it would be a mistake to argue that such Cold War issues excluded other global phenomena, since they occurred in a changing international context that included a growing and ever more integrated global economy; an increasing interdependence between societies and states; a growing divide between rich and poor societies, and between rich and poor within societies; the increasing activity of nonstate actors such as multinational corporations and nongovernmental organizations; rapid techno-logical advances; and a growing concern over environmental degradation. Nevertheless, the politics of the superpower rivalry, attended by the threat of global nuclear war, was the pri-mary subject of attention in the realm of international affairs.

To most Canadians, it appears as though the focus of global politics has been reoriented toward a more complex set of issues. These include efforts (often the object of vociferous protest) to manage the global economy, a vital subject to a trade-dependent state such as Canada. Of course, over 80 percent of Canadian trade is with one partner, the United States, and this relationship continues to dominate foreign policy considerations. The democratiza-tion process in Eastern Europe, Latin America, and Africa is of great interest to Canadians, as other states embark on experiments similar to our own. Regional ethnic, religious, and fac-tional conflicts; gender issues; the proliferation of conventional weapons and weapons of mass destruction; threats to the global commons; refugee and population movements; terrorism; and the information and communications revolution are all on the agenda of the cos-mopolitan Canadian. And yet a cautionary voice must be raised here. Though it is tempting to speak of the end of the Cold War or the events of September 11, 2001, as the beginning of a new age of global politics, much remains the same. The world is still politically divided into a system of territorial states; conflict and cooperation between states and within states con-tinues; and despite developments in economic interdependence and global communications, the world remains divided between rich and poor, between different civilizations, religions, and ethnicities, and between different modes of domestic governance. In this text we have tried to situate the immense change occurring around us within an understanding of these elements of continuity.

The central aim of *Global Politics: Origins, Currents, and Directions* is to introduce readers to the rich and diverse enterprise that is the study of contemporary international relations, encouraging an appreciation of the theoretical roots of divergent perspectives on how the international system operates. The text also establishes the vital historical context required for any understanding of international relations. Furthermore, the book intends to stimulate thoughtful analysis and critical thinking and to promote a healthy skepticism for established wisdom and prevailing assumptions. *Global Politics* also reveals the human element of inter-national relations by providing insights and biographies of individuals who have made an impact on the world in which we live. Finally, many recently published textbooks are revised editions of works originally published during the Cold War, structured in a manner that reflects Cold War issues and priorities. This text was conceived in a post–Cold War context and designed from the beginning to reflect the contemporary global environment and the issues faced by today's scholars, policy makers, students, and citizens. The Cold War is history (albeit important history), and this book is structured around this fact. To this end, *Global Politics* gives equal attention to the theoretical developments and historical events of the past, the key issues facing us today, and the emerging agenda that confronts us all. As the full title indicates, this book looks to the future as much as it looks to the past and the present. The book does not claim to be a crystal ball but it does identify trends and themes, and challenges the reader to think about the issues and theoretical approaches that loom on the horizon.

THE STRUCTURE OF THE BOOK

As our subtitle suggests, *Global Politics* is organized into three parts: origins, currents, and directions. Part One, "Origins," examines the theoretical perspectives that are fundamental to any understanding of the debates and controversies in the discipline, and the evolution of the international system to the end of the Cold War. The development of the key contending perspectives in international relations theory is discussed in historical context. Part One reveals how these contending perspectives tend to focus on different types of historical events or have different interpretations of history. For example, realists emphasize the history of empires, great powers, and wars, while liberals emphasize economic history and the development of interdependence. Critical theorists emphasize historical patterns of hierarchy and dominance and the processes that perpetuate poverty and disempowerment. In short, Part One looks at the history of war, the state, the Cold War, international political economy, international institutions, and law, and it gives us the theoretical background necessary to understand it.

In Part Two, "Currents," readers are introduced to some of the key issues on the contemporary international security and economic agenda. We look at today's varied conflict management efforts, the divisive impact of globalization on the world economy, and some principal human rights questions. Part Two is designed to give the reader a snapshot of the contemporary international situation and an improved understanding of the issues that confront today's world. Key themes include civil warfare, weapons proliferation, terrorism, arms control, humanitarian intervention, poverty and marginalization, relativist versus universalist human rights, international criminal law, and many others.

In Part Three, "Directions," items of growing importance on the international agenda are explored. We begin with a discussion of contemporary global environmental problems. Next, we look at population growth and movements, the impact of the information revolution, and possible future trends. These admittedly selective subjects are discussed because, in the view of the authors, they will dominate the future agenda of global politics over the long term, and presumably the lives of many if not all of our students. Of course, all of these issues are interlinked not only with each other, but with the security, economy, and human rights context established in Part Two. Not all these issues will affect Canadians directly, but the connections between Canada's future and the complex trends outside the country are genuine.

An overarching theme knits the subject matter of the book together. The past, present, and future of global politics can be characterized in terms of political *convergence* and *divergence*. Trends of convergence, or what some prefer to label *integration*, can be identified in economic globalization and interdependence; regional zones of peace, international organizations, and the expansion of international law; the growing volume of international transactions, communication, and travel; the so-called development of a global culture; democratization; and reduced friction between the great powers. Trends of divergence, often termed *fragmentation*, can be identified in the uneven globalization between rich and poor and the information haves and have-nots; the fragmentation of states and intrastate conflict; ethnic, religious, and factional warfare; the development of regional trading blocs;

the persistence of interstate conflicts; and the friction between world cultures. The convergence/ divergence theme is revisited throughout the book.

TO THE STUDENT

It is an exciting, and no doubt anxious, time to be studying global politics. You are one among a growing generation of students who have been exposed to a new global political environment that is quite different from the environment faced by students of international relations during the Cold War. However, as you look to the future of the world in which you live, it would be wrong to ignore the past. Despite changes in the global political scene and advancements in technology and communications, in some respects little has changed. Many of the issues and problems that have plagued the world for decades and even centuries persist today. Discovering that a hot topic today was also a hot topic a generation ago can be a humbling experience, but much can be understood from past events and from how current issues are both similar to and different from those events.

Studying global politics is also a demanding undertaking, for the subject matter is broad, deep, and multidimensional, and many points of dispute and controversy exist. It is tempting for students to focus on certain issues (the environment, war, or technology, for example) to the exclusion of others. However, this narrow focus is a mistake, for virtually all subjects in global politics are closely interrelated, and it is impossible to understand one issue in isolation from others. Furthermore, an appreciation of different perspectives is an absolute must. Part of the challenge of any scholarly pursuit is to understand perspectives that differ from your own. When you do this, you gain in two ways: first, you improve your understanding of the basis for disagreements between individuals, groups, and states; and second, you are forced to examine your own personal perspectives and why you believe what you do. In some cases, this process will cause you to change your mind, while in other cases it will not. In any event, you will have gained a critical understanding of different views and ideas about the world.

This book is best viewed as a guide that can direct you through the interrelated subject matter of the subfields of global politics. The text introduces the specialized terms and jargon that international relations scholars use to describe different phenomena and contending perspectives. We have put the significant terms, which are defined in the glossary, in **bold** type. Of course, a large and rich literature exists on every subject discussed in this text, and you may want to learn more about a particular topic or find materials for research papers. At the end of each chapter, we supply a list of suggested readings and Internet resources to assist you in this task. Further, take care to read the endnotes that accompany each chapter, for they include some of the better-known and valuable sources, and we do not list them all again among the suggested readings."

As a guide, this textbook is only an introduction to the vast topic of global politics. Your instructor may cover other issues, and you may find that you or your instructor do not agree with many of the points made in this book. However, we have tried to be as inclusive and balanced as possible in presenting the subject matter. As individuals, we differ on many aspects of our discipline and agree on many more. While it may be impossible to be completely balanced in such an undertaking (as we learned from preliminary reviews of this book), we have tried to incorporate as many diverse perspectives as possible while retaining content that is traditionally expected of an international relations textbook. Ultimately, it is up to you to develop your own informed opinions and ideas. We are both very interested in receiving any comments you may have regarding the present edition of *Global Politics*, and we invite you to write or e-mail us with them.

pstoett@alcor.concordia.ca
asens@politics.ubc.ca

We completed our bachelor's and master's degrees in the late 1980s and obtained our doctorates in the early 1990s at Canadian universities. Our careers as students and professionals straddle the Cold War and post–Cold War eras. Our studies have taken us to Western and Eastern Europe, West and East Africa, northern and southern Asia, Latin and Central America, and of course the United States. We have taught in several Canadian universities before finding homes in Vancouver and Montreal, and we are both frequently involved with the foreign policy–making process in Ottawa. Our experience is one of change and flux, and we, like you, look with excitement and deep concern at the future. Though our views often differ, we have strived to achieve a workable and, we hope, fair balance between them. We hope that this experience and dedication gives us ample qualification as the authors of a text on global politics, and we hope that you are inspired to pursue similar paths of discovery and engagement after reading *Global Politics: Origins, Currents, and Directions.*

ACKNOWLEDGMENTS

Many friends, colleagues, and scholars have contributed to the development, writing, and editing of this book. It would be impossible to list all those who have touched our lives and work in meaningful ways over the years, so any attempt that follows is necessarily partial.

We would like to thank the following colleagues whose expertise and assistance have been invaluable: Abbie Bakan, Robert Boardman, Max Cameron, Andrew Cooper, David Cox, Simon Dalby, Gerald Dirks, Bill Graf, David Haglund, Kal Holsti, Horst Hutter, Rosalind Irwin, Bob Jackson, Brian Job, Eric Laferrière, Jayent Lele, Don Munton, Jorge Nef, Kim Richard Nossal, Kwasi Obu-Fari, Angela O'Mahony, Charles Pentland, Richard Price, Norrin Ripsman, Patricia Romano, Doug Ross, Heather Smith, Lisa Sundstrom, Yves Tiberghien, Claire Turenne Sjolander, Henry Wiseman, and Mark Zacher. Our apologies to the many we have left off our list.

We owe a special debt of gratitude to our invaluable research assistants. For the first edition, Dan Wolfish took time from a busy doctoral studies schedule to assist in the preparation of the penultimate draft; and the second edition would not have been possible without the resourcefulness and dedication of Roberta Abbott. This third edition benefited from the efforts of Scott Watson and Elayne Carslie.

We owe special thanks to the many reviewers commissioned by Thomson Nelson, including Alistair David Edgar, Wilfrid Laurier University; Charmaine H. Enger, University of British Columbia; Maria Peluso, Dawson College; Vincent Della Sala, Carleton University; David Winchester, Capilano College; and Yuchao Zhu, University of Regina. Their comments not only enriched the text and filled gaping holes but also gave us a sense of the current state of the discipline across Canada today. We would also like to thank the invaluable administrative assistance provided by staff in the Political Science departments at the University of British Columbia and Concordia University.

For the exhaustive editorial, production, and marketing effort at Thomson Nelson we thank all those who worked on the third edition, including, but not limited to, Rebecca Rea, Chris Carson, and Bob Kohlmeier. Special thanks go to Karen Rolfe and Vivien Leong for their comprehensive copyediting and proofreading, respectively. Most important of all, we would also like to express our appreciation for the comments offered by our students over the years. Students are the lifeblood of any scholarly enterprise, and ours have provided a wealth of critical insights and suggestions.

Special thanks go to Pam Baldwin and Cristina Romanelli, our better halves, life companions, and beacons of light during the dark early morning hours spent finishing this edition. As always, Peter thanks his daughter Alexandra for her smiles and hope. We dedicate this book to these three extraordinary sources of inspiration.

Any errors, of course, are our responsibility alone.

A NOTE ON MAPS AND NAMES

In global politics, conflicts (especially territorial conflicts) are often symbolized by disputes over the name of a country or territory. For example, Macedonia is called "the Former Yugoslavian Republic of Macedonia" (FYROM) because the Greek government objects to the use of a name that distinguishes an area within Greece. In addition, the names of many countries change over time, often because of a change in government. For example, the Khmer Rouge changed the name of Cambodia to Kampuchea (today, Cambodia is the common usage once again); Burma has been renamed Myanmar by the military regime in power there (although it is commonly referred to as Burma); and following a revolution in 1997 the African country of Zaire was renamed the Democratic Republic of Congo. Furthermore, separatist or nationalist movements that want to create or re-create their own states often refer to an area of land as their territory. For example, the representatives of the Kurdish people claim parts of Turkey, Syria, and Iran as the territory of Kurdistan, while the leadership of the Palestinian people wants to re-establish an independent state of Palestine in an area now occupied by the state of Israel. The politically sensitive nature of names is compounded by the fact that the use of one name over another is often taken as an indication of political support. This book seeks to make the student aware of such disputes and changes, although space considerations often make this impractical. We have strived to be as balanced and respectful as possible.

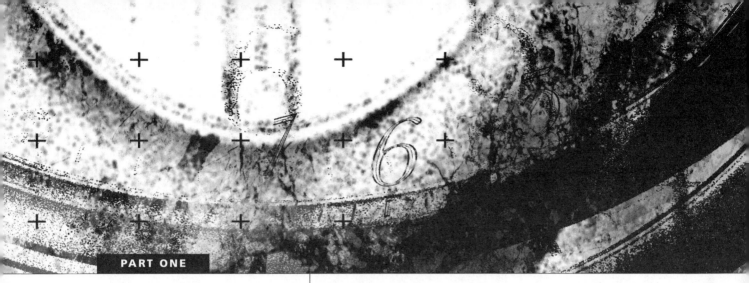

PART ONE

Origins

This section of the book lays the foundation for subsequent discussions of contemporary and future issues in global politics. It begins with an introduction to the academic field of inquiry widely known as international relations, and the prevalent theoretical perspectives that guide researchers in the discipline. In Chapter 2, we turn to a brief history of the evolution of the international political system, including the rise and fall of empires, the prominent role of the state in the Westphalian system, and the impact of major war on global politics. The next chapter discusses the Cold War and the study of how foreign policy decisions are made. Chapter 4 discusses the evolution of the world economy, with an emphasis on liberal economic theory and the origins of globalization. Finally, Chapter 5 examines the evolution of international law and international institutions. This foundation will allow us to pursue more contemporary topics in Part Two.

CHAPTER 1

An Introduction to the Study of Global Politics

Let us not imitate the historians who believe that the past has always been inevitable, and thus suppress the human dimension of events.

—*Raymond Aron*[1]

ON THE MENU: COMPLEXITY, INSECURITY, AND TRADITION

The student of global politics today deserves some pity. He or she faces an enormous volume of contested information, historical interpretations, daunting international issues, and growing anxiety about the future. Indeed, the task of understanding the international system seems almost futile. For those studying global politics, efforts to adjust to the end of the Cold War have given way to frantic attempts to cope with the post–September 11, 2001, era. In the midst of ongoing debates over the meaning and value of globalization, more traditional concerns about military security have resurfaced with a vengeance, and war is once again a prominent phenomenon in world affairs. Furthermore, the choices any student or scholar of global politics must make when conducting research—concerning epistemology (the nature of knowledge), methodology, topic selection, geographic focus, and other factors—remain as relevant as ever. Issues that have raised eyebrows in preceding decades, such as ethnic conflict, environmental degradation, economic crises, global poverty, and intellectual property rights, continue to attract attention. Students today must also add to this menu exciting new conceptual approaches and emerging issues, and the global fallout of a major terrorist attack on the United States.

As individuals, our relationship with global politics is an interactive one. At the most basic level, you are alive and reading this text because you have not been killed in a nuclear war. At the height of the Cold War, almost four decades ago, such an Armageddon-like calamity seemed possible, indeed plausible, to many. Through a horrible accident or dramatic political change, nuclear war could become a predominant threat once again in the near future. Today, depending on where we live, we are more immediately threatened by global environmental change, the spread of infectious diseases, terrorist acts (and military responses to them), the dislocation associated with the globalization of the economy, and many other threats to human security. Anyone with a son or daughter in the Canadian military, with investments in international markets, or with vacation plans abroad realizes how susceptible we are to world events.

You need not be a professional diplomat, corporate executive, or social activist to interact with global politics on a daily basis; our everyday decisions impact the world economy, environment, and political landscape. This statement is as true for someone living in Canada as it is for someone living in Germany, Pakistan, Uganda, Peru, or Micronesia, although within and among these countries the range of choice available to any given individual (and the relative impact that choice may have) is remarkably varied. Furthermore, we face daily exposure to the realm of global politics through media images. We need only recall the antiglobalization protests in Quebec City in 2000, the hijacked planes slamming into the World Trade Center on September 11, 2001, and the military invasion and occupation of Iraq in 2003 to realize the significance of media coverage. Canadians have witnessed the trials and tribulations in the 1990s of their cherished peacekeepers, taken hostage in Bosnia and accused of human rights violations themselves during an earlier mission in Somalia. Images of starving children from around the world flood our living rooms—and our eyes, with tears—while images of world leaders meeting in Group of Eight (G-8) summits reinforce our understanding of who constitutes the global elite. To make matters worse, such events "come wrapped in representations, bundled in ideology, edited by the media, warped by official stories."[2]

Indeed, we are often directly affected by global events, regardless of where we live. Changes in world oil prices have an impact on people in Alberta as well as Nigeria; the SARS epidemic killed people in both East Asia and southern Ontario. The shift to Chinese rule in Hong Kong has affected the demographic character of Vancouver. The sustained violence in the Middle East has prompted heated demonstrations in the streets of Montreal. Over 15 000 people died in the scorching European summer of 2003 in France, and many observers would attribute this to global warming. Canada's far-northern Inuit have long suffered the health affects of pollution from industries in countries thousands of kilometres away. September 11 has resulted in a new American foreign policy of a preventive "War on Terrorism," forcing all other states to respond with support, opposition, or resignation. Anyone boarding an airplane in North America or Europe knows that September 11 has changed the security environment in dramatic ways, and people of Arab origin in the United States and elsewhere face new challenges due to an old tendency toward ethnic stereotyping.

Although the "War on Terror" (the George W. Bush Administration's self-styled label for a heavily militarized campaign against terrorism) has dominated the early 2000s, along with the continued crisis in the Middle East, other issues are also central to the discipline today. We are currently concerned with subjects as varied—though often interconnected—as the crisis in the Middle East; the investment activities of multinational corporations; the pandemic of AIDS in Africa, Asia, and more recently Russia; and forestry practices in British Columbia, Brazil, and Indonesia. In the late 1990s and early 2000s, the Canadian government has pursued issues such as war-affected children and the ban on land mines as part of a larger effort to promote human security. Indeed, threats to human security are widespread. Despite the action (or, some would argue, because of the inaction) of the United Nations, violent conflict continues to rage throughout the world, from Colombia to Chechnya to Sudan. The war in the former Yugoslavia and the genocide in Rwanda stand out as two clear examples of gross violations of human rights in the 1990s, and NATO justified its massive display of military force in Serbia in 1999 as a response to ethnic cleansing. Many nuclear weapons have been dismantled, but many remain, and new designs are being contemplated. Furthermore, the

absolute poverty in which billions of people live may be seen as a form of structural violence in itself. Violence against women is a major concern, organized crime is flourishing, and environmentalists often portray the assault on global ecosystems as ecocidal. Add to this dizzying menu the newfound concern with acts of mass terror, and it becomes apparent we have a full plate indeed.

We might be inclined to agree with the frustrated student who declares global politics a field of such newfound complexity that it quite literally boggles the mind. But the claim that global politics has been radically and irreversibly altered is unfounded: rather, we have witnessed the further complication of an already complex subject. Furthermore, complexity itself is nothing new. Though some analysts lament the passing of the good old bad days of the **Cold War** (the **bipolar** era), things were hardly simple then either, as Chapter 3 indicates. However, the period between the end of World War II (1945) and the fall of the Soviet Union (1991) did permit us to take certain factors for granted. The United States and the Soviet Union were the two principal **state** powers, and although other states had nuclear weapons, the two **superpowers** possessed a clear advantage in terms of firepower and delivery capability. Similarly, before the economic rise of Japan and the development of the European Union, the Soviet Union and the United States had the two largest economies in the world. The United Nations was split along a relatively clear ideological dividing line between the capitalist West, led by the United States, and the centrally planned economies of the East, led by the Soviet Union. Many other countries, such as India and Tanzania, tried to pursue a third or **nonaligned** path in an effort to remain independent of either superpower, with varying degrees of success.

This basic division of humanity, itself simplified for the purpose of illustration, largely evaporated in the late 1980s and early 1990s, as the Eastern bloc and the Soviet Union collapsed and so-called intrastate conflicts assumed centre stage. Not only did the geopolitical landscape change but also other issues, such as environmental integrity, human rights abuses, and the perpetuation of poverty, became even more visible. All the while, economists spoke of the increased globalization of the world economy, giving rise to visions of a borderless system in which capital (though not labour) moved freely, and where cultural differences were vanishing with the spread of market-based economies and liberal democracy. Indeed, it may be argued that two simultaneous trends have emerged as one of the central paradoxes of our time: *convergence* and *divergence*. While economic, technological, and network integration (labelled **globalization** by many) is taking place, so is political fragmentation in the form of separatist movements, competition for scarce resources, religious animosity, and other sources of conflict.

This concept is not a novel one, and many other authors have touched on these apparently contradictory trends.[3] Much debate has ensued over whether one of these trends predominates. It would be simpler for all of us if one clearly prevailed, but we must deal with the confusing fact that both are happening simultaneously. While it is obvious that there are major military conflicts underway, the movement toward a global marketplace continues. The horrors of genocide during World War II provided the impetus for the establishment of a universal human rights regime to protect individuals from persecution conducted by the state. However, to varying degrees, ethnic minorities within states (from the Québécois in Canada to the Kurds in Turkey, Iraq, and Syria) continue to feel insecure in political systems dominated by other ethnic groups. Their efforts to protect their culture and gain political influence can spark confrontation and conflict. As you read this text and follow world events, you might look for evidence of convergence and divergence, so as to make up your own mind as to which, if either, is prevailing.

PROFILE 1.1 Canada and Global Politics

Canada (population 32 million), with the second largest land-mass on earth (Russia has the largest), found itself in an enviable position after the Cold War ended in 1990.

It faced no traditional military threats to its territory or political independence, possessed a virtually unequalled standard of living, and was largely free of the violent conflict that characterized many states in the 1990s. However, this position is no excuse for complacency. Canada depends on a generally peaceful and stable international order for its physical security and its economic health. The Canadian economy is heavily dependent on trade (in particular, trade with the United States, the destination for approximately 85 percent of all Canadian **exports**), and Canada, along with the United States and Mexico, is a member of **North American Free Trade Agreement (NAFTA)**. Beyond trade, Canada's foreign policy stresses various international security issues, including the promotion of human security: the protection of people caught in the middle of civil wars and other calamities; the establishment of a land mines treaty; and the promotion of women's rights abroad are all mainstays of this agenda. Perhaps more visible, however, has been Canada's need to adapt to the post–September 11 environment,

since this impacts both troop commitments abroad in places such as Afghanistan, as well as the security of Canadian borders, coastal zones, and airspace. Canada is a significant diplomatic actor, and it belongs to many major international forums and institutions, including the **Group of Eight (G-8)**, the **North Atlantic Treaty Organization (NATO)**, the **Commonwealth, La Francophonie**, and the United Nations, to name only a few. Successive Canadian governments have been strong supporters of **multilateralism**; within international organizations and coalitions Canada can at least have its voice heard. And yet Canada's close proximity to the world's only superpower often overshadows these concerns. In 2003, Canada's decision not to play an active role in the U.S.–U.K. invasion of Iraq presented a serious challenge to Canadian–American relations; other issues, such as the U.S. construction of a missile defence system, remain contentious. Any change in government leadership may lead to changes in Canada's international direction, although for the most part Canadian foreign policy has remained remarkably consistent. The three "pillars" of Canadian foreign policy—security, prosperity, and the promotion of Canadian values—have not been altered for many years.

WHY STUDY GLOBAL POLITICS?

Global politics is a complex, and often surreal, congruence of physical and intellectual power, political structures and institutions, ideas, and personalities. Commonly, the study of International Relations or "IR" has been considered a part of the larger field of political science, and most political science departments have international relations specialists. However, many universities are moving toward a much more explicitly interdisciplinary approach by, for example, granting degrees in international studies or international relations. Students of business, medicine, law, geography, history, and many other disciplines need a solid background in international relations to understand the parameters of, and changes in, their own disciplines. It is not necessary to label them political scientists to achieve this, though most of the theories advanced to explain the complex phenomena of IR are derived from political philosophy and science. A basic education in IR can also open and supplement career opportunities. Most large-scale businesses are engaged in some form of international activity. Many foreign firms hire domestic nationals to work in their branch companies. Increasingly, many young people are travelling to work or study abroad and are finding opportunities to learn (and teach) languages and establish careers in other countries. Still others are working with nongovernmental organizations (NGOs) such as humanitarian aid agencies, or as journalists

Canadian troops land on Towr Ghar in Tora Bora, on May 4, 2002. Canada was the largest troop contributor to the NATO-led, UN-sanctioned International Security Assistance Force (ISAF) in Afghanistan until August 2004. (CP Picture Archive/Stephen Thorne)

or international lawyers. Regardless of one's eventual career path, it is likely that it will involve contact with people in other countries.

Beyond the instrumentalities of the job market, there are other reasons for today's student to study global politics, not least of which—and here we reflect our personal bias without apology—is the sheer excitement of studying politics at the international level and learning more about the world in which we live. Every day, newspapers, television, and the Internet carry news items, features, and discussions on a bewildering array of events happening around the world. Indeed, knowledge may be power, but it must make sense to be of any use. Many Canadian students are from immigrant families, most with direct connections abroad, and they are concerned about the life circumstances of family and friends in other parts of the world. Many students also plan to travel to far-flung destinations, and need to have a solid educational foundation to help them adapt to new environments. While IR as a general field does not provide sufficient detail on its own, it does advance one's understanding of the context in which other states and peoples exist.

To some extent, all academic disciplines suffer from what we term the *irrelevancy disease.* In many cases, academics prefer to rely on abstract thinking, which many students find difficult to relate to their daily lives. While some of the theories floating around the discipline seem rather abstract at first glance, the people who study IR today are often engaged in work that is highly relevant to politicians and the public alike. As greater numbers of people live and work in countries other than their birthplace, the applications of IR theory have become more

PROFILE 1.2 Individual Actors on the Stage of World Politics

Members of the Brazilian Air Force, left, salute as Sergio Vieira de Mello's coffin is loaded aboard a Brazilian presidential plane by UN officials at Baghdad International Airport, Iraq, 22 August 2003. Vieira de Mello, the top UN official in Iraq, was killed in a suicide truck bombing attack on UN headquarters on August 19, 2003, that killed at least 22 other people and left more than 100 injured. (AP Photo/Manish Swarup/CP Archive)

SERGIO VIEIRA DE MELLO

Sergio Vieira de Mello was born in Rio de Janeiro in 1948. He joined the United Nations in 1969 while studying at the University of Paris. In the course of his impressive career at the UN, Vieira de Mello served as United Nations Assistant High Commissioner for Refugees, Under-Secretary-General for Humanitarian Affairs, and Emergency Relief Coordinator. For a short time he was the Special Representative of the Secretary-General in Kosovo, and he also served as United Nations Transitional Administrator in East Timor. On September 12, 2002, Vieira de Mello was appointed United Nations High Commissioner for Human Rights. In May 2003, he was asked by Secretary-General Kofi Annan to take a four-month leave of absence from his position as High Commissioner to serve in Iraq as Special Representative of the Secretary-General. It was there that Sergio Vieira de Mello was tragically killed on August 19, 2003, when the UN head-quarters in Iraq fell victim to a terrorist attack. Following the tragedy, Kofi Annan appointed an Independent Panel on the Safety and Security of UN personnel in Iraq, and work continues to assure that UN personnel are protected in such circumstances.

varied than ever, as has its sources: academics from states outside Europe or North America are also leaving their mark on the field.

Furthermore, ours is a dangerous world filled with a great deal of human suffering, and many people want to make it better, to make a difference (see Profile 1.2), perhaps by working with intergovernmental organizations (IGOs) or nongovernmental organizations (NGOs). In many locales, civil wars, famines, harsh structural adjustment policies, chronic **malnutrition**, epidemics, pollution and environmental degradation, illiteracy, and many other hardships make life harder than ever. Though working on the ground in these areas can be very fulfilling, it comes with unique dangers. For example, Nancy Malloy was a Canadian Red Cross nurse and a specialist in hospital administration. A resident of Vancouver, she joined the Red Cross in 1987 and took her first international assignment in 1990, motivated by a personal desire to help alleviate suffering in war-torn areas. She worked in five war zones over the next six years, in Ethiopia (1990), Kuwait (1991), the former Yugoslavia (1993), Zaire (1995), and Chechnya (1996). On December 17, 1996, gunmen broke into a Chechen hospital complex during the night and killed six Red Cross workers, including Nancy Malloy. (She was the first Canadian Red Cross worker killed in the field. Also killed were Spanish head nurse Fernanda Calado, New Zealand nurse Sheryl Thayer, Norwegian nurses Gunnhild Mykleburst and Ingeborg Foss, and Dutch construction technician Johan Elkerbout.) A person need not be a ruling politician to be a hero in world politics, nor to be a victim to its vicissitudes.

Undoubtedly, all these problems have important international dimensions, and addressing them requires international solutions. And most important, knowledge enables us to challenge, question, and doubt the position and rationales of governments, political leaders, and prevailing orthodoxy on international issues. So the question is not so much how the discipline can be relevant but, rather, whether today's citizens can afford not to know a good deal about the international system.

THE INTERDISCIPLINARY, YET DIVIDED, DISCIPLINE

Formally, and according to academic convention, the field of IR is divided into several subfields, or what some prefer to term subdisciplines. In this way, IR scholars can break an enormous amount of material and topics into more digestible sections for investigation and analysis. For the sake of brevity, we will assume that the study of international relations has four major subfields.

International relations theory is a body of literature that seeks to explain the nature of the international system and the behaviour of the actors within it.[4] *International security* has traditionally involved the study of conflict and war and attempts to prevent or control it. Recently, international security specialists have been examining ethnic and religious conflicts, the proliferation of weapons, and the link between the environment and security.[5] The study of *international political economy* grew in the 1960s and 1970s as issues such as trade, finance, foreign debt, and underdevelopment became increasingly prominent in international affairs.[6] Finally, the subfield that examines institutions such as the United Nations is generally referred to as *international organization*, which focuses on means of cooperation such as the establishment of regimes or agreements among states, groups, or individuals, including international law.[7]

This division of the field into subfields is admittedly arbitrary. Some would argue that other subfields exist, such as foreign policy analysis, international ethics, or development studies, or that many issue-areas, in particular gender studies and global environmental problems, have attained the rank of subfields themselves. Yet others would argue that these divisions are superfluous, because such a large overlap exists between the subfields that to separate them is misleading. Provided that we are aware of these objections, however, the divisions allow us to conceptualize the overall project of the study of global politics. Moreover—and this will become increasingly obvious as you read this text—those engaged in this project benefit from the collaboration of a large number of specialists from other well-established fields, including experts in comparative and domestic politics, world and local history, physics, economics, geography, psychology, sociology, and anthropology.

When we move beyond the descriptive and analytical into more prescriptive areas, we engage in normative work, in which writers are as interested in putting forth their vision of how the world should be as they are in telling us how it is. Normative projects reflect the moral and ethical judgments of the scholar or demonstrate how ethics are acted on by world leaders and diplomats.[8] Importantly, some scholars argue further that it is misleading to separate the analytic from the normative, since all investigators have their own biases, and all theories have their value-laden assumption bases. Explicitly normative work borrows heavily from the vast literature on ethics and philosophy and ventures into questions concerning the just causes of war, the true meaning of human rights, religious differences, and environmental values. Finally, in this technological age, we also borrow from the applied and natural sciences, such as robotics and bioengineering, to describe international developments. In short, the student of global politics must become adept not only at taking a broad approach, but also at practising considerable **synthesis** as well.

The discipline is divided further into differences over what primary level of analysis should demand our attention. Three main levels of analysis exist—the *individual* level, the *state* or *group* level, and the *systemic* level—although this rough division is open to dispute.[9] The *individual* level of analysis focuses on the decisions of individuals, and the perceptions, values, and experiences that motivate those decisions. Generally, the individual level of analysis emphasizes the role of political leaders, for it is often assumed (perhaps erroneously) that those individuals most influence the course of history.[10] While it is clear that powerful leaders such as Napoleon and Hitler changed the course of history, they could hardly have done so alone, without the right conditions to aid them. The *state* or *group* level of analysis focuses on the behaviour of individual states, which is often attributed to the form of government one finds at a particular time. We will return to the debate over democratic peace theory later, but the argument here is that liberal democracies do not fight wars against each other, and thus the explanation for war may be found through analyzing different political modes of governance at the state level. Of course, it remains necessary to look within states as well to determine which groups are influencing foreign policy. For example, **free trade** agreements are supported by the industrial sectors within states that will benefit most from lowering restrictions on trade in their products, and opposed by labour groups and others fearful of the impact on jobs and competitiveness.

At the *systemic* level of analysis, the actions of states are seen as the result of external influences and pressures on them in relation to their attributes or position in world politics. In other words, the nature of the environment, or system, in which actors find themselves explains their behaviour. The capabilities and resources the actors have at their disposal establish the range of options they might have in any given situation. This emphasis on global structures leads us to an age-old debate within the social sciences concerning the relative causal weight assigned to systems and actors, otherwise known as structures and agents. Does the structure of the system predetermine the actions of actors? Or do humans shape events of their own accord? Many people today view this dichotomy as a false one, forcing us to reduce complex interactions to two essential forces. Rather, one can argue that continual interaction occurs between the individual and group or state units of action and the structures within which they operate. In the political world, each influences the other, although limitations exist as to how much influence can be projected by units into their environment, and by the environment onto units. For example, a state such as Canada cannot expect to be a dominant influence in the current international system, since it has a limited amount of power and is effectively overshadowed by the influence of its southern neighbour, the United States. However, in certain areas, such as peacekeeping and humanitarian assistance, certain Canadians have made extraordinary contributions to multilateral efforts. The modern state's extensive ties to the international system (or, to put it in more controversial terms, the outside world) not only limit its abilities to take autonomous actions but they also provide opportunities (see Profile 1.3).

When we examine the behaviour of actors within a system, as political scientists we are often most interested in discerning their relative influence; that is, we seek to identify who the dominant actors are, be they states, socioeconomic classes, organizations, corporations, or individuals. However, this identification is but half the story, for every form of dominance or control generates opposition. Thus, we seek also to identify and explain the motivations of counterdominant actors, which could refer to the Ogoni resisting oppression by the Nigerian government, or people protesting the World Trade Organization in Seattle. It could refer to ambitious entrepreneurs introducing innovative products to the global market, or it could refer to environmentalists chaining themselves to trees to prevent clear-cut logging. However,

PROFILE 1.3 Political Leadership: Pierre Elliott Trudeau, 1919–2000

Searching for peace. Canadian Prime Minister Pierre Trudeau meets with China's Chairman Deng Xaoping in the Great Hall of the People in Beijing in 1983. Trudeau met with Deng to discuss his peace proposals. (CP Picture Archive/Andy Clark)

In the summer of 2000, Canadians mourned the passing of one their most beloved—and controversial—political leaders, Pierre Elliott Trudeau. Trudeau was prime minister from 1968 to 1979, and again from 1980 to 1984. While he was always occupied with matters of national importance such as the separatist movement in Quebec and the evolution of the Canadian constitution, he was also exceptionally visible on the international stage. Early in his term as prime minister, Trudeau halved Canada's commitment of troops to NATO. He became a friend of Fidel Castro, despite the American embargo on Cuba. His government recognized the People's Republic of China in 1970. At one point, and against widespread public opposition, Trudeau allowed the Americans to test cruise missiles over Canadian soil. Soon after, he undertook an international peace mission that saw him meet with world leaders to discuss disarmament and other issues. Widely respected for his intellect, Trudeau was known as a charming and, initially, novel statesman when he travelled abroad. As did any Canadian prime minister, he dealt constantly with the prospects of internal division at home and of external absorption by the United States. Thousands of Canadians paid tribute after his death in 2000, in Ottawa, during a last train ride home, and at a large public funeral in Montreal.

it is too simple to say that dominant actors are conservative and support the status quo and counterdominant actors are progressive and support positive change. After all, neo-Nazi groups in Germany would certainly consider themselves counterdominant actors. Each sphere of human activity differs, and since the political playing field is neither level nor stable, the question of just who is dominant and who is counterdominant is not amenable to an eternal formula. To further confuse the issue, it may be argued that the influence of some actors will be greater than others in times of flux.[11]

We also have to be careful regarding the nature of influence itself. It is impossible to define power—one of the most contested terms in all of political science—here, but many analysts have argued power has hard and soft dimensions.[12] Hard-power capability refers to the more obvious: military hardware, technological capabilities, and economic size. In many cases hard power is still put to the test today, as we saw with the American-led military assaults on Afghanistan and Iraq in 2002 and 2003. Soft power refers to the role of ideas, persuasion, culture, and innovation, which possess less tangible qualities. Within the international system, some states have more hard and soft power than others. There are limitations, however; even the United States could not pressure the government of India to sign a new treaty banning nuclear weapons testing in 1996. But the agent–structure debate noted above continues: should we focus on the power of states per se or on the power of a larger structure, or system, such as the capitalist world economic system, where the soft power of prevailing ideas becomes even more important? Neo-Gramscians, discussed later in this chapter, argue that hegemony is not just about the power of potential force, but the gradual acceptance of orthodoxy in the realm of ideas. Ultimately, this is one of the many analytic questions students need to answer for themselves.

Below we discuss some of the more prevalent basic perspectives that have been generated by international relations theorists. However, keep firmly in mind the interdisciplinary contributions, and methodological divisions, discussed above. Some have even suggested that we have moved into a world of "post-international" politics, an age characterized by the "decline of long-standing patterns" leaving us uncertain about "where the changes may be leading."[13] However, an unmistakable continuity exists: the international system remains fundamentally competitive, as different states, economic players, and ideas battle to secure or advance their interests or their dominance. To gain even a cursory understanding of all this, we need to impose clarity, and this is done by referring to the various theoretical perspectives we have outlined below. Even to the well-initiated, global politics is a strange and heady conceptual brew, to be sipped with caution. However, if we proceed with a basic understanding of the main conceptual ingredients, we will drink with greater confidence.

IR THEORY: A BRIEF SURVEY

Charles Lindblom, in the introduction to his book on the purpose and effects of contemporary social science, readily admits that "classical nineteenth-century liberalism is my prison. It is not the most inhumane of prisons; its cells are by far larger than those of any other prison I know. Indeed, its construction is such that inmates often succeed in persuading themselves that they are wholly free."[14] This admission acknowledges an important point: we are all, to some degree, trapped within our own particular way of seeing and making sense of the world. As Kenneth Boulding warned us back in 1959, "It is what we think the world is like, not what it is really like, that determines our behaviour."[15] The constructivist school described further below echoes this sentiment today. Textbook writers are hardly free of this circumstance; the perspectives of the authors, their origins, and the assumptions they make become part of the book, though we have made every effort to be as inclusive as possible. We might add also that our own perspectives differ sufficiently to add what we hope is a good measure of balance. However, we must keep in mind that all these perspectives are best viewed as fluid conceptions, subject to change, reinterpretation, manipulation, and other exercises. Further, none of them emerged from an intellectual vacuum: they took shape in an historical context that informed their development. As the historian Arthur Schlesinger Jr. has observed, traumatic events (such as war, acts of terror, and environmental decay) often lead to "skeptical reassessments of supposedly sacred assumptions."[16] We might ask ourselves whether such an event—the attack on the World Trade Center in 2001—is forcing us to rethink things yet again.

IDEALISM

An idealist perspective assumes the best of human nature: we are essentially cooperative political animals who are occasionally led astray by evil influences into war and conflict, and we have a natural affinity toward the communal, as opposed to the individual, good. When people behave violently, it is because of the institutional or structural setting in which they live. International relations is teleological in that we move either toward some form of world government or toward a self-controlled **anarchy** in which peace will reign.

The death and destruction caused by World War I resulted in a condemnation of the way international politics had been conducted in the past. The war also created a reaction against power politics, secret diplomacy, arms races, and what was seen as the abuse of unchecked power by the monarchs who led the Central Powers into war. For many, the horrors of World War I served as the final exhibit of the folly of war in human history. A change was required, a change that would alter the international environment in a way that would prevent future wars and eliminate the practices and policies that had made the history of humanity a history of conflict and war. This sentiment prompted the search for a theory of international politics that provided an explanation for all wars and offered directions and policies for preventing them in the future. What emerged from this search was the theoretical framework known as political idealism.

Political idealism has its origins in the philosophical tradition of liberalism, which emerged in Europe in the 16th century, although many of the moral principles of liberalism and idealism can be found in earlier works. This philosophical tradition emphasizes the liberty of the individual and the need to protect this liberty from the state. Liberalism, with its focus on individuals as the centre of moral virtue, regards the pursuit of power, authoritarian governance, and intolerance as obstacles to human progress. Some liberal philosophers place their emphasis on building a tolerant, liberal society as the only humane response to pluralism and diversity. Others place more emphasis on the development of capitalism, free trade, and republican democracy as the answer to global problems and the absence of global order. Liberal philosophers include John Locke, Immanuel Kant, Benjamin Constant, John Stuart Mill, Montesquieu, David Hume, Adam Smith, T.H. Green, L.T. Hobhouse, and Thomas Jefferson.

Postwar idealists such as G. Lowes Dickinson, Alfred Zimmern, **Norman Angell**, James T. Shotwell, and U.S. President **Woodrow Wilson** drew on the liberal philosophical tradition, criticized by E.H. Carr and others as an attempt to impose an illusory world-view on the international system. Although idealists differed on many issues, they all shared a number of assumptions about the nature of humanity, the nature of world politics, the experience of World War I, and the road to the future. To varying degrees, idealists assumed the following:

- *Human nature is essentially good.* As a result, assistance and cooperation are possible and natural, motivated by the human qualities of altruism, philanthropy, and humanitarianism.

- *Evil is not innate to humanity.* Evil activity or harmful behaviour is the result of bad institutions, states, and structures that motivate individuals to act in a self-interested, distrustful, or aggressive fashion.

- *Social progress is possible.* Human society has developed and improved and will continue to do so.

- *The main problem in international relations is war.* International society must reform itself with the aim of preventing future wars.

- *War can be prevented.* Eliminating bad institutions, states, and structures will eliminate the root causes of war.

- *International cooperation will promote peace.* International organizations and international law will help prevent war.

The policy program of the idealists—their proposed solutions to the problem of war and the issues facing the international system—was expansive and ambitious. Idealists regarded the structure of international relations as a war-making structure that promoted distrust, hostility, conflict, and confrontation. The history of international relations, idealists believed, proved their argument that war was endemic because of the nature of the international system. Idealists believed that by changing the latter it would be possible to reduce or eliminate war. Their answer was the **collective security** system. Within such a system, all states would agree that in the case of aggression by any state against any other state in the system, all other states would respond to defend the attacked state. In effect, a collective security system sought to make any aggression against any member of the system an act of aggression against all members. As a result, any potential aggressor, faced with the prospect of having so many enemies, would not engage in aggression in the first place. In this way, peace would be preserved. Idealists also believed that international peace could be encouraged through the development of international organizations, international law, and arms control.

The principles and hopes of political idealism did serve as a guide for postwar efforts to remake the international system, most famously in the creation of the League of Nations and in U.S. President Woodrow Wilson's famous **Fourteen Points**, which influenced the post–World War I settlement. The Covenant of the League of Nations was drafted at the Paris Peace Conference in 1919. The League comprised an assembly and a council of permanent members, which included Great Britain, France, Italy, and Japan, and later Germany (1926) and the Soviet Union (1934). We discuss the operations of the League in more detail in Chapter 5. Between 1920 and 1939, the League considered 66 disputes between states and contributed to peaceful outcomes in 35 of them. The League reflected the idealist perspective's assumption that international organizations would serve to maintain peace and promote cooperation among states on a wide variety of international issues and problems. Peace would be strengthened by the development of international law, including efforts to make war illegal, such as the 1928 **Kellogg–Briand Pact**. Peace would also be strengthened through **arms control**, such as the 1922 Washington Naval Treaty, which restricted the number and armament of battleships in the fleets of the great powers. However, the treaty is also an example of how states pursue their own interests in arms control negotiations; under the treaty some states could have more battleships than others, and naval competition continued in the aircraft carrier and cruiser classes of ships.

The principles of political idealism were neither universally shared nor admired, and the immediate postwar period was characterized by "power politics" as much as by idealist behaviour. The events of the interwar period and the erosion or failure of many of the key elements of the idealists' reform program removed much of the enthusiasm for idealist assumptions and solutions. Political idealism as a view of the world receded. However, it did not vanish. As we will see in later chapters, many of the key elements of the idealist program remained in place and were employed in the international system long after idealism's golden years had faded. Today, the legacy of political idealism lives on in the principles that form the foundation for arms control, international organizations, and international law.

REALISM

Classical realism, as it has come to be called, is less generous regarding human nature. People are generally viewed as nasty self-serving creatures, and political power merely corrupts them further. Political relations are fundamentally about conflict, as unitary rational actors seek their own self-interest. In the case of global politics, the relevant actors are states, which seek their national interest at all times. Military power is the most important expression and guarantor of survival, and the most important issue-area in the field is the threat or actual use of force (everything else is "low politics"). When it comes to foreign policy and security, states must choose what to do in certain situations purely based on their own self-interest, and we should not be surprised when they choose to go to war. The only way to change this situation would be to make the world system nonanarchic; but this system would require a world government, and realists reject that prospect as a virtual impossibility.

Not surprisingly, the realist perspective developed within IR as a discipline following World War II, which many felt provided clear evidence that idealist claims about the progressive inclination of human nature were hopelessly naïve. However, the intellectual roots of realism lay in early writings about war and statecraft in the work of the ancient Greek historian Thucydides, in the writings of Kautilya, in the advice of Sun Tzu, in the philosophies and advice on statecraft of Niccolo Machiavelli, and in the reflections of the English theoretician

PROFILE 1.4 — The Idealist Perspective and the Realist Perspective Compared

ISSUE	IDEALISM	REALISM
Human nature	Good; altruistic	Evil; selfish
Central problem	War and the establishment of peace	War and security
Key actors	States and individuals	States
Motives of actors	Mutual assistance; collaboration	Power; national interest; security
Nature of international politics	Cooperation and community	Anarchy
Outlook on future	Optimism	Pessimism; stability
Policy prescriptions and solutions	Reform the system; develop institutions	Enhance power; protect national interests

Thomas Hobbes. These and other writings emphasized the importance of power and self-interest above all other considerations. The realist perspective was thus built on the intellectual heritage of *realpolitik*. As writes David Boucher in his excellent exposition on classical political philosophy and international relations, "Hobbes does not believe that there is any higher law ordained by a force outside of human will ... morality is equated with expediency ... In the international sphere, in the absence of a sovereign, there is no justice or injustice, but there are principles relating to honourable and dishonourable acts which serve to restrain excessive acts of cruelty or recklessness."[17]

Early exponents of political realism include E.H. Carr, Hans J. Morgenthau (see Profile 1.5), Kenneth W. Thompson, and Reinhold Niebuhr. As a group, realists made several assumptions about the character of international politics. States were the principal actors in international politics since no authority in international politics superseded the authority of the state. For the purposes of analysis, states were also taken to be rational, unitary actors, interested above all else in their security and in maximizing their power. The pursuit of power—the ability to make other actors do what they would not otherwise do—was the core aim of international politics.[9] Although most realists would find the following to be an oversimplification of their world view, to varying degrees, realists assumed that

- People are essentially selfish and acquisitive by nature.
- The desire for power is instinctive to all individuals and cannot be eliminated.
- As a result, international politics is a struggle for power.
- The international system is anarchic in nature as no central authority or world government exists that is capable of enforcing rules.
- In such an environment, the primary objective of all states is to follow their national interests, defined in terms of power.
- In such an environment, states must ultimately rely on their own efforts to ensure their own security.
- Military power and preparedness is the most important factor in determining state power and security.

PROFILE 1.5 Hans J. Morgenthau

Hans J. Morgenthau was born in Germany in 1904. He received his university education in Germany and practised law in Frankfurt before moving to the United States in 1937, where he was appointed to the University of Chicago in 1943. His most famous work was entitled *Politics among Nations*, first published in 1948. Morgenthau presented a theory of international politics in the book, and his "six principles of political realism" became one of the foundations of the realist perspective:

1. Politics is governed by objective laws that have their roots in human nature, which has not changed since the time of classical China, India, and Greece.

2. States, and their leaders, think and act in terms of interest defined as power, and to understand their actions observers of international politics must think the same way.

3. The idea of interest is the essence of politics and is unaffected by time and place; efforts to transform politics without considering this basic law will fail.

4. Tension exists between moral command and the requirements of successful political action. Morality cannot be applied universally in the abstract but must be filtered through the circumstances of time and place.

5. The moral aspirations of a particular nation are not to be confused with the moral laws that govern the universe.

6. Intellectually, realism maintains the autonomy of the political sphere, as economists, lawyers, or doctors maintain theirs.

Morgenthau, then, argued that international relations is characterized by states pursuing their national interests defined in terms of power. The world is the result of forces inherent in human nature, and is characterized by opposing interests and conflicts among them. For Morgenthau, international politics was governed by universal principles or laws based on the pursuit of the national interest.

SOURCE: HANS J. MORGENTHAU, *POLITICS AMONG NATIONS* (NEW YORK: KNOPF, 1948). COPYRIGHT © 1985 BY ALFRED A. KNOPF, A DIVISION OF RANDOM HOUSE, INC.

- Alliances can increase the security of a state, but the loyalty and reliability of allies should always be questioned.

- International organizations and international law cannot be relied on to guarantee security, as state actions are not bound by enforceable rules.

- Order can be achieved only by the balance of power system in which stability is maintained by flexible alliance systems.

If power is as important as realists suggest, we need to know how to measure it. This task is not easy, conceptually or empirically, since much emphasis has been placed on the tangible, measurable capabilities of states. Such factors include the base assets of a state, such as its territory, population, geography, natural resources, and **gross domestic product (GDP)**. These elements of power are long-term attributes that generally change slowly over time. They represent the foundation of state power, or what Canadian foreign policy analyst Kim Richard Nossal has termed "relative invariates."[18] Some states are more endowed with these elements than others by virtue of location or conquest. Frequently, though not exclusively, these states become great powers. Other states stand little or no chance of attaining such status.

For realists, military power is the principal means through which states exercise power in the short term. Military capabilities are the most important measure of state power in war when other power elements are not directly engaged. However, if a war is long, the states with the greater power resources to mobilize and commit to military ends will have the advantage. Estimating the power—especially the military power—of others is a crucial element of international politics, realists argue. As Sun Tzu wrote: "Know the enemy and know yourself; in a hundred battles you will never be in peril." However, tangible, measurable factors of **hard**

power are not the entire story. Power encompasses intangibles, elements that are not easily measured or compared. A state must be able to deploy hard-power capabilities in an effective fashion. This ability depends on the unity of purpose within the state, which can be influenced by public opinion, religion, ideology, or nationalism (the conscription crisis in Canada during World War I is an example of such a difficulty, as was the American war effort in Vietnam). The effective deployment of power can also depend on the support a state has obtained in the international system, which may depend, in turn, on the moral legitimacy of its cause, the loyalty of its allies, and the diplomatic and political skills available to the state. Power can also lie in the ability of an actor to set agendas, establish norms of behaviour, and gain wider agreements on rules and regulations that others agree to obey.

The less tangible elements of power (**soft power**) reflect the appeal or attraction of ideas and values. If a state's ideas and values are seen as attractive, they will provide that state with opportunities to exert influence and leadership. For example, some have argued that the United States leads the world in terms of soft power because of its position as the world's leading capitalist marketplace and liberal democracy. Some Canadians (such as former Foreign Affairs Minister Lloyd Axworthy) have suggested that Canada has influence in the world beyond its capabilities (especially its military capabilities) because of its emphasis on international cooperation and institutions over the use of military force and coercion. In this view, soft power has enabled Canada to provide limited leadership on issues such as peacekeeping, the movement to ban land mines, and sanctions against South Africa during the **apartheid** era. This view of soft power rejects the hard-power perspective advanced by realists. For their part, realists argue that soft power flows from the ability to exert hard power, and, therefore, hard power remains the central currency of all power in global politics.

Anarchy and the Security Dilemma

Realism is not a monolithic theory, and has evolved considerably from its early origins. Classical realists such as Morgenthau and Niebuhr emphasize the role of human nature. Structural realists such as Kenneth Waltz emphasize the anarchic nature of the system as a determinant of state behaviour. The term *anarchy* implies not complete chaos or absence of law but rather the lack of a central authority or government capable of enforcing rules.[19] Within states, governments can deter participants from breaking legal restrictions, can enforce contracts, and can use their monopoly on the use of coercion to compel citizens to obey the law. In contrast, no central authority exists to enforce and ensure state compliance with international rules or norms. Consequently, states must become self-reliant if they are to survive. All states must, therefore, be prepared to use force in their own defence, for in an anarchic environment, a state may use coercion or force at any time if the benefits to be gained outweigh potential costs (see the discussion of the stag hunt in Profile 1.6). So, in the absence of an effective security system, states arm themselves for protection against such an eventuality, following the advice of the Latin phrase *Si vis pacem, parabellum*—"If you want peace, prepare for war."

In doing so, however, states can find themselves in a situation that scholars have called the **security dilemma**. In this situation, when states take unilateral measures to ensure their own security (such as increasing the capabilities of their military forces), they decrease the security of neighbouring states. Neighbouring states will perceive these measures as threatening and will take countermeasures (increasing the capabilities of their own armed forces) to enhance their own security. These military enhancements will provoke insecurity in other states, which will increase their military capabilities as well. This action–reaction cycle occurs when states increasingly spend resources on military capabilities but make no real gains in the way of security. This dynamic is the basis of the many arms races that have occurred between states. Characterized by periods of high tension and the rapid escalation of the military capabilities of the states engaged, they promote hostility and mistrust and create the conditions in which a crisis could easily lead to misunderstanding, miscalculation, and war. In Chapter 3, we will examine in detail the evolution of what was, arguably, the greatest security dilemma of all time, the Cold War.

For realists, the existence of an anarchic self-help system does not mean that the international system lacks order or cooperation. In fact many, such as Hedley Bull, argued that the international system is far from chaotic. In an anarchic system, states can cooperate and do so all the time; states reach trade agreements and form alliances. However, realists argue that this cooperation occurs not for altruistic reasons but because it is in the interests of states to cooperate. Cooperation is simply another reflection of self-help. Furthermore, when states interact they follow international norms and conventions most of the time. Norms are shared expectations about what constitutes appropriate behaviour in the international system. An example of such a norm is the concept of sovereignty, the principle that a state has control over affairs within its own territory, free from external interference by other states. In principle, states are therefore autonomous in that they answer to no higher authority in the international system. Another prominent norm is respect for internationally recognized borders. Despite the fact

PROFILE 1.6 The Trouble with Cooperation: The Stag Hunt

Jean Jacques Rousseau (Copyright © Bettman/ Corbis)

The stag hunt is an allegory that originated in the writings of the Geneva-born 18th-century philosopher **Jean Jacques Rousseau**. In this allegory, five individual hunters exist in a state of nature, with no government or social structure to determine their behaviour. The hunters have a choice of cooperating to attain a mutually desired goal or defecting from such cooperation if their own individual short-term interests can

be satisfied. They can collaborate to encircle and subsequently capture a stag, which will satisfy the food needs of all five hunters if they share it. However, in doing so, it is possible that one of the hunters will encounter a tempting hare, which will satisfy that individual hunter's food needs. That hunter then faces a choice: let the hare go and serve the common interest by continuing the effort to capture the stag, or take the hare and defect from the group, thus ruining the hunt for the other four hunters, who will not have their food needs satisfied.

The allegory raises several questions about incentives and disincentives for cooperation. If a hunter prefers to cooperate to capture the stag, can the other hunters be trusted to do the same? Is it not in the rational self-interest of a hunter to take the hare? If this is the case, how can the hunters trust each other to cooperate on a hunt for the stag? And if they cannot trust each other, is it not in their interests to take the hare before any of the other hunters do? Indeed, what is the incentive to cooperate at all? The stag hunt allegory illustrates the difficulty of establishing cooperation in an anarchic environment and the corrosive effect short-term self-interest can have on collaborative efforts. Rationality, competition, and trust are all subjective terms.

that most borders in the world today are the result of past wars and international agreements or the legacy of colonial occupation, the territorial integrity of states is regarded as one of the foundations of international stability. Attempts to revise these borders—through conquest or succession—are generally regarded as dangerous or destabilizing events, because a challenge to an existing border is in principle a challenge to borders everywhere. Other norms regulate the conduct of diplomatic relations between states. For example, embassies are considered to be the territory of their home states, rather than that of the host country, and are therefore not subject to interference or the laws of the host country. Finally, as we will see, governments obey a wide variety of international norms, procedures, regulations, and laws every day.

Since cooperation and norms do provide the basis for some order in the international system, anarchy does not mean the absence of order. However, realists emphasize that when it comes to security issues, or so-called high politics concerns, states rely on power to manage relations between them. This reliance has led to the development of the concept of the balance of power, discussed in greater detail in our next chapter.

LIBERALISM: COMPLEX INTERDEPENDENCE, LIBERAL INSTITUTIONALISM, AND LIBERAL DEMOCRATIC PEACE THEORY

As mentioned in our description of idealism, a liberal perspective suggests people can rationally cooperate in the name of self-interest (since what is good for one may be good for another as well, contrary to a zero-sum world perspective in which a gain for one is a loss for another). Liberals emphasize the importance of private property, law, free markets, democracy, and justice. Great importance is placed on economic growth, both domestically and internationally. It is believed that more trade leads to fewer wars, since trade instills a sense of cooperation and mutual interest even though it occurs in a competitive environment. In addition, so-called transnationalist avenues for international cooperation, such as the creation of international organizations and cultural exchanges, can reduce the chances of war and increase global wealth. Three popular variants of liberalism remain in circulation today: complex interdependence, liberal institutionalism, and liberal democratic peace theory. They are all highly relevant for foreign policy analysis, studies of globalization, and international political economy.

If we blend realism's concern with power and state conflict with liberalism's optimism and emphasis on transnationalist phenomena, we get what Robert Keohane and Joseph Nye Jr., in a seminal work of the 1970s, termed "complex interdependence theory."[20] In a prelude to our more current concerns with globalization, they argued that economic factors were fast becoming as important as military matters, and that nonstate actors such as **multinational corporations (MNCs)** and **nongovernmental organizations (NGOs)** play important roles alongside states. Further, states are not always rational, coherent actors, since they respond to internal discord. Keohane and Nye intended their theory to be a modification, not a refutation, of realism, but much of what they argued has been subsumed under the liberal banner.

Idealists and liberals have much in common, including the desire for stronger institutions to facilitate global cooperation. These institutions are often called **regimes**, sets of principles, norms, rules, and decision-making procedures around which actors' expectations converge. They reduce uncertainty and allow people to get on with important transnational business, such as trade, investment, or pursuing human rights improvements. The essential argument here is that the anarchism so instrumental in a structural realist understanding of global politics need not prevent states and individuals from achieving a more harmonious world; in some cases international institutions could actually replace the state as a provider of goods to citizens. This gives rise to neo-functionalist theory, exemplified by the evolution of the

European Union, a supranational institution that has substantial impact on the daily lives of citizens in states as diverse as Belgium and Greece. We return to these themes in Chapter 5.

Finally, liberal democratic peace theory asserts that historically, liberal democracies rarely if ever go to war against each other. This view was an important component of the work of Immanuel Kant (see Profile 1.7). The key to global stability is not necessarily a balance of power, or even increased trade, but rather the spread of Western-style liberal democracies, whose executives are constrained in their autonomy and cannot get away with the hazardous act of starting wars against other democracies. People will throw expansionist politicians out of office if their designs on international power exceed the willingness of the population to sacrifice. More to the point, there is little incentive for one liberal democracy to attack another, as neither will regard the other as a threat to its way of life. Democratic peace theory has come under considerable scrutiny for several reasons: it is based on a Eurocentric definition of democracy; there are methodological problems with the measurement of war; and the fact that republics such as the United States are obviously quite willing to wage war is undeniable. The theory leads some to suggest the key to peace is the spread of not only democracy per se but the market institutions that often accompany it. More nuanced explorations of the theory ask questions about the relative autonomy of the executive decision-making units in democratic states, and take into account the abilities of even democratically elected leaders to deceive civilians into accepting the need for warfare.[21] Again, we return to this theory in later chapters, but the utility of a perspective based on what Kenneth Waltz labelled the "second image"—that the nature of the state can largely determine the nature of its foreign policy—remains a contested proposition.

CRITICAL PERSPECTIVES

There are two central ways critical theories challenge the more mainstream variations of realism and liberalism described above. The first involves a rejection of the central values, or lack of values, posited by the realist and liberal ontologies, emphasizing concerns with social justice that neither mainstream approach can adequately embrace. The second is an epistemological rejection of the orthodoxy of positivism, or the belief that we can take adequate stock of the world through empirical observation and the testing of hypotheses. This does not mean critical theorists are on a different page altogether: if Christian Reus-Smit is correct, then the main debate animating IR theory today "revolves around the nature of social agency, the relative importance of normative versus material forces, the balance between continuity and transformation in world politics, and a range of other empirical-theoretical questions."[22] These same questions inspire theorists of all stripes; however, the different strands of critical theory discussed below are united by their common rejection of realism or liberalism as ideological justifications for an unjust status quo.

In this view, global politics is not only about relations among states; nonstate actors and social forces, such as entrenched classes and popular movements, are also agents of change. History can be seen in terms of the domination, exploitation, and marginalization of one group over another: of the Southern Hemisphere by the northern European imperialist powers; of women by men; of some races by others. Of course, remarkably different viewpoints exist within this general critical perspective. A very cursory treatment of four of them follows.

NEO-MARXISM, DEPENDENCY THEORY, AND NEO-GRAMSCIAN PERSPECTIVES

The central assumption behind these perspectives is that economic classes are the primary units of analysis in world affairs and that the economic growth experienced by the rich Northern world has come at the cost of others, namely those in the poor Southern world.

PROFILE 1.7 Immanuel Kant (1724–1804)

Immanuel Kant (Copyright © Archivo Iconografico, S.A./Corbis)

Immanuel Kant was a German philosopher who wrote as the Enlightenment was sweeping through Germany in the 18th century. He wrote his most famous work, *Perpetual Peace*, in 1795. Based on the experience of the wars of the French Revolution, Kant argued that there were two possible futures for humanity: the end of all hostilities through international agreements, or the perpetual peace of the cemetery of humankind after an annihilating war. *Perpetual Peace* is written as a contract similar to the diplomatic documents of the day; in this sense, it is a model for the establishment of international peace through international agreements between states. In it Kant proposes the following: the establishment of a system of conduct among states, including the principles of sovereignty, noninterference, and eventual disarmament; the conversion of authoritative states into republican states (which are less likely to go to war than the former); the development of an international federation of free states with a republican constitution that respects the sovereignty of its members; and the creation of conditions for universal hospitality and growing commerce across state borders. Kant believed that these measures would lead to peace among all peoples, a peace that would be reinforced by the natural tendency of states to engage in commerce rather than war with one another: "In connection with the life of the agriculturalist, salt and iron were discovered which were perhaps the first articles that were sought far and near, and which entered into the commercial intercourse of different peoples. Thereby they would be first brought into a peaceful relation to one another; and thus the most distant of them would come to mutual understanding, sociability and pacific intercourse."

SOURCE: "IMMANUEL KANT," IN M. FORSYTH ET AL., EDS., *THE THEORY OF INTERNATIONAL RELATIONS: SELECTED TEXTS FROM GENTILI TO TREITSCHKE* (LONDON: GEORGE ALLEN AND UNWIN, 1970), 220.

Economic relations are determined by geography and colonial history. Thus, states rich in natural resources, such as Canada, have gained from exporting them abroad and in particular to large markets such as the United States. At the same time, however, this traps states such as Kenya, Argentina, Zambia, and Peru into dependencies based on staple exports such as tea, bauxite, coffee, tobacco, and wood. Reliance on staple products is exacerbated by relative political weakness. Within underdeveloped states, the upper classes participate in the North–South exploitative relationship, not only reinforcing global inequality but also benefiting from it. Thus, most Neo-Marxist analysis in IR has focused on theories of imperialism.

The origins of Marxism lie in the writings of **Karl Marx** (1818–83), who studied law and philosophy and wrote about history. In league with Friedrich Engels (1820–95), Marx campaigned for a socialist Germany. Marxism itself is a branch of thought emerging from the French Revolution, the British Industrial Revolution, and German philosophy. Marx insisted on a materialist world-view, implying that the world is constructed in our minds by the economic structure of society and that the means of production (technology, invention, natural resources, property systems) determine our religious, philosophical, governmental, legal, and

PROFILE 1.8 Lenin and Monopoly Capitalism

Revolutionary leader Vladimir Ilyich Lenin is seen in this February 1897 picture in St. Petersburg. Russians listed Lenin as their No. 1 choice of "man of the century" for their country, followed by dictator Josef Stalin, the Interfax news agency reported 26 December 2000. Lenin (1870–1924) founded Bolshevism and was the Soviet leader from 1917 until his death in 1924. (AP Photo/CP Archive)

Though Lenin's place in history is well known, his role in the formation of an intellectual perspective on international political economy is less celebrated. In a treatise published at the end of World War I ("Imperialism: The Highest Stage of Capitalism"), Lenin argued that the war had resulted from competition among the major capitalist powers, which had reached the target of monopoly capitalism, "in which the division of all territories of the globe among the great capitalist powers has been completed." Imperialism resulted from the concentration of production in combines, cartels, syndicates, and trusts; the competitive quest for sources of raw materials; and the development of banking oligarchies. Under these conditions, imperialism was inevitable and not a matter of choice. The principal exporters of capital would be the dominant powers in the international system. Critics argue that this essentially economic explanation does not take into account other causes of imperialism, such as the search for glory and recognition. However, Lenin did explain nationalism as part of the false consciousness that guided the working classes to the battlefield and perpetuated their mutual slaughter; the sentiment of futility that eventually characterized participation in World War I worked in the Bolshevik's favour immediately prior to the Russian Revolution in 1917. Lenin's ultimate creation, the Soviet Union, is dead, but to many concerned with the plight of the Southern Hemisphere, his ideas still form the core of their thinking.

moral values and institutions. What the *bourgeoisie* had done in France, Marx believed, the *proletariat*, or working class, could do elsewhere. According to Marxism, then, classes are the social engines of history. The state is conceived as a vehicle of the ruling economic class; it exists primarily to serve their interests and not those of the public. Marxist thinkers such as **John Hobson**, **Rosa Luxemburg**, and **Vladimir Lenin** wrote about the international impact of capitalism, which they considered to be the primary cause of imperialism (see Profile 1.8 for Lenin; Luxemburg is very significant also, since she was a prototypical Marxist feminist intellectual). As the domestic economies of the European powers ran out of markets, it became necessary to expand into the colonial areas to find new markets, natural resources, and a place to export capital.

International thinking along Marxist lines has taken many paths. One of the more influential modern variants has been **dependency theory**, which argues that Southern states have become trapped in a system of exploitation, one that forces them to be dependent on the North for capital and locks them into an unfair trading relationship. Inspired largely by the Latin American states' relationship to the United States, dependency theory suggests that the world system evolved from European imperialism to the disadvantage of those in the periphery. The wealth of the North was derived in part from the poverty of the South. States in the South were complicit, because the ruling classes in the periphery also benefited from the system. An important link existed between local capitalists, the underdeveloped state apparatus, and multinational corporations (or, put another way, transnational capital). In addition, even the working classes in the North gained from this exploitative relationship. Thus, some theorists, such as Andre Gunder Frank, proclaimed that the real choice was between underdevelopment and revolution. The world was not interdependent; it was hierarchical and exploitative. We will explore dependency theory in more depth in Chapter 4.

Neo-Marxists and dependency theorists share several assumptions and views regarding global politics:

- The most important actors in global politics are dominant economic interests or socioeconomic classes; Marxists differ considerably on the importance of structures.

- Both the state and war are largely (though not exclusively) instruments of the ruling economic classes.

- States (and their ruling elites) are bound into a hierarchical structural relationship characterized by patterns of dominance and dependence.

- A wide differential in power exists between the rich and the poor, and this is related to their relationship to the means of production in national and global economies.

- For the marginalized and dependent states and peoples everywhere, revolution and the overthrow of the world capitalist system are the only hope for change. However, since this prescription of "delinking" from the world economy has proven elusive, many advocate major reform in both domestic and international systems instead.

The Marxist origins of this theoretical perspective are important, since Karl Marx and other revolutionary thinkers argued that the state was essentially an instrument of domination, keeping the lower classes, or proletariat, in place as providers of labour. Though multinational corporations have come to dominate the global economy, they cannot do so without the protection of the modern state, a theme we revisit in chapters 4 and 8. However, we should point out that many scholars today adopt the work of the Italian Marxist scholar Antonio Gramsci in their own work. Gramsci argued that hegemony should be seen as the impact of the socialization of the masses, the educational effort to convince them that their lives are better off under capitalism than could be otherwise, and the idea that they should aspire to imitate the upper classes in order to live the good life—a life most will never achieve. Similarly, one can argue that the dominant states and elite capitalist centres of the world economy have also ensured that the development of global politics protects their wealth not only with guns and warships, but with the spread of conducive ideology and aspirations, reflected perhaps most visibly in the idea that globalization will be good for all, and not just a select few. The Neo-Marxist project calls for sustained attention to a critical reading of such ideology, and reform of the system that allows its perpetuation.[23]

FEMINISM

The primary focus of feminism is gender inequality and the critique of the patriarchal systems that perpetuate it. Feminists who study global politics argue that a patriarchal system exists at the international level. Further, as J. Ann Tickner argues, dominant academic perspectives (in particular realism) have served only to reinforce the system with gender-specific language and the cult of masculinity surrounding political and military discourse.[24] However, quite distinct versions of feminism exist. Liberal feminists argue that women's participation in world affairs has been too silent or marginalized and that this situation must be corrected; feminists who are more radical argue this correction would be insufficient and that deeper changes are necessary. There is a large divide here: while liberal feminists argue the central injustice is the lack of women in positions of authority, radical feminists argue the entire state and international apparatus is based on patriarchal ideologies that perpetuate cycles of violence and environmental destruction (recall the mention of Rosa Luxemburg, above). As Jean Bethke Elshtain writes, "received notions of sovereignty incorporated in their absolutist heart of hearts a demand for blood-sacrifice: *pro patria mori.* This sacrificial demand got encoded into modern identities, male and female, with the triumph—the very bloody triumph—of the modern nation-state."[25] This is certainly an applicable theme today as well. Other concerns, such as women's access to health care, family planning, and education, and freedom from violence, are also on the feminist agenda.

The feminist perspective operates at two levels: First, the argument is made that the role women play in the global economy is essential and must be recognized in any salient analysis, whether the researcher is looking at structural adjustment programs, the international sex trade, the microelectronics production industry, the generation of intellectual capital, or any other field. Similarly, the role women have played in historical developments, including the great ages of imperialism, should not be overlooked simply because history has not, by and large, been written by them. Second, there is a rejection of the dominant realist values and an emphasis on the values of self-worth, community development, cooperation, peace, and sustainable development. While it remains to be seen whether some of these values can infiltrate the halls of academia and become dominant in the field, there can be little doubt that the feminist critique of traditional international relations theory has had a profound impact on the thinking of both younger and older scholars. The larger question may well be whether, in an economic world still dominated by males and masculinized discourse, feminist perspectives can have a serious impact on actual policy decisions. We return to feminist approaches to specific issue-areas throughout this book.

GLOBAL ECOPOLITICAL THEORY

Although environmental approaches are not unified in any coherent body of theory, environmentalists do agree that liberal theories do not adequately account for the ecological costs of global economic growth, while realism ignores the role played by the state in perpetuating environmental exploitation. The multitude of ecological crises afflicting the world at present did not appear without warning: the misuse of agricultural land, for example, has long been known to have dire consequences, and pollution was a prevalent theme in the 1960s in North America and Europe. The historic connection between industrial development and environmental decay, in all hemispheres, has become for many the overwhelming theme of human history. In 2004, things look as problematic as ever; though there have been improvements in certain areas, such as protection of the ozone layer, there remains great uncertainty about the eventual consequences of global warming, species extinctions, and the harmful effects of chemicals.

Again, many varieties of global ecopolitical theories exist, some of which stress dealing with overpopulation, overconsumption, pollution, or the threat to endangered species with an institutionalist, regime management approach. This line of thinking, with its liberal pedigree, dominates the policy process and much of mainstream political science. More radical approaches advocate reconceptualizing capitalism or redefining human relations. Ecofeminists link patriarchy with **ecocide**. Nonstate actors are often seen as the most important agents of change, although some radical environmentalists believe in direct action through protest or even acts of violence. Others argue that stronger states are necessary to preserve what is left of the natural world, even if it means limiting human personal freedoms in the process. We address this issue in greater detail in Chapter 10. In general, one can argue that all the forms of theory discussed here, including realism and liberalism, begin with certain premises about the relationship between humans and nature, though it is evident that radical ecological thought has the most in common with critical approaches.[26]

Some commentators suggest that the terrorist acts of 9-11 can serve as a cataclysmic event, forcing those in high-consumption societies to rethink our priorities and re-examine the impact of our own behaviour. For example, Western dependence on foreign oil supplies leads to the support for many "petro-tyrannies," which fail to foster democracy and encourage anti-Western sentiment. Some point to the failure of several Western oil companies to build a trans-Afghanistan pipeline as one of the causes of further Taliban–United States hostility. Those taking a critical international political economy perspective would stress the importance of American and Western efforts to secure oil access in the Middle East and elsewhere, and this may be viewed as all the more regrettable as renewable energy sources are available but underfunded. In chapters 10 and 13 we return to this theme, which is highly relevant for people living in a resource-dependent state such as Canada.

PROFILE 1.9 — Realism, Liberalism, and Critical Theories Compared

ISSUE	REALISM	LIBERALISM	CRITICAL THEORIES
Human nature	Evil; selfish	Good; willing to cooperate for mutual gain	Variable
Central problem	War and security	Encouraging cooperation on global issues	Marginalization and imperialism; gender inequality; ecocide
Key actors	States	Individuals; MNCs; "penetrated" states; international institutions; NGOs	Classes; groups; MNCs; NGOs
Motives of actors	Power; national interest; security	Rational self-interest; justice; peace; prosperity	Power; greed; liberation; justice
Nature of international politics	Anarchy; economic growth will not overcome state conflicts	Interdependent; economic growth will promote peace	Hierarchy; dominance; exploitation; resistance
Outlook on future	Pessimism; stability; states will pursue neomercantilist policies	Optimism; progress is possible; economic growth is good for all	Pessimism unless paradigmatic change is achieved
Policy prescriptions and solutions	Enhance power; protect national interests	Develop institutions and regimes to encourage cooperation	Engender revolution, transformation, and social change

THE POSITIVIST/POSTPOSITIVIST DISTINCTION AND CONSTRUCTIVISM

As mentioned above, critical theories are separated not only by more explicit concerns with social justice issues, but also by their tendency to reject the positivist foundations of liberalism and realism. We need to be cautious here, since many Marxists, for example, base their analyses in historical materialism, which claims empirical validity, and it would be improper to label all feminists or environmentalists postpositivist. Postmodernists are primarily concerned with how people interpret the world around them and how they act on this understanding; they are critical of the positivist aspirations of the traditional theories. Postmodernists reject the idea that realists, liberals, or Marxists (all positivist and materialist theories) can ever really know anything concrete about global politics (or build objective knowledge about the world), since their personal biases will invariably influence their conclusions. For postmodernists, we cannot truly understand reality because how we see the world is socially constructed by subjective images that have their origins in our formative experiences, our cultures, our educations, our languages, and our political perspectives. "Reality" is, therefore, inherently intangible and sub-jective and is dependent on the nature of the viewer, not on the existence of an objective world; and all viewers are ensconced in power relations previously socially constructed by others.

The more critically inclined postmodernists argue that individuals who have inherited the Western tradition have performed the bulk of research work in the sciences and humanities. This hegemonic intellectual tradition serves to marginalize other perspectives and non-Western thought. At the heart of the postmodern research agenda is an investigation into how power distribution in a relationship affects policy and scholarship. Every analysis, or policy, is constructed in such a way as to perpetuate or enhance a power relationship. As such, the tra-ditional approaches contribute to the present social injustice brought about by the develop-ment of modernity, the scientific revolution of the West. Postmodernist thought has many strands as well: deconstructionists emphasize the importance of breaking down popular texts or discourses to understand the power relations they perpetuate, while feminist postmod-ernists look for gender bias in traditional discourse. It is not fruitful to contrast these more interpretive approaches with the positivist orientations, since neither can claim to actually "better" the other. Their sets of assumptions and aims are fundamentally different. Where they do converge, however, is in the effort to contribute to the intellectual debate over the need and possibility of avoiding mass violence.

Another approach, broadly labelled *constructivism*, depicts global politics (or any social subject, for that matter) as intersubjective. That is, "material resources only acquire meaning for human action through the structure of shared knowledge in which they are embedded."[27] For constructivists, meaning is derived from collective understandings of the material world: it is on the basis of such collective understandings that human action, group action, and social action is based. Stefano Guzzini described the "common ground" of contructivist theory as the social construction of knowledge and the construction of social reality.[28] In other words, what we attempt to understand in global politics is not independent, or separate, from our interpretation of global politics and the language we use to describe it. Constructivism stresses the impact of intersubjective understandings among political actors on constituting their own identities. This social construction of the self, be it by national leaders (I am the leader of the free world), members of international organizations (I am a neutral international civil ser-vant), environmental scientists (I am a citizen of the world), or others, determines the nor-mative acceptability of practices and discourses within issue-areas. Some or all of the practices and discourses considered acceptable and even normatively positive in one social context (I will lead the free world in a war against terrorism) will be less positive in another (I believe only the UN can legitimize a "War on Terrorism") or unacceptable in others (I reject the "War on Terrorism" as shortsighted and counterproductive). In short, "it is collective meanings that constitute the structures which organize our actions."[29]

In this sense, constructivism builds on the work of theorists such as Michel Foucault, Anthony Giddens, and others. How is constructivism distinguished from other theories? Emanuel Adler puts it this way:

> Unlike positivism and materialism, which take the world as it is, constructivism sees the world as a project under construction, as becoming rather than being. Unlike idealism … and postmodernism, which take the world *only* as it can be imagined or talked about, constructivism accepts that not all statements have the same … value and that there is consequently some foundation for knowledge.[30]

Constructivists thus like to argue that there is much more room for actors to effect change in global politics. They are skeptical of the idea that enduring realities or continuities or structures determine the behaviour of actors. For example, take the realist concept of anarchy, which according to realists exerts pressure on decision makers to act in a certain way. For constructivists, this idea of anarchy is not a material condition of global politics, but a social construct. Anarchy does not make states act the way they do: anarchy is what states make of it.[31] We hesitate to include constructivism as a distinct theory since it is in essence a way of understanding change that borrows from postmodernism and can be applied by a wide range of analysts with roots in all the perspectives outlined above. In particular, constructivism can be applied by those interested in studying international institutions, many of whom come from the liberal institutional school.[32]

EMBRACING THEORETICAL DIVERSITY

At this point it would be inaccurate to say that any one perspective dominates the study of global politics. Realism certainly held sway in the United States for much of the Cold War era, but liberal perspectives are at least as prominent today and have often been so in England, Australia, and Canada. Critical perspectives are as popular as ever, especially among graduate students and in the Southern Hemisphere. For example, the 2002 annual meeting of the International Studies Association in Portland, Oregon, which involved thousands of participants, was organized around the theme "The Social Construction of Knowledge." While the debates between theoreticians can be fascinating, and often quite overwhelming, we will not devote significant sections of this text to them, but attempt to integrate various perspectives in our own treatment of the subject matter. It will be clear to most readers, for example, that the next chapter, focusing mostly on historical conflicts and empire-building, has a realist context; subsequent chapters no doubt display liberal, institutionalist, critical theory, and environmentalist perspectives as well.

There are good reasons to insist on your own perspective being the right one. At the same time, however, we would encourage you to proceed in this complex field with an open mind, and try to arrive at new conclusions regarding which perspective best explains and suggests global politics to you. There is no need to impose a rigid orthodoxy on the field; one of its attractions is the eclectic nature of the work it has inspired amongst generations of scholars and practitioners.

ONWARD!

This book intends to introduce students to the discipline of international relations (IR) in the 21st century, and from a distinctly non-American viewpoint. Put bluntly, most IR textbooks are written by Americans, from an American perspective, for American students. The key examples and foreign policy dilemmas offered are American ones, reflecting that state's obviously unique position in world affairs. Students living in **middle powers** such as Canada, however, appreciate an approach that takes the circumstances of their country (as well as their own personal interests) into account. The task before citizens of smaller states such as Canada, Norway, Australia, Brazil, South Africa, Thailand, and many others is to better understand the global political environment and all that it entails, rather than to maintain national pre-eminence within it. Some may think of themselves not as citizens of states at all, but as global citizens with planetary concerns. None of this denies the significance of the question of American power and influence in today's global political theatre. One of Paul Martin's first steps as Prime Minister of Canada in 2004 was to visit U.S. President George W. Bush, in an effort to patch up relations strained by Canada's nonparticipation in the Iraq War. However, there are issues in the world beyond those that concern the United States, and these are as valid and central to both everyday life and the bigger picture of global politics but are often neglected or given peripheral treatment in other texts.

This chapter has introduced the field of global politics and has argued that an approach that escapes the American focus typical of most texts is needed. But the most central rationale for a new look at this topic is that, as the new century evolves, history is moving on. Though the older concepts that have shaped the field—such as state, war, and diplomacy—have retained their significance, we face an era when nonstate actors are often as important, when market forces are changing millions of lives on a daily basis, and when people are attempting to forge new definitions of human rights and dignity. This idea generates a lengthy set of questions—an agenda for study—that requires looking into both traditional and nonconventional areas. A partial list of such questions includes the following:

1. Which theoretical perspective best describes and explains the world? This question is a fundamental one, because different theoretical perspectives provide very different explanations of events and have different sets of priorities. Does a postpositivist approach add to our understanding?

2. What are the lessons of the past? This is an enduring question in the field, but in the contemporary and future context it involves the examination of periods in history that more closely approximate our own. The hope is that we can avoid the repetition of mistakes.

3. Is the international system fragmenting or integrating? Two phenomena seem to exist side by side in the international system: the breakup and collapse of empires and states, and increasing interdependence and political and economic amalgamation. Is there a trend in one direction or another?

4. Are states becoming obsolete? One trend in international affairs has been the increased permeability and penetrability of state borders. Has the **sovereignty** of the state eroded to the point where we may speak of the imminent demise of the state in world politics?

5. What are the implications of the "War on Terrorism" for the international system and our understanding of it?

6. What are the causes of war, and how can conflicts be managed or prevented? This is also a question of enduring importance in international relations, but today efforts are concentrated on addressing the problem of ethnic or religious wars within states, as well as the protection of civilians during conflict, part of the broader human secu-

rity agenda adopted by Canada during the late 1990s under the guidance of the then Minister for Foreign Affairs, Lloyd Axworthy.

7. How can the proliferation of conventional weapons and weapons of mass destruction be stopped? The flow of weapons of mass destruction, sophisticated conventional weapons, and small arms to areas of tension and conflict is a pressing international concern.

8. What is the future of the international economy? Are we heading toward an increasingly liberalized world economy characterized by global free trade, or is the world economy heading toward the development of regional trading blocs? Will the global economy be characterized by continued growth or by crisis and economic downturn?

9. Are international organizations getting stronger or weaker? International organizations are a key manifestation of cooperation in international affairs. Some would argue that they serve to enhance and reinforce cooperation. Yet the invasion of Iraq in 2003, and the bombing of Serbia in 1999, proceeded without United Nations approval.

10. How will environmental issues affect global politics? Environmental degradation has emerged as a serious issue between states and within them. The question is whether environmental pressures such as climatic change and resource scarcity contribute to increased cooperation or increased conflict among states and peoples.

11. What will be the impact of the information revolution on global politics? Does the information revolution promise a world of improved communication, understanding, and sharing of knowledge leading to a global community, or a world of the information rich and the information poor?

12. How will increasing migration of people affect global politics? People are on the move around the world, in the form of emigrants, refugees, and migrant workers. Increasing hardship and population pressures in the developing world suggest that even larger population movements will occur in the future, posing hard questions for immigration and refugee policy. Human smuggling is a growing international organized-crime activity.

13. What will be the future impact of the power differential between the developing and developed world? An ever-widening gap in economic and political power exists between the richer countries of North America and Europe and the poorer countries of Latin America, Asia, and Africa. This question has given rise to the North–South debate.

14. What are the best strategies for development and aid? This issue has been a pressing one since the 1960s, and as the divide between the world's rich and the world's poor continues to widen, the debate over development strategies has taken on a new urgency. Placing more priority on the role of women in development has led to opportunities and new challenges.

Arguably, all these issues are linked by the pursuit of security. And, if global politics is largely about the pursuit of security (or the freedom from harm), security must be understood in terms of individual, community, national, and even global survival. Responding to this broad agenda is the greatest challenge we face in global politics. More generally, states often perceive neighbouring states as threats to their continued existence. Such fears continue to ignite arms races, particularly in the South Asia, Asia-Pacific, and Middle East regions, though these military buildups have very willing suppliers in arms-exporting states, such as the United States, China, and Russia. The introduction of nuclear weapons, which have the ability to destroy all life on earth (**omnicide**), made us think in terms of global security. As recent nuclear tests by India and Pakistan demonstrate, these weapons are still with us, along with the fear of accidents, wars of miscalculation, and weapons proliferation by states such as North Korea.

These are but a few of the many questions challenging students of global politics today as they embark on a journey of overwhelming complexity, frustration, and discovery. Above all, this text is designed to provide interested readers with a rough guide for that journey, one that encompasses origins, currents, and directions. Some aspects of the study of global politics are timeless. As one author contends, "diplomacy, in the sense of the ordered conduct of relations between one group of human beings and another group alien to themselves, is far older than history."[33] Some theorists argue that human nature has always been with us and will not change; others insist it can change for the better, or worse, according to circumstances. As our historical discussions in Part One of this book suggest, war and trade—two primary modes of human interaction—have both been around a very long time. We begin with a look at the formation of the nation-state and the problem of war. Although this subject no longer dominates the field as it once did, it remains the most vivid example of the potential consequences of the nation-state system. Chapter 3 explores the Cold War era and the nature of state decision making. Next, we examine political perspectives pertaining to the global economy and its evolution. Our final chapter in "Origins" deals with international institutions and international law.

Part Two of the book is devoted to "Currents" in global politics, those issues that may have deep roots but have emerged as more significant in the contemporary era. These issues include the spread of weapons of mass destruction, terrorism, peacekeeping and peacemaking, globalization and marginalization, and human rights questions. Finally, Part Three is devoted to "Directions" in global politics, forcing us to look ahead, however tentatively, at trends that are unfolding. Such trends include various environmental problems, increasing human migration, and the role of emerging technologies on global politics. We have chosen these themes because they help convey an understanding of the complex convergence/divergence paradox outlined above, and because readers will no doubt relate to most of them in their everyday lives. Onward!

Endnotes

1. *Peace and War: A Theory of International Relations* (1966; Garden City, NY: Anchor, 1973), 9.
2. J. Der Derian, "A Reinterpretation of Realism: Genealogy, Semiology and Dromology," in same, ed., *International Theory: Critical Investigations* (New York: New York University Press, 1995), 363–96, 366.
3. One of the most cited examples is Kal Holsti's article "Change in the International System: Interdependence, Integration, and Fragmentation," in O. Holsti, R. Siverson, and A. George, eds., *Change in the International System* (Boulder, CO: Westview Press, 1980), 23–53; more popularly, see B. Barber, "Jihad vs. McWorld," *Atlantic* 269 (March 1992), 53–63.
4. See, for example, J. Dougherty and R. Pfaltzgraff Jr., *Contending Theories of International Relations: A Comprehensive Survey*, 3rd ed. (New York: Harper & Row, 1990); P. Viotti and M. Kauppi, *International Relations Theory: Realism, Pluralism, Globalism*, 2nd ed. (Toronto: Maxwell, 1993); T. Taylor, ed., *Approaches and Theory in International Relations* (Essex: Longman, 1978); C. Kegley, ed., *Controversies in International Relations Theory: Realism and the Neoliberal Challenge* (New York: St. Martin's Press, 1995); R. Keohane, ed., *Neorealism and Its Critics* (New York: Columbia University Press, 1986); O. Holsti, "Models of International Relations and Foreign Policy," *Diplomatic History* 13 (1989), 15–43; and J. Der Derian, op. cit.
5. See D. Dewitt and D. Leyton-Brown, eds., *Canada's International Security Policy* (Scarborough, ON: Prentice Hall, 1995). A classic text on conflict management is R. Matthews, A. Rubinoff, and J. Gross Stein, eds., *International Conflict and Conflict Management: Readings in World Politics* (Scarborough, ON: Prentice Hall, 1984). Another subfield, known formally as peace studies, has focused on theories related to cooperation. In fact, the study of peace has a technical name: *irenology*. See J. Starke, *An Introduction to the Study of Peace (Irenology)* (Leyden: A.W. Sijthoff, 1968).

6. A popular text is K. Stiles and T. Akaha, eds., *International Political Economy: A Reader* (New York: HarperCollins, 1991); for a recent Canadian perspective, see D. Drache and M. Gertler, eds., *The New Era of Global Competition: State Policy and Market Power* (Montreal/Kingston: McGill-Queen's University Press, 1991).

7. See R. Riggs and J. Plano, *The United Nations: International Organization and World Politics* (Chicago: Dorsey Press, 1994); J. Ruggie and H. Milner, eds., *Multilateralism Matters: New Directions in World Politics* (New York: Columbia University Press, 1993); S. Krasner, ed., *International Regimes* (Ithaca, NY: Cornell University Press, 1983); and A. Cassese, *International Law* (Oxford: Oxford University Press, 2001).

8. For example, see M. Walzer, *Just and Unjust Wars* (New York: Basic Books, 1992); F. Kratchvil, *Rules, Norms, and Decisions: On the Conditions of Practical and Legal Reasoning in International Relations and Domestic Affairs* (Cambridge, UK: Cambridge University Press, 1989); R. Jackson, *The Global Covenant: Human Conduct in a World of States* (Oxford: Oxford University Press, 2000); and T. Pogge, ed., *Global Justice* (Oxford: Blackwell, 2001).

9. See J.D. Singer, "The Level of Analysis Problem in International Relations," *World Politics* 14 (1961), 77–92; K. Waltz, *Man, the State, and War* (New York: Columbia University Press, 1959); and R.C. North, *War, Peace, Survival: Global Politics and Conceptual Synthesis* (Boulder, CO: Westview Press, 1990).

10. In fact, much of this work is termed *diplomatic history*, and continues today.

11. For example, John Naisbitt argues that the larger the system, the more powerful and important are its smaller parts. See his *Global Paradox: The Bigger the World Economy the More Powerful Its Smallest Players* (New York: William Morrow, 1994).

12. These two dimensions are outlined in more detail in Joseph S. Nye Jr., *Bound to Lead: The Changing Nature of American Power* (New York: Basic Books, 1990).

13. J. Rosenau, *Turbulence in World Politics: A Theory of Change and Continuity* (Princeton: Princeton University Press, 1990), 6.

14. C. Lindblom, *Inquiry and Change: The Troubled Attempt to Understand and Shape Society* (New Haven: Yale University Press, 1990), x.

15. K. Boulding, "National Images and International Systems," *Journal of Conflict Resolution* 3 (June 1959), 120–31.

16. See A. Schlesinger Jr., *The Cycles of American History* (Boston: Houghton Mifflin, 1986).

17. D. Boucher, *Political Theories of International Relations: From Thucydides to the Present* (Oxford: University Press, 1998), 162–63.

18. See his *The Politics of Canadian Foreign Policy*, 2nd ed. (Scarborough, ON: Prentice-Hall, 1989).

19. See H. Bull, *The Anarchical Society: A Study of Order in World Politics* (London: The Macmillan Press, 1977).

20. For the most recent edition of this work, see *Power and Interdependence*, 3rd ed. (New York: Longman, 2001).

21. A wealth of literature has emerged on this theoretical proposition; for an excellent overview and sophisticated application see N. Ripsman, *Peacemaking by Democracies: The Effect of State Autonomy on the Post-World War Settlements* (University Park, PA: Pennsylvania State University Press, 2002). See also J. Owen, "How Liberalism Produces Democratic Peace," *International Security* 19, no. 2 (1994), 87–125.

22. C. Reus-Smit, "Constructivism," in S. Burchill et al., *Theories of International Relations* (London: Palgrave, 2000), 209–30, 221–22.

23. See M. Rupert and H. Smith, eds., *Historical Materialism and Globalization* (London: Routledge, 2002), for a series of sophisticated essays.

24. For a review of feminist approaches to IR see J. Ann Tickner, "Feminist Perspectives on International Relations," in Walter Carlsnaes, Thomas Risse, and Beth A. Simmons, eds., *Handbook of International Relations* (London: Sage, 2002), 275–91.

25. "Feminist Themes and International Relations," in J. Der Derian, op. cit., 340–62, 353. On Luxemburg, see R. Dunayevskaya, *Rosa Luxemburg, Women's Liberation, and Marx's Philosophy of Revolution*, 2nd ed. (Chicago: University of Illinois Press, 1991).

26. See E. Laferriere and P. Stoett, *International Relations Theory and Ecological Thought: Towards a Synthesis* (London: Routledge, 1999); and same, eds., *Global Ecopolitical Theory: Reflections and New Directions* (Albany, NY: SUNY Press, forthcoming).

27. A. Wendt, "Constructing International Politics," *International Security* 20 (Spring 1995), 73.

28. S. Guzzini, "A Reconstruction of Constructivism in International Relations," *European Journal of International Relations* 6 (Summer 2000), 149.

29. A. Wendt, "Anarchy Is What States Make of It: The Social Construction of Power Politics," *International Organization* 46, no. 2 (1992), 391–25.

30. E. Adler, "Constructivism and International Relations," in Walter Carlsnaes, Thomas Risse, and Beth A. Simmons, eds., *Handbook of International Relations*, 95.

31. Thus the title of Wendt's seminal article; see note 29.

32. For a spirited discussion and defence of this broad yet emergent thinking, see especially J. Der Derian, "Post-Theory: The Eternal Return of Ethics in International Relations," in M. Doyle and J. Ikenberry, eds., *New Thinking in International Relations Theory* (Boulder, CO: Westview, 1997), 54–76. For a general treatment of constructivism, see I. Hacking, *The Social Construction of What?* (Cambridge, MA: Harvard University Press, 1999).

33. Sir Harold Nicolson, *Diplomacy*, 3rd ed. (London: Oxford University Press, 1963), 5.

Suggested Readings

Note: Readers are reminded to consult the endnotes in each chapter for additional relevant readings.

Amstutz, M. *International Conflict and Cooperation: An Introduction to World Politics.* Madison: Brown and Benchmark, 1995.

Art, R., and R. Jervis, eds. *International Politics: Enduring Concepts and Contemporary Issues.* 3rd ed. New York: HarperCollins, 1992.

Brown, M., S. Lynn-Jones, and S. Miller, eds. *The Perils of Anarchy: Contemporary Realism and International Security.* Cambridge, MA: MIT Press, 1995.

Bull, H. *The Anarchical Society: A Study of Order in World Politics.* London: Macmillan, 1977.

Calvocoressi, P. *World Politics Since 1945.* 6th ed. London: Longman, 1991.

Carlsnaes, Walter, Thomas Risse, and Beth A. Simmons, eds., *Handbook of International Relations.* London: Sage, 2002.

Clark, I. *Globalization and IR Theory.* Oxford: Oxford University Press, 1999.

Cox, R. *Approaches to World Order.* Cambridge, UK: Cambridge University Press, 1996.

Dougherty, J., and R. Pfaltzgraff Jr. *Contending Theories of International Relations: A Comprehensive Survey.* 3rd ed. New York: Harper and Row, 1990.

Doyle, M. *Ways of War and Peace.* New York: Norton, 1997.

Gabriel, J.M. *Worldviews and Theories of International Relations.* New York: St. Martin's Press, 1994.

Galtung, J. "A Structural Theory of Aggression." *Journal of Peace Research* 1, (1964), 95–119.

Gill, S., and J. Mittelman, eds. *Innovation and Transformation in International Studies.* Cambridge, UK: Cambridge University Press, 1997.

Holsti, K.J. *The Dividing Discipline: Hegemony and Diversity in International Theory.* Boston: Allen and Unwin, 1985.

Katzenstein, P., ed. *The Culture of National Security: Norms and Identity in World Politics.* New York: Columbia University Press, 1996.

Kegley, C., and E. Wittkopf, eds. *The Global Agenda: Issues and Perspectives.* 4th ed. New York: McGraw-Hill, 1995.

Kennedy, P. *The Rise and Fall of the Great Powers: Economic Change and Military Conflict from 1500 to 2000.* New York: Random House, 1987.

Kratochwil, F. *Rules, Norms and Decisions.* Cambridge, UK: Cambridge University Press, 1989.

Kuhn, T. *The Structure of Scientific Revolutions.* Chicago: University of Chicago Press, 1962.

Lapid, Y., et al. "Exchange on the 'Third Debate.'" *International Studies Quarterly* 33 (1989).

Linklater, A. *Beyond Realism and Marxism: Critical Theory and International Relations.* London: Macmillan, 1990.

Little, R., and M. Smith. *Perspectives on World Politics.* 2nd ed. London: Routledge, 1991.

Machiavelli, N. *Machiavelli: The Chief Works and Others.* Edited by A. Gilbert. 3 vols. Durham: Duke University Press, 1989.

Mansbach, R. *The Global Puzzle: Issues and Actors in World Politics.* 3rd ed. Boston: Houghton Mifflin Company, 2000.

Morgenthau, H. *Dilemmas of Politics.* Chicago: University of Chicago Press, 1958.

Niebuhr, R. *The Structure of Nations and Empires.* New York: Scribner, 1959.

Ponton, G., and P. Gill. *Introduction to Politics.* Oxford: Martin Robertson, 1982.

Rourke, J., ed. *Taking Sides: Clashing Views on Controversial Issues in World Politics.* 7th ed. Guilford: Dushkin, 1996.

Said, A., C. Lerche, and C. Lerche III. *Concepts of International Politics in Global Perspective.* 4th ed. Englewood Cliffs, NJ: Prentice Hall, 1995.

Spegele, R. *Political Realism and International Theory.* Cambridge, UK: Cambridge University Press, 1996.

Steans, J. *Gender and International Relations: An Introduction.* New Brunswick, NJ: Rutgers University Press, 1998.

Sylvester, C. *Feminist International Relations: An Unfinished Journey.* Cambridge, UK: Cambridge University Press, 2002.

Walt, S. *The Origins of Alliances.* Ithaca, NY: Cornell University Press, 1987.

Weigall, D. *International Relations: A Concise Companion.* London: Arnold, 2002.

Suggested Websites

Note: The websites listed here both are general in nature (i.e., are broad resources for the study of IR) and pertain to IR theory in particular.

Libraries
Berkeley Sunsite Library Links Libweb
   http://sunsite.berkeley.edu/Libweb
Carrie: A Full Text Electronic Library
   http://kuhttp.cc.ukans.edu/carrie
Gabriel: Gateway to European Libraries
   http://portico.bl.uk/gabriel/en/welcome.html

General Political Science and International Relations Resources
ACUNS home page
   http://www.acuns.wlu.ca
Berkeley Institute of International Studies
   http://globetrotter.berkeley.edu
Canadian Institute of International Affairs (CIIA)
   http://www.ciia.org/index.htm
Foreign Affairs Canada (FAC)
   http://www.fac-aec.gc.ca/menu-en.asp
Foreign Policy
   http://www.foreignpolicy.com

International Affairs Resources Library
http://www.etown.edu/vl

International Relations and Security Issues: University of Oregon documentation center
http://libweb.uoregon.edu/govdocs/cat-ir.html

International Trade Canada (ITC)
http://www.itcan-cican.gc.ca/menu-en.asp

Policy.ca: A Non-Partisan Resource for the Public Analysis of Canadian Policy Issues
http://www.policy.ca

SACIS International Relations Resources
http://www.library.ubc.ca/poli/international.html

Social Science WWW Virtual Library
http://www.clas.ufl.edu/users/gthursby/socsci

United Nations Homepage
http://www.un.org

The Virtual Library: International Affairs
http://vlib.org/InternationalAffairs.html

Weatherhead Center for International Affairs
http://www.wcfia.harvard.edu

Yale University, International Affairs: Internet Resources
http://www.library.yale.edu/ia-resources/resource.html

CHAPTER 2

History and Global Politics: War and Peace

Even the ordinary, the "impartial" historiographer, who believes and professes that he maintains a simply receptive attitude; surrendering himself only to the data supplied him—is by no means passive as regards the existence of his thinking powers. He brings his categories with him, and sees the phenomena presented to his mental vision, exclusively through those media.

—*Georg Wilhelm Friederich Hegel*[1]

AN INTRODUCTION TO THE ROLE OF HISTORY

When the Cold War ended, it was tempting to proclaim that a new historical epoch had dawned. Certainly, much had changed: the Soviet Union had collapsed, Europe was no longer divided, and the threat of global nuclear war had receded. However, well into the second decade of the "post–Cold War" period it is abundantly evident that many things have not changed: the world remains divided into states, war still plagues many regions and peoples, and challenges such as poverty and infectious disease continue to confront us. And so, the end of the Cold War brought enormous changes to the edifice of global politics but few changes to its foundations. As we look further back into history, we can see how other dramatic events (such as the French Revolution and World War II) left both changes and continuities in their wake. This historical record is crucial to our understanding of contemporary global politics, because we need to understand the past in order to comprehend the present. The study of history can help us identify patterns of continuity and change, and divergence and convergence. History can provide case studies and examples for research into any number of questions, such as the origins of war, revolutions, and terrorism. For example, any attempt to understand or address the conflicts surrounding the disintegration of Yugoslavia would be incomplete without an examination of the long history between the Slovenian, Croatian, Serbian, and Bosnian Muslim (Bosniak) peoples. The same must be said of the conflict between Israel and the Palestinian people. The division of the Korean peninsula must be understood with reference to World War II and the **Korean War**. An understanding of the September 11, 2001, terrorist attacks against the United States cannot be understood without an awareness of the history of the Middle East or

American foreign policy. It is impossible to understand the persistent national unity question or First Nations issues in Canada without some knowledge of the colonial legacy in North America. In short, history is all around us, and we ignore it at our peril.

However, we must raise a few caveats about the use of historical material. As our opening quote suggests, rarely is the importance of perspective more evident than when examining history, since many different interpretations of past events exist. States tend to have official versions of historical events, often glorifying the importance and righteousness of their country's actions, or perhaps minimizing the harm caused in their name. For example, Japanese textbooks still omit many of the facts about Japanese foreign policy during World War II (see Profile 2.1). Indeed, many states have suffered collective amnesia after particularly traumatic events, including war-related atrocities.[2] Groups of individuals unified by race, religion, or clan ties also have their own interpretations of history, which are frequently at odds with the interpretations of other groups or state governments. Scholars of international relations also have divergent views of historical events, depending on their educational and social background, as well as their theoretical orientation. Furthermore, as feminists and postmodernists often argue, historical perspectives are inherently exclusionary. Many groups—including women and ethnic and religious minorities—argue, quite correctly, that they have been underrepresented in mainstream histories. Finally, history is vulnerable to radical revisions for political ends. For example, those who deny that the Holocaust ever took place are not interpreting history; they are trying to rewrite it for their own ends. Vigilance against this sort of manipulation is as important as respect for different perspectives (see Profile 2.1).

In this chapter, we will briefly examine world history with a view to highlighting three key themes in the relationship between history and global politics. First, history is most often presented, as it is here, as the history of war and conflict and the rise and fall of civilizations, states, and empires. This is the historical interpretation of the realist perspective on global politics, which emphasizes the continuity of power politics and the inevitability of war. Although this view of history is not necessarily inaccurate, as we will see in future chapters, it is incomplete. Second, developments in history have had a defining impact on the development of theories of war and peace. The two are inseparable, and the changing nature of global politics has stimulated the development of new theories and the adaptation of old ones. As we shall see, the theories we discussed in Chapter 1 are all grounded in historical developments and interpretations of those developments. Third, history reveals the importance of ideas as driving forces of change and transformation. History can also be interpreted as the history of ideas. Of course, historical interpretations are always undergoing revision, often by theories that seek to challenge prevailing assumptions. Hindsight is seldom 20/20, and the lessons of history are always subject to critical reassessment.

THE ANCIENT LEGACY: THE RISE AND FALL OF CIVILIZATIONS AND EMPIRES

In the Middle East, civilization first developed around 3500 B.C.E., in the basins of three great river systems. The river basin of the Tigris and Euphrates was the cradle for the early Mesopotamian city-states and the Assyrian (1244–605 B.C.E.) and Persian (550–331 B.C.E.) empires. The Nile River basin sustained the great Egyptian empires of the Pharaohs, which rose to the heights of the age of the pyramids (c. 2590 B.C.E.) and the XII (1991–1786 B.C.E.) and XVIII (1570–1320 B.C.E.) dynasties. The Indus River basin and the plain of Ganges was the cradle of India's early Harappa and Mohenjo-Daro civilizations (c. 2550–1550 B.C.E.). By this time, organized warfare was already a common phenomenon: civilization and war have a symbiotic relationship. Once individuals settle in a given area, and their very survival becomes tied to the land around them, the idea of ownership and the protective instinct become very

PROFILE 2.1 Abusing History

CONTENT OMISSION IN JAPANESE SCHOOL TEXTBOOKS

In 1997, a Japanese historian named Saburo Ienega won a landmark case before the Japanese Supreme Court. The court ruled that the Japanese Education Ministry broke the law when it removed certain material from a high school textbook written by Ienega. Since the 1950s, the Education Ministry has screened Japanese textbooks, removing references to the atrocities committed by the Japanese military in World War II. As a result, generations of Japanese school children have gone through school with only a general or highly sanitized account of Japan's war record, with key events and facts omitted or treated in an incomplete manner. One of the references removed from Ienega's textbook concerned biological warfare experiments conducted by the Japanese military on Chinese subjects during the war. Opposition to such references comes from nationalists (who regard such references as an attack on Japanese pride) and widespread ignorance of Japan's war record (largely a result of the education policy). Others hoped that the Ienega case might finally signal an end to this practice. Successive generations of Japanese textbooks have included more information and facts concerning Japan's role in the war. For example, most textbooks now mention the infamous "comfort women" who were forced into prostitution to serve the soldiers of the Japanese military. However, references to atrocities remain brief, and serious omissions are often made. Most textbooks acknowledge only partial responsibility, a key element of the Japanese government's position on Japan's wartime misdeeds. Japan provides an important example of how states and governments can abuse history through censorship and the suppression of unpopular ideas or facts.

Because of the court's decision, the material on biological warfare experiments was restored to Ienega's textbook. However, other references in his book were not restored.

JIM KEEGSTRA AND HOLOCAUST DENIAL

In 1985, an Alberta schoolteacher named Jim Keegstra went on trial in Red Deer, Alberta. Keegstra was charged with willfully promoting hatred against an identifiable group—Jewish people—from 1978 to 1982 while he taught social studies at Eckville High School in Alberta. Keegstra taught his students that Judaism was an evil religion that perverted the laws of God and condoned the harsh treatment of non-Jewish peoples. He implicitly taught his students that the Holocaust was a hoax and that an international Jewish conspiracy—called the "hidden hand"—was working behind the scenes with the support of Jewish financiers to establish a new world order in which there would be one government. According to Keegstra, Jews had infiltrated every institution of society, and this demanded that non-Jews be aware and watchful. Keegstra taught his students that conventional history books had lies in them, and in his classes he used books and pamphlets from his own library. Class exams and essays were based on these readings and class notes. In most respects, Keegstra's teachings were typical of anti-Semitic views, full of conspiracy theories based on historical distortions and outright inaccuracies, suppression and denial of evidence and fact, and barely concealed hatred. He passed these views on to students in a high school social studies class as fact, one example among many of the abuse of history by individuals or groups. Jim Keegstra was found guilty, was fined $5000, and was prohibited from teaching high school.

strong. As John Keegan suggests, "Pastoralism, and agriculture even more so, make for war."[3] Furthermore, large-scale warfare can be conducted only by systems of government that possess the organizational capacity to marshal surplus resources for war. In ancient civilizations, revenues from taxes and rents tended to go to war, worship, or welfare.[4]

Civilization in the Mediterranean was dominated by successive waves of Greek peoples, who established control over much of the Mediterranean (c. 1150–550 B.C.E.). In Asia Minor (present-day Turkey) the Greek advance clashed with the Persian Empire of Darius and Xerxes. Although Greece resisted conquest, the unity of the Greek city-states collapsed and the resulting

Peloponnesian War (431–404 B.C.E.) between Athens and Sparta enabled Macedon, under Philip, to dominate the Greek peninsula. The Peloponnesian War is regarded as an important case study in global politics (see Profile 2.2). Philip's son, **Alexander the Great**, conquered a dominion that stretched from Macedon to the Indus River. After Alexander's death in 323 B.C.E., a new power centre developed around Rome in central Italy, and soon expanded over the entire Italian peninsula (510–264 B.C.E.). Bolstered by an extremely effective military and administrative system, Roman rule (first as a republic and then as an empire) eventually stretched from present-day Spain to Mesopotamia. However, the Roman Empire declined due to internal decay, civil war, and barbarian invasions. The Roman Empire was divided in 330 C.E. when an Eastern Empire was created under the control of Constantinople (Byzantium). The Western half of the empire fell to invasion in the fifth century, but the Eastern half, known as the Byzantine Empire, survived another 1000 years. The Byzantine Empire eventually fell to Ottoman conquest with the fall of Constantinople in 1453 C.E. When the power of Rome collapsed, most of the infrastructure, knowledge, and security its rule had provided decayed, diffused, or disappeared as a Dark Age enveloped much of Europe and the Mediterranean. Many observers of our own time have argued that the United States exerts a greater hegemonic influence today than Rome at the height of its power: the decline and fall of Rome is therefore studied with great interest. Could American power fail, as did Rome's, and what would be the consequences?

In northern Europe, distinct cultural groups had developed by 800 B.C.E. Much of northern Europe came under Celtic domination by 450 B.C.E. The Slavic peoples established a centre of civilization in what is today central Russia. The decline and fall of the Western Roman Empire in the fourth and fifth centuries exposed Europe to numerous invasions from nomadic peoples living in

Remembering Rome. Will tourists of the future learn about the decline and fall of the American empire, as these tourists are learning of the decline and fall of the Roman Empire? (AP Photo/Plinio Lepri/CP Archive)

PROFILE 2.2 Thucydides (460–400 B.C.E.)

Thucydides is regarded as the greatest of the classical Greek historians because of his unfinished account of the Peloponnesian War between Athens and Sparta (Lacedaemon). Thucydides himself was an Athenian general who was exiled from Athens. In exile, he wrote a history of the war that was taking place all around him. His exhaustive and dramatic account can be read as a Greek tragedy, a story of human virtue and human deceit, and an exploration of the origins of war. Many contemporary students of global politics maintain that the themes in the book are applicable across time, culture, and place. Thucydides sought to draw themes and generalizations about the origin of all wars and to offer historical lessons for those who might read his work in the future. For Thucydides, "the growth in the power of Athens, and the alarm this inspired in Lacedaemon, made war inevitable." Thucydides thus identified the cause of war in the fear provoked by shifts in the distribution of power across the Greek city-states. His focus on the importance of power is most graphically illustrated in the famous Melian Dialogue, in which the powerful Athenians say to the less powerful Melians, "for you know as well as we do that right ... is in question only between equals in power, while the strong do what they can and the weak suffer what they must." Thucydides also reflected on the role of prominent individuals in the course of events, and he is considered one of the intellectual founders of political realism.

SOURCE: THUCYDIDES, *THE PELOPONNESIAN WAR*, THE CRAWLEY TRANSLATION (NEW YORK: THE MODERN LIBRARY, 1982), 14, 351.

northern and southern Europe (Goths, Vikings, Vandals, and Magyars), and from larger incursions that originated in central Asia (Huns, Avars, and, later, Mongols). These nomadic peoples also invaded Mediterranean Europe, China, India, and Persia, throwing all of these centres of civilization into ruin or near collapse. In northern Europe, the slow recovery from the fall of Rome began with the Carolingian empire (751–888 C.E.). However, this empire fragmented, and power devolved to local nobles, ushering in the era of European feudalism and the Middle Ages. Warfare, like political and economic life, was highly localized and in the hands of small numbers of nobles and knights who exerted a measure of political independence derived largely from the defensive strongholds of their castles. As political life was fragmented, so were economic and social life: loyalties were given to lord, religion, town, and guild. The unifying forces of nationalism and citizenship were far off. For Karl Marx, the development of feudalism was an important step in the evolution of society toward Communism. Nomad invasions continued: from 1206 to 1696 C.E. the Mongol empire launched repeated invasions into Europe, the Middle East, and Asia under Genghis Khan and his sons and grandsons. However, the unity of the Mongol empire broke down, and Mongol power receded in the face of an expanding Russia and China.[5]

Medieval Europe saw the spread of Christianity and the emergence of settled kingdoms, whose monarchs competed for territory and power. Through expansion, larger kingdoms ruled by dynastic monarchies began to consolidate themselves in Europe between the 10th and 13th centuries in what are today the British Isles, Germany, France, and Eastern Europe. Gunpowder facilitated this process of political consolidation: cannon could blow down castle or city walls, and with them went the ability of the knight or the town to resist a monarch with the wealth to purchase the new weapons. Cannons helped to make kings. This process of political consolidation, as well as the process of agricultural, industrial, and intellectual development, was slowed by climatic change, famine, plague, and war (in particular, the Hundred Years' War between England and France). European recovery from these events began in 1450, as the empires of France, the **Hapsburgs**, Muscovy/Russia, Sweden, and Lithuania all grew through the 15th and 16th centuries. However, resistance to amalgamation was widespread; for example, the Scots and Irish resisted the expansion of English rule. This resistance left a legacy felt to this day in the independence movements of Scotland and the violence in Northern Ireland. Italy was divided into city-states, and this period is often regarded as a case study in power politics (see Profile 2.3). Finally, the religious wars of the Reformation, culminating in the devastating **Thirty Years' War** (1618–48), dominated political, intellectual, and religious affairs (see Profile 2.4).

Despite this instability, this era was one of European exploration and expansion. European exploration by Portugal and Spain, and then by France, England, and Holland, was originally motivated by a desire to circumvent the controlling influence of the commercial cities (primarily Venice and Genoa) that dominated the medieval trade routes to central Asia and the Middle East. This brought a European presence to virtually all the inhabited continents. These events produced several lasting outcomes. The focus of political and commercial activity shifted from the Mediterranean to the trading empires of Western Europe. Trade and commerce became truly global in scope. The political and economic life of Europe was extended throughout the world, particularly in the form of growing rivalries between the trading empires, and the colonization of millions. Trade and political violence became inseparable. As

---

PROFILE 2.3 **Niccolo Machiavelli (1469–1527)**

Niccolo Machiavelli (Copyright © Bettman/Corbis)

Machiavelli was a civil servant and diplomat in the republic of Florence during the Italian city-states period of the 15th and 16th centuries. These city-states vied for power and influence, and advising the rulers of Florence during this struggle was Machiavelli's profession. When Florence fell in 1512, Machiavelli was without a job, and he spent the final years of his life writing books, including his most famous works, *The Prince* and *The Discourses*. Drawing heavily

on his examination of Greek and Roman writings as well as his own experience as a diplomat, he wrote of power, alliances, and the causes of conflict in the Italian city-state system. Much of what he wrote was aimed at the leaders—or princes—of states, advising them on the principles of statecraft, the conduct of their affairs with other princes, the importance of military force, and the lessons of historical experience. For Machiavelli, the security and survival of the state was the paramount concern of the prince; all other concerns were subordinated to this objective. The ends—the security of the state—justified the means necessary to achieve that objective. This Machiavellian approach to politics has often been criticized as amoral. However, Machiavelli argued that rulers must do what is in the best interests of the state; to do otherwise would in fact be immoral. Machiavelli also stressed that his advice to princes was based not on ethical principles or visions of the world as it should be or ought to be, but rather on the way the world was, according to historical and contemporary evidence. To act based on how one felt the world ought to be, as opposed to how the world really was, would be a recipe for disaster. In international relations, Machiavelli's emphasis on interests, power, and the conduct of statecraft is inseparable from the realpolitik tradition of political realism.

SOURCES: NICCOLO MACHIAVELLI, *THE PRINCE* AND *THE DISCOURSES* (NEW YORK: THE MODERN LIBRARY, 1950).

Jeremy Black argues, "Violence was employed in order to influence or even dictate the terms of trade, in particular by excluding rivals, rather than to gain territory."[6] Slowly but steadily, the age of European empire was beginning.

In the Middle East, the spectacular rise and expansion of Islam dominated the period after the fall of Rome. Established by the prophet Muhammad (c. 570–632 C.E.), Islam expanded within a century from the Arabian Peninsula to include North Africa and southern Spain, and the western reaches of China and India. After a period of great prosperity and cultural and intellectual development, internal dissension weakened the Arab Empire, which lost some of its territories in southern Europe and the Mediterranean to crusading Christians from Europe in the 10th century. However, Islam experienced a resurgence between 1300 and 1639, led by the Ottoman Empire. By 1354 the Ottoman Empire expanded through the Balkans east of the Adriatic and south of the Danube, and all around the Black Sea. By the time of Suleiman the Magnificent (1520–66), the Ottoman Empire was one of the great empires of the world. In the East, Islam spread through Persia, expanding to central Asia, southern Asia and the outlying provinces of China, as well as present-day Indonesia (see Map 2.1). However, the Islamic world began to fracture politically (as the Mughal Empire in India and Safavid Persia clashed with each other and the Ottoman Empire) and religiously (as the **Sunni** and **Shiite** branches of Islam came into conflict). Nevertheless, the Ottoman Empire remained a world power until World War I.[7]

PROFILE 2.4 **Thomas Hobbes (1588–1679)**

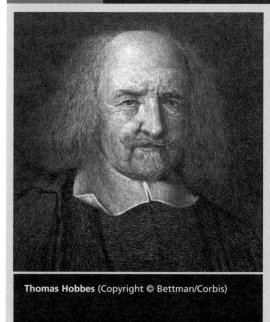

Thomas Hobbes (Copyright © Bettman/Corbis)

Hobbes was an English political philosopher who wrote in the turbulent years of the early 17th century, which were dominated by the Thirty Years' War in Europe. In England, Parliament was asserting its power against the monarchy, which would eventually lead to the English Civil War, and Hobbes, a royalist, was compelled to flee to France for eight years. In his writings, Hobbes's primary focus was politics within the state. In his most famous work, *Leviathan*, he depicted the condition of humanity in a hypothetical "state of nature" that would exist in the absence of governmental authority. This condition, he argued, would be characterized by anarchy, "a war of every one against every one," in which there would be "continual fear and danger of violent death; and the life of man, solitary, poor, nasty, brutish, and short." This condition could be avoided only by the creation of the "Leviathan," a state that or ruler who would establish and maintain order. Without order, there could be no civilization. Realists often describe international relations as a Hobbesian state of nature that lacks a Leviathan in the form of a world government or a dominant power to impose order. Like individuals in a state of nature, states exist in an anarchic environment, in a war of everyone against everyone, in which suspicion, distrust, conflict, and war are inevitable. In such a world, states must pursue their individual self-interests.

SOURCE: THOMAS HOBBES, *LEVIATHAN*, EDITED BY MICHAEL OAKESHOTT (NEW YORK: COLLIER MACMILLAN, 1974).

Map 2.1 The Extent of the Islamic World in 1500

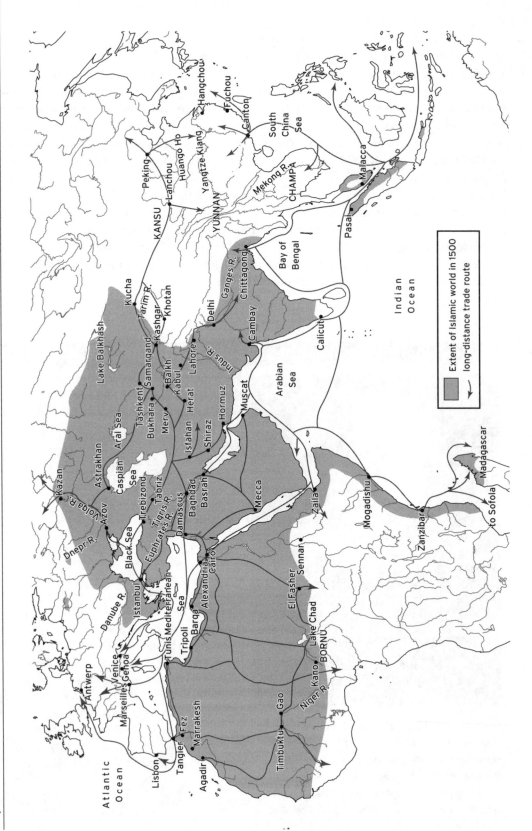

Extent of Islamic world in 1500

long-distance trade route

Atlantic
Ocean

Lisbon
Antwerp
Marseilles
Venice
Genoa
Tangier
Fez
Marrakesh
Agadir
Tunis
Tripoli
Barqa
Alexandria
Cairo
Timbuktu
Gao
Niger R.
Kano
BORNU
Lake Chad
El Fasher
Sennar
Zaila
Mogadishu
Zanzibar
to Sofola
Madagascar

Istanbul
Danube R.
Mediterranean Sea
Black Sea
Dnepr R.
Azov
Kazan
Volga R.
Astrakhan
Aral Sea
Lake Balkhash
Caspian Sea
Trebizond
Tabriz
Damascus
Baghdad
Basrah
Mecca
Euphrates R.
Tigris R.
Isfahan
Shiraz
Hormuz
Muscat
Herat
Merv
Bukhara
Samarqand
Balkh
Kabul
Tashkent
Kashgar
Khotan
Kucha
Tarim R.
Indus R.
Lahore
Delhi
Cambay
Calicut
Ganges R.
Chittagong
Arabian Sea
Indian Ocean
Bay of Bengal
Pasai
Malacca
CHAMPA
Mekong R.
YUNNAN
KANSU
Lanchou
Peking
Huango Ho
Yangtze-Kiang
Hangchou
Fuchou
Canton
South China Sea

SOURCE: *ATLAS OF THE ISLAMIC WORLD SINCE 1500* (OXFORD: PHAIDON PRESS LTD., 1982), 88.

In Asia, civilization began with the development of the first agricultural, hunting, and fishing communities around 4000 B.C.E., in what are today northern China, Southeast Asia, and India. The Shang Dynasty (1700–1100 B.C.E.) was the first historical dynasty in China, but like the enormous Harappa and Mohenjo-Daro civilizations of India (c. 2550–1550 B.C.E.), it succumbed to foreign invasion. A period of consolidation and fragmentation of political units in both China and India followed. In India, Chandra-Gupta seized the Magadhan throne, and his dynasty (297 B.C.E.–236 C.E.) succeeded in unifying most of the Indian peninsula under one ruler (see Profile 2.5). Invasion from the north fragmented the empire, which was re-established under the Gupta empires (320–410 C.E.). In China, the Chou Dynasty (1122–221 B.C.E.) replaced the Shang Dynasty. Between 1122 and 771 B.C.E., the empire maintained stability and order based on a feudal system. However, after 771 B.C.E. the empire increasingly fragmented into independent kingdoms engaged in almost continual conflict, culminating in the Warring States period of 403–221 B.C.E. (see Profile 2.6 and Map 2.2). This period in Chinese history is often used to illustrate the themes of power politics, in much the same way as the Italian city-state period. The victorious Ch'in Empire in turn collapsed and was replaced by the Han Dynasty (206 B.C.E.–220 C.E.), which established a prosperous and well-administered empire. Invasions of nomadic peoples prompted the Ch'in Empire and the Han dynasty to build the Great Wall of China. However, the Great Wall could not protect the Han Empire from internal disintegration, and nomadic invaders breached the wall in 304. Recovery was slow, but under the Sui (581–617 C.E.), T'ang (618–907 C.E.), and Sung (960–1279 C.E.) dynasties, China expanded and became prosperous, stable, and intellectually and scientifically advanced beyond any other civilization. Mongol invasion brought a period of decline, but under the Ming dynasty (1386–1644) Chinese power and prosperity were restored. In Japan, feudal warlords dominated politics until the Tokugawa shogunate unified Japan for 250 years before the forced opening of Japan by the European powers.

PROFILE 2.5 Kautilya (350–275 B.C.E.)

Also known as Chanakya or Vishnugupta, Kautilya was councillor and chief minister to Chandra-Gupta, the founder of the Mauryan Empire. His views survive in the form of the *Arthasastra (The Book of the State)*, a treatise on the science of politics, which is summarized in 6000 verses. Written primarily for rulers, the *Arthasastra* is essentially a compendium of reflections on human nature and the conduct of political activity. The *Arthasastra* contains advice to rulers on the conduct of war, foreign policy, and empire building. Kautilya argued that war must serve political objectives. The purpose of war is to strengthen an empire, not merely to destroy an enemy. Weakening an enemy before fighting was the key to success in battle and was more important than the force of arms. He advised that rulers should fight weaker states and ally with stronger ones. Kautilya warned that the natural enemies of a ruler were the rulers of bordering empires. However, the rulers of the empires that bordered one's neighbours were natural friends, a piece of advice more commonly captured by the phrase "the enemy of my enemy is my friend." Kautilya also commented on the qualities of the ideal ruler, who, he argued, had to possess good character and a willingness to listen to advisers (like Kautilya). The character of the ruler affected the character of the ruled. Kautilya warned about the corrosive effects of injustice and advised the ruler that it was his responsibility to keep the people content if rebellion, chaos, and violence were to be avoided. Kautilya is sometimes called the Indian Machiavelli, but it would be more accurate to call Machiavelli the Italian Kautilya. Many of the themes familiar to the power politics approach can be found in the *Arthasastra*, far removed from the time and context of Machiavelli's Italy.

SOURCE: ARADHANA PARMAR, *TECHNIQUES OF STATECRAFT: A STUDY OF KAUTILYA'S "ARTHASASTRA"* (DELHI: ATMA RAM AND SONS, 1987).

PROFILE 2.6 Sun Tzu

Sun Tzu was a warrior philosopher in fourth-century (B.C.E.) China. His *Art of War*, one of the greatest classical Chinese texts, is one of the most influential books on strategy ever written. *The Art of War* was evidently composed during the Warring States period in ancient China. The period was characterized by competition, shifting alliances, and warfare between the kings who struggled for power in Chou China. Sun Tzu drew heavily on Chinese philosophy—in particular, the Taoist works *I Ching* (*Book of Changes*) and the *Tao-te Ching* (*The Way and Its Power*)—and Chinese military practices in writing what is in essence a study of the conduct of competition and conflict on any level, from the interpersonal to the international. Most popularly known for its general advice that to win without fighting is best, *The Art of War* emphasizes shunning battle except when victory is assured, avoiding risk, dom-

inating an opponent through psychological means, and using time rather than force to wear an enemy down. The book also includes advice on preparations for war, battle tactics, sieges, manoeuvres, and the use of terrain. Much of the advice emphasizes the importance of achieving advantage over one's enemy before any military engagement. Today, military leaders, politicians, and business executives study *The Art of War* as a window on the political and business approaches of Asian countries and businesses. For international relations scholars, and realists in particular, the themes in Sun Tzu's work reflect the nature of politics and power in anarchic environments. Along with Kautilya, Sun Tzu offers evidence of the existence of power politics themes across time, place, and culture.

SOURCE: SUN TZU, *THE ART OF WAR*, TRANSLATED BY THOMAS CLEARY (BOSTON: SHAMBALA, 1988).

Map 2.2 China and the Warring States Period (300 B.C.E.)

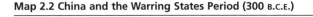

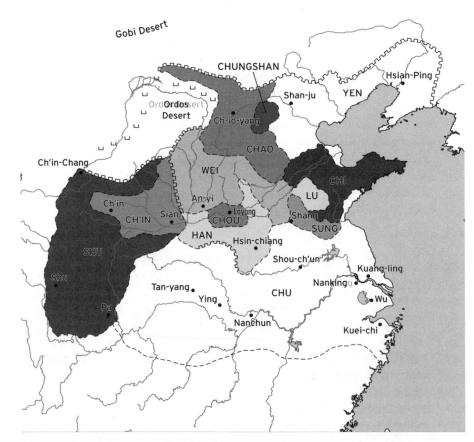

SOURCE: MARTIN VAN CREVELD, *THE ART OF WAR AND MILITARY THOUGHT* (LONDON: CASSELL AND CO., 2000).

In Africa, civilization developed in the Nile tributaries and in eastern Africa, where the Kingdom of Kush dominated from c. 900 B.C.E. to 400 C.E. Settlers moved through present-day Ethiopia into southern Africa, and **Iron Age** civilizations developed in central and southern Africa by 100 C.E. Great trading empires developed in Africa over the next 1000 years in what are today Zimbabwe, the Democratic Republic of Congo (formerly Zaire), and Ghana. The influence of Islamic expansion into North Africa contributed to the wealth of the Mali, Songhay, and the Kanem Borno empires, as Arab merchant colonies spread along Africa's north and east coasts (see Map 2.3). By the arrival of the first Europeans (the Portuguese in 1448), Africa had a thriving trading system based on gold, ivory, copper, and slavery. Portuguese, and later British and Dutch, trading stations spread rapidly in Africa. Trade with Europeans, at first based on gold, shifted to slaves, who were in demand for the colonial sugar plantations in South America and the West Indies. Between 1450 and 1870, some 15 million Africans were shipped across the Atlantic, 90 percent of them to South America and the Caribbean. Some regions of Africa suffered heavily from this trade; others profited. In 1800, most of Africa (except the northern areas held by the Ottoman Empire) remained independent.

In the Americas, the first large civilizations emerged in Mesoamerica (present-day southern Mexico) in the form of the Olmecs and Zapotecs and in the central Andes around 1000 B.C.E. In the fifth century C.E., the Olmecs and Zapotecs were conquered by the invading Maya (300–900 C.E.), who left an enduring cultural legacy in Mesoamerica. In North America, large trading and agricultural centres emerged in Hopewell territory (300 B.C.E.–550 C.E.) around

Map 2.3 African Empires in History

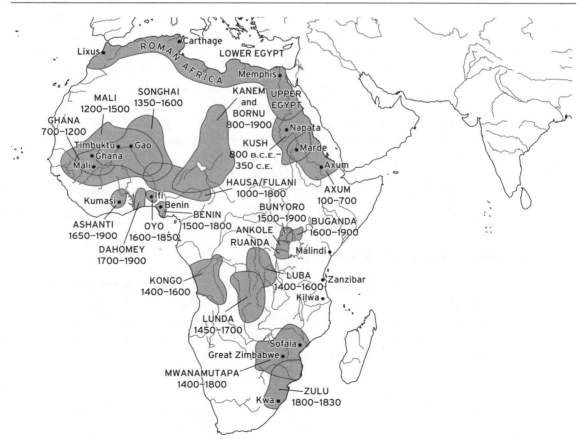

SOURCE: MARTIN GLASSNER AND HARM J. DE BLIJ, *SYSTEMATIC POLITICAL GEOGRAPHY*, 4TH ED. (NEW YORK: JOHN WILEY AND SONS, INC., 1989). REPRINTED WITH PERMISSION OF JOHN WILEY AND SONS, INC.

the southern Great Lakes. In Central America, Mayan civilization was followed first by the Toltecs in the 11th century, and then the Aztecs in the 13th century. Aztec expansion, conducted through a combination of alliance and conquest, reached its zenith under Montezuma II (1502–20). In South America, several diverse civilizations developed in the Andes and were unified under the Huari and Tiahuanaco empires (600–800 C.E.). These empires collapsed, and unity in the Andes was not achieved until the Inca civilization of the 15th century. The Inca Empire expanded between 1438 and 1525 to an area 4000 kilometres long and more than 300 kilometres wide, with a hereditary dynasty and an advanced bureaucracy and infrastructure (see Map 2.4). However, the Spanish on their arrival in the beginning of the 16th century overthrew the Aztec and Inca civilizations. The defeat of such large, established empires by small bands of Spanish soldiers has been explained by a combination of superior military technology, different cultural approaches to war, the introduction of disease, the assistance of native allies, Aztec and Incan political weakness, and even a superior Western way of war.[8] Elsewhere, the Portuguese slowly expanded into Brazil, establishing an extensive sugar industry worked by slaves. In North America, colonization was slower, and economic and political activity was based on a wide range of cultural traditions (see Map 2.5).

So far, the principal actors in this narrative have been the mighty civilizations and empires. The fate of less powerful actors in the evolution of human society is often rather stark. In a history defined by power politics, the less powerful (whether groups, city-states, or small empires) have been at a disadvantage. The weak have indeed suffered what they must. The less powerful have often disappeared from history altogether, been assimilated into larger political units, been forced to accept humiliating terms of surrender or tributary status, or been conquered and had their populations killed, scattered, or sold into slavery. For realists, this history confirms the centrality of power in the world, and the importance of those who wield the greater share of it. Across time and place, say realists, history is made by the powerful. The other, weaker actors, far more numerous though they may be, are largely irrelevant to the course of history. However, many weaker groups survived, maintaining their language, cultures, and traditions, only to re-emerge later to find independence or some measure of autonomy. Furthermore, weaker actors have made an impact in history, and even shaken empires and mighty civilizations through resistance and revolution.

At this point in history, the rise and fall of civilizations and empires came to be dominated by the slow but steady rise of Europe to a position of global dominance. The legacy of this historical development (also referred to as the rise of the West) remains with us in many forms today, including the nature of the modern state, the formalities of diplomacy, the spread of Western legal principles, and the impact of colonialism. The military and commercial power of Europe was to leave an indelible imprint on rest of the world.

THE MODERN STATE AND THE PEACE OF WESTPHALIA

The modern international system is often called the Westphalian state system. The Peace of Westphalia ended the Thirty Years' War in Europe in 1648 (see Map 2.6) and established a new order in Europe. From its origins in Europe, this system was extended throughout the world through the expansion of the European empires. With the virtual collapse of the European empires in the second half of the 20th century, what was left behind was a world of sovereign states that inherited the territorial, legal, and administrative structures and practices of the European tradition. However, it is important to recognize that the global expansion of the European state system does not provide a complete picture of the modern international system. After all, civilization existed in other regions of the world long before it existed in Europe, and these historical and cultural traditions continue to exert a profound influence on contemporary international relations, just as they did in the past.[9] Nevertheless, the Peace of

Map 2.4 The Peoples and Civilizations of Central and South America

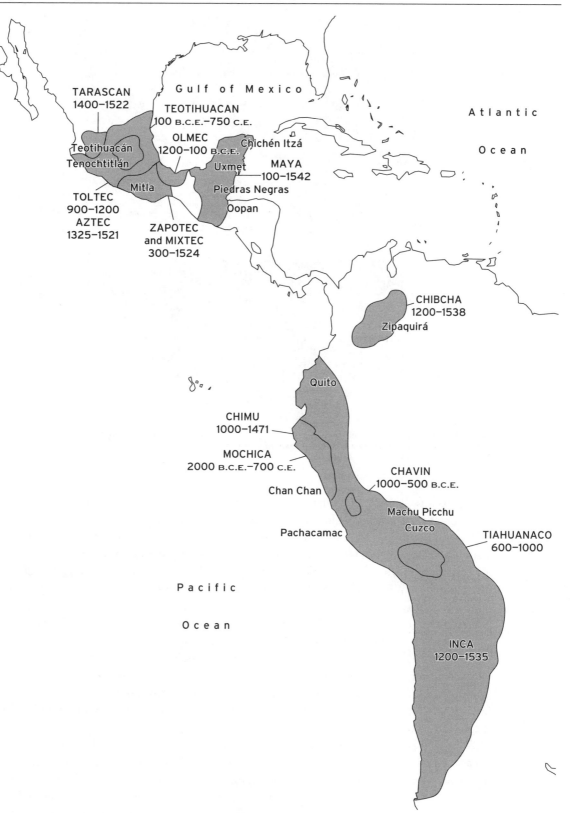

SOURCE: MARTIN GLASSNER AND HARM J. DE BLIJ, *SYSTEMATIC POLITICAL GEOGRAPHY*, 4TH ED. (NEW YORK: JOHN WILEY AND SONS, INC., 1989). REPRINTED WITH PERMISSION OF JOHN WILEY AND SONS, INC.

Map 2.5 The Peoples of North America (c. 1500)

SOURCE: "NATIVE AMERICAN PEOPLES," IN PATRICK K. O'BRIEN, ED., *ATLAS OF WORLD HISTORY* (NEW YORK: OXFORD UNIVERSITY PRESS, 1999). REPRINTED WITH PERMISSION OF OXFORD UNIVERSITY PRESS.

Westphalia is a significant benchmark, for it established the foundations of the modern state. Although the principles behind the sovereign state had begun to emerge before 1648, this date is a useful point of differentiation between medieval Europe and modern Europe, and "kingly states" and "territorial states."[10] In medieval Europe, kingly states were not fully autonomous or sovereign; they were under the authority (in spirit if not always in practice) of the Pope or the Holy Roman Emperor. Interference in the domestic politics of these states was commonplace, primarily in the form of efforts to convert the rulers or the people to one or another Christian denomination (a cause of the devastating Thirty Years' War). The Peace of Westphalia established the constitutional, legal status of states as territorial entities. The territorial state was sovereign, free to determine and practise its domestic affairs (meaning the religious denomination followed by the ruler and the people), and free from interference from the outside. The year 1648 thus marked the beginning of the supremacy of the state as a sovereign, territorial actor and the beginning of the end of the church's leading political role in European affairs.

This change occurred for a number of reasons. First, the power of the church had been weakened by the splits in Christendom, in particular during the Reformation. The horrors of the Thirty Years' War (in what is today Germany, two-thirds of the population was killed or displaced) revealed the fragility of Christian Europe. The answer was the sovereign state, which in principle was to be free from foreign interference in its domestic affairs. The hope

Map 2.6 Westphalian Europe, 1648

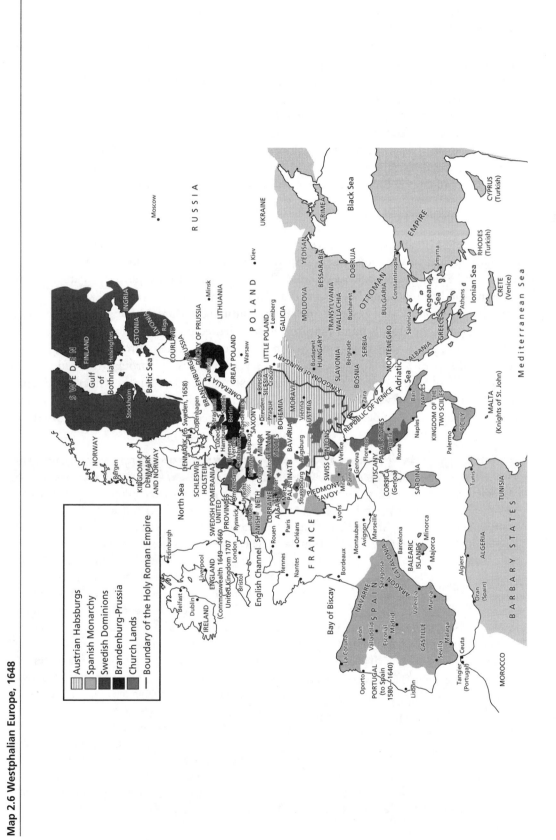

Legend:
- Austrian Habsburgs
- Spanish Monarchy
- Swedish Dominions
- Brandenburg-Prussia
- Church Lands
- — Boundary of the Holy Roman Empire

SOURCE: R. PALMER AND J. COLTON, *A HISTORY OF THE MODERN WORLD*, 8TH ED. (NEW YORK: McGRAW-HILL, 1995). REPRINTED WITH PERMISSION OF THE McGRAW-HILL COMPANIES.

was that devastating religious conflicts such as the Thirty Years' War might be prevented if the domestic affairs of territorial units were recognized as the exclusive reserve of the rulers of states. Second, some of the monarchs of medieval Europe had been slowly acquiring increased economic and military power, which enabled them to expand their territories through the amalgamation and conquest of less powerful political units. Furthermore, the establishment of hereditary monarchies promised increased stability with respect to leadership transition. The expansion of administrative and legal systems, with their power derived from the monarch, improved the capacity of rulers to exert control over their territories and subjects. For these reasons, the state emerged as the dominant political actor in international affairs and took on the distinctive characteristics that we recognize today (see Profile 2.7). As these developments occurred, European monarchies were embarking on the first period of European exploration and empire building. The world was entering the age of the European empires.

THE RISE OF THE EUROPEAN EMPIRES

In Europe, the 17th and 18th centuries were characterized by the territorial expansion of certain states in Europe and the overseas imperial conquests of the Spanish, Portuguese, Dutch, English, and French empires. Under Louis XIV, France was the most powerful state in Europe in the mid- to late 1600s, but Louis's territorial ambitions provoked repeated alliances against France, which soon became weakened by almost continual warfare. Although formally in existence until 1806, the **Holy Roman Empire** had fragmented into some 300 small principalities and city-states, which were vulnerable to conquest. Prussia (largely through the conquests of Frederick the Great) and Austria under the Hapsburgs (largely through the conquests of Prince Eugene of Savoy) emerged as the dominant states in central Europe. Great Britain, protected from continental wars by the English Channel, carved out a global empire that was the envy of the rest of Europe. The Russian Empire (especially under **Peter the Great** and

---

PROFILE 2.7 **The Nature of the Modern State**

Different theories abound in social science regarding the formation and present role of the state, but in typical international relations discourse, the term *state* refers to political entities with the following qualities:

- They occupy a defined territory.
- They possess a permanent population.
- They are sovereign with respect to other states (that is, they are, in principle, free from interference in their internal affairs).
- They are diplomatically recognized by other states.
- They possess a monopoly on the legitimate use of force, both within and outside their territories.

The terms *nation* and *state* are often used interchangeably in discussions of global politics. However, nation is not the same as state. The state refers to an autonomous institutional and legal structure that controls a defined territory. The state is a political and legal concept. Nation refers to a people who possess a shared sense of common descent and unifying ethnic, religious, or linguistic characteristics. Nation is an ethnic and cultural concept. A nation may exist without a state: two contemporary examples are the Kurdish and the Palestinian nations. A state that has essentially one nation living within its borders is called a nation-state. In practice, very few nation-states exist, because most states in the world today have many nations living within their borders. Canada and the United States are examples of multination-states. The distinction between state and nation is becoming increasingly important in international politics, as in many cases disputes between the nations living within multination-states have led to domestic instability, turmoil, and, in extreme cases, violence.

Catherine the Great) expanded to the borders of the Prussian and Austrian Empires in the west, the Ottoman Empire to the south, and China and the Pacific Ocean to the east.

However, revolts rocked the European empires in the second half of the 18th century. While the character of the revolts varied—from peasant unrest to a desire for independence in some regions—their origins lay in the spread of the Enlightenment, with its emphasis on the rights of individuals and its rejection of traditional authority. Enlightened monarchs, seeking reform, provoked a backlash of resistance from their aristocrats and provincial rulers. Provinces such as the Austrian Netherlands and Hungary rebelled against the centralization and reform policies imposed by Enlightened monarchs. Overseas colonies, such as those in Spanish America and Haiti, rebelled against imperial rule and demanded more autonomy or outright independence. The most significant revolution occurred in the Thirteen Colonies in America, and the independence of the United States of America would later be recognized as one of the most significant developments in world history. Many European regions, such as Corsica, Sardinia, Ireland, Serbia, and Tyrol, also sought independence. However, the most significant revolution in Europe occurred in France.

The French Revolution (1789–94) changed the face of Europe. The revolution began as a middle-class phenomenon but spread to worker and peasant uprisings. When Austria and Prussia threatened invasion, combining external threat with internal chaos, the monarchy collapsed. A republic was established that ruthlessly suppressed its enemies at home and defeated its enemies abroad. The ideals of the French Revolution spread across Europe: equality before the law, the abolition of feudalism, and the "rights of man." The French Revolution sparked the beginning of the development of modern nationalism, and while nationalism was initially rejected by monarchs (and unknown to the poor), it was to become one of the driving forces behind events in Europe and around the world. Nationalism would be a motive force for soldiers in battle, would enable the establishment of the first true national armies of citizen soldiers, would prove to be the inspiration for revolution, and would become inextricably linked with the institutional and legal apparatus of the emerging nation-state.

However, the French Republic did not survive. In 1799 a 30-year-old general named **Napoleon Bonaparte** seized power. During the subsequent **Napoleonic Wars**, Napoleon was practically unbeatable, defeating the armies of Austria and Prussia (see Profile 2.8). By 1810 most of western Europe was controlled by France. However, Napoleon could not subdue England, nor could he completely conquer the Iberian Peninsula. His invasion of Russia (1812) was a disaster, destroying most of the best formations in the Grand Army. Napoleon's final defeat at Waterloo in 1815 ended French dominance in Europe. The **Congress of Vienna** and the formation of the **Concert of Europe** followed, an attempt by the great powers to manage their relations and prevent a recurrence of the Napoleonic Wars. For almost 100 years, no continent-wide war occurred between the European great powers. However, it is inaccurate to say that peace prevailed, for several wars took place in this period, such as the Wars of Italian Unification, the **Crimean War**, and the Franco-Prussian War. Nationalism experienced a revival in the 1830s, and Greece, Belgium, and Norway obtained independence. Italy was unified in 1861 and Germany (as the German Empire) in 1871. In both cases, the union was accomplished through a combination of war and the use of nationalism as a political instrument.

The European empires also continued to expand abroad. However, by the 19th century the nature of European imperialism was beginning to change. As the Industrial Revolution took hold in Europe, imperial expansion was driven less by the search for trade goods and more by the search for raw materials and markets for products and by territorial competition between the imperial powers. Between 1880 and 1914 the European empires added more than 13.6 million square kilometres (approximately one-fifth of the world's surface) to their colonial possessions (see Profile 2.9). Much of this was acquired in the so-called scramble for Africa, which began in

PROFILE 2.8 Karl von Clausewitz (1780–1831)

Karl von Clausewitz was a Prussian military officer, instructor, and strategist who rose to the rank of general in the Prussian army and served on the Prussian general staff during the Napoleonic Wars. His famous work, *On War*, was written after the Napoleonic Wars and his recall to duty in East Prussia in 1830 (he died of cholera in 1831, leaving *On War* unfinished). Virtually unknown when he was alive, Clausewitz had a major influence on all subsequent intellectual thought on war; he viewed it as a timeless phenomenon with its own elements and dynamics. Written in the dialectical and comparative style associated with German idealist philosophy, *On War* is often misunderstood or misinterpreted. For Clausewitz, war is distinguished from other social activity by its large-scale violence, which tends toward absolute war—the highest degree of violence. However, wars usually fall short of this level, because they are mitigated by political goals and the characteristics of societies and their economies and governments. Clausewitz believed that even military force had to be subordinate to the political aims and objectives of the state. War, Clausewitz argued, should not be regarded as separate and distinct from peacetime politics among states. Rather, war should be seen as "a continuation of political activity by other means." In international relations theory, realists regard *On War* as an illuminating treatise of the prominence of the military instrument in the conduct of statecraft.

SOURCE: KARL VON CLAUSEWITZ, *ON WAR*, EDITED AND TRANSLATED BY MICHAEL HOWARD AND PETER PARET (PRINCETON: PRINCETON UNIVERSITY PRESS, 1976), 87.

earnest in 1882; by 1914, only Ethiopia and Liberia were independent. For peoples across the world, colonial rule meant the imposition of arbitrary political boundaries, a profound dislocation in local patterns of commerce, and the dominance of colonial administrations. These administrations ruled through a combination of political and economic coercion and reward, often co-opting local elites into the colonial system of governance. This period was the beginning of the expansion of capitalism, both in Europe and across the European empires around the world. For Marx, this was another key development in the social history of human society.

Because of the worldwide expansion of the European empires, wars in Europe quickly became global in scope. Wars in Europe between France, England, and Spain broke out in 1744 and 1754, and the supremacy of British naval power resulted in the loss of the French colonial empire in North America and the weakening of the Spanish empire. However, the rebellion of the 13 colonies in 1776 (aided by France) and the American War of Independence compelled Great Britain to recognize American independence in 1783. American expansion proceeded rapidly after independence (largely through the Louisiana Purchase, war with Mexico, and war against indigenous peoples). The **American Civil War** interrupted the territorial expansion of the United States. The American Civil War was notable as it foreshadowed the destruction of World War I, and illustrated the battlefield power of large mass armies equipped with the weapons of the Industrial Revolution. After the war, the United States continued to expand with the purchase of Alaska from Russia, and territorial gains through annexation or conquest in the Pacific (Hawaii, Samoa, Midway, and the Philippines) and in Latin America (Cuba and Puerto Rico). The hope of some in the United States for expansion into British North America had been thwarted in the War of 1812, and subsequently with the formation of Canada in 1867 and its expansion to include western territories. Nevertheless, by 1914 the United States was one of the world's leading powers.

In South America, Napoleon's invasion of the Iberian Peninsula enabled the Spanish and Portuguese colonies to attain independence. These revolutions were carried out by a colonial aristocracy that sought independence, but with minimal social change. For the most part,

PROFILE 2.9 The Colonial Legacy

Many of the states that we consider independent today were at one point colonized by imperial powers or listed as protectorates. Here we list just some of them. Note that some were colonized by more than one empire over time. For example, the Philippines, a Spanish colony from 1565, became a U.S. possession after 1898 (it was occupied by the Japanese during World War II, then achieved independence in 1946). Note also that many names have changed over time. For example, what is now known as Zimbabwe was once called Rhodesia; while under British control, Sri Lanka was known as Ceylon. What follows is a partial list of the imperial powers and some of their possessions over the course of the past few hundred years.

BRITAIN
Anguilla, Antigua and Barbuda, Australia, Bahamas, Bahrain, Botswana, Brunei, Canada, Ceylon, Dominica, Fiji, Gambia, Ghana, Grenada, Hong Kong, India, Ireland, Kenya, Malawi, Malaysia, Maldives, Malta, Nigeria, Papua New Guinea, Sierra Leone, South Africa, Uganda, Zambia, Zimbabwe

FRANCE
Algeria, Benin, Burkina Faso, Cambodia, Chad, Comoros, Dakar, Djibouti, French Cameroon, French Congo, Gabon, Haiti, Ivory Coast, Laos, Madagascar, Mali, Mauritania, Morocco, Niger, Senegal, Vietnam

THE OTTOMAN EMPIRE
Albania, Algeria, Anatolia (Turkey), Armenia, Bosnia-Herzegovina, Bulgaria, Cyprus, Egypt, Iraq, Jordan, Lebanon, Libya, Qatar, Yemen

SPAIN
Argentina, Bolivia, Chile, Colombia, Cuba, Ecuador, El Salvador, Equatorial Guinea, Guam, Guatemala, Honduras, Mexico, Nicaragua, Paraguay, Peru, Philippines, Puerto Rico, Venezuela

PORTUGAL
Angola, Azores, Brazil, East Timor, Equatorial Guinea, Guinea-Bissau, parts of India, Macao, Mozambique

GERMANY
Burundi, Cameroon, Namibia, Rwanda, Tanganyika (Tanzania), Togo, Western Samoa, other occupations during World War II

ITALY
Ethiopia, Libya, Somalia

THE NETHERLANDS
Dutch Borneo, Dutch East Indies, Dutch West Indies, Suriname

BELGIUM
Burundi, Rwanda, Zaire

DENMARK
Faroe Islands, north Germany, Greenland, Iceland, parts of Norway, Sweden

JAPAN
Bonin Island, Korea, other occupations during World War II

THE UNITED STATES
Guam, Hawaii, Midway, Panama, Philippines, Puerto Rico, Samoa, Cuba

colonial administrations were replaced by military dictatorships, which were to become an enduring feature of political life in Central and South America. In 1823, revolution created the Republic of Mexico. In South America, Spanish power was broken by revolt and military defeat at the hands of Simón Bolívar. Portugal agreed to Brazilian independence in 1822. In post-revolutionary Central and South America, territorial disputes between the newly independent countries were frequent and violent, and efforts to unite South America into a union failed at the Congress of Panama (1826). Export-driven economic growth and control of land increased the wealth of elites, but the bulk of the population lived in poverty (and still does).

In China, dominated by the Ch'ing (or Manchu) dynasty since 1644, trade with Europe—primarily in textiles, tea, porcelain, and opium—had flourished, although the empire was beset with rebellions and internal unrest. By the 1830s, China was the world's largest and most populous empire, but economic and administrative difficulties brought on by its growing population left China vulnerable to the Western powers, which sought to open the Chinese market to their products. The British won the Opium War (1839–42), seized Hong Kong as an imperial possession, and opened five (later many more) treaty ports. Inside these treaty ports, foreigners enjoyed exemption from Chinese law and rule. Other powers—especially Russia, France, and Japan—then expanded their authority in China, seizing territory and opening more treaty ports. The failure of the Manchu leadership to institute reform and resentment of foreign influence in China led to the so-called Boxer Rebellion in 1900. This strife was suppressed by the foreign powers in China, who in retribution seized more territory and privileges. These actions did not quell the rebellion and disaffection, and on the eve of World War I, China remained unstable and dominated by foreign colonial powers.

PATTERNS IN THE HISTORY OF WAR AND PEACE

Many themes and generalizations have been drawn from this conventional account of global history up to the world wars of the 20th century. As we will see, these themes formed the foundation of the realist approach to international relations.

- *The recurrence of war and conflict between civilizations, peoples, and empires.* The history of the world is a history of armed struggle. When cooperation does occur, it is in the form of alliances based on short-term need or convenience. War is a historical inevitability, and the prudent are prepared for it, even in times of peace. The price for those who are not able or willing to prepare for war is political domination or outright conquest.

- *The rise and fall of civilizations and empires.* The explanations for the rise and fall of the great world civilizations and empires are many and varied. First, the fate of these empires is often linked to the emergence and the decline of a single great ruler or the dynasty established. Second, empires have repeatedly been subject to conquest, either at the hands of other empires or from invasion by barbarian peoples. Third, many empires suffer from internal decline due to a combination of economic failure, social decay, and the costs associated with protecting a growing territory. The fortunes of civilizations, empires, and great powers are, therefore, historically fleeting; all eventually decline, to be superseded by others.[11]

- *The recorded political history of the world is primarily the history of the activities of great civilizations, empires, and states.* History is made by the powerful. For some, history can be described in terms of the machinations of **hegemonic powers**, civilizations, great powers, or empires that dominated all others. As a result, smaller or weaker civilizations, empires, and states have not been considered significant in history except as allies or pawns of the powerful.

- *The development of an intellectual tradition on statecraft, drawn from historical experience.* Advice to leaders—kings, princes, or emperors—was the privilege of only a very few individuals, but these individuals represent the beginning of thought on international relations, offering insights into the perspectives of those who lived hundreds and even thousands of years ago. What is revealing about these writings is the extent to which they share common themes about the nature of the conduct of international politics. Writers such as Sun Tzu, Kautilya, Thucydides, and Machiavelli established the intellectual foundation of the realist perspective in international relations. Meanwhile, as we will see, writers such as Mo Ti, Thomas Aquinas, Immanuel Kant, and John Locke established the foundation of the liberal perspective.

- *The rise of political geography and geopolitics.* Before World War II, diplomatic historians conducted most of the research on international affairs. These historians studied historical patterns and the leaders and officials of empires and states. Political geographers developed theories that promoted the decisive influence of geography on state power in general and the calculations of decision makers in particular. The use of geographic explanations or arguments to characterize political decisions or advocate certain policies became known as political geography or geopolitics. The most famous of these political geographers were Sir Halford Mackinder and Alfred Thayer Mahan (see Profile 2.10). Geopolitical thought has had a profound influence on the conduct of many states and has served as the cornerstone for many national security strategies, including those of the European imperial powers, Nazi Germany, and the United States during the Cold War.

The beginning of the 20th century was a time of general peace—with a few exceptions, most notably the Russo-Japanese War (1904–05)—and growing prosperity. International developments suggested that long-term peace was in the offing. No major war had occurred in Europe since 1870, and international law on armaments and war had been strengthened at

---

PROFILE 2.10

Sir Halford Mackinder and Alfred Thayer Mahan

SIR HALFORD MACKINDER (1861–1957)

Sir Halford Mackinder was a British geographer who wrote a famous paper on "the geographical pivot of history," which he presented to the Royal Geographical Society in 1904. Mackinder argued that the world could be divided into three regions: the Heartland (at the centre of Eurasia); the Interior or Marginal Ring (Europe, the Middle East, and southern and northern Asia); and the Ring of Islands or Outer Continents (North and South America, Africa, and Australia). For Mackinder, the geographic pivot in world politics was the Heartland. From this view he derived the following geopolitical calculation: whoever controls the Heartland controls the World Island (Europe, Asia, and Africa); whoever controls the World Island controls the world. He concluded that Russia must not be permitted to expand into the lands of the Interior Ring as this would lead to Russian world domination. His theory was influential in Europe, particularly in Germany, where it contributed to the geopolitical views of Karl Hausofer, who advocated *Lebensraum*, German territorial expansion eastward. Mackinder's theory also influenced U.S. strategy to contain the Soviet Union, which already dominated the Heartland, during the Cold War. However, Mackinder's many critics have pointed out that his theory could not explain why tsarist Russia and the Soviet Union had not dominated the world despite controlling the Heartland. Nor

could his theory explain the dominance of the United States for most of the 20th century. Others criticize his view as a thinly veiled rationale for the maintenance of the British Empire, which controlled territories in the Middle East and southern Asia and so served as the guardian of the Interior Ring against aggression from the Heartland.

ALFRED THAYER MAHAN (1840–1914)

Alfred Thayer Mahan was an American naval strategist. His most famous work, *The Influence of Sea Power on History 1660–1783*, influenced the naval doctrines of the United States and the European imperial powers. His central conclusion was that naval powers, rather than land powers, were dominant in history. For Mahan, the principles of naval strategy and naval warfare remained constant, and these principles pointed to one historical theme. Contrary to land power explanations of world politics, the key to state power lay in powerful naval forces supported by a network of overseas possessions and naval bases. From these possessions and bases, naval forces could dominate the seas, and with that dominance came control of the merchant traffic of the world. The influence of Mahan's views was felt in Europe in the struggle for naval mastery between Great Britain and Germany, and in the United States, where it provided a rationale for American imperial expansion during and after the Spanish–American War.

Map 2.7 The World According to Mackinder

SOURCE: GERARD CHALIAND AND JEAN-PIERRE RAGEAU, "THE WORLD ACCORDING TO MACKINDER," FROM *STRATEGIC ATLAS: COMPARATIVE GEOPOLITICS OF THE WORLD'S POWERS*, 3RD ED. (NEW YORK: HARPERCOLLINS, 1993), 21. COPYRIGHT © 1993 BY GERARD CHALIAND AND JEAN PIERRE RAGEAU. REPRINTED BY PERMISSION OF HARPERCOLLINS PUBLISHERS. INC.

the Hague Peace Conferences of 1899 and 1907. The prevailing sentiment was that increasing trade and industrialization was making war more costly and less likely (this argument is often made by liberals today). However, this sense of optimism began to erode as disputes between the European great powers and their alliances intensified. Nationalist rhetoric grew, an arms race broke out, and war flared in the Balkans (1912–13). Nevertheless, few sensed the impending disaster that would soon befall Europe.

WORLD WAR I

The beginning of World War I is generally marked by the assassination of the heir to the throne of the Austro-Hungarian Empire, Austrian Archduke Franz Ferdinand, at Sarajevo, on June 28, 1914. The assassination of the archduke set in motion a series of actions and reactions that led the European powers to war. However, while this event may indeed have been the spark that set Europe ablaze, the fuel for the conflict had been accumulating for years. Europe had divided into two hostile alliances: the Triple Alliance of Germany, Austro-Hungary, and Italy; and the Triple Entente of Great Britain, France, and Russia. The latter was wary of the increasing power of Germany and its desire for a place in the sun with the other established imperial powers. The Triple Alliance feared encirclement and the expansion of Russian power in the Balkans. Commercial rivalry, disputes over colonial possessions, and a naval arms race between Great Britain and Germany intensified the antagonism between these two countries. (The naval arms race would later become one of the most studied arms races in history, as analysts sought to learn lessons that could be applied to the nuclear arms race between the superpowers during the Cold War.) In all countries, enormous national armies could be created rapidly through the mobilization of the citizenry, trained for war through **conscription**. Most European military establishments believed that success in a future war would go to the country that mobilized most rapidly and launched its offensive first. This "cult of the offensive" existed in most countries.[12] In particular, German planning sought to avoid a two-front war against Russia and France simultaneously by attacking and quickly defeating France before turning against Russia.

The mood in most societies was one of extreme nationalism (which was often explicitly racist) and faith in the superiority of one's own country and people.

After the assassination of the Archduke, Europe began its slide toward war. The assassination, planned in Belgrade by Serbian nationalists, intensified Austro-Hungarian concerns about the threat Serbia posed to Austro-Hungarian power in the Balkans. Germany, hoping to deter Russian intervention in the Balkans in support of its Serbian ally, issued its famous "blank cheque" of support to Austria. Austria then delivered an ultimatum to Belgrade and declared war on July 28, 1914. Russia, fearing Austrian hegemony in the Balkans, mobilized to support Serbia, a fellow Slavic country. Germany then mobilized and, as called for in prewar planning, attacked France through neutral Belgium. Germany's violation of Belgian neutrality brought Great Britain into the war. The war took on a global aspect with Japan's declaration of war on Germany, the outbreak of fighting between British and German colonial forces in Africa, and the entry into the war of the Ottoman Empire. For many, war was welcome; nationalist fervour brought cheering crowds into the streets and long lines at recruiting stations. Before its horrors were common knowledge, war held an air of adventure. The mood among decision makers was more sombre. On August 3, following a speech to Parliament in which he confirmed British intentions to enter the war, British Foreign Minister Sir Edward Grey remarked: "The lamps are going out all over Europe; we shall not see them lit again in our lifetime."[13] And yet, throughout Europe, the expectation was that the war would be a short one, with the recently mobilized soldiers home by Christmas.

The German offensive into France was conducted according to the carefully crafted **Schlieffen Plan**, which saw Germany's armies in the west move through Belgium and northern France toward Paris. In doing so, Germany violated Belgian neutrality, another testament to the fate of weaker powers in great-power politics. However, Germany failed to defeat France quickly. The firepower of modern weapons soon brought manoeuvres to a standstill, and by October 1914 a front line of trenches, barbed wire, and machine guns extended from the Swiss border to the English Channel. Offensives designed to break the stalemate by punching through these defensive lines with massive infantry attacks failed repeatedly, with great loss of life (see Profile 2.11 for Canada's experience). Germany embarked on a submarine warfare campaign against merchant ships at sea. With the exception of the Battle of Jutland, the massive battleship fleets that had been built during the Anglo-German naval arms race saw little action (the British battle fleet did impose a naval blockade against Germany, blocking German access to products and materials from abroad). The German decision to expand the submarine campaign also brought the United States into the war against Germany on April 6, 1917.

In the east, military defeat and economic chaos had led to the collapse of the Russian war effort and the Bolshevik Revolution of October 1917. The Romanov dynasty was overthrown, and the new **Bolshevik** government sued for peace. With the eastern front secured, Germany transferred its forces west for a final great offensive aimed at defeating Britain and France before the United States could mobilize. The offensive, launched on March 21, 1918, failed with heavy losses, and in July the French, British, and Americans began their counteroffensive, which was to be the decisive turning point of the war. By September, Germany was near defeat. Its armies were exhausted, and its economy was in shambles from the war effort and the British naval blockade. Austria was near collapse. Fearful of domestic unrest and the possibility of a Bolshevik revolution in Germany, the German government sued for an **armistice**, which went into effect on November 11, 1918. Seven months later, on June 28, 1919, Germany signed the Treaty of Versailles.

PROFILE 2.11 Canada and World War I

We will always remember. Lance Corporal Iden Herbert Baldwin when he was 22 years old and waiting to return to Canada after fighting in World War I. There are very few Canadian World War I veterans left alive. Iden Baldwin died on January 31, 2003, at the age of 105. (CP Photo/Globe and Mail)

Canada entered World War I when Great Britain declared war on August 4, 1914. Canadian Prime Minister Robert Borden had promised Canadian support for the empire's war effort. Little dissent existed in Parliament as the Liberals under Wilfred Laurier supported Canada's entry into the war. However, dissent was expressed in French Canada, where many French Canadians opposed Canada's involvement in the war and the increasing sacrifices the war effort entailed. The First Canadian Division entered the battle lines in France in February 1915, although most of the senior commanders were British. Canadian troops performed admirably in the field during the

Battle of Ypres in April 1915. The Canadian contingent in Europe grew rapidly, and a Canadian Corps (composed of three divisions) was established in mid-1915. However, the war had settled into a costly stalemate, and losses at the front made conscription an issue in 1917. The conscription crisis was very divisive, encountering strong opposition in French Canada and among workers and farmers. In April 1917, Canadian troops seized Vimy Ridge at a cost of 3598 lives after repeated Allied efforts had failed. This success was followed by the Passchendaele offensive, a sobering experience in which the Canadian Corps occupied a few square kilometres of mud and water-filled craters at a cost of 8134 lives. By this time Canadian officers under General Arthur Currie commanded the Canadians. By the end of the war, 56 634 Canadians had been killed and more than 150 000 wounded.

Some maintain that Canadian nationalism was born at Vimy Ridge in 1917—that Canada's service and sacrifice developed a sense of Canadian independence. Sir Robert L. Borden himself was to argue that the war had made Canada an international personality and entitled Canada to a certain independent status. Canada was a signatory to the **Versailles Treaty**, and it received a seat in the League of Nations. Others would point to the political and workplace advances of Canadian women during the war years. Others, however, caution that the conscription crisis and labour disputes divided the country and that, for many, the war meant lost loved ones and shattered lives.

The consequences of World War I were enormous. More than 13 million people had died, and millions more were wounded. In 1918, the German general Erich Ludendorff coined the term "total war" to capture a qualitatively different form of warfare. The state, nationalism, and the Industrial Revolution had combined to create a lethal mix. Large, conscripted armies, motivated by nationalism and equipped, transported, and supplied by the technologies of the Industrial Revolution, were guided by the unparalleled strategic planning capacities of the modern state into organized slaughter by the killing machines of modern war. Entire societies, and not just militaries, became targets in total war. As Richard Overy has remarked, "To be able to wage total war states would have to mobilize all the material, intellectual, and moral energies of their people; by implication the enemy community as a whole—its scientists, workers and farmers—became legitimate objects of war."[14] Three empires had collapsed—the Austro-Hungarian, Russian, and Ottoman—and new independent nations emerged in

Map 2.8 Territorial Changes in Europe after World War I

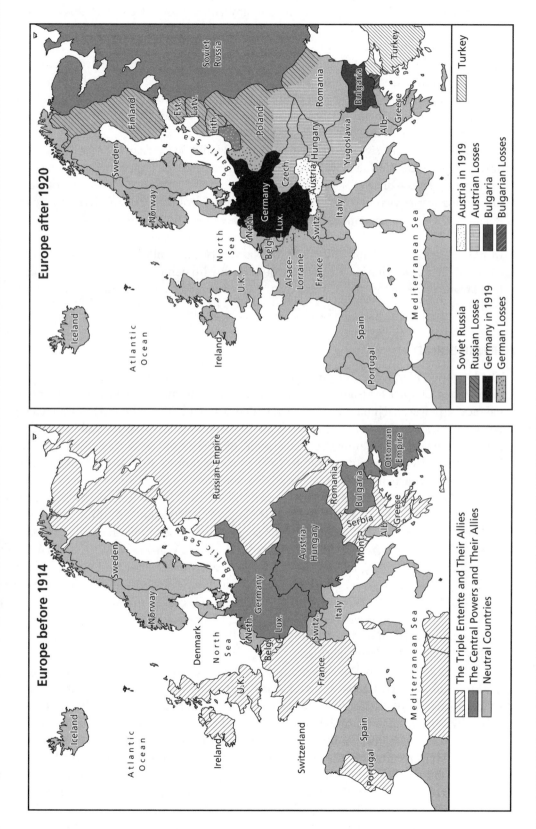

Europe after 1920

Soviet Russia
Russian Losses
Germany in 1919
German Losses

Austria in 1919
Austrian Losses
Bulgaria
Bulgarian Losses

Turkey

Europe before 1914

The Triple Entente and Their Allies
The Central Powers and Their Allies
Neutral Countries

SOURCE: GERARD CHALIAND AND JEAN-PIERRE RAGEAU, *STRATEGIC ATLAS: COMPARATIVE GEOPOLITICS OF THE WORLD'S POWERS*, 3RD ED. (NEW YORK: HARPERCOLLINS, 1993), 34. COPYRIGHT © 1993 BY GERARD CHALIAND AND JEAN-PIERRE RAGEAU. REPRINTED BY PERMISSION OF HARPERCOLLINS PUBLISHERS, INC.

Czechoslovakia, Poland, Yugoslavia, Finland, Estonia, Latvia, and Lithuania (see Map 2.8). The Russian Revolution had brought a change in government and ideology to Russia that would shape international politics in the years to come. Fear of the Russian Revolution was widespread, as was concern over the emergence of **fascism** as a major political movement. Nationalism, far from eroding in the face of the war, intensified, and the peace settlement left dissatisfied minorities across Europe. The United States emerged as a global power but slowly turned to **isolationism** with respect to European affairs. Finally, dissatisfied revisionist powers emerged on the continent; the Soviet Union sought to regain lost territories, and Italy and Hungary sought revisions of borders.

However, the most significant revisionist state would be Germany. Under the terms of the Treaty of Versailles, Germany was prevented from possessing a large army or modern military equipment, the province of Alsace-Lorraine was returned to France, Germany's colonies were distributed to the victors, East Prussia was separated from the rest of Germany by the new Poland, the German government was forced to pay reparations, and war guilt was assigned to Germany. The legacy of Versailles would cause much bitterness in Germany, bitterness that would be exploited by Adolf Hitler and the Nazi Party. The ambitions of the revisionist countries and their authoritarian ideologies would clash with democratic, antirevisionist countries that favoured the status quo. Ultimately, the war to end all wars had merely set the stage for World War II.

THE INTERWAR PERIOD

The horror of World War I inspired efforts to make that war "the war to end all wars." As we discussed in Chapter 1, idealism gained credence as an alternative to the realpolitik behaviour, balance of power machinations, and secret alliances that had led the world to such a disaster. For idealists, such as U.S. President Woodrow Wilson, the hope was to establish a new order, based on the League of Nations, collective security, the rule of law, and arms control. However, behind the outward unity displayed by the victorious powers after World War I were serious disagreements, particularly among Great Britain, France, and the United States, over the treatment of Germany. France was the most uncompromising. It had been devastated during the war: 1 355 800 French citizens had been killed and 4 260 000 wounded; almost 300 000 homes had been destroyed; and the country was heavily in debt due to the financial costs of the war effort.[15] The French were not willing to place their faith in Wilson's collective security concept (see Chapter 1), deciding instead that a system of alliances built against Germany would be the best guarantee of peace. Another matter of dispute was the issue of reparations. France and Great Britain wanted Germany to pay for the entire cost of the war, and Germany began to default on reparations payments as early as 1920. In response, the French government acted unilaterally and occupied the Ruhr Valley in 1923. Within Germany, popular resentment against the Versailles Treaty increased.

In the interwar period, Russia went through the throes of revolution to resurface as a major actor in Europe. Increased economic hardship, growing hunger, and the clear incompetence of the Russian political and military leadership in the war led to the overthrow of the tsar in February 1917. The Duma, or Parliament, assumed power, but its decision to continue the war alienated the people, leaving it vulnerable to revolutionary organizations of workers, called Soviets, and the return from exile of Vladimir Lenin, who promised peace, land, bread, and all power to the Soviets (see Chapter 1). The provisional government collapsed, and Lenin's Bolsheviks seized power in the October revolution. Lenin's first task was to obtain peace, and despite opposition he accepted unfavourable terms from Germany in return for peace in the Treaty of Brest–Litovsk (1918). Peace, however, was short lived. Civil war broke out as the

White Russian movement, hoping to restore the monarchy, attacked Bolshevik forces with support from intervening armies from Britain, France, and the United States. War weariness broke the spirit of the intervening powers, and by 1921 the Bolsheviks prevailed. The Union of Soviet Socialist Republics (U.S.S.R.), often called the Soviet Union, was established in December 1922. By 1925 the Soviet Union had recovered economically and was reaching out internationally, even obtaining diplomatic recognition from France, Great Britain, and other European countries. Lenin's death in 1924 eventually brought Josef Stalin to power, who, with his doctrine of "socialism in one country," embarked on a massive program of industrialization and agricultural collectivization, as well as purges of the Communist Party and the Red Army that left millions dead. However, the Soviet Union was firmly established as a great power.

In the Middle East and Asia, the interwar period saw the fall of an empire, chaos in another, and the rise of a new great power. As one of the defeated powers, the Ottoman Empire was partitioned by the victorious states. These humiliations sparked a nationalist uprising led by Mustapha Kemal (Ataturk) that marked the beginning of a secular Turkish state, the heir to the Ottoman legacy. China experienced a period of chaos, instability, and invasion in the interwar period. Successive central leaderships proved incapable of addressing economic problems or the issue of foreign interference in China. Central rule broke down, and provincial warlords assumed local power. Under the leadership of Sun Yat-sen and then Chiang Kai-shek, the Nationalist (Koumintang) Party, allied with the Chinese Communists, attempted to suppress the warlords, end foreign power in China, and reunify the country. After initial success in the north of the country, the alliance between the Koumintang and the Communists broke down. However, Japan intervened in Manchuria in 1931, and Chiang now had to meet two threats simultaneously: the Japanese; and the Communist movement in the countryside, led by Mao Tse-tung. Chiang's efforts to crush Mao's Communists forced Mao and his supporters into the famous Long March of 1934–35. The Nationalist and Communist forces were to battle the Japanese until the end of World War II.

The interwar period saw the rise of a new power in Asia: Japan. The Meiji Restoration of 1868 reopened Japan to the world after 200 years of isolation. Japan embarked on a period of rapid industrialization and established an empire on the mainland. Japan was recognized as a victorious power at the Paris Peace Conference and was given great-power status and a permanent seat on the Council of the League of Nations. However, the Great Depression hit Japan hard as the rise of trade barriers around the world hurt the trade-dependent Japanese economy. The government fell, and was replaced by a military government. These changes, coupled with China's efforts to recover Manchuria (an important source of raw materials and industrial production) from Japan, led to the Japanese fabrication of an attack on a Japanese railway line, which provided the pretext for a Japanese military intervention in Manchuria in 1931. The League failed to respond forcefully, issuing a report in 1933 calling for Chinese control of Manchuria with protection of Japanese interests. The collective security provisions of the League were not invoked. In response to the League report, Japan walked out of the League of Nations. In 1937, Japan invaded China, and tensions between Japan and the United States escalated over the invasion and trade issues.

The interwar period also saw the rise of two revisionist powers in Europe. In Italy, fascist leader Benito Mussolini came to power in 1922, and in 1935, Italy attacked Ethiopia. The League responded quickly, identifying Italy as the aggressor and voting to implement an embargo on armaments against Italy. However, all other products (including oil, coal, and steel) could still be traded to Italy, and the enforcement of the embargo was never effective. The collective security principle was never activated. The Italian venture was successful, and in 1936 Mussolini proclaimed Ethiopia a province of Italy. In 1937, Italy withdrew from the League of

Nations and annexed Albania in 1939. In Germany, economic disaster struck. A combination of a weakened economy and the onset of the **Great Depression** in Europe devastated the value of the German mark as inflation spiralled out of control. It was in this economic and political context that the Nazi Party rose to prominence in Germany, on a platform of resentment toward the Versailles Treaty, renewed German nationalism, and **anti-Semitism**. Under Hitler, Germany began to rearm, with no forceful response from Great Britain or France. In 1938 Germany annexed Austria into the Third Reich, and demanded a solution for the Sudetenland Germans, who lived in Czechoslovakia. At Munich, the British and French governments sought to appease Hitler and accepted the incorporation of the Sudetenland into the Third Reich. This region was also Czechoslovakia's main line of defence; when it was annexed, the country was in a hopeless position to resist any further German expansion. In April 1939, Hitler occupied the rest of Czechoslovakia, and once again a small state had fallen victim to the power politics of the great powers. Subsequent German demands for territory around Danzig from Poland prompted the British and the French to become allies to protect Poland.

In the face of increasing international diplomatic and economic tensions, the League was increasingly unable to act effectively. For most of its history, the League counted only four of the seven great powers among its membership, and as a result it could not serve as the universal organization it was intended to be. The League was further damaged when it could not take effective action against Italian aggression in Ethiopia, Japanese aggression in Manchuria, and later German and Soviet aggression in Europe. The aims of the revisionist powers of the 1930s were fundamentally at odds with the principles of the Covenant. Although some League committees continued to operate during the war, the League was irrelevant as an instrument of peace and security. In April 1946, the League was formally disbanded. The experience of the League would be remembered after World War II, and the lessons of the League's shortcomings would play an important role in the design of the United Nations Charter.

The revisionist powers of the interwar period—Germany, Italy, and Japan—encountered limited resistance to their territorial gains and aggressive acts. Why? The experience of World War I was clearly a factor; no one wanted to risk another world war. The neutralist position of the United States also weakened the strength of nonrevisionist states. Without U.S. support and active involvement in world affairs, countries such as Great Britain and France lacked the support to decisively respond to aggression, or so they believed. In addition, all countries in the world were grappling with enormous domestic economic problems, especially after the stock market crash of 1929. In the face of huge domestic economic hardships, international aggression in Manchuria and Ethiopia seemed very far away. Countries had turned inward: the United States had retreated into isolationism, the British behind the English Channel, and the French behind the supposedly impregnable fortifications of the Maginot Line. As a result, the policy toward revisionist countries, in particular toward Germany, became known as **appeasement**: giving in to the demands of revisionist states in the hope that they would soon be satisfied with their gains. Munich, and appeasement, would later be vilified as a naïve and idealistic failure. The lesson to be learned was never to appease dictators, a lesson that would be applied toward the U.S.S.R. during the Cold War and to Iraqi dictator Saddam Hussein. However, appeasement was not a policy of blind subjection to threats. The publics in Great Britain, France, and the United States were opposed to war, and all countries were unprepared for it. Appeasement might satisfy Hitler and Mussolini; if not, it would at least buy time to rearm.

WORLD WAR II: TOTAL WAR

In August 1939, Nazi Germany and the Soviet Union signed the Nazi–Soviet nonaggression pact. The pact was a surprise, since German National Socialism and Soviet Communism were self-declared ideological enemies. A month later, the motivation for the pact would become clear. Hitler invaded Poland on September 1, 1939, and would later split the gains with the Soviet Union, which would invade Poland and the Baltic States only a few weeks later. By then, Britain and France had honoured their pledge to Poland by declaring war on Germany on September 3, 1939. World War II had begun. The war rapidly expanded. Utilizing the new tactics of the *blitzkrieg* (lightning war), and seizing command of the air, German forces invaded and conquered Denmark, Norway, the Netherlands, and Belgium. France succumbed as German forces swept around the Maginot Line, circumventing the fortified line that had been built at great effort and cost. Paris fell in June 1940. The Battle of Britain then began, an air campaign in which the German Luftwaffe unsuccessfully attempted to bomb Britain into submission. In the Mediterranean, Mussolini's Italy had invaded Greece, but the failure of the campaign brought Germany into the conflict, and Germany conquered Yugoslavia and Greece in early 1941. German and Italian troops in Africa moved toward Egypt, with the aim of wresting the Suez Canal from British control. In what we might with retrospect label the greatest strategic blunder of all time, in June 1941, Hitler invaded the Soviet Union. Having achieved total surprise, German forces swept through Russia, destroying much of the Red Army in the process. By December, German troops had advanced to within a few kilometres of Moscow. However, the German advance was halted by the Russian winter, lack of supplies, and stiffening Russian resistance around Moscow and Leningrad as Russia began to mobilize its superior resources and population.

In another notable strategic blunder, on December 7, 1941, Japan launched a surprise attack on the United States at Pearl Harbor, home of the American Pacific Fleet. Japan also mounted a swift campaign of conquest in the western Pacific, seizing the Philippines, French Indochina, the Dutch East Indies, Singapore, much of New Guinea, and the Bismarck and Solomon Islands in the South Pacific in the course of a few months. American isolationist sentiment collapsed in the face of the Pearl Harbor attack, and the democratic United States forged an alliance with democratic Great Britain and the Communist Soviet Union—the Allied powers—to oppose Nazi Germany, fascist Italy, and Imperial Japan—the Axis powers. In 1942 and 1943, the fortunes of war began to turn against the Axis powers. German and Italian forces were repulsed from Egypt. The 1942 German offensive in southern Russia ended in German defeat at Stalingrad. In the Atlantic, after heavy losses to German submarines, more and more merchant ships carrying supplies from Canada and the United States began to get through to Britain. In the Pacific, the Japanese Imperial Navy was defeated at the Battle of Midway and at the Battle of the Coral Sea. The United States then began to embark on a series of campaigns to retake the South Pacific from the Japanese. In May 1943, German and Italian forces in North Africa were defeated. At the decisive battle of Kursk in July 1943, the German summer offensive was defeated, and the Red Army forced the Germans on to the defensive on the entire eastern front. American and British strategic bombing raids against Germany began, damaging German industry and transportation, killing many civilians, and complicating the German war effort.

The decisive blows of the war were struck against the Axis powers in 1944. In June, British, Canadian, and U.S. troops landed in northern France, broke through German defences, and liberated France, Belgium, and the Netherlands. The Soviet Union launched an offensive on the eastern front a few weeks later and by late 1944 had pushed German forces back into eastern Europe. In 1945, after an unsuccessful German counteroffensive in the west, British and American forces advanced into Germany (see Map 2.9). In January 1945, the Red Army launched a final offensive aimed at Berlin. Adolf Hitler committed suicide on April 30, and on May 7 Germany surrendered unconditionally. Thus would end the career of one of the most influential and darkly troubling politicians in modern history. Indeed, one might argue that

Map 2.9 The War in Europe

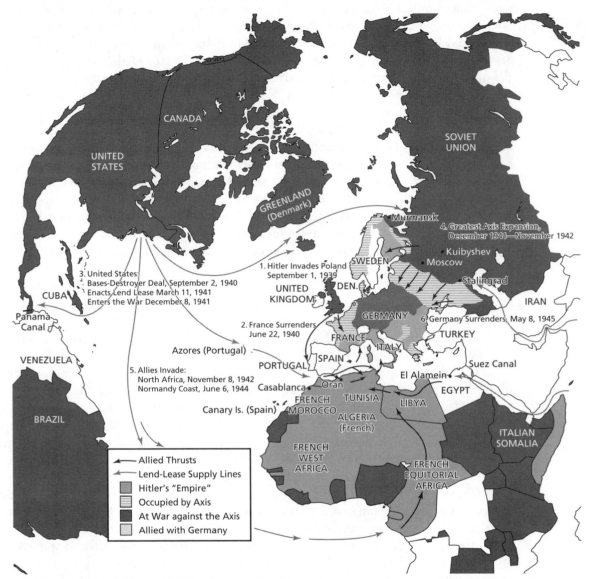

SOURCE: R. PALMER AND J. COLTON, *A HISTORY OF THE MODERN WORLD*, 8TH ED. (NEW YORK: McGRAW-HILL, 1995). REPRINTED WITH PERMISSION OF THE McGRAW-HILL COMPANIES.

World War II would not have occurred without the existence of this single man, lending credence to the value of the individual level of analysis discussed in Chapter 1.

In the Pacific, American forces began the reconquest of the Philippines, and the Japanese Imperial Navy was eliminated as an effective fighting force at the Battle of Leyte. British and Indian troops retook Burma, and Japan came under air attack from American bases in China and the Marianas Islands. In 1945, the American capture of Iwo Jima and Okinawa secured air bases closer to Japan, enabling the air offensive to be accelerated. Despite the devastation of most Japanese cities and Japan's industrial capacity, the Japanese still resisted, and preparations were made to invade the home islands of Japan (see Map 2.10). The war soon ended but not in a conventional manner. Throughout the war the United States had been engaged in top-secret research to develop an atomic weapon. Such a device had been successfully tested near Alamogordo, New Mexico, in the spring of 1945. In a controversial decision, President

Map 2.10 The War in the Pacific

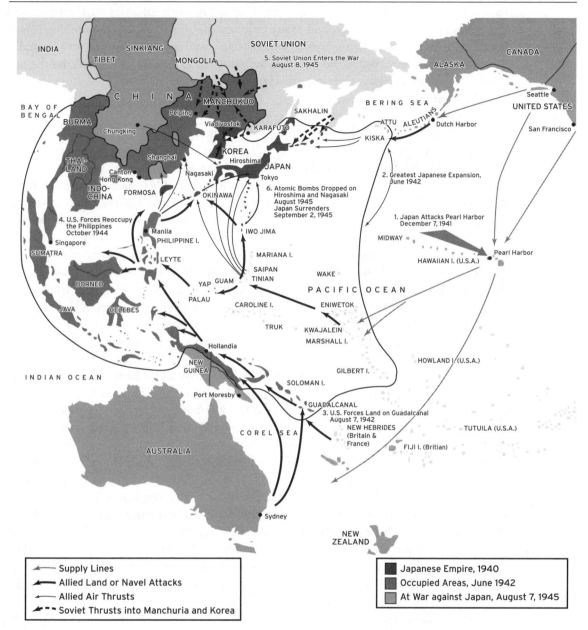

SOURCE: R. PALMER AND J. COLTON, *A HISTORY OF THE MODERN WORLD,* 8TH ED. (NEW YORK: McGRAW-HILL, 1995). REPRINTED WITH PERMISSION OF THE McGRAW-HILL COMPANIES.

Truman authorized the first military use of the **atomic bomb**, which was dropped on Hiroshima on August 6, 1945; its short-term and long-term effects killed more than 140 000 people. A second bomb was dropped on Nagasaki on August 9, one day after the Soviet Union declared war on Japan and invaded Manchuria. On September 2, 1945, Japan capitulated, and the war was over.

The use of the bomb remains controversial even today. Was it necessary? Defenders of the decision cite the enormous casualties that American service personnel would have suffered in any invasion of Japan. Others suggest the atomic bomb was dropped primarily to demonstrate American military might to the Soviet Union. Many argue that the decision to use the bombs against densely populated civilian targets was inhumane, as well as unnecessary. However, the saturation bombing of cities had long been practised by both sides during the war. London, Rotterdam, Dresden, Hamburg, and many other cities suffered extensive bombing. The fire-bombing of Tokyo caused more casualties than those suffered at Hiroshima and Nagasaki. In this context, the atomic bomb did not seem very different. Nevertheless, to this day the bombings of Hiroshima and Nagasaki retain special symbolic importance, since the atomic era began with the destruction of those cities.

World War II was the most destructive conflict in history. Approximately 15 million combatants and 35 million civilians were killed. The Soviet Union alone suffered 20 million casualties—more than the entire population of Canada at the time (for Canada's role in the war, see Profile 2.12). Six million Jews and more than 5 million others were murdered in the concentration camps of Nazi-occupied Europe (see Chapter 9 on human rights for a discussion of genocide, the Holocaust, and the important **Nuremberg war crimes trials**). Cities and industries across Europe and Asia had been reduced to rubble. A massive rebuilding task faced the survivors. Never before had war so fundamentally affected the lives of civilians. They had become targets of bombing campaigns and had participated in war production to an unprecedented degree.[16] The concept of total war had reached its apogee: industrialization, nationalism, and the power of the state had combined with the increased firepower of new technologies to truly devastate whole societies.[17] World War II was the ultimate war of attrition: the societies that could bring the greatest human and material resources to bear were victorious, but at a terrible price.

World War II also had enormous political consequences. The victory of the Allied powers over the Axis powers altered the distribution of power in the world. Borders in Europe changed in accordance with agreements made between **Winston Churchill** and Josef Stalin in 1944 and at the "big three" conference of Roosevelt, Stalin, and Churchill at Yalta in February 1945. The Soviet Union absorbed some 600 square kilometres of territory, which included the Baltic States and land from Poland, Finland, Czechoslovakia, and Romania, recovering what had been lost under the Treaty of Brest–Litovsk. Poland was compensated with land from Germany, which was divided into four occupation zones. Austria was separated from Germany. In the Far East, Japan lost control over Manchuria, Taiwan, and Korea (which was divided into Soviet and U.S. zones) and suffered the loss of the Kurile Islands, which were seized by the Soviet Union. The war had also ushered in the nuclear era; to say the least, the atomic bomb was to have an enduring impact on international relations. The war also weakened the European colonial powers, and a great wave of decolonization swept the world in the decades that followed, leading to an explosion of the number of independent states. Finally, the end of World War II saw the emergence of two powers—the United States and the Soviet Union—that possessed capabilities far greater than those of any other country. The emergence of these superpowers, as they came to be called, would define international politics in the postwar era, and suspicion and distrust between them grew rapidly. World War II had ended, but the Cold War, which we will turn to in Chapter 3, had just begun.

HISTORY, ALLIANCES, AND THE BALANCE OF POWER CONCEPT

Realists argue that the historical record from the ancient period to today speaks to the continuity of world politics. For realists, war and the rise and fall of states and empires is a universal experience, and the writings of thinkers from Thucydides to Clausewitz confirm that political responses to this universal experience are common across time and culture. In essence, these responses champion the importance of military power and the utility of **alliances**. Military power and alliances are at the core of what realists argue is the ordering mechanism of international politics since the ancient world: the **balance of power**.

PROFILE 2.12 Canada and World War II

Tears for the fallen. An unidentified Royal Canadian Navy veteran wipes his eyes during the 2002 commemorations to honour Allied soldiers killed in the Dieppe raid. There are 904 Canadians buried at the Cemetery of Virtues in Dieppe. (AP Photo/str/CP Archive)

Canada declared war on Nazi Germany on September 10, 1939, seven days after Great Britain. The government of Mackenzie King had envisioned a limited overseas commitment when it entered the war. Opinion in Canada was not as deeply divided as it had been in World War I, and although conscription was once again an issue in 1944 due to battlefield losses, the divisive debates of 1917 were not repeated. By June 1940 only Great Britain, Canada, and the other Commonwealth countries stood against the Axis. Canada was now committed to a total war and produced vast amounts of ammunition and military equipment in cities such as Hamilton, Toronto, and Montreal. The Royal Canadian Navy bore most of the convoy escort duty early in the war, providing security for the vital merchant shipping lanes to Great Britain. More than 1 100 000 Canadians served during the war, and at its peak, the Canadian Army fielded nearly 500 000 soldiers; most students are surprised to learn that, at this time, the Canadian Air Force and the Navy were among the largest in the world after those of the great powers.

Canadians first fought together in large numbers in the disastrous Dieppe raid in August 1942. The circumstances of the raid are a subject of controversy to this day, since some suggest Allied commanders sent the Canadians to their slaughter. Canadians first saw mass service in the Italian campaign in 1943 and were assigned their own landing beach (along with the United States and Great Britain) in the Normandy invasion of 1944. The Canadian Army fought in the Normandy campaign and then liberated much of the Netherlands (to this day, the people of the Netherlands have a deep respect for the sacrifice made by Canadians in liberating their country in the war). More than 42 000 Canadians died in World War II. It may seem surprising now, but Canada ended the war as one of the most powerful countries in the world. This position was the foundation of Canada's postwar middle-power status and the basis for Canada's postwar internationalism.

The term *balance of power* can be used in several ways. The balance of power can be used as a descriptive term to denote the state of the power balance between certain states or groups of states in a certain region of the world (it was not until the 20th century and the superpower confrontation that the concern with a global balance of power arose). The term can be used to describe a particular policy of states that may be seeking a balance of power. Most commonly, it refers to a historical phenomenon in which empires and states have repeatedly formed alliances against other states or groups of states. The balance of power is a system of order in an anarchic international system in which states act to ensure that no one state or group of states can come to dominate the system or conquer all other states in the system. This balancing behaviour preserves the system of sovereign states because no one state or group of states can acquire the power to control the entire region (or the world). This balancing behaviour can also preserve peace, by redistributing power in an effort to maintain an equilibrium, or balance, in the system. However, the balance of power does not necessarily mean the preservation of peace. In fact, the balance of power does not exist to ensure peace, but rather to ensure the survival of the state system. The preservation of the balance of power system often requires war to defeat the efforts of certain states to dominate the system.

The concept of the balance of power suggests that if the power of a state or a group of states grows, other states in the system will balance against this growing power. States can balance in one of two ways. They can increase their own power (generally through military spending) or they can engage in alliances with other states. Alliances are formal agreements between states that commit them to a common purpose, such as military security against a common threat. Alliances are often referred to as **collective defence** arrangements. Arrangements that are not formalized in treaties and that tend to be of shorter duration are often called *coalitions*. Alliances are a quick and relatively cheap method of supplementing one's own power with the power of another. Alliances, then, are a form of self-interested cooperation (another term we might use is *marriage of convenience*). Realists argue that the historical frequency of alliances reveals the universality of the balance of power concept.

Generally, alliances form when two or more states share a perceived threat and agree to coordinate their efforts to meet that threat.[18] This agreement may take the form of treaty obligations to assist the other state if it is attacked. In other cases, agreements may extend to high levels of cooperation on political and military issues, including the formation of joint institutions and joint military forces. Alliances are notoriously fluid and changing, and alliance commitments are often broken. When the threat common to alliance members disappears, alliances tend to break up as well, although as our discussion of the North Atlantic Treaty Organization (NATO) in subsequent chapters suggests, some alliances have persisted over time, and in many cases states have been reluctant to dissolve them. A state might be reluctant to defect from an alliance relationship because of concerns that it would acquire a reputation as an unreliable ally. In the future, other countries might be less willing to form an alliance with a state that has a poor reputation for maintaining its commitments and obligations. Alternatively, alliances might survive because self-interested states want to maintain the advantages of the cooperative relationship they have built.

Alliances vary with respect to the commitment of their members and their internal unity, often called **alliance cohesion**. Cohesive alliances have a high degree of shared interests and coordination among their members, and tend to be formally institutionalized. NATO is an example of a highly cohesive alliance that has developed a complex system of political and military cooperation since its inception in 1949. Alliances that are less cohesive have lower levels of coordination and have divergent interests among their membership. Cohesion is important because the ability to form a strong united effort against a threat is the key to a credible alliance; potential enemies are far less likely to attack a cohesive alliance because it seems certain that the members will all honour their commitments. Similarly, efforts by a potential enemy to create rifts in an alliance may not succeed if an alliance is cohesive.

For realists, because states will act to balance the power of other states, the distribution of power in the international system or in regional systems is extremely important. The distribution of power is defined by concentrations of power in a region or in the entire international system and by how many of these concentrations exist. These concentrations of power are called poles, and the distribution of power is often described in terms of **polarity** (a term borrowed from physics). Polarity describes the number of independent centres or concentrations of power in the system. These poles of power, and the relations between them, determine the polarity of the system; other actors may exist, but they are not decisive in determining system polarity. Changes in the distribution of power may take place slowly, the result of different economic growth rates and technological innovation among states. Some changes in the distribution of power may be very dramatic, the result of a sudden shift in alliances across the states in the system or the sudden weakening of one or more of the powers in a system through internal collapse or defeat in war. When this happens, the polarity of the system may change, and a different kind of system may emerge. For the purposes of study, realist scholars have identified three different kinds of polarity in the history of international relations: multipolar systems, bipolar systems, and unipolar systems. Each system type has a certain distribution of power (polarity), and each is the subject of debate as to its relative advantages and disadvantages.

Multipolar systems consist of three to seven independent centres, or poles, that are relatively equal in power. These systems can be global in scope (the global balance of power), regional in scope (such as the historical European balance of power systems), or localized (such as the Warring States period in China). The stability of multipolar systems is a major issue of debate among realists. Morgenthau argued that such a system is stable (and therefore more peaceful) because enough centres of power always exist to prevent a single power or group of powers from dominating. However, some realists, such as Kenneth Waltz, warn that multipolar systems are inherently unstable, precisely because they are so flexible.[19] In such a system, the actions of one centre of power (such as an attack on another centre of power or a decision to expand its military) can reverberate throughout the system and have unintended consequences (such as system-wide war or an arms race). A special kind of multipolar system is the tripolar system in which three centres of power exist. Tripolar systems are very unstable as there is a tendency for two of the power centres to ally against the third, with no prospect of achieving a power balance to deter war. Historical examples of such power distributions are rare, although some of the characteristics of such systems can be found in the "strategic triangle" between the United States, the Soviet Union, and China during the Cold War.[20]

In **bipolar** systems, two centres of power, either in the form of two predominant states or two great rival alliance blocs, dominate the international system, such as in Greece during the height of the Athenian and Spartan empires, and during the early Cold War between the superpowers and their respective allies. As the Cold War wore on, however, other countries attained more flexibility, largely because of their recovery from the devastation of World War II. As a result, while the superpowers remained militarily and economically predominant, other states increasingly embarked on their own foreign policy agendas and relationships, although these rarely challenged the policy of the superpowers. (In practice, the major allies of the United States maintained more freedom of manoeuvre than did the allies of the Soviet Union.) This system is sometimes referred to as **bipolycentrism**. Realists also disagree on the stability of bipolar systems. Some, such as Kenneth Waltz, argue that bipolar systems are stable because the two centres of power deter each other from rash actions, and they can develop a familiarity that will reduce the chances of miscalculation. Others argue that such a system is inflexible because of the lack of balancing potential; each state sees its position with respect to the other as a **zero-sum game**.[21] As a result, even small changes in the distribution of power between the two centres of power can have destabilizing effects that could lead to war. As we shall see in the next chapter, this became particularly dangerous in the nuclear age, when an all-out war between the two poles could have resulted in the destruction of most life on the planet.

The third configuration is a **unipolar** system, characterized by a single centre of power: a state or a powerful state and its allies dominate the forums, rules, and arrangements governing political and economic relations in the system. Such actors are often called hegemons. Most often, **hegemony** is a reflection of one state's preponderant power in traditional economic and military terms. However, hegemony can also refer to the dominance of certain ideas or certain cultures.[22] The theory of **hegemonic stability** holds that a hegemon can have a stabilizing or ordering influence on a regional system or the international system by performing some of the functions a central government would perform. It can deter aggression or use political and economic pressure to prevent or stop wars between smaller countries. It can provide hard currency for use as a world standard. Two prominent examples of hegemonies in history are Great Britain in the 19th century and the United States in the 20th century. Great Britain's period of dominance occurred after the defeat of France in the Napoleonic Wars. The United States' period of hegemony began with the defeat of Nazi Germany and Imperial Japan at the end of World War II, and, arguably, persists to this day.

It is important to note that scholars of international relations do not always agree on which states have achieved hegemonic status in the past and how long this position lasted. Some scholars would include 17th-century Netherlands and 16th-century Spain as examples of hegemony. It is also important to note that in practice a hegemon may exist in a multipolar setting (as did Great Britain in the 19th century) and in a bipolycentric setting (as did the United States during the Cold War). In such cases, the term *hegemony* merely describes the existence of a state that is more powerful than all others in the system but is not so powerful that one can speak with empirical confidence of a unipolar system. For example, the Cold War is described as a period of bipolarity, as there were two clearly pre-eminent centres of power in the system. However, it was also clear that the United States was the more powerful in terms of the influence it exerted over international institutions, rules, and the world economy. As a result, the American role was often described as hegemonic, despite the broader bipolar context.

States that achieve hegemonic status do not retain this status indefinitely. Hegemonic decline will eventually occur over decades or centuries. A combination of domestic internal decay and costly military overextension weakens the hegemonic state. The hegemon will then face the efforts of a challenger to overthrow the hegemon's pre-eminent position. The transition from one hegemon to another may take the form of a hegemonic war or a peaceful transition in which the first hegemon will be compelled to pass on its status to a rising power.[23] Alternatively, the challenger may fail and the hegemon survive. As we shall see in Chapter 4, the status of the United States today is a point of debate among scholars, who disagree as to whether the United States is a hegemon in decline.[24]

HISTORY AND ASYMMETRIES IN POWER

The historical record also reveals that across time and place most political units (whether they be groups or states) do not possess anything like the power wielded by the strongest political units. For the most part, history is characterized by a small number of very powerful political units and a large number of less powerful units. Realists tend to focus on the most powerful actors, or **great powers**, because these actors define the character of the system (the distribution of power and the polarity of the system), and their actions are, therefore, the most important. There is no question that great powers are tremendously important. Few of them exist at any given point in history, and yet they possess most of the world's power resources at that time. Great powers possess the strongest military forces and the largest economies. Often these capabilities are based on natural endowments of large populations and plentiful resources, as in the case of the United States, Russia, and China. In other cases, these resources might be acquired through expansion, as was the case with the British Empire, or through economic growth and trade, as is the case with Japan. As a result, great powers tend to endure. Only great powers can decisively defeat other great powers militarily. They also tend to have global interests and commitments. And on occasion, great powers are formally recognized as such by international structures such as the Concert of Europe or the UN Security Council.

However, the bulk of state actors in the history of international politics have not been great powers. For the most part, historical systems have been composed of a small number of large (powerful) states and a large number of smaller (less powerful) states. The latter states vary widely in terms of their characteristics, resources, and capabilities, and, as a result, classifying them has been very difficult. The term *middle power* has been used to refer to a group of states that rank below the great powers in terms of power resources and influence in international politics. These states may exert influence within their respective regions, or they may have an international profile on certain specific issues, but for the most part their ability to influence the larger global setting is limited. Some middle powers may be geographically large, such as Canada or Australia, while others may be quite small, such as South Korea or Sweden. Small powers, or **small states** as they are more generally known, are countries that have less power capabilities than middle powers and little or no influence on international politics. Small states have smaller economies (although many small states are very wealthy on a per capita basis), tend to have small populations and territories, and tend to have limited power capabilities (such as small militaries) as a result. Small states are generally considered significant only to the extent that they become important in the schemes of the great powers. For example, Belgium has been a small state in Europe since its creation, but it has been important because of its status as a buffer state between Germany and France. Vietnam might be far less well known today but for the engagement of the United States in the Vietnam War and its historical conflicts with China. In addition, regional context is an important factor in judging the importance of states. Some small states in Europe or Asia would be among the most powerful states if they were relocated in different regions of the world. And Brazil, South Africa, and India all have a claim to great-power status in their respective regions.

Canada provides a good example of the difficulty inherent in classifying states according to their power. Canada has been described variously as a small state, a satellite of the United States, a middle power, and even a "principal power."[25] Canada has one of the leading economies of the world but has a very small military. The country is rich in resources but has a small population. And yet, Canada consistently is ranked amongst the top 10 countries in the world in which to live, and is a member of the G-8 group of countries. Classifying states according to their power therefore raises the question of how power is measured. For realists, military and economic indicators (hard power) determine a state's power and its associated diplomatic status. However, power can also be measured in terms of the power to persuade without coercion, the power of ideas and values, and the power of social stability and a high quality of life. In this sense, small states can be significant actors in global politics, often serving as a source of ideas, as mediators, and as contributors to multilateral institutions. Furthermore, in an increasingly interdependent world, classifying states may become increasingly problematic in the face of the permeability of borders, the significance of multinational corporations, and the evident limitations on the use of force as experienced by the United States in Vietnam and the Soviet Union in Afghanistan. Nevertheless, the classification of states continues. The United States is invariably described as the world's only superpower. The United Kingdom, France, China, Russia, and sometimes Germany and Japan are frequently referred to as great powers. Some countries are described as *regional powers*, such as India, Israel, Indonesia, and Brazil. Almost all other states are called small states. And some states are so small (often literally) they are called *micro-states*. The symbolism of state equality is maintained in the principles of diplomatic formality (see Chapter 7) and in organizations such as the UN General Assembly (see Chapter 5), where the United States has the same number of votes (one) as does Nauru. However, that is where the equality ends, and the reality of power asymmetry begins.

CONCLUSIONS

In this chapter we have provided a necessarily brief history of global politics, focusing on the rise and fall of civilizations and empires, the formation of the modern state system, and the enduring problem of war. This historical experience reminds us of the need to be aware of both continuities and changes in the course of human affairs, and to be careful when proclaiming the dawning of a new era or a transformation in the nature of world politics. We also explored some of the core questions surrounding the issue of war and peace in global politics up to 1945 and how these questions influenced the development of ideas and theories, such as geopolitics, realism, idealism, collective security, and the balance of power. All of these ideas, derived from historical developments and interpretations of those developments, maintained their relevance into the Cold War period. The next chapter examines in detail the most protracted power struggle in recent history, one that affected all states, small and large: the epic confrontation between the West and the East during the Cold War.

Endnotes

1. Georg Wilhelm Friederich Hegel, "An Introduction to the Philosophy of History," in Jacob Loewenburg, ed., *Hegel Selections* (New York: Scribner's, 1929).

2. For an engaging read on this topic see Erna Paris, *Long Shadows: Truth, Lies and History* (Toronto: Vintage Canada, 2001).

3. John Keegan, *A History of Warfare* (New York: Alfred A. Knopf, 1993), 122.

4. See William H. McNeill, *The Pursuit of Power: Technology, Armed Force, and Society since A.D. 1000* (Chicago: University of Chicago Press, 1982), 5.

5. For a history of Mongol power, see Robert Marshall, *Storm from the East: From Genghis Khan to Kublai Khan* (Berkeley: University of California Press, 1993).

6. Jeremy Black, *War and the World: Military Power and the Fate of Continents, 1450–2000* (New Haven: Yale University Press, 1998), 32.

7. See Albert Hourani, *A History of the Arab Peoples* (Cambridge, MA: Belknap Press, 1991).

8. See Victor Davis Hanson, *Carnage and Culture: Landmark Battles in the Rise of Western Power* (New York: Anchor Books, 2001), esp. 193–232; and Mark Cocker, *Rivers of Blood, Rivers of Gold: Europe's Conquest of Indigenous Peoples* (New York: Grove Press, 1998).

9. See Adda B. Bozeman, *Politics and Culture in International History* (Princeton: Princeton University Press, 1960).

10. Philip Bobbitt, *The Shield of Achilles: War, Peace, and the Course of History* (New York: Alfred A. Knopf, 2002), 118–43.

11. On the theme of the overextension and decline of empires, see the popular text by Paul Kennedy, *The Rise and Fall of the Great Powers: Economic Change and Military Conflict from 1500 to 2000* (London: Unwin Hyman, 1988).

12. See Stephen Van Evera, "The Cult of the Offensive and the Origins of the First World War," *International Security* 9 (1984), 58–107; and Jack Lewis Snyder, *The Ideology of the Offensive: Military Decision Making and the Disasters of 1914* (Ithaca, NY: Cornell University Press, 1984).

13. Quoted in Barbara W. Tuchman, *The Guns of August* (New York: Bantam Books, 1962), 146.

14. Richard Overy, "Total War II: The Second World War," in Charles Townshend, ed., *The Oxford History of Modern War* (Oxford: Oxford University Press, 2000), 139.

15. See William L. Shirer, *The Collapse of the Third Republic* (New York: Simon and Schuster, 1969).

16. It is important to note that as Canadian and American men fought abroad, women were recruited into wartime production at home, continuing a fundamental shift in the economic role played by women in advanced capitalist economies that began under similar circumstances during World War I.

17. See Gabriel Kolko, *Century of War: Politics, Conflicts, and Society Since 1914* (New York: The New Press, 1994).

18. See Stephen Walt, *The Origins of Alliances* (Ithaca, NY: Cornell University Press, 1987).

19. See Kenneth Waltz, "The Stability of a Bipolar World," in D. Edwards, ed., *International Political Analysis* (New York: Rinehart and Winston, 1970), 340. See also John Mearsheimer, "Why We Will Soon Miss the Cold War," *Atlantic Monthly,* August 1990, 37.

20. See Alan Ned Sabrosky, ed., *Polarity and War: The Changing Nature of International Conflict* (Boulder, CO: Westview Press, 1985).

21. See K.W. Deutsch and J.D. Singer, "Multipolar Power Systems and International Stability," in J. Rosenau, ed., *International Politics and Foreign Policy*, rev. ed. (New York: Free Press, 1969), 315–24. In a zero-sum game, one state's gain is automatically perceived as another's loss. Therefore, the outcome of the game is still zero (+1 for the winner, –1 for the loser = 0).

22. The Marxist (Gramscian) tradition in international political economy refers to hegemony as ideational domination by transnational class interests; see Chapter 4. See also S. Gill, *American Hegemony and the Trilateral Commission* (Cambridge, UK: Cambridge University Press, 1990).

23. The most famous treatment of this theory of hegemonic stability and transformation is probably Robert Gilpin's *War and Change in World Politics* (Cambridge, UK: Cambridge University Press, 1981). See also R. Keohane, *After Hegemony: Cooperation and Discord in the World Political Economy* (Princeton: Princeton University Press, 1984).

24. This debate is crystallized in two popular works: Paul Kennedy, *The Rise and Fall of the Great Powers: Economic Change and Military Conflict from 1500 to 2000* (London: Unwin Hyman, 1988); and Joseph S. Nye Jr., *Bound to Lead: The Changing Nature of American Power* (New York: Basic Books, 1990).

25. See D. Dewitt and J. Kirton, *Canada as a Principal Power: A Study in Foreign Policy and International Relations* (Toronto: John Wiley and Sons, 1983). For further discussion, see Kim Richard Nossal, *The Politics of Canadian Foreign Policy*, 3rd ed. (Scarborough, ON: Prentice-Hall, 1997), 52–68; and Andrew Cooper, *Canadian Foreign Policy: Old Habits and New Directions* (Scarborough, ON: Prentice-Hall, 1997), 9–21.

Suggested Readings

Archer, C., et al. *World History of Warfare*. Lincoln: University of Nebraska Press, 2002.

Asimov, I. *Asimov's Chronology of the World: The History of the World from the Big Bang to Modern Times*. New York: HarperCollins, 1991.

Barraclough, G., ed. *The Times Atlas of World History*. Maplewood, NJ: Hammond, 1978.

Black, Jeremy. *War and the World: Military Power and the Fate of Continents, 1450–2000*. New Haven: Yale University Press, 1998.

Bobbitt, Philip. *The Shield of Achilles: War, Peace, and the Course of History*. New York: Alfred A. Knopf, 2002.

Brown, M., S. Lynn-Jones, and S. Miller, eds. *The Perils of Anarchy: Contemporary Realism and International Security*. Cambridge, MA: MIT Press, 1995.

Bull, H. *The Anarchical Society: A Study of Order in World Politics*. London: Macmillan, 1977.

Cocker, Mark. *Rivers of Blood, Rivers of Gold: Europe's Conquest of Indigenous Peoples*. New York: Grove Press, 1998.

Dockrill, M. *Atlas of Twentieth Century World History*. New York: HarperCollins, 1991.

Doyle, M. *Ways of War and Peace*. New York: Norton, 1997.

Gabriel, J.M. *Worldviews and Theories of International Relations*. New York: St. Martin's Press, 1994.

Gianfranco, P. *The State: Its Nature, Development, and Prospects*. Stanford: Stanford University Press, 1991.

Hanson, Victor Davis. *Carnage and Culture: Landmark Battles in the Rise of Western Power*. New York: Anchor Books, 2001.

———. *The Dividing Discipline: Hegemony and Diversity in International Theory*. Boston: Allen and Unwin, 1985.

Holsti, K.J. *Peace and War: Armed Conflicts and International Order 1648–1989*. Cambridge, UK: Cambridge University Press, 1990.

Keegan, John. *A History of Warfare*. New York: Alfred A. Knopf, 1993.

Knutsen, T. *The History of International Relations Theory: An Introduction.* Manchester: Manchester University Press, 1992.

McNeill, William H. *The Pursuit of Power: Technology, Armed Force, and Society since A.D. 1000.* Chicago: University of Chicago Press, 1982.

Rothstein, R.L., ed. *The Evolution of Theory in International Politics.* Columbia, SC: University of South Carolina Press, 1991.

Spegele, R. *Political Realism and International Theory.* Cambridge, UK: Cambridge University Press, 1996.

Tilly, Charles, ed. *The Formation of National States in Western Europe.* Princeton: Princeton University Press, 1975.

Townshend, Charles, ed. *The Oxford History of Modern War.* Oxford: Oxford University Press, 2000.

Young, J., and J. Kent. *International Relations Since 1945: A Global History.* Oxford: Oxford University Press, 2004.

Suggested Websites

The History Guide: Resources for Historians
http://www.historyguide.org/resources.html

The History Net
http://www.thehistorynet.com

Internet Resources for Historians
http://www.ksu.edu/history/resources

CHAPTER 3

The Nuclear Era, the Cold War, and Foreign Policy Analysis

To the extent that the nuclear threat has deterrent value, it is because it in fact increases the risk of nuclear war.

—Robert S. McNamara[1]

Restraint? Why are you so concerned with saving their damn lives? The whole idea is to kill the bastards. At the end of the war if there are two Americans and one Russian left alive, we win.

—General Thomas Power, Commander of U.S. Strategic Air Command in the 1960s[2]

THE COLD WAR: POWER POLITICS ASCENDANT

The Cold War seems distant now, but just a decade ago it dominated our understanding of global politics.[3] Citizens of every state on earth were put at risk by the nuclear arms race. Canadians would have been caught in a horrific crossfire if nuclear war had occurred. A high level of animosity existed between East and West, between the ideologies of the Communist command economies (the so-called Second World) and democratic liberal capitalism (the so-called First World), between the red scare and the American imperialists, between the "commies" and the "Yankees," between the "pinkos" and the "fascists"—the list of quaint phrases depicting each side seemed endless. The Cold War was a comprehensive ideological, geopolitical, military, and international rivalry between the two superpowers (and their respective allies and **client states**) that became increasingly global in scope as the postwar era matured. Thankfully, as its name implies, the Cold War never became a global hot war; the vast military capabilities of the superpowers never directly fought each other. Instead, the Cold War was fought in the international arena through diplomacy, ideological rhetoric, arms races, regional **proxy wars** and interventions, and the competition for allies and military bases around the world. Although the Cold War was sometimes called the "long peace," this somewhat misleading label only applies to the absence of great-power war between 1946 and 1991.[4] Millions of people died in the regional wars and related human rights outrages of this period. The Cold War may have been a long peace for some, but it was certainly not so for others.

We can destroy you. The testing of nuclear weapons by the United States and the Soviet Union was the most visible expression of Cold War animosity. This was the U.S. test at the Bikini Atoll in the Marshall Islands on July 24, 1946. The dark spots in the foreground are old naval vessels placed near the blast to test the effects of nuclear explosions on ships. Such technology introduced a new possibility: omnicide. (AP Photo/ CP Archive)

The Cold War was not the only issue in post–World War II international relations. Decolonization greatly increased the official number of states, and development became a major international issue. There was growing interest in the protection and promotion of human rights. The global economy grew dramatically. Nonstate actors, especially multinational corporations and nongovernmental organizations, became more prominent. Nevertheless, the dominant characteristic of this era was the superpower rivalry; the international politics of this period cannot be addressed or examined in isolation from this fact. An examination of the history of the relationship between the superpowers reveals several themes that persisted until the collapse of the Soviet Union:

- *A cyclical pattern of confrontation and cooperation.* The Cold War was characterized by periods of high tension and crisis between the superpowers, alternating with periods of a relative relaxation of tensions and increased levels of cooperation. Good relations reached a high point between 1968 and 1978, a period sometimes called **détente**, in which both countries sought restraint and increased cooperation in their relations with each other.

- *The nuclear stalemate.* For most of the Cold War, especially after the late 1960s, each superpower was vulnerable to complete destruction by the nuclear arsenal of the other. Nuclear deterrence became the dominant military strategy of the Cold War.

- *The development of informal rules and mutual understandings.* Over time, the superpowers established formal and informal understandings and agreements that often guided relations between them. When these agreements or understandings were violated in the view of one of the superpowers, tensions between the countries increased.

- *Political pragmatism versus ideological rhetoric.* During the Cold War, both superpowers professed the superiority of their respective ideologies. However, both superpowers sacrificed the principles of their respective ideologies if geopolitical considerations demanded it. For example, both superpowers supported allies with political systems antithetical to their own.

- *Superpower involvement in regional wars.* Although the two superpowers avoided direct warfare, both used or supported allies and client states in wars directed against their opponent's allies and clients. These wars are referred to as proxy wars. For example, Cuba's involvement in the Angolan Civil War was a proxy for direct Soviet involvement. For the many people caught up in these regional conflicts, the Cold War was hardly a period of stability.

For other countries in the international system, the Cold War was the context for much of their foreign policy decision making. Many countries voluntarily sought security arrangements and alliances with the superpowers. Most of the countries of Western Europe joined the

United States and Canada in the North Atlantic Treaty Organization (NATO), which bound its members to come to the assistance of any member should it be attacked. This alliance, of course, was built against the threat posed by the Soviet Union. The Warsaw Treaty Organization (WTO), more commonly called the **Warsaw Pact,** joined the countries of Eastern Europe with the Soviet Union in an alliance against NATO. The Warsaw Pact, however, was much more tightly controlled from Moscow; Poland, Hungary, the former Czechoslovakia, and other Eastern European states were expected to be compliant partners and suffered ill consequences if they objected. Twice the Soviet Union used force to keep its Eastern European allies in line: in Hungary in 1956, and in Czechoslovakia in 1968.

Around the world, states established relationships with the superpowers based on a combination of ideological affinity and pure self-interest. Both superpowers established a network of client states around the world to which they gave varying degrees of diplomatic, economic, and military assistance. The United States gave large amounts of assistance to countries such as Israel, Iran (before the Iranian Revolution), Pakistan, and South Korea. The Soviet Union supported North Korea, Cuba, Vietnam, and Syria. Very few countries succeeded in following a neutral path, such as Switzerland, Austria, and Sweden. Some countries such as India, Indonesia, and Egypt sought to distance themselves from the Cold War by forming the Nonaligned Movement (NAM) but never succeeded in becoming a major political force, since few if any countries could escape the fact that international issues were invariably affected by the behaviour of one or both superpowers. To varying degrees, all countries had to accommodate this fact when making foreign policy decisions.

The aim of this chapter is to explore the origins, character, and collapse of the Cold War. This task is a crucial one because our own time is often defined as the "post–Cold War era." This identification begs the question of what has changed since the end of the Cold War and what has not. This chapter also examines an important area of study within global politics: the study of decision making. This area developed dramatically during the Cold War, because the consequences of intentional or accidental nuclear war were so great. Today, these decision-making theories are valuable tools in our search for how the decisions that shape global politics are made.

THE ORIGINS OF THE BIPOLAR ERA

The Cold War began with the swift erosion in cooperation between the Western Allies and the Soviet Union during 1946 and 1947. However, the seeds of the Cold War were planted in the latter half of World War II, when distrust and friction began to develop between the Western Allies (primarily the United States and Great Britain) and the Soviet Union. Each side was suspicious of the other's ultimate intentions, although distrust was held in check by the larger interest in continued cooperation to defeat Nazi Germany and Imperial Japan. However, when the war ended, their differences became more evident and tensions quickly escalated. In a short time, the former allies had become adversaries.

Was the superpower rivalry inevitable? After all, the Western Allies and the Soviet Union had cooperated during World War II despite their differences, and both had expressed a desire to maintain that cooperation in the postwar period. Suggestions were made that coexistence might have been possible through the establishment of spheres of influence in which the other side would agree not to interfere. The membership of the United States and the U.S.S.R. in the newly created United Nations (UN), which was mandated to preserve world peace, offered hope that cooperation would continue. Nevertheless, relations between the West and the East deteriorated to open hostility and rivalry and paralyzed the principal organ for conflict resolution in the UN, the **Security Council**. This hostility and rivalry had several origins and took on many forms. The Cold War had an ideological dimension, a geopolitical dimension, a strategic dimension, and an international dimension. Together, these established the character of the Cold War.

THE IDEOLOGICAL DIMENSION

The Cold War had an important ideological content, for the superpower rivalry was characterized not only by military or geopolitical competition but also by a confrontation between two antagonistic political, economic, and social systems. In a sense, the Cold War was a confrontation between two different ways of life, a competition to determine which system performed best and which could build a better and more just society. On the one hand, the majority of Western countries and their peoples perceived Marxism-Leninism as a fundamentally authoritarian political ideology that stifled the political and economic freedom of the individual. Communism threatened the overthrow of Western liberal democracy and the free market economic system. On the other hand, the ideological pronouncements of the Soviet Union characterized the West as a bastion of capitalist interests that controlled the world economy and was bent on surrounding and then destroying the Marxist-Leninist revolution in Russia. Capitalism and Communism could not coexist, and the Soviet Union had to do what it could to accelerate the historical inevitability of Communist revolutions around the world. U.S. Secretary of State James Byrnes once argued that "there is too much difference in the ideologies of the U.S. and Russia to work out a long term program of cooperation."[5]

During the Cold War, a persistent and intense debate raged in government and academic circles (as well as in the general public) about whether the U.S.S.R. was an expansionist power. For many, particularly early in the Cold War, the answer to this question was yes: the Soviet Union was a messianic, expansionist power bent on expanding its power and influence in the world through direct aggression and the support of Communist national liberation movements abroad. For these **hawks**, Marxist-Leninist ideology was a blueprint, a guide, for Soviet actions. Just as Hitler's book *Mein Kampf* had outlined the plans and world view of that dictator, the ideological writings of Lenin and Stalin and the pronouncements of Soviet leaders outlined the plans and world-view of the Soviet leadership. However, many argued otherwise. These **doves** argued that the foreign policy of the Soviet Union was essentially defensive, concerned primarily with preserving and protecting the Soviet state. While the Soviet Union would take advantage of opportunities to increase its power or expand its influence, it would not take undue risks in the pursuit of such opportunities. Ideology was not a guide to Soviet policy; at best, it was a perceptual lens through which the Soviet leaders saw the world. Soviet behaviour actually had more in common with the policies of Russia's tsars. It was power politics that drove Soviet policy, not ideology.

As the Cold War dragged on, the ideological intensity of the superpower competition receded, as did the hostility of the rhetoric between the two countries. However, ideology remained the cornerstone of the confrontation between the United States and the Soviet Union. The competition between the two systems manifested in extreme nationalism (or patriotism) in both countries. Even in periods of détente, it surfaced in sports, the arts, scientific achievement, and space travel. In the 1980s, the ideological rhetoric of the Cold War intensified when Ronald Reagan became president of the United States. Reagan took a hawkish view of the U.S.S.R., believing that the Soviet Union was the root of all evil in the world. The ideological animosity of the Cold War also existed between allies of the United States and other Communist countries in the world. The ideological rivalry of the Cold War was not uniform across all countries, however. Canada, for example, had better relations with

Romania and Cuba than did the United States. In fact, Canada's relatively friendly relations with Cuba remain a central point of contention in Canada–U.S. relations today.

THE GEOPOLITICAL DIMENSION

As indicated above, ideological rivalry does not provide a complete characterization or explanation for the events of the Cold War. Just as important was the geopolitical rivalry between the superpowers. The pre-eminence of the United States and the Soviet Union at the end of World War II led them naturally to regard each other with suspicion. As Robert Tucker has observed, "The principal cause of the Cold War was the essential duopoly of power left by World War II."[6] In other words, the structure of the international system at the end of World War II led each superpower to regard the other as a rival. The ideological differences between the two countries only exacerbated this situation. As the Cold War intensified, geography played an important role in the strategic and foreign policy decisions of Washington and Moscow.

In the United States, the Soviet threat was cast in the geopolitical context of Halford Mackinder and his view of the world (see Chapter 2). The Soviet Union, after all, seemed to occupy the "heartland," and was poised to expand along the "interior ring" along the way to dominating the "world island"—and thereafter the world. From this position, the Soviet Union had the tremendous geopolitical advantage of the interior lines of transport and was thus poised to expand anywhere along a wide perimeter (see Map 3.1). To contain the U.S.S.R., the United States and its allies were forced to defend this wide perimeter all around the heartland of Eurasia. This prompted the United States to form multilateral and bilateral alliances with countries around the perimeter of Eurasia. The United States found many willing partners. The governments of Western Europe saw the Soviet Union as a direct (and geographically close) threat. Common threat perceptions shared by most Western European countries and the United States led to the creation of NATO in 1949. Japan also felt threatened, not least because the U.S.S.R. had occupied several Japanese territories at the end of WWII. Japan and the United States would sign a bilateral security treaty in 1951. In Canada, concern arose about the threat the Soviet Union represented to the postwar order.[7] This would prompt the Canadian government to join NATO as a founding country and to establish a wide array of security agreements with the United States, most notably the North American Air Defence Agreement (NORAD) in 1958.

However, in its search for allies the United States also found willing partners that capitalized on the anti-Communist passions of U.S. foreign policy by accepting U.S. aid and using it for their own purposes. In its desire to geographically contain the Soviet Union and prevent the spread of Communism, the United States would assist not only democratic countries that felt threatened by the U.S.S.R., but also dictatorial and military regimes, which used U.S. assistance to maintain their power, often through repression and human rights violations. Realists would proclaim that such alliances were natural if unfortunate manifestations of power politics. For successive U.S. governments, the enemies of Communism and the U.S.S.R. were automatically perceived as friends of the United States. However, for liberals, constructivists and feminists alike, U.S. support for regimes such as those in Chile, Guatemala, South Africa, Iran, and the Philippines were perversions of the principles and values espoused by the United States. Furthermore, by supporting such regimes diplomatically, financially, and militarily while ignoring the brutal treatment that many citizens of these countries endured at the hands of their governments, the United States was complicit in some of the worst human rights abuses perpetrated during the Cold War. Ultimately, unlike NATO and the U.S.–Japan security treaty (which are still in place today), some of the alliances built by the United States would not endure: the Central Treaty Organization (CENTO) in the Middle East and the

South-East Asian Treaty Organization (SEATO) both collapsed early in the Cold War. Nevertheless, **geopolitics** would continue to play an important role in the foreign policy of the United States in the Cold War period.

In the Soviet Union, the geopolitical position of the country was regarded in a rather different fashion. We can simulate a Soviet geopolitical view of the world by using a polar projection of the world (see Map 3.2). The difference is striking. No longer does the Soviet Union seem poised to strike out in any direction with the advantage of the interior lines. Instead, the Soviet Union is encircled, and the long border of the Soviet Union is threatened by enemies and security concerns. Any potential effort to break out of this encirclement or to conduct military operations from the U.S.S.R. would encounter some of these enemies or threats. In Europe are the NATO countries, backed by the power of the United States. In southern Europe are the NATO countries of Greece and Turkey, which dominate the straits between the Black Sea and the Mediterranean. In the Middle East lies the Muslim world, a security concern because of the fear that this region could have an influence in the Islamic republics of the Soviet Union. To the east is China, a great ideological competitor by the second half of the Cold War, and Japan, a close ally of the United States. From the perspective of Soviet planners, then, the geopolitical position of the U.S.S.R. was not an enviable one.

THE STRATEGIC DIMENSION

Both superpowers and their respective allies maintained large conventional military forces throughout the Cold War. An immense amount of time, money, and effort was devoted to the maintenance of these forces and their training, equipment modernization, and deployment around the world. By the late 1980s the size of these conventional military forces was immense. In particular, Europe was host to the large armies of NATO and the even larger armies of the Warsaw Pact. However, the strategic character of the Cold War was defined by nuclear weapons and the nuclear arms race between the United States and the Soviet Union. The nuclear weapon was a revolutionary development in the history of warfare, a fact dramatically punctuated by the two bombs dropped on Japan at the end of World War II.[8] Ironically, the weapons were so destructive, and the consequences of their use so enormous, that the military usefulness of such weapons came under question. But if nuclear weapons could not be usefully employed on the battlefield, what could they be used for? In short, they were useful only for preventing their use by others. In other words, nuclear weapons were instruments of **deterrence**, not warfighting.

Deterrence is a policy of preventing or discouraging an action by confronting an opponent or opponents with risks they are unwilling to take. The actor doing the deterring is a *deterrer*, and the actor being deterred is a *deterree*. A potential aggressor will likely be deterred when the probability of victory is low or the costs of a war (whatever the outcome) are high. Two broad types of deterrence strategies are

- *Deterrence by denial.* A deterree will not start a war because it is convinced it cannot achieve its objectives. Deterrence by denial was a prenuclear phenomenon, based on the view that powerful military forces and high levels of military preparedness could discourage an attack by one country against another.

- *Deterrence by punishment.* A deterree will not start a war because of the threat that it will receive unacceptable damage in return. The enormous destructive power of nuclear weapons, coupled with advanced delivery systems, made deterrence by punishment feasible.

Nuclear deterrence defined the military relationship between the superpowers during the Cold War. Even though the nuclear arsenal of the United States was superior to that of the

Map 3.1 The Western Geopolitical View of the World during the Cold War

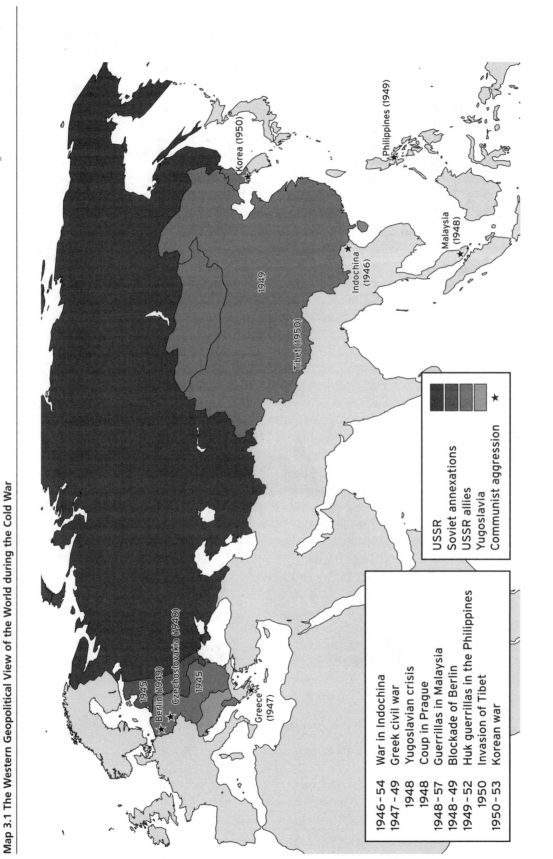

Philippines (1949)

Korea (1950)

Malaysia (1948)

1949

Indochina (1946)

Tibet (1950)

1945

Berlin (1949)

Czechoslovakia (1948)

1945

Greece (1947)

1946–54	War in Indochina
1947–49	Greek civil war
1948	Yugoslavian crisis
1948	Coup in Prague
1948–57	Guerrillas in Malaysia
1948–49	Blockade of Berlin
1949–52	Huk guerrillas in the Philippines
1950	Invasion of Tibet
1950–53	Korean war

★

USSR
Soviet annexations
USSR allies
Yugoslavia
Communist aggression

SOURCE: GERARD CHALIAND AND JEAN-PIERRE RAGEAU, *STRATEGIC ATLAS: COMPARATIVE GEOPOLITICS OF THE WORLD'S POWERS*, 3RD ED. COPYRIGHT © 1993 BY GERARD CHALIAND AND JEAN-PIERRE RAGEAU. REPRINTED BY PERMISSION OF HARPERCOLLINS PUBLISHERS, INC.

Map 3.2 The Soviet Geopolitical View of the World during the Cold War

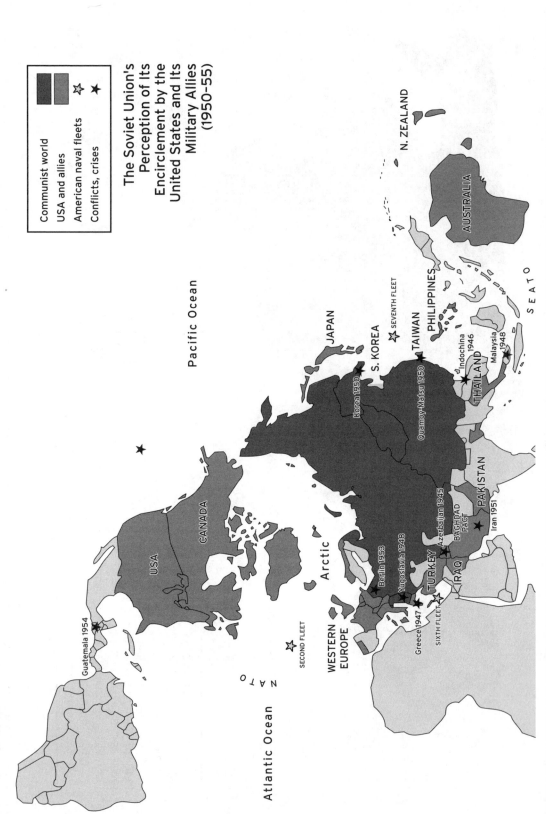

Legend:
- Communist world
- USA and allies
- ☆ American naval fleets
- ★ Conflicts, crises

The Soviet Union's Perception of Its Encirclement by the United States and Its Military Allies (1950–55)

Labels on map: Pacific Ocean, Atlantic Ocean, Arctic, USA, CANADA, Guatemala 1954, WESTERN EUROPE, NATO, SECOND FLEET, Greece 1947, SIXTH FLEET, TURKEY, IRAQ, BAGHDAD PACT, Azerbaijan 1945, Iran 1951, PAKISTAN, Yugoslavia 1948, Berlin 1953, Indochina 1946, Quemoy-Matsu 1950, Korea 1950, S. KOREA, JAPAN, SEVENTH FLEET, TAIWAN, PHILIPPINES, THAILAND, Malaysia 1948, SEATO, AUSTRALIA, N. ZEALAND

SOURCE: GERARD CHALIAND AND JEAN-PIERRE RAGEAU, *STRATEGIC ATLAS: COMPARATIVE GEOPOLITICS OF THE WORLD'S POWERS*, 3RD ED. (NEW YORK: HARPERCOLLINS, 1993), 44. COPYRIGHT © 1993 BY GERARD CHALIAND AND JEAN-PIERRE RAGEAU. REPRINTED BY PERMISSION OF HARPERCOLLINS PUBLISHERS, INC.

U.S.S.R. at least until the mid-1960s, the explosion of the Soviet atomic bomb in 1949 had ended America's nuclear monopoly, and forced both leaderships to confront the consequences of a nuclear war between them. By the mid-1960s, a rough parity, or equivalence, existed between the arsenals of the two superpowers. The nuclear arsenals of the United States and the Soviet Union were capable of inflicting unacceptable damage on the military forces and civilian population of the other in the event of a nuclear war. And so the logic of deterrence by punishment suggested that if both superpowers could annihilate each other in a war, neither would start such a war by launching a first strike. This ability of both superpowers to destroy the other in the event of a nuclear war was referred to as **mutual assured destruction (MAD)**. During the Cold War both superpowers devoted massive resources to the development and maintenance of enormous nuclear forces so there could be no doubt that their arsenals possessed an assured retaliatory capability, which made each country capable of devastating the other under any possible set of circumstances. The result was a nuclear arms race (see Figures 3.1a and b). To this end, both countries built and deployed their arsenals so that even if a large portion of their nuclear forces were destroyed, enough weapons would survive to devastate the other country.

As the Cold War progressed, the size and destructive potential of the nuclear arsenals of both superpowers led to a growing realization that all-out nuclear war between the two countries would be devastating to more than just the superpowers. Not only would the United States and the Soviet Union be destroyed, the effects of nuclear radiation and the possibility of nuclear winter (the cooling of the global climate from the ejection of dust and debris into the atmosphere) raised the question of whether humanity itself would survive a nuclear war. This fear of omnicide, coupled with the enormous expenses of the nuclear arms race, fostered the development of large peace movements and antinuclear movements in most Western countries during the Cold War, dedicated to stopping the nuclear arms race and promoting arms control and disarmament.

During the Cold War, superpower arms control focused on nuclear weapons and on ways to reduce the prospects for nuclear war. The signing of arms control agreements often accompanied larger efforts to improve the relationship between the United States and the Soviet

Figure 3.1a Nuclear Warhead Stockpiles, 1945–2002

YEAR	U.S. (1945)	RUSSIA (1949)	U.K. (1953)	FRANCE (1964)	CHINA (1964)	TOTAL
1945	6	–	–	–	–	6
1950	369	5	–	–	–	374
1955	3 057	200	10	–	–	3 267
1960	20 434	1 605	30	–	–	22 069
1965	31 642	6 129	310	32	5	38 118
1970	26 119	11 643	280	36	75	38 153
1975	27 052	19 055	350	188	185	46 830
1980	23 764	30 062	350	250	280	54 706
1985	23 135	39 197	300	360	425	63 417
1990	21 211	33 417	300	505	430	55 863
1995	10 615	14 978	300	500	400	27 131
2000	10 615	10 201	185	470	400	21 871
2002	10 600	8 600	200	350	400	20 150

Note: Date in brackets is year of acquisition. Israel is believed to have a stockpile of some 200 warheads, the first of which may have been assembled as early as 1967.

SOURCE: "GLOBAL NUCLEAR STOCKPILES, 1945–2002," *BULLETIN OF THE ATOMIC SCIENTISTS* 58 (NOVEMBER/DECEMBER 2002), 103–104.

Figure 3.1b Nuclear Warhead Stockpiles, 1945–2002

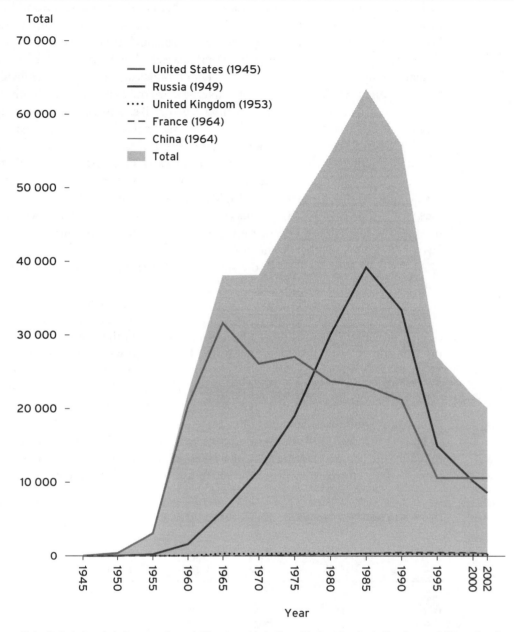

Note: Date in brackets is year of acquisition. Israel is believed to have a stockpile of some 200 warheads, the first of which may have been assembled as early as 1967.

Union in periods of détente. In addition, some arrangements were made in an informal manner: U.S. President Jimmy Carter and Soviet Foreign Minister Andrei Gromyko promised each other that their countries would never be the first to use nuclear weapons. This pledge was never made formal in an agreement, despite the efforts of "no first use declaration" advocates. NATO maintained the right to retaliate with nuclear weapons throughout the Cold War. In 1993 the new Russia confirmed the right to use nuclear weapons to defend itself.

Profile 3.1 reflects the impressive scope of bilateral arms control agreements between the United States and the Soviet Union/Russia (Russia has assumed the U.S.S.R.'s treaty obligations). Among the most important formal agreements were the **Strategic Arms Limitation**

Treaty (SALT) and the **Strategic Arms Reduction Treaty (START)**. Signed in 1972, SALT I placed limits on the number of **intercontinental ballistic missiles (ICBMs)** and **submarine-launched ballistic missiles (SLBMs)** deployable by both sides for five years. SALT I also placed limits on the deployment of **antiballistic missiles (ABMs)** in the so-called ABM Treaty. In 1979, the more comprehensive SALT II agreement placed a ceiling of 2250 on the number of ICBMs, SLBMs, heavy bombers, and air-to-surface ballistic missiles (ASBMs) permitted by each side. After the 1979 Soviet invasion of Afghanistan, the United States Senate never ratified SALT II, although both countries continued to abide by the basic provisions of the treaty. The criticism of both SALT I and SALT II was that neither agreement actually reduced the number of weapons held by the superpowers; the agreements simply introduced restrictions on the numbers of weapons that could be deployed in the future.

In June 1982, the Reagan administration initiated a new round of arms control talks, called the START negotiations. However, any progress on nuclear arms control through START was quickly overshadowed when the Reagan administration embarked on a new course. In a speech on March 23, 1983, President Reagan announced a program to develop a defence against ballistic missiles. The idea was not a new one: by the 1960s both the United States and the U.S.S.R. had developed antiballistic missile systems. However, these systems were of doubtful reliability and effectiveness, and in a world of nuclear deterrence, defences could threaten the logic of MAD. Indeed, the 1972 ABM Treaty ensured the dominance of deterrence by banning the development and deployment of missile defences (with the exception of one installation of 100 interceptors). President Reagan proposed a much more ambitious scheme. His Strategic Defense Initiative (SDI) envisioned the deployment of ground and space-based missile and energy weapons of sufficient capability to shoot down incoming missiles and nuclear warheads. SDI would completely protect the United States and would render nuclear weapons, as Reagan put it, "impotent and obsolete."[9] Due to the high-technology aspects of the program, SDI became known popularly as "Star Wars" after the famous 1977 science fiction movie.

SDI had many supporters. As hard as it is to believe today, some analysts in the United States believed that the U.S.S.R. was surpassing the United States in military power. Missile defences promised to restore U.S. dominance. Others hoped to escape the immorality of MAD and the prospects for a devastating nuclear war. U.S. defence contractors, and many scientific researchers, were naturally supportive of SDI for the billions of dollars in contracts the program promised. Others argued that SDI would strengthen deterrence: faced by both assured destruction and U.S. strategic defences, the U.S.S.R. would never contemplate war. However, there were also many critics of the program. Many charged that SDI was technically infeasible. Energy weapons research had simply not advanced to the point where a deployable weapon could be envisioned. More conventional technologies such as missiles were difficult to guide to their targets with sufficient accuracy: after all, both the incoming warhead and the interceptor missile would be travelling faster than a bullet out of the barrel of a gun. Furthermore, critics argued that since the U.S.S.R. could launch thousands of warheads at the United States, no defensive shield could ever be 100 percent effective. Some warheads would inevitably get through, and these few warheads would cause incalculable damage. There was also the concern that SDI would stimulate an arms race in space. If the United States developed a defensive shield, the U.S.S.R. would respond in kind. Of course, the 1972 ABM Treaty would have to be abrogated as well.[10]

Critics also argued that SDI was destabilizing and could, contrary to its intentions, increase the risk of nuclear war. If a U.S. shield were only partially effective (as it certainly would be) then both the United States and the U.S.S.R. would have an incentive to strike first in a crisis. The U.S.S.R. could strike first, firm in the knowledge that a U.S. shield could not stop a massive first attack. However, if the United States were to strike first and damage the Soviet

Major Bilateral Arms Control Agreements between the United States and the Soviet Union/Russia

PROFILE 3.1

DATE	AGREEMENT	PRINCIPAL AIMS
1963	Hotline Agreement	Establishes a direct radio and telegraph communications link between Moscow and Washington (updated with a satellite communications link in 1971)
1971	Nuclear Accidents Agreement	Creates a procedure for notification of a nuclear accident or unauthorized detonation and establishes safeguards to prevent accidents
1972	SALT I Interim Agreement	Limits number of ICBMs and SLBMs allowed by each side
1972	Anti-Ballistic Missile Treaty	Limits deployment of antiballistic missile systems to two sites (later reduced to one in a protocol in 1974) and prohibits development of space-based ABM systems
1973	Agreement on the Prevention of Nuclear War	Commits superpowers to consult in the event of the threat of nuclear war
1974	Threshold Test Ban	Restricts underground testing of nuclear weapons over the yield of 150 kilotons; broadened in 1976
1977	Convention of the Prohibition of Military or Any Other Hostile Use of Environmental Modification Techniques	Bans weapons that threaten alteration or modification of the environment
1979	SALT II (not ratified)	Restricts number of strategic delivery vehicles permitted by both sides
1987	Nuclear Risk Reduction Centers Agreement	Establishes facilities in both capitals to manage nuclear crisis
1987	Intermediate-Range Nuclear Force Treaty (INF Treaty)	Eliminates U.S. and Soviet ground-launched intermediate-range nuclear weapons in Europe
1990	Chemical Weapons Destruction Agreement	Bans further production of chemical weapons and calls for reduction in weapons stockpiles to 5000 tons each by 2002
1991	START (Strategic Arms Reduction Treaty)	Reduces nuclear arsenals by approximately 30 percent
1992	START I Protocol	Commits Russia, Belarus, Ukraine, and Kazakhstan to strategic weapons reductions specified in START I
1993	START II	Reduces strategic nuclear arsenals to 3000 (Russia) and 3500 (United States) by 2003; bans multiple-warhead land-based missiles

nuclear arsenal, weakening its striking power, SDI might be able to protect the United States from this smaller, less coordinated retaliatory attack. The United States could thus "win" a nuclear war, unless the U.S.S.R. struck first! SDI thus undermined the logic of MAD and, said its critics, made nuclear war more likely. Finally, critics charged that SDI would be too costly and ultimately ineffective. The price tag for a deployable system ran into the hundreds of billions and even trillions of dollars. For far less money, the U.S.S.R. could build more missiles and warheads and develop decoys to overwhelm any strategic defences by sheer weight of numbers. In addition, SDI would be useful (maybe) against only ballistic missiles, and the U.S.S.R. could simply deploy more cruise missiles and bombers. SDI, the critics charged, would end up being the Cold War equivalent of the French Maginot Line.

However, political events began to undermine the SDI program. As superpower relations improved between the Reagan Administration and the new Soviet government of Mikhail Gorbachev, arms control once again became the focus of bilateral relations. In 1987, the superpowers signed the Intermediate-Range Nuclear Forces (INF) agreement, eliminating all U.S. and Soviet medium-range nuclear missile systems in Europe. SDI was quietly shelved, but some research continued, and as we shall see in Chapter 6 the debate over ballistic missile defences would re-emerge in the late 1990s. In July 1991 the START talks, heavily criticized by arms control advocates through the 1980s for their lack of productivity, finally bore fruit when the superpowers signed START, which committed both sides to reducing their nuclear arsenals by one-third. This dramatic agreement was made possible largely by the changing climate brought about by the tail end of the Cold War. Critics charged that the agreement would reduce the nuclear arsenals of the superpowers only to the levels that existed in 1982, the year the START negotiations began. However, by 1989–91 events were in motion that would dramatically alter the context of nuclear arms control. We will explore post–Cold War arms control issues in Chapter 7.

THE INTERNATIONAL DIMENSION

The Cold War rapidly became a fixture of international politics. Not only was the Cold War an immediate concern in North America and the Soviet Union, it had a visible impact in Latin America, Europe, Africa, the Middle East, and in South and East Asia (for the impact of the Cold War on Canada, see Profile 3.2). Indeed, no region was uninfluenced by the superpower confrontation, and crises and confrontations occurred with startling frequency. In the early years of the Cold War, tensions were high and confrontations were numerous, including the Soviet refusal to pull out of Iran in 1946 and reports of Soviet involvement in the Greek Civil War. These events prompted U.S. President Harry S. Truman to adopt the policy suggestions put forward by **George Kennan**. Kennan, a junior official in the United States' embassy in Moscow, decisively influenced postwar U.S. attitudes toward the Soviet Union. Instructed to analyze the postwar intentions of the Soviet Union, Kennan responded with a famous "long telegram," in which he argued that the U.S.S.R. regarded the United States as its foremost international opponent, and that as long as the United States remained strong, Soviet power could not be secure. In an anonymous published statement of his beliefs in the influential journal *Foreign Affairs* in 1947—the famous "X" article—Kennan argued that the Soviet Union represented a dangerous blend of an autocratic ruler (Stalin), a revisionist and messianic ideology (Marxism-Leninism), and a violent and expansionist history. Kennan recommended the political containment of the Soviet Union until the internal nature of the Soviet Union changed and along with it, its foreign policy.[11]

Truman soon declared "that it must be the policy of the United States to support free peoples who are resisting attempted subjugation by armed minorities or outside pressures."[12] This commitment came to be called the **Truman Doctrine**, and was the first articulation of what was to become America's grand strategy during the Cold War: the **containment** of the perceived expansionist and revisionist power of the Soviet Union. The aim of containment was to prevent the spread of Communist ideology around the world, to prevent any direct aggression by the U.S.S.R., and to prevent the Soviet Union from expanding its influence in the world. Virtually all U.S. foreign policy action, from foreign assistance to military intervention to diplomacy, was directly related to or influenced by the objectives of containment. Kennan, however, did not support the emphasis placed on military containment. He felt that the Soviet threat was primarily political and that it could not be met entirely by military means.[13] As tensions between the United States and the Soviet Union escalated, further crises followed, including the American decision to establish the Federal Republic of Germany, a Communist coup in Czechoslovakia in 1948, the Soviet blockade of West Berlin of June 1948, the Communist victory in China in 1949, Chinese behaviour in Tibet, numerous Taiwan Strait crises, and the Korean War in 1950. The Cold War era was also characterized by mass decolonization as the former European empires finally crumbled, and both superpowers competed for allies among newly independent countries.

Europe, which would be the focal point of the superpower competition for much of the Cold War, was divided. The concern of the United States and other Western governments was that the Soviet Union might gain control of Western Europe, either through direct conquest or by having Communist parties taking control in the war-devastated region. To prevent this, the United States launched the **Marshall Plan**, a program of U.S. financial assistance to rebuild the economies of Western Europe. The most prominent confrontations of the early Cold War were centred on the status of Berlin. Germany was split into what would become the Federal Republic of Germany (FRG) or West Germany and the German Democratic Republic (GDR) or East Germany. West Berlin, a small enclave of the city controlled by West Germany, was surrounded by East German territory. The Berlin crises of 1948 and 1961, in which the Soviet Union attempted to gain full control of the city, led to armed confrontations, but not to war. Across Germany, a fenced and guarded line—which Winston Churchill called

Attention. You are now leaving West Berlin. The Berlin Wall, seen here from West Berlin looking into East Berlin in the background, was a symbol of the Cold War division of Europe and the East–West confrontation. The Brandenburg Gate, at the centre of the picture, was in the zone dividing Berlin.

the "iron curtain" in 1946—dramatically symbolized the division of Europe. In 1961, East Germany built the **Berlin Wall**, separating East and West Berlin, and forcibly preventing Berliners from communicating or travelling across this divide.

In 1949, the United States, Canada, and several European allies established NATO, a formal alliance arrangement that solidified the American and Canadian commitment to Western Europe. Throughout the Cold War, half the world's total defence spending would be devoted to the superpower standoff in Europe. It was along the inter-German border that the military forces of NATO (including soldiers from European NATO countries and the United States and Canada) would face the military forces of the Warsaw Pact. In this respect, NATO was a classic alliance, a collective defence arrangement made to counter a common threat. However, NATO also served other functions. First, it guaranteed that U.S. forces would be involved immediately if the Soviet Union attacked Western Europe. NATO thus bound Western Europe and the United States together. Second, NATO also provided for the safe, albeit slow, reintegration of West Germany back into European politics. West Germany would become a member of NATO in 1951. NATO thus served a collective security purpose, providing confidence that Germany did not pose a threat in Europe. And so, in the words of NATO's first Secretary-General, Lord Ismay, NATO was established to "keep the Russians out, the Americans in, and the Germans down."

In China, the nationalists under Chiang Kai-shek and the Communists under Mao Tse-tung had battled invading Japanese forces during World War II. However, the evacuation of the forces of the defeated Japanese left the nationalists and the Communists to battle over control of China. Despite assistance from the United States, Chiang Kai-shek was defeated by the Communists and forced to flee to the island of Formosa, which is today known as Taiwan. On October 1, 1949, the People's Republic of China (PRC) was proclaimed. To the capitalist West, the "loss" of China to Communism was the first of what have been called the two shocks of 1949 (the second shock was the explosion of the first Soviet atomic bomb). Continued fighting between the nationalists and the Communists on mainland China led to a U.S.–Taiwan defence pact in 1954, which was put to the test when nationalist possession of the two small islands of Quemoy and Matsu were threatened by mainland China in 1954–55 and 1958.

Ideological differences, distrust, and Chinese resentment of what they perceived as domineering Soviet attitudes led to the Sino-Soviet split of the early 1960s. Thereafter, the Soviet Union and China were geopolitical and ideological competitors in the world. The two countries engaged in direct although relatively minor military clashes along the disputed common border. During the rest of the Cold War, the Soviet Union devoted approximately one-third of its military resources to guarding the Sino-Soviet frontier. The two countries also engaged in rhetorical sparring matches, each claiming to represent the true path to Communism. The threat posed by Soviet power prompted China to establish a rapprochement with the United States, which culminated in a visit by U.S. President Nixon in 1972. The Sino-Soviet split led to debate over whether the split was fundamentally ideological or geopolitical, similar to the debate over the origins of the Cold War.

In June 1950 the Korean War broke out when Communist North Korea attacked South Korea. In response, the United States and 15 allied countries sent military forces to South Korea. This deployment was done under the collective security provisions of the United Nations, although in practice the United States dominated both the political and military direction of the war. The U.S.S.R. had walked out of the Security Council over the issue of Chinese representation and so was absent (and could not cast a **veto**) when the decisive vote was taken to give UN authorization to the U.S.-led collective security operation. (The Soviet Union would never walk out of the Security Council again!) As the war progressed, allied forces pushed the North Koreans back toward the Chinese border, with the intent of unifying the country. China then intervened, sending more than 300 000 "volunteers" into North

PROFILE 3.2 Canada and the Cold War

Canadian Prime Minister Lester Pearson and American President Lyndon Johnson. Though they had some differences over American foreign policy, particularly with regard to the war in Vietnam, Canada was for the most part a firm ally during the Cold War. (CP Photo)

Canada was a close ally of the United States and a member of the Western club of countries. Some have argued that Canada was a close American ally because it was largely controlled by American interests and capital; essentially, a satellite economy with little real foreign policy autonomy. However, although the flexibility of Canadian governments was limited, Canada adopted the foreign policy it did during the Cold War largely based on an appraisal of Canadian interests in the Cold War world. The reality was that Canada was strategic territory, as any attack on the continental United States would devastate Canada as well. As a result, Canada joined in combined efforts to deter or prevent war by participating in NATO and the North American Air Defence (later Aerospace) Agreement. Canada's economy was heavily dependent on a stable international trading system (built by the United States) and on trade with the United States itself. Since Canada is a democratic country, Canadian governments and the majority of the Canadian people were suspicious and even hostile to Communism as a political and economic system. In other words, Canada was a status quo state, comfortable with its position in the world under the *Pax Americana* and interested in the prevention of instability or war.

However, this comfort did not mean that Canada did not exert an independent foreign policy. Canada was a strong supporter of the UN throughout the Cold War and was a key contributor to United Nations peacekeeping (which contributed to efforts to prevent regional wars from becoming larger conflagrations that might draw in the superpowers). Canada consistently advocated multilateralism during the Cold War, largely because multilateralism gave it an opportunity to participate in cooperative efforts and institutions, giving Canada a voice in international affairs. Canada also took an independent stand toward Cuba, and established good diplomatic relationships and a positive reputation in much of the developing world. However, successive Canadian governments took care not to alienate the United States; Canadian criticisms of U.S. policy in Central and South America and Vietnam were muted as a result.

Korea, who pushed allied forces back in retreat. A stalemate followed near the original border along the 38th parallel, and the war ended in a truce in 1953 (see Profile 3.3). The Korean War heightened Western fears of Communism and revealed that conventional wars could still occur in an era of nuclear weapons and that clashes between the West and the Communist world could occur in the form of proxy wars.

After this period of crisis and the death of Stalin in 1953, the Cold War thawed to some extent. Nikita Khrushchev emerged as the new General Secretary of the Communist Party of the Soviet Union. The first U.S.–Soviet Summit meeting was held at Geneva in 1955. However, the spirit of Geneva did not last long. In 1956, the Soviet Union crushed a rebellion in Hungary. In the Suez Crisis of the same year, Israel, France, and Great Britain invaded Egypt. The European states were clinging to imperial prestige and resented Egypt's **nationalization** of the Suez Canal. The Soviet Union threatened to intervene on behalf of Egypt, one of its allies in the region. The United States, which opposed the actions of its allies in Egypt, com-

PROFILE 3.3 Canada and the Korean War

On June 25, 1950, North Korea invaded South Korea. The next day, under U.S. request, the UN Security Council passed a **resolution** calling on member states to respond to halt North Korean aggression. The Canadian government agreed in principle with the U.S. position, but was noncommittal about sending troops. Initial Canadian contributions involved naval vessels and transport planes. Not until August 7 did the St. Laurent government, under criticism at home for its inaction, commit ground troops to Korea. Canada was anxious that the operation in Korea be controlled and managed by the UN. It was thought that multilateral management of the conflict would restrain American impulsiveness. However, the Korean War was fought largely by American and South Korean forces, and the political decision making was dominated by Washington. This situation led to some criticism in Canada that the Canadian government was too closely tied to that of the United States, a critical theme that persisted throughout the Cold War. Canadian troops joined the 27th Commonwealth Infantry Brigade in February 1951 and later formed the 25th Canadian Infantry Brigade Group operating as part of a Commonwealth Division. Canadian troops took part in a number of battles, and by the war's end on July 27, 1953, Canadian troops had suffered 312 killed and 1577 wounded in what came to be known as Canada's "forgotten war."

pelled them to accept a proposal forwarded by Canadian Foreign Minister Lester B. Pearson for a ceasefire and a UN interpositionary force in the region. Great Britain and France withdrew, and Israel pulled its forces back. Though peace in the region would be short lived, the Suez Canal crisis signalled the end of European dominance in world affairs, the beginning of superpower management of crises, and the introduction of modern peacekeeping.

Cold War intrigue also spread to the Caribbean. The United States attempted to overthrow Fidel Castro's revolution by supporting the **Bay of Pigs** invasion by Cuban exiles. The invasion failed and served to drive Castro further into the Soviet camp. In 1960, an American U-2 spy plane was shot down over the Soviet Union. These incidents culminated in the 1962 Cuban Missile Crisis in which the United States and the Soviet Union came closer to all-out conflict than they would at any time during the Cold War. The crisis was precipitated by the construction of medium-range ballistic missile launch sites on the island of Cuba. These sites, built to offset Cuba's strategic inferiority and to help deter another invasion of the island, were detected

The visual evidence, 1962. The scene in the United Nations Security Council on October 25, 1962, as U.S. Ambassador Adlai Stevenson provides evidence of missile launch sites being built in Cuba. The launch sites were intended for Soviet ballistic missiles aimed at the United States. (AP Photo/CP Archive)

by U.S. aerial reconnaissance. Soviet merchant vessels carrying missiles were also detected as they sailed to Cuba. U.S. President John F. Kennedy imposed a naval blockade of Cuba to prevent the landing of the missiles and to force the removal of the bases. The world seemed headed toward war when the U.S.S.R. agreed not to station missiles in Cuba in return for an American promise not to invade the island. The fear prompted by the Cuban Missile Crisis led both superpowers to establish closer ties, agreeing in 1963 to a Limited Test Ban Treaty that banned atmospheric nuclear tests, as well as to a Moscow–Washington hotline, and a variety of scientific, cultural, and space and aviation agreements.

However, Cold War competition continued around the world (see Profile 3.4). Both superpowers supported allied and client states in the developing world with political, financial, and military assistance. In addition, both the United States and the Soviet Union supported insurgency movements in the allied and client states of the other superpower. The pattern of support did not necessarily reflect ideological positions. In many cases, the United States supported governments and movements that were authoritarian and undemocratic (though not opposed to the investment of American capitalists), while the Soviet Union often supported governments and movements that could scarcely be called Communist. Proxy wars continued, the largest of which occurred in Vietnam, where warfare had persisted since World War II during the painful retreat of French colonialism.

In the Vietnam War, the United States backed a succession of authoritarian governments in Saigon against an internal insurgency mounted by the Viet Cong and supported by Communist North Vietnam (which in turn was supported by the Soviet Union and China). The United States, concerned with expanding Communist influence in Asia, committed itself to preventing a Communist takeover in Vietnam. In the face of continued Communist successes in South Vietnam, what was initially a small U.S. involvement (in the form of military advisers) soon escalated to the deployment of more than 540 000 U.S. troops by 1968. The Americans engaged in massive saturation bombing campaigns of North Vietnam and Cambodia. The United States also introduced the large-scale use of defoliants, such as Agent Orange, to remove the jungle canopy in parts of Vietnam, and engaged in other forms of environmental destruction in a policy known ironically as "Operation Ranch Hand." This was a modern variation of an ancient practice called ecocide: the deliberate destruction of the environment to root out enemy forces. However, the United States failed to defeat the insurgency in South Vietnam or to prevent supplies and reinforcements from the North from reaching the South. The Vietnam War divided the American public and compelled the Nixon Administration to seek an end to the war. The Paris Peace accords of 1973 led to a pullout of all American troops from South Vietnam, which fell to the North in 1975. Approximately 58 000 Americans were killed in Vietnam, and more than 1 million Vietnamese perished. The Vietnam War, often billed as the first war the United States lost, had a profound impact on the American psyche, as many questioned the rightness of the war and were hesitant to support the deployment of U.S. forces to future crises. The failure in Vietnam was compounded by the energy crisis of the 1970s, created by the 1973 Arab oil embargo against the United States and the fall of the U.S.-backed Shah of Iran at the hands of a rebellion led by Islamic clerics in 1979.

However, both superpowers had begun to recognize the wisdom of improving their relations. The foundation for détente had been laid by the development of strategic nuclear parity between the United States and the Soviet Union. By 1969, tensions between the two superpowers had begun to relax. Both superpowers also had domestic rationales for cooperating with the other: U.S. President Richard Nixon had been seeking Soviet assistance to end the Vietnam War, while Leonid Brezhnev (who had come to power in 1964) had hoped that trade and technology transfers from the West would help invigorate a stagnating Soviet economy. The trade relationship

PROFILE 3.4 The Domino Theory and Other Zero-Sum Views

During the Cold War, successive American administrations committed the United States to combating the spread of Communism whenever and wherever it took place, a perspective that was shared to varying degrees in many other Western capitals. This commitment grew from the fear that if one country in a region fell under Communist rule, then the other countries in that region would also be at risk. Therefore, Communism had to be prevented from taking root in even the smallest and remotest of countries. This concept came to be called the *domino theory*, after the practice of lining domino pieces on end one after the other, close together. Tipping over one domino causes the rest of the dominoes to fall. The domino theory suggested that Communism could spread in the same way: once one country fell, its neighbours would inevitably fall as well. This fear contributed to American efforts to prevent the spread of Communism around the world, most prominently in Korea and Vietnam. Another analogy was *salami tactics,* in which the world was represented as a salami. Communism was taking over the world slice by slice, country by country. Yet another instrument was the use of world maps that showed Communist countries in red. As more countries fell to Communism, more red appeared on the map. This method contributed to the fear that the Soviet Union was "painting the map red." All these conceptualizations were based on a zero-sum view of the Cold War; the perception was that a gain for one side was an equivalent loss for the other side, so both superpowers found themselves engaged in struggles for countries whose citizens often knew or cared little about the broader Cold War context.

between the two countries expanded. Visits and cultural exchanges increased. And the superpowers reached new agreements on arms control, including the Strategic Arms Limitation Treaty (SALT) I in 1972 and SALT II in 1979. These agreements placed limits on the size of the superpowers' nuclear arsenals. However, tensions between the superpowers began to increase. And the United States voiced its opposition to continued Soviet involvement in the developing world, which the Soviet leadership resented. And the Soviet Union was disappointed with the economic benefits détente was supposed to bring.

The final blow to détente was the Soviet invasion of Afghanistan in 1979. U.S. President Jimmy Carter responded by enunciating the Carter Doctrine, which committed the United States to protecting its interests in the Persian Gulf by any means necessary, including military force. He also organized a **boycott** of the 1980 Moscow Olympics, suspended U.S. grain exports to the Soviet Union, and dramatically increased defence spending. The invasion of Afghanistan was to prove as much of a quagmire for the Soviet Union as Vietnam had been for the United States. The Soviet Union was unable to fully suppress Afghan resistance to the invasion, and the Soviet army was to suffer 13 000 dead and 35 000 wounded by the resistance fighters, who were given financial and weapons support from the United States through Pakistan. Some of this support would later come back to haunt the United States. Among some of the benefactors of U.S. assistance were those who would later rule Afghanistan in the Taliban government. It was this government that provided sanctuary to terrorists, including Osama Bin Laden and Al-Qaeda, the group believed to be responsible for the September 11, 2001, terrorist attacks. If the invasion of Afghanistan soured U.S.–Soviet relations, the election of President Ronald Reagan in 1980 ushered in a period sometimes referred to as Cold War II. President Reagan and his supporters came to power with a very hostile view of the Soviet Union, which was reflected not only in his public speeches and proclamations (most famously, he repeatedly labelled the U.S.S.R. an "evil empire") but also in the policies of his administration. The Reagan Administration accelerated the military buildup initiated by President Carter, proposed the development of the Strategic Defense Initiative, and enhanced U.S. support to insurgency movements in Soviet client states (particularly in Nicaragua and Angola). Escalating tensions between Washington and Moscow fuelled increasing concerns about the possibility of war and growing opposition to the nuclear arms race in the form of a growing antinuclear movement.

THE END OF THE COLD WAR: POWER POLITICS DESCENDANT?

The combination of the superpower confrontation during the Cold War, the regional wars that broke out around the world, and the nuclear arms race all served to provide ample ammunition to realists. The Cold War seemed to confirm much of the premise and dynamics of the power politics approach to explaining the international system and international relations. However, as we will explore over the next few chapters, some significant new trends began to take shape in the Cold War world, including the development of an increasingly interdependent world economy, the growth of international institutions and organizations, heightened concern over the environment, increased international travel and communication, and the widening gap between the rich and the poor. These trends began to challenge the accuracy of the realist framework. Nevertheless, it was the end of the Cold War that removed the shadow of the superpower rivalry and brought these trends from the back burner of international relations to the front of the international agenda. Few international events have been as dramatic as the end of the Cold War. The revolutions against Communist rule in Eastern Europe, the reunification of Germany, and the collapse of the Soviet Union itself took place within a startlingly short time—from mid-1989 to the end of 1991—and changed the face of global politics. The Cold War ended not with a hegemonic war (as many had feared and anticipated) but with the disintegration of one of the two poles of power. It is crucial to explore the question of why this occurred.

The Soviet Union experienced increased economic stagnation during the rule of Leonid Brezhnev. By the time Mikhail Gorbachev came to power in 1985, the problems facing the Soviet Union were enormous. The economy was performing poorly and in some sectors was actually shrinking. By the 1980s Japan had overtaken the U.S.S.R. as the world's second-largest economy. Soviet central planning had created an economic structure that was inefficient, obsolete, and incapable of meeting the demand for food and even basic consumer items. The Soviet Union's two vital energy resources, coal and oil, were becoming more difficult to extract. The U.S.S.R. had become the world's largest importer of grain, with a quarter of its own crops rotting in the fields because of a poor distribution system. The military budget was absorbing approximately 20 to 25 percent of the country's gross national product (GNP), as well as 33 percent of the country's industrial force, 80 percent of its research and development personnel, and 20 percent of its energy output. In addition, the Soviet Union subsidized its allies, spending more than U.S.$20 billion a year. The workforce suffered from poor morale, with strikes and demonstrations taking place in many cities. Food rationing had to be reintroduced. Life expectancy and infant mortality compared unfavourably with the West. The closed nature of the Soviet system, which restricted access to information and controlled television, newspapers, and books, was unable to take advantage of the computer and information revolution.[14]

Gorbachev's solution to these problems was to implement a reform program based on three elements: **glasnost** (openness) to broaden the boundaries of acceptable political discussion; **perestroika** (restructuring) to reorganize the old economic system by introducing limited market incentives; and democratization to increase the involvement of the people in the political process. It was Gorbachev's hope that this program would revitalize the Soviet economy while the Communist Party remained in power. Gorbachev never envisioned that his reforms would fundamentally alter the nature of political power in the U.S.S.R.; he was a reformer, not a revolutionary (see Profile 3.5). To embark on this program of domestic reform, Gorbachev required a favourable international environment. He required good relations with the West to obtain Western aid so that resources could be diverted from military spending to the civilian economy. Gorbachev embarked on a foreign policy that saw him reach out to the West with arms control proposals and summits with Western leaders. He also withdrew Soviet forces from Afghanistan. In so doing, Gorbachev changed the tone of the East–West relationship, and even became something of a celebrity in the West. Gorbachev's arrival on the international scene marked the beginning of the end of the Cold War.

However, Gorbachev's domestic program did not yield the desired results. In fact, the opposite occurred, as the living standard of the average Soviet citizen actually began to fall. By the end of the 1980s, the contradictions in the Gorbachev reform program were evident. In the attempt to reorganize the economy, the old system was dismantled, while no new legal or reformed banking system was put in place to allow market forces to operate. The result was

PROFILE 3.5 Mikhail Gorbachev

Hailed in Canada. Former Soviet Union President Mikhail Gorbachev presents the James S. Palmer Lecture at the University of Calgary, 12 October 2000. (CP Picture Archive/ Adrian Wyld)

The last leader of the Soviet Union (from March 11, 1985, to December 25, 1991), Mikhail Gorbachev was the architect of the reform program that initiated a chain of events that was to culminate in the collapse of the U.S.S.R. After studying law in Moscow (graduating in 1955), Gorbachev worked his way through the ranks of the Communist Party organization, eventually becoming responsible for agriculture. He became a full **Politburo** member in 1980, and after the deaths of Brezhnev's successors (Yuri Andropov and Konstantin Chernenko), Gorbachev became General Secretary of the Central Committee of the Communist Party of the Soviet Union. He embarked on an ambitious program of political

and economic reform, what he called "the new political thinking" on domestic and foreign policy issues. This reform was dramatically displayed in Gorbachev's approach to arms control, a cooperative relationship with Europe, and a hands-off approach to the Eastern European countries (even when they were throwing off Communist rule).

While Gorbachev's international diplomacy earned him international acclaim and the Nobel Peace Prize in 1990, at home he was increasingly unpopular, and his reform program had unleashed forces that were soon spiralling out of control. Central control over the economy was lost, nationalism spread and intensified, the constituent republics of the U.S.S.R. began to agitate for more autonomy, and the political spectrum in the U.S.S.R. diverged into radical reformers and conservatives. Ultimately, the reform program was rendered obsolete by the political events surrounding the breakup of the Soviet Union.

In retrospect, Gorbachev was one of the great reformers in world history, but his efforts were inadequate in the face of a system that required transformation rather than mere reform. Outside contemporary Russia, Gorbachev is remembered as the Soviet leader who did more than any one individual to make the end of the Cold War peaceful by acquiescing to the freedom of Eastern Europe. However, within Russia, Gorbachev is vilified as the man who caused the collapse of the Soviet Union and increased the misery of the average citizen. The last leader of the Soviet Union remains far more popular abroad than in his own country.

economic decline, unemployment, and a drop in production. Glasnost served to expose the inefficiencies and corruption of the economic system and increasingly of the government and the Communist Party itself. Within the U.S.S.R., some wanted to slow reform and maintain many of the characteristics of the old economic system, while others wanted to accelerate reform and remove the old system entirely. Gorbachev was increasingly isolated politically between these two factions, and his credibility and influence began to wane.

By the late 1980s the end was near. The last gasps of the Soviet Union began in 1989. In a series of revolutions in Eastern Europe—some peaceful, others violent—the ruling Communist parties in those states were swept away with no response from Gorbachev. The Berlin Wall, the symbol of the Cold War division of Germany and the division of Europe, was officially opened on November 7, 1989, although citizens of both countries had been singing and dancing on the wall and taking picks and hammers to the Cold War symbol for days. Germany, divided during the Cold War, was reunified on October 3, 1990. The Warsaw Pact, the Soviet Union's alliance system in Eastern Europe, was dissolved. Although Germany and Eastern European countries would now have to struggle with political and economic reform and the legacy of more than 40 years of Communist rule, the Europe of the Cold War had vanished.

Within the U.S.S.R., increasing disaffection with the central leadership in Moscow led to demands for an increased devolution of powers to the constituent republics. A new Union Treaty was to be signed on August 20, 1991, that would have weakened the power of the centre. However, on August 19, a coup attempt was mounted while Gorbachev was away on vacation,

People power defeats the Berlin Wall. Germans from East and West Berlin celebrate the fall of the Berlin Wall, 10 November 1989. The wall was removed and the Brandenburg Gate was restored. (AP Photo/CP Archive)

and an eight-person council took power.[15] The coup was based in three overlapping groups in the central leadership: the state bureaucracy, military and industrial interests, and the security forces, which all felt threatened and marginalized by the reforms and devolution of powers to the republics. However, the coup failed, largely because key elements of the internal security apparatus and the military refused to support it. Instead, many backed Boris Yeltsin, a former Communist Party official who had been elected Chairman of the Supreme Soviet of the Russian Republic in May 1990 and President of the Russian Republic (the largest of the 15 republics) in June 1991. Faced with public opposition and without control of the army, the junta caved in, and Gorbachev was brought back to Moscow. However, the central government began to simply wither away as governments in the republics gathered increasing power in their own jurisdictions. Gorbachev was quite literally president of a federal bureaucracy detached from the republics and possessing little real authority. The final blow fell with the Ukrainian vote for independence on December 1, 1991, which effectively scuttled the attempts to revive a Union Treaty. Declarations of independence from other republics followed. On December 8 the **Commonwealth of Independent States (CIS)** was formed as a coordinating framework for most of the former republics of the U.S.S.R. (only the Baltic States are non-members). In the last week of December 1991, the Soviet flag was taken down from the Kremlin in Moscow. The Soviet Union had disintegrated, and the Cold War was over.

PONDERING THE END OF THE COLD WAR

For almost half a century, the Cold War defined global politics. Virtually everything deemed internationally newsworthy was directly or indirectly related to the Cold War, whether it was the announcement of new defence spending projects, the negotiation of a new arms control agreement, or the outbreak of a war somewhere in the world. Everyone feared the ever-present threat of nuclear war and the unspeakable yet certain devastation such a war would bring. Indeed, it is possible to speak of a Cold War generation for whom nuclear annihilation was a constant possibility (it still is, but the threat is much less intense). The Cold War affected domestic politics as well. In the democratic industrialized world, the fear of Communism led to suspicion and often suppression of domestic Communist movements. In some countries, witch-hunts were conducted to purge government, the arts, and society of Communist influences. The most famous of these efforts took place in the United States in 1952–53 under Senator Joseph McCarthy, whose use of accusation and innuendo with no substantial evidence gave rise to the term *McCarthyism*, an extreme example of the general tendency during the Cold War to regard with suspicion those who were sympathetic to or supportive of Communism and the Soviet Union (or China). In other countries, anti-Communism was used as an excuse to suppress dissident movements, Communist or non-Communist, often with the larger purpose of maintaining a political and military elite in power. For example, hundreds of thousands of people died in Indonesia as a result of a bloody anti-Communist purge by the Suharto government in 1965. In Communist countries, political freedoms were almost nonexistent, and state-controlled media emphasized the evils of the capitalist West. Reports of international events, when they occurred, were invariably cast in terms of Western plots against the Communist world.

The Cold War was the foundation of the foreign policies of most states. Patterns of tension and conflict around the world either originated in the Cold War or were influenced by it. Events such as the Berlin Airlift and the Cuban Missile Crisis were a direct result of Cold War tensions between the superpowers. Conflicts in Africa, the Arab–Israeli wars, the conflicts between India and Pakistan, and wars such as those in Vietnam and Afghanistan had local or regional origins but took on a Cold War dimension through the direct or indirect involvement of the superpowers. At the same time, Cold War considerations also formed the basis for much cooperation among states. This cooperation took a variety of forms, including the creation of alliances aimed at a common enemy (such as NATO and the Warsaw Pact), the sale of arms to client countries, and arms control agreements between the principal antagonists, the United States and the Soviet Union.

Intellectually, the Cold War contributed to a sense of predictability and order in world affairs. The most predominant concern was maintaining a stable superpower relationship and keeping the Cold War cold. A general consensus (although by no means universal) emerged in most countries with respect to foreign affairs and defence policy. Broadly supported by their publics, governments maintained their alliance commitments and a certain level of defence spending. In scholarly circles, the Cold War seemed to vindicate much of the realist perspective, and academic work concentrated on issues such as strategic stability, deterrence, and arms control. The Cold War fed an interest in the history and politics of the Soviet Union, and Kremlinology became an important area of study. This does not imply that scholarship during the Cold War was stale or uniform. On the contrary, major theoretical debates took place. Most prominent perhaps was the clash between behaviouralists, who wanted to quantify global politics, and traditionalists, who maintained that history, not data analysis, was still the best teacher. This debate ended in an agreement to disagree. An increased interest in economic interdependence fostered the rise of liberal perspectives, and a growing academic voice for and from the Southern Hemisphere pushed theories about imperialism and dependency to the fore. However, when it came to the study of international security issues, the discourse was dominated by the superpower standoff.

The Cold War was characterized by periods of high tension, crises, proxy wars, and a conventional and nuclear arms race between the superpowers and their allies. Why did these differences and confrontations not lead to a global war between the United States and the Soviet Union? First among the reasons was the nuclear stalemate between the two countries. The leaders of both countries knew that if a conflict between them developed into a war, there was a very good chance that the war would escalate to the use of nuclear weapons, resulting in a strategic nuclear war that would at the very least devastate both societies. The Cuban Missile Crisis proved to be the catalyst for a growing realization that to avoid a nuclear war, the superpowers would have to manage their relationship rather than engage in eternal conflict. As a result, both countries exercised caution in their relationship because the consequences of miscalculation were so significant. The superpowers established a hotline between Washington and Moscow to facilitate communication in a crisis. Over time, informal rules were established between the two countries, such as the acknowledgment of spheres of influence in which the other would not overtly interfere and consultation and communication during times of war or crises in regions such as the Middle East and Asia. The leaders of both countries met in summits, arrived at cooperative arrangements such as cultural exchanges and trade agreements, and signed several arms control treaties. All these efforts served to enhance the communication and cooperation between the United States and the Soviet Union and were a reflection of the awareness of both countries that the Cold War had to be kept cold.

Because the end of the Cold War meant the end of conditions that had been so pervasive and all encompassing, it left a conceptual and intellectual aftershock. Political leaders, scholars, and the public began to ask fundamental questions about the nature of global politics, questions that were seldom asked during the Cold War. Little thought had been devoted to what a post–Cold War world would be like. No plans were made for such an eventuality, and some, like John Mearsheimer, suggested that we would come to miss the Cold War, with its familiarities and certainties.[16] In contrast, Francis Fukuyama suggested that the end of the Cold War represented the final triumph of liberal democracy and market economics over authoritarianism and central planning. For Fukuyama, this meant the "end of history," the end of the historical ideological struggle over how human society would be organized.[17] However, in the former Communist world, the end of the Cold War has been much more traumatic. Economic hardship, social decay, and environmental problems abound in many of the countries that are trying—with various degrees of enthusiasm—to restructure their economies and open their political systems.

The collapse of the Soviet Union left many people in Russia wondering what had happened. Post-Soviet Russia embarked on a rapid program of economic reform designed to bring capitalism to the country. The reforms, coupled with the resistance of powerful bureaucratic and industrial interests, have caused massive disruptions in the economy. While a few new rich prosper, life for most Russians has improved only slightly, and for many it has become worse. The sense of pride associated with being citizens of one of only two superpowers has vanished, replaced by the realization of the country's fragmentation and the humiliation of declining standards of living and an erosion of personal safety in the face of growing crime rates. The formerly well-funded sectors of Russian society and industry are also deeply troubled. A poorly led, poorly prepared, and cash-starved military performed poorly in the suppression of Chechnya, a small region in the Caucasus that sought independence. Scientists who worked in the huge Soviet military-industrial complex have struggled to support their families; some have resorted to suicide. The military and the arms industry are willing to sell arms to generate revenue, and a recent trend toward the sale of advanced weapons systems—including a controversial nuclear technology sale to Iran—raises concerns about the proliferation of sophisticated weapons, including weapons of mass destruction.

Some fear that the state of affairs in Russia could lend itself to extremist leadership. Conditions in Russia today are disturbingly similar to those that existed in **Weimar Germany**, and those conditions were instrumental in enabling Adolf Hitler to rise to power. Russian President Vladimir Putin was popular largely for his forceful approach to Chechen separatists. Putin won power in presidential elections in March 2000 (in elections marred by fraud), but many worry that his government shows too much enthusiasm for centralized power, suppression of dissent, and control of the media, and too little enthusiasm for the rule of law. In addition, old patterns of suspicion and hostility remain intact in Russia. When a Russian nuclear submarine sank in the Barents Sea in August 2000, some Russian military officials were quick to blame Western military operations for the accident, though this was unfounded. More significantly, the expansion of NATO in the post–Cold War era is often viewed as a serious threat by Russian nationalists and moderates alike.

WHY DID THE SOVIET UNION COLLAPSE?

Realism has been attacked for its failure to predict the end of the Cold War. In truth, however, none of the theoretical frameworks employed by international relations scholars can claim a better record in this regard. Nevertheless, with the benefit of hindsight, we can isolate several factors that offer potential explanations for the fall of the Soviet Union. In general, these factors point to a superpower that was in increasingly dire straits, a superpower that had become a "Potemkin Village" and was facing an unpromising future (see Profile 3.6).

In retrospect, many observers in the West were well aware of the problems facing the U.S.S.R. However, they underestimated the extent to which these forces were undermining the Communist Party of the Soviet Union, which after all could call on massive military forces, a large internal security apparatus, and state control of political and economic life to maintain its power and keep order in the country. The autopsy following the collapse of the U.S.S.R. has yielded the following perspectives and explanations for this dramatic event:

PROFILE 3.6 The Potemkin Village Analogy

The Potemkin Village analogy originates with the story of a Russian prince named Grigori Potemkin, a favourite of the famous tsarina of Russia, Catherine the Great. Potemkin had helped organize her imperial tour of the southern provinces of the Russian Empire in 1787, taking great efforts to make the tour as spectacular as possible. This effort included the construction of attractive false fronts, or façades, for many of the buildings and towns along the tsarina's route, to impress Catherine with the prosperity of the empire, a prosperity that was at least in part an illusion manufactured by Potemkin. This story is used as an analogy for the state of the Soviet Union by the 1980s, a Potemkin Village, a super-power that was in truth a superpower in military terms only. This façade of strength, while signifi-cant, obscured the fact that the Soviet Union was sliding deeper into economic decline, with most of its citizens cynical about the political and eco-nomic system and struggling to maintain their meagre standard of living.

- *Containment and the arms race.* One explanation is that the grand strategy of containment by the United States worked. The cost of the nuclear arms race, the cost of maintaining a massive military establishment, and the cost of supporting allies in Eastern Europe and overseas bankrupted the Soviet Union. Unable to devote resources to the revitalization of its civilian economy and boost sagging consumer and agricultural production, the U.S.S.R. simply spent itself into its grave. Many realists in the West (particularly in the United States) take this position and argue that the policy of firm containment and high defence spending contributed to the end of the Cold War and a Western victory. In con-trast, liberals argue that, in fact, the containment policies of the West may have prolonged the Cold War. Soviet leaders could use the threat posed by the West as a rallying point for political support and as an excuse to maintain high levels of defence spending and cen-tralized control over the economy. Without an external threat to distract attention from domestic hardships, the U.S.S.R. may have embarked on reform (or even collapsed) far earlier. George Kennan, the original author of containment, argued in 1992 that "the gen-eral effect of Cold War extremism was to delay rather than hasten the great change that overtook the Soviet Union at the end of the 1980s."[18]

- *Imperial overstretch.* Another explanation can be found in the theories of power transi-tion and imperial decline. Using the theories publicized by Yale historian Paul Kennedy, this explanation suggests that empires tend to expand until they overstretch themselves. The costs of these commitments burden the economy at home, which undercuts the long-term capacity of the economy to sustain itself. By this explanation, the U.S.S.R. took on too many commitments in the world, which forced it to devote scarce resources to client states such as Cuba, Syria, and Vietnam. The Soviet Union supplied such countries with financial assistance, preferential trade terms, and weapons. The war in Afghanistan burdened the economy even more in the early 1980s. The costs of these commitments drew already scarce resources out of the country, resources that could have been used to reinvigorate the Soviet economy.

- *Domestic decline.* The most widely accepted explanation of the collapse of the Soviet Union is that the Communist system simply did not work very well. The command economy that had been so successful in guiding the rapid industrialization of the Soviet economy later served to hinder reform and innovation. Consumers suffered from shortages of even basic goods and endured long lineups for food items. Industries in the civilian sector turned out poorly manufactured goods developed and built not for the consumer but to fulfill production **quotas** set by the state. Agricultural techniques stagnated and led to poor distribution and massive waste. Worker morale declined, as exhibited in the famous Soviet workers' proverb: "They pretend to pay us, and we pretend to work." New technologies and techniques could not be absorbed into the Soviet economic system, which became increasingly entrenched in a heavily bureau-cratized political system that favoured the elite few—the *nomenklatura*—but was resis-tant to change. More important, the ruling elites had lost their legitimacy, a legitimacy based at least in part on the idea of building toward a better future. In many of the Soviet Union's regions, nationalism and ethnic identity were growing out of disaffection with the political centre. The collapse of the Soviet Union was therefore the result of a failed economic system, one that could not sustain itself, let alone compete with the West, which was entering the electronic and information age.

- *Gorbachev's reforms.* Another explanation argues that the reform program of Mikhail Gorbachev was the most important reason behind the collapse of the U.S.S.R. Gorbachev sought a middle way to reform between the command economy and market forces. However, no middle way was to be had, and the poorly conceived reform program was doomed from the beginning. This misdirected reform effort made an already bad situation worse, creating such desperation and discontent that the centre lost its grip on power. A different reform program might have succeeded. Alternatively, the old system might have been kept in place, despite its inefficiencies, and the Soviet Union would still exist. The Soviet system was badly run down, but in trying to fix the system, Gorbachev broke it.

- *The triumph of democracy and the market.* Finally, liberals argue that the collapse of the Soviet Union represented a victory for democracy and the market as systems of gover-nance. The virtues and advantages of an open political system, the efficiencies of a market economy, and the capacity to innovate and adapt to changing conditions and technology served as a standard against which all other systems were measured. Clearly, the Communist system did not measure up. The average Soviet citizen was becoming increasingly aware of the living standards enjoyed in the West, and this was a source of increasing concern and embarrassment to the Soviet leadership. This explanation argues that soft power played an important role in the end of the Cold War.

It is tempting to argue that everything changed when the Cold War ended. However, as we saw in the previous chapter, major historical tidal waves leave both changes and continuities in their wake. The end of the Cold War can be described as the third defining event of the 20th century, following the shocks of World War I and World War II. Just as the interwar period and the Cold War years saw changes and continuities, so have the post–Cold War years. We will turn to the issues of contemporary global politics in Part Two of this book.

THE STUDY OF FOREIGN POLICY DECISION MAKING

During the Cold War, international relations scholars began to take an interest in how states (and, to a lesser extent, other actors) made foreign policy decisions. This growing interest cre-ated a distinct area of study in international relations that continues to fascinate.[19] Scholars had a natural interest in how governments reached decisions that could have devastating con-sequences and in how the breakdown of decision-making systems, and the possibility of mis-calculations and errors, might lead to crises or even wars. Scholars working in this area of study borrowed ideas and concepts from psychology (with its interest in motives and percep-tion), economics (which examines the decisions of consumers in terms of tradeoffs and pref-erences), and business administration (with its interest in efficiency and organizational culture). The field was grounded in rational choice theory, which makes certain controversial assumptions about the decision maker.

In general terms, foreign policy is "the concrete steps that officials of a state take with respect to events and situations abroad." Foreign policy is "what individuals representing the state do or do not do in their interactions involving individuals, groups, or officials elsewhere in the world."[20] Foreign policy, then, is the public policy of a state, implemented in the environment external to the state. However, this definition excludes nonstate actors and the influence of domestic politics. Of course, we must remember that nonstate actors, such as the Holy See, multinational corporations, and humanitarian relief organizations, can make decisions relevant to events and situations abroad, as can nonstate militants that resort to orchestrated violence. We must also be aware that domestic decisions can have foreign policy consequences; in fact, the boundary between domestic and international issues has been eroding steadily. The spread of diseases such as severe acute respiratory syndrome (SARS), bovine spongiform encephalopathy (BSE or mad cow disease), and the avian flu have raised questions about the domestic safety and regulatory practices of states in international forums. In addition to domestic government and medical officials, these international discussions have also included scientific groups, nongovernmental organizations, and officials of the World Health Organization (WHO). In short, foreign policy decision making often involves more than just the consideration of state actors.

As defined by James Dougherty and Robert Pfaltzgraff Jr., "decision making is simply the act of choosing among available alternatives about which uncertainty exists."[21] The primary concern of decision-making theory is process, rather than outputs or actual decisions. When actors make decisions, these decisions are made in a larger context, which influences the nature of the decision. This context includes

- *The external environment.* The broader setting in which the decision must be made includes the kind of issue confronting the actor, the position and power of the actor with respect to others, and the influences and pressures that are being exerted on the actor by others.

- *The internal environment.* The domestic setting in which the decision must be made concerns the nature and structure of the political system, the role of key decision makers, the influence of public opinion or interest groups, the influence of domestic political factors (such as elections), and the role of certain bureaucracies in foreign policy decision making.

- *The perceptions of the decision makers.* The perceptual lenses of individual decision makers can have a major influence on decision making. How individuals in the process see the world and the actors in it is a key determinant of actor behaviour.

- *The decision-making process.* The rules governing how decisions are made can be a crucial influence. Is one individual making the decision? Is the decision made by majority vote or the achievement of consensus among a leadership group? Was the decision taken with wide consultation and democratic input?

- *The time constraints.* The temporal setting (the amount of time the decision makers have in which to reach a decision) is crucial. If a decision is required quickly, it will be made in a different way than if the decision involves long-term planning.

In order to analyze foreign policy decisions, students and scholars of global politics must account for this context if they are to have a complete picture of why a decision was made.

An important constraint on students of decision making is access to information. In many cases, vital documents may be held as state secrets, sometimes for decades. Interviews with key decision makers may yield self-serving interpretations of events. Incomplete media reports can lead to erroneous conclusions or the development of conspiracy theories. Propaganda and misinformation may lead analysts astray. As a result, the study of decision making often involves revisions to supposed facts and truths, and reassessments of explanations once thought to be above reproach. Of course, all of this makes it very difficult to engage in analysis of recent decisions. The more recent the decision under analysis, the less information will be available on how the decision was made.

In order to make sense of how decisions are made, a variety of different models have evolved. Two main models of decision making are used, and they offer alternative explanations of how decisions are made by actors in the international system (although they are primarily focused on states). The **rational actor model** argues that decision makers make decisions in a rational fashion. The **bureaucratic politics model** suggests that decision outputs are the result of competition and bargaining among different organizations within government.

THE RATIONAL ACTOR MODEL

Recall that the realist perspective, which dominated academic discourse on international relations during the Cold War, assumes that states are rational, unitary actors. Liberals make the same basic assumption about individuals. In the rational actor model of decision making (also called the *classical model*), decisions are regarded as the product of a largely unified and purposeful process based on considerations of available alternatives aimed at selecting the best option. In other words, decisions are the result of a rational process of choice designed to maximize outcomes. The rational choice process has four steps:

1. *Recognize and identify the problem.* Recognizing that a decision must be made, and identifying the nature of the problem, is the first step in any rational process of decision making.

2. *Establish objectives and aims.* The next step involves considerations of one's goals with respect to the issue at stake. These goals must be established based on judgments about interests and preferences, in addition to expectations about prospects for success.

3. *Establish options.* Next, possible alternative decisions must be formulated and considered in the context of available resources, capabilities, and potential reactions by other actors.

4. *Select an option.* Finally, the best option available—in terms of satisfying the goals of the actor and having the best chance of success—will be selected.

As a result, this model contends that decisions are—or, certainly, should be—the product of a careful cost–benefit analysis process.

As an example, take the decision of the Canadian government under Brian Mulroney to pursue and then sign the Canada–U.S. Free Trade Agreement, which came into force on January 1, 1989. The rational actor model would explain this decision beginning with the belief of the Canadian government that it faced a problem. The problem was a looming crisis in the Canadian economy: the economy could not be competitive in the future or sustain a high living standard for Canadians by serving the small Canadian market. In fact, this was the conclusion of the Macdonald Royal Commission in 1985. With the problem established, the rational actor model suggests the Canadian government would then have developed its objectives, which included developing markets for Canadians products abroad (in order to expand the demand for Canadian products). The government would then have examined its options. Canada could have pursued increased trade liberalization through multilateral trade negotiations. However, multilateral negotiations were slow and cumbersome. Canada might have pursued bilateral trade agreements with Europe or Japan. However, the limited demand for Canadian products in Europe or Japan and the constraint of transportation costs reduced the viability of this option. Another option was to seek a free trade agreement with the United States, the largest market in the world and already the destination of the vast majority of Canadian products. A free trade agreement would secure Canada's access to the U.S. economy, and pre-empt economic nationalists in the United States from erecting protectionist trade barriers that would shut Canadian products out of the U.S. market. However, there was concern across Canada that signing a free trade agreement would threaten Canadian sovereignty and cultural distinctiveness, and compromise Canadian policies on health and environmental regulations. Finally, the rational actor model suggests that the Canadian government would have weighed the advantages and disadvantages of each option, and then selected the option that it considered best: that option was pursuing a free trade agreement with the United States. The rational actor model thus provides us with one possible explanation of the decision making process. The next step for the analyst is to test the accuracy of the model, by conducting research to determine whether the Canadian government really did act in this "rational" manner.

However, decision making in the real world can seldom exist in such a pure or comprehensive theoretical form. In practice, decision making is impeded or constrained by a number of factors. This phenomenon is known as **bounded rationality**.[22] The ability of individuals to process information and operate effectively under pressure varies. The information that decision makers receive may be incomplete or inaccurate. Decisions may also be made based on **satisficing**,[23] which occurs when decision makers examine their available alternatives until they encounter one that meets their minimum standards of acceptability. They then select that alternative without proceeding to examine any further options, even though better ones may be available. Other decision makers may choose to make small, incremental decisions and so avoid having to undertake a fundamental review of an existing policy or make a decisive decision on a current issue. Finally, decision makers will seldom select an option that carries a high level of risk. Instead, decision makers will bypass such options and decide on those that entail fewer prospects for gains but also fewer risks.[24]

Decision makers are risk averse rather than risk acceptant; even Saddam Hussein's decision to invade Kuwait in 1990 may be explained with reference to the idea that he did not realize he risked an American counteroffensive. Time constraints may also force decision makers to make choices under pressure without the advantages of careful deliberation. Indeed, during crises rational decision-making processes tend to break down.[25] Very little time is available to gather information and test it for accuracy, and communications between individuals and groups may be disrupted. Insufficient time may be available to formulate a comprehensive set of options and to consider their advantages and disadvantages. Decision makers tend to fall back on prevailing views or assumptions and ignore or dismiss contrary opinions or information. Stress and sleep deprivation may affect the ability of decision makers to make reasoned choices. Emotions become more intense and are a greater factor in decisions. Mistakes and errors are made with greater frequency, with fewer opportunities to catch and correct them. As a result, at a time when the issues at stake are very important and when the need for an effective decision is most urgent, the decision-making procedures and systems designed to make effective, reasoned outputs might break down. All of these factors suggest that human and organizational variables will compromise the extent to which decisions can be made in a perfectly rational manner. However, decision makers may still be acting rationally, in accordance with the four steps outlined above. The idea that rationality may be bounded does not challenge the rational actor model; it simply reminds us that there are limits to what decision makers can know and how perfectly rational they can be.

Furthermore, government officials do not make decisions in vacuums; the external environment is often of crucial importance. In liberal democracies such as Canada, two variables often have immense influence: interest groups and public opinion. Interest groups comprise individuals who share common perspectives and goals on particular issues and seek to influence the decisions made on such issues. For the leaders of states, these societal interests must often be accommodated, although in practice the influence of various groups and the openness of the political system to such groups vary considerably. Interest groups can take a wide variety of shapes and forms, including political parties, professional associations, business coalitions, labour unions, churches, senior citizens, veterans' groups, and activist organizations such as human rights or environmental groups. These groups engage in two levels of activity: lobbying and public awareness campaigns.

Lobbying occurs when representatives of interest groups meet with decision makers in an attempt to change or influence their views on an issue. In some cases rewards may be offered to the decision maker in return for taking a particular stand on an issue. In countries where corruption is a serious problem, rewards may take the form of bribes or favours of various illicit kinds. In other cases, interest groups may take their case directly to the public in an effort to influence public attitudes and wishes about certain issues. In this way, interest groups can achieve their aim by compelling decision makers to respond to larger public pressure. Public awareness campaigns can take the form of written or electronically disseminated material, protest rallies and marches, and seminars. For example, nongovernmental organizations raised international awareness of the global land mines problem by using the Internet. The profile of this campaign compelled governments of states such as Canada to respond to the issue with the creation of a global land mines treaty. In practice, interest groups may have goals or views that clash with the interests of broader society (however those might be defined), and wealthy clients can hire lobbyists who are more effective. To return to our example of Canada and free trade with the United States, during the private and public deliberations leading up to the Canada–U.S. Free Trade Agreement, interest groups lobbied the Canadian government in an effort to influence the outcome of the decision. Most (though not all) corporations, business associations, and provincial governments were prominent supporters of free trade, and lobbied the government to reach an agreement. On the other hand, most labour unions, social activist groups, and environmental nongovernmental organizations were opposed to a free trade agreement, or wanted it to address their key concerns (this would occur, to some extent, with NAFTA, signed several years later). And so, one interpretation of the Canadian government's decision to enter a free trade agreement with the United States is the superior lobbying power of Canadian business interests. The influence of interest groups has often been derided as counterproductive and a threat to representative decision making in a democratic society.

Public opinion is a general reference to the range of attitudes held by the people in society. Public opinion is especially important in democratic political systems, although it is not irrelevant in authoritarian systems. To win public support for their foreign policies, governments will launch information or propaganda campaigns. These campaigns can vary considerably, from efforts by governments to explain and justify their actions to blatant distortions and falsifications of evidence. In democratic political systems, public opinion can be gauged through polls, which can influence government action. In some cases, autocratic and democratic governments may embark on a foreign policy venture to increase their popularity or to distract the public from domestic problems. This has been called the "diversionary theory of war" or "wagging the dog," after a popular movie released in the 1990s.[26] An example of this phenomenon is the 1982 Falklands War, in which the military government of Argentina seized Las Malvinas (the Falklands) in an effort to revive its sagging popularity at home. It worked, but only for a short time as Great Britain retook the islands by force. The Argentine government fell shortly thereafter. The same argument could be applied to the British government of Margaret Thatcher, which was low in the polls before the crisis and may have used the British military response to bolster its domestic popularity.

As any pollster knows, public opinion is rarely monolithic. Frequently, public opinion can be uninformed and tend toward simplistic views and beliefs, which can complicate the efforts of decision makers to explain their policies or the constraints facing the country on a certain issue. As a result, public opinion can send mixed or contradictory signals to government decision makers. Public opinion can also change and, therefore, compel governments to act in haphazard and unpredictable ways. For example, in 1992, media coverage of the war and famine in Somalia created public opinion pressure on the U.S. government to lead a multinational force (which included Canada) to support the relief effort and end the war. Less than a year later, 18 U.S. soldiers were killed in an ambush and one soldier's body was dragged through the streets of Mogadishu. U.S. public opinion shifted dramatically against U.S. involvement in Somalia, and the U.S. withdrew shortly thereafter. However, it would be a mistake to assume that governments are always at the mercy of swings in domestic public opinion; governments can (and often do) pursue foreign policy actions that either lack a broad base of support or are deeply unpopular.[27] For example, the Spanish and Italian governments both supported the invasion of Iraq in 2003, despite widespread domestic protests. However, the Spanish government was voted out of office in March 2004, as public opposition to its domestic policies grew, especially in the wake of a series of bombings against commuter trains in Madrid, which left 191 people killed and over 1800 injured.

Nevertheless, public opinion does not have the same level of influence over foreign policy issues that it does over domestic issues. Foreign policy decision makers generally have more autonomy from both public scrutiny and public input, because diplomacy tends to be both less visible and more secretive. Therefore, international affairs is often regarded as the exclusive reserve of a foreign policy elite, composed of elected and unelected government officials, some business elites, journalists, lobbyists, and experts. For this reason, advocates of the rational actor model argue that it remains the best explanation of how decisions get made.

THE BUREAUCRATIC POLITICS MODEL

The bureaucratic politics model makes very different assumptions about the nature of the decision-making process. This model suggests that decision-making outputs do not reflect a process of the rational consideration of alternatives by individuals but rather are the result of the process of competition or bargaining among bureaucratic units with divergent perspectives on the issues.[28] One of the most famous works on decision making was *Essence of Decision: Explaining the Cuban Missile Crisis*, written by Graham Allison in 1971.[29] In his discussion of the bureaucratic politics model, Allison argued that state decisions would be the result of "pulling and hauling" between government agencies. What bureaucratic interests are involved in this process? Governments have become increasingly dependent on foreign policy bureaucracies, which provide a source of expertise on the issues and have the staff and instruments at their disposal to execute the decisions of governments. Many of these bureaucratic units are engaged in the decision-making process. In Canada, for example, the Prime Minister's Office, the Department of Foreign Affairs and International Trade, the Department of National Defence, the Department of Finance, and parliamentary committees have input into foreign policy decision making.

The assumption of the bureaucratic politics model is that those who represent different bureaucratic interests within the decision-making structure will hold different views on the issue confronting the decision makers. This assumption is premised on the idea that where an individual stands on an issue depends on where that individual sits; individuals representing the Department of Foreign Affairs and International Trade may have a very different view of how the Canadian government should act than individuals from the Department of Finance or from the Canadian International Development Agency. Also at stake in this bureaucratic process—whether it involves struggling or bargaining—are the prestige, influence, and perhaps the budget, of the bureaucratic agency.

Another influence that organizations can exert on decision making is through the organizational process by which they implement or execute decisions. The organizational process model suggests that decisions are neither the result of a rational process of choice nor the result of competition or bargaining among bureaucracies. Instead, decision-making outcomes are the result of the constraints imposed on decision makers by the bureaucratic organizations that execute the decisions of policymakers. These constraints come in the form of standard practices or routines called standard operating procedures (SOPs). Because these SOPs reflect what an organization is prepared or equipped to do, they can limit the range of choices available to the decision maker. In other words, the organization responsible for executing a decision may not be capable of performing the desired tasks. In effect, the capabilities, preparedness, and contingency plans of an organization often determine the range of choice available to decision makers.

Returning to our example of the Canadian government's decision to pursue a free trade agreement with the United States, the bureaucratic politics model would explain the decision making process very differently than the rational actor model. The decision of the Canadian government would have been the outcome of "pulling and hauling" between organizational units of the Canadian government. The Department of Foreign Affairs and International Trade, the Department of Finance, Industry Canada, Natural Resources Canada, the Prime Minister's Office, and a myriad of other departments and agencies of the Canadian government would have advanced their own positions on the issue of free trade depending on their bureaucratic interests. At the end of the day, the bureaucratic units in favour of a free trade agreement with the United States prevailed. This perspective thus challenges the notion that foreign policy decisions are the result of a process of rational deliberation. Instead, they are the result of bureaucratic and organizational interests engaged in a process characterized by a lack of unity among the key departments and agencies in state governments.

THE INDIVIDUAL, THE GROUP, AND THE ROLE OF PERCEPTION

Perception plays a crucial role in the decision-making process. Perception can have an impact on decision making on two levels: the level of the individual and the level of the group or organization. At the level of the individual, all decision makers have different and often unique life experiences, preconceptions, personal beliefs, value systems, prejudices, and fears that influence their perspective of the world and how they process information about it. As a result, considerable attention has been devoted to the perceptions of individual decision makers and the link between these perceptions and their decisions.[30] This study can be done through content analysis (the exploration of themes in speeches and writings), examinations of personal histories, or the discovery of operational codes in which routine and method act as an influence on personal beliefs.[31] In addition, leadership style can be an important influence on decisions, especially when a single leader dominates the decision-making process.[32]

In short, we all possess perceptual lenses through which we view the world. Individuals examine and process information through these perceptual lenses, which leads to some of the following tendencies in decision making:

- *Worst-case analysis.* Decision makers tend to regard their own decisions as objective responses, while attributing hostile motives to the decisions of others.

- *Mirror imaging.* Decision makers can form similar images of each other ("we are peaceful, they are warlike," etc.) that reinforce mutual hostility. Decision makers can also make the mistake of believing that other decision makers are mirror images of themselves and that they will act in the same manner.

- *Wishful thinking.* Decision makers may have a personal attachment to a certain outcome, and may overestimate the chances of achieving that outcome.

- *Historical analogy.* Frequently, decision makers will employ history as a guide to policy, a process that can be beneficial or counterproductive, depending on the appropriateness of the analogy and the similarities with the current issue.

- *Affective bias.* All decision makers have learned or intuitive preconceptions of issues or actors. Decision makers tend to be more accepting of information that confirms their predispositions and less accepting of information that challenges those preconceptions.

- *Grooved thinking.* Decision makers may categorize information or events into a few basic types, and in some cases information and events may be unsuitably categorized, which can lead to inappropriate foreign policy responses.

- *Uncommitted thinking.* Decision makers may have no opinions on certain issues and questions and may vacillate or flip flop among different views of the issue and the different options available to respond to it.

- *Committed thinking.* Alternatively, decision makers may have a strong commitment to certain beliefs and views that remain consistent over time and are difficult to change.

At the group level, the dynamics that take place between individuals within a decision-making body (whether it be the foreign policy team of a state, or the decision-making body of a nonstate actor) can also influence the decision-making process. In some circumstances, the influence of group dynamics can promote a rigorous and systematic approach to the problem by accounting for a number of individual differences expressed by those in the group. In effect, the group can promote rationality by encouraging deliberation and debate. However, group dynamics may also interfere with the rationality of a decision-making process. Groups can develop shared mindsets or belief systems—in essence, dominant views—that individuals within the group are afraid to challenge. Psychology experiments have shown that when a group of six people are shown two lines on a screen and five of the six people (who are accomplices to the experiment) say that the lines are of equal length when in fact they are not, the sixth individual is likely to agree with the group rather than make the correct assessment. This phenomenon is called **groupthink**.[33] In extreme cases, those who advocate policies at odds with the prevailing view may be ostracized or isolated from the group.

In addition, groups and organizations have their own cultures, perceptual lenses, and value systems, and information and ideas that are in accordance with these belief systems are passed up the organizational ladder. Those ideas that are not in accordance with prevailing views are discarded, subjected to intense scrutiny, and perhaps never passed up the organizational ladder by junior officials, who may try to anticipate what senior decision makers want to hear or read. This is called **anticipatory compliance**.[34] In the wake of the Iraq War, questions have arisen in both the United States and the United Kingdom concerning prewar intelligence reports on Iraqi weapons of mass destruction. Iraq did possess chemical weapons in the 1980s and in fact used them on numerous occasions, especially during the Iran–Iraq War. However, as of mid-2004 no evidence had come to light that Iraq had possessed the vast stocks of chemical and biological weapons that U.S. and British intelligence dossiers claimed it did. This intelligence was a crucial component of the case for war presented by U.S. President George Bush and British Prime Minister Tony Blair. Some have accused the two leaders of engineering a deliberate deception in order to gain domestic and international support for the war. Others have suggested that political interference from senior government officials distorted the intelligence reports, and this distorted evidence was presented to the leaders as accurate information. It is also possible that decision makers in both governments experienced groupthink. It is also possible that intelligence officials engaged in anticipatory compliance when passing intelligence information up the ladder to senior government officials. In any case, this example is likely to occupy the attention of many analysts for a long time.

These conceptual models of decision making can be valuable instruments for students of international relations, as the models can be used to derive alternative explanations for why decisions were made. To use another example, in May 1998, India tested a series of nuclear warheads, tests that established India as a declared nuclear power. Why did India conduct these tests? One explanation is derived from the rational actor model. India tested nuclear warheads because the government felt that it was the best option in the face of India's security concerns about Pakistan and China and that the tests would bolster India's power and prestige in the world. The bureaucratic politics model suggests that the tests were the outcome of competing interests within the Indian state, with the pro-test factions led by the military and nuclear science establishments emerging victorious. Alternatively, the tests could have been an effort (and a successful one at that) to rally public support behind the new government led by the Bharatiya Janata party. In other words, the tests were driven by domestic political considerations. By using these decision-making models to analyze historical and contemporary events, we can gain a richer understanding of the nature of the decisions made in the arena of global politics.

How did this group make decisions? President George W. Bush and his National Security Council meet on September 12, 2001. From left to right, CIA Director George Tenet, Secretary of Defense Donald Rumsfeld, Secretary of State Colin Powell, President Bush, Vice President Dick Cheney, Chairman of the Joint Chiefs of Staff Gen. Henry Shelton, and National Security Advisor Condoleezza Rice. Were these individuals rational actors or bureaucratic actors? What were their views of the world, and their perceptions of the attacks that had taken place the day before? (AP Photo/Doug Mills/CP Archive)

PLAYING GAMES

Yet another instrument used to study the decisions of policy makers is **game theory**, which is further derived from a rational choice model. Game theory is a branch of mathematics concerned with modelling behaviour and outcomes under certain prescribed conditions. Two or more actors are provided with a set of alternative policy choices, and each is provided with a set of payoffs that are dependent on both their policy choice and the policy choices of others. In other words, the expected utility (the payoff or gain) is influenced by the decisions of others. Therefore, the policy choices of the players are influenced not only by their policy preferences but also by their expectations about the policy preferences of others. Game theory attempts to predict the outcomes of games by anticipating the preferences of the players. The outcomes of games can also be affected by altering the payoffs or gains that the actors receive. Some games are zero-sum games in which a loss by one actor is considered a gain for the other. Other games are non-zero-sum games in which it is possible for both players to gain (or to lose).[35]

Game theory is employed by some scholars in international relations to model the behaviour of states under certain conditions. It should not surprise us that realists often employ models that assume rationality and utility maximization. In particular, a game called **Prisoner's Dilemma** is used by realists to demonstrate how the character of an environment can lead actors to make rational, self-interested choices that will actually leave them worse off than if they were to cooperate with one another. The actors in the game do not cooperate because no basis for trust exists among them; this situation is roughly equivalent to the security dilemma discussed in the previous chapter.

Prisoner's Dilemma is the most common games model; it centres on a story of two prisoners who have jointly committed a crime, such as armed robbery. The two prisoners are placed in their own cells and are unable to communicate with each other. The prosecutor knows that the two prisoners have committed the crime but requires a confession to get a conviction on the charge of armed robbery. Otherwise, the prosecutor has enough evidence only to get a conviction on the lesser charge of possession of a gun. The prosecutor offers the following deal to each prisoner:

> If you confess, and your partner does not, you will go free and your partner will go to jail for armed robbery for 10 years. If your partner confesses, and you do not, your partner will go free and you will go to jail for armed robbery for 10 years. If you both confess, you will split the penalty for armed robbery, and you will each go to jail for 5 years. If you both do not confess, you will both be convicted for gun possession and will serve a penalty of 1 year.

The game assumes there is no possibility for retaliation, that this is an isolated case, and that the prisoners care only about their own individual interests. Given these payoffs, the outcome of the game is clear: both prisoners will confess to the crime of armed robbery. The logic for such a decision is based on the following calculation of individual interest by each prisoner:

> I should confess, because if I confess and my partner does not, I will go free and my partner will go to jail. If I confess and my partner also confesses, I will still go to jail, but for a shorter term than I would if I didn't confess and my partner did. Under no circumstances should I not confess, for I cannot trust my partner to do the same.

Both prisoners will serve fairly long sentences when they could have served a short one by trusting each other to keep quiet. The Prisoner's Dilemma game can be represented by the following chart:

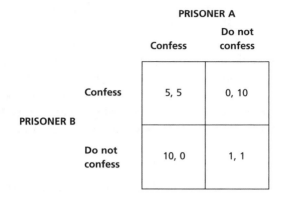

PRISONER A

		Confess	Do not confess
	Confess	5, 5	0, 10
PRISONER B			
	Do not confess	10, 0	1, 1

This chart is called a *payoff matrix* and illustrates the choices and payoffs facing each prisoner. Therefore, if both prisoners confess, they each get 5 years in prison. If prisoner B confesses and prisoner A does not, prisoner B goes free while prisoner A receives 10 years in prison for armed robbery. If both prisoners do not confess, they receive one year in prison for gun possession charges. In international relations theory, this game has been used to illustrate how countries may find themselves in arms races. It is in the interest of both countries not to engage in an arms race, for they will expend vast sums of money and yet end up no more secure than they were before. However, neither country can afford to trust the other by not arming itself, for if one country armed and the other did not, then the country that did not arm would be at a disadvantage. So both countries arm, even though both states would do better to avoid an arms race altogether.

Another game often employed by international relations scholars is called Chicken, drawn from a practice allegedly popular among North American teenagers in the 1950s and immortalized by James Dean in the movie *Rebel Without a Cause*. Two cars are driven toward one another, on a collision course, at high speed on a narrow stretch of road. The first to swerve to avoid the imminent collision is "chicken" and suffers a corresponding drop in prestige. The driver who does not swerve wins an increase in prestige at the cost of the other driver's reputation. If both drivers swerve, they both lose prestige but not as much as they would have if they had swerved alone. If they both do not swerve, they will collide and be killed or seriously injured. As they approach each other, the two drivers may take actions that are designed to signal their commitment to stay on course, such as accelerating, raising their hands off the steering wheel, or removing the steering wheel and throwing it out the window (thus entirely removing the ability to swerve).[36] The following payoff matrix applies:

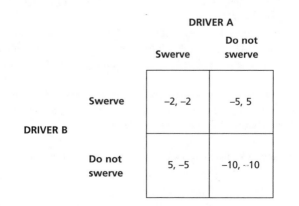

DRIVER A

		Swerve	Do not swerve
	Swerve	−2, −2	−5, 5
DRIVER B			
	Do not swerve	5, −5	−10, −10

This game is used to model international crises in which countries are on a collision course toward war; the country that blinks or backs down first "loses." If neither country backs down, the outcome may be a costly or devastating war.

As mentioned earlier, the study of decision making grew rapidly in popularity among scholars during the Cold War. This interest grew largely because the decisions made in Washington and in Moscow were so significant for the international system. Because decisions made in these capitals could have led to conflict or even nuclear war, a natural interest in the character and dynamics of decision making emerged. The study of foreign policy decision making remains of vital importance today, as states grapple with the tortuous dilemma presented by the American "War on Terrorism." More than ever, we seek to understand the causes and implications of foreign policy decisions in an uncertain world.

CONCLUSIONS

This chapter began with an examination of the various themes and dynamics of the Cold War, an omnipresent reality in global politics after World War II, which influenced virtually every aspect of international life. The tense relationship between the superpowers and the nature of the nuclear arms race fuelled the growth of decision-making analysis as a subfield of the study of international relations. However, as we will see in later chapters, the international system began to experience some significant changes in the latter half of the Cold War period, changes that served to challenge the accuracy and applicability of the power politics approach. We now turn to an examination of one of these changes: the growth of economic interdependence in the global economy.

Endnotes

1. "The Military Role of Nuclear Weapons: Perceptions and Misperceptions," *Foreign Affairs* 62 (1983), 59–80.
2. Jeremy Isaacs and Taylor Downing, *Cold War: An Illustrated History* (Toronto: Little, Brown, and Company, 1998), 232.
3. The term *Cold War* originates in the 14th century and refers to the long conflict between Muslims and Christians for the control of Spain.
4. See John Lewis Gaddis, *The Long Peace* (New York: Oxford University Press, 1987); and John Lewis Gaddis, "Great Illusions, the Long Peace, and the Future of the International System," in Charles W. Kegley Jr., ed., *The Long Postwar Peace* (New York: Harper Collins, 1991), 25–55.
5. Quoted in Charles W. Kegley Jr. and Eugene R. Wittkopf, *World Politics: Trend and Transformation,* 5th ed. (New York: St. Martin's Press, 1995).
6. Robert W. Tucker, "1989 and All That," *Foreign Policy* 69 (Fall 1990), 94.
7. See Denis Smith, *Diplomacy of Fear: Canada and the Cold War 1941–1948* (Toronto: University of Toronto Press, 1988).
8. Lawrence Freedman, *The Evolution of Nuclear Strategy* (London: The Macmillan Press, 1983).
9. Ronald Reagan, "Speech on Military Spending and a New Defense," in Douglas P. Lackey, ed., *Ethics and Strategic Defense* (Belmont, CA: Wadsworth, 1989), 36.
10. For a review of some of the contending perspectives on SDI see Craig Snyder, ed., *The Strategic Defense Debate: Can "Star Wars" Make Us Safe?* (Philadelphia: University of Pennsylvania Press, 1986); and Hans Binnendijk, ed., *Strategic Defense in the 21st Century* (Washington, DC: Center for the Study of Foreign Affairs, 1986).
11. X [George F. Kennan], "The Sources of Soviet Conduct," *Foreign Affairs* 25 (July 1947), 566–82.
12. Quoted in John Lewis Gaddis, *Strategies of Containment: A Critical Appraisal of Postwar American National Security Policy* (New York: Oxford University Press, 1982), 64–65.
13. Ibid., 40.
14. David Mackenzie and Michael W. Curran, *A History of the Soviet Union,* 2nd ed. (Belmont, CA: Wadsworth, 1991), 474–75.

15. In a rather embarrassing episode, Canadian government officials decided to reach out to the coup leaders, stating they would communicate with them in the near future.

16. John Mearsheimer, "Why We Will Soon Miss the Cold War," *Atlantic Monthly*, August 1990, 35–50.

17. See Francis Fukuyama, *The End of History and the Last Man* (New York: Free Press, 1992).

18. George Kennan, "The G.O.P. Won the Cold War? Ridiculous," *New York Times,* 21 October 1992, A21.

19. For a discussion of the development of foreign policy analysis see Walter Carlsnaes, "Foreign Policy," in Walter Carlsnaes, Thomas Risse, and Beth A. Simmons, eds., *Handbook of International Relations* (London: Sage, 2002), 331–49.

20. James N. Rosenau, "The Study of Foreign Policy," in James N. Rosenau, Kenneth W. Thompson, and Gavin Boyd, eds., *World Politics: An Introduction* (New York: Free Press, 1976), 16.

21. James E. Dougherty and Robert L. Pfaltzgraff Jr., *Contending Theories of International Relations: A Comprehensive Survey*, 4th ed. (New York: Longman, 1996), 457.

22. Herbert A. Simon, *Models of Bounded Rationality* (Cambridge, MA: MIT Press, 1982).

23. See Herbert A. Simon, *Models of Man* (New York: Wiley, 1957).

24. Jack S. Levy, "An Introduction to Prospect Theory," *Political Psychology* 13 (June 1992), 171–86. See also Yaacov Vertzberger, *Risk Taking and Decision-making: Foreign Military Intervention Decisions* (Stanford: Stanford University Press, 1998).

25. Michael Brecher, *Crises in World Politics: Theory and Reality* (New York: Pergamon Press, 1993).

26. See Jack S. Levy, "The Diversionary Theory of War: A Critique," in Manus I. Midlansky, ed., *Handbook of War Studies* (Boston: Unwin Hyman, 1989), 259–88.

27. For more on public opinion and U.S. foreign policy, see Eugene R. Wittkopf and James M. McCormick, eds., *The Domestic Sources of American Foreign Policy* (Lanham, MD: Rowman and Littlefield, 2003).

28. David A. Welch, "The Organizational Process and Bureaucratic Politics Paradigms: Retrospect and Prospect," *International Security* 17 (1992), 112–46.

29. Graham T. Allison, *Essence of Decision: Explaining the Cuban Missile Crisis* (New York: Harper and Row, 1971). See also Graham T. Allison and Philip Zelikow, *Essence of Decision: Explaining the Cuban Missile Crisis*, 2nd ed. (New York: Longman, 1999); and Jonathan Bendor and Thomas H. Hammond, "Rethinking Allison's Models," *American Political Science Review* 86 (1992), 301–22.

30. For a discussion of psychological factors in the study of decision making see Janice Gross Stein, "Psychological Explanations of International Conflict," in Walter Carlsnaes, Thomas Risse, and Beth A. Simmons, eds., *Handbook of International Relations* (London: Sage, 2002), 292–308.

31. See Robert G.L. Waite, "Leadership Pathologies: The Kaiser and the Fuhrer and the Decisions for War in 1914 and 1939," in Betty Glad, ed., *Psychological Dimensions of War* (Newbury Park: Sage, 1990), 143–68; and Alexander George, "The 'Operational Code': A Neglected Approach to the Study of Political Leaders and Decision-Making," *International Studies Quarterly* 13 (1969), 199–222.

32. See Margaret G. Hermann, Thomas Preston, Baghat Korany, and Timothy M. Shaw, "Who Leads Matters: The Effects of Powerful Individuals," *International Studies Review, Special Issue* 3 (Summer 2001), 83–131.

33. Irving L. Janis, *Victims of Groupthink: A Psychological Study of Foreign-Policy Decisions and Fiascoes* (Boston: Houghton Mifflin, 1972). See also Paul A. Kowert, *Groupthink or Deadlock: When Do Leaders Learn from Their Advisors?* (Albany, NY: State University of New York Press, 2002).

34. E.K. Stern and Bengt Sundelius, "Understanding Small Group Decisions in Foreign Policy: Process, Diagnosis, and Procedure," in P. t'Hart, E.K. Stern, and Bengt Sundelius, eds., *Beyond Groupthink: Political Dynamics and Foreign Policy Making* (Ann Arbor: University of Michigan Press, 1997), 123–50.

35. Pierre Allan and Christian Schmidt, *Game Theory and International Relations: Preferences, Information, and Empirical Evidence* (Brookfield, VT: Edward Elgar Pub., 1994).

36. In the movie, James Dean and his opponent race toward a cliff in separate cars; the one who jumps out of the car first loses. The other driver is killed when his door jams and he goes over the cliff; this may be a more appropriate analogy, after all.

Suggested Readings

Note: See also the detailed bibliography in J. Young and J. Kent, *International Relations Since 1945: A Global History* (Oxford: Oxford University Press, 2004).

Allan, P., and C. Schmidt. *Game Theory and International Relations: Preferences, Information, and Empirical Evidence.* Brookfield, VT: Edward Elgar Pub., 1994.

Allison, Graham T., *Essence of Decision: Explaining the Cuban Missile Crisis.* New York: Harper and Row, 1971.

Allison, Graham T., and Philip Zelikow. *Essence of Decision: Explaining the Cuban Missile Crisis.* 2nd ed. New York: Longman, 1999.

Binnendijk, Hans, ed. *Strategic Defense in the 21st Century.* Washington, DC: Center for the Study of Foreign Affairs, 1986.

Bottome, E. *The Balance of Terror: A Guide to the Arms Race.* Boston: Beacon Press, 1971.

Carlsnaes, Walter, Thomas Risse, and Beth A. Simmons, eds. *Handbook of International Relations.* London: Sage, 2002.

Catudal, H. *Nuclear Deterrence: Does it Deter?* Atlantic Highlands, NJ: Humanities Press, 1985.

Craig, P., and J. Jungerman. *Nuclear Arms Race: Technology and Society.* New York: McGraw-Hill, 1986.

Gaddis, John Lewis. *The Long Peace.* New York: Oxford University Press, 1987.

——. *The United States and the Origins of the Cold War, 1941–1947.* New York: Columbia University Press, 1972.

George, A. *Bridging the Gap: Theory and Practice in Foreign Policy.* Washington, DC: United States Institute of Peace, 1993.

Geva, N., and A. Mintz, eds. *Decision Making in War and Peace: The Cognitive Rational Debate.* Boulder, CO: Lynne Rienner, 1997.

Harvard Nuclear Study Group. *Living with Nuclear Weapons.* Toronto: Bantam Books, 1983.

Hess, G. *Presidential Decisions for War: Korea, Vietnam, and the Persian Gulf.* Baltimore: Johns Hopkins University Press, 2001.

Kowert, P. *Groupthink or Deadlock: When Do Leaders Learn from Their Advisors?* Albany, NY: State University of New York Press, 2002.

Lafeber, W. *America, Russia and the Cold War, 1945–1990.* 6th ed. New York: McGraw-Hill, 1991.

McKeown, T., and D. Caldwell, eds. *Diplomacy, Force, and Leadership: Essays in Honor of Alexander George.* Boulder, CO: Westview Press, 1993.

Neack, L., J. Hey, and P. Haney, eds. *Foreign Policy Analysis: Continuity and Change in Its Second Generation.* Englewood Cliffs, NJ: Prentice-Hall, 1995.

Nogee, J., and R. Donaldson. *Soviet Foreign Policy Since World War II.* 4th ed. New York: Macmillan, 1992.

Reiss, E. *The Strategic Defense Initiative.* Cambridge, NY: Cambridge University Press, 1992.

Renshon, S., and D. Welch Larson, eds. *Good Judgment in Foreign Policy: Theory and Application.* Lanham, MD: Rowman and Littlefield, 2003.

Reynolds, D. *One World Indivisible: A Global History Since 1945.* London: Allen Lane, 2000.

Roberts, J. *Decision-Making during International Crises.* New York: St. Martin's Press, 1988.

Robertson, C. *International Politics since World War II: A Short History.* 2nd ed. New York: John Wiley and Sons, 1975.

Sakwa, R. *Gorbachev and His Reforms, 1985–1990.* New York: Prentice Hall, 1990.

Smith, D. *Diplomacy of Fear: Canada and the Cold War, 1941–1948.* Toronto: University of Toronto Press, 1988.

Smith, H. *The New Russians.* New York: Random House, 1990.

Snyder, Craig, ed. *The Strategic Defense Debate: Can "Star Wars" Make Us Safe?* Philadelphia: University of Pennsylvania Press, 1986.

t'Hart, P., and E.K. Stern, and Bengt Sundelius, eds. *Beyond Groupthink: Political Dynamics and Foreign Policy Making.* Ann Arbor: University of Michigan Press, 1997.

Vertzberger, Y. *Risk Taking and Decision-making: Foreign Military Intervention Decisions.* Stanford: Stanford University Press, 1998.

Vertzberger, Y. *The World in Their Minds: Information Processing, Cognition, and Perception in Foreign Policy Decisionmaking.* Stanford: Stanford University Press, 1990.

Wittkopf, E, and J. McCormick, eds. *The Domestic Sources of American Foreign Policy.* Lanham, MD: Rowman and Littlefield, 2003.

Suggested Websites

Center for Defense Information: Nuclear Weapons
http://www.cdi.org/issues/nukef&f/database

Cold War Hot Links
http://www.stmartin.edu/~dprice/cold.war.html

Cold War International History Project
http://wwics.si.edu/index.cfm?topic_id=1409&fuseaction=topics.home

President Reagan's "Star Wars" Speech
http://www.cnn.com/SPECIALS/cold.war/episodes/22/documents/starwars.speech/

U.S. Diplomatic History Resources Index
http://faculty.tamu-commerce.edu/sarantakes/stuff.html

CHAPTER 4

Political Perspectives on the World Economy

The British taste for tea ... could not have been cultivated in that damp little island had it not been able to export its cheap textiles to Southern Asia, albeit to sell them in captive colonial markets, along with common law, cricket and railways.

—*Malcolm Waters[1]*

AN INTRODUCTION TO INTERNATIONAL POLITICAL ECONOMY

The global economy we so readily refer to today has been a long time in the making. Historians, economists, and anthropologists alike remind us that long before the advent of the modern state era, the spread of ideas, technology, and culture was facilitated first and foremost by the growth of trade between groups, nations, and empires. The development of modern capitalism in Europe and its expansion around the world established European dominance in the global economy by the 17th century. Following the two world wars and the decline of European imperial power, the United States became the dominant state actor in the world economy, and the leading proponent of liberal economics. Today capitalism remains the primary socioeconomic system in the world, and the principles of liberal economics guide the theory (if not always the practice) behind the economic policies of most states, **International Financial Institutions (IFIs)** and banks, and corporations. Trade agreements, financial flows, technology, IFIs, and increased communications traffic all suggest the world economy is a place of great convergence. World economic output continues to expand: world economic growth was estimated at 4.8 percent in 2000, 2.4 percent in 2001, and 3 percent in 2002.[2] The value of world exports was estimated at U.S.$6.4 billion in 2002.[3] There were an estimated 500 million Internet users in 2002, a number expected to grow to over 1 billion by 2005.[4] In the face of such developments, it is not surprising that analysts continue to speak of the process of "globalization" and a "borderless world."[5]

For advocates of liberal economics, the spread of capitalism is seen as a positive phenomenon, bringing greater wealth and quality of life to the world's population and reducing the prospects for war as trade and investment promote international interdependence and cooperation. However, many analysts, students, and activists dispute this view. Critics argue that the world economy is unfair, unstable, and unsustainable; the growth of wealth in some highly protected locales has come at the expense of poverty, dislocation, and violence in other areas, and has uniformly damaged the natural ecosystems on which it is based. The world is increasingly polarized between the generally rich states of the Northern Hemisphere and the generally poor states of the Southern Hemisphere. This polarization is at the root of the North–South debate, which is reflected in different opinions about IFIs and in diplomatic disputes at international conferences on environmental and development issues.

Trade has certainly increased international contact and cooperation throughout human history, but it has also produced trade disputes, empires, economic coercion, and warfare. Economically powerful states have tended to dominate weaker ones. The attempt by poor Southern states to "catch up" to the North and achieve the same level of affluence has not been particularly successful, although there are notable exceptions. For critics, the 1997 Asian financial crisis, the bursting of the "dot-com" stock bubble in 2000, and the costly fallout from a culture of greed and mismanagement in several major corporations in 2003 (such as Enron in the United States and Parmalat in Italy) all serve notice that the world economy is not stable. According to this negative view of the global economy, the future looks bleak as well, not only because the technological advances (including genetic science) of the industrialized world will disproportionately benefit the richest portion of the world's population, and economic growth worldwide has been pursued with little regard for environmental sustainability, but because of the continued cultural divide between Western commercial culture and those communities determined to resist its seemingly inexorable expansion. Some would argue the violent events of September 11, 2001, may be at least partially explained in this context.

These wildly different visions of the future are, of course, extremes, drawn to illustrate the divides that exist within the field of International Political Economy (IPE). Those who study the vast field of IPE are interested in the relationship between economics and politics at the international level. For example, Robert A. Isaak defines IPE as "the study of the politics behind the economic relations among peoples and nations in order to assess their relative wealth and power."[6] Theodore H. Cohn suggests that IPE is "concerned with the interaction between 'the state' and 'the market.' The state and the market, in turn, are associated with the (political) pursuit of power and the (economic) pursuit of wealth."[7] Thomas Oatley defines IPE as "the study of how economic interests and global processes interact to shape government policies."[8] Students of IPE examine the evolution of the global economy, its current structure, and the strain between the state and an increasingly interdependent world economy. This chapter will begin with an examination of the ascendance of IPE in the study of global politics. We will then return to some of the theoretical perspectives introduced in Chapter 1 and examine the foundations of liberal economic theory, as well as some of the alternative approaches to IPE.[9] The chapter will briefly review the evolution of the world economy, setting the stage for our examination of contemporary IPE issues and debates in Chapter 8. This chapter thus explores the conceptual and historical foundations of our modern world economy, and the origins of globalization and marginalization.

ECONOMIC POLITICS ASCENDANT?

We make no attempt here to educate the reader on purely economic matters, be they macro- or microeconomic in nature; a wealth of literature written by economists is readily available.[10] Rather, our focus is on the interaction between political and economic forces, forces that are so interwoven that it is often difficult to discern between the two. In fact, any debate on whether politics drives economics or economics drives politics is at least partially artificial. The realm of politics and the realm of economics almost always overlap.[11] The United

Nations, for example, is well known as a political institution. Yet, through the work of its development agencies, the **World Bank**, and the associated **International Monetary Fund (IMF)**, it is certainly an economic actor as well. When the Prime Minister of Canada personally promotes increased trade in the Pacific region, he or she is acting in the capacity of a political actor, although an economic agenda is being followed. At the same time, economic matters can transcend political ones and vice versa. A particularly dramatic example of the separation of commerce from politics occurred in the Crimean War of 1854–56. While England was at war with Russia, London banks floated loans for the Russian government! In 2004, even as tensions rose between the governments of Taiwan and China over the ongoing issue of Taiwanese independence, Taiwanese corporations were continuing to expand their business operations on the mainland. In contrast, in the late 1960s and early 1970s the United States fought a ruinous war in Vietnam, a country in which it had little economic interest but considerable ideological and strategic interest in the context of the Cold War.

As we discussed in chapters 2 and 3, much of the attention devoted to the study of international affairs has focused on warfare and military security concerns. This focus does not mean that economics was ignored in the conduct of international affairs or in the study of global politics. In fact, it has long been recognized that economic power is a necessary foundation for military power. Nevertheless, economics was often categorized as one of the concerns of low politics rather than high politics for several reasons. The two world wars focused attention on military security issues, and the Cold War was largely defined as the geopolitical and ideological competition of superpower states, conveniently subsuming popular focus on their economic interests. Nuclear weapons were thought to have transformed international politics, and it was believed that both conventional weapons and economic dimensions of power would be less important as a result. American domination of the global capitalist economy offered limited stability and set the majority of rules and norms of the postwar order. However, by the latter half of the Cold War, the profile of international economic issues began to increase, and by the 1990s economic issues were the leading priority for most states. The ascendance of economic issues in global politics can be attributed to the following factors:

- *Increasing global interdependence.* It became increasingly evident by the 1960s that economic activity in the form of trade, financial flows, and monetary policies, facilitated by advances in communications technology, was linking the economies of states to an unprecedented extent. This interdependence was reflected in the increased importance of the economic institutions, organizations, and agreements designed to promote economic transactions across states. These organizations became just as prominent as international institutions built around military security objectives (and in some instances more so).

- *The decline of the U.S. economy.* For much of the early Cold War, the United States was the world's only economic superpower (the closest competitor was the Soviet Union, with an economy half the size of the U.S. economy). However, in the latter half of the Cold War, the U.S. economy entered a period of what some describe as decline, and many observers concluded that the era of U.S. economic dominance was over. The implications of this decline are still hotly debated, even as a general consensus emerged that the United States was no longer in as dominant an economic position as it had been when the postwar international economic system was established.

- *The rise of other state economies.* During the Cold War, other states recovered from the devastation of World War II and became increasingly important actors. The economies of Western Europe and Japan emerged as economic centres of power, and several countries in East Asia—led by the Four Tigers of Hong Kong, Taiwan,

Singapore, and South Korea—experienced high levels of economic growth. China's emergence as an economic power in the late 1980s has led to much speculation that the Chinese economy may one day rival the United States', with dramatic implications for global politics.

- *The rise of multinational corporations (MNCs).* The emergence of MNCs—corporations with operations in several countries—as major economic actors in the world challenged prevailing views about the dominance of states as economic actors. There are over 60 000 MNCs in the world economy, accounting for approximately one-third of world trade. As the size and resources of MNCs grew, so did debates about their impact on global trade and their role in the economic development of poor countries.

- *The oil shocks.* In 1973 and 1980 the oil-rich states of the Middle East (and Venezuela) had a profound influence on international politics through their manipulation of the supply of oil. The heightened international significance of the oil-producing states increased the attention paid to the economic dimension of international relations and increased the external debt of many southern states in the process. The supply of oil remains a strong factor in global politics today.

- *European integration.* In 1951, France, West Germany, Italy, Belgium, the Netherlands, and Luxembourg formed the European Coal and Steel Community (ECSC) to coordinate their production and trade policy in these sectors. Buoyed by their success, and mindful of the ongoing need to reinforce cooperation to prevent Franco-German conflict and to strengthen Western Europe against the Soviet threat, in 1957 these six countries established the European Economic Community (EEC). In 1993, an expanded community of 15 states renamed itself the European Union (EU), and on May 1, 2004, 10 new states joined the EU, continuing a process that remains the leading example of economic and political integration in the world.

- *Growing awareness of global disparities.* While poverty and wealth disparity predate the modern world economy, the wave of decolonization in the post–World War II period led to the creation of a large number of newly independent countries that for the most part were ill-prepared to meet the economic challenges they faced. Beset by high levels of poverty, poor infrastructure, economies dislocated by colonialism, a lack of modern technology, and political instability, these countries were automatically at a disadvantage in the world economy. The wide disparity between the wealth and power of the rich industrialized countries of "the North" and the great majority of **less-developed countries (LDCs)** in "the South" emerged as one of the most serious challenges in global politics, remaining so today.

- *The collapse of the Soviet Union.* The fall of the Soviet Union dramatically illustrated the importance of economics as a foundation for state power. As discussed in Chapter 3, the U.S.S.R.'s decline and eventual collapse were due largely to the failure of its economic system. As well, the fall of the U.S.S.R. removed the military and ideological threat to the West, and as a result economic issues became more prominent on the global stage.

Chapters 2 and 3 focused on a historical and political perspective that emphasized the politics of war and peace. IPE scholars (of all different perspectives) see global history differently. They focus on economic developments and on the relationship between economics, politics, society, and power. However, while this focus on the interaction between the political realm and the economic realm unites all scholars of IPE, there are vast differences in their theoretical orientations, and therefore vast differences in how they describe and explain events in the global economy. In Chapter 1, we explored the core differences between these theoretical perspectives, and we now turn to an explanation of how these different theoretical perspectives approach the subject of IPE.

THINKING ABOUT THE INTERNATIONAL POLITICAL ECONOMY

The importance of theory as a guide for action is powerfully illustrated in the study of IPE, because the principles of economic liberalism form the foundation of the contemporary global economy. Liberal economic principles form the basis of the international trade system and its related organizations such as the **World Trade Organization (WTO)**. Liberal economics have also determined the shape of the international monetary system. MNCs, as well as smaller firms, conduct their global economic affairs in accordance with liberal market principles. The predominant development strategy directed at LDCs is based on liberal approaches to the generation of wealth and the promotion of economic growth. In the first three chapters of this book, we have seen how theoretical perspectives can be influenced by historical events. We also have seen how theory can be the basis of political action. In particular, realism was informed by the events of the interwar period and a certain interpretation of world history. In turn, realism informed much of the security policy decision making of the Cold War period. It is not an exaggeration to suggest that a liberal orthodoxy has dominated the theoretical and policy discourse on global economic affairs.

However, the liberal approach has been subject to sustained criticism from other theoretical approaches, which have very different views of the global economy and subsequent policy prescriptions. In Chapter 8, we shall see how some of this criticism of liberalism has intensified in recent years in the form of antiglobalization perspectives, and how many liberals themselves are critical of how the global economy has developed. For now, we will examine the three broad theoretical perspectives in IPE: economic nationalism (rooted in realism), liberalism, and Marxism. We will explore the foundations of liberal economic theory as it developed out of a reaction against economic nationalism. We will then turn to Marxist perspectives, and then to a hybrid approach called hegemonic stability theory.

REALIST APPROACHES TO IPE: MERCANTILISM AND ECONOMIC NATIONALISM

In Chapter 1, we explored the foundations of realist thought, with its emphasis on the state and the survival and security of the state in an anarchic international environment. Realist approaches to IPE are consistent with this view of global politics. The state is the most important actor in international economic affairs, and states act to secure and advance their economic interests defined in terms of economic power. This is critical because economic power is regarded primarily as a foundation of state power. Realists argue that states are concerned with **relative gains** in economic strength across states. So, if country A and B both experience gains in wealth (that is, they both experience **absolute gains**) but state A experiences a greater gain in wealth than state B, it is this *relative* gain that matters in terms of the power relationship between these two states. Realists thus tend to see the world economy as a **zero-sum** competition: gains experienced by one state are a proportionate loss to another. Relative gains and economic competition are therefore crucial components of the struggle for survival and power among states.[12]

This focus on the state in IPE does not mean realists completely dismiss the relevance of nonstate actors such as MNCs or NGOs. However, these actors must operate in an international system with regulations defined by states. As a result, nonstate actors do not possess the kind of power or significance that liberals would ascribe to them. Similarly, realists argue that international economic organizations are built and managed by states, especially the most powerful states, and as such are primarily forums for state action and arenas for state competition. Why then do states cooperate on trade and financial matters? For realists, states cooperate out of the need for self-help: when the interests of states converge, cooperation is possible. When the interests of states diverge, cooperation is not possible.

The origins of the contemporary realist perspective on IPE can be found in **mercantilism**. Mercantilism is a term derived from the writings of Adam Smith, who criticized the economic practices of the mercantile system that prevailed in Europe between 1500 and 1750. Mercantilism is a set of economic practices that emphasize the connection between state wealth and state power and the necessity of state intervention in economic affairs. Specifically, mercantilists argued that the accumulation of gold and silver in a state treasury would provide the foundation for military strength and political influence. In order to accumulate such wealth, states had to export more goods than they imported. If they could achieve this, more money would flow into the state compared with that flowing out, as foreigners bought more of its goods than its own population bought of foreign goods. Mercantilists were therefore early advocates of **balance of trade** surpluses. The desire to accumulate gold and silver to increase state power also drove European colonialism, as trade surpluses with colonial economies and the precious metals of the colonies helped fill the treasuries of the European imperial states. Today, states remain concerned about the status of their trade balance as well as their balance of payments (see Profile 4.1).

In the wake of the Industrial Revolution, when industrialization and the development of manufacturing capabilities were seen as crucial to state power, mercantilist practices evolved into what today are generally referred to as neomercantilist or economic nationalist practices. Neo-mercantilists and economic nationalists emphasize the building of state power not through the accumulation of precious metals, but entirely through economic practices aimed at generating balance of trade surpluses. This is achieved through the stimulation of domestic production and the promotion of exports.[13] However, a balance of trade surplus can come only at the expense of one's trading partners (who must then have a trade **deficit**). As a result, neomercantilism is often referred to as a **beggar-thy-neighbour** economic policy. As a result, Richard Rosecrance suggests that states have evolved into "trading states," intervening in economic affairs to secure trade surpluses and to ensure that national economic interests are protected and promoted.[14] Neomercantilists and economic nationalists also emphasize the importance of advanced industrial development and technological innovation. Put simply,

PROFILE 4.1 The Balance of Payments

The **balance of payments** is an accounting system for recording a state's financial transactions with the outside world. The balance of payments comprises two accounts: the current account and the capital account. The first includes exports and imports of merchandise (cars, radios, CD-ROM drives), exports and imports of services (management consulting, information), investment income and payments (dividends and interest income earned from foreign investments along with payments to foreigners who have invested in the home country), and foreign aid and other transfers (humanitarian relief, loans and grants,

the sale of military weapons). The capital account includes short-term and long-term investment inflows (foreign investment in the home state) and outflows (investment abroad). States with a highly troubled balance of payments may borrow money from the International Monetary Fund or sell bonds to make up the difference. One other account is important: a state's official reserves, which represent the foreign currencies, gold, and other financial assets accumulated by its central bank to pay for imports and meet other financial obligations.

there is a hierarchy of economic activity in the global economy: high-technology industries are preferable to steel or textile industries, which are in turn preferable to agricultural production and natural resource exports. Those states that position themselves as industrial and technological leaders in the world economy will be best placed to maintain and increase their power in global politics.

How do neomercantilists and economic nationalists translate these principles into government practice? In general, states pursuing this approach employ a combination of **protectionism** and export promotion. States may employ **tariffs** to restrict or reduce imports. Tariffs are essentially taxes charged to goods as they enter a country, and the cost of the tariff is generally passed on to the consumer, thus making that product more expensive and therefore less desirable compared with a domestically produced alternative. Domestic producers thus benefit, and consumer money stays in the country rather than going to a foreign producer of a good. Today, tariffs are still an instrument of import controls, but international trade agreements between states have eliminated or lowered tariffs on most products as states try to derive greater economic benefits from trade. This has led to the use of nontariff barriers to trade, which include safety, health, labelling, or environmental standards that may serve to exclude foreign products and shield domestic firms from foreign competition. Nontariff barriers to trade have been a major issue in global trade negotiations, with champions of free trade arguing that international rules need to be put in place so government rules cannot be used as barriers to trade. However, critics of globalization have argued that placing restrictions on government powers threatens the ability of governments to set appropriate rules for safety, health, and other social standards. For mercantilists, nontariff barriers can be effective instruments for restricting imports.

Members of the Team Canada trade mission prepare to take part in an official dinner hosted by Bavarian President Edmund Stoiber at the Antiquarium der Residenz in Munich, Germany, Febuary 2002. (CP Photo/Fred Chartrand)

States following neomercantilist practices also employ **subsidies**, government programs that provide direct financing, low-cost loans, or tax exemptions to particular high-value industries in order to encourage their development and their international competitiveness or to protect them from foreign competition. The extensive use of subsidies in the world economy today has led to the use of countervailing duties (taxes imposed on imports from a state accused of using illegal subsidies) and anti-dumping duties (taxes imposed on imports that are allegedly being exported into a foreign market and sold at a price below the cost of production). States can also impose **quotas** on imported products, which serve to limit the number of any given product that is imported into the country. A common practice is for states to negotiate "voluntary" export quotas, in which exporting states essentially agree to voluntarily restrict their exports to a particular country, usually in return for similar concessions from their negotiation partners. Taken together, all of these measures are tools (or weapons) employed by states as they seek economic survival and economic gain in an anarchic world. Of course, states with the greatest economic power will have a structural advantage when wielding these instruments, and will have a greater capacity to influence international organizations and use coercion and reward to further their economic objectives. In reality, most states in the global economy pursue some neomercantilist or economic nationalist policies some of the time. Some states, such as Japan, have been known as especially mercantilist because they strongly protect their domestic markets, allowing limited goods and services in, while they actively promote their products abroad. Even less mercantile countries such as Canada have maintained high levels of protectionism on some products while promoting exports abroad. Canada's former Prime Minister, Jean Chrétien, frequently took groups of government and business representatives ("Team Canada") abroad to pursue business contracts.

Despite the limited success of the **General Agreement on Tariffs and Trade (GATT)** negotiations in reducing tariffs, the 1970s ushered in a new era of protectionism, which resulted from several events. The boom in oil prices brought on by the OPEC cartel, the shift from fixed to flexible **exchange rates** that occurred as the United States finally gave up its role as the guarantor of international monetary stability, rising competition from export-led industrializing states such as Japan and the newly industrialized countries (NICs), and increased trade subsidies and barriers imposed by the European Economic Community all created a climate of economic uncertainty. A major recession in the early 1980s, brought on partly by another steep rise in the price of oil, further contributed to this uncertainty. Those threatened by job displacement in the industrialized Northern states put considerable pressure on governments to slow the pace of trade liberalization and impose protectionist measures to preserve sectors of the economy. A notable example was the agricultural sector in Western European states. Economic nationalist practices therefore have a powerful domestic constituency in many countries. In difficult economic times, economic nationalist policies become more popular as groups in society look to governments for protection.

As we shall see in Chapter 8, economic nationalism remains an influential perspective in most states, despite growing international trade and regional and global free trade agreements. Anti–free trade movements have maintained or increased their popularity in most countries, supported by individuals and groups concerned about jobs, social programs, and culture. In response, neomercantilists insist that the state is still the primary actor in the global political economy and that MNCs are simply instruments of the states in which they house their headquarters. Neomercantilists claim that the opening of the world economy to increased trade has led not to a borderless world, as the proponents of globalization proclaim, but to one in which the state continues to act as a protectionist force. Free trade agreements simply reflect the fact that certain states believe that free trade will benefit them and increase, rather than decrease, the power they wield in the world.

LIBERAL APPROACHES TO IPE: CLASSICAL LIBERALISM, KEYNESIANISM, AND INSTITUTIONALISM

In Chapter 1, we examined how the liberal perspective describes and explains global politics. For liberals, international affairs are characterized by increasing interdependence, a decline in the utility of military power, an erosion of the state, and the rise of nonstate actors. The foundation of the liberal approach to IPE rests on the work of Adam Smith (1723–90), specifically in his classic work *An Inquiry into the Nature and Causes of the Wealth of Nations*. Smith's writings were motivated by his opposition to mercantalism, which he argued was not only poor economics, but also a source of "discord and animosity" in international affairs.[15] In contrast, Smith supported the establishment of open markets in which individuals would be free to engage in commerce. The "invisible hand" of unfettered markets could maximize prosperity, and free trade would create "a bond of union and friendship" among nations.[16] From these intellectual beginnings, liberal approaches to IPE emphasize the market and the promotion of individual wealth over protectionism and the accumulation of state power. For liberals, economic actors (whether individuals, firms, or households) will engage in mutually beneficial exchange if given the freedom to do so. While states and their governments will be required to establish laws and enforcement provisions concerning private property and economic transactions, liberals argue that resources are allocated most efficiently through free market activity unburdened by excessive state regulation. Therefore, governments should pursue a hands-off or *laissez-faire* (literally: let do) approach to economic management, allowing individuals, households, and firms the freedom to make their own decisions on economic matters.

At the global economic level, liberals argue that states will gain from increased free trade. In contrast to neomercantilist and economic nationalist thought, liberals argue that trade can benefit everyone, not just states that successfully maintain balance of trade surpluses. By pursuing mutually beneficial exchange, all states can benefit from free trade and it is this benefit that matters, not the relative gains made by some states over others. Liberals thus reject the zero-sum-game characterization of realist approaches to IPE. However, although liberals agree on the basic principles underpinning liberal economic theory, there are significant differences of opinion within the liberal perspective on IPE.[17] We describe these differences in terms of classical liberalism, Keynesianism, and liberal institutionalism.

Classical liberals, like Adam Smith, emphasize *laissez-faire* economic policies and the efficiency of the market in determining the exchange and allocation of money, goods, and resources. Classical liberals are champions of free trade in global politics. In a market-driven international economy every state will find an economic niche by specializing in the production of goods it can produce most efficiently and trading for those goods it cannot produce efficiently. This **absolute advantage** would mean that every state would gain from free trade with other states. Why waste resources producing goods inefficiently, when you can trade for those goods by selling the goods you do produce efficiently? For example, if Canada can produce wood products more efficiently than India, but India can produce cloth more efficiently than Canada, both countries will benefit from specialization and trade. Each country would no longer be wasting resources on inefficient production. As more and more states engaged in such trade, the collective use of their resources would become more and more efficient, and they would all accumulate greater wealth as a result.

Another classical liberal, David Ricardo (1771–1823) took Smith's logic a step further. Ricardo's work *On the Principles of Political Economy, and Taxation* (1817) outlined his theory of **comparative advantage**, which remains the foundation of trade theory to this day.[18] Ricardo's theory of comparative advantage is crucial because it demonstrates why states will (and should, say liberals) trade, even if no absolute advantage exists between them. What if state A and state B contemplated a trade relationship, only to find that state A produced *all* goods more efficiently than state B? Would this not mean that neither state would benefit from trade? Ricardo argued that both states could in fact benefit from trade, because state B would still produce some goods comparatively more efficiently than state A. In other words, even though state A produces all goods more efficiently than state B, not all of these goods will be produced with the same margin of efficiency over the goods produced in state B. It is this comparative margin, or difference, that is the basis for a mutually beneficial trade relationship (see Profile 4.2).

PROFILE 4.2 Comparative Advantage: An Illustration

To illustrate the theory of comparative advantage, we will use a hypothetical example involving Canada and Mexico (in his *On the Principles of Political Economy, and Taxation*, Ricardo used the example of England and Portugal). We will pick two products (wheat and cloth) and one production input (labour). The table below provides the hypothetical amount of labour (hours of work) required to produce one bushel of wheat and one roll of cloth in Canada and Mexico.

	ROLL OF CLOTH	BUSHEL OF WHEAT
Canada	9 hours	7 hours
Mexico	3 hours	6 hours

Mexico therefore has absolute advantage over Canada in the production of both wheat and cloth, because it requires fewer labour hours to produce both products. However, Canada has a comparatively small labour disadvantage in wheat production, and therefore Canada has a comparative advantage in wheat and Mexico has a comparative advantage in cloth. The two countries can specialize and achieve gains from trade by emphasizing what they produce most efficiently. If Canada were to divert 100 hours of labour from cloth production to wheat produc-

tion, wheat production would rise by approximately 14 bushels (100 divided by 7), and cloth production would fall by approximately 11 rolls (–100 divided by 9). If Mexico were to divert 50 hours of labour from wheat production to cloth production, cloth production would increase by nearly 17 rolls (50 divided by 3) and wheat production would fall by approximately 8 bushels (–50 divided by 6). So, through greater specialization and trade, Canada and Mexico together produce 6 more rolls of cloth and 6 more bushels of wheat!

	ROLL OF CLOTH	BUSHEL OF WHEAT
Canada	–11	+14
Mexico	+17	–8
Gain	+6	+6

Of course, this is a simplified example. In the complex world of global economics, states have many trading partners, not just one. There are many goods produced, not just two. And there are more inputs into production costs than labour time expended, including social and environmental costs. Nevertheless, this basic concept of comparative advantage forms the foundation of liberal trade theory: in theory, all states benefit from free trade.

The single greatest challenge to liberal trade theory and its classical liberal foundations is the distribution of the gains from trade. Liberals acknowledge that not all individuals, firms, households, or states will gain equally from free trade. Everyone will benefit, but some will benefit more than others. Liberals emphasize absolute gains (everyone benefits) but as we have seen, realists emphasize relative gains (some benefit more). As we shall see, other critics of liberal economics emphasize the widening gap between those who benefit least (the poor) and those who benefit the most (the rich); Smith's work was completed before the advent of mobile, transnational capital, which today can relocate production processes while seeking the lowest wages and environmental standards.

In contrast to classical liberalism, **Keynesian liberalism** is based on the ideas of John Maynard Keynes (1883–1946). One of the most influential liberal economists of his time, Keynes was critical of both neomercantilism and classical liberal economics.[19] In his view, the classical liberal argument that the pursuit of mutually beneficial exchange in a largely unregulated market would lead to gains for all and society as a whole was flawed. Keynes drew his argument from the experience of the Great Depression, which he believed demonstrated that unregulated market activity would lead to economic instability (such as the 1929 stock market crash) and perpetuate high levels of unemployment (which persisted well into the 1930s). This unemployment in turn would lead to a downturn in the economy (because people had less to spend) and a consequent fall in production and investment. In his most important

The more, the better? Trade has increased dramatically over the decades, and ports such as Vancouver and Halifax are busier than ever. However, while some economies have benefited from trade, others have not. Gains from trade are unevenly distributed, and environmentalists question the ecological sustainability of economic growth. (CP Photo/ Chuck Stoody)

book, *The General Theory of Employment, Interest, and Money* (1936), he challenged the conventional economics of the time, arguing that governments needed to intervene in economic activity to a much greater extent than classical liberals would ever contemplate. Keynes argued that a *laissez-faire* philosophy was harmful during economic downswings and that the state should intervene in the economy, encourage low interest rates, and adopt a fiscal policy that injects money into the economy through increased public expenditure or lower taxes. Keynes's solution to the Depression was for governments to stimulate demand through large public works projects. While this might require running budget deficits in the short term (in effect, governments would borrow money to spend on public works projects) this would benefit society in the long run by increasing employment, and therefore demand, production, and investment. The increased tax revenue generated by a growing economy could then be used to pay off the deficits incurred by government borrowing. In effect, Keynes argued that government intervention in the economy was required to ensure economic stability and the larger social good, which could not always be guaranteed by classical liberal economic policy.

Keynes extended his idea to include international economic affairs. He was a critic of the harsh economic prescriptions of neomercantilism. In *The Economic Consequences of the Peace* (1919), Keynes questioned the wisdom of the postwar settlement that imposed heavy reparations on Germany. Although he was generally supportive of free trade, he argued that governments had to be willing to manage such trade, and intervene when necessary to ensure that free trade did not damage domestic employment levels. Keynes thus saw a positive role for restrictions on imports under certain circumstances. International economic activity, he argued, should be managed and planned through multilateral negotiations, in order to ensure international economic stability and the effective coordination of macroeconomic policies. As an economic adviser to the British government, Keynes drafted proposals for the establishment of an International Clearing Union after World War II. In this system, nations with trade deficits would be able to maintain participation in the global economy by drawing on the union, which other states would help fund. The IMF and the **International Bank for Reconstruction and Development** (now known as the **World Bank**) perform a function similar to that of Keynes's proposed union. Although the Keynesian outlook fell into serious disrepute among industrial countries when it was discovered that undisciplined deficit spending by governments led to high levels of public debt, the idea that it is the government's responsibility to create jobs to keep an economy healthy survives, advocated by famous economists such as Canadian-educated John Kenneth Galbraith. Keynes thus established the principles for a more interventionist, managed approach to liberal economics. As Theodore H. Cohn has argued,

> Despite his divergence from liberal orthodoxy, Keynes remained firmly within the liberal-economic tradition, believing in the importance of individual initiative and the inherent efficiency of the market. Greater management, in Keynes's view, would facilitate rather than impede the efficient functioning of world market forces. Thus, Keynes favoured intervention by the government, not to replace capitalism but to rescue and revitalize it. Keynes's views, calling for greater government intervention in the economy, gave rise to the interventionist strand of liberalism.[20]

Finally, **liberal institutionalism** emphasizes the importance of international organizations and **regimes** in the global economy. We discuss international organizations and regimes in greater detail in Chapter 5, so here we will focus only on the significance of liberal institutionalism in IPE. Regimes are "sets of implicit or explicit principles, norms, rules, and decision-making procedures around which actors' expectations converge."[21] In other words, over time sets of principles, norms, and rules can be established that serve to regulate and guide state behaviour in some issue areas, such as transportation and communication.[22] Liberal institutionalists argue that this desire for coordinating instruments is a logical consequence of cooperation. As states experience gains from cooperation, it is to their mutual benefit to develop mechanisms to govern and regulate their relationship. In IPE, liberal institutionalists point to the creation and rapid growth of regimes established since World War II to regulate economic affairs between states. This wide array of rules determines what kinds of economic activities are allowed or disallowed. Of course, it helps to have these principles, norms, and rules written down, and so it should be no surprise that the world economy is also characterized by a wide array of international agreements, treaties, regulatory agencies, and organizations that serve to manage global economic activity. The relationship between regimes and IGOs is symbiotic. For example, today the WTO and regional trade organizations are part of the global trade regime. These organizations also contribute to the deepening and widening of this regime, as organizations establish new rules and invite new states as members.

For liberal institutionalists, these regimes and organizations matter a great deal, because they serve to entrench liberal economic practices. The greater the cooperation between states, and the more states that participate, the stronger regimes become. States are increasingly bound together in an ever-deepening and ever-widening interdependence, reinforcing the benefits of economic cooperation and the prospects for peace. However, realists and Marxists are less complimentary about the role of regimes. For realists, regimes are merely instruments created and employed by the most powerful states to control international economic activity to their advantage. It is not a coincidence that the United States was the founder and principal maintainer of most of the economic regimes in the world today. On the other hand, Marxists argue that regimes are merely part of the mechanisms of control wielded by economic elites in service of their efforts to exploit others. Like states themselves, regimes and organizations serve the interests of dominant economic classes.

MARXIST APPROACHES TO IPE: LENINISM, DEPENDENCY THEORY, AND WORLD-SYSTEM THEORY

In our discussion of Marxism in Chapter 1, we outlined the core elements of the Marxist approach to global politics. As we have seen, Marxism is grounded by a historical materialist view: economic developments have driven political developments in world history. Marxism is an evolutionary perspective based on transitions from one mode of production to another, holding in common the exploitation of a poor, politically subordinate peasant or working class by a rich, politically dominant land-owning or factory-owning class.[23] History hinges on class struggle, as the subordinate class struggles to achieve its liberation from oppression and exploitation. In capitalist systems—the dominant mode of production in modern times—the *bourgeoisie* (the capitalist class) dominates and exploits the *proletariat* (the workers). The state is merely an instrument of the bourgeoisie, used to maintain their power and privilege.[24] This exploitation cannot end until the capitalist system, the economic foundation of the political order, is overthrown in a revolution of the proletariat that will usher in a classless society free from inequality and therefore free of social conflict.

Karl Marx (1818–83) never developed a comprehensive theory of international politics, and as a result others developed Marxist theories of IPE. It was left to Vladimir Lenin (1870–1924) to build on the work of Marxist and non-Marxist economists (such as John A. Hobson) to develop the theory of imperialism.[25] Marx had predicted that capitalist systems would collapse because of overproduction. As production exceeded demand, employment and wage prospects for the working class would diminish. The proletariat would thus live in growing hardship, and this would eventually spark revolution and the overthrow of the bour-

Still influential: though few states espouse Marxism as an ideology today, its central proponents continue to inspire political activity around the world. Here, members of the leftist People's Liberation Front carry placards of Communist icons (from left) Karl Marx, Friedrich Engels, and Vladimir Lenin in a procession to commemorate international workers on May Day 1998 in Colombo, Sri Lanka. (AP Photo/Gemunu Amarasinghe CP Archive)

geoisie in the advanced capitalist countries (most notably Germany). However, the revolution did not seem imminent, and Lenin explained this by arguing that the age of European imperialism had delayed the revolution. The colonies of the capitalist states of Europe had brought new sources of cheap labour, raw materials, capital, and new markets to consume products. As a result, the predicted crisis in capitalism had not occurred. However, Lenin argued that once the imperial powers had divided the world between them, their desire for more labour, resources, and markets would drive them into competition and war with each other. In this zero-sum game of competition for imperial possessions, the imperial powers would come into conflict and then engage in war, a war that would precipitate the revolution and overthrow capitalism. Although it was not his own idea, Lenin's theory of imperialism was the foundation for subsequent Marxist work on IPE. The idea that capitalism was extended around the world, and the idea that there was a dominant set of capitalist imperial states that dominated and exploited their colonies, would establish the foundation for dependency theory and world-system theory.

Dependency theory developed in Central and South America in the 1960s, and was almost exclusively concerned with development in developing countries (specifically those in Latin America). An important authorial link between Marxism and dependency theory was Paul Baran, who argued that the economic elites in advanced capitalist states used developing states as "source countries" for raw materials and opportunities for corporate profit and investment.[26] Dependency theorists agreed with Baran, pointing to the position of Latin American economies within the economic orbit of the United States. Dependency theorists argued that economic elites in "core" countries such as the United States kept "periphery" countries such as those in Latin America in a subordinate position of "underdevelopment."[27] This dominance was facilitated by the cooperation between economic elites in the United States and economic elites in Latin America. These Latin American elites were landowners and export merchants, whose economic wealth and political power were tied to U.S. elites. What dependency theorists called a *comprador* class thus controlled Latin American countries. The interests of these *compradores* were not in the economic development of their country but in the maintenance of their own power and privilege, which was directly linked to the subordinate and exploited status of their country.[28] Although some countries might develop more than others in this environment, poor countries remained poor by virtue of their subordinate roles in an international capitalist system run by economic elites in core countries, in cooperation with compradores in the periphery countries.

Dependency theory was powerfully influenced by the economic and political role of the United States in Latin America before and during the Cold War. This role frequently took the form of outright intervention in the affairs of Caribbean and Central and South American countries. For example, the U.S. military occupied the Dominican Republic between 1916 and 1924. Although the occupation came in the wake of successive dictatorships, the occupation created a political climate favourable to U.S. investment.[29] In another example, the United States engineered the overthrow of the Guatemalan government of Jacobo Arbenz in 1954. Arbenz had been elected in 1950 on a platform of socioeconomic reforms. Fearing (with little justification) that a nationalist, Communist regime was taking root, the U.S. Central Intelligence Agency embarked on a campaign of subversion that eventually forced Arbenz to resign and flee the country. The CIA installed Castillo Armas in power, beginning a long period of successive Guatemalan dictators who would be responsible for some of the worst human rights abuses in the Americas. However, the most famous example of U.S. intervention in Latin America involved Chile. In 1970, Salvador Allende Gossens, a self-proclaimed Marxist, was elected president over a candidate favoured by the U.S. government and U.S. business in Chile (including Kennecott Copper, International Telephone and Telegraph, and

Pepsi-Cola, among others). The Allende government was reviled by the Nixon Administration, both for its rhetoric (which was highly critical of the United States) and for its economic policies (which included the nationalization of foreign businesses and factories). With the cooperation of U.S. firms, the United States began a campaign to destabilize the Allende government, by cutting off sources of finance and pressuring other countries not to purchase Chilean products. The Chilean economy weakened, and protests began to grow against the government. Finally, in 1973 Allende was overthrown and killed in a military coup led by Augusto Pinochet. The Pinochet regime (which would receive the support of the United States) would go on to become one of the most brutal in South America.[30] Given this record, and the example set by the Cuban revolution, it is not hard to see why dependency theory developed in Latin America, and why it received considerable support in a region that could see for itself what the "core" could do to countries in the "periphery."

World-system theory shares many similarities with dependency theory. The focus of analysis is the world-system, a world economy organized according to the logic of capitalism. Much of world-system theory is drawn from the work of Immanuel Wallerstein, who argued that "there is one world system. It is a world-economy and it is by definition capitalist in form."[31] Like dependency theorists, world-system theorists argue that the world is divided between a dominant "core" and an exploited "periphery." As Wallerstein went on to argue that "capitalism involves not only appropriation of the surplus value by an owner from a labourer, but an appropriation of surplus of the whole world-economy by core areas."[32] World-system theorists thus argue that the world economy mimics domestic capitalism on a global scale. Economic elites in the rich industrialized world, using the power of states that they control, dominate and exploit the poor of the world. The instruments of control are the institutions and nonstate actors of the global economy: international organizations and agencies, multinational corporations, and regimes.

World-system theory does differ from dependency theory in several respects. First, while dependency theory tends to focus on periphery states, especially those in Latin America, world-system theory examines the entire system, including relations among the core countries. Second, world-system theory allows for some movement by states across the categories of core, periphery, and what world-system theorists call "semi-periphery" countries. These semi-periphery countries are more powerful and economically advanced than periphery countries, and enjoy more autonomy from the core. While semi-periphery countries are still dependent on the core, world-system theorists suggest that countries can on occasion move across these categories, while dependency theorists argued that no periphery countries could escape their subordinate status without revolution. Dependency theory and world-system theory, grounded in the Marxist approach, continue to be relevant perspectives in the contemporary study of IPE. As we shall see, these perspectives play a powerful role informing the views of those critical of liberal theories of progress in developing countries. Many of the antiglobalization perspectives we will explore in Chapter 8 are informed by dependency or world-system interpretations of the global economy.

HEGEMONIC STABILITY THEORY AND IPE: IS THE UNITED STATES IN DECLINE?

In Chapter 2, we introduced the theory of hegemonic stability, which holds that a dominant state can exert a stabilizing influence over international affairs, including the management of the world economy. This theory has been one of the most hotly debated and politically significant concepts in the study of global politics since the end of World War II, largely because it has profound implications for the policies (and the very future) of the United States. Although hegemonic stability theory is grounded in realism, there are liberal scholars who support and criticize the theory. In other words, hegemonic stability theory is something of a special case, having won praise and condemnation across theoretical boundaries.

Hegemonic stability theory is grounded in the realist concept of the distribution of power. When one state is so powerful compared to all the others in the system, that state is described as "hegemonic" or a "hegemon." Robert Gilpin characterizes a hegemonic system as one in which "a single powerful state controls or dominates the lesser states in the system."[33] However, the concept of hegemony has been extended beyond the traditional measures of power employed by realists. Immanuel Wallerstein describes a hegemonic environment as one in which "one power can largely impose its rules and wishes (at the very least by effective veto power) in the economic, political, military, and diplomatic and even cultural arenas."[34] Gramscian, postmodern, and constructivist thought extends the idea of hegemony even further to include the dominance of certain ideas and belief systems (such as capitalism and liberal economic theory). Hegemonic ideas are part of the power structure of global politics. Hegemonic states and hegemonic ideas have a symbiotic relationship, each serving to reinforce the dominance of the other. In this way, the status quo is maintained, both in the realm of state power and in the realm of ideas.

In the study of IPE, hegemonic stability theory holds that the existence of a dominant state, willing and capable of exerting leadership in international economic affairs, is essential for the development and maintenance of a stable international economic order. The hegemon uses its preponderance of power in the system to establish rules, institutions, and regimes, and provides the **public goods** necessary for the maintenance of the system. The implications of hegemonic stability theory are therefore quite stark: when there is no hegemon, or when a hegemon is in decline, the prospects for the creation or maintenance of a stable, open international economic system are poor. As Robert Keohane has argued, "hegemonic structures of power, dominated by a single country, are most conducive to the development of strong international regimes whose rules are relatively precise and well obeyed … [T]he decline of hegemonic structures of power can be expected to presage a decline in the corresponding international regimes."[35] This is why many liberals are supportive of hegemonic stability theory. While realists tend to see the hegemon as more coercive, and Marxists tend to see the hegemon as exploitative, liberals regard hegemons as a benevolent presence because the hegemon must be willing to pay a price for its dominant position, and bears a disproportionate share of the burden of maintaining the system.[36]

For liberals, hegemons perform two valuable functions that serve to maintain an open and stable international economic order. First, liberals argue that hegemons will provide public goods in order to maintain an open trading system. Public goods (sometimes referred to as collective goods) are goods that, once created, benefit everyone, including those who do not pay to create or maintain the good. Public goods can be used by anyone, and it is difficult or impossible to restrict their use to some while excluding others. Public parks and sidewalks are examples of domestic public goods. For liberals, an open international economy is a public good established and maintained by the current hegemon (the United States) from which all states derive benefit, whether they contribute to its maintenance or not. Second, because public goods can be used by everyone and exclusion is difficult, the natural tendency of all users is to free ride; that is, to continue to use a public good while contributing nothing to maintain it. Of course, if everyone adopted this approach, the public good (whether a public park, a sidewalk, or the international economic system) could decline into disrepair until it was no longer usable. For liberals, the corrosive impact of free riding on public goods is minimized when a hegemon takes it upon itself to maintain the public good. A hegemon can also reduce free riding by encouraging or threatening other states to bear at least some of the burden of maintaining the good. Therefore, hegemons help to reduce the harmful effects of self-interested free riding. If there is no hegemon, or a hegemon disappears, free riding becomes more likely, and the prospects for maintaining public goods become rather poor.

And so, for most liberal economists, the United States bears a disproportionate share of the burden of maintaining the public good of an open, international economic order, from which all other states benefit. Liberals argue that the United States supplies its currency as the central unit of account and reserve in the world economy, and must therefore maintain a money supply that benefits all, not just U.S. interests. The United States must also maintain a relatively open domestic market, even though more cheaply produced goods are free to enter the United States from abroad, thus threatening domestic interests and jobs. In other words, the United States must tolerate balance of trade deficits in order to maintain a global free trade regime. The United States has also had to take the lead coordinating the macroeconomic policies of the world's largest economies, and providing credit as a lender of last resort when states need to finance deficits or when economic shocks threaten to destabilize the world economy. In short, for liberals a hegemon gives as well as receives in its role, and without U.S. hegemony an open international trading system may never have been built or maintained. However, realists and Marxists have less benevolent views of hegemons. For realists, hegemons maintain their dominant position through the power of reward and threat, and derive a highly disproportionate advantage from this status as compared with any burdens they need to bear. For Marxists, the provision of public goods is merely another instrument of hegemonic control over world capitalism. The hegemon establishes and maintains an open trading system because it is the mechanism through which its dominant elites exert their dominance over poor countries and poor classes, and transnational economic elites in the periphery collude in this system.

Historically, hegemons rise and decline. The period of British hegemony began to decline in the 1870s and disappeared after World War II. The period of U.S. hegemony began during World War II. Today, the question is whether the United States' hegemonic power is beginning to erode. The question is extremely significant, for two reasons. First, debate over U.S. decline obviously strikes a chord in America, as it calls into question the future of American power, American foreign policy, and America's role in the world. Second, the debate over U.S. decline calls into question the future of the international economy, for if the hegemon is in decline, would this not mean the future of the global economic system is in question?

Why do hegemons decline? Periods of hegemony are temporary because of slow but steady changes in the economic fortunes of the most powerful states. Changes in the international distribution of economic power arise from technological innovation and changes in economic efficiency, production costs, and economic competitiveness between states. Eventually, the economic position of a hegemon begins to erode relative to new centres of economic growth and dynamism. Robert Gilpin concludes that "with the inevitable shift in the international distribution of economic and military power from the core to the rising nations … the capacity of the hegemon to maintain the system decreases."[37] In addition, in their effort to maintain the international order, hegemons suffer from what Paul Kennedy has termed "imperial overstretch."[38] Hegemons tend to take on a large number of international commitments, especially military commitments. The investment in these military capabilities draws resources away from economic revitalization and domestic economic development, thus contributing to and even accelerating hegemonic decline. Paul Kennedy's 1987 book titled *The Rise and Fall of the Great Powers* began the enduring debate over U.S. hegemonic decline.

Kennedy and other "declinists" argue that the United States is showing the early symptoms of hegemonic decline. The U.S. share of global economic output fell from 50 percent in 1947 to 20 percent in the 1990s.[39] The United States is now the world's largest debtor nation, has failed to invest in public infrastructure and education, and has overstretched itself with large military budgets and extensive overseas military commitments. However, those who dispute the notion that the United States is in decline have criticized the declinist thesis. "Revivalists" or "renewalists" argue that the drop in the U.S. share of global output can be explained by the recovery of the war-devastated economies of Europe and Japan after World War II. The U.S. economy is more than twice as large as any other in the world. As for high levels of U.S. debt, the U.S. economy remains large and robust enough to sustain such a debt burden. U.S. military spending (historically maintained at approximately 3 percent of GDP) is not an unbearable burden (though recent deficit-financed increases related to the "War on Terrorism" are certainly cause for concern). Furthermore, the United States leads the world in cultural influence, innovation, and ideas, and is therefore the world leader in "soft" power.[40] We can expect the declinist–revivalist debate to continue. The 2003 U.S.-led war on Iraq is viewed by declinists as another example of costly imperial overstretch, while revivalists see it as an expression of the continued dominance of U.S. power.

As the declinist–revivalist debate continues, we can expect the debate between realist, liberal, and Marxist interpretations of IPE to continue as well. Globalization has brought a new energy to theoretical debates in IPE, and concern over the future of the global economy has never been more widespread. In Chapter 8, we will explore globalization and the theoretical debates that surround it in more detail. But to get there, we need a rough composite of from whence we came. We now turn to a discussion of how the modern world economy developed, and how the principles of liberal economics, in particular, became embedded in the structure and institutions of the contemporary world economy. The usual caveat about the inevitability of bias and exclusion on our part fully applies.

THE EVOLUTION OF THE GLOBAL ECONOMY

Throughout history, groups of people have traded with one another. Trade over wide geographic areas developed around 200 B.C.E. with the rise of the Roman and Han Empires. Trade flourished within these empires, and luxury goods traded between the empires via the famous Silk Route and by sea routes connecting Indian and Persian ports with those in the Mediterranean. Trade nearly collapsed after the fall of the Roman Empire and the invasion of India and China by "barbarian" peoples. Long-distance trade routes were reopened between 570 and 1000 C.E. With increased trade came the rise of merchant cities such as Bruges, Venice, Baghdad, Samarkand, and Hangchow. A variety of products, ranging from Asian spices to Flemish woollens, were in heavy demand, and merchants began travelling to sell them. As economic activity and wealth grew, demand for exotic luxury items increased. By 1100 C.E., trading centres had been established all over Europe, from Italy to the Baltic, from England as far east as Bohemia. In 1317 the Venetians produced the Flanders galleys, commercial flotillas that made regular passage between the Adriatic and the North seas. In the 1400s, trade flourished in Europe, and financial empires based on international banking rose in importance (for example, the Fuggers of Augsburg and Medicis of Florence).

Extensive long-distance trade did not begin until about 1500. With the adoption of the mariner's compass and improvements in ship design and building, it became possible to sail the open seas, out of sight of land, and still get—roughly—where one wanted to go. The Portuguese were the first to build a sea-based commercial and political empire, but all the major European nations, including the Spanish, Dutch, French, and others, would soon follow. As a result, just as the Westphalian state system was extended around the world through the expansion of the European empires (see Chapter 2), the economic system of Europe was extended around the world in a similar fashion. Through the 1500–1750 time period, the economic principles of mercantilism prevailed, as states sought balance of trade surpluses and the accumulation of gold and silver. Colonialism and mercantilism were thus closely linked, as some overseas colonies provided markets, cheap labour, and resources, and others (especially in Central and South America) provided gold and silver. The economic and trading systems of non-European empires and civilizations initially survived (and even thrived), but increasingly they were reduced to colonial status by the political and economic dominance of the European empires. In this way, the seeds of the current North–South debate were sown.

Asia had long been a source of many highly valued commodities, such as silk and cotton fabrics, rugs, jewellery, porcelains, sugar, and spices (the remarkable rise of Asia-Pacific trade in the late 1900s is not as surprising when we take this historical context into consideration). But the new sea route to the East and the discovery of America in the late 1400s brought a vast increase in trade not only in luxury items but also in bulk commodities such as rice, sugar, and tea. Older commercial activities were transformed by the widening of markets. Spain increasingly drew cereals from Sicily, the Netherlands drew food from Poland, and the French wine districts ate food from northern France. Russia and the Baltic States entered the commercial scene with the growth of shipping and related industries. Trade had become a way of life for many people by the middle of the past millennium.

Arguably, the opening of the Atlantic in the 16th century was the real beginning of a global economy. In this period, the economic dominance of the Mediterranean and the Middle East receded, as western and northern Europe became the new centres of economic activity with trade links to the Americas, Africa, and Asia. The Portuguese and Spanish were the first to profit, and they retained a near monopoly through most of the 16th century, but their eventual commercial and military decline made room for the British, French, and Dutch empires. However, this economic activity had a dark side. First, the slave trade was one of the largest activities in the world economy. The arrival of European traders in Africa greatly increased the traditional sub-Saharan and Arab slave trades; between 1500 and 1850, White traders forced almost 10 million Africans to the Americas, most of them to the newly opened plantations of the Caribbean, Brazil, and the United States. Second, the colonial powers were adamant about protecting their trade routes and markets. For example, the famous Opium War (1839–42) was caused primarily by British traders, who insisted on trading opium to addicts of the drug in China despite official Chinese protestations. In 1839, opium in British warehouses was destroyed, and in retaliation the British sent warships and troops to attack China's coastal cities (such as Hangchow, Hong Kong, and Canton). Eventually, the victorious British received a $20 million indemnity and temporary colonial possession of Hong Kong, and they opened ports to the opium trade. The Opium War also weakened Imperial China, leaving it vulnerable to demands for treaty ports and trading concessions by Russia, Japan, France, and Germany. Hong Kong was finally returned to Chinese rule at the end of June 1997.

Another great expansion of international trade took place when systems of delivery—ships and trains—acquired new capabilities in the 19th century. As a result of the innovations of the Industrial Revolution, world trade grew threefold between 1870 and 1913, before being curtailed by World War I. Most trade at that time took place between imperial powers and their colonies; the latter would export primary products such as natural resources, and the parent country would export finished products (this pattern of trade persists today in many sectors). Opening up borders to trade was not an easy development, since governments were highly protective of domestic markets and could use the colonies to attain raw materials instead of trade with each other. The defeat of the Corn Laws, which had imposed high tariffs on imports of grain into England, was one of the first major victories for free trade. The Anti–Corn Law League, established in 1838, was composed mostly of industrialists and wage earners, all of whom sought to establish lower corn prices with freer trade. The British landowning aristocracy, however, wanted to protect English agriculture from the onslaught of cheaper, continental products. Pressure from the League and a famine in Ireland ultimately led to the Corn Law's repeal in 1846. Great Britain, by that time an emerging economic state, would become dependent on imports for food and was thus committed to an interdependent global economic system of increased free trade.

However, it was not just the movement of goods that was shaping the emerging global economy. Between 1845 and 1914, some 41 million people migrated to the Americas, especially the United States, from Europe. Others went to Australia and South Africa (see Chapter 11). This migration and the stagnation of industrialized European economies led to the development of the export of capital. British, Dutch, French, Belgian, Swiss, and eventually German investors tried to increase their incomes by buying the stocks of foreign business enterprises and the bonds of foreign businesses and governments. They organized companies of their own to operate in foreign states; and banks began granting loans to each other across the Atlantic. As early as the 1840s, half the annual increase of wealth in Great Britain was going into foreign investments. By 1914 the British had U.S.$20 billion in foreign investments, the French about U.S.$8.7 billion, and the Germans about U.S.$6 billion (these were huge sums of money at the time). The sums went into the Americas, the less affluent regions of Europe, and then after 1890 to Asia and Africa. However, in World War I the British lost about a quarter of their foreign investments, the French about a third, and the Germans lost everything.

Investment, trade, and monetary policy in the 18th, 19th, and 20th centuries were largely influenced by capitalist principles. Capitalism involves the ownership of means of production and the employment of labourers to produce goods that are then sold on domestic and international markets. As an economic system, capitalism is prone to cycles of boom and depression, the most notable example of the latter being the long depression that set in about 1873 and lasted to about 1893. The growth of capitalism depended partly on the technological changes that ushered in the Industrial Revolution, but in the strict economic sense it was contingent also on a willingness to grant credit and gamble with it. Sometimes this gamble works, in the sense that profits are realized and loans are paid back; other times it does not, and the willingness to loan and gamble recedes. During times of recession, governments began to take a more active role in the economy. Previously, governments had adopted a hands-off or *laissez-faire* approach to their economies, except in the case of tariffs. Governments began taking measures to combat the essential insecurity of private capitalism, adopting additional protective tariffs and social insurance and welfare legislation, and allowing trade unionism to grow in some areas. After 1880, the old orthodoxy of 19th-century unregulated, *laissez-faire* capitalism diminished in an era of interventionist governments.

Investment and trade were both facilitated by the near-universal adoption of the gold standard. England had adopted the gold standard in 1816, when the pound sterling was legally defined as the equivalent of 113 grains of fine gold. This standard led many investors to keep money in London in the form of sterling on deposit. This money, and the military defeat of Napoleon in 1815, established London's reputation as the centre of the world economy and signalled the beginning of Britain's hegemonic status. Western Europe and the United States (the latter was growing into a major economic power, though the American Civil War would forestall this) adopted an exclusively gold standard in the 1830s; a person holding any *civilized* money (pounds, francs, dollars, marks, etc.) could turn it into gold at will, and a person holding gold could turn it into money. Thus citizens from states with different currencies could trade with confidence that the money changing hands could be transformed. Until 1914 exchange rates between the currencies remained very stable, though the gold standard was hard on countries with little gold, and it produced a gradual fall in prices, especially between

1870 and 1900, because (until the gold discoveries in South Africa, Australia, and Alaska in the 1890s) the world's production of gold lagged behind the expanding production of industrial and agricultural goods.

In the 15 years before World War I, world trade increased dramatically. German exports grew more rapidly than British exports at this time, and some historians feel this severe economic competition was one of the primary factors leading to the "war to end all wars." The war would help usher in another economic system, put in place by Lenin's Bolsheviks after the Russia Revolution in 1917 (see Chapter 2). This rejection of capitalism by Russia produced a wave of fear that other states in Europe or North America might experience a similar revolution. The new Soviet state would pronounce itself owner of all the means of production and, after World War II, would participate in an alternative trade system involving itself and other states based on the socialist economic model.

After World War I, production was at an all-time high, due especially to the mass production of the automobile. However, much of the postwar boom was based on credit and stock market speculation. The Great Depression began as a stock market crisis in New York in October 1929. The crisis was related to speculation; stockbrokers (and many ordinary citizens as well) had purchased large amounts of stock on credit, pushing up stock prices. When prices began to fall, owners of stock had to sell off enough stock to pay back the money they had borrowed, and this snowballed into a huge sell-off: between 1929 and 1932, the average value of 50 industrial stocks traded on the New York Stock Exchange dropped from $252 to $61, and 5000 American banks shut down.[41]

As Americans stopped exporting capital and buying foreign goods, world trade decreased. The failure of a leading European bank in Vienna in 1931 sent shock waves across Europe. Massive unemployment was experienced across the globe, and states adopted policies designed to protect themselves. The gold reserve in Britain that had supported the pound sterling declined, and investors converted their pounds into other currencies they felt would be safer. By 1931 Britain had devalued the pound and gone off the gold standard, and other countries soon followed suit. Governments manipulated their currencies to keep up exports (i.e., they devalued their currencies, making it cheaper to buy their goods). In response to this global economic crisis, states turned away from multilateral free trade to protectionism, in an effort to insulate their hard-hit industries and labour forces from foreign competition. Tariffs were raised, first by the United States in the famous Smoot–Hawley tariff of 1930 (see below) and then by other countries, which had the effect of almost eliminating trade in some products (such as agricultural products), while quotas were introduced for others. World trade fell from U.S.$35.6 billion in 1929 to U.S.$11.9 billion in 1932. This decline in trade exacerbated the economic crisis and made economic recovery much more difficult and much slower than it could have been. An International Monetary and Economic Conference met in London in 1933, but participants were unable to negotiate a reversal of these restrictions on trade as the world sank deeper into the Depression.

In Germany, Adolf Hitler rode to power on a wave of post-Versailles discontent and tremendous inflation rates. The German economy, in shambles after World War I, did begin to recover as a result of the Dawes Plan. In 1924 an American banker, Charles G. Dawes, proposed a plan under which war reparations would be lowered and bank loans would be extended to Germany to enable it to pay the reduced reparations. Money flowed into Germany from the United States, financing economic recovery and the payment of reparations to Great Britain and France. These reparation payments were in turn used to pay off the debts these countries owed to the United States. The importance of the U.S. economy in this arrangement was highlighted in 1929, when the stock market crash stopped the flow of U.S. dollars to Europe. When the Germans could no longer pay their reparations, the British and French

On to Ottawa! Canada did not escape the hardships of the Depression. Thousands of unemployed "rode the rails" in search of jobs. In 1935, many unemployed rode the rails in protest against the conditions in government work camps. Then, as now, there is a direct relationship between economic hardship and political instability. (CP Photo/Toronto Star)

could no longer pay their war debts to the United States. To pay these debts, the British and French governments sought to increase their exports to the United States to obtain the needed currency. However, protectionist sentiment (to protect domestic industry) in the United States was high, and the Smoot–Hawley tariff of 1930 raised tariffs against foreign imports to the United States to their highest levels ever. The result was that British and French exports were shut out of the United States. The Smoot–Hawley tariff hampered international trade, blocked collection of war debts, and initiated a chain reaction of protectionism around the world, including the 1932 Ottawa Agreements, which established favourable tariff agreements for the Commonwealth. The Smoot–Hawley tariff also exported the depression to Europe, which, without U.S. dollars, could not finance its debt burdens. The result was economic disaster; businesses closed and unemployment soared. Just as it did in Germany, economic nationalism contributed to political nationalism and the rise of extremist movements, which capitalized on the frustration and resentment over high unemployment and falling living standards. Democratic governments fell in Japan, Austria, and Eastern Europe (with the exception of Czechoslovakia).

The rise of fascism in Spain, Germany, and Italy, and Japanese expansionism in Asia would eventually lead to World War II, but many analysts argue that the effect of the Great Depression and the fall of the multilateral trading system as it had evolved to that point were also partly responsible for the war. During World War II, economic production became war oriented. According to Alvin and Heidi Toffler, the United States manufactured nearly 6 million rifles and machine guns, more than 300 000 planes, 100 000 tanks and armoured vehicles, 71 000 naval vessels, and 41 billion rounds of ammunition.[42] The United States had built up considerable gold reserves during the 1930s and benefited further from trade with the Allies. As a result, the most powerful military power emerged as the most powerful economic power after the war. Theorists of imperialism and neomercantilists alike would argue that this legacy of economic dependence on military production is still a major factor in contemporary international political economy.

BRETTON WOODS AND THE DEVELOPMENT OF THE WORLD MONETARY SYSTEM

The instability that characterized the interwar period is often attributed to U.S. reluctance to join the League of Nations and provide a leadership role in the world economy. The United States refused to accept the mantle of leadership and fill the void left by the diminishment of the British Empire, which had previously wielded great power within the world economy through the common use of the pound sterling.[43] After World War II the United States emerged as the most powerful economic and military power in the world, especially given the devastation and war-exhaustion of most European and Asian economies. In contrast to the interwar period, the United States was willing to assume the role of a hegemonic power, and to exert leadership in establishing postwar monetary and trade institutions and regimes. In July 1944, even before the end of World War II, representatives of 44 countries met at Bretton Woods, New Hampshire, to construct a stable postwar international economic system. This system came to be called the **Bretton Woods system**, and until 1971 the plans developed at Bretton Woods were to form the foundation of what would be called the **Liberal International Economic Order (LIEO)**, the international economic system of the non-Communist world.

The first priority of the Bretton Woods conference was to establish an international financial structure based on fixed currency rates. Floating exchange rates were blamed for the instability and ultimate collapse of the international economy in the interwar period. At Bretton Woods, all countries agreed to fix (or peg) their currencies to the U.S. dollar at a specified rate of exchange and to maintain that rate. The U.S. dollar, in turn, was fixed (or pegged) to gold, at an exchange rate of U.S.$35 an ounce. The United States pledged that it would exchange dollars for gold at any time. As a result, all countries knew the value of their currency in U.S. dollars (and ultimately in gold). They knew this value would not fluctuate unpredictably, because states could borrow from the International Monetary Fund (IMF) (see below) to prevent a weakening of their currency and because any change in exchange rates required international negotiations. As a result, the international monetary system would be predictable and stable. The U.S. dollar became the central unit of account in the international system, used by states to maintain the value of their currency (by using dollars to sell or buy their own currency internationally), to purchase products needed for postwar reconstruction, and to store financial reserves.

The Bretton Woods negotiations also established two institutions to help manage the system and perform central banking functions. The IMF was created to facilitate trade. The IMF had to approve changes in the fixed exchange rate system and possessed a credit fund of U.S.$8.8 billion to lend to countries that were experiencing downward pressure on the value of their currencies. The IBRD, also known as the World Bank, was created to assist war-torn countries in rebuilding their economies by providing short-term financing (see Profile 4.3). Later, both the IMF and the World Bank became prominent lenders to developing countries, a role they still perform today, although not without criticism. Together, the IMF and the IBRD are known as the "twin institutions" of the Bretton Woods system. It was clear soon after the war that the Soviet Union, with its commitment to a noncapitalist path, would not participate in the building of the LIEO. It was also clear that all the other states with large economies, most of which required a great deal of reconstruction, were willing to accept American leadership. The United States provided much of the funding for the creation of the United Nations, the IMF, and the IBRD and came to the aid of the Bretton Woods system when it was threatened in 1947.

PROFILE 4.3 The IBRD (the World Bank)

The IBRD (or the World Bank) was established at the Bretton Woods conference in 1944 and is located in Washington, D.C. After the postwar reconstruction of Europe, the Bank began to focus on Southern development. It has supported more than 6000 projects in 140 countries, offering over U.S.$300 billion in financing. The Bank operates on a weighted voting system, meaning that the more a state contributes, the more say it has in what the Bank does and does not do. Obviously, then, Bank decisions are dominated by the United States, Japan, Germany, and other wealthy states. In 1957 the Bank established the International Finance Corporation (IFC) to assist poorer states in obtaining finance from private lenders, and in 1960 the International Development Association (IDA) was established. The IDA made 50-year interest-free loans to poorer states. In the 1970s the activities of the Bank accelerated under a campaign to eliminate poverty, and aid was linked to economic and social reforms, many of which harmed the most vulnerable members of society. Critics charge that the Bank has contributed to the perpetuation of poverty by favouring large-scale infrastructure projects that benefit the wealthy and cause environmental damage. The Bank has attempted to reform its previous approaches, but a public campaign (entitled "Fifty Years Is Enough!") waged in the mid-1990s called for its dissolution. Today, the Bank is active in assisting the former Communist states and lending to the Middle East to support the peace process.

In 1947, the international problem was a dollar shortage. Quite literally, too few U.S. dollars were circulating in the international system. As discussed above, dollars were in demand for a number of crucial functions, but if enough dollars were not available, what then? More dollars had to be disbursed into the international system if Bretton Woods was to survive. The answer was a massive program of aid to foreign countries so that they would be able to buy the U.S. goods they required for reconstruction. The most famous of these programs was the Marshall Plan under which 16 Western European countries received more than U.S.$17 billion between 1948 and 1952. The United States also tolerated trade protectionism in Europe and Japan to revive the European and Japanese economies (and thus create more consumers for U.S. products in the future). As a result of the Marshall Plan and trade protectionism abroad, the United States experienced massive balance of payments deficits; that is, more money was flowing out of the country than was coming in. Although this deficit was not a concern in the late 1940s and early 1950s, by the late 1950s the balance of payments deficit was becoming a problem, and by 1960 the Bretton Woods system was again in trouble.

GATT AND THE DEVELOPMENT OF THE WORLD TRADING SYSTEM

Negotiations on the principles and structure of the postwar trading system began between the United States and Great Britain in 1942, with multilateral discussions beginning in 1945. As was the case at Bretton Woods, the United States dominated the proceedings. An open trading system was naturally in U.S. interests because it would allow the United States to export products overseas. An open trading system would also allow European and Asian economies to export products to the United States, thus facilitating postwar economic development. There was also an additional interest. Most governments believed the Depression had been prolonged and deepened by protectionism. An open trading system, established by treaty and maintained by the hegemonic United States, would prevent protectionism from stalling economic recovery after World War II. And so, in 1947 the General Agreement on Tariffs and Trade (GATT) was established. GATT was a treaty binding its members to certain rules concerning international commerce. Only 23 countries attended the first GATT conferences in

1947. Originally, the authors of the Bretton Woods system had intended to establish a powerful International Trade Organization (ITO). However, the U.S. Congress objected to an exception for imperial trading systems, which effectively killed the ITO proposal. The GATT system proceeded without the ITO, focusing on a series of trade negotiations. The aim of GATT was to increase trade liberalization. For its part, Canada was an avid supporter of the GATT regime.[44]

GATT was initially designed to promote trade liberalization in two ways. First, because it was an intergovernmental process, GATT provided an important forum for states to negotiate reductions in barriers to trade. GATT was an ongoing process and provided a steadily expanding body of rules and agreements to build upon as more states joined the GATT process (see Profile 4.4). Second, GATT established (and continually developed) sets of norms and rules governing international trade. For the first 30 years of GATT's existence, these norms and rules focused on the reduction of tariffs. Tariffs are essentially taxes imposed by governments on goods originating in another country. In other words, tariffs are taxes on imports. The costs of these taxes are passed on to the domestic consumer in the form of a higher price for the good, making the imported good more expensive and therefore less desirable. Tariffs thus discourage trade. And so GATT emphasized the negotiated reduction of tariffs. The average tariff on a manufactured good among the governments belonging to GATT after World War II was 40 percent. After successive negotiations in GATT, in the early 1970s the average tariff on manufactured goods had fallen to 9 percent.[45] The result was an increase in trade among GATT countries as falling tariffs led to falling prices for imported manufactured goods, which in turn increased demand for imported and exported products.

In order to ensure that the GATT system was fair, GATT rules included the principles of **nondiscrimination** and **reciprocity**. The principle of nondiscrimination specifies that all members of GATT must treat all other members of GATT the same with respect to trade policy. For example, a GATT member could not have a low tariff on a good imported from country A and impose a higher tariff on the same good imported from country B (assuming both state A and state B are members of GATT). The tariff would have to be the same for both countries, and any changes to the tariff would have to be applied equally to all members of GATT who produced that good. In principle, this ensures there is no discrimination in how states treat one another in GATT. This convention is also known as the Most Favoured Nation (MFN) principle. The principle of reciprocity specifies that all members of GATT should make approximately the same value of concessions to each other when making trade policy. For example, if Canada was to reduce its tariffs on rice imported from Japan, Japan should reciprocate by reducing its tariffs on a product it imports from Canada, such as wood products. Moreover, this Japanese reciprocity should lead to approximately the same value of increased trade for Canada in wood products as the Canadian tariff reduction did for Japanese

PROFILE 4.4	**Multilateral Negotiations under GATT and Number of Participants**
1. Geneva, 1947: 23 states	5. Dillon Round, 1960–61: 26 states
2. Annency (France), 1949: 13 states	6. Kennedy Round, 1964–67: 62 states
3. Torquay (Britain), 1950–51: 38 states	7. Tokyo Round, 1973–79: 99 states
4. Geneva, 1955–56: 26 states	8. Uruguay Round, 1986–94: 107 states

rice. These two principles were crucial for GATT, because they entrenched the idea that all members should benefit from trade, and they should all benefit as equally as possible. In this way, it was hoped that neomercantalist temptations would be minimized.

As GATT evolved and expanded, and world economic activity grew in scope and complexity, member states began to negotiate and implement measures on a variety of other issues related to trade liberalization. One of the first issues to be addressed was **dumping**, the practice of exporting goods to a country and selling them at below the cost of production (in order to seize market share by bankrupting competing producers prior to increasing prices). Dumping was made illegal under GATT, although accusations of dumping remain commonplace in the global economy. By the 1980s, **nontariff barriers** to trade were under discussion. There was growing concern that countries were using health and safety regulations, labelling laws, and government contracting rules as barriers to trade (that is, to exclude foreign products from their market to favour domestic producers). This of course led to debates on whether such regulations were unfair trade practices or justifiable efforts by governments to regulate their economies and societies. Under the Tokyo and Uruguay Rounds of GATT, some progress was made on the issue of nontariff barriers but, as we shall see, this debate continues to rage today. The Uruguay Round also began to create rules governing intellectual property rights. Intellectual property involves creations of the imagination, including artistic works, literature, symbols and logos, among many others. The holder of the patent or copyright for such creations has the exclusive right to profit from a piece of music, computer software, image, or brand name. Since the 1980s, an international problem has emerged surrounding the issue of copyright infringement and piracy. Companies in some parts of the world turn out counterfeit, unlicensed versions of these creations at low cost for their own profit, thus costing the patent holder thousands, millions, or billions of dollars in lost revenue and reducing the incentives to produce creations of imagination in the first place. As we shall see in Chapter 8, the negotiation of **Trade-Related Intellectual Property Rights (TRIPs)**, which require member states to create and enforce copyright rules, has been a controversial issue in IPE. Some critics charge that TRIPs agreements protect the profits of large firms, and high licensing or user fees prevent developing countries from using technology and ideas that could improve their social condition.

The Uruguay Round also created a **General Agreement on Trade in Services (GATS)** to govern the growing international trade in the service sector. Services are economic activities such as banking, insurance, tourism, and transportation, to name a few. The expansion of the service sector in the 1980s was addressed in GATT because service sector companies were finding it very difficult to operate in other countries. The GATS agreement began the process of liberalizing trade in services, an effort that continues today, though not without controversy. GATT was also forced to confront a growing problem in the world economy: the divide between rich countries and poor countries. Decolonization brought a large number of new (and generally poor) states into the international system, and large numbers of these states joined GATT. The poor states of the developing world called for greater access to the markets of rich states, through the lowering of tariffs on products exported by developing countries. Greater access to rich world markets would enable poor countries to generate increased revenues through increased exports. For the most part, rich states were reluctant to do this because of the threat the (generally cheaper) goods of the developing world posed to domestic industries and agriculture. While a **Generalized System of Preferences** was established in GATT in the 1960s (allowing industrialized states to lower tariffs on imports from developing countries to levels below the tariffs imposed on the same goods from developed countries), this system never succeeded in addressing the North–South divide in the global economy. As we shall see in Chapter 8, this issue has only intensified in contemporary debates over global-ization.

Agreements in GATT were not reached without considerable debate at the intergovern-mental level, and of course most governments faced domestic political opposition to many GATT measures. GATT agreements reached at the end of each round always reflected what was possible through negotiation. States sought to protect their economic and social interests in the GATT negotiations, and realists would remind us that GATT agreements reflected these interests. States negotiated exemptions for certain sectors of economic and social activity. For example, many countries (including Western European states, the United States, and Canada) protected their agricultural sector from high levels of trade liberalization in the early rounds of GATT, enabling them to maintain subsidies and high tariffs in this politically sensitive sector. Canada and other countries (especially France) fought to protect their cultural sector against the perceived threat of U.S. cultural influences. Of course, states also found themselves in trade disputes with other GATT members. Trade disputes arise when one or more states feel that other GATT states are engaging in economic or public policy that is against the letter or the spirit of GATT rules. Trade disputes became a central feature of global politics. Major dis-putes, such as those between the United States and Japan over automobile imports, and the United States and the EEC over agricultural trade, received considerable media and public attention.

Though the successive rounds of GATT succeeded in reducing tariffs and facilitating increased levels of world trade, the 1970s and 1980s saw a rise in protectionism. The final round of GATT negotiations (the eighth) may have been the most difficult. The Uruguay Round began in 1986 and involved 107 countries (including the individual members of the EEC). Only the Soviet Union and China sat out the negotiations. On April 15, 1994, at Marrakesh, Morocco, the final result of these lengthy negotiations (some refer to GATT as the "General Agreement to Talk and Talk") was released to the public. Under this new world trade agreement, 123 countries (the membership of GATT by 1994) agreed on a set of rules that would reduce tariffs by approximately one-third. Since 1994, more states have signed the agreement, and the countries that are party to the Uruguay Round agreement account for 90 percent of world trade. Finally, the agreement also established the **World Trade Organization (WTO)** and appointed Peter Sutherland as the first director-general of the WTO. We will explore the WTO further in Chapter 8.

THE DECLINE AND FALL OF THE BRETTON WOODS SYSTEM

By 1960, the problems facing the Bretton Woods system were in many ways different from the ones it faced in 1947. The persistent balance of payments deficits experienced by the United States meant that more and more dollars were in circulation in the international system. The deficits, caused by U.S. military activities around the world, military and economic aid, and private investment in foreign countries, were increasingly out of control. The dollar shortage had turned into the dollar glut. In 1960, for the first time, more dollars were in circulation than there was gold in U.S. reserves. This imbalance meant that the United States would not be able to exchange gold for dollars at $35 an ounce. Not surprisingly, many began to ques-tion the strength of the U.S. dollar as a reserve currency and feared that it would be devalued. As a result, many holders of U.S. dollars began to convert their dollars into gold, creating the first dollar crisis.

Other developments also threatened the position of the dollar. The economies of Western Europe and Japan had recovered from the war, and the need for U.S. dollars and U.S. products lessened. The IMF was moving away from reliance on the U.S. dollar toward Special Drawing Rights (SDRs), a basket of major currencies that could be drawn on by countries in search of financing. (Because SDRs were a blend of currencies, they were seen as more stable than gold or U.S. dollars.) The expenditures of the Vietnam War and President Lyndon Johnson's War on Poverty had also eroded the competitiveness of the U.S. economy. And finally, in 1971, the United States experienced a balance of trade deficit (with more goods imported into the country than were exported) for the first time. This deficit threatened jobs at home and increased international tensions as the U.S. government blamed Western Europe and Japan for maintaining undervalued currencies (currency values that did not reflect the true cost of goods and services in those countries). This undervaluing in turn made foreign products more attractive for consumers in the United States, which contributed to the U.S. balance of trade deficit.

On August 15, 1971, the Nixon Administration responded to the eroding position of the U.S. economy by announcing that it would no longer exchange dollars for gold. A tariff was placed on goods entering the United States, and the U.S. dollar was devalued to increase exports.[46] For all intents and purposes, the Bretton Woods system had collapsed. This collapse had two general consequences. First, the international monetary system was transformed. With the collapse of the fixed exchange rate system, the value of currencies now floated freely in international financial markets. The value of a currency was now based on perceptions of the strength and health of a state's economy. Market forces, rather than government intervention, determined a currency's value. The financial predictability of Bretton Woods vanished, replaced with the volatile financial markets we are familiar with today (see Profile 4.5). Second, it was apparent by 1971 that the United States could no longer unilaterally regulate the global economic system. Economic power had become more dispersed in the international system, and although the United States was still by far the world's largest economy, it was no longer capable of exerting leadership unilaterally, and other countries were no longer willing to unconditionally accept that leadership. The management of the international economy began to shift from a hegemonic management system to an increasingly multilateral management system. Of course, this shift to a new international monetary system had implications for other countries, including Canada (see Profile 4.6).

THE POLITICS OF OIL

The global economy faced another challenge in the wake of the collapse of Bretton Woods: the formation of the **Organization of the Petroleum Exporting Countries (OPEC)**. In 1960, four Middle Eastern states and Venezuela had formed OPEC, initially to fight proposed oil price cuts by oil companies and later to pressure transnational oil corporations to give host-country governments a greater share of the immense profits being made. By the early 1970s OPEC was winning significant concessions and had raised the price of oil. It is important to keep in mind that oil has been the predominant fuel of industrialization since the latter half of the 20th century, especially in the United States, Western Europe, and Japan. As two analysts have noted, "one of the great anomalies of nature is the immense concentration of huge, easily accessible, and cheap oil supplies in the Middle East and particularly in the Gulf region. Saudi Arabia alone is conservatively estimated to be endowed with over 25 per cent of the world's proven reserves. On the other hand, consumption is concentrated in the industrialized West and Japan."[47] OPEC is a **cartel**, a producer's organization that seeks to raise the price of a good by reducing its supply through controls on production. In 1973, in reaction to U.S. support for Israel in the 1973 Arab–Israeli War, OPEC countries initiated a cutback in oil production and

Money and Floating Exchange Rates

Toronto Stock Exchange. *Star* photo by Gordon Powley, taken circa June 1952. (Copyright © Toronto Star Syndicate 2003. All rights reserved.)

Money performs several different functions in the international economy. Currencies must be accepted and recognized so that actors possessing currency can use it to purchase goods and services from other actors. Money serves as a store of value, and money must be a standard of deferred payment so that actors will be willing to lend money knowing that the money will still have purchasing power when the loan is repaid. This belief is important because the value of money can erode through inflation. Inflation occurs when the supply of money exceeds the value of goods and services produced in an economy. As a currency becomes inflated, it loses purchasing power and becomes a poor store of value and less acceptable as an exchange for the payment of debts. As a result, governments around the world try to keep inflation as low as possible.

Changes in currency exchange rates occur when international evaluations of a country's economy and its ability to maintain the value of its money change due to political or economic events or trends. If a country has a healthy and growing economy, its currency will rise relative to other currencies (one unit of the currency will buy more of another currency) because it becomes more desirable as a store of value or a medium of exchange. If, however, a country's economy is performing poorly, its currency will fall relative to other currencies (one unit of the currency will buy less of another currency)

because it is less desirable as a store of value or a medium of exchange. Of course, since all currencies are floating relative to each other, the exchange rates between them are dependent on the relative performance of their economies. Who makes these international evaluations of the performance of state economies? International organizations, governments, banks and financial institutions (such as investment houses), corporations, and individuals all contribute to the general appraisal of a state's economy (although certain institutions play a greater role than others). Much of the activity in international financial markets is based on currency speculation, an effort to make money by buying it and selling it at a profit. In essence, speculators gamble (based on economic and political indicators) that the value of a currency will increase in the future: they will buy the currency, store it, and sell it when the value of the currency is higher (thus making a profit).

As a result, the capacity of a state government to influence the value of its own currency is limited, because the value of the currency is based on what others think of the state's economy. However, governments will try to act in support of their currencies, because the value of a currency (and especially its stability relative to other currencies) is extremely important for exporters and importers of goods and services, since they must purchase or sell their goods and services across state borders in accordance with current exchange rates. Governments will therefore try to follow responsible fiscal policies so as not to damage the value of their currency. Governments intervene by buying or selling their own currency in the international system, thereby increasing or decreasing the value of the currency by affecting the international demand for it. One of the great challenges of the post–Bretton Woods system was adjusting to the fact that the value of currencies could fluctuate quite dramatically and that this fluctuation was due to forces largely out of state control. Today, changes (even small changes) in the value of currencies are important knowledge, whether you are planning a holiday or managing a government's financial reserves.

PROFILE 4.6 Canada and Floating Exchange Rates

Like most other currencies, the value of the Canadian dollar is largely determined by financial markets. Currency traders, buyers, speculators, banks, and foreign governments evaluate the attractiveness of the Canadian dollar on the basis of the health of the Canadian economy, the economic policies of Canadian federal and provincial governments, and political developments in Canada. If the Canadian economy shows disappointing trends (such as lower growth), the Canadian dollar is less attractive to foreign currency holders and the value of the Canadian currency will decline. Similarly, if the Canadian government follows economic policies that are viewed as fiscally irresponsible (such as increased budget deficits), the value of the Canadian dollar will decline. Political developments may also cause the value of the Canadian dollar to fluctuate. For example, in the 1997 federal elections in Canada, early returns indicated a possible minority government for the Liberal Party. A minority government may have meant instability in Canada's political scene, and the value of the Canadian dollar dropped as speculators, banks, and governments found the Canadian dollar less attractive. As the election

results showed a slim Liberal majority government, the dollar rebounded somewhat on international markets. Canada, like most countries, is faced with two dilemmas in this market-oriented monetary environment. Canadian governments must make economic policy with an eye on the possible reaction of international financial markets, which constrains the government's ability to make decisions based on domestic needs. The Canadian government must also decide when to intervene to prop up the dollar by buying Canadian dollars on international markets (thus creating a demand for Canadian dollars, which increases the value of the currency). Doing this, of course, costs money. Because Canada is a major exporter and importer, currency fluctuations are of tremendous importance to the Canadian economy. In late 2003 and early 2004, the increasing value of the Canadian dollar relative to the U.S. dollar caused consternation among Canadian exporters, as the higher Canadian dollar made Canadian exports more expensive to consumers (especially consumers in the United States). On the other hand, many imported products dropped in price, to the pleasure of many Canadian consumers!

imposed an oil embargo against the United States. World oil prices rose dramatically, from $2.50 a barrel in 1973 to $11.65 in 1974 (a barrel is a standard measure for petroleum, equivalent to 42 U.S. gallons or 159 litres). The oil shock created havoc in the West and particularly in the United States, the world's leading importer of oil. World recession followed, as countries had to spend more for energy. Dollars also flowed to OPEC countries in such huge amounts ($70 billion in 1974 alone) that the supply of dollars in the international system depressed the value of the dollar still further.

Some equilibrium was achieved when oil prices began to decline in the late 1970s due to a fall in demand through conservation efforts, reduced consumption, the discovery of new deposits elsewhere, and a shift to alternative sources of energy. However, another oil shock followed after the Iranian revolution in 1979, as world prices of oil shot up to $50 a barrel. Global recession once again followed, although, again, conservation measures and the exploitation of new sources of oil eventually reduced pressure on world oil prices. However, to this day many of the world's leading industrial economies (especially those in Europe and Asia) are heavily reliant on Middle Eastern oil. In fact, many would argue that the war in the Persian Gulf in 1991 and the Iraq War in 2003 were related directly to the strategic importance of oil. Oil is also a key factor in the politics of export-dependent states such as Nigeria and Venezuela. It can also be argued that the sudden influx of petrodollars to Western banks encouraged the latter to make hazardous loans to Southern state governments, bringing on the developing countries' debt crisis.

THE GROUP OF SEVEN (AND THEN THERE WERE EIGHT)

Since 1975, a very exclusive forum has met to discuss and reach agreement on economic issues. The Group of Seven (G-7) countries are Canada, France, Germany, Great Britain, Italy, Japan, and the United States. Initially known as the Group of Five (G-5) before the admission of Canada and Italy in 1976, the G-7 is not an international organization. Rather, it is a forum for discussion and coordination on a wide range of political and economic issues. In short, the G-7 has a deliberative function (members meet to create understanding and awareness), a directive function (summits establish agendas and priorities), and a decisional function (members reach joint agreements on programs, targets, and timetables). Summits of the leaders of the G-7 countries are held on a yearly basis. In the early years of the G-5/G-7, the primary role of the forum was to coordinate the management of exchange rates and domestic interest rates. This role is significant because it signalled the inability of the United States to manage the global economic system on its own, and it committed the largest economies of the free world to cooperation on economic policy to attempt to manage the international economy. In addition, the early meetings marked the return of Japan to global prominence.

The G-7 summit in 1994 was held in Naples, where leaders agreed to revitalize international economic institutions and integrate the former Communist countries into the global economic system more rapidly. This summit was also notable for the fact that Russian President Boris Yeltsin was invited. Although Russia was not invited to become a full economic member of the forum, it has attended the G-7 summits every year since Naples (leading some to refer to the G-7 as the G-8 or simply the Eight). In 1995 the G-8 summit was held in Halifax, where leaders discussed the collapse of the Mexican peso and the progress achieved

The 2003 G-8 Summit meeting in Evian, France. The leaders are (clockwise from centre foreground) EU President Romano Prodi, Italian Prime Minister Silvio Berlusconi, German Chancellor Gerhard Schröder, Canadian Prime Minister Jean Chrétien, Russian President Vladimir Putin, French President Jacques Chirac, U.S. President George W. Bush, British Prime Minister Tony Blair, Japanese Prime Minister Junichiro Koizumi, and Greek Prime Minister Konstantinos Simitis. Although not a member of the G-8, Greece and many other countries were invited to attend a variety of other meetings with G-8 leaders in an expanded version of the traditional G-8 Summit format. (CP Photo/ Tom Hanson)

in creating new financial institutions. In recent years the G-8 summits have addressed a wide range of political issues, including wars and security challenges, the environment, and development. For example, the 2003 G-8 Summit in Evian, France, addressed a number of issues from African development to terrorism. This raises questions about whether the G-8 is becoming something akin to an elitist concert of powers. Membership in the G-8 has also become an issue. As a forum for the world's largest democratic market economies, the G-8 membership is rather anachronistic. If economic size were the sole measure of membership, for example, Canada would no longer be a member of the group. Canada's continued membership in the G-8 is a reflection of Canada's international diplomatic profile, its tradition of involvement in international economic and political issues, and the unwillingness of other G-8 countries to discuss the politically sensitive issue of membership criteria. In another relatively exclusive forum, the **Trilateral Commission**, economic experts from North America, Europe, and Japan meet to discuss future relations. The 29 states in the **Organisation for Economic Co-operation and Development (OECD)** carry out research and consultations on promoting free trade and economic efficiency. OECD countries produce two-thirds of the world's goods and services. The organization is often criticized as a rich countries' club, though Mexico and South Korea have both won admission.

As we have seen, the global economy has evolved considerably since the end of World War II, through a combination of long-term trends (such as economic growth, trade, technological innovations, and the decline of U.S. dominance, or hegemony, in the system) and short-term shocks (such as the collapse of Bretton Woods, the oil shocks, and the fall of the Soviet Union). In general, the politics of the global economy have evolved from a largely unilateral or hegemonic management of the system to a multilateral management effort. The global economy we live in today is the product of a conscious effort to create an open trading system at the end of World War II based on liberal economic principles, and of the subsequent political and economic events that shaped the 20th century.

CONCLUSIONS

As the Cold War ended, the global economy was as complex as ever. A clear dividing line remained between rich and poor, largely in North–South terms. However, it was becoming quite apparent that the Soviet Union and the Eastern European states were in economic disarray. They had to be integrated into the world economy somehow, and they embarked on a program of privatization that, initially at least, caused a great deal of hardship. China was charting a new course toward greater privatization and was experiencing rapid economic growth based on cheap labour and increased exports. Other Asian countries were also continuing down the export-led development path with record growth, although the Asian financial crisis of 1997 (see Chapter 8) would slow this. The United States had entered into NAFTA with Canada and Mexico, and Europe was forging ahead with its problematic economic and political integration. Sub-Saharan Africa and Latin America were still mired in development dilemmas related to debt and democracy. The environmental problems that had resulted from years of global industrialization and population growth became topics of great concern as the world prepared for the United Nations Conference on Environment and Development, held in Rio de Janeiro, Brazil, in 1992. MNCs were growing in number and in size, and raised questions about the impact such firms were having on trade and development.

Poverty and wealth, the two central themes of economic history, continue to coexist. So, too, do the central perspectives on IPE we have outlined. In this chapter, we have emphasized several divergent perspectives: neomercantilism, liberalism, Marxism, and hegemonic stability theory. We have provided a brief outline of the recent evolution of trade and finance in the international economy and the principles on which this system is based. In Chapter 8, we will look at the modern world economy and discuss some of the prevalent concerns facing those who study IPE today. We turn now to an examination of what many analysts feel are the principal potential facilitators of both peace and economic progress on a global scale: international institutions.

Endnotes

1. Malcolm Waters, *Globalization* (London: Routledge, 1995), 66–67.
2. *World Economic Outlook, September 2003* (Washington, DC: International Monetary Fund, 2003), 173.
3. *Handbook of Statistics 2002* (New York: United Nations Conference on Trade and Development, 2003), 2.
4. *Human Development Report 2002: Deepening Democracy in a Fragmented World* (New York: Oxford University Press, 2002), 10.
5. Kenichi Ohmae, *The Borderless World: Power and Strategy in the International Economy* (New York: Harper Perennial, 1990).
6. Robert A. Isaak, *Managing World Economic Change: International Political Economy*, 3rd ed. (Upper Saddle River, NJ: Prentice-Hall, 2000), 2.
7. Theodore H. Cohn, *Global Political Economy: Theory and Practice*, 2nd ed. (Toronto: Longman, 2003), 6.
8. Thomas Oatley, *International Political Economy: Interests and Institutions in the Global Economy* (New York: Pearson Education, 2004), 3.
9. Liberalism, economic nationalism, and Marxism are widely accepted as representative of the basic schools in the subdiscipline of international political economy; perhaps the best-known account of this is produced in Robert Gilpin's *The Political Economy of International Relations* (Princeton: Princeton University Press, 1987).
10. See, for example, P. Krugman and M. Obstfeld, *International Economics: Theory and Policy* (New York: HarperCollins, 1991); and J.D. Richardson, *Understanding International Economics: Theory and Practice* (Boston: Little, Brown and Company, 1980). For a study of the interaction between politics and economics see Joseph M. Grieco and G. John Ikenberry, *State Power and World Markets: The International Political Economy* (New York: W.W. Norton, 2003).
11. Charles E. Lindblom, *Politics and Markets: The World's Political Economic Systems* (New York: Basic Books, 1977).
12. Robert Gilpin, *The Political Economy of International Relations* (Princeton: Princeton University Press, 1987).
13. See Robert S. Walters and Robert H. Blake, *The Politics of Global Economic Relations*, 4th ed. (Englewood Cliffs, NJ: Prentice-Hall, 1992).
14. For what has fast become a classic text, see R. Rosecrance, *The Rise of the Trading State: Commerce and Conquest in the Modern World* (New York: Basic Books, 1986).
15. Adam Smith, *An Inquiry into the Nature and Causes of the Wealth of Nations*, vol. 1, bk. 4 (London: Dent and Sons, 1910), 436.
16. Smith, 436.
17. Theodore H. Cohn suggests there are three variants of liberalism: orthodox, interventionist, and institutional. Cohn, 93.
18. For a discussion of international trade theory and its evolution, see Douglas Irwin, *Against the Tide: An Intellectual History of Free Trade* (Princeton: Princeton University Press, 1996).
19. For a discussion of the impact of Keynes's ideas, see Peter A. Hall, ed., *The Political Power of Economic Ideas: Keynesianism across Nations* (Princeton: Princeton University Press, 1989).
20. Cohn, 98.
21. Stephen D. Krasner, "Structural Causes and Regime Consequences: Regimes as Intervening Variables," in Stephen D. Krasner, ed., *International Regimes* (Ithaca, NY: Cornell University Press, 1983), 2. See also M. Zacher, "Toward a Theory of International Regimes," *Journal of International Affairs* 44, no. 1 (1990), 139–58; and O. Young, "The Politics of International Regime Formation: Managing Natural Resources and the Environment," *International Organization* 43, no. 3 (1989), 349–75.
22. See, for example, Mark W. Zacher with Brent A. Sutton, *Governing Global Networks: International Regimes for Transportation and Communication* (Cambridge, UK: Cambridge University Press, 1996).

23. Karl Marx and Friedrich Engels, *The Communist Manifesto* (New York: International Publishers, 1948). Much more important, from a theoretical viewpoint, was Marx's landmark study, *Das Capital*, and his earlier, more philosophical work.

24. Ralph Miliband, *The State in Capitalist Society* (New York: Basic Books, 1969).

25. Vladimir I. Lenin, *Imperialism: The Highest Stage of Capitalism*, rev. trans. (New York: International Publishers, 1939).

26. See Paul A. Baran, *The Political Economy of Growth* (New York: Monthly Review Press, 1962), 12.

27. See, for example, André Gunder Frank, *Latin America, Underdevelopment or Revolution: Essays on the Development of Underdevelopment and the Immediate Enemy* (New York: Monthly Review Press, 1970). For an excellent review of dependency theory, see M. Blomstrom and B. Hettne, *Development Theory in Transition, The Dependency Debate and Beyond: Third World Responses* (London: Zed Books, 1984); and Peter Evans's classic, *Dependent Development: The Alliance of Multinational, State, and Local Capital in Brazil* (Princeton: Princeton University Press, 1979). See also Samir Amin, *Accumulation on a World Scale: A Critique of the Theory of Development*, vols. 1 and 2 (New York: Monthly Review Press, 1974).

28. See Fernando Enrique Cardoso and Enzo Faletto, *Dependency and Development in Latin America*, translated by Marjory Mattingly Urquid. (Berkeley: University of California Press, 1979).

29. See Piero Gleijeses, *The Dominican Crisis: The 1965 Constitutional Revolt and American Intervention*, translated by Lawrence Lipson (Baltimore, MD: Johns Hopkins University Press, 1978).

30. See Robinson Rojas Sandford, *The Murder of Allende and the End of the Chilean Way to Socialism*, translated by Andree Conrad (New York: Harper and Row, 1976). For more on U.S. foreign policy in Latin America, see Robert A. Pastor, *Exiting the Whirlpool: US Foreign Policy Toward Latin America and the Caribbean* (Boulder, CO: Westview Press, 2001).

31. Immanuel Wallerstein, "The Rise and Future Demise of the World Capitalist System: Concepts for Comparative Analysis," in Immanuel Wallerstein, *The Capitalist World-Economy* (New York: Cambridge University Press, 1979), 35.

32. Wallerstein, 18–19.

33. Robert Gilpin, *War and Change in World Politics* (Cambridge, UK: Cambridge University Press, 1981), 29.

34. Immanuel Wallerstein, "The Three Instances of Hegemony in the History of the Capitalist World Economy," in Immanuel Wallerstein, *The Politics of the World-Economy: The States, the Movements, and the Civilizations* (Cambridge, UK: Cambridge University Press, 1984), 38.

35. Robert Keohane, "The Theory of Hegemonic Stability and Changes in International Economic Regimes, 1967–1977," in Ole Holsti, Randolph M. Siverson, and Alexander L. George, eds., *Change in the International System* (Boulder, CO: Westview Press, 1980), 132.

36. See Charles Kindleberger, *The World in Depression, 1929–1939* (Berkeley: University of California Press, 1973).

37. Gilpin, *The Political Economy of International Relations*, 78.

38. Paul Kennedy, *The Rise and Fall of the Great Powers* (New York: Random House, 1987).

39. Donald W. White, "Mutable Destiny: The End of the American Century?" *Harvard International Review* 20 (Winter 1998), 42–47.

40. For examples of revivalist writings, see Joseph S. Nye Jr., "The Changing Nature of World Power," in Charles W. Kegley Jr. and Eugene R. Wittkopf, eds., *The Global Agenda*, 6th ed. (Boston: McGraw Hill, 2001); Joseph S. Nye Jr., *Bound to Lead: The Changing Nature of American Power* (New York: Basic Books, 1990); and Susan Strange, "The Persistent Myth of Lost Hegemony," *International Organization* 41, no. 4 (Autumn 1987), 551–74.

41. On the causes and consequences of Black October 1929, see J.K. Galbraith, *The Great Crash: 1929* (1954; Boston: Houghton Mifflin, 1988).

42. A. Toffler and H. Toffler, *War and Anti-War: Survival at the Dawn of the 21st Century* (Boston: Little, Brown and Company, 1993), 40. See also N. Polmar and T. Allen, *World War II: America at War, 1941–1945* (New York: Random House, 1991).

43. Kindleberger.

44. See Frank Stone, *Canada, the GATT and the International System* (Montreal: Institute for Research on Public Policy, 1984).

45. Oatley, 20.

46. See F. Block, *The Origins of International Economic Disorder* (Berkeley: University of California Press, 1977). This tariff increase especially angered Ottawa, since Canada and the United States had such a close trading relationship by that time.

47. A.A. Kubursi and S. Mansur, "The Political Economy of Middle Eastern Oil," in R. Stubbs and G. Underhill, eds., *Political Economy and the Changing Global Order* (Toronto: McClelland and Stewart, 1994), 313–27, 324. See also D. Yergin, *The Prize: The Epic Quest for Oil, Money and Power* (New York: Simon and Schuster, 1991).

Suggested Readings

Amin, S. *Accumulation on a World Scale: A Critique of the Theory of Underdevelopment.* New York: Monthly Review Press, 1974.

Ashworth, W. *A Short History of the World Economy Since 1850.* London: Longman, 1991.

Baran, P. *The Political Economy of Growth.* New York: Monthly Review Press, 1967.

Black, J.K. *Development in Theory and Practice: Bridging the Gap.* Boulder, CO: Westview, 1991.

Braudel, F. *Civilization and Capitalism: 15th–18th Century.* 3 vols. New York: Harper and Row, 1981, 1982, 1984.

Brawley, M. *Turning Points: Decisions Shaping the Evolution of the International Political Economy.* Peterborough, ON: Broadview, 1998.

Cohn, T. *Global Political Economy: Theory and Practice.* 2nd ed. Toronto: Longman, 2003.

Cox, R. *Production, Power, and World Order.* New York: Columbia University Press, 1987.

Doyle, M., and G. John Ikenberry, eds. *New Thinking in International Relations Theory.* Boulder, CO: Westview, 1977.

Elsenhans, H. *Development and Underdevelopment: The History, Economics, and Politics of North-South Relations.* New Delhi: Sage, 1991.

Gill, S., and D. Law. *The Global Political Economy: Perspectives, Problems, and Policies.* Baltimore: Johns Hopkins University Press, 1988.

Grant, R., and K. Newland, eds. *Gender and International Relations.* Bloomington: Indiana University Press, 1991.

Grieco, Joseph M., and G. John Ikenberry. *State Power and World Markets: The International Political Economy.* New York: W.W. Norton, 2003.

Hall, Peter A., ed. *The Political Power of Economic Ideas: Keynesianism across Nations.* Princeton: Princeton University Press, 1989.

Irwin, Douglas. *Against the Tide: An Intellectual History of Free Trade.* Princeton: Princeton University Press, 1996.

Isaak, Robert A. *Managing World Economic Change: International Political Economy.* 3rd ed. Upper Saddle River, NJ: Prentice-Hall, 2000.

Johnson, H., ed. *The New Mercantilism.* Oxford: Oxford University Press, 1974.

Jones, R.J.B., and P. Willetts, eds. *Interdependence on Trial: Studies in the Theory and Reality of Contemporary Interdependence.* New York: St. Martin's Press, 1985.

Keenes, E. "The Myth of Multilateralism: Exception, Exemption, and Bilateralism in Canadian International Economic Relations." *International Journal* 50, no. 4 (1995), 755–78.

Kennedy, Paul. *The Rise and Fall of the Great Powers.* New York: Random House, 1987.

Kindleberger, Charles. *The World in Depression, 1929–1939.* Berkeley: University of California Press, 1973.

Knorr, K. *Power and Wealth: The Political Economy of International Power.* New York: Basic, 1973.

Oatley, Thomas. *International Political Economy: Interests and Institutions in the Global Economy*. New York: Pearson Education, 2004.

Petras, J., and H. Veltmeyer. *System in Crisis: The Dynamics of Free Market Capitalism*. London: Zed, 2003.

Polanyi, K. *The Great Transformation: The Political and Economic Origins of Our Time*. New York: Beacon Press, 1944.

Spero, J.E. *The Politics of International Economic Relations*. New York: St. Martin's Press, 1977.

Strange, S. "Protectionism and World Politics." *International Organization* 39 (Spring 1982), 233–59.

Strange, S., ed. *Paths to International Political Economy*. London: George Allen and Unwin, 1984.

Wilber, C., and K. Jameson, eds. *The Political Economy of Development and Underdevelopment*. 5th ed. New York: McGraw-Hill, 1992.

Suggested Websites

G-8 Information Centre
http://www.g7.utoronto.ca

Global Exchange
http://www.globalexchange.org/index.html

History of Economics Internet references
http://home.tvd.be/cr27486/hope.html

International Monetary Fund
http://www.imf.org

International Trade Canada (ITC)
http://www.itcan-cican.gc.ca/menu-en.asp

OPEC: Organization of the Petroleum Exporting Countries
http://www.opec.org

Organisation for Economic Co-operation and Development
http://www.oecd.org/home

Routledge Journal: Review of IPE
http://www.tandf.co.uk/journals/titles/09692290.asp

University of Puget Sound International Political Economy Program
http://www.ups.edu/ipe/home2.htm

WebEc
http://www.helsinki.fi/WebEc/webecf.html

World Bank Group
http://www.worldbank.org

World Trade Organization
http://www.wto.org

WWW Virtual Library: Resources on International Economics and Business
http://www.etown.edu/vl/intlbus.html

CHAPTER 5

International Institutions and Law

*We the Peoples of the United Nations, determined to save succeeding gen-
erations from the scourge of war, which twice in our lifetime has brought
untold sorrow to mankind, and to reaffirm faith in fundamental human
rights, in the dignity and worth of the human person, in the equal rights
of men and women and of nations large and small, and to establish conditions under which justice and respect for the obligations arising from
treaties and other sources of international law can be maintained, and to
promote social progress and better standards of life in larger freedom ...
Have Resolved to Combine Our Efforts to Accomplish These Aims.*

—Preamble, The Charter of the United Nations, 1945

*The globalization of law is an integral aspect of the globalization of cap-
italism. The law globalizes rules that facilitate transnational patterns of
capital accumulation, attenuating certain regulatory capacities of states,
while advancing others.*

—A. Claire Cutler[1]

INTRODUCTION

There are many ways of looking at international organizations (IOs) and international law
(IL), and some truth to all of them. IOs and IL can be seen as the conceptual and regulatory
core of the international society of states. In this view, the famous UN building in New York
is the diplomatic centre of world politics. Here, one can witness a remarkable range of activity:
the gathering of representatives from every recognized state on earth in the General Assembly;
the daily business of specialized agencies and programs aimed at implementing the UN's goal
of increasing the standard of living of all peoples; the power politics intrigues among the often
divergent permanent five (P-5) members of the Security Council ; and the expression of world
opinion through the resolutions adopted by the General Assembly. Today, many high school
and university students participate in Model United Nations Conferences, held in places as
diverse as Toronto and Cairo, which provide a highly educative experience. UN-related websites are popular, and generally considered authoritative, destinations on the Internet. It is still
a defining moment of statehood to become a member of the General Assembly: since 1989,

more than 30 new states have joined the UN, from Andorra to Uzbekistan to the Democratic Republic of Timor Leste (Timor Lorosa'e to the locals). Every September, various heads of state or their foreign ministers find the time to visit New York and deliver a speech to the General Assembly. Not only the UN, but also many regional organizations such as the European Union (EU) and the Organization of American States (OAS) influence the national and daily lives of millions of people. Obviously, this is a view most favored by liberal institutionalists (see Chapter 1).

Realists are rather less enthusiastic about the purpose and prospects of international institutions and law, which they view primarily as vessels or forums for the pursuit of national interests. They ascribe little autonomy to IOs, and little causal significance to IL. This said, realists certainly recognize the potential of IOs to intervene in conflict situations, and to present both obstacles and opportunities to rational decision makers. Most critical theorists, meanwhile, would argue that what Marx would call the "superstructure" of the capitalist system—the institutions and ideologies enforcing and justifying the socioeconomic order—can be found at the IO and IL level. Historically, law has protected property, including of course the territorial right to sovereignty held by states or those who determine the national interest for states. At the same time, however, many critical theorists see the UN, and IL more generally, as a possible forum for serious reforms of the global economy. International institutions and law could become the path to a more equitable world order; they could become instruments for enhancing the observation of human rights standards, and they could become conduits for some form of global redistribution of wealth. Constructivists argue that by participating in IOs such as the European Union (EU), states slowly change their own self-identities, and thus their estimation of self-interest in the process.

However, even a tentative understanding of the contemporary UN system necessitates a broader examination of the role of IOs in global politics today. The UN, though one of the most developed and multifunctional international organizations, is but one example of a wide variety of institutions that have been created around the convergence of interests and ideas. Despite futuristic and probably impulsive predictions, the UN has not evolved into a world government, complete with standing armies, powers of jurisprudential enforcement, demo-cratic legitimacy, or the ability to redistribute the world's wealth. Nor has it disintegrated (as pessimists assumed was inevitable) like its predecessor, the League of Nations, despite recent turmoil caused by the American decision to invade Iraq without a final Security Council resolution (which was vigorously opposed by France and Russia).

An international organization (IO) is what Plano and Olton term a "formal arrangement transcending national boundaries that provides for the establishment of institutional machinery to facilitate cooperation among members in security, economic, social or related fields."[2] Generally, two types of IOs exist: **intergovernmental organizations (IGOs)** and **nongovernmental organizations (NGOs)**. All IGOs share a number of characteristics. First, they comprise states and only states (although in

A challenging occupation. UN Secretary-General Kofi Annan speaks at a news conference on February 2004. At this time he was negotiating a settlement between the Greek and Turkish Cypriots, just one example of his many challenging roles. (AP Photo/Osamu Honda/CP Archive)

some cases nonstate actors may be represented, or have "observatory status"). Second, IGOs are created by treaties between states and, therefore, have legal standing under IL; they have, for example, the right to immunity from jurisdiction of state courts for acts and activities performed by the organization. Third, they hold regular meetings attended by delegates from member states. Those delegates represent the policies and interests of their respective countries. Fourth, IGOs have permanent headquarters and an executive secretariat that runs the day-to-day activities of the organization; IGOs hold legal status, and are entitled to certain rights and privileges according to IL. Finally, IGOs have permanent administrative employees who work for the organization and do not represent their governments; rather, they are international bureaucrats. Although these employees do not renounce their citizenships, they serve the organization, not their respective states. Such organizations have proliferated in number, especially in the 20th century. In 1909, there were 37 IGOs. In 1960, there were 154; in 1987, there were 381; and there are currently more than 400 IGOs. As we will see, these organizations perform a wide variety of functions in the international system, and states have increasingly interacted and cooperated with each other through the mechanisms provided by IGOs. In addition, such institutions are vital to smaller states, such as Canada, that have many connections to the international diplomatic scene but a limited capacity to influence international events on their own. Many Canadians, such as Yves Fortier, Stephen Lewis, Elizabeth Dowdeswell, Lester Pearson, Douglas Roche, and Maurice Strong, have played high-profile roles at the United Nations, and continue to do so. In early 1998 another Canadian, Louise Fréchette, made headlines when she was appointed to the post of deputy secretary-general, a key Secretariat administrative post.

It is important to recognize the wide scope of activities in which international organizations engage. The UN, for example, is involved in issue-areas as diverse as international and civil war, technology, gender relations, humanitarian assistance and disaster relief, literacy, pollution abatement, decolonization, human rights and IL, disarmament, important treaties such as the **Non-Proliferation Treaty**, and significant conferences such as the Population Summit in Cairo in fall 1994. The various specialized agencies and programs of the UN are rough indicators of the range of activity that converges in the political space of the UN system alone. This includes the International Research and Training Institute for the Advancement of Women, the United Nations Population Fund, the United Nations Office for the Coordination of Humanitarian Affairs, the International Civil Aviation Organization, the World Intellectual Property Organization, all of the UN-mandated peacekeeping operations in effect around the globe, UNAIDS, and many others. As well, we have seen the rise of a particular single actor, the **secretary-general**, from the preconceived role of an international bureaucrat to that of a globetrotting mediator, and an often controversial one at that.

Several types of IGOs exist. The UN is a *multipurpose, universal membership* organization. It serves many functions and can be joined by all states in the international system, providing the Security Council's permanent members and two-thirds of the General Assembly agree.[3] Importantly, the UN universe includes more than 30 major agencies and programs such as the International Labour Organization (ILO), the **Food and Agriculture Organization of the UN (FAO)**, the **UN Educational, Scientific and Cultural Organization (UNESCO)**, the International Maritime Organization (IMO), the **UN Conference on Trade and Development (UNCTAD)**, and the **UN Development Programme (UNDP)**, in addition to those mentioned earlier. Multipurpose, universal membership organizations may be contrasted with *regional* and *functional* organizations, which manage issues at a regional level or are designed for a specific purpose. In fact, most IGOs fall into the latter category. The most famous regional IGO is the European Union, which was known as the European Community (EC) before 1994; indeed, the EU has coordinated policies to such a degree that it is often called a *supranational* institution. Other multipurpose regional organizations include the Organization of American States (OAS), the Association of Southeast Asian Nations (ASEAN), and the **Arab League**. Single-purpose, or functional, regional organizations include the **Asian Development Bank**, the North Atlantic Treaty Organization (NATO), the **Northwest Atlantic Fisheries Organization (NAFO)**, and the Organization of the Petroleum Exporting Countries (OPEC). Lest we think only the UN has potential global membership, we should keep in mind the existence of open-membership organizations that have single functions, such as the various UN agencies[4] mentioned above, the International Organization for Migration (IOM), and the International Whaling Commission (IWC). Not all states have joined these organizations, but they may if they desire.

INTERNATIONAL ORGANIZATIONS AND REGIMES IN HISTORY

International organizations have been around for a long time in the form of religious or political institutions such as the powerful Roman Catholic Church. Indeed, the political administration of territories occupied by the Roman Empire and, much later, of the European great powers, could technically be labelled embryonic forms of IOs, since they involved political interaction and structure across frontiers. The Olympic Games, which organized peaceful competition among Greek city-states, were another early ancestor of the modern IO.[5] We could include in this historical list arrangements among states to maintain power and order, such as the Concert of Europe (see Chapter 2). But when we speak of modern, formal IOs, such as the League of Nations (1919–46) and the current UN system (1945–present), we are discussing relatively recent development. The League and the UN were established for two primary reasons. The first is practicality. Once the nation-state system was established and contacts between states expanded, it became clear that governments would have to maintain linkages that facilitated communication and coordination. As economic interdependence between states grew, it became necessary to establish new lines of communication and to reduce the probability of unexpected events. Trade relations are very dependent on order, the ability to expect payment for goods, fair treatment in foreign markets, freedom from piracy, and other factors.

Second, IOs can be set up to serve a much broader purpose, such as the establishment or maintenance of world order and peace—this is the official mandate of the UN itself, which was established following the most destructive war in global history. However, we should stress how these rationales complement each other. Simply put, most functional organizations are based on some set of guiding principles (or ideals), but their creation is also necessitated by the practical circumstances surrounding them. For example, two early IOs still in operation today are the **International Telecommunication Union** (1865) and the **Universal Postal Union** (1874), both created for rather specific purposes (telegraphs and postage between nations).[6] Another early IO with a clear functional purpose was the **International Office of Weights and Measures**, established in 1875. Yet behind this functional cooperation was a belief, held by participating government and industry representatives, that telegrams, mail, and common measurement standards were good for business, if not for world peace itself. Liberal values on international political economy, as discussed in the previous chapter, surface again here: increased trade and communication is assumed by many to be the best path toward a peaceful international system, and IOs provide the regulatory framework of predictability.

We can see, then, that it is tempting to conclude that IOs are similar in their wide range of functions to domestic governments, though they do not often disrupt the cardinal principle of state sovereignty. IL, on which we focus later in this chapter, evolved alongside the IO, though it has a much more complex history predating the contemporary era. International treaty law is especially important, since it often establishes the legality of IOs themselves. The first major effort at IO in the 20th century was the League of Nations, the result of the infamous Treaty of Versailles.

THE LEAGUE OF NATIONS

As discussed in Chapter 2, the **League of Nations** was created at the end of World War I. Two basic principles underlay the League's system of peace maintenance. First, members agreed to respect and preserve the territorial integrity and political independence of other states. Second, any war or threat of war was considered a matter of concern to the entire League. While the major emphasis of the League's Covenant was on maintaining international peace and stability, some recognition was also given to promoting economic and social cooperation. The Covenant did not provide any special machinery for overseeing these efforts, though a commitment was included for the establishment of one or more organizations to secure "fair and humane conditions of labor for men, women and children" (Article 23), and an autonomous International Labor Office (ILO) was established as part of the Treaty of Versailles (the ILO is still in existence as the International Labour Organization).

League organization centred around three major organs: the Assembly, to which all member-states belonged; the Council, to which a select few belonged; and the **Secretariat**. The League also established a Permanent Court of International Justice in 1921 to resolve disputes between members of the international community. From the outset the Permanent Court's role was not considered of primary importance, mirroring the present International Court of Justice in the UN system, which retains some symbolic significance but is not a decisive factor in world affairs. The League Assembly and the Council were the two main deliberative organs of the League. In both organs, each state possessed one vote. The Assembly was primarily responsible for discussing important issues confronting either individual members of the League or the international community as a whole. The Council was primarily responsible for discussing the maintenance of peace.

Originally, the Council was to be composed of five permanent and four elected members. However, since the United States never joined (the U.S. Senate did not ratify the Treaty of Versailles, preferring its old isolationist foreign policy), Great Britain, Italy, Japan, and France were the original permanent members. Germany was given Permanent Council status on its admission to the League in 1926, and the Soviet Union was given the same status in 1934. Germany and Japan would eventually withdraw from the League, and the Soviet Union was expelled in 1939 for its invasion of Finland.

Despite the failure of the League to prevent war, it did enjoy some success. The operations of the Secretariat, which was charged with administrative duties, were widely regarded as a success. As Egon Ranshofen-Wertheimer has observed, "The League has shown that it is possible to establish an integrated body of international officials, loyal to the international agency and ready to discharge faithfully the international obligations incumbent upon them. It was not for lack of executive efficiency that the League system failed."[7] Beyond this administrative precedent, the League of Nations established or incorporated bureaus and committees dealing with disease, communications, traffic in arms, slavery, drugs, labour, women, and children. In 1925, it played an important role in bringing about the peaceful resolution of the Greek–Bulgarian border dispute. By 1921, 48 members had joined the League and by mid-1929, 46 states had ratified the 1928 Kellogg–Briand Pact, in theory committing signatories to the peaceful settlement of disputes. The League considered 66 disputes and conflicts between 1920 and 1939, and in 35 of them, it was able to contribute to a peaceful resolution. The League was linked to several semiautonomous organizations, such as the Economic and Financial Organization, the Health Organization, the Organizations for Communications and Transit, the High Commissioner for Refugees, and the Intergovernmental Committees on the Drug Traffic, Traffic in Women, the Protection of Children, and Intellectual Co-operation. Nevertheless, despite the Wilsonian idealism that surrounded the formation of the League, its "primary purpose, like that of the Concert of Europe, was to assist in the management of a multipolar balance of power, not to replace it with a universal system."[8]

Unfortunately, the League's ability to alleviate serious disputes was limited. As discussed in Chapter 2, when the Japanese launched a series of attacks against Manchuria in 1931, some Council members, including Great Britain and France, were unwilling to apply economic and military sanctions, which seriously undermined the League's ability and willingness to discourage members of the international community from resorting to arms to achieve their objectives. Another serious blow to the League's credibility came in 1935, when the League was unable to deter Italy's invasion of Ethiopia, although the economic sanctions imposed on Italy were the first on behalf of the international community, setting an important precedent for the use of economic sanctions by the UN.

Several reasons have been advanced for the League's demise. Some attribute it to the absence of the United States and, during shorter periods, to the absence of the Soviet Union and Germany (this lack of leadership helped give rise to theories about hegemonic stability discussed in previous chapters). Its collapse can be linked to the inherent deficiencies of its Covenant, including Article 5, requiring unanimity on all major Assembly and Council decisions. Yet, in the critical tests, such as Japan and Ethiopia, it appeared to be the lack of political will among the members of the League, rather than the available machinery, that was primarily responsible for the League's failings. Finally, the aggressive foreign policies of the Axis powers made a successful League impossible; the League of Nations, reduced to insignificance by the cataclysm of World War II, was officially disbanded in April 1946.

THE UNITED NATIONS ORGANIZATION

It is common knowledge that plans for the establishment of the UN had begun far before the end of World War II. The term "United Nations" originated in the Washington Declaration of 1942 in which 26 Allied countries pledged to fight Germany, Japan, and Italy; before that, the Declaration of Principles (the **Atlantic Charter**) expressed similar concerns. By October 1943, the governments of the United States, Great Britain, the Soviet Union, and China were prepared to issue a clear statement of their intention to establish a general IO. That year, further steps were taken to create several agencies that would eventually fall under the auspices of the UN or that would come to be closely associated with it. The Food and Agriculture Organization (FAO) would be established in 1945, and, as a result of the Bretton Woods conference in 1944, the IMF and the IBRD were created.

However, it was not until the Dumbarton Oaks Conference of August 21, 1944, that representatives from the United States, Great Britain, and the U.S.S.R. (China participated in the second phase of negotiations) began to map out a blueprint for a new world body. At the famous Yalta Conference of February 1945, progress was made on filling several of the technical gaps that remained open at the Dumbarton Oaks Conference. Two important conferences took place before the eventual historic meeting in San Francisco, where the organization was officially born. In February and March 1945, representatives from the United States and its Latin American allies met in Mexico City to discuss their plans for a general IO. At the same time, a committee of jurists representing virtually all the states that would attend the San Francisco conference met in Washington to discuss the creation of an **International Court of Justice (ICJ)**, which would replace the Permanent Court of International Justice established under the League of Nations.

Inis Claude states that it was important to begin discussing plans for the creation of the United Nations before the end of war for two main reasons. First, as former U.S. Secretary of State Cordell Hull pointed out, if negotiations for an IO had been left to the end of the war, it

Canadian delegation to the United Nations conference in London, January 1946. Vincent Massey, Canadian High Commissioner to the United Kingdom (left), stands next to Minister of Justice Louis St. Laurent, Secretary of State Paul Martin Sr., and Associate Under-Secretary of State for External Affairs Hume Wrong. (CP Picture Archive)

Paul Heinbecker, Canadian Ambassador to the UN, speaks to the media in New York on March 3, 2002. Canada has traditionally placed strong emphasis on the UN in its foreign policy design and is often elected a nonpermanent member of the Security Council. (AP Photo/Osamu Honda/ CP Archive)

would have been much more difficult to reach a consensus on how to create the organization, since politicians would be too preoccupied with political, economic, and social issues at home. Second, it was extremely important to avoid creating an unnecessarily close relationship between the UN and the peace settlement. In other words, the founders of the UN did not want it to appear as if the rights and obligations contained in the UN Charter were being imposed on states as part of the peace settlement, which appeared to be the case with the League. Rather, the UN was to be created expressly for "all peace loving nations," which opened the possibility of accepting postwar Germany and Japan to join in the hope of bringing about lasting peace.[9]

In addition, it is important not to dismiss the psychological and political factors motivating diplomats from countries such as Canada to support the creation of the UN. Canadians, for example, believed that—in contradistinction to the League of Nations experience—the United States had to be engaged in postwar affairs, and saw the UN as a means to ensure this. A great deal of support existed among several governmental and nongovernmental bodies in the United States for the UN, although to gain support for the organization, several American leaders had to emphasize that the UN was an entirely new organization. Yet a close reading of the UN Charter indicates that although this document is approximately four times longer than the League's Covenant, it nonetheless contains many of the same features. Not unlike the Covenant, the Charter refers to the principal organs of the UN and the functions each should perform. Moreover, it clearly sets out the primary purpose of the UN, the maintenance of international peace and security, and how this commitment can be fulfilled. Furthermore, like the Covenant, the Charter emphasizes the inherent responsibility of all member states to deter aggression.

The climactic event in the long and arduous process of building a new IO took place in San Francisco in the spring of 1945. Representatives from 50 nations deliberated for two months before they could agree on the final version of the UN Charter. On June 26, 1945, the Charter was signed, but it was not until January 10, 1946, that the first session of the General Assembly was held in London. Eventually, UN headquarters would be moved to its permanent home in New York City, a building now easily recognized around the world (see Profile 5.1). Although initial hopes for the organization were high (especially in Canada), the superpower confrontation effectively paralyzed the UN's capacity to mount collective security efforts. This incapacity did not mean that the UN was inactive. On the contrary, the UN performed many other crucial functions, most prominently in the process of decolonization, peacekeeping, and aid and development.

The UN has six principal organs (see Figure 5.1). At the heart of the UN is the General Assembly (GA), a forum in which all states can send representatives to sit in session, present opinions, and vote on resolutions, which need a two-thirds majority to pass (see Profile 5.2). It is true that GA resolutions cannot force other UN members to act; however, since those resolutions are considered by many to carry the weight of world opinion, they remain significant. The GA also makes key decisions regarding who gets to join the organization, what the Economic and Social Council (ECOSOC) does, and the spending powers of the organization. The GA has exclusive authority over the budget of the UN and elections to the Security Council and ECOSOC but needs a recommendation from the Security Council to take action on the appointment of the secretary-general, UN membership, and amendments to the Charter. The Assembly and Security Council are jointly responsible for electing the judges of the International Court of Justice (ICJ).

The Security Council includes 5 permanent members, including the People's Republic of China, France, the Russian Federation, the United Kingdom, and the United States. Each of these states has a veto over any substantive matter that comes before the Council. There are also 10 nonpermanent members (originally there were 6), elected by the General Assembly in accordance with an agreed geographical formula for two-year terms. A substantive matter (as opposed to a procedural one) requires nine positive votes and the absence of a veto to pass in the Council. The Council meets whenever the secretary-general decides a matter has come up

---

PROFILE 5.1 **Locating the United Nations**

What if you had built a world organization on which a new global order was to be based but didn't know where to put it? Locating the UN was, in fact, one of the first problems faced by the organization. This issue was obviously important since it was initially believed that a truly global organization could hardly be located anywhere closely affiliated with a major power, such as in Washington or Moscow, and it would be unsafe to locate it in an unstable state where political authority itself was contested, such as in China or soon-to-be-independent India. In all probability, the idea of locating the UN in a Southern state was never taken seriously; the first Southern Hemisphere location of a UN agency was in Nairobi, Kenya, and this was the headquarters of the UN Environment Programme established in the early 1970s. Germany, Japan, and Italy were (of course) out of the question as hosts of the new UN, as was any truly neutral place, such as the inaccessible Antarctic. The Swiss, hosts to the League of Nations and the first temporary location of the General Assembly of the UN, were reluctant to assume the responsibility of long-term UN involvement; they refused to host a UN capable of making decisions related to the use of force, which is of course precisely what Chapter 7 of the UN Charter authorizes the Security Council to do. (Switzerland joined the UN in 2002.) Europe was in a state of financial chaos and most of its capital cities were literally in physical ruin. The only country in a position of relative economic strength was the United States, and it was the American philanthropist John Davison Rockefeller Jr. who supplied the initial capital to build the UN in New York City. After the September 11, 2001, attack on the World Trade Center, there was some concern that the UN building was under similar threat, but it has yet (2004) to be either attacked or relocated.

Figure 5.1   The United Nations System

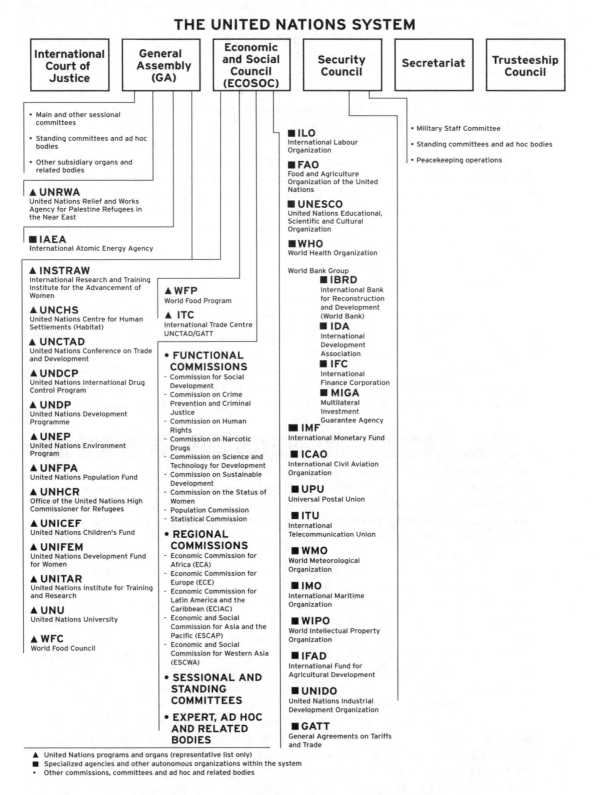

THE UNITED NATIONS SYSTEM

▲ United Nations programs and organs (representative list only)
■ Specialized agencies and other autonomous organizations within the system
• Other commissions, committees and ad hoc and related bodies

SOURCE: *THE CANADIAN REFERENCE GUIDE TO THE UNITED NATIONS* (OTTAWA: FOREIGN AFFAIRS CANADA, 2000). REPRODUCED WITH THE PERMISSION OF THE MINISTER OF PUBLIC WORKS AND GOVERNMENT SERVICES CANADA, 2004.

PROFILE 5.2 — Member States of the United Nations as of July 2004

MEMBER (DATE OF ADMISSION)

Afghanistan (19 Nov. 1946)

Albania (14 Dec. 1955)

Algeria (8 Oct. 1962)

Andorra (28 July 1993)

Angola (1 Dec. 1976)

Antigua and Barbuda (11 Nov. 1981)

Argentina (24 Oct. 1945)

Armenia (2 Mar. 1992)

Australia (1 Nov. 1945)

Austria (14 Dec. 1955)

Azerbaijan (9 Mar. 1992)

Bahamas (18 Sep. 1973)

Bahrain (21 Sep. 1971)

Bangladesh (17 Sep. 1974)

Barbados (9 Dec. 1966)

Belarus (24 Oct. 1945)

Belgium (27 Dec. 1945)

Belize (25 Sep. 1981)

Benin (20 Sep. 1960)

Bhutan (21 Sep. 1971)

Bolivia (14 Nov. 1945)

Bosnia and Herzegovina (22 May 1992)

Botswana (17 Oct. 1966)

Brazil (24 Oct. 1945)

Brunei Darussalam (21 Sep. 1984)

Bulgaria (14 Dec. 1955)

Burkina Faso (20 Sep. 1960)

Burundi (18 Sep. 1962)

Cambodia (14 Dec. 1955)

Cameroon (20 Sep. 1960)

CANADA (9 NOV. 1945)

Cape Verde (16 Sep. 1975)

Central African Republic (20 Sep. 1960)

Chad (20 Sep. 1960)

Chile (24 Oct. 1945)

China (24 Oct. 1945)

Colombia (5 Nov. 1945)

Comoros (12 Nov. 1975)

Congo (20 Sep. 1960)

Costa Rica (2 Nov. 1945)

Côte d'Ivoire (20 Sep. 1960)

Croatia (22 May 1992)

Cuba (24 Oct. 1945)

Cyprus (20 Sep. 1960)

Czech Republic (19 Jan. 1993)

Democratic People's Republic of Korea (17 Sep. 1991)

Democratic Republic of the Congo (20 Sep. 1960)

Denmark (24 Oct. 1945)

Djibouti (20 Sep. 1977)

Dominica (18 Dec. 1978)

Dominican Republic (24 Oct. 1945)

Ecuador (21 Dec. 1945)

Egypt (24 Oct. 1945)

El Salvador (24 Oct. 1945)

Equatorial Guinea (12 Nov. 1968)

Eritrea (28 May 1993)

Estonia (17 Sep. 1991)

Ethiopia (13 Nov. 1945)

Fiji (13 Oct. 1970)

Finland (14 Dec. 1955)

France (24 Oct. 1945)

Gabon (20 Sep. 1960)

Gambia (21 Sep. 1965)

Georgia (31 July 1992)

Germany (18 Sep. 1973)

Ghana (8 Mar. 1957)

Greece (25 Oct. 1945)

Grenada (17 Sep. 1974)

Guatemala (21 Nov. 1945)

Guinea (12 Dec. 1958)

Guinea-Bissau (17 Sep. 1974)

Guyana (20 Sep. 1966)

Haiti (24 Oct. 1945)

Honduras (17 Dec. 1945)

Hungary (14 Dec. 1955)

Iceland (19 Nov. 1946)

India (30 Oct. 1945)

Indonesia (28 Sep. 1950)

Iraq (21 Dec. 1945)

Ireland (14 Dec. 1955)

Islamic Republic of Iran (24. Oct. 1945)

Israel (11 May 1949)

Italy (14 Dec. 1955)

Jamaica (18 Sep. 1962)

Japan (18 Dec. 1956)

Jordan (14 Dec. 1955)

Kazakhstan (2 Mar. 1992)

Kenya (16 Dec. 1963)

Kiribati (14 Sept. 1999)

Kuwait (14 May 1963)

Kyrgyzstan (2 Mar. 1992)

Lao People's Democratic Republic (14 Dec. 1955)

Latvia (17 Sep. 1991)

Lebanon (24 Oct. 1945)

Lesotho (17 Oct. 1966)

Liberia (2 Nov. 1945)

Libyan Arab Jamahiriya (14 Dec. 1955)

continued

Member States of the United Nations as of July 2004 (cont'd)

PROFILE 5.2

MEMBER (DATE OF ADMISSION)		
Liechtenstein (18 Sep. 1990)	Paraguay (24 Oct. 1945)	Swaziland (24 Sep. 1968)
Lithuania (17 Sep. 1991)	Peru (31 Oct. 1945)	Sweden (19 Nov. 1946)
Luxembourg (24 Oct. 1945)	Philippines (24 Oct. 1945)	Switzerland (10 Sep. 2002)
Madagascar (20 Sep. 1960)	Poland (24 Oct. 1945)	Syrian Arab Republic (24 Oct. 1947)
Malawi (1 Dec. 1964)	Portugal (14 Dec. 1955)	Tajikistan (2 Mar. 1992)
Malaysia (17 Sep. 1957)	Qatar (21 Sep. 1971)	Thailand (16 Dec. 1946)
Maldives (21 Sep. 1965)	Republic of Korea (17 Sep. 1991)	The former Yugoslav Republic of Macedonia (8 Apr. 1993)
Mali (28 Sep. 1960)	Republic of Moldova (2 Mar. 1992)	Timor-Leste (27 Sep. 2002)
Malta (1 Dec. 1964)	Romania (14 Dec. 1955)	Togo (20 Sep. 1960)
Marshall Islands (17 Sep. 1991)	Russian Federation (24 Oct. 1945)	Tonga (14 Sept. 1999)
Mauritania (7 Oct. 1961)	Rwanda (18 Sep. 1962)	Trinidad and Tobago (18 Sep. 1962)
Mauritius (24 Apr. 1968)	Saint Kitts and Nevis (23 Sep. 1983)	
Mexico (7 Nov. 1945)	Saint Lucia (18 Sep. 1979)	Tunisia (12 Nov. 1956)
Micronesia (Federated States of) (17 Sep. 1991)	Saint Vincent and the Grenadines (16 Sep. 1980)	Turkey (24 Oct. 1945)
Monaco (28 May 1993)	Samoa (15 Dec. 1976)	Turkmenistan (2 Mar. 1992)
Mongolia (27 Oct. 1961)	San Marino (2 Mar. 1992)	Tuvalu (5 Sep. 2000)
Morocco (12 Nov. 1956)	Sao Tome and Principe (16 Sep. 1975)	Uganda (25 Oct. 1962)
Mozambique (16 Sep. 1975)	Saudi Arabia (24 Oct. 1945)	Ukraine (24 Oct. 1945)
Myanmar (19 Apr. 1948)	Senegal (28 Sep. 1960)	United Arab Emirates (9 Dec. 1971)
Namibia (23 Apr. 1990)	Serbia and Montenegro (1 Nov. 2000)	United Kingdom of Great Britain and Northern Ireland (24 Oct. 1945)
Nauru (14 Sept. 1999)	Seychelles (21 Sep. 1976)	United Republic of Tanzania (14 Dec. 1961)
Nepal (14 Dec. 1955)	Sierra Leone (27 Sep. 1961)	United States of America (24 Oct. 1945)
Netherlands (10 Dec. 1945)	Singapore (21 Sep. 1965)	
New Zealand (24 Oct. 1945)	Slovakia (19 Jan. 1993)	Uruguay (18 Dec. 1945)
Nicaragua (24 Oct. 1945)	Slovenia (22 May 1992)	Uzbekistan (2 Mar. 1992)
Niger (20 Sep. 1960)	Solomon Islands (19 Sep. 1978)	Vanuatu (15 Sep. 1981)
Nigeria (7 Oct. 1960)	Somalia (20 Sep. 1960)	Venezuela (15 Nov. 1945)
Norway (27 Nov. 1945)	South Africa (7 Nov. 1945)	Viet Nam (20 Sep. 1977)
Oman (7 Oct. 1971)	Spain (14 Dec. 1955)	Yemen (30 Sep. 1947)
Pakistan (30 Sep. 1947)	Sri Lanka (14 Dec. 1955)	Yugoslavia (24 Oct. 1945)
Palau (15 Dec. 1994)	Sudan (12 Nov. 1956)	Zambia (1 Dec. 1964)
Panama (13 Nov. 1945)	Suriname (4 Dec. 1975)	Zimbabwe (25 Aug. 1980)
Papua New Guinea (10 Oct. 1975)		

that demands its attention. Simultaneous translation allows it to operate in six official languages: Arabic, Chinese, English, French, Spanish, and Russian. Sydney Bailey and Sam Davis write that one diplomat, Victor Andres Belaunde of Peru, "used to choose a language to suit his mood: French when he wanted to be precise, English when he wanted to understate, Spanish when he wanted to exaggerate."[10] The Security Council is still the primary organ dealing with questions of international peace and security, and in particular collective security, a concept embraced originally by the UN's founders despite its apparent failure during the interwar period (see Profile 5.3). Canada has been elected six times to a nonpermanent seat on the Council: 1948–49, 1958–59, 1967–68, 1977–78, 1989–90, and 1999–2000.

The Economic and Social Council (ECOSOC) comprises 54 members elected by the General Assembly for a term of three years. ECOSOC has established several regional and functional commissions and other bodies, considers general policy questions regarding economic and social development, and makes recommendations.

A third UN council, the Trusteeship Council, was set up to help manage trust territories after World War II but is no longer a relevant body.

The Secretariat is the administrative arm of the organization, comprising the secretary-general and staff appointed by that person. Staff members are supposed to act as truly international civil servants, discarding any national obligations they may have toward their home state. The Secretariat has been trusted with increasingly important matters since the formation of the UN, and the secretary-general has participated in, or has had representatives participate in, many diplomatic missions through the "good offices" function.

The other important organ of the UN, the International Court of Justice (ICJ), is discussed in our examination of IL later in the chapter.

Despite the UN's profile in the world, and despite the wide variety of political, economic, and social functions it performs, the organization operates in a state of permanent financial crisis. Many people hoped that the end of the Cold War would free the UN to act as an instrument of global conflict management and collective security as its founders had intended. However, the UN was beset by problems in the 1990s, and continues to be beset by problems in the early 2000s. The most serious of these problems is the funding crisis. The regular annual budget of the UN is approximately U.S.$1.2 billion, and the money is paid to the UN in the form of dues from member states (peacekeeping costs are assessed separately). Yet, many members have not paid their dues; the biggest debtor, the United States, has, however, paid back much of its debt—after prolonged negotiations.

The United States has argued that it has no obligation to fund programs of which its government disapproves; and that the current weighting mechanism to determine contributions is unfair. Member states are generally expected to contribute a certain percentage of the UN budget based on the size of their gross national product (GNP). As a result, because the United States has typically generated from a third to a quarter of world GNP, it is expected to pay much more than other states. However, with the increased growth in the economies of Europe and Japan over the past two decades, the United States has argued that it pays more than its share, and began to demand that its contribution be capped at 22 percent. In addition, over the last few decades the United States has on occasion unilaterally withdrawn funding for various agencies, such as the United Nations Population Fund, which promotes family planning and contraception.[11] Despite current friction between the Bush Administration and the UN, things have improved since 1999, when the United States made a payment of $264 million. Yet, the United States still owed 65 percent of the total $2.51 billion owed the UN that year ($1.831 billion for peacekeeping, $644 million for the regular budget, and $35 million for the criminal tribunals for the former Yugoslavia and Rwanda).[12] Without this money, the UN is virtually bankrupt, and lack of funds has severely constrained UN activities. The UN has also

PROFILE 5.3 Collective Security and the UN

Collective security is a system of international order in which all states respect recognized territorial boundaries and in which aggression by any state is met by a collective response. In other words, an attack on one will be considered an attack on all and dealt with accordingly. This ideal differs from collective defence systems, which are traditional alliances aimed at potential aggressors outside the membership of the system. Collective security is an ideal system that has yet to be fully realized by the international community. The League of Nations was a collective security organization, as is the United Nations. The United Nations rarely exercised its collective security provisions during the Cold War, due to the use (or threatened use) of the veto. It came close to doing so in the Korean War, but the Soviet Union was absent from the Security Council vote on Korea. Some argue that the response to Iraq's invasion of Kuwait in 1990–91 was an instance of collective security in action; others insist it was merely an example of American-orchestrated power. NATO chose to avoid the Security Council altogether when it launched its air war over Serbia in 1999, aware that the Russians and Chinese would most likely veto military action; and the United States did not seek final Security Council authorization before it and the United Kingdom launched the invasion of Iraq in 2003.

been criticized for being unrepresentative, with the composition of the Security Council reflecting the old distribution of power and excluding emergent countries (especially Japan and Germany, as well as developing countries), and for being overly bureaucratic and resistant to reform. Finally, the UN can be only as effective as its members want it to be. National interests, concerns over protecting sovereignty, and economic and political disputes between states continue to plague the UN. Indeed, many countries (especially in the developing world) want to avoid a stronger UN; they are concerned that the UN could become an instrument used by rich states to dominate or intimidate others. Contrary to the blatantly erroneous allegations of some individuals, the UN is nowhere close to becoming a world government with any kind of supranational powers.

For the most part, smaller states such as Canada tend to be supportive of the UN, showing generally consistent dedication to paying their dues and contributing to peacekeeping missions.[13] Many countries view the UN as the cornerstone of an international legal system, and Security Council authorization is often seen as the most important form of legitimation for collective security–related military operations. However, a large rift has grown between theory and practice, since neither NATO's attack on Serbia in 1999, nor the "coalition" invasion of Iraq in 2003, were given explicit Security Council approval (vetos from Russia over Serbia and from France over Iraq were almost certain). Beyond this, and despite the fact that the UN has not succeeded in achieving all the goals that its advocates would like, the UN and its agencies perform so many valuable functions that if it did not exist, it would likely have to be created. However, in the end the UN does what its members allow it to do, and, much like the League of Nations, the political will of its members sets its limitations.

NON-UN IGOS

The UN, of course, is not the only IGO in the international system. Arguably, the most advanced supranational institution is the European Union: it can be seen as an ongoing experiment in political integration, challenging many aspects of the sovereign statehood that characterized the European system for so long. The EU is a much more demanding institution than the UN, since it has more regulatory and legal powers within member states. But there are other IGOs of great significance as well. While space does not permit an exhaustive survey, here is an overview of some other prominent IGOs that have special relevance for Canada and other middle powers.

- *The North Atlantic Treaty Organization.* NATO (also informally called the Atlantic Alliance) was established in 1949 to deter a Soviet invasion of Western Europe and to solidify American leadership (Canada was a founding member.) After the Cold War, NATO adopted a New Strategic Concept, which reduced its standing military forces and created a force structure oriented toward crisis response. NATO has established close relationships with other European institutions and has become actively involved in peacekeeping operations in the former Yugoslavia. In a controversial action, NATO embarked on a bombing campaign against Serbia in 1999 in response to human rights abuses in the Serbian province of Kosovo. NATO has also strengthened its cooperation with countries in Eastern Europe and has been involved in arms control on the continent, especially the Conventional Forces in Europe (CFE) Treaty. NATO had had 16 members since 1982, but Poland, Hungary, and the Czech Republic joined by 1999. Seven more countries—Bulgaria, Estonia, Latvia, Lithuania, Romania, Slovakia, and Slovenia—joined in 2004, bringing NATO membership to 26 states. NATO's headquarters are in Brussels, Belgium.

- *The Commonwealth.* The origins of the Commonwealth lie in the British Empire. World War I, the adoption of the famous Balfour Declaration at the 1926 Imperial Conference, and the institution's formal creation in 1931 under the Statute of Westminster were the defining events in the formation of the Commonwealth and the independence of its early members (which included Canada and Newfoundland). The Commonwealth expanded during the decolonization era, though South Africa was expelled, and in 1965 a Secretariat was established. A major issue facing the Commonwealth during the Cold War was the apartheid regime in South Africa; its eventual collapse led to the readmission of South Africa in 1994. Today, human rights, democracy, and development are the major concerns of the Commonwealth (see Profile 5.4), with Nigeria and Zimbabwe both presenting major problems and Commonwealth suspensions (Zimbabwe withdrew in late 2003; Pakistan, South Africa, and Fiji all quit at some point but have rejoined). Another important cultural and political organization with ties to Canada's colonial past is La Francophonie.

- *The Organization of American States.* According to its own literature, the OAS is the oldest regional intergovernmental organization in the world, with its origins in the 1826 Congress of Panama. The Charter of the present OAS was signed in 1948 and entered into force in 1951. The OAS has a troubled history, both because of the political instability of Central and South America and because of the disturbing tendency of the United States to engage in unilateral action (including invasions and interventions) in the region. As a result, the OAS has been frequently maligned as ineffective and dominated by Washington. Today, the principal activities of the OAS are focused on democratic values, trade, and economic development. The OAS has also played a minor role in political oversight and mediation, frequently deploying election observers and negotiating teams. The OAS had 35 members in 2004 (Canada joined in 1990) and is headquartered in Washington, D.C.

PROFILE 5.4 Membership in the Commonwealth

The 53 Commonwealth states have an estimated 1.7 billion citizens. Members are listed below:

Antigua & Barbuda	Jamaica	St Vincent & the Grenadines
Australia	Kenya	Samoa
The Bahamas	Kiribati	Seychelles
Bangladesh	Lesotho	Sierra Leone
Barbados	Malawi	Singapore
Belize	Malaysia	Solomon Islands
Botswana	Maldives	South Africa
Brunei Darussalam	Malta	Sri Lanka
Cameroon	Mauritius	Swaziland
CANADA	Mozambique	Tanzania (United Republic of)
Cyprus	Namibia	Tonga
Dominica	Nauru	Trinidad & Tobago
Fiji Islands	New Zealand	Tuvalu
The Gambia	Nigeria	Uganda
Ghana	Pakistan	United Kingdom
Grenada	Papua New Guinea	Vanuatu
Guyana	St Kitts & Nevis	Zambia
India	St Lucia	

NONGOVERNMENTAL ORGANIZATIONS

In Chapter 4, we mentioned the growing importance of international nongovernmental organizations (INGOs) in world affairs—those run for profit, which are more typically termed multinational corporations (MNCs), as well as those dedicated to a particular cause or representing social movements. Not only are NGOs significant actors in their own right, but they also often interact, sometimes on a permanent basis, with multilateral intergovernmental venues.

Scholar James Rosenau has written of the "bifurcation of global structures into the old state-centric world and the relatively ascendant multicentric world, composed of sovereignty-free actors including MNCs, ethnic minorities, subnational governments and bureaucracies, professional societies, and transnational organizations."[14] Most visibly, the rising influence of groups such as Amnesty International, CARE, Médecins Sans Frontières, and the International Committee of the Red Cross/Red Crescent is viewed by many as a positive development in human rights and humanitarian issues. While INGOs may not have the military power or diplomatic resources of states, they do possess an inherent ability to change shape, to submerge and resurface, and to make decisions rapidly, all important tools of survival. Meanwhile, the IOs that form the core of state-centric diplomacy, in particular the immense UN system, can act as channels or conduits between the state and the NGO community.

While NGOs may not have access to the same resources as states, they are increasingly important and visible actors in the global system. In 1972 about 2100 NGOs existed; in 1982 more than 4200 had been established, and by 1993 more than 4800 had been registered with the Union of International Associations in Geneva. Remarkably, current estimates run as high as 40 000 international nonprofit NGOs. Most are private organizations, founded by individuals or groups and funded from donations, grants, IGO budgets, or governments. These individuals or groups do not formally represent their states or governments, although they continue to be citizens of states, and many do collaborate extensively with governments. It is impossible to list the wide variety of NGO activities here, but a partial list would include the following:

- *Humanitarian NGOs.* These NGOs undertake aid efforts to assist in the alleviation of human suffering. The **International Committee of the Red Cross** (ICRC; "Red Crescent" in Muslim societies) provides medical assistance to victims of war and armed conflict. CARE International provides developmental and emergency care to poor peoples and victims of natural disasters and conflicts. Save the Children focuses on alleviating child poverty.

- *Human rights NGOs.* Human rights NGOs monitor and investigate human rights abuses worldwide and put pressure on governments to improve their human rights records or take action against other governments with poor human rights records. The most prominent example is Amnesty International.

- *Corporate lobby groups.* Corporations typically pool their money and expertise to create lobby groups with international reach. Examples include the Trilateral Commission, the European Roundtable of Industrialists, the Canadian Business Council on National Issues, the Davos World Economic Forum, and the International Chamber of Commerce.

- *Scientific and technical organizations.* Scientific and technical NGOs work to increase scientific cooperation, achieve standardization, and promote research and development. Examples include the Council of Scientific Unions, the International Peace Research Institute, and the European Space Agency.

- *Sports bodies.* Sporting organizations manage international sporting events and frequently find themselves involved in world politics, as sport is often employed for political purposes (such as the former ban on South African athletes or boycotts of the Olympics). The International Olympic Committee (IOC) is the most prominent sport-related NGO.

- *Professional associations.* Professional associations exist to promote the interests of their members and interaction among them. Examples include the International Federation of Airline Pilots and the International Studies Association.

- *Environmental groups.* Environmental NGOs promote awareness on environmental issues and often mount protests and publicity campaigns to this end. Two well-known environmental INGOs are Greenpeace and Friends of the Earth.

- *Women's issues NGOs.* These NGOs exist to promote the political and economic advancement of women. Examples include the parallel Women's Forum of the ECOSOC Commission on the Status of Women, and the Associated Country Women of the World.

- *Philanthropic organizations.* A large number of trusts and foundations provide grants and sponsor projects on a variety of international issues. Although not strictly INGOs because they are chartered under the domestic law of one state, organizations such as the Ford Foundation and Rockefeller Foundation have supported the NGO community and continue to do so.

- *Religious organizations.* A large number of religious INGOs exist, including the Roman Catholic Church and the World Jewish Congress. Multifaith INGOs include the International Association for Religious Freedom and the World Congress of Faiths. They promote religious activities and are often directly involved in political campaigns related to lifestyle and other moral choices.

INGOs perform many functions in global politics: they facilitate communication between interested individuals; act as pressure groups to change government policies; offer information-gathering resources, often when no other reliable source exists; distribute aid and knowledge; and play an important role in the formulation of state or IGO policy in cooperation with governments. Indeed, there is a growing tendency toward institutionalized interaction between official multilateral organizations and NGOs with more specific agendas. Such hybrids include the Arctic Council, which is composed of eight Arctic states—Canada, Denmark (for Greenland), Finland, Iceland, Norway, the Russian Federation, Sweden, and the United States—as well as six initial permanent participant groups—the Inuit Circumpolar Conference; the Saami Council; and the Russian Association of Indigenous Peoples of the North; the Aleut International Association; the Arctic Athabascan Council; and the Gwich'in Council International (see Profile 5.5). It is not insignificant that these groups have been guaranteed a permanent status on the Council, even if they will have less influence than the formal governments involved. The Council is supposed to be a "high-level permanent intergovernmental forum to provide for co-operation, co-ordination and interaction among the Arctic states, the Arctic indigenous communities and other Arctic inhabitants on common Arctic issues [including] economic and social development, improved health conditions and cultural well-being."[15] In another somewhat ironic example, even legislators have an NGO, the Parliamentarians for Global Action. Here we see the ultimate meshing of the public sector and the nonprofit NGO.

At the UN, INGOs have consultative status in many agencies. As A. LeRoy Bennett writes,

> The most sought-after consultative status is granted by the Economic and Social Council. The breadth of ECOSOC's mandate explains the large number of NGOs that have been granted consultative status, including more than 800 organizations divided into three categories according to the extent of their involvement in ECOSOC's program ... The relationships between United Nations agencies and hundreds of NGOs demonstrates the impossibility of effectively separating public from private organizations.[16]

Bailey and Daws argue that NGOs play an important role within ECOSOC, "so long as they do not try to usurp the functions of governments."[17] Meanwhile, David Keen, who is concerned with refugees' rights, argues that while NGOs can contribute immensely to such UN-related activities as humanitarian relief, "this trend nevertheless carries risks. It represents a shift in welfare responsibilities away from government-funded bodies in the UN towards organizations largely funded from private contributions ... Linking the welfare of millions with private charity—which is unpredictable and makes planning difficult—seems a poor alternative to establishing an international system in which refugees' rights to welfare are guaranteed by regularized public contributions and clear legal obligations."[18]

Some analysts even suggest that transnational environmental activist groups, such as the World Wildlife Fund, Friends of the Earth, Greenpeace, Conservation International, and Earth Island Institute are formative agents in the development of a new world civic politics.[19] A wide

PROFILE 5.5 Jack Anawak, Ambassador for Circumpolar Affairs

Jack Anawak, born in 1950, served as a Liberal M.P. from 1988 to 1993. He was known for putting his constituents' interests ahead of strict allegiance to the party. He was criticized for frequently using the Inuktitut language during his speeches in the House of Commons.

The Arctic Council is an example of intergovernmental cooperation based on a distinct regional link: proximity to the Arctic. The origins of the Arctic Council can be found in efforts by circumpolar countries to cooperate on environmental issues in the region as part of a broader goal of achieving Arctic security. The Arctic Environmental Protection Strategy was established n 1991, and the Arctic Council was established in the Ottawa Declaration of 1996, broadening cooperation to include all aspects of sustainable development. Canada's first Ambassador for Circumpolar Affairs was Mary Simon, an Inuk from Nunavik. An active citizen of the North and environmental activist, Mary Simon retired in 2004 and Jack Anawak was appointed as Canada's second Ambassador for Circumpolar Affairs. Born in Repulse Bay in what is today Nunavut, Ambassador Anawak has served as Mayor of Rankin Inlet, a Member of Parliament for Nunatsiaq, and was Interim Commissioner of Nunavut. In 1999 he was elected to the Nunavut Legislative Assembly, where he served until his appointment as Ambassador on January 19, 2004.

SOURCE: GOVERNMENT OF CANADA, CANADA AND THE CIRCUMPOLAR WORLD. http://www.dfait-maeci.gc.ca. circumpolar/sec02a_jack_anawak-en.asp (Ottawa, 2003)

variety of actors cluster around certain issue-areas; for example, the annual meeting of the International Whaling Commission habitually attracts representatives from more than 90 NGOs. Similarly, in the political arena, groups such as Amnesty International and Human Rights Watch play a key role in monitoring and exposing violations of human rights by governments. Others, such as CARE International, play a constructive role in both long-term and emergency development and relief efforts. And NGOs, domestic and international, have always been the active force behind what has been broadly labelled the *peace movement* in both the international and domestic contexts.[20] However, the tendency to equate NGO activity with the broader political concept of civil society may be criticized as an oversimplification, as we would then have to include organizations such as the National Rifle Association and even pro-racist groups with internationally organized memberships. One can also include transnational criminal activity, since drug smuggling, money laundering, and other illicit activities are clearly international and, just as clearly, highly organized; we revisit this theme in Chapter 6.

Throughout the remainder of this text we will refer often to various NGOs that have been involved in global politics. Whether we are on the verge of a new global civic politics is highly debatable, but we are undeniably living in an era in which nonstate actors have increased their ability to influence the work of governments and IOs alike.

INTERNATIONAL LAW

Many would argue that IL has its origins in the Roman Empire, when Roman judges settled disputes between persons of different regions with conflicting local customs. Roman law held that no custom was necessarily right, that a higher universal law existed that was inherently fair and would apply to all. This *natural law*, or *law of nature*, would arise from human reason and nature itself, and it would derive its force from being enacted by a proper authority. This authority, attributed (not surprisingly) to the emperor, was called *majestas*, or sovereign power. Thus the central question of IL remains the achievement of global standards that can be applied within the context of respect for the individualism of different localities and geographic areas of the world (see Profile 5.6). In addition, the international legal system, like the Westphalian state system and the international economic system, resulted from the expansion of the European empires. As a result, Western values and legal concepts dominate IL and are often the source of considerable friction between Western countries and the Islamic and Asian world.

IL is often dismissed as a strong force in world politics because it is based on voluntarism, on states' willingness to commit themselves to its realization, rather than on any body capable of enforcing it. Though no legal authority exists that can enforce IL in the same way domestic courts can enforce national laws, as A. LeRoy Bennett writes, an assessment "of the deficiencies of IL may lead erroneously to the conclusion that no legal principles operate across national boundaries, but an inadequate system does not signify the absence of any system."[21] In the study of IL, formal *public* IL encompasses the affairs of states, while *private* IL largely concerns the transactions of companies doing business in the international arena. The latter is the more lucrative for aspiring lawyers, while the former is, arguably, the more important for its implications for global politics. We should further distinguish between what some authors label *progressive development* and *codification*. The first aims at developing new law (*lex ferenda*), while codification aims essentially at clarifying existing law (*lex lata*). In practice, a bit of both occurs. Finally, many analysts distinguish between *hard law*, codified by treaties and enforced by some sort of punishment mechanism, and *soft law*, which consists mainly of declaratory statements emerging from the GA and elsewhere.

PROFILE 5.6 **Hugo Grotius (1583–1645)**

Grotius was a Dutch jurist and diplomat (in Swedish service). His most famous work, *De jure belli ac pacis* (*On the Law of War and Peace*), is regarded as one of the intellectual foundations of IL. Grotian thought offers an alternative perspective on international relations from that of Machiavelli or his English contemporary, Thomas Hobbes. This perspective, referred to as the *Grotian tradition*, seeks to establish order and escape anarchy in the international system through the creation of IL. For Grotius, the origins of IL rested in natural law principles and in treaties and covenants established between states. In addition, Grotian thought recognizes the existence of values and norms that influence the behaviour of states and help to maintain order among them. Grotius believed that IL should be binding on states even in the absence of a central authority to enforce them. In this sense, Grotius was advocating the building of a world as it ought to be, rather than describing the world as it existed.

Four key Grotian ideas have had an enduring legacy in international relations:

1. States should refrain from interference in the internal affairs of others, by not seeking to impose their ideologies (in Grotius's time, Catholicism and Protestantism) on others.

2. A law of nature exists that is higher than human affairs but can be known through reason.

3. Acceptance of the principles of this natural law is the only escape from anarchy.

4. An assembly of nations ought to be created to enforce such laws.

In international relations theory, Grotius is recognized as one of the key founders of the concepts behind IL and IOs.

IL is derived from many sources, including treaties, customs, and legal scholarship. Of these, treaties are the most important, since they are largely seen to bind states to agreements. Tens of thousands of bilateral and multilateral agreements exist today, a sign of the spread of diplomatic activity as well as faith in IL. Treaties are assumed to be binding on successor governments, no matter how those governments come into power. Many treaties, however, have escape clauses that permit states to withdraw their obligations without penalty, and other clauses that allow disputants to use the International Court of Justice (or the World Court) to settle arguments over their interpretation.

Arguably, the most important treaty is the Charter of the United Nations, which enshrines the primacy of the principle of state sovereignty, the most important principle in contemporary IL. The UN Charter attempts to strike a balance between the principle of state sovereignty and the need for collective responses to international issues. For example, although states that sign the UN Charter do commit themselves to collective security and in theory surrender some of their sovereign authority to make foreign policy decisions to the greater body called the United Nations, it is the Security Council, comprising a mere 15 members (5 of which, we will recall, have disproportionate power as permanent members), that ultimately decides when collective security has been breached and when the UN can take action. In addition, in practice many states have not contributed to collective security or peacekeeping efforts by the UN. Participation is largely voluntary, and no system exists to force or compel states to contribute to UN operations. Another example of the protection of sovereignty in the Charter is the contrast between supranational jurisdiction and two conflicting perspectives on the legitimate prosecution of crimes. The *territorial principle* suggests that courts in the country where the crime is committed should have first crack at prosecution. The *nationality principle* implies that states can assert their jurisdiction over the conduct of nationals anywhere, including outside their home state.

IL is also derived from customary law, which stresses the validity of repeated modes of interaction over time; in what is known as the positivist sense, customs that occur over time can be said to constitute some form of lawlike behaviour, while natural or divine law (said to have come from the heavens) is rejected. Customary law has an important psychological element in the sense that it requires "a conviction felt by states that a certain form of conduct is *permitted* by international law."[22] For example, in the so-called Fisheries Case in the International Court of Justice (*United Kingdom vs. Norway, 1949–51*), the United Kingdom complained that Norway had reserved an exclusive fishing zone for its nationals within a four-mile zone (about 6.5 kilometres) that had been drawn according to several fixed points along the coastline instead of using the configuration of the actual coastline itself. The Court found that Norway had been using this method for decades without any objections by other states and that, therefore, it was permissible under customary IL. The ICJ can also refer to legal scholarship, the judgments of international arbitrational bodies such as itself, as well as the writings of highly respected experts in the field, when arriving at decisions.

If no global police force exists to enforce IL, are there mechanisms at least to encourage compliance? The short answer is yes. States that reject or deliberately disobey IL can be subject to **reprisals** (actions that would have been illegal under IL may be legal if taken in response to the illegal actions of another state). The most extreme example of this action is the outright declaration of war on a state, as was seen when Iraq violated the sovereignty of Kuwait, and the Security Council voted in November 1990 to authorize the use of force against Iraq. (Cuba and Yemen voted against the relevant resolution, and China abstained.) Bilateral or multilateral sanctions can also be applied.[23] In the bilateral case a state will suspend or reduce its customary trade relationship with another state, and in the multilateral case a number of states will join to impose sanctions on a target state. As we will see in Chapter 7, it is debatable how effective sanctions really are. For example, some say sanctions helped change apartheid South Africa, while others (such as former British Prime Minister Margaret Thatcher) argue that South Africa changed despite them. Less doubt remains, however, that multilateral sanctions will have a greater impact on the offending state than will bilateral sanctions. A sanctioned state can, over time, assume the status of a pariah in the world community. Nigeria, Burma, Iraq, Iran, Serbia, Sudan, Zimbabwe, and Libya are examples of states that have achieved this dubious distinction (though Libya has rehabilitated itself by renouncing weapons of mass destruction in 2004). When more powerful states violate IL, however, much less is done by the world community. Russia's activities in Chechnya, China's actions in Tibet, and the American/British invasion of Iraq are all, arguably, examples of breaches of global norms without direct legal responses.

Certain conventions related to international diplomacy must be mentioned at this stage. Embassies in foreign states are considered part of the embassy state's territory. As such, the laws of the embassy state apply there, not the local laws of the land. When Iranian students seized and occupied the American embassy in Iran in 1979 following the Islamic revolution there, it was widely considered a breach of IL. Since host governments are expected to use force to protect the sanctity of embassies, the Iranian government was condemned as an accomplice. Another important convention is the extension of diplomatic immunity to foreign diplomatic staff (though there are some constraints on their right to travel). Because this means the law of the local state does not apply to foreign diplomats, the worst a state can do to a diplomat suspected of engaging in criminal acts is expel that person from the country. This treatment opens up room for espionage activities and can elicit a rather indignant response among the local population.

International criminal law has been defined as a "complex set of norms and conflict-resolving mechanisms adhered to by sovereigns within a particular jurisdictional unit, through agreement or the use of sanctions."[24] As such, it encompasses slavery, terrorism, hijacking, drug trafficking, genocide, piracy, acts against the peace, acts of aggression, and war crimes. Obviously, a great deal of overlap exists between many of these crimes, and jurisdictional overlap between them and domestic legal systems also exists. We deal with many of these potential breaches of IL in the other chapters in this book since it is a continual—and controversial—aspect of any issue-area in world affairs. The recent establishment of the International Criminal Court, which has the unique ability to prosecute individuals under IL, pushes the debate forward.

Sometimes, the concerns of private and public IL converge in a single case. For several years, three judges from the United States, three from Iran, and three from other countries have been quietly negotiating the issue of financial compensation following the Iranian revolution in 1979. The Iran–United States Claims Tribunal meets in an unmarked building on the outskirts of The Hague. As Abner Katzman writes, "despite the backdrop of political bitterness, the daily hearings in the marble and wood-paneled chambers have resolved almost 4000 cases arising from expropriations, the freezing of assets, and broken contracts. That has meant about $2.1 billion (U.S.) for American claimants and about $9 billion to Iranians, with a billion more in interest." The tribunal also facilitated the settlement of a $61.8 million payment the Americans made to Iran after the cruiser USS *Vincennes* shot down an Iran Air A-300 Airbus over the Persian Gulf on July 3, 1988. The Airbus case had been before the ICJ for years before both sides agreed that it would be easier to deal with through the tribunal.[25]

However, this case is by no means typical, since political divisions will often undermine attempts to achieve consensus and healthy compliance levels with IL. The prevalent cynicism about the efficacy of IL is understandable. However, that a body of legal thought and historic precedents pertaining to international relations exists at all is impressive. In a speech to the

General Assembly of the UN in New York, the former president of the ICJ, Judge Nagendra Singh, argues we should not be

> mesmerized by the simplistic notion of politics and law as antipoles. On the contrary, the law made by treaties is a law made by political decisions; the law codified in conventions is a law confirming the *opinio juris* of political entities; while the law of custom registers the regularity of State conduct. But in all three the keynotes are balance and reconciliation, tolerance and mutual regard: in a nutshell, the evidence that politics can, and must, transcend the partisan, the provisional, and the parochial.[26]

Others, such as Theodore Couloumbis and James Wolfe, are less sanguine:

> Without worldwide consensus on vital international issues, without central global authorities, without a legislature, without effective courts, given the existence of large autonomous subjects with powerful military establishments, given further the permanent companion of human history called war ... in these circumstances, all that international law can hope to accomplish is to limit violence [and] to substitute for it at times.[27]

The UN has developed a complex network of international legal specialists and governmental representation over the years. Two important bodies are the International Law Commission, which is an independent body of 34 legal experts who meet once a year in Geneva to work on the codification of existing laws, and the Sixth Committee of the General Assembly, the Legal Committee. The Legal Committee is filled with governmental representatives who report to the GA on current developments in IL and also draft conventions. More recently, the Treaty of Rome of 1997 established the **International Criminal Court** to try individuals with crimes against humanity, but it has yet (2004) to begin trials (we return to this court in Chapter 9). Although many other parts to the giant puzzle of contemporary IL exist, the most prominent institution is the International Court of Justice, also known as the World Court.

THE INTERNATIONAL COURT OF JUSTICE

Established in 1946, the ICJ is the principal judicial organ of the UN and meets at The Hague in the Netherlands. Its 15 judges are elected by separate votes (simple majorities required) in the Security Council and the General Assembly, and they are intended to reflect the world's leading civilizations and judicial systems. The judges serve nine-year terms. Decisions are taken in private by a majority vote, the quorum being nine. Cases are brought before the ICJ voluntarily when both states seek a ruling, but the Court also provides **advisory opinions** at the request of the General Assembly, individual states, or any of the specialized agencies. All members of the UN belong to the Court, although many have opted out of accepting its compulsory jurisdiction (the ability to call states before it at will and enforce decisions). Article 36 of the ICJ Statute says that states may agree in advance to adhere to compulsory jurisdiction. In 1946 the United States made a reservation (known as the Connally Amendment) that asserts the right to exclude disputes believed to fall under domestic jurisdiction, and most states have adopted similar reservations. Thus the ICJ is nothing like a domestic court of law.

Most states have signed the treaty establishing the Court, but only about one-third have signed the Optional Clause, which would give the Court unconditional jurisdiction in certain cases.[28] The United States withdrew from the Optional Clause when it refused to allow the Court's 1986 decision regarding the mining of Nicaraguan harbours to affect its foreign policy. Israel has withdrawn its acceptance of the Optional Clause as well. Canada put forth a reservation over the issue of extending Canadian sovereign jurisdiction in Arctic waters in the early 1970s.[29] However, literally hundreds of bilateral and multilateral treaties contain clauses agreeing that the parties will submit any disputes over the terms of the treaty to the ICJ. And the Court has jurisdiction over a number of specialized human rights conventions, including the Convention on Genocide; the Supplementary Convention on the Abolition of Slavery, the Slave Trade and Institutions and Practices Similar to Slavery; the Convention on the Political Rights of Women; the Convention Relating to the Status of Refugees; and the Convention on the Reduction of Statelessness. The ICJ also works in conjunction with other legal bodies. For example, the European Convention for the Protection of Human Rights and Freedoms (1950) allows individuals to petition the European Commission on Human Rights, which may ask the European Court of Human Rights to enforce the relevant UN convention.

In some cases, states employ the ICJ as a mediator. For example, in 1992, El Salvador and Honduras used the Court to settle territorial disputes along six stretches of border, three islands, and territorial waters. The disputes had been one of the causes of a war in 1969. The commonly accepted five-judge panel was headed by a Brazilian, and included judges from El Salvador, Honduras, Britain, and Japan. The Court drew borders in the ruling that gave about two-thirds of the total land to Honduras and split the territorial waters among both countries and Nicaragua, and all the relevant governments pledged to abide by the decision. Thus, a potentially violent conflict was avoided by the use of the ICJ. Canada and the United States have similarly used the Court to determine fishing rights off the East Coast.

The Court has also gone beyond its role as mediator and passed commentary. It recently found that the use or threat to use nuclear weapons is "generally illegal under international

The ICJ was asked to deliver a difficult advisory opinion on the international legality of Israel's efforts to construct a "security fence" within the Occupied Territories. Pictured here are, Nasser al-Kidwa, left, head of the Palestinian delegation, and Amre Moussa, right, secretary-general of the League of Arab States, during a press conference at the Peace Palace in The Hague, Netherlands, February 2004. (AP Photo/Serge Ligtenberg/CP Archive)

law." The Court added that it was impossible to say whether the weapons would be illegal to use in self-defence, however. This hardly challenges the theory of deterrence, which, as we saw in Chapter 3, is based on the idea that nuclear weapons would be used only in self-defence anyway. This opinion was also a nonbinding one sought by the General Assembly, and the presiding judge, Mohammed Bedjaoui of Algeria, had to break a 7–7 tie on crucial paragraphs of the ruling. Yet, despite all this ambiguity, many have interpreted the Court's ruling as a strong push toward the negotiation of a Comprehensive Test Ban Treaty, which has so far escaped the nuclear weapons states despite the indefinite extension of the Non-Proliferation Treaty in 1995. Canada's former disarmament ambassador, Douglas Roche, believes the Court was telling the nuclear five "to get on with it."[30] However, it is rather contestable whether an ICJ ruling on such a matter will have any significant influence when it comes to a topic state leaders tend to hold so dear to national security. Another controversial advisory opinion is unfolding at the time of writing: Palestinians have asked the Court to rule on the legality of the Israeli "security fence" being constructed in the Occupied Territories. Canada abstained from the GA vote calling for the trial, claiming it was asking the Court to render a political, and not a legal, decision. However, the distinction between these two modes of decision remains unclear.

THEORY AND INTERNATIONAL ORGANIZATIONS

Three interpretations of the role and influence of IOs stand out in the literature on IOs. The central question pursued here is how much influence and autonomy IOs have in the contemporary world system. We have seen already that both IGOs and NGOs have increased in size and scope. But has this change resulted in a commensurate increase in their abilities to affect human behaviour? Are they actually capable of making independent decisions, free from the constraints of members' objections? Are they places where the interests and expectations of various actors merely converge, or have they assumed a causal role in global politics themselves?

First, MNCs and INGOs have some automatic freedom from governments since they are not official representatives of states and exist to pursue their own objective, be it profit, charity, or value promotion. However, powerful though they may be, they are still subject to the national laws that exist where they operate, as well as the constraints imposed by the international system. But what about intergovernmental organizations themselves? The three main perspectives regarding the role of IGOs are simplified immediately below. Keep in mind that one can view the question of the effect of IL in much the same manner.

1. IGOs are seen as mere instruments of foreign policy: they are little more than political arenas in which members (states) pursue their self-interests.

2. IGOs are seen as "intervening variables"; that is, IGOs and international regimes intervene between causes and outcomes in world politics. As a result, they have some limited influence in global politics.

3. IGOs can be seen as autonomous and influential actors, able to command their own resources and significantly alter the international system.[31]

As mentioned in the introduction to this chapter, both neorealists and critical theorists tend to reject the notion of IO autonomy.

Liberals tend to see the most potential for IOs, so much so that the literature refers to *liberal institutionalism* as a genuine perspective. The core belief held by liberal institutionalists is that international regimes and institutions can facilitate agreements among rational utility maximizers. IOs operate as modifiers of state behaviour or, as Stephen Krasner and others put it, as "intervening variables." Although diplomacy is still the prerogative of states, the IOs to which they belong (and, in the broader sense, the regimes) at least partially shape their behaviour. Some would suggest that IOs are perhaps even supplanting the state in importance. In other words, IOs are gaining autonomy from the governments that send representatives to them and have an independent voice in world affairs. Within the liberal perspective we may identify at least two prevalent strains of theory: *functionalism* and *regime analysis*.

FUNCTIONALISM

Integration theorists have written of the gradual establishment of supranational governments, be they along federal or confederal lines. **Functionalism**, with roots in the writings of David Mitrany, emerged as a branch of such thinking following World War II.[32] Functionalists envisioned such integration as a process arising out of technical cooperation among nation-states, and in the behaviouralist era (1960–70) neo-functionalists stressed the role of mutual self-interest in the construction of institutions whose success would "spill over into other areas of interaction."[33] In the development of larger political communities, form should follow function. IOs should be constructed according to the specific needs they can satisfy for the citizens of states, and eventually those citizens will come to realize that their loyalty to the nation-state is itself misplaced. The European Union has been the traditional source of empirical inspiration for functionalism and neo-functionalism (see Profile 5.7). Regional economic arrangements are heralded as embryonic political communities, since a "regional market's institutional machinery, its harmonization of economic policies, and the spillover effect of its successes may help create an awareness within the region of the advantages of the integrative process."[34]

For functionalism to make sense, it must be manifested at the institution-building level: the granting of authority to supranational entities in which a scientific or technocratic consensus determines policy. Although examples of this authority occur in limited areas, it is impossible to talk seriously of apolitical international relations. First, policies will reflect the operative ideologies of the decision makers, regardless of how objective their research and suggestions might be. Second, the sacrifice of state sovereignty such institutions demand can be viewed as a short-term commitment, rather than the kind of permanent obligation required to transform global politics. Third, aware of the possibility that political interests will usually interfere with scientific or technocratic calculations, political scientists have been rather skeptical about the idea of functionalist bodies capable of freeing themselves from the political demands of individual members. Neo-functionalists argue that, in some cases, self-interest will be best pursued by such cooperation, which will then spill over into other areas. However, the evidence in terms of a neo-functionalist trend in the continuing evolution of the European Union (often considered the most fertile proving ground for neo-functionalism) seems rather bleak.[35]

One observation that flows from the functionalist literature has a special resonance for global politics today: the notion that the modern state is unequipped to deal with the daily needs of contemporary citizens. In a certain sense, little doubt exists that a growing number of states, due to ecological and other problems, are incapable of effective governance. Lynton Caldwell writes of the potential spread of what he terms *socioecological insolvency*, wherein "a state has exhausted its material means of self-support and no longer provides to its people the elementary services of government."[36] Furthermore, functionalism stresses the possible emergence of some form of global technocratic social democracy and predicts the formation of groups of international scientists acting in concert to influence policy. These groups are commonly referred to as "epistemic communities."[37] However, none of these developments necessarily means the end of the sovereign state system or the end to conflicts between states.

REGIME ANALYSIS

It is more common today for students of IOs to discuss institutionalism rather than integration, accepting the inconvenient fact that the nation-state just will not go away. Oran Young's differentiation between institutions ("social practices consisting of easily recognised roles coupled with clusters of rules or conventions governing relations among the occupants of those roles") and organizations ("material, extant entities that possess legal sovereignty and physical artifacts, such as office buildings") is helpful.[38] The first category is currently manifested in academic inquiry by what has been popularly labelled *regime analysis*, stemming from the neoliberal preoccupation with the concept of interdependence in world politics. To cope with this interdependence, states form regimes, defined succinctly by Stephen Krasner as sets of norms, principles, rules, and decision-making procedures around which actors' expectations converge. Regimes do not change the fundamental structures of political power, but they may influence the ultimate outcome of behaviour emanating from the international system.[39] Of course, one may be more or less enthusiastic about just how "intervening" these variables are. This intervention does not always seem to matter in its current usage; the term *regime* has acquired fantastic flexibility. A loose definition of what exactly constitutes a regime or institution—a tight definition would be unnecessarily constraining—leads to the conclusion that most areas of international collaboration are regimes whether or not some hegemonic leader provides the "public good" of leadership. What were once functionalist projects, for example, have become regimes.[40]

Regime analysis may seem a shallow, even cosmetic, perspective by those obsessed with grand theories that attempt to explain everything. Others argue that any study of regimes must reflect the social constructions or normative contexts that influence these interactive activities. The identification of the latter can be only an imprecise enterprise, perhaps largely determined by the intellectual perspective of the observer. This contribution belongs to the social constructivists mentioned in preceding chapters, who suggest that agents and structures co-evolve as participants acquire intersubjective understandings of each other and themselves. Prolonged exposure to certain institutions will affect the perceptions of policy makers and thus their policies, for better or for worse.

International institutions do help us define acceptable behaviour, though this is not an inherently progressive function. This process of definition may involve delegitimization: redefining certain types of behaviour as illegitimate and attempting to proscribe them. In these cases we see the development of *global prohibition regimes*: they are guided by norms that "strictly circumscribe the conditions under which states can participate in and authorize these activities and proscribe all involvement by nonstate actors."[41] Slavery is often used as an example of an international activity that came to be viewed as inhumane by key actors in the global system, which led to a global prohibition regime outlawing the world slave trade. At the same time, regulatory regimes have a corresponding positive function, to legitimize behaviour that is taking place. This legitimization could include, for example, behaviour that is arguably hazardous to environmental health, such as the spread of nuclear power, which is one of the stated goals of the **International Atomic Energy Agency**. The tendency to equate regime formation with a progressive evolution in world affairs overlooks the dual nature of institutions and organizations that have both promotional and regulatory roles. Finally, mainstream regime analysis is often criticized for overlooking the contemporary role of nongovernmental actors, despite the fact that the rise of such actors helped promote thinking about inter-dependence.

PROFILE 5.7 **The European Union**

The EU is widely regarded as the most advanced case on contemporary political integration among states. It began with three largely functional "communities" established by post–World War II Western European states: the European Coal and Steel Community (1952), the European Economic Community (1957), and the European Atomic Agency (EURATOM) (1957). In 1967 these three institutions merged and became the European Community. Increased integration at the economic and political level prompted the establishment of the European Union in 1993. The original membership included France, Germany, Italy, Belgium, the Netherlands, and Luxembourg. The United Kingdom, Denmark, and Eire (Ireland) joined in 1973; Greece in 1981; Spain and Portugal in 1986; Austria, Finland, and Sweden in 1995. In May 2004, a group of 10 states joined the EU: Estonia, Lativa, Lithuania, Poland, the Czech Republic, Hungary, Slovakia, Slovenia, Malta, and Cyrpus. Even Turkey might join in the future. The consideration of Turkey raises interesting questions about what, exactly, it means to be "European." Within the EU, economically weaker regions are, traditionally, supplanted with assistance from the stronger regions, though this is a contested concept when even the stronger economies, such as Germany, are having serious problems. There is the ongoing question of the extent of Britain's commitment. Also, regional nationalists, such as the Basques in Spain, see the EU as an opportunity to express themselves directly on the international stage, without the mediating capital city of their states.

The EU can be seen as a bold experiment in political integration, involving the forging of a new identity that supersedes the identities of its collected units. This has resulted in reluctance, and even denunciation, expressed by nationalist elements, who feel that Brussels has acquired too much influence over national affairs. Indeed, EU regulations cover everything from recycled beer cans to the enforcement of the European Convention on Human Rights, though the principle of subsidiarity suggests that the European Council should intervene only when lower jurisdictions cannot deal adequately with issues. The adoption of the euro as a single currency (see Chapter 8) further unifies and divides Europeans, as does the enlargement of the EU itself. Many argue that the Eastern European states will harm the EU's economy, as potentially millions of labourers flood into the West looking for work.

CONCLUSIONS

This chapter has argued that IOs are highly relevant in global politics. We offered a brief historical look at international institutions in history, including the development of the League of Nations and the United Nations. Next, we discussed IL and some of its key terminology before turning to the International Court of Justice. Though IL has limited direct utility and relies on consent rather than any strong coercive powers, it contributes to the popularization of important issues, such as the validity of nuclear weapons, and can promote human rights and compliance with regime agreements designed to preserve the environment. However, certain states will consider themselves above the law, and this belief leads to a crisis of legitimacy for institutions such as the ICJ. As the noted scholar Martin Wight once commented, IL has a tendency to "crawl in the mud of legal positivism."[42] Yet IL remains a core component of efforts to build a more tightly knit global society—for better or for worse.

We finished the chapter by discussing theoretical perspectives pertaining to the role of IOs and IL. Realist and critical theorists feel that IOs and IL serve the interests of the more powerful states or classes. Neoliberal institutionalists hold a more positive view of institutions and organizations, regarding them as important actors that can be used to lower levels of conflict and promote greater understanding and well-being. Students might reflect on this question of the influence and autonomy of IOs when reading the remainder of this book, since IOs (and

IL) factor into all of the issue-areas we examine. One of the more fundamental questions concerns what IOs—and their context, the global political system—look like in the post–Cold War era, which is remarkably different from the bipolar system that preceded it. The next section of this book provides an overview of the issues that dominate contemporary global politics.

Endnotes

1. "Historical Materialism, Globalization, and Law," in M. Rupert and H. Smith, eds., *Historical Materialism and Globalization* (London: Routledge, 2002), 230–56, 231.

2. J. Plano and R. Olton, *The International Relations Dictionary*, 4th ed. (Santa Barbara: ABC-CLIO, 1988), 416. This dictionary has become standard in the international relations field.

3. States can also be expelled, though this is rare. It is still a matter of some contention regarding which states belong to the UN, since China has resolutely disallowed the Republic of Taiwan from joining, claiming it is still part of mainland China. Despite hosting many of its key institutions, Switzerland refused to join the UN for many years, protecting its policy of neutrality (collective security would commit it to taking sides in a UN-approved war). However, after a national referendum on the subject, Switzerland finally officially joined in 2002.

4. This difference may lead to understandable confusion for the nonspecialist. The agencies of the UN (WHO, UNESCO, etc.) are in and of themselves IOs, with working constitutions and general and executive assemblies. However, they are generally considered part of a larger organizational entity, the UN Organization.

5. The games were held from 776 B.C.E. to 393 C.E., every four years at Olympia, in honour of Zeus; they resumed in their present format in 1896. At present, the International Olympic Committee is a universal-membership, single-purpose IO, with headquarters in Lausanne, France. Recent corruption scandals have plagued the IOC.

6. The ITU was originally created as the International Telegraph Union; the title was changed in 1934. The ITU became a UN specialized agency in 1947. Headquarters are in Geneva. See G. Codding and A. Rutkowski, *The International Telecommunication Union in a Changing World* (Dedham, MA: Artech House, 1982). The UPU was established when the first International Postal Convention was signed, creating the General Union of Posts; its name was changed to the UPU four years later. Stamp collectors will recognize the importance of the Convention, which gave every member-state full use of postal services throughout the world. Headquarters are in Bern, Switzerland, where the International Copyright Union is also stationed. See G. Codding, *The Universal Postal Union* (New York: New York University Press, 1964).

7. *The International Secretariat* (Washington, DC, 1945), 428.

8. Barry Hughes, *Continuity and Change in World Politics: The Clash of Perspectives*, 2nd ed. (Englewood Cliffs, NJ: Prentice-Hall, 1994), 73.

9. Claude's classic text is *Swords into Ploughshares*, 4th ed. (New York: Random House, 1971).

10. *The United Nations: A Concise Political Guide*, 3rd ed. (London: Macmillan, 1995).

11. See *Crisis and Reform in United Nations Financing*, Report of the United Nations Association—USA Global Policy Project (United Nations Association of the United States of America, 1997), 1.

12. *New York Times*, 11 June 1997; and United Nations "Secretary-General and Under-Secretary-General for Management Address 5th Committee as It Takes Up Improving UN Financial Situation," press release GA/AB/3310, 5 October 1999.

13. See F.H. Suward and E. McInnis, "Forming the UN, 1945," in D. Munton and J. Kirton, eds., *Canadian Foreign Policy: Selected Cases* (Scarborough, ON: Prentice-Hall, 1992), 4–18, for more on the initial Canadian position.

14. For a concise summary, see Rosenau's article "Normative Challenges in a Turbulent World," *Ethics and International Affairs* 6 (1992), 1–20. A (much) lengthier exposition is found in his *Turbulence in World Politics: A Theory of Change and Continuity* (Princeton: Princeton University Press, 1990).

15. Canada, Department of Foreign Affairs and International Trade, press release, 19 September 1996.

16. A. LeRoy Bennett, *International Organizations: Principles and Issues*, 6th ed. (Englewood Cliffs, NJ: Prentice Hall, 1995), 272.

17. S. Bailey and S. Daws, *The United Nations: A Concise Political Guide*, 3rd ed. (Lanham, MD: Barnes and Noble, 1995).

18. *Refugees: Rationing the Right to Life* (London: Zed, 1992), 40.

19. P. Wapner, "Politics beyond the State: Environmental Activism and World Civic Politics," *World Politics* 47 (1995), 311–40; J. Fisher, *The Road from Rio: Sustainable Development and the Nongovernmental Movement in the Third World* (Westport: Praeger, 1993); J. McCormick, *Reclaiming Paradise: The Global Environmental Movement* (Bloomington: Indiana University Press, 1989); and P. Willetts, ed., "*The Conscience of the World*": *The Influence of Non-Governmental Organizations in the UN System* (Washington, DC: Brookings, 1996).

20. R. Angell, *Peace on the March: Transnational Participation* (New York: Van Nostrand Reinhold, 1969); for a Canadian history, see T. Socknat, *Witness against War: Pacifism in Canada 1900–1945* (Toronto: University of Toronto Press, 1987).

21. Bennett, 180.

22. M. Akehurst, *A Modern Introduction to International Law,* 3rd ed. (London: George Allen and Unwin, 1977), 35.

23. On sanctions, see especially M. Doxey, *Economic Sanctions and International Enforcement,* 2nd ed. (New York: Oxford University Press, 1980).

24. C. Bassiouni and V.P. Nanda, eds., *A Treatise on International Criminal Law: Crime and Punishment.* vol. 1 (Springfield, IL: Charles Thomas, 1973), 5.

25. A. Katzman, "U.S., Iran Claims Settled Quietly," *The Globe and Mail,* 20 March 1996.

26. Reprinted in *The International Court of Justice,* 3rd ed. (The Hague: ICJ, 1986), 144.

27. *Power and Justice: Introduction to International Relations,* 3rd ed. (Englewood Cliffs, NJ: Prentice-Hall, 1986), 259.

28. This is Article 36 of the Statute of the ICJ, which provides in Section 2 that any party can recognize as compulsory the jurisdiction of the Court in legal disputes concerning the interpretation of a treaty; any question of international law; the existence of any fact that, if established, would constitute a breach of an international obligation; and the nature or extent of the reparation to be made for the breach of an international obligation. By July 1993, only 56 states had filed declarations of acceptance of the Optional Clause.

29. See K. Kirton and D. Munton, "Protecting the Canadian Arctic: The Manhattan Voyages, 1969–1970," in K. Kirton and D. Munton, eds., *Canadian Foreign Policy: Selected Cases* (Scarborough: Prentice-Hall, 1992), 205–26, 220.

30. *The Globe and Mail,* 9 July 1996, A8. For a broad discussion of this important theme, see N. Singh and E. McWhinney, *Nuclear Weapons and Contemporary International Law,* 2nd ed. (Dordrecht: Martinus Nijhoff, 1989).

31. For another summary, see Charles Pentland, "International Organizations," in J. Rosenau, K.W. Thompson, and G. Boyd, eds., *World Politics* (New York: The Free Press, 1976), 624–39.

32. Mitrany's classic text is *A Working Peace System: An Argument for the Functional Development of International Organisation* (London: RIIA, 1943).

33. Most famously, see E. Haas, *Beyond the Nation-State* (Stanford: Stanford University Press, 1964); and A. Groom and P. Taylor, eds., *Functionalism: Theory and Practice in International Relations* (London: University of London, 1975).

34. R. Riggs and J. Plano, *The United Nations: International Organizations and World Politics* (Chicago: Dorsey, 1988), 290.

35. See, in particular, M. Huelshoff and T. Pfeiffer, "Environmental Policy in the EC: Neo-Functionalist Sovereignty Transfer or Neo-Realist Gate-Keeping?" *International Journal* 47, no. 1 (1992), 136–58.

36. L. Caldwell, *International Environmental Policy: Emergence and Dimensions,* 2nd ed. (Durham: Duke University Press, 1990), 328. We expand on this theme in Chapter 11.

37. See Peter Haas, "Introduction: Epistemic Communities and International Policy Coordination," *International Organization* 46, no. 1 (1992), 1–35.

38. O. Young, *International Cooperation: Building Regimes for Natural Resources and the Environment* (Ithaca, NY: Cornell University Press, 1989), 32. For example, the University of British Columbia is an organization, and the Canadian postsecondary school system is an institution; the International Atomic Energy Agency is an organization, and the non-proliferation regime is an institution; the Las Vegas Wedding Chapel is an organization, and marriage is an institution.

39. For standard texts, see S. Krasner, "Structural Causes and Regime Consequences: Regimes as Intervening Variables," in S. Krasner, ed., *International Regimes* (Ithaca, NY: Cornell University Press, 1983), 1–22; R. Keohane, *After Hegemony: Cooperation and Discord in the World Political Economy* (Princeton: Princeton University Press, 1984); M. Zacher, "Toward a Theory of International Regimes," *Journal of International Affairs* 44, no. 1 (1990), 139–58; and O. Young, "The Politics of International Regime Formation: Managing Natural Resources and the Environment," *International Organization* 43, no. 3 (1989), 349–75.

40. For example, see P. Sands, "EC Environmental Law: The Evolution of a Regional Regime of International Environmental Protection," *Yale Law Journal* 100, no. 8 (1991), 2511–23.

41. E. Nadelmann, "Global Prohibition Regimes: The Evolution of Norms in International Society," *International Organization* 44, 4 (1990), 481–526.

42. M. Wight, "Why Is There No International Theory?" in H. Butterfield and M. Wight, eds., *Diplomatic Investigations* (Cambridge, MA: Harvard University Press, 1968), 29.

Suggested Readings

Archer, C. *International Organizations.* 2nd ed. London: Routledge, 1992.

Baehr, P., and L. Gordenker. *The United Nations Reality and Ideal.* New York: Praeger, 1984.

Boyd, A. *Fifteen Men on a Powder Keg: A History of the United Nations Security Council.* New York: Stein and Day, 1971.

Brownly, A. *Principles of Public International Law.* 4th ed. New York: Oxford University Press, 1990.

Byers, M., ed. *The Role of Law in International Politics: Essays in International Relations and International Law.* Oxford: Oxford University Press, 2000.

Cassese, A. *International Law.* Oxford: Oxford University Press, 2001.

Cox, R., and H. Jacobsen. *The Anatomy of Influence: Decision Making in International Organization.* New Haven: Yale University Press, 1973.

Drezner, D. *Locating the Proper Authorities: the Interaction of Domestic and International Institutions.* Ann Arbor: The University of Michigan Press, 2003.

Falk, R. *Law in a Merging Global Village: A Post-Westphalian Perspective.* Ardsley: Transnational Publishers, 1998.

Falk, R. *The State of Law in International Society.* Princeton: Princeton University Press, 1970.

Falk, R., with S. Kim and S. Mendlovitz, eds. *The United Nations and a Just World Order.* Boulder, CO: Westview, 1991.

Fasula, L. *An Insider's Guide to the UN.* New Haven: Yale University Press, 2004.

Franck, T. *Judging the World Court.* New York: Priority, 1986.

Goldberg, G. *The Peace to End Peace: The Paris Peace Conference of 1919.* New York: Harcourt, Brace and World, 1969.

Goodrich, L. "From League of Nations to United Nations." *International Organization* (February 1947), 3–21.

Grieco, J. "Anarchy and the Limits of Cooperation: A Realist Critique of the Newest Liberal Institutionalism." *International Organization* 42 (Summer 1988), 485–507.

Haas, E. *Why We Still Need the United Nations: The Collective Management of International Conflict, 1945–1984.* Berkeley: Berkeley Institute of International Studies, University of California, 1986.

Haggard, S., and B. Simmons. "Theories of International Regimes." *International Organization* 41 (Summer 1987), 491–517.

Henkin, L. *How Nations Behave: Law and Foreign Policy.* New York: Praeger, 1970.

Higgins, R. *The Development of International Law through the Political Organs of the United Nations.* Oxford: Oxford University Press, 1963.

Hoffmann, S., and K. Deutsch, eds. *The Relevance of International Law.* Garden City, NY: Doubleday–Anchor, 1971.

Huntington, S. "Transnational Organizations in World Politics." *World Politics* 25 (April 1973), 333–68.

Jacobsen, H. *Networks of Interdependence.* 2nd ed. New York: Alfred Knopf, 1984.

Kratochwil, F. *Rules, Norms, and Decisions on the Conditions of Practical and Legal Reasoning in International Relations and Domestic Affairs.* Cambridge, UK: Cambridge University Press, 1989.

Kratochwil, F., and J.G. Ruggie. "International Organization: A State of the Art on the Art of the State." *International Organization* 40 (Autumn 1986), 753–75.

Martin, L., and B. Simmons, eds. *International Institutions: An International Organization Reader.* Cambridge, MA: MIT Press, 2001.

Rosenau, J., and E.-O. Czempiel, eds. *Governance Without Government Order and Change in World Politics.* Cambridge, UK: Cambridge University Press, 1992.

Ruggie, J.G. "International Regimes, Transactions, and Change Embedded Liberalism in the Postwar Economic Order." *International Organization* 36 (1982), 379–415.

Simmons, P., and C. de Jonge Oudraat, eds. *Managing Global Issues: Lessons Learned.* Washington, DC: Carnegie, 2001.

Strange, S. "Cave Hic Dragones: A Critique of Regime Analysis." *International Organization* 36 (Spring 1982), 479–96.

Van Someren, L. *Umpire to the Nations: Hugo Grotius.* London: Dennis Dobson, 1965.

von Glahn, G. *Law Among Nations: An Introduction to Public International Law.* New York: Macmillan, 1965.

Walters, F. *A History of the League of Nations.* London: Oxford University Press, 1952.

Weber, S. "Institutions and Change." In *New Thinking in International Relations Theory*, edited by M. Doyle and G.J. Ikenberry. Boulder, CO: Westview, 1997.

Wicker, H-R., ed. *Rethinking Nationalism and Ethnicity: The Struggle for Meaning and Order in Europe.* Oxford: Berg, 1997.

Suggested Websites

Amnesty International
  http://www.amnesty.org

European Union Newsweb
  http://www.eurunion.org/states/home.htm

The Fletcher School of Law and Diplomacy
  http://fletcher.tufts.edu

The Global Policy Forum
  http://www.globalpolicy.org

International Court of Justice
  http://www.icj-cij.org

International Monetary Fund
  http://www.imf.org

Union of International Associations
  http://www.uia.org

United Nations (the best place to begin any search for IOs)
  http://www.un.org

WashLaw Web
  http://www.washlaw.edu

World Bank Group
  http://www.worldbank.or

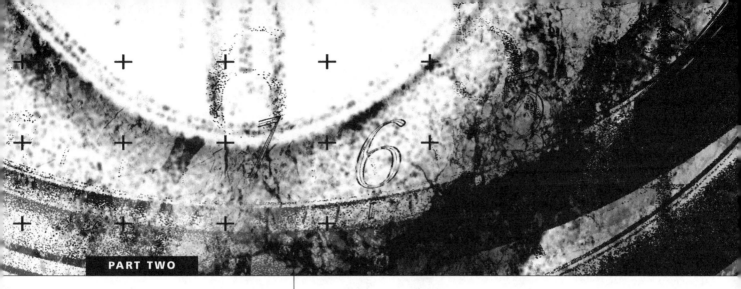

PART TWO

Currents

This section explores the issues and debates that characterize contemporary global politics. In the preceding section we presented an overview of the historical and intellectual roots that have contributed to the evolution of the international system and our understanding of it. Although we will still make use of historical reflection, we move now into more contemporary matters, such as current security concerns and conflict management techniques; the globalized world economy and its many environmental, cultural, and poverty-related concerns; and the debate over human rights in international affairs. As we will see, the dual process of convergence/divergence continues to define the political landscape. We have tried to provide as complete an overview of current world affairs as possible but make no claim to have captured them all in the brief space of four chapters. Readers are, as usual, encouraged to look further using the suggested readings, endnotes, and websites provided at the end of each chapter.

CHAPTER 6

International Security after the Cold War

The supreme importance of the military instrument lies in the fact that the ultimate ratio of power in international relations is war.

—Edward Hallett Carr[1]

Not since Rome has one nation loomed so large above the others. Indeed, the word "empire" has come out of the closet. Respected analysts on both the left and the right are beginning to refer to the "American Empire" approvingly as the dominant narrative of the twenty-first century. And the military victory over Iraq seems only to have confirmed this new world order.

—Joseph S. Nye Jr.[2]

INTRODUCTION: THE CHANGING NATURE OF SECURITY STUDIES

Students and scholars interested in international security focus on how individuals, groups, and states conceptualize security and how they act to increase their security. They are also interested in how the actions of individuals, groups, and states affect the security of regional subsystems and ultimately the international system as a whole. Naturally, this leads us to a fundamental query: what is security? What does it mean to be secure? Dictionary definitions suggest that security is freedom from threats or dangers, but who or what is being threatened or endangered? And who or what is doing the threatening and endangering? Traditionally, international security has focused on the security of states, and as a result security is most frequently conceptualized as the security of a state from external threats to its territorial integrity, political independence, and way of life. Traditionally, the most important challenge has been assumed to be the military threat posed by other states, although revolutionary movements, secessionist movements, and terrorist groups have also been long regarded as threats to state security. However, this rather restrictive view of security has been challenged in recent decades, both by theoretical schools that do not accept a state-centric interpretation of global politics, and by changes in the structure of the international system itself—its demographic, economic, and environmental characteristics.

As a result, there has been a vigorous debate over the concept of "security" in contemporary global politics.[3] On the one hand, there is an argument for broadening the scope of security studies to include a range of threats that are not state-centric or military in nature. For example, environmental degradation, the intrusion of outside cultural influences, modernization, economic integration, and migration of peoples may represent threats to the well-being or even the survival of societies. On the other hand, there is an argument for deepening the agenda of security studies, to focus on actors and forces other than the state. For example, certain ideologies, individuals, groups, or socioeconomic conditions existing within or across state boundaries may represent a threat to states and societies. Of course, states are still highly relevant actors in international security studies. Peter Andreas has argued that "clandestine transnational actors" are shifting conceptions of borders and security away from military defence and toward policing, and therefore "territoriality is persisting—but with a shift in emphasis."[4] Furthermore, states themselves may threaten the security of individuals or groups, through a variety of repressive measures including the use of military or police force, legislation, or economic policies. Nevertheless, in moving the reference point of security away from a focus purely on the state and military power, liberal, Marxist, and feminist scholars have all contributed to an expansion of the concept of security long dominated by realist interpretations of international politics. Constructivists have also made a significant contribution to security studies in the form of *securitization theory*, emphasizing that security is not an objective term but is constructed through social processes. Certain issues are "securitized" though speech, the media, and other forms of social dialogue, becoming security issues because they are represented as such in a society, thus influencing how people subsequently approach these these issues.[5]

In many respects, the study of international security is a post–World War II phenomenon. As we saw in Chapter 2, philosophers, historians, and advisers throughout history have addressed security issues. What distinguished strategic studies in the bipolar Cold War period was the inescapable prominence of nuclear weapons in the discourse. In the early Cold War period, much attention was devoted to the implications of the atomic bomb and what it meant for military strategy and for international relations. When nuclear parity developed between the superpowers, the focus turned to the study of nuclear deterrence and the theory and practice of implementing nuclear weapons into national security strategies. As the Cold War progressed, arms control became a more prominent issue, as did peace studies, which emphasized conflict resolution and conflict prevention strategies. As a result, four main questions of inquiry were pursued in international security studies during the Cold War:

- What is the best way to prevent war, especially nuclear war, between the superpowers?
- How can deterrence be made more effective and stable?
- How can limited regional wars be kept limited and regional, so that they do not become catalysts for a superpower war?
- How can arms control processes serve the goal of a stable and peaceful world?

While bipolarity and nuclear weapons were the central subjects of concern, attention was also directed toward conventional (non-nuclear) warfare, regional wars (especially in the Middle East and South Asia), the proliferation of nuclear and conventional weapons, and the study of so-called low-intensity conflicts (LICs), largely in the Southern Hemisphere. For the most part, American scholars and practitioners dominated the formal study of international security during the Cold War.

The end of the Cold War had a profound effect on the study of international security. Concerns about the nuclear balance and arms control between the superpowers have now largely faded into the background. Today, a wide range of other security issues has moved to centre stage. The subject matter of international security studies is now much broader, but several consistent lines of inquiry occupy the attention of most scholars and analysts:

- *The origins and causes of conflict in the international system.* This work now includes a growing literature on the origins of civil wars and ethnic conflicts, as well as research into the link between poverty and war, environmental degradation and war, economic incentives for war, and criminal motivations and war.

- *National security and research on potential threats.* Interstate security concerns have not vanished, and state governments continue to grapple with a broad range of security threats to their territorial integrity, the independence of their political institutions, and their way of life. Other interests may include strategic territory and allies abroad, and access to vital resources such as oil.

- *Group security.* The focus of this growing area of study is ethnic, religious, clan, or factional groups. The issues of group security revolve around minority rights, economic and political grievances, **self-determination**, and in some cases separatism. In most violent conflicts today, some or all of the actors involved are groups.

- *Nuclear weapons safety and nuclear weapons proliferation.* While issues such as the safety and security of nuclear arsenals in the U.S. and Russia continue to receive some attention, the bulk of the focus on nuclear weapons is now directed to the possibility of a nuclear war between India and Pakistan, the spread of nuclear weapons technology, and the remote though much feared prospect of a terrorist attack using nuclear weapons.

- *Chemical and biological weapons terrorism.* The spread of chemical and biological weapons and their use by states and/or terrorist groups is now one of the most prominent security concerns in global politics.

- *The spread of conventional weapons.* While a great deal of attention is placed on nuclear, chemical, and biological weapons (sometimes collectively referred to as "weapons of mass destruction" or WMD), the fact remains that conventional arms buildups are a major point of concern in many regions, and most organized political violence in the world is conducted with so-called conventional weapons, mostly small arms such as assault rifles or rocket-propelled grenades.

- *Asymmetric threats.* Asymmetric threats are threats that are not easily deterred or fought through conventional military means. Terrorism and transnational criminal organizations are two high-profile examples of asymmetric threats.

- *Human security.* The focus of human security is on the individual as the object of security. The objective is the freedom of individuals from violent or nonviolent threats to their rights, safety, and lives. The human security agenda has developed considerably in recent years, led by countries such as Canada that have pursued a wide range of policies and programs including the Ottawa Treaty to ban land mines, the International Criminal Court, and international agreements on war-affected children and child labour, to name a few. We will explore human security in more depth in Chapter 7.

- *Regional security studies.* Much more attention is now devoted to regional security dynamics, especially in West Africa and sub-Saharan Africa, the Middle East, the Persian Gulf, South Asia, Central Asia, Southeast Asia, and Balkan Europe.

- *Environmental security.* Here, the object of security is the ecology of the earth. Environmental security concerns include global and local ecological degradation and its impact on human communities. Environmental security can be achieved only through sustainable economic and social development. This concept of security is an important element of the ecopolitics approach we discuss in Chapter 10.

Profile 6.1 illustrates how the security agenda has shifted since the end of the Cold War and highlights the major issues that occupy the attention of scholars today. Generally, the new international security agenda is far more diverse and varied than in the past. It is important to note that most contemporary security issues are not really new; most (such as regional conflicts and terrorism, to name only two) were issues during the Cold War period as well. However, the end of the Cold War served to bring these issues to the immediate concern of governments, publics, and scholars.

Our aim in this chapter is to explore the problem of interstate and intrastate war, a traditional concern of security studies that remains relevant today. This chapter will then address the secu-

PROFILE 6.1 The International Security Agenda: Cold War and Post–Cold War

COLD WAR		CONTEMPORARY	
East–West	Preoccupation with superpower confrontation as the source of the next world war	North–South	Growing awareness of global disparities and poverty as a source of conflict
Interstate	Study of wars between states	Intrastate	Study of wars within states: ethnic, religious, and factional conflicts between substate actors
Nuclear strategy	Focus on deterrence and nuclear weapons programs	Nuclear, biological, and chemical (NBC) proliferation	Concern with the spread of nuclear weapons to substate groups
Alliances	Study of alliance formation, East and West blocs	Zones of peace and instability	Study of actors and structures (especially institutions) in peaceful regions as compared with warring regions
Military	Focus on military security and military as foreign policy instrument	Economic, social, and environmental	Examination of economic conflict, resource wars, and environmental degradation as a root cause of wars
High-intensity conflict (HIC)	Focus on large-scale wars between powerful states and development of sophisticated weapons	Low-intensity conflict (LIC/ conventional weapons proliferation)	Focus on insurgency wars and spread and production of conventional armaments around the world
War in Europe	Concern with NATO/ Warsaw Pact HIC in Europe	Regional conflicts	Concern with outbreak and spread of war and instability in the world's regions
Superpower arms control	Effort to control superpower arms race especially with agreements on nuclear weapons	Global arms control	Effort to control spread of weapons around the world
Escalation	Concern that conventional war would escalate to nuclear war	Spillover	Concern that regional conflicts could spread to neighbouring areas

rity challenges that have grown in prominence with an increasingly interdependent world; the proliferation of weapons, terrorism, and the growth of international organized crime.

THE NATURE OF WAR IN GLOBAL POLITICS

One of the defining texts on warfare in the study of global politics is the famous work *On War* by Karl von Clausewitz. Clausewitz characterizes war as a "continuation of politics by other means" and therefore focuses on war as a political act. However, war may originate from economic motives, or be more deeply rooted in cultural, as opposed to purely political, objectives.[6] War is a period of armed hostilities within or between states or other collectivities (such as ethnic groups or political factions). In war, killing and physical destruction are both expected and condoned, although the participants are expected to follow the boundaries and constraints established by existing laws or norms. War is distinguished from other forms of organized political violence by casualty rates: in this respect, a commonly accepted definition of war is an armed conflict in which there are 1000 or more combat-related deaths. However, this rather arbitrary measure of war has been challenged by the existence of persistent armed conflicts that generate fewer than 1000 battle-related deaths but in every other respect must be considered wars. Furthermore, these armed conflicts can cause immense human suffering among civilians (noncombatants), who may die in large numbers from the indirect effects of armed conflict.

In an effort to identify larger patterns in the history of warfare, the Correlates of War (COW) Project, directed by J. David Singer, collected data on warfare from 1816 to 1980. The COW Project identified 216 interstate wars in that period. The conclusion of Singer and his associates is that no identifiable trend in the frequency of interstate wars exists. However, Jack S. Levy suggests that if the historical period under examination is widened, a clear trend is identifiable. Levy examined warfare over five centuries and found that the number of wars has declined steadily since the 16th century, with a slight increase in the 20th century.[7] The latter half of the 20th century has a seen a shift from major power wars to minor power wars, a shift from wars in Europe to wars in other regions, and a shift from wars between states to wars within states.[8] Wars have become more destructive as technological advances increased the firepower of successive generations of weapons, taking an increasingly enormous toll in human life. Between 1500 and the end of the Cold War, there were approximately 589 wars in the world, which caused approximately 141 901 000 deaths.[9] In the 20th century alone, four times more people have died in wars than in all wars in the previous 400 years.[10] Patterns in war-related deaths and the frequency of war between 1900 and 1995 are shown in Figure 6.1.

In the post–World War II era, several trends can be identified. Between 1946 and 2002, 226 armed conflicts took place in the international system.[11] During this period there were no wars between great powers, although great powers have been involved in wars (such as Korea, Vietnam, the Falklands, and the Gulf). Instead, the bulk of these wars have taken place between or within smaller countries and more confined geographic regions. Interstate wars have been remarkably absent in North America (none since 1913–15), Western Europe (none since 1945), and South America (none since 1941, with the exception of the Falklands war, which was fought between Argentina and Great Britain). However, interstate wars have been frequent and destructive in other regions, most notably in the Middle East and in Asia. Another trend is the frequency of intrastate conflicts. In his study, Kalevi Holsti observed that of the 187 wars between 1945 and 1995, only 58 (31 percent) were interstate conflicts.[12] Between 1990 and 2002, there were 58 major armed conflicts in the world, and all but 3 (just over 5 percent) were internal (intrastate) conflicts.[13] The rest took place within states, and most of these conflicts occurred outside Europe and North America. In the 1990s the magnitude of war has been on the decline, in terms of the toll on human life, the size of war-affected

Figure 6.1 Twentieth-Century Wars and War-Related Deaths, 1900–95

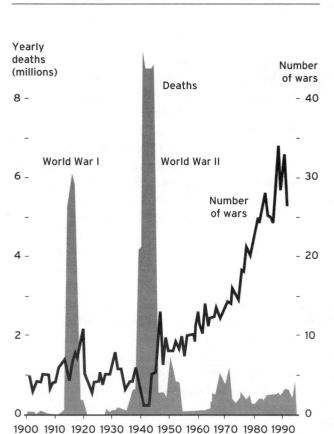

areas, dislocated populations, and the extent of infrastructure damage. However, increasingly the victims of war are civilians. In World War I, 15 percent of the fatalities were civilians. In World II, this percentage rose to 65 (including Holocaust victims). In wars since 1945, more than 90 percent of casualties have been civilians.[14]

In the years immediately following the end of the Cold War, there was an encouraging decline in global military spending. In 1998, world military spending totalled U.S.$690 billion, the lowest level of expenditure since 1966 and a decline from the peak of U.S.$910 billion in 1988 (all prices in 2000 dollars). Most of this post–Cold War decline came from the dramatic fall in military expenditures in Eastern Europe and the former Soviet Union.[15] Of course, the sum of U.S.$690 billion is still seen by some as a tragic waste of valuable financial resources better spent elsewhere (for example, the entire annual UN budget, including peacekeeping operations, has rarely exceeded $5 billion). However, since 1998 world military spending has increased. In 2002, world military spending totalled U.S.$784 billion. This represented 2.5 percent of world GDP and U.S.$128 per human being. Much of this increase was due to a surge in U.S. military spending following the September 11, 2001, attacks and the war in Afghanistan. The United States accounted for 75 percent of the increase in military spending between 2001 and 2002, a year in which world military spending increased by 6 percent, and increased by 14 percent from the post–Cold War low of 1998.[16] The United States accounts for 43 percent of world military expenditures, a figure that will rise as the costs of the Iraq War and the aftermath are calculated. The top five countries (the United States, Japan, the United Kingdom, France, and China) account for approximately 62 percent of world military spending.[17]

THEORIZING ABOUT THE ORIGINS OF WAR

Not surprisingly, many efforts have been made to understand the phenomenon of war and to explain its cause. The difficulty with this enterprise is our inability to confidently generalize from one war to the next. After all, every war has unique multifaceted causes; monocausal explanations tend to be oversimplistic. Wars have started over tangible issues such as territory, wealth, colonies, economic interests, freedom of navigation, the destruction of enemies, and independence. Wars have also been fought over intangibles such as ethnic, religious, cultural, and ideological values; national pride; and revenge. The obstacle to establishing the universal origins of war has been captured effectively by Quincy Wright: "A war, in reality, results from a total situation involving ultimately almost everything that has happened to the human race up to the time the war begins."[18] A daunting analytic task!

We can, however, build narrower categories of possible explanations of war by exploring the three levels of analysis introduced in Chapter 1: causes of war at the individual level, the state or group level, and the systemic level. Using the *individual level* of analysis, we would find the cause of war in ourselves, in our nature as a species. But where does this nature come from? Most of the world's religions have an explanation for the origins of evil acts by human beings. Early psychologists suggested that humans are inherently aggressive, and, therefore, war is inevitable. In a letter to Albert Einstein, Sigmund Freud suggested that humans possess a death instinct, a desire to destroy and kill.[19] Konrad Lorenz, an anthropologist, referred to humans as killer apes, one of very few species that kills its own kind.[20] Social Darwinists once argued that aggression was a function of the survival of the fittest, with the weak peoples of the world conquered by the strong. This explanation has been discredited, as it was inextricably linked to the racism that characterized the Social Darwinist perspective in the late 19th and early 20th centuries. On the other hand, behavioural sociologists suggest that aggressive and violent behaviour is not innate but learned. Human society developed in such a way as to reward aggressive individuals and social organizations. These traits were in turn passed on to future generations. Some feminists have argued that aggression is related to gender, with most males being more aggressive than females (whether through biology or social conditioning). Still other theories suggest that the origins of war lie in individual personalities and misperception.[21] The problem with these explanations of war is that human behaviour is often cooperative or philanthropic (even more often than aggressive or violent). Most conflicts are resolved peacefully, and most humans are not at war with others all, or even most, of the time.

The *state* or *group level* of analysis suggests that the cause of war is to be found in the social and political characteristics of states or groups. Put simply, some states or groups are more prone to war than others. Cultural determinists such as anthropologist Margaret Mead argue that war is an invention and that some cultures never experienced war, such as some of the Indigenous peoples of the South Pacific.[22] However, most societies and civilizations have experienced war. An enduring debate exists over what kinds of states or groups are inherently more warlike, and, not surprisingly, the prevailing consensus has changed over time. Today, it is generally held that states or groups with authoritarian internal structures are more warlike. Authoritarian states are often referred to as "bad states" or "rogue states"; the leaders of such states are isolated from the will of their peoples and lack any checks or controls on their exercise of power. The authoritarian leaders of substate groups are often called *warlords*. In contrast, democratic states are regarded as inherently peaceful, an assumption we will examine further in the next chapter. However, in the past, monarchies were regarded as stable and responsible forms of government, while republics were seen as impetuous, aggressive, and dangerous. During the Cold War, capitalist states regarded themselves as inherently peaceful and Marxist states as inherently aggressive, while Marxist states regarded capitalist states as warlike, seeking markets abroad through imperialism and combating other imperialist states in the process. On other occasions, great powers have been seen as aggressive actors, while small states, lacking such power, were less war-prone. Echoes of this sentiment can be found in some Canadian attitudes toward the United States. In other words, the conception of what is a war-prone form of social organization has changed over time and according to political or ideological perspectives.

Finally, the *system level* or *structural theory explanation* finds the origins of war in the nature of international politics itself. As discussed in Chapter 1, this view is widely held by structural realists. The principal source of war is anarchy (the absence of central authority) and the distribution of power (the number of poles in the system). Individual aggressiveness and the internal character of states and groups are less important as explanatory factors. Wars arise not necessarily from belligerence, but because, as Kenneth Waltz argues, "There is nothing to prevent them."[23] The insecurity of an anarchic environment will lead to the security dilemma, arms races, and competing alliances (see Chapter 2). One of the more popular systemic-level explanations of war has been the concept of hegemonic war. Some realist scholars have suggested that history oscillates between **long cycles** of war and peace between great powers, with a general war breaking out approximately every 100 years.[24] Long-cycle theory is based on the rise and decline of hegemonic powers; at their height, they maintain systemic stability by establishing order, usually in the form of rules governing trade and security. However, as these hegemonic powers decline due to overextension, costs of empire, and the rise of challengers to their position, the pre-eminence of the hegemon is delegitimized, and war breaks out between the declining hegemon and its challengers. At the conclusion of the war, a new hegemon emerges and the cycle begins anew. In this view, the outbreak of war is linked to the fortunes of hegemonic powers. Smaller wars, such as the Vietnam conflict in the 1960s and 1970s, are seen as proxy wars amongst competing hegemons.

INTERSTATE WARFARE AFTER THE COLD WAR: FROM THE GULF WAR TO THE IRAQ WAR

On August 28, 1990, Iraq invaded and occupied neighbouring Kuwait. Although the precise motives for doing so remain unclear, Iraq had claimed (with little justification) a right to Kuwait as a province of Iraq. It is more likely that Iraq's dire economic situation at the end of its war with Iran prompted Iraqi leader Saddam Hussein to seize the oil-rich country of Kuwait for both immediate economic gain and long-term control over a significant portion of Middle East oil reserves. Almost every country in the world condemned the Iraqi invasion of Kuwait, and at the UN a series of resolutions called for Iraqi withdrawal, imposed severe economic sanctions against Iraq, and eventually authorized the use of force against Iraq. An American-led military coalition assembled by U.S. President George Bush began to deploy military capabilities to the Gulf, initially to defend Saudi Arabia against Iraqi attack but then to prepare for an offensive military operation should it be required. Great Britain, France, Saudi Arabia, Syria, Egypt, Canada, and many other countries joined the coalition (which received its mandate from the UN Security Council). By the time war broke out, the coalition had amassed 750 000 personnel in the Gulf, three-quarters of them American. Public opinion in most coalition countries was not solidly behind the war; antiwar demonstrations took place in many countries. However, once the war began, public support increased. This change has been attributed to the "rally around the flag" effect and to carefully managed (and controversial) media coverage of the war.

In response, the Iraqi government took Western civilians in Iraq hostage and attempted to mobilize Islamic sentiments against the coalition. Saddam Hussein attempted to link his withdrawal from Kuwait to Israeli withdrawal from the Occupied Territories. He attempted to widen the war by involving Israel, hoping to break the coalition between Western and Middle Eastern countries. Iraq also deployed more than 400 000 troops to defend its gains in Kuwait. However, in terms of troop and equipment quality, the Iraqi army, though formidable, was no match for the modern armies fielded by the United States, Great Britain, and France. In the end, diplomacy failed; Saddam Hussein was unwilling to meet coalition demands that he withdraw unconditionally from Kuwait, and economic sanctions were judged (prematurely in the minds of many critics) as too slow by an impatient Bush Administration in Washington. The military campaign began on January 17, 1991, with a 40-day air campaign against Iraq and Iraqi forces in Kuwait. Iraqi air defences were destroyed, and the coalition controlled the air for the rest of the war. Iraq responded by launching Scud missile attacks against Saudi Arabia and Israel, which failed to cause serious damage or bring Israel into the war. The war ended with a 100-hour ground offensive into Iraq and Kuwait, which succeeded in routing Iraqi forces. A ceasefire was called on February 27, 1991.

Iraq was expected to abide by all UN Security Council resolutions, including the renunciation of claims to Kuwait, the payment of reparations for the war, and the destruction of its weapons of mass destruction program. The costs of the war were high. In monetary terms, the war cost more than U.S.$150 billion, most footed by Saudi Arabia, Kuwait, Germany, and Japan. The coalition suffered approximately 240 casualties, while estimates of Iraqi military casualties range between 20 000 and 85 000. Estimates of Iraqi civilian deaths range between 2300 and 20 000. The war also caused the displacement of 4 to 5 million people, mostly migrant workers living in Iraq, Kuwait, and Saudi Arabia.[25] During the war, Kurds in the north of Iraq and Shiite Muslims in the south both rebelled against Saddam Hussein's rule. These uprisings were brutally suppressed by Saddam Hussein until large parts of northern and southern Iraq were declared to be safe havens, protected by coalition airpower. The environmental impact of the war was also enormous. Iraq intentionally released vast quantities of crude oil into the Gulf in an effort to foul Saudi Arabian coastal areas, destroying fish and wildlife habitat. During their retreat from Kuwait, Iraqi forces blew up hundreds of Kuwaiti oil wells, which sent black smoke into the atmosphere over a wide area.

The Gulf War was successful in that it achieved its stated objective: the removal of the Iraqi military from Kuwait and the restoration of the Kuwaiti government. However, the war also left a number of unresolved issues. First, Saddam Hussein remained the leader of Iraq, and although the Iraqi military was crippled, the most loyal elements of the Iraqi military, the Republican Guard, were strong enough to keep the regime in power through force and intimidation. Second, UN weapons inspectors entered Iraq to begin destroying Iraq's weapons of mass destruction programs. However, these inspectors encountered a systematic effort by Iraq to hide its weapons of mass destruction programs. Third, coalition airpower remained in place over northern and southern Iraq, enforcing the no-fly zones over these safe havens. Periodically, air strikes were launched to punish Iraqi forces for threatening the no-fly zones and to compel Iraq to cooperate fully with UN weapons inspectors. This continued military presence of coalition airpower (particularly that of the United States) contributed to an increasing anti-American sentiment in the region. Fourth, UN sanctions remained in force against Iraq, aimed at pressuring Saddam Hussein to completely destroy his weapons of mass destruction program. These sanctions became increasingly controversial, as they crippled Iraq's economy and caused hardship to Iraqi civilians, who faced shortages of basic goods and medical and safety equipment (we examine the issue of sanctions in Chapter 7). The Iraqi population suffered from increased rates of disease, malnutrition, poverty, and infant mortality. In response, a growing protest movement argued that the sanctions should be lifted or modified to alleviate human suffering in Iraq. Supporters of the sanctions regime argued that lifting the sanctions would simply permit Saddam Hussein to rebuild his military and his weapons of mass destruction programs. These issues would keep Iraq high on the list of international crisis points through the 1990s and the years of the Clinton Administration. Combined with the highly controversial election of George W. Bush, they would precipitate another confrontation that would lead to another war.

After the terrorist attacks of September 11, 2001, terrorism became the primary security threat to the United States (we examine terrorism and September 11 later in this chapter). Terrorism, and the states that supported it, became the focus of a "War on Terrorism" launched by the new administration of George W. Bush, the son of former U.S. President George Bush. Initially supported by widespread public and government opinion, and backed by UN Security Council resolutions, the United States identified Al-Qaeda and its leader,

Osama Bin Laden, as the group responsible for the attacks. A United States–led coalition, which included Canada, launched a war to overthrow the Taliban government in Afghanistan, which had harboured and aided Al-Qaeda activities. However, the "War on Terrorism" would not stop in Afghanistan. On January 29, 2002, in his State of the Union address, President Bush referred to North Korea, Iran, and Iraq as an "axis of evil" that threatened the United States and world peace. The speech was uncompromising in tone, despite the fact that there had been some improvement in relations with Iran and an ongoing, if painfully slow, process of discussion with North Korea. However, relations with Iraq had been steadily deteriorating. For many senior officials in the new Bush Administration, Saddam Hussein was an unresolved piece of business and the most important security threat facing the United States. In their view, "Saddam" had a record of starting wars, he was producing and using chemical weapons and trying to acquire nuclear weapons (weapons that could be placed in the hands of terrorists), he supported terrorism in the Middle East, and he had a habit of attacking his enemies (demonstrated by his assassination of his sons-in-law in 1995 and the attempted assassination of former U.S. President George Bush in 1993).[26] Despite the lack of evidence suggesting a substantive link between Al-Qaeda and Saddam Hussein, the Iraq agenda and the "War on Terrorism" began to converge in Washington.

By the late 1990s, the Saddam Hussein regime had become increasingly less cooperative with the conditions imposed on it by UN resolutions.[27] Since the end of the Gulf War, Iraq had defied 10 UN resolutions related to arms inspections, sanctions, safe havens, and no-fly zones. The Iraqi military had shot at coalition aircraft enforcing the no-fly zones, and compliance with UN weapons inspectors had been poor. Although large quantities of weapons of mass destruction–related materials had been destroyed since the end of the Gulf War, serious questions remained about what capabilities were still hidden or unaccounted for. The weapons inspection teams faced increased opposition to their activities from Iraqi authorities and were ultimately withdrawn in 1998. In December 1998, U.S. and British aircraft bombed suspected weapons of mass destruction sites. Dubbed "Operation Desert Fox," the bombings were not authorized by the UN and drew considerable international criticism. France withdrew from the coalition enforcement of the no-fly zones, which proved to be the beginning of a widening rift between Washington and Paris on the issue of Iraq. Efforts to reinstate inspections failed in 1999 and 2000 as the Iraqi regime continued to place conditions on its cooperation with UN inspections. In the wake of President Bush's "axis of evil" speech, the U.S. government began an effort to build international support against Iraq. The U.S. received considerable diplomatic support from the United Kingdom, and British Prime Minister Tony Blair would be a forceful and (unlike Bush) eloquent spokesman for the case against Iraq and the decision to go to war.

However, there was considerable opposition to U.S. efforts, and support was not as forthcoming as it had been over Afghanistan, or in the 1990–91 Gulf War. Many governments simply did not agree that Iraq was an immediate threat to United States or world security and did not see any connection between the September 11 attacks and Saddam Hussein. There was widespread suspicion of American motives, particularly in the Middle East, where American policy was seen as an expression of a U.S. desire to remove Saddam Hussein and control Iraqi oil. Moreover, domestic politics were also in play. The prospect of American-led military action against Iraq was deeply unpopular in almost all countries. As the threat of war grew so did antiwar protests, which culminated in a global "Day of Action" on February 15, 2003, a worldwide protest of millions of people coordinated over the Internet. Public opposition was especially deep in Europe and specifically Germany, where the government was facing an election and proved to be a staunch opponent of U.S. policy on Iraq. A stake in Iraq's future may also have influenced some governments' policies toward America's anti-Saddam stand: French and

Russian companies in particular had a large number of contracts with the Iraqi government that had been suspended by the UN sanctions regime and would be void if a new regime took power in Baghdad. There was also a growing concern over the policies of the Bush Administration and the direction the "War on Terrorism" was taking. At a speech at West Point Military Academy in June 2002, President Bush stated that U.S. security would require Americans "to be ready for preemptive action when necessary ..."[28] The United States released a new national security strategy document in September 2002, which in its discussion of terrorism stated that "while the United States will constantly strive to enlist the support of the international community, we will not hesitate to act alone, if necessary, to exercise our right of self-defense by acting preemptively against such terrorists, to prevent them from doing harm against our people and our country ..." The security strategy also called for "proactive counter-proliferation" efforts, to "deter and defend against the threat before it is unleashed."[29] In October 2002, the U.S. Congress authorized the Bush Administration to use force against Iraq. These proclamations increased suspicion that the United States was moving toward a unilateral, preemptive approach to its security priorities in general and Iraq in particular.

It was in this context that the frantic and often acrimonious diplomacy surrounding the prelude to the Iraq war was conducted. The United States, unwavering in its conviction that Iraq represented a threat to the United States and world peace, sought to persuade the UN Security Council to adopt a harder line against Iraq, backed by the threat to use military force. The United States sought to obtain a Security Council resolution authorizing force against Iraq because of the legitimacy that resolution would provide to any war, and because domestic and international opinion was much more supportive of a war that had UN approval. Even as a U.S. and British military buildup began in the region, in November 2002, the UN found Iraq in material breach of prior UN resolutions on arms inspections. The United States proposed a draft resolution with a strict deadline and an authorization to use force if Iraq did not comply fully with its weapons inspection obligations. France was opposed to such a resolution, and instead proposed a resolution that would call for the return of inspectors to Iraq, but with no firm deadline and no commitment to use force. The UN Security Council passed Resolution 1441, an awkward compromise between the French and U.S. positions, and weapons inspectors did return to Iraq in November. However, by January 2003 the head of the UN inspection commission, Hans Blix, estimated that their work would take another year to complete, and that the Iraqi government was once again not fully cooperative.[30] Seeking to speed the process and obtain UN authorization to use force, in February the United States, Spain, and the United Kingdom drafted a resolution explicitly authorizing force against Iraq. The United States and the United Kingdom presented intelligence dossiers on Iraqi weapons of mass destruction to

Making the case against war. A peace march moves through London's Piccadilly toward Hyde Park on February 15, 2003, as part of the global "Day of Action" in protest against a possible invasion of Iraq. (AP Photo/Kirsty Wigglesworth/CP Archive)

the UN. U.S. Secretary of State Colin Powell made a lengthy presentation to the Security Council on February 5, 2003, in which he outlined the suspected Iraqi weapons of mass destruction programs, circumventions of UN sanctions, connections to Al-Qaeda, and human rights violations by the Iraqi government.[31] France, Russia, and China, all veto-wielding members of the Security Council, along with Germany, a nonpermanent Council member, were opposed to the draft resolution, believing that Iraq should be given more time to comply with UN resolutions. France even threatened to use its veto to stop any resolution authorizing force against Iraq. When it became clear that a resolution authorizing force against Iraq would not be passed by the Security Council and would not receive majority support from nonpermanent members, the proposed resolution was withdrawn. The diplomatic effort at the UN was over. On March 17, 2003, U.S. President George Bush gave Saddam Hussein 48 hours to leave Iraq.

The military campaign against Iraq began on March 19, 2003. Unlike the Gulf War in 1990–91, there were significantly fewer states willing to assist the United States militarily or financially. Of the 30 countries that openly supported the effort diplomatically, only the United States, Britain, and Australia contributed military forces, while some countries in the Gulf allowed their airspace or territory to be used by coalition forces. Turkey, a traditional ally of the United States, refused to permit coalition forces to use Turkish land bases for the attacks on Iraq. Canada, another traditional ally of the United States, also refused to participate in the war in the absence of a UN Security Council resolution. Unlike the 1990–91 Gulf War, no Middle Eastern or Muslim countries contributed military forces. The lack of broad support for the United States–led war was an indication of the diplomatic isolation of the United States. Nevertheless, the military campaign was swift and successful. With air supremacy gained almost immediately, U.S. and British forces moved into Iraq from Kuwait on March 20. In the north, U.S. Special Forces, airborne troops, and Kurdish fighters advanced on regime strongholds north of Baghdad. Despite some resistance and bad sandstorms, U.S. forces advancing from the south reached Baghdad by April 3. The Iraqi army proved unwilling to

Making the case for war. The scene in the United Nations Security Council on February 5, 2003, as U.S. Secretary of State Colin Powell presents evidence of Iraq's weapons of mass destruction program. (CP/Actionpress)

fight for Saddam Hussein. The Republican Guard put up more resistance, but it was swept away in a series of one-sided battles. By April 9, the regime in Baghdad had ceased to function, Saddam Hussein had fled, and U.S. troops controlled the city. By April 16, the last pockets of organized resistance in towns loyal to the Saddam Hussein regime had collapsed. On May 1, President Bush declared the war to be over. Saddam Hussein was captured in a small, underground hideaway on December 13.

The Iraq War leaves any student or analyst of global politics with many questions and unknowns. In so many ways, the Iraq War may prove to be a watershed event, and yet we cannot be sure of the ultimate consequences or outcomes of this conflict, any more than any of the observers of past wars could be sure. However, we can with confidence raise the following questions, issues, and criticisms:

- *What were the human and monetary costs of the war?* At its peak, the United States–led coalition deployed over 500 000 personnel, with over 90 percent of these being American. By May 1, the coalition had suffered 172 fatalities. However, by late June 2004, the coalition had suffered 968 fatalities (851 American) due to ongoing anti-coalition violence inside Iraq. One early estimate of Iraqi casualties suggested that between 1500 to 2500 civilians and between 5000 and 20 000 military personnel were killed or wounded, but any estimates may prove to be inaccurate.[32] By mid-July 2003 ongoing violence in Iraq since the war was declared over had claimed more coalition casualties than had been suffered during the war itself. Continued bombings, assassinations, and attacks on coalition soldiers, foreign aid and UN workers, and Iraqi civilians have made the process of stabilizing Iraq slow and dangerous. The monetary costs of the war are uncertain, because estimates depend on accounting practices. But, estimates of the direct costs of the war range from approximately U.S.$60 billion to U.S.$100 billion. On November 6, 2003, President Bush approved an U.S.$87 billion package for occupation-related expenses and reconstruction. This was in addition to a U.S.$79 billion package approved earlier. These costs, and the costs of a continued U.S. presence in Iraq, belie the prewar estimates that the war was affordable: spending on Iraq, a U.S.$400 billion defence budget, and tax cuts increased the U.S. budget deficit to over U.S.$500 billion in 2004.

- *What was the Bush Administration's motive for going to war?* It seems likely that the administration was motivated by a number of factors, and we should appreciate the caution of decision-making theories that remind us that different theories lead to different explanations, and that accurate information is often hard to come by. The perceived threat of weapons of mass destruction may have unified the administration, but others also felt that a message had to be sent to regimes in the Middle East. Certainly, Iraq was unfinished business for a number of leading figures in the administration that had been in government during the 1990–91 Gulf War, and dealing with Saddam Hussein was an early priority for President Bush. Many critics of the administration have charged that the Bush Administration was so focused on Iraq that it ignored the threat posed by Al-Qaeda prior to September 11.[33] Still others saw a war as an opportunity to reorder the Middle East, by affecting regime change in Baghdad and installing a "democracy" in the region.[34] Much was made of the U.S. desire to control Iraqi oil (the "No War for Oil" slogan was a popular feature of the antiwar protests) and of the Bush Administration's connections with the oil industry. Certainly, controlling Iraq would make the politics of the international oil market much more favourable to the United States. However, although oil was a motive it is unlikely that oil was the only motive: if it had been, America might have reasonably decided to cut a deal with Saddam Hussein. After all, earlier U.S. governments had done so, and had made similar arrangements with other authoritarian regimes the world over. While it is likely that the desire to deal with Iraq was the predominant driving force in White House decision making (particularly among Bush and his senior advisers), all of these motives seem to have combined to take Bush and his senior advisers, including Secretary of Defense Donald Rumsfeld, National Security Advisor Condoleezza Rice, Vice President Richard Cheney, and Secretary of State Colin Powell, toward war.

• *Was the Iraq War a "war of necessity"?* In making the case for war, the Bush Administration maintained that the war was necessary, but this is a contentious issue and a debate that will be renewed whenever new information comes to light. Perhaps the weapons inspectors were not given enough time to complete their tasks, and more international support for military action may have been forthcoming if Saddam Hussein's intransigence had continued. (However, the failure to actually find any weapons of mass destruction suggests the inspections may have worked after all.) Alternatively, a policy of "vigilant containment" may have been more appropriate.[35] Above all else, Saddam Hussein was interested in maintaining his own power, and therefore it was unlikely that he would support or initiate an attack against the United States with weapons of mass destruction that would invite his own destruction in return. Another option was to remove Saddam Hussein through covert action, although there is some evidence to suggest such an effort may have been in place since 1991, to no avail. The Iraq War also diverted enormous resources and extensive diplomatic energy away from more immediate terrorist threats and the ongoing effort to rebuild Afghanistan. Certainly, the failure to obtain UN Security Council authorization was a major blow to the legitimacy of the war. For all of these reasons, the Iraq War may have been, as one of its critics suggested, "the wrong war, in the wrong place, at the wrong time, against the wrong enemy."[36]

• *What happened to the weapons of mass destruction?* The primary stated rationale for the war on Iraq was the danger posed by Iraqi weapons of mass destruction (WMD). Bush Administration officials had repeatedly stated that there was "no doubt" that Iraq possessed chemical weapons, and was close to acquiring biological and nuclear weapons. Therefore, Iraq was an "immediate threat" to U.S. and global security. The case presented to the UN Security Council and the world was almost exclusively devoted to the WMD issue. And yet, a full year after the war was over, inspectors had found no evidence that Iraq possessed weapons of mass destruction. There was, of course, evidence of past weapons possession and past efforts to acquire such weapons, but these were well known. Charges that President George Bush and Prime Minister Tony Blair had engaged in a deliberate deception abounded, and of course the two leaders bear ultimate responsibility for their decisions. Attention has focused on the U.S. National Intelligence Estimate on Iraq that proved to be systematically inaccurate for a number of reasons. First, the starting assumption was that Iraq would never give up its weapons of mass destruction, as evidenced by a systematic campaign of obstruction against UN inspectors. However, by the mid-1990s it appears that Saddam Hussein had decided to scale down his WMD program to avoid detection. This change in policy was apparently missed by intelligence agencies. Second, when UN inspectors left Iraq in 1998 the primary source of intelligence gathering and verification dried up, leaving intelligence officials relying on suspect information that could not be independently confirmed. Lacking good data, they began to rely on their assumptions concerning Iraqi intentions. Third, the Bush Administration was clearly receptive to information that confirmed its beliefs about Saddam Hussein, and doubted or rejected contrary intelligence information. Efforts appear to have been made to manipulate intelligence by "cherry picking" certain information for reports to senior officials. Fourth, the Bush Administration has been accused of distorting intelligence reports to enhance the public case for war. Administration officials would cite "worst-case" estimates from intelligence reports, but not the estimates considered most likely by the intelligence community. This is an especially damaging accusation for, if true, it represents a deliberate effort to mislead not only the American public, but also world governments and world opinion.[37]

- *Why was the United States so poorly prepared to stabilize and rebuild postwar Iraq?* The United States and its coalition partners encountered enormous problems dealing with stability in postwar Iraq. There was no clear transition government ready to put in place, there were an insufficient number of troops available to maintain order and prevent theft and looting, there were insufficient resources available to repair infrastructure, institutions and government agencies had ceased to function, and few good communications channels had been opened with the local population. Critics charged that the Bush Administration was unprepared for the magnitude of the rebuilding project and the challenges of governance. However, the criticisms were wide of the mark. In fact, a great deal of planning for the challenges of rebuilding Iraq had been done in the U.S. government. As early as late 2001, what would become the Future of Iraq Project was already underway in the U.S. State Department, preparing for a possible postwar Iraq scenario. In the year prior to the war, experts inside and outside government had warned Congressional committees that the challenges of postwar Iraq would be greater than the challenges of defeating the Saddam Hussein regime. The United States Agency for International Development formed an Iraq Working Group that accumulated the experience of U.S. nongovernmental organizations in postwar environments. The U.S. Army conducted studies on the numbers of soldiers necessary to invade Iraq and maintain order afterward. The problem was not that these studies had never been carried out, or that the studies had failed to anticipate the postwar challenges correctly. The problem was that senior officials in the Bush Administration routinely and systematically ignored or dismissed these studies and reports. Supremely confident in their approach, Bush Administration officials—through a combination of arrogance, ignorance, and carelessness—chose to treat warnings about the challenges of postwar Iraq as antiwar sentiment.[38] The failure to adequately prepare for governing and rebuilding postwar Iraq has been costly. The United States lost a great deal of credibility both inside and outside Iraq, and the Iraqi people endured a great deal of unnecessary suffering.[39]

- *The image of the United States in the world.* Perhaps the greatest criticism that can be brought to bear on the decision to launch the Iraq War is the damage it has done to the legitimacy, prestige, and image of the United States. In the wake of September 11, the United States received the sympathy and support of most governments and most peoples around the world. Unprecedented advances in cooperation on counter-terrorism and intelligence gathering followed. The war in Afghanistan, though not without controversy, was supported by the vast majority of the world's governments and sanctioned by the UN. And yet, in less than two years, the United States had effectively squandered that sympathy and political support, had alienated most of its key allies, and was deeply unpopular around the world.[40] The depth of this anti-American sentiment was very strong in 2004: in an annual poll of global attitudes toward the United States (conducted by the Pew Global Attitudes Project), discontent with the

United States intensified in the year following the Iraq War. In the United States, the poll found that Americans generally think the war helped the "War on Terrorism," and demonstrated U.S. trustworthiness and support for democracy. However, the majority of people in Germany, Turkey, and France (and half of respondents in Britain and Russia) believed the war in Iraq undermined the "War on Terrorism." Majorities in most countries found the United States less trustworthy as a result of the war, with 82 percent of Germans and 78 percent of French respondents expressing less confidence that the United States is trustworthy. Majorities in six of the nine European countries surveyed did not believe that the United States–led "War on Terrorism" was a sincere effort to reduce terrorism, and large majorities in almost every country surveyed believed that President Bush and Prime Minister Blair lied about Iraqi weapons of mass destruction. In the Muslim countries surveyed, discontent toward the United States was even deeper, with large majorities believing the war on Iraq was an effort to control oil and dominate the world. More ominously, majorities in Jordan and Morocco believed suicide bombings against Americans and Westerners in Iraq were justified. In Pakistan, 46 percent of respondents thought such attacks were justified, and in Turkey, 31 percent believed they were justified.[41] The Iraq prison abuse scandal, which centred on the mistreatment and torture of Iraqi prisoners by U.S. personnel in 2003 and 2004, caused even more damage to image of the United States around the world.

The future of Iraq is uncertain. The end of the Saddam Hussein regime should not be lamented. However, the future of Iraq may be characterized by ongoing violence and social upheaval, the division of the country into Kurdish, Shiite, and Sunni blocs, or the emergence of another authoritarian ruler. Interference from neighbouring states seeking influence in post-Saddam Iraq is also likely. Of course, one must dare to hope that the future of Iraq will be a better one, where fear of Saddam Hussein's regime or a similar facsimile is banished, and where a democratic system and economic development can offer a better choice than

Loss of credibility. U.S. President George Bush is depicted with a Pinocchio nose on a float in the annual carnival parade in Düsseldorf, Germany, in February 2004. The writing on the nose reads: "Iraq possesses weapons of mass destruction." (CP Photo/Frank Augstein/CP Archive)

extremism and violence. The challenges are formidable, and depend on the willingness of countries (especially the United States) to commit the resources necessary for the length of time necessary to consolidate peace and stability.[42] In a global context, perhaps the United States will be able to repair the damage to its legitimacy and image abroad, and rebuild its relations with both its allies and more mistrustful countries. This will require a more concerted effort to engage in multilateral forums and compromise for the sake of achieving a broader consensus on postwar Iraq and the "War on Terrorism." The Bush Administration has chosen a course that emphasizes military paths to security and foreign policy. Perhaps this is the prerogative of empire, but critics have pointed out that such a policy can alienate allies and undercut the power that America can wield through international support for its ideas and leadership. Once again, sound policies, political commitment, and the wise expenditure of resources will be necessary if the positive possibilities are to be realized.[43]

The Gulf War of 1990–91 and the Iraq War of 2003 remind us that interstate wars may still occur in an era of intrastate conflict and transnational security concerns. However, we must avoid thinking of interstate war in terms of only these two conflicts. Examples abound of high levels of tension and rivalry between states in the contemporary international system that could lead to future wars:

- *Greece and Turkey* both claim control over islands in the Aegean Sea and have clashed over the control of Cyprus, an island divided between Greek Cypriots and Turkish Cypriots. A recent settlement was rejected by referendum.

- *India and Pakistan* have fought three wars since the end of World War II and continue to clash over territorial and religious issues. In 1998, both countries tested nuclear weapons, raising the prospect of a nuclear war in South Asia.

- *China, Vietnam, Malaysia, Brunei, and the Philippines* are the principals in a dispute over the Spratly Islands, a chain of small volcanic outcroppings in the South China Sea. Small violent clashes have occurred over the possession of these islands and the right to exploit fishing and mineral resources and conduct oil exploration in the territorial limit around them. China and *Taiwan* also have an unresolved conflict over the status of Taiwan.

- *Israel and Syria* have fought each other in the Arab–Israeli wars, and continue to dispute possession of the **Golan Heights**. Their interests and allies also clash in Lebanon.

- *North Korea and South Korea* have not fought each other since 1953, but despite an improvement in relations in 2000 (including a meeting between the leaders of the two states), a very high level of tension remains on the Korean peninsula.

- *Peru and Ecuador.* Since the last major war between these two countries in 1941, they have clashed over their disputed border. The latest border skirmishes took place in 1995.

- *Ethiopia and Eritrea.* Between 1998 and 2000, Ethiopia and Eritrea fought a war over territory and economic issues. The civilian population in the war zone suffered horribly from drought, famine, disease, ethnic cleansing, and mass deportations. The war killed between 70 000 and 100 000, and displaced more than 650 000 civilians. The battles of the war were reminiscent of World War I: "The death toll is high because the combatants use the weaponry of the Korean War, the tactics of the first world war, and the medical establishments of the 19th century."[44] The war ended in December 2000, and a UN peacekeeping force was deployed to the border between the two states. However, the underlying territorial and economic issues have not been resolved, and there are concerns that another war could break out in the future.

- *Cameroon and Nigeria.* These countries nearly went to war in 1981 over two long-standing territorial disputes over the Bakassi peninsula and the border around Lake Chad. Tensions have increased in recent years, exacerbated by disputes over offshore oil resources in the Gulf of Guinea.

Warfare between these states remains a very real possibility, and of course other interstate wars could break out almost anywhere with virtually no warning. Many states continue to regard their neighbours with suspicion, have unresolved territorial or political disputes, and have a history of conflict.

Another use of force by states also remains relevant in contemporary international politics: the use of coercive diplomacy and military intervention during crises. Threatening to employ military force to achieve political objectives remains a prominent tool of state diplomacy. Military forces do not actually have to be employed in war to be useful; the threat of their use can compel, or coerce, other states into a certain course of action. In strategic studies parlance, crises occur when states attempt to force other states to alter their behaviour to the point where the risk of war is real. Crises have been frequent and widespread in the international system, with 390 crises erupting between 1918 and 1988. Almost all states have been involved in international crises.[45] Furthermore, states also employ military force in a limited fashion, through military intervention in ongoing conflicts and wars between other actors. Between 1945 and 1991, 690 cases of direct military intervention occurred in the world.[46] By their very nature, military interventions carry the risk of precipitating war or widening an existing war. We must, therefore, be cautious in proclaiming the post–Cold War world an era of intrastate war and transnational security issues. Wars between states remain possible, even if relatively few examples have occurred in recent years. Nevertheless, the problem of intrastate war is more immediately relevant in light of the vast majority of wars being fought in the world today, and the concern over transnational security threats has risen dramatically. We now turn to an examination of these contemporary security issues.

ETHNIC, RELIGIOUS, AND FACTIONAL CONFLICT

As indicated earlier in this chapter, one of the most noticeable trends in international security is the extent to which traditional conflicts between states—interstate conflicts—have been less frequent, while conflicts within states—intrastate conflicts—have been numerous. In fact, the vast majority of recent conflicts have occurred at the substate level. These conflicts are often generically referred to as *ethnic conflicts*, but not all intrastate conflicts are ethnic conflicts. In many cases, they may be conflicts between religious communities, clans, or political factions, and some would argue that class relations are central factors in most of them. As a result, in this chapter we use the term *communal conflicts* to describe wars that take place between communal groups of all types at the substate level.[47] Intrastate conflicts have been a feature of international politics for a long time. Those causing at least 1000 civilian and military deaths have occurred 162 times from 1816 to 1992.[48] Since World War II, intrastate wars have broken out more often than wars between states. In the 187 military conflicts in the world between 1945 and 1995, 129 were internal conflicts (69 percent).[49] Another study has estimated that between 1945 and 1991, 258 identifiable cases of ethnic conflict occurred in the world.[50] Of the 58 major armed conflicts in the world between 1990 and 2002, all but 3 (just over 5 percent) were internal, intrastate conflicts.[51] What is new is that communal wars are virtually the only kind of wars currently being fought, and so ethnic, religious, and factional groups are arguably the most important source of conflict in the contemporary international system.[52]

THE NATURE OF COMMUNAL GROUPS

Communal groups come in many forms (see Profile 6.2), but they all share one important quality: a sense of common identity. Ted Robert Gurr calls this shared sense of identity a "psychological community" that is enduring and differentiates the group from others.[53] This sense of identity gives the group the internal solidarity and the capacity for collective action. Without this quality (if group identification is weak) there is seldom the potential for organized collective action by the group. Communal identities can be based on one or more of the following characteristics:

- Ethnicity (race, custom)
- Historical experience or myth
- Religious beliefs
- Region of residence
- Familial ties (clan systems)

It is important to note that communal group identity is not a menu or checklist of items that identify a group. Communal identity is bestowed on individuals by virtue of birth, but it is not a fixed or permanent characteristic of all individuals within a group. Communal identity may be more or less active in some individuals at any given time, depending on the issues at stake. Communal identity also has a voluntary element, in the sense that individuals within a group have a certain element of choice over how much they want to identify themselves by communal group loyalty. Some of these communal characteristics are more subject to individual choice than others. Obviously, physical characteristics are not a matter of choice. However, observing religious beliefs or social customs is more subject to individual choice, though it is irresponsible to generalize across cultures in this respect.

Communal groups are also not static or unchanging. The self-identity of communal identities may vary over time. Some communal groups may assimilate into other groups and

---

PROFILE 6.2 Types of Communal Groups

NATIONAL PEOPLES

Ethnonationalists: regionally concentrated peoples with a history of autonomy and independence objectives (Kurds, Croats, and Québécois)

Indigenous peoples: descendants of conquered original inhabitants with cultures sharply different from dominant groups (Aboriginals in Canada and Australia, Masai in Africa, Dayaks in Borneo)

MINORITY PEOPLES

Ethnoclasses: ethnically or culturally distinct peoples descended from immigrants or slaves, usually of low-status economic position (descendants of African slaves in North America and Latin America, North Africans in France, Koreans in Japan, Romany in Europe)

Militant sects: groups that derive their status and activities from religious belief (Sunni, Shiite, Druze in Lebanon, Jewish peoples, Baha'i in Iran)

"Communal contenders": distinct peoples, tribes, or clans in heterogeneous societies

Disadvantaged: groups subject to political or economic discrimination (apartheid South Africa)

Advantaged: groups with a preponderance of political or economic power (Sunni in Iraq, Tutsi in Rwanda, Anglo-Saxons in the United States)

SOURCE: ADAPTED FROM TED ROBERT GURR, *MINORITIES AT RISK: A GLOBAL VIEW OF ETHNOPOLITICAL CONFLICTS* (WASHINGTON, DC: UNITED STATES INSTITUTE OF PEACE, 1993). COPYRIGHT © 1993 BY THE ENDOWMENT OF THE UNITED STATES INSTITUTE OF PEACE, WASHINGTON, D.C.

---

become less distinguishable as a separate group. The unity of some groups may be influenced by their position within a larger society. On the one hand, if a group comes under external pressure (for example, a threat to its religious beliefs or social customs), its sense of identity and capacity for communal action may increase. On the other hand, if the group has its basic desires accommodated within a larger social structure, the identity and capacity for action may decline. Communal identity can also be affected over time by other social constructions. Myth and legend, passed down from generation to generation, can keep beliefs, values, and shared history alive. Communal identity can also be reinforced and even constructed through schooling and social life. Nation-states aspire to communal status; the modern state spends time and money on fostering group coherence at the national level. In some cases, such as the former Yugoslavia or the former Czechoslovakia, the effort fails completely because substate communal loyalties persevere and triumph over state nationalism.

EXPLAINING COMMUNAL CONFLICT

Why do communal conflicts break out? It is tempting to point to a particular causal factor and declare that it is the cause, and the only cause, of that conflict. In some cases, this declaration may be accurate. However, in most cases, multiple causal factors are behind the outbreak of a communal conflict, and while some may be more readily apparent than others, no one factor is solely to blame. Communal conflicts may originate in one or more of the following situations.

1. *Grievances.* One communal group within a society may have a grievance against other groups or against the state itself. These grievances may take several forms, including

   - *Economic grievances.* Communal conflicts can be conflicts over entitlements and resources and the right or power to control them. In this sense, communal conflicts are struggles against entrenched economic discrimination. Often, one communal group will control these resources and the means of distributing them, and this control will lead to conflict between the advantaged and the disadvantaged groups.

   - *Political grievances.* Communal conflicts may be conflicts over political rights and freedoms. In this sense, these conflicts are struggles against political discrimination, which may take the form of efforts to gain the right to vote, practise a religion, travel, organize, or secure protection from human rights abuses. In addition, the conflict may be a struggle for representation in the institutions of the state, government, the army, the police, or the bureaucracy.

2. *Autonomy and independence.* In other cases, conflict may develop out of the desire of a communal group for greater political and cultural autonomy or independence. It is perhaps ironic that many intrastate conflicts are motivated at least in part by a desire by one or more communal groups to establish a state. Most communal groups regard a certain defined territory (which they may or may not occupy) as part of their ethnic endowment or as their natural homeland. Conflict may develop over territorial rights and interpretations of possession between rival communal groups that claim the same stretches of territory.

3. *Social change.* In other cases, conflict may erupt when a communal group feels threatened by change, such as modernization. This change may take the form of the threat posed by industrialization or commercialization or by government policies that threaten their political, economic, territorial, or cultural position in society. In such cases, communal groups will mobilize in defence of their way of life. Because this way of life is at the core of self-identity of the individuals within a group, emotions run high; individuals are committed to the issues at stake in a very personal manner.

4. *Primordialism.* Another explanation is that communal conflicts develop out of the hatreds that various particular communal groups feel for one another. These hatreds usually have a long historical record, and the communal groups involved have long memories of past injustices perpetrated generations before. This explanation suggests that communal conflicts start at the grassroots level between peoples and that these hatreds drive political events.

5. *Incitement by leaders.* Another explanation suggests that self-aggrandizing nationalist leaders, who incite nationalist, ethnic, or religious bigotry for their own political ends, can spark ethnonational conflict. Such leaders may attempt to mobilize public support for their goals of territorial expansion or ethnic purification by vilifying other communal groups. Alternatively, nationalist leaders may create scapegoats for economic and social hardships at home. This "instrumental" explanation suggests that communal conflicts begin at the *elite* level, not at the grassroots level.

6. *State nationalism versus ethnonationalism.* Conflicts can originate in a clash between the state and ethnic groups. The nation-state is built on an internal tension between the sovereignty of the state based on territorial demarcation and the imposition of this sovereignty on the ethnic, cultural, and religious divisions of the world. Only 10 percent of all states in the world are ethnically homogeneous. Only half of all states in the world have one ethnic group that makes up as much as 75 percent of the population. All other states are far more diverse. In the effort to achieve domestic social unity, political leaders have sought to emphasize a sense of common identity based on loyalty to the state; this loyalty is challenged by loyalty to a communal group.

7. *The loss of the political centre.* The structural explanation for communal conflict suggests that when state, regional, and international forces are too weak to maintain order and protect the security of individual groups within the country, communal groups are plunged into a condition of anarchy. In the contemporary international system, this cause has taken a number of forms. One is the collapse of old imperial systems and colonial orders, which left behind weak and unstable states that continue to be beset with internal problems. A second explanation is the recent collapse of states, such as the Soviet Union and Yugoslavia, both of which left a patchwork of newly independent states and peoples in their wake. A third explanation is the phenomenon of weak states and the collapse of failed states. When states and empires collapse, the human geography of their territory resembles a quilt, a patchwork of peoples with islands and enclaves of one group often surrounded by others. In such situations, a security dilemma can develop among peoples as it has developed among states. Other groups are seen as potential threats, and attempts to protect group security become interpreted as hostile acts by neighbours, starting (or renewing) a cycle of mistrust or hostility.

8. *Symbolic politics.* The symbolic politics approach suggests that symbols and myths are the key to understanding ethnic conflicts. Symbolic politics is "any sort of political activity focused on arousing emotions rather than addressing interests."[54] Ethnic conflicts begin when symbolic politics involving hostile myths and ethnic fears are mobilized within ethnic groups in the absence of a political centre willing and capable of stopping this mobilization. When this happens, people make decisions based increasingly on emotional attachments to ideas and values, preconceptions of enemies and heroes, and interpretations of right and wrong. Symbolic politics can be mobilized at either the grassroots level (primordialism) or the elite level (instrumentalism): in either case, emotions, myths, and symbolism carry the group toward confrontation

and war. The symbolic politics explanation thus tries to unify the various explanations for ethnic conflict covered above, by arguing that the emergence of symbolic politics is a necessary precondition for ethnic conflict.

THE NATURE OF COMMUNAL WAR

Intrastate wars have a very different profile than the wars of the past. As Kalevi Holsti has observed, "There are no declarations of war, there are no seasons for campaigning, and few end with peace treaties. Decisive battles are few. Attrition, terror, psychology, and actions against civilians highlight 'combat.' Rather than highly organized armed forces based on a strict command hierarchy, wars are fought by loosely knit groups of regulars, irregulars, cells, and not infrequently by locally based warlords under little or no central authority."[55] In particular, the violence and brutality of contemporary communal conflicts has shocked and appalled most observers, and this sentiment is in no small part responsible for the many international efforts to terminate or manage these conflicts. However, wars have always been brutal; even so-called good or just wars have been extremely destructive and characterized by brutal attacks on noncombatants. In World War II, for example, entire cities were laid waste in an effort to destroy manufacturing facilities and to weaken the morale of the civilian population. Massacres and rapes were not uncommon. What is it about communal conflicts that strike such a chord of repulsion? Is it the way these wars have been presented to viewers on television? Is it because the relatively small number of casualties involved enables us to sympathize with the victims on an individual level in a way that we cannot with the abstraction of high casualties? Or is there a qualitative difference between these wars and interstate conflicts?

One significant difference may be the extent to which civilians are intentional targets in communal conflicts. Attacks on civilians are widespread for several reasons. Civilians are the centre of group power, the source of soldiers, food, and support, and so they are attacked to weaken the military potential of the communal group. In addition, because communal groups are often closely intermingled, the early stages of communal conflicts tend to involve violence or open warfare between close neighbours. Finally, and perhaps most insidiously, because territorial gain is reflected in the composition of people living in that territory, forcing populations to leave is, therefore, a cornerstone of military campaigns. A new term, **ethnic cleansing**, has been coined to refer to this practice. Ethnic cleansing is the forced removal of peoples from their area of residence (see Chapter 9). In communal conflicts, territory is really conquered only when all members of the other ethnic group have been removed, and people of the victor's ethnic group have been brought in to replace them. Then, and only then, is the territory considered "cleansed."

The instruments of ethnic cleansing include forced deportation, mass murder, and the destruction of homes and property—spreading terror and compelling people to flee the area in search of safety. Fear and terror are, therefore, weapons in communal conflicts. Rape has also been used as an instrument of terror in such conflicts, most notably in the former Yugoslavia and in Rwanda. Beyond the pain and trauma to individuals, rape spreads fear among the female population, compelling the women of a communal group to flee; it also contributes to the spread of AIDS and other sexually transmitted diseases. Once the women are gone, communities are completely uprooted. In addition, in many societies, women and teenage girls who have been raped are considered undesirable as a mate, reducing the chances that they will have children. Or, if a pregnancy results from the rape, that child will be of mixed heritage. Therefore, rape is also an attack on the very ability of a communal group to reproduce itself. For all these reasons, the violence of communal conflicts is regarded as especially brutal, even by the standards of behaviour found in the history of warfare. The case studies below provide vivid illustrations of the dynamics of communal conflict. What is evident is that many similarities exist between intrastate conflicts around the world but that understanding the origins and dynamics of each conflict requires careful consideration of the circumstances and societies unique to each war.

Finally, ethnic conflicts often have a powerful economic component that is sometimes overlooked. While the tendency of the observer is to focus on political, territorial, and religious aspects of the conflict, these may in fact be secondary to the economic gains the continuation of a war can bring to certain groups or individuals. Mats Berdal and David M. Malone suggest that civil wars of all kinds, including ethnic wars, have been "driven not by a Clausewitzian logic of forwarding a set of political aims, but rather by powerful economic motives and agendas."[56] For example, a rebel leader in Liberia was estimated to have made more than U.S.$400 million a year from the war between 1992 and 1996. In Angola, the rebel group controlled 70 percent of the country's diamond production, creating an international reaction against "conflict diamonds" that financed an ongoing war. In Cambodia, senior commanders in the rebel groups and the government's army alike were often more interested in reaping the profits of illegal logging and trading in gems than in the politics of the war.[57] As David Keen has suggested,

> Conflict can create war economies, often in the regions controlled by rebels or warlords and linked to international trading networks; members of armed gangs can benefit from looting; and regimes can use violence to deflect opposition, reward supporters or maintain their access to resources. Under these circumstances, ending civil wars becomes difficult. Winning may not be desirable: the point of war may be precisely the legitimacy which it confers on actions that in peacetime would be punishable as crimes.[58]

This connection between ethnic conflict, civil wars, and economic gain must of course be addressed in any conflict management efforts designed to end such wars.

THE CASE OF YUGOSLAVIA: COMMUNAL CONFLICT IN A FRAGMENTED STATE

The violence in the former Yugoslavia is one of the great tragedies of the post–Cold War period. The Yugoslavian state was created following the disintegration of the Austro-Hungarian and Ottoman empires, with Serbia and Montenegro forming the core of the new state and Slovenians and Croatians joining out of concerns over Italian expansionism. In World War II, Yugoslavia was conquered by Nazi Germany, but during the occupation numerous acts of violence and brutality were perpetrated by all ethnic groups against each other, as well as those perpetrated by occupation forces. Memories of this violence resurfaced in the 1990s. Yugoslavia was a federal state composed of eight republics and provinces, presided over by the dictator Josef Tito. When Tito died in 1980, the federal structure and the federal army became dominated by Serbia, alienating Slovenia and Croatia, which sought to leave the federation and declare independence. Violence broke out in 1990, with skirmishes between Serbian minority militia and the Croatian police. Both Slovenia and Croatia declared independence in June 1991. The Serbian-dominated federal army was instructed by Serbian President Slobodan Milosevic to use force to keep Slovenia and Croatia in the federation, but the army failed and withdrew from Slovenia in 1991 and from Croatia in 1992.

In April 1992, war spread to Bosnia, where the Bosnian Muslim government, having declared independence, wanted to preserve a multiethnic state. However, nationalist movements in the Serbian and Croatian regions of Bosnia sought independence and eventual amalgamation with Serbia and Croatia respectively. Months of savage fighting followed, characterized by ethnic cleansing, artillery bombardment of cities, and battles for control of ethnic enclaves. The initial success of the Bosnian Serbs, supported by the Milosevic government in Belgrade, was reversed by a combination of a Muslim–Croat alliance, the withdrawal of Serbian support (the result of UN sanctions), and the intervention of NATO in support of the UN. At the end of 1995, after more than three years of war, a peace was brokered in Bosnia, leading to the Dayton Agreement and the deployment of 60 000 heavily armed NATO troops authorized to use force to maintain the peace. The long-term success of Dayton is still uncertain, but at the very least, it has brought relative peace to a region torn apart by the violent disintegration of a state at the hands of warring ethno-religious communal groups. A number of ominous events have kept international attention on the region. Slobodan Milosevic was put on trial at the International Criminal Tribunal for the Former Yugoslavia, although procedural issues have delayed the trial. In many of the recent elections held in the region, nationalist parties have gained office or increased their popular support, raising concern about the prospects for long-term reconciliation. The murder of Serbian Prime Minister Zoran Kjindic in March 2003, apparently by a powerful criminal organization with ties to Milosevic, was another blow to stability in the region. With the number of NATO troops in Bosnia steadily declining, the prospects for disruptions in the peace may increase, even as the prospects for long-term reconciliation look grim.

THE CASE OF SOMALIA: CLAN CONFLICT IN A FAILED STATE

Somalia emerged as an independent state out of colonial Africa in July 1960. However, it was a state deeply divided along clan lines. In 1969, Major-General Mohammed Siad Barre seized power and attempted to establish a socialist state. Opposition to Barre's rule grew in the 1970s and 1980s, and he was forced to rely on his own clan to maintain power. In January 1991 Barre was ousted by a coalition of opposition clans after a long period of strife that devastated much of the country. The opposition clans soon fell to bickering among themselves over the question of who was to rule in post-Barre Somalia. Warfare between rival clans broke out, and 16 months of war followed, destroying what was left of the infrastructure of Somalia. A humanitarian disaster of enormous proportions, originating in drought and war, gained the attention of the international community, which responded in an effort to bring humanitarian relief and peace to Somalia. Yet while the humanitarian relief effort was largely successful, the peace efforts were not. Clan conflict continued in Somalia, with UN peacekeepers and American-led coalition forces engaging in armed clashes with local warlords. The international presence was withdrawn in March 1995, and sporadic violence between the rival clan factions has continued. The country remains deeply divided, with no central government and poor prospects for long-term peace and development, and is a continuing source of regional instability in the form of arms trafficking, refugees, and possibly terrorism.

THE CASE OF CHECHNYA: THE RUSSIAN STATE AGAINST AN ETHNIC GROUP

A centuries-old history of conquest, repression, and deportation has left a legacy of bitter relations between Moscow and the peoples of the Caucasus region. This bitterness was especially true of Chechnya, the most homogeneous Muslim republic in the Russian Federation. When the Soviet Union collapsed in 1991, Chechen leaders claimed the right of self-determination and independence for Chechnya. The Russian government maintained that Chechnya was part of Russia. Neither demonstrated any willingness to compromise, and Chechens increasingly ran their own affairs in defiance of the political authority of Moscow. In 1993, the Russian government under Boris Yeltsin decided to use military force to crush Chechen independence. The first round of violence lasted two years, resulting in 100 000 casualties and nearly 400 000 refugees. Most of the major cities and towns of Chechnya were devastated by indiscriminate artillery and air bombardment, including the capital, Grozny. The war was very unpopular in Russia. A ceasefire in August 1996 saw the withdrawal of Russian troops from Chechnya and an agreement to defer the status of Chechnya for five years. During the ceasefire, the Chechen leadership continued to defy Moscow, and Russia continued its attempts to destabilize the Chechen leaders.

In August 1999 war returned to Chechnya as the Russian government under President Vladimir Putin sought an end to the conflict. The so-called Second Chechen War received more popular support in Russia after a series of bombings in Moscow was attributed to Chechens. The Chechen people (and indeed all people of the Caucasus) have been demonized in Russia as criminals or radical Islamists. Through the indiscriminate use of firepower and the deployment of 90 000 troops, Russia now controls most of Chechnya, although it has been unable to eliminate Chechen resistance or to impose complete authority over the entire breakaway republic. Despite the evident horrors of the war, international reaction to the Russian campaign was muted. Most countries verbally condemned the Russian government but, in an effort to maintain good relations with Russia, cited the right of the Russian government to maintain internal order in its own territory. A controversial referendum was held on a new republic constitution in March 2003. The referendum was run by the Russian government, and asked Chechens to confirm that Chechnya was part of the Russia in return for greater local autonomy. Despite widespread irregularities in the voting, it appears that a majority of Chechens supported the referendum in the hopes it would end the violence. However, a year later Chechnya still faced the legacy of both Chechen wars: a destroyed civilian infrastructure; a countryside ridden with land mines; and a population living in destitution with a fierce hatred of Moscow. Chechnya requires a massive reconstruction effort, and it is unlikely to receive such an effort from the very government that waged war on it.[59]

These examples are only a few of the ongoing and potential intrastate communal conflicts in the world. Other important conflicts with a communal dimension include

- *Israel and the Palestinian people.* This decades-old conflict between the Jewish and Palestinian peoples, who both claim the same territory as their own, has defied efforts to build a permanent peace. In September 1993, a peace process known as the Oslo track culminated in the signing of an agreement between Israel and the Palestine Liberation Organization (PLO). However, the peace process began to unravel after the assassination of Israeli Prime Minister Yitzhak Rabin in November 1995. Violence began to escalate in 1996 and has increased dramatically since 2000. Little progress has been made on outstanding issues such as the future of Jerusalem, the return of refugees, Israeli settlements, and division of territory and land. A number of Palestinian terrorist groups have employed suicide bombers against civilian and military targets in Israel. The Israeli government has responded with a hard-line policy of doubtful legality including air strikes, military incursions into Palestinian self-rule areas, economic coercion, and restrictions on Palestinian freedom of movement. These policies have in turn inflamed Palestinian sentiment toward Israel. In 2002, Israel began construction of a "security fence," which has become another source of tension between Israel and Palestinians.

- *The Kurds.* The Kurdish people are an ethnic group living in a large territory currently controlled by Turkey, Iraq, Iran, and Syria. Kurdish efforts to establish their own state

(Kurdistan) have led to periodic violence and terrorism by Kurdish separatist groups and brutal suppressions of Kurds by the governments of Turkey and Iraq. The Kurds in northern Iraq have had considerable autonomy over their own affairs since the 1990–91 Gulf War. The future of the Kurds living in post-Saddam Iraq is unclear. Separatist sentiment already runs high, and if the government of Iraq fails to satisfy Kurdish desires for regional autonomy and input into central government positions, renewed calls for separatism are likely, and the possibility of violence will increase.

- *The Sudan.* The intrastate war in Sudan has waged since 1956, apart from a nine-year break in the 1970s. The country is extraordinarily diverse, but in general the war has pitted an Arab Muslim government in the north against African Christian and animist militias in the south and west. The conflict has been waged over territory, religious practices, separatist claims, and oil. In 2002, peace talks began between the government and rebel groups, and significant progress was made by 2003 when the two sides had agreed on regional autonomy for the south, the sharing of oil revenues, and religious practices. A peace agreement was finally signed on May 26, 2004. However, in mid-2004 violence intensified in western Sudan, raising concerns that the peace process in the south might be derailed. In the summer of 2004 it became clear that yet another humanitarian disaster was looming in Dafur.

- *Indonesia.* In Indonesia, conflicts between separatist movements and the Indonesian government have occurred in several regions of the country. East Timor, long a point of international controversy because of the Indonesian government's invasion and occupation of the territory in 1976, became independent in 2002 after an international intervention in 1999. However, a violent separatist movement in Aceh continues to smolder after the collapse of peace talks in 2003. Separatist movements also exist in Irian Jaya and Kalimantan, while ethnic violence has broken out in Maluku. These conflicts continue to cause fears that the Indonesian state might disintegrate.

The cases we have examined here represent only a small percentage of the number of ongoing intrastate, communal conflicts in global politics. Every year, new conflicts emerge and many descend into violence. As a result, one of the core questions facing international conflict management is how such conflicts can be avoided and stopped. We will explore this question in Chapter 7. Of course, even a casual observer of the world's interstate and intrastate conflicts cannot help but notice the presence of weapons. The proliferation, or spread, of weapons around the world is a major international security concern, especially in the wake of September 11. It also seems as if conventional weapons, from missiles and tanks to small arms and land mines, are readily available everywhere on the post–Cold War map. We turn now to a discussion of the weapons proliferation problem in global politics.

THE PROLIFERATION OF WEAPONS

The proliferation of weapons comes in two forms. Vertical proliferation refers to increases in the number of weapons possessed by individual states; horizontal proliferation refers to the spread of military capabilities across states. In the contemporary international system, the most prominent proliferation concern is with the horizontal spread of weapons of mass destruction (nuclear weapons, chemical weapons, and biological weapons). Also of concern is the horizontal spread of conventional weapons, which include a wide variety of weapons systems such as fixed-wing and rotary aircraft, naval vessels, missiles, and armoured vehicles, as well as individual "light" weapons or "small arms" such as assault rifles, rocket-propelled grenades, and land mines. The proliferation of weapons is regarded with anxiety because regional arms races can exacerbate existing tensions or raise levels of distrust and hostility. In addition, should war break out, the parties to the conflict will be equipped with more modern weapons technology capable of high levels of destruction. Concern also exists that substate groups such as terrorist organizations are acquiring increasingly sophisticated weapons systems, including chemical and biological weapons. The control of the spread of weapons systems and weapons technology is, therefore, regarded as an important contribution to both preventing war and reducing the level of violence in future wars.

THE PROLIFERATION OF NUCLEAR WEAPONS

One of the greatest concerns today is the prospect of the spread of nuclear weapons capabilities to more states and perhaps to substate actors. In the 1960s it was thought that as many as 20 countries would have the bomb within a decade. Today, 8 countries possess nuclear weapons, with 4 more acquiring them but subsequently giving them up. However, these facts are no cause for complacency. As many as 30 countries in the world now have the requisite level of technological expertise and economic development to become nuclear weapons states. Currently, 7 states are *declared* nuclear powers, with the 8 (Israel) maintaining an *undeclared* status. Several other states have been attempting to develop a nuclear weapons capability as well (see Profile 6.3).

Some scholars—in particular, structural realists—have argued that nuclear weapons can have a steadying effect on regional stability.[60] As Kenneth Waltz argues, "the presence of nuclear weapons makes states exceedingly cautious. Why fight if you can't win much and might lose everything?"[61] Thus, nuclear proliferation may increase regional stability, by creating a multilateral nuclear peace. However, the prevailing view is that the spread of nuclear weapons is inherently dangerous.[62] Simply put, if more decision makers have the option of using nuclear weapons, then nuclear weapons are more likely to be used. The prospects for accidental or unauthorized nuclear release will increase, especially as many new nuclear

PROFILE 6.3	**Nuclear Weapons States:** **Past, Present, and Future**	
NUCLEAR WEAPONS STATES	**FORMER NUCLEAR WEAPONS STATES**	**FUTURE NUCLEAR WEAPONS STATES?**
United States (1945)	South Africa[b]	Iran
Russia (1949)	Ukraine[c]	Syria
United Kingdom (1952)	Belarus[c]	Iraq[d]
France (1960)	Kazakhstan[c]	Libya
China (1964)		Japan[e]
Israel (1969)[a]		North Korea[f]
India (tested 1974) (tested 1998)		
Pakistan (1992) (tested 1998)		

[a] Undeclared nuclear weapons state.
[b] South Africa developed nuclear weapons in the 1970s but unilaterally dismantled the weapons and the program.
[c] Ukraine, Belarus, and Kazakhstan all inherited the nuclear weapons on their soil after the collapse of the Soviet Union, but all three relinquished possession of those weapons.
[d] A significant nuclear weapons program was disrupted by the 1990–91 Gulf War. Ceasefire terms required Iraq to eliminate all nuclear-related facilities and materials. No nuclear weapons were found at the conclusion of 2003 Iraq War. Iraq can no longer be considered an imminent nuclear proliferation threat.
[e] Regarded as a very distant threat at this stage.
[f] In April 2003, North Korea informed U.S. officials it possessed a nuclear bomb.

weapons states may not invest the same effort or resources into the development of effective command and control systems. In addition, small nuclear arsenals may be more vulnerable to pre-emptive strikes, thus increasing the incentives to use nuclear weapons first in crisis or war. The social and environmental costs of nuclear arms races are tremendous, as the Russians and Americans are well aware.

Several rationales may motivate state leaders to develop a nuclear weapons capability. First, they may want to acquire nuclear weapons for security reasons, perceiving a threat from another country and seeking the bomb to act as a deterrent, as a war-fighting instrument, or as a weapon of last resort. Certainly, these reasons were important considerations in the respective decisions by the Soviet Union and by Pakistan to develop a nuclear capability. Second, state leaders may seek the prestige such a capability would bring to a country: nuclear weapons are equated with modernization and development. This idea was a factor in the Chinese and Indian nuclear weapons programs. Others might be seeking security, autonomy, and independence—the ability to be self-reliant when it comes to nuclear weapons. These factors were important in the motivation behind the development of France's Force de Frappe. Alternatively, some countries might develop (or attempt to develop) nuclear weapons because of isolation (South Africa) or ambition (Iraq). As we saw in Chapter 3, another possible explanation is the influence of domestic politics: nuclear weapons may be acquired to advance the interests of domestic groups, industries, and bureaucracies.[63]

What is required to become a nuclear weapons state? For any country seeking to develop nuclear weapons, several steps must be taken. First, the political will to develop the weapons must exist. Canada, for example, could build nuclear weapons tomorrow, but successive Canadian governments have decided not to do so. Second, a country must acquire the knowledge base required to build nuclear weapons. A country must develop its own nuclear scientists and technicians or purchase the services of foreign scientists and technicians. Some worry today that nuclear expertise from the former Soviet Union may be available to would-be nuclear weapons states. Working conditions and opportunities for scientists and technicians in the former Soviet Union are poor, and the concern is that they will be willing to sell their services and knowledge to the highest bidder. Third, a country must build the nuclear, industrial, and manufacturing infrastructure required to build a bomb. This infrastructure may involve the construction of a nuclear reactor, processing plants for nuclear material, and laboratories and manufacturing facilities. All this infrastructure takes time to build, is costly, and may be detected if the program is a clandestine one. Fourth, the country must acquire fissile material—highly enriched uranium or plutonium—for the bomb. This acquisition is often the most difficult challenge for would-be nuclear states, for this material is rare and must be purchased from abroad or mined and processed at home. Finally, a bomb design must be adopted and a decision made to assemble and deploy the weapons. A test may be necessary, although computer modelling has improved to the point where a country can have a high expectation that its bomb will work even if it is not tested. We will explore international efforts to prevent the proliferation of nuclear weapons in the next chapter, but the greatest obstacles to the spread of nuclear weapons remain the technical difficulty, costs, and long time frame associated with a nuclear weapons program.

While the Iraq War in 2003 removed Iraq from the list of nuclear proliferation concerns, the profile of the North Korean case has escalated dramatically. The isolated country began its nuclear weapons program in 1964, and efforts accelerated in the 1980s. Under increasing international suspicion, North Korea was suspected of having produced plutonium for a nuclear bomb by the early 1990s. The international response was to call for inspections of North Korea's nuclear facilities, which North Korea refused to permit. The Clinton

Administration began preparations to use force against North Korea. In October 1994 negotiations between the United States and North Korea led to a Framework Agreement in which the North Korean government agreed to stop its nuclear weapons program and give international inspectors leave to enter, in return for assistance in building replacement reactors for civilian use and regular supplies of fuel oil. In October 2002 North Korean officials admitted to having a program to enrich uranium for use in nuclear weapons, a violation of the 1994 agreement. Negotiations continued, and during a trilateral meeting between the United States, China, and North Korea in April 2003, a North Korean official informed U.S. representatives that North Korea had at least one nuclear weapon.[64] There was no independent verification of this claim, but if true it represents a dangerous development on the Korean peninsula and complicates future efforts at preventing the spread of nuclear weapons.

Of course, states are not the only actors who may be interested in acquiring nuclear weapons. Concern is increasing that nuclear weapons may fall into the hands of substate groups, especially terrorist organizations. This fear has been magnified by over a decade of concern over the security of weapons grade materials, technology, and warheads from the former Soviet Union and Russia.[65] While the concern is considerable, the likelihood of a terrorist organization acquiring a nuclear device or the capability to produce one is remote. Terrorist organizations may not be able to achieve their goals with a weapon so destructive, and its use (or the threat of its use) might be counterproductive. Developing such weapons is not easy and is beyond the resources of most substate actors. Stealing a weapon is also a difficult proposition, but even if a warhead could be obtained, the terrorists would still have to find someone with the knowledge to detonate the bomb, which is a rare talent. Nevertheless, the threat of nuclear terrorism cannot be ignored, because the use of even trace amounts of plutonium in a "radiological" or "dirty" bomb is a possibility and because the implications are so enormous.

A NUCLEAR SOUTH ASIA

One of the most significant developments in nuclear weapons proliferation after the Cold War took place in May 1998. From May 11 to 13, India conducted five nuclear tests, and Pakistan followed suit with six tests between May 28 and 30. While India had tested a nuclear device in 1974 and Pakistan was thought to have nuclear weapons by 1992, these tests heightened tensions in South Asia and increased awareness of the dangers of nuclear proliferation. International condemnation was swift, as countries such as the United States, Japan, Australia, and Canada imposed sanctions on India and Pakistan. The sanctions hurt both economies (especially Pakistan's), but neither country showed any indication of renouncing its nuclear weapons program. Although both countries were accused of violating international norms on nuclear testing and damaging the non-proliferation regime, Indian and Pakistani officials argued that such accusations were hypocritical. After all, they argued, most of their accusers possess nuclear weapons or benefit from the security provided by them. Did not India and Pakistan have the same right as sovereign states to respond to their own security requirements?

As we indicated in Chapter 3, the relevance of nuclear deterrence did not end with the Cold War. Nuclear deterrence is alive and well in South Asia, with concerns that two countries that have fought three wars might fight a fourth war with nuclear weapons. These concerns were exacerbated by the development of ballistic missiles by both countries. However, the nuclear tests might have imposed the same threat of mutual annihilation on India and Pakistan that existed between the superpowers during the Cold War. Indeed, on February 20, 2000, the leaders of India and Pakistan inaugurated the first bus service between the two countries in

50 years, using the occasion to reinforce their desire for peace and to avoid a nuclear war. It seemed that the nuclear weapons might compel the two states toward a closer political relationship, much in the same way the United States and the U.S.S.R. established a closer (though still antagonistic) relationship as the Cold War progressed. However, in the summer of 2000, a border skirmish in Kashmir between Pakistani-backed separatists and the Indian military increased tensions between the two countries and illustrated that the possession of nuclear weapons would not necessarily prevent conflict between them.

In Chapter 3 we discussed some varying explanations for why India and Pakistan tested nuclear weapons in 1998. Several factors played a role in India, including the enthusiasm of nuclear scientists, the Indian government's desire to increase domestic support, the threat from Pakistan and China, and the desire to be seen as a great power. Pakistan's government was under enormous pressure to respond to the Indian tests and not appear weak. Growing conventional military inferiority meant nuclear weapons promised security from India. And the Pakistani military, a strong force in Pakistani politics, was largely in favour of the tests. Public opinion in both countries was solidly behind the tests, with large crowds celebrating in an atmosphere of national fervour. Yet there were dissenters: in 1998, thousands of protestors marched in India and Pakistan to oppose the tests. It is possible that these groups will be the beginning of growing regional antinuclear movements similar to those that existed in the West during the Cold War. As one Indian commentator lamented, "A country that has nearly half its population living in absolute poverty, that has an illiterate population more than 2.5 times that of Sub-Saharan Africa, that has more than half its children over the age of four living in malnourishment can never be a superpower."[66] To outsiders, foreign governments, and opponents of nuclear weapons, the tests were sadly inappropriate for two countries mired in poverty and struck a serious blow to efforts to reduce the stockpile of nuclear armaments.

THE PROLIFERATION OF CHEMICAL AND BIOLOGICAL WEAPONS

Although the proliferation of nuclear weapons has attracted much of the attention of scholars, government officials, and the public, the proliferation of chemical and biological weapons may be a more urgent and pressing concern. Chemical and biological warfare involves the dissemination of chemicals or living organisms over military or civilian targets. The primary vector—that is, the medium through which the chemical or biological warfare agent reaches a human being—is the atmosphere, although these weapons can be transmitted to humans through water and surface contact as well. Chemical agents include mustard gas, phosgene, cyanide, and the nerve agents sarin, soman, and tabun, among many others. Biological weapons are living organisms that multiply within the host, eventually killing it. Biological agents include plague, dysentery, typhus, anthrax, smallpox, yellow fever, and botulism. Research and development have produced newer and deadlier chemicals, and biotechnology has led to the development of various engineered bacteria and viruses.

Chemical weapons were used extensively in World War I. The Japanese Imperial Army used chemical and biological weapons in China during World War II. Chemical weapons were used by the United States in Vietnam, in the form of napalm, defoliants, and tear gas. There were persistent allegations of chemical weapons use in Afghanistan and in Cambodia. During the Iran–Iraq War (1980–88), Iraq used chemical weapons at the front against Iranian troops and also used chemical weapons against a Kurdish rebellion in northern Iraq. In 1995, nerve gas was used in a terrorist attack in the Tokyo subway system. Chemical weapons have limited utility against well-trained and well-equipped military personnel. Against such forces, they are largely of nuisance value, forcing soldiers to wear hot, cumbersome, and restrictive protective clothing. Biological weapons have a limited battlefield utility, as they take time to incapacitate

PROFILE 6.4	**States with Chemical and Biological Weapons**		
CHEMICAL WEAPONS		**BIOLOGICAL WEAPONS**	
Known:	Iran, Libya, North Korea, Syria	Known:	
Probable:	China, Egypt, Ethiopia, Israel, Myanmar, Pakistan, Taiwan	Probable:	China, Cuba, Egypt, Iran, Libya, North Korea, Russia, Syria
Possible/ Suspected:	Algeria, Cuba, Sudan, Vietnam	Possible/ Suspected:	Algeria, India, Israel, Pakistan, Sudan, Taiwan
Former:	Canada, France, Germany, India, Italy, Japan, South Africa, United Kingdom, United States, Yugoslavia (Federal Republic of)	Former:	France, Germany, Iraq, Japan, South Africa, United Kingdom, United States

SOURCE: "CHEMICAL AND BIOLOGICAL WEAPONS: POSSESSION AND PROGRAMS PAST AND PRESENT," CENTER FOR NONPROLIFERATION STUDIES, MONTEREY INSTITUTE OF INTERNATIONAL STUDIES, http://cns.miis.edu/research/cbw/possess.htm (ACCESSED 28 JUNE 2004).

or kill. However, both chemical and biological weapons can be devastating against unprotected military personnel or civilians, which is why they are classified as weapons of mass destruction.

Why would political or military leaders want to acquire chemical or biological weapons? Some countries may acquire such weapons for use on the battlefield, particularly if their prospective opponent is not well equipped with protective clothing. The use of gas by Iraq during the Iran–Iraq War demonstrated the utility and effectiveness of such weapons against unprepared opponents. Other countries may acquire these weapons for deterrent purposes, reasoning that if they possess such weapons, other countries will be reluctant to attack them. Compared with the costs associated with nuclear weapons, chemical and biological weapons are relatively inexpensive to develop and produce. As a result, chemical and biological weapons have been called "the poor state's nuclear weapon." Furthermore, the technology to produce such weapons is readily available and accessible; much of the equipment used does not vary widely from fertilizer or chemical industry technology. The materials required are also not difficult to obtain; the precursors, or component chemicals, for most chemical weapons are common industrial compounds that can be purchased openly on the international market. Research facilities need not be large or expensive: one U.S. study managed to build a small biological weapons facility for U.S.$1.6 million.[67] In short, countries unwilling to invest the time and expense of developing nuclear weapons may find chemical or biological weapons an effective and economical alternative (see Profile 6.4).

THE PROLIFERATION OF CONVENTIONAL WEAPONS

Although weapons of mass destruction receive more publicity, conventional weapons have been responsible for the overwhelming majority of deaths and casualties in the world's wars since 1945. For the most part, these casualties are caused by small arms and light weapons, such as military rifles, grenades, rocket launchers, and land mines. The problem of conventional weapons proliferation has three dimensions: the legal international arms trade, the covert arms trade, and the indigenous development and production of weapons. The bulk of conventional weapons that change hands in the international system do so through the perfectly legal international arms trade, consisting of arms deliveries between governments and between corporate manufacturers and governments. The world arms trade has contracted considerably from Cold War levels, but that contraction seems to have slowed, and the arms trade has stabilized for the last few years. In 2002 the value of world arms transfers totalled U.S.$16.5 billion (at constant 1990 prices), a decline from the 1998 total of U.S.$23.2 billion. Between 1998 and 2002, world arms transfers totalled U.S.$92.544 billion.[68] Traditionally, the bulk of the arms trade has consisted of transfers from the industrialized countries to the developing world. Since the 1970s, three-quarters of all weapons shipments were transfers to the developing world. In the last decade of the Cold War, developing states spent U.S.$430.6 billion on weapons purchases. Most major weapons systems—armoured vehicles, naval craft, aircraft, and missiles—were delivered to the Middle East. In 2002, arms transfers to the developing world accounted for 65 percent of the global arms trade. Between 1998 and 2002, Asia imported 40 percent of all arms transfers. During that same time period, the Middle East accounted for 24 percent of imports, Europe 20 percent, Africa 6 percent, and Latin America 5 percent. China overtook Taiwan as the leading arms importer in the world between 1998 and 2002, importing U.S.$8.82 billion worth of arms.[69] The leading supplier states remain the industrialized countries, with Russia surpassing the United States as the world's leading arms supplier in 2000. In 2002, Russia accounted for 36 percent of all arms exports. Between 1998 and 2002, the United States was the leading arms supplier in the world (see figures 6.2 and 6.3).

The fall in arms sales after 1991 was the result of three factors. The end of the Cold War and the collapse of the Soviet Union greatly reduced the availability of armaments from that country (which had been responsible for three-fifths of world arms exports between 1985 and 1989). Strained budgets in the South, even among the relatively wealthier countries of the Middle East, mean that less money is available for the purchase of weapons systems. Indigenous weapons production in an increasing number of countries has reduced the extent to which they are reliant on weapons purchased from abroad. Nevertheless, the global trade

Figure 6.2 Leading Suppliers of Major Conventional Weapons by Value, 1998–2002

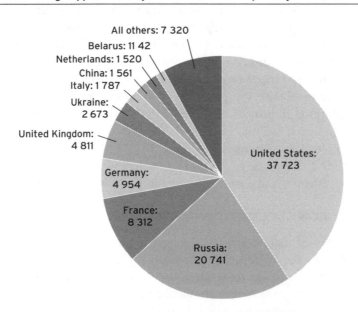

All others: 7 320
Belarus: 11 42
Netherlands: 1 520
China: 1 561
Italy: 1 787
Ukraine: 2 673
United Kingdom: 4 811
Germany: 4 954
France: 8 312
Russia: 20 741
United States: 37 723

Total value: 92 544
(U.S.$ millions, 1990 prices)

SOURCE: B. HAGELIN, M. BROMLEY, AND S.T. WEZEMAN, "THE VOLUME OF TRANSFERS OF MAJOR CONVENTIONAL WEAPONS: BY RECIPIENTS AND SUPPLIERS, 1999–2003," IN *SIPRI YEARBOOK, 2004: DISARMAMENT AND INTERNATIONAL SECURITY* (OXFORD UNIVERSITY PRESS, 2004), PP. 475–480 (PRE-PRINT VERSION).

in armaments remains very lucrative and a subject of considerable dismay to those concerned with the economic development of these countries and the improvement of the quality of life for their citizens.

Another point of concern is the quality of many weapons now being purchased. Because of the shrinking nature of the international arms market, the level of competition has escalated. As a result, many of the very best weapons are up for sale, and many countries are purchasing weapons that represent significant improvements over their past inventories. Particular concern exists over the spread of ballistic missile capabilities, which could be used to deliver nuclear, chemical, or biological weapons in various regional settings. In addition, many countries are acquiring sea-skimming antiship missiles, modern tanks, new fighter aircraft, and submarines. Competition has also led most arms companies to offer generous offset packages to prospective buyers, which take a variety of forms. The importing country might be permitted to manufacture certain components of the weapon domestically under licence (and perhaps in time the entire weapon). Some offset packages permit the permanent transfer of technology to the recipient country. Governments may assist their own arms industries by lifting export restrictions on certain armaments. In other cases, governments may offer financing or credit to prospective buyers to secure the contract for their own arms industry.

The arms industry itself is also in the process of transformation. Just as global economic interdependence has facilitated the internationalization of civilian business, finance, and manufacture, it has also facilitated the internationalization of the arms industry. Weapons systems can now use components and technology from a variety of different countries and corporations. Why do governments allow, encourage, and help weapons manufacturers sell their product abroad? In some cases, hard currency is the main motivation, especially if that country is in dire need of cash. For some countries (such as Russia), military hardware is a significant export and hard-currency earner in the country's economy. Jobs are another incentive to secure

Figure 6.3 Leading Recipients of Major Conventional Weapons by Value, 1998–2002

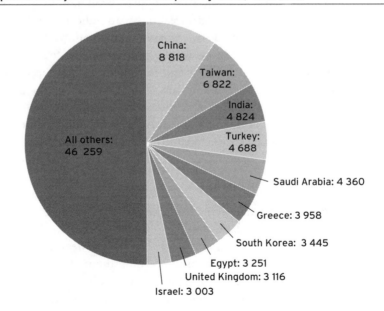

China: 8 818
Taiwan: 6 822
India: 4 824
Turkey: 4 688
Saudi Arabia: 4 360
Greece: 3 958
South Korea: 3 445
Egypt: 3 251
United Kingdom: 3 116
Israel: 3 003
All others: 46 259

Total value: 92 544
(U.S.$ millions, 1990 prices)

SOURCE: DATA FROM STOCKHOLM INTERNATIONAL PEACE RESEARCH INSTITUTE, *SIPRI YEARBOOK, 2003* (OXFORD: OXFORD UNIVERSITY PRESS, 2003), 466.

arms deals abroad. Producing states will encourage arms exports to maintain production activity and the employment that activity brings. Producing states may also want to maintain their manufacturing capability (sometimes called the defence industrial base) and keep their production lines open for future sales. As long as the production line is busy, the skilled workforce, design teams, and manufacturing facilities will remain intact. If the production line has to close down, these assets may be lost. Finally, producers may want to encourage sales abroad to lower the unit cost of the weapon. If a weapons system has a long production run and large numbers are produced, the costs of that weapon on a per unit basis will be lower than if the weapons system was manufactured in lower quantities. The larger the production run, the lower the costs of each individual weapons system, making the weapons system more affordable, both for foreign buyers and for domestic purchasers.

In comparison to the legal arms trade, the covert arms trade is harder to track. The value of the covert trade in armaments (or *gunrunning*, as it is sometimes called) is estimated at between U.S.$2 billion and U.S.$10 billion per year.[70] International arms dealers purchase weapons and stockpile them for sale on the black market, or broker sales between sellers and buyers. The weapons may have been purchased legitimately, stolen from military stocks, diverted from their original destinations, or purchased in war-torn regions from individuals or groups that have a large surplus of weapons available for sale to any bidder. In some cases, weapons available for illegal sales may be sold by companies that failed to observe embargoes or export rules, sometimes with the tacit approval of governments. The weapons are then transported through transshipment points to their buyers. During the war in the former Yugoslavia, despite a UN arms **embargo**, more than U.S.$2 billion worth of armaments was covertly shipped into the country in 1993 alone.[71]

Another characteristic of conventional weapons proliferation is the development of indigenous production of weapons systems, which has occurred for several reasons. Many countries have developed the technological infrastructure and expertise to manufacture more modern weapons systems. Other countries have manufactured certain weapons or components under licence and have acquired production rights over time. For other countries, the ability to produce modern weapons is an indicator of their technical and industrial expertise. This phenomenon has two worrying implications. First, efforts to increase controls over the proliferation of weapons will be complicated by the fact that more and more states are producing their own weapons and relying less on purchases from abroad. Second, the growth of indigenous production means that more countries are producing weapons for export, increasing the number of producer states in the world. As we will see in the next chapter, concern over the proliferation of all types of weapons systems has led to the creation of a number of international efforts to control the global spread of armaments.

INTERNATIONAL TERRORISM

Few international events have the emotional impact that incidents of terrorism generate. In many cases, incidents are often broadcast around the world, even as they transpire, by the global media. Images and stories of horror, death, injury, and kidnapping are paralleled by revelations or speculations concerning the motive for the attacks. The surprise that attends most acts of terrorism contributes to this international impact; without warning, a plane is hijacked, a bomb explodes, or individuals are kidnapped or taken hostage. And yet, many more cases go unnoticed or unreported. Terrorism directly or indirectly affects the policies of all actors in global politics, and terrorist activity often stretches across borders and regions. In this sense, it is a transnational security concern. It affects the decisions of governments and the way multinational corporations do business and is on the agenda of both IGOs and

NGOs. Military and police forces must be equipped and prepared to respond to terrorist acts. Huge sums are spent every year on counterterrorism and security measures at airports and public places. Terrorism influences the travel decisions of tourists and causes a perpetual state of anxiety in many societies. The terrorist attacks committed against the United States on September 11, 2001, have thrown all of the debates about terrorism and counterterrorism into sharp relief and raised the profile of international terrorism to a level never witnessed before. The United States and many other countries now regard international terrorism as the most important security threat they face. People living in Canada have been fortunate as Canada has been relatively unscathed by terrorist attacks. Although 25 Canadians died in the September 11 attacks, and there can be no doubt that international terrorists use Canada as a travel conduit, a location for fundraising, and a place where a small minority of sympathetic individuals might be found, incidents of terrorism in Canada have been rare. The FLQ Crisis and the activities of Direct Action are the exceptions rather than the rule (see Profile 6.5).

Terrorism is far from a recent phenomenon. Terrorist incidents, or the causes that motivate them, often have deep historical roots. Traditionally, terrorism has been the weapon of the weak, employed as a political instrument by individuals or groups seeking to reject authority, generate social change, promote revolution, or spread fear. Historical examples of the use of terrorism include the Zealots, a Jewish sect that appeared in B.C.E. 6 and used assassinations in an effort to force the Roman Empire out of Palestine. In the Middle East between 1090 and 1275 C.E., Muslims known as *hashashin* (from which the word "assassin" originates) carried out many political and religious killings on behalf of their political and spiritual leaders. In 1605, a group of English Catholics conspired to blow up James I of England, in the failed "gunpowder plot." At the end of the 19th century, political assassinations by anarchists claimed U.S. President William McKinley, French President Sadi Carnot, the Empress Elizabeth of Austria, and Spanish Prime Minister Antonio Canovas. World War I began with an act of terrorism— the assassination of Austrian Archduke Franz Ferdinand—by a Serbian terrorist organization called the Black Hand. In an eerie precursor to contemporary car bombings, in 1920 a horse-drawn cart exploded on Wall Street in New York City, killing 40 and injuring 300 in an attack that remains unsolved. In 1946, the Jewish Irgun Tsvai-Leumi bombed the King David Hotel, the headquarters of the British Secretariat in Palestine, killing 91 people. At the 1972 Olympics in Munich, the Palestinian group Black September killed 11 Israeli athletes. Also in 1972, "Bloody Friday" claimed 9 lives and injured 130 as 22 bombs planted by the Irish Republican Army exploded in and around Belfast. In 1980, government-backed death squads in El Salvador killed a Catholic priest and four U.S. nuns. In 1985, a bomb placed on board Air India Flight 182 by Sikh extremists at Vancouver International Airport killed 329 people. North Korean agents planted a bomb on Korean Airlines Flight 858 in 1987, killing all 115 on board. In 1993, a car bomb exploded in the underground parking lot of the World Trade Center Towers in New York, killing six. In 1995, a Japanese cult named Aum Shinrikyo released sarin nerve gas in the Tokyo subway system, killing 12 and injuring 5000. In the same year, 168 people were killed when Timothy McVeigh and his associates detonated a truck bomb outside the federal building in Oklahoma City. In 1999, Ahmed Rassam, an Algerian national, was arrested crossing the Canada–United States border with explosive materials for a bomb intended to attack Los Angeles International Airport. These incidents are but a small fraction of the terrorist acts perpetrated over the years, and illustrate how terrorism as a historical phenomenon cuts across countries, regions, and cultures.

There is no universally accepted definition of terrorism in international law. Definitions of terrorism are notoriously difficult to construct, in part because terrorism is a politically charged word, and is often used inappropriately for political purposes. The familiar adage "one person's terrorist is another's freedom fighter" illustrates the relative nature of the term.

PROFILE 6.5 The FLQ Crisis

Although it is not a case of international terrorism, the FLQ Crisis in Canada is the most prominent example of terrorism on Canadian soil. The Front du Libération du Québec (FLQ), a self-styled revolutionary movement advocating independence for an "oppressed Québec," engaged in a series of bombings in Montreal in 1969. The FLQ kidnapped the British Trade Commissioner for Quebec, James Cross, and Quebec Minister of Labour Pierre Laporte (who was subsequently murdered). In response, Prime Minister Pierre Trudeau invoked the War Measures Act, calling in the Armed Forces, which patrolled Montreal streets, restricting travel and movement. The Royal Canadian Mounted Police, using broad local powers of seizure and arrest to locate the FLQ, arrested more than 400 suspects, of whom 62 were brought to trial and 20 convicted. The FLQ was eliminated as an organized group. Trudeau's decision remains controversial, with some calling it a scar on Canada's civil liberties record and an abuse of state power over its citizens. Others argue that the government had to respond forcefully to terrorism. The FLQ was crushed, and all civil liberties were swiftly restored. After the crisis, the federal government embarked on measures to address some of the grievances of the French community, including increased investment in French-speaking areas.

Many different types of terrorism occur, and it is difficult to establish a single definition that accounts for all of them. Walter Laqueur defines terrorism as "the substate application of violence or threatened violence intended to sow panic in a society, to weaken or even overthrow the incumbents, and to bring about political change."[72] Cindy Combs defines terrorism as "a synthesis of war and theatre, a dramatization of the most proscribed kind of violence—that which is perpetrated on innocent victims—played before an audience in the hope of creating a mood of fear, for political purposes."[73] Paul Wilkinson's definition is more comprehensive:

> Terrorism is the systematic use of coercive intimidation, usually to serve political ends. It is used to create and exploit a climate of fear among a wider target group than the immediate victims of the violence, often to publicize a cause, as well as to coerce a target into acceding to terrorist aims. Terrorism may be used on its own or as part of a wider conventional war. It can be employed by desperate and weak minorities, by states as a tool of domestic and foreign policy, or by belligerents as an accompaniment or additional weapon in all types and stages of warfare. A common feature is that innocent civilians, sometimes foreigners who know nothing of the terrorist's political quarrel, are killed or injured.[74]

Definitions of international terrorism introduce an additional element. As Suman Gupta argues, in cases of international terrorist acts "the motives and/or agencies and/or effects cross the boundaries of nation-states, and are not necessarily conducted (certainly seldom directly) at the behest of any nation-state."[75]

Paul Wilkinson's definition reminds us that individuals and groups are not the only perpetrators of terrorism. Although the image of the small terrorist cell operating in a clandestine fashion in the city or countryside is the most popular conception of terrorism, much of the terrorism in the world is planned and executed by states against their own citizens. **State terrorism** is employed by states within their own borders to suppress dissent and silence opposition. Such campaigns frequently involve massive human rights violations, an issue we shall return to in later chapters. State terrorism also has deep historical roots. The Roman emperor

Nero killed large numbers of suspected political opponents, including members of his own family. In the French Revolution, state terrorism was employed as a tool of the French Republic to get rid of its enemies. During the years of racial segregation, or apartheid, in South Africa, government hit squads killed political opponents of the regime to spread fear and to intimidate others. In the late 1970s, the Khmer Rouge in Cambodia systematically murdered approximately 1.5 to 2 million people in an effort to fulfill a bizarre ideological purification of the country. The military government of Argentina was responsible for the deaths of almost 10 000 people in 1976–77 alone. In the 1980s, the government of Guatemala used death squads to conduct assassinations and kidnappings of political opponents. Accusations of state terrorism have been directed against Israel for its actions against Palestinians. Such state terrorism differs from **state-sponsored terrorism**, which is the support of international terrorist individuals or groups by a government. Libya once provided sanctuary and assistance to the Abu Nidal Organization, and Iran has supported the operations of Hamas and Hizbollah, among others. Many accusations of state-sponsored terrorism have been directed against the United States: the arming and training of the Contras in Nicaragua in their effort to overthrow the Sandinista government is but one example.

THE ORIGINS AND CAUSES OF TERRORISM

State terrorism is designed to eliminate political opposition, and the killers and torturers who engage in it are paid for their work, which can even become routine for them. But what causes the nonstate terrorist to commit acts of violence against innocent people? In most cases, terrorist acts will be committed for a number of motives. If appropriate and effective counterterrorist strategies are to be developed, an understanding of these motives is essential. Studies of terrorism and terrorists suggest that terrorism can be explained by the following factors:

Individual Psychology

Some researchers suggest that the root cause of terrorism is the psychological makeup of the individuals who participate in terrorist activities. In particular, psychologists and psychiatrists suggest that personality disorders or even mental illness may explain terrorist activity.

Ideological Fanaticism

Terrorism can originate from the commitment of individuals and groups to a particular political idea and their efforts to promote this political idea through violence. Ideologies such as Marxism-Leninism, fascism, and extreme racism offer a framework for interpreting social injustice and inequality and identifying those responsible, and provide a program of action to build a better society. Terrorists are thus committed to the idea of social change through violence.

Religious Fanaticism

Terrorist acts may originate in religious extremism, drawn from literal interpretations of religious beliefs. Often, religious fanaticism employs a belief system that is in fact a perversion of the principles of that religion. Terrorist acts are carried out by individuals or groups seeking to advance their religious views, secure religious rights or freedoms, or wage a holy war against their religious enemies.

Grievance and Cycles of Violence

Terrorist acts may originate with the grievances of a particular group. This group may be the target of discrimination and repression, which may include economic, political, or religious persecution. In some instances, this persecution may be violent. Although the relationship between poverty and terrorism is uncertain, the combination of economic and political grievances can create angry and resentful individuals, who can then be recruited and indoctrinated to carry out acts of violence against the perceived enemy.

Nationalism and Separatism

Terrorism may also originate from the desire of individuals within a larger community for greater political autonomy or even full independence. While this desire often originates with a history of grievances, the specific aim of the terrorist activity is to advance the political independence of a group.

Activist Fanaticism

Terrorist activity may also originate from a very specific issue or controversy that provokes certain individuals or groups to violence. The aim of such violence is to prevent certain political or social activity or to force their belief systems on others. Such issues include abortion, animal rights, racial superiority, and environmental protection.

Despite the shock and horror that terrorism evokes, terrorism is seldom successful in achieving its stated objectives. While terrorist activity is designed to promote a cause, it can often have the opposite effect. Terrorist activity can alienate other supporters of the cause who do not believe that violence is the appropriate instrument for advancing their interests or beliefs. Terrorism can also discredit moderates, who become associated with the violence even though they have no connection to it. While a harsh backlash against terrorists by a central authority can drive more people to the terrorists' cause, these measures can also lead to persecution and repression of the people or group the terrorist organization is supposedly fighting for.

SEPTEMBER 11, 2001

On the morning of September 11, 2001, 19 terrorists used box cutters and verbal threats to hijack four civilian airliners in the United States. They overpowered the crews and commandeered the planes. On board each plane was one hijacker who had taken flight training lessons in the United States. Two of the aircraft were deliberately crashed into the two towers of the World Trade Center in New York, which subsequently collapsed due to the structural damage and fire caused by the collisions. The third hijacked plane was crashed into the Pentagon, the headquarters of the American military establishment. The fourth plane, whose target was believed to have been either the Capitol Building or the White House, crashed into a field in Pennsylvania when the passengers tried to overpower the hijackers. Over 3000 people were killed that morning. The images of the attacks were transmitted around the world on television and the Internet. For most, it was a day of profound shock and dismay, as well as fear and uncertainty of what might happen next. All civilian airline traffic in the United States was grounded, and most flights inbound from other parts of the world were diverted to Canada. The Canada–United States border was closed, bringing cross-border travel and commerce to a halt. In the following days, as transportation systems in North America resumed operation and cleanup efforts started to remove rubble and human remains, the funerals of the victims began, and expressions of sympathy and support were extended to the United States from around the world. Many questions were also being asked: Who committed these attacks? And why?

The September 11 attacks were the result of years of planning and preparation by a small group of terrorists associated with Al-Qaeda, a terrorist group lead by Osama Bin Laden. As early as two days after the attacks, official suspicion fell on Al-Qaeda, as the organization had been responsible for the bombing of the World Trade Center in 1993, the bombings of U.S. embassies in Africa in 1998, and an attack on a U.S. warship in 2000. The Clinton

9:03 a.m., September 11, 2001. United Airlines Flight 175 strikes the south tower of the World Trade Center in New York, just 18 minutes after American Airlines Flight 11 hit the north tower. Both towers subsequently collapsed. (AP Photo/Moshe Bursuker/CP Archive)

Administration had identified Al-Qaeda as the number one enemy of the United States, and had attempted to disrupt its operations and capture Osama Bin Laden. Al-Qaeda was a formidable network of loosely associated terrorist cells, controlled by a leadership group under Osama Bin Laden. With operations in over 50 countries, Al-Qaeda engaged in the planning and execution of terrorist attacks; fund-raising and revenue-generating efforts including charities, businesses, and smuggling operations; and the training of thousands of terrorist fighters, primarily in bases in Afghanistan. Investigation of the September 11 hijackers revealed that some had entered the United States legally on student visas, though not through Canada as some earlier reports had suggested. Cell phone and transaction records revealed that some of the hijackers had been in contact with known Al-Qaeda operatives in Europe and the Middle East. The case against Al-Qaeda grew, and on September 17, Osama Bin Laden was formally accused as the perpetrator of the attacks. A great deal of criticism was directed against the U.S. intelligence community, which failed to detect preparations for the attack despite some early warning signs that an attack was imminent. The Bush Administration has also been criticized for focusing on Iraq and failing to take Al-Qaeda as seriously as it should have upon entering office.

The motive for the attacks has been the subject of considerable debate and controversy. The increasing resentment directed against the United States in large parts of the world in general and the Islamic world in particular was well understood by observers of global politics (though not the American population at large). Anti-American sentiment was built on a wide array of grievances that include U.S. support for Israel (and therefore complicity in the repression of the Palestinian people), U.S. assistance to repressive regimes in the Islamic world, the growing cultural influences of the United States, and a reaction against Western modernization and globalization, which is led in large part by Washington. The world perspective of Osama Bin Laden and the Al-Qaeda ideology used an extreme interpretation of these grievances, and combined them with a particular brand of Islamic fundamentalism, to recruit and train young volunteers for a perverse form of *jihad* or holy war against America and the West. However, there may also have been a broader political purpose behind the attacks. Al-Qaeda had long regarded most Middle Eastern governments as enemies of Islam. The September 11 attacks may have been intended to precipitate an American reaction that would lead to a general uprising and revolution across the Arab world. Critics of U.S. foreign policy also pointed out that Bin Laden (virtually unknown at this time) and other extremists had received U.S. assistance during the Cold War in their fight against the Soviet occupation of Afghanistan. Of course, any suggestion that the United States may have been even partially responsible for the September 11 attacks was rejected by Washington, which chose to cast the attacks as an act of unjustified aggression by extremists. In one sense, this sentiment is understandable, as none of the 3000 people who were killed in the attacks had any hand in the real or imagined grievances of the attackers, and it is hard to imagine any political leader acknowledging that a terrorist attack might have been understandable. Moreover, one cannot blame U.S. foreign policy in isolation from other factors, including the hate- and ambition-inspired motives of terrorist leaders and the propaganda and invective they employ to guide others to kill in the name of faith or politics. It is difficult to imagine any political initiatives that could satisfy Al-Qaeda, whose spokesman, Suleiman Abu Ghaith, stated that there could be no truce until 4 million Americans had been killed.[76] However, in another sense this rejection of responsibility by the United States government is a counterproductive sentiment, for it absolves the United States of any critical reflection on its role in the world. The United States cannot detach itself or its policy decisions from the political and economic grievances that even now are being used to preach hatred and violence against it, and to recruit future generations of poor, desperate, ignorant, angry, and easily misled youth to be the next generation of terrorists.

Once Al-Qaeda was identified as the perpetrator, the United States began to move against the group's primary base of operations in Afghanistan, which was controlled by the Taliban, a predominantly ethnic Pashtun group that had seized power over most of Afghanistan in 1997, with the exception of the north of the country where groups opposed to the Taliban continued to fight against Taliban forces. Composed largely of students of religious schools preaching an extremist form of Islam, the Taliban government was already isolated from the international community for its harsh imposition of Islamic law and its treatment of women. The United States accused the Taliban government of harbouring Al-Qaeda terrorists and Osama Bin Laden and demanded they be handed over to the United States. The Taliban government refused, and the diplomatic efforts of Pakistan and Saudi Arabia to change the Taliban government's position were unsuccessful. The Bush Administration began a war against Afghanistan on October 7, 2001. The war in Afghanistan received considerable international support, including a UN Security Council resolution authorizing force. Thirty-three countries offered military forces, and many others offered political support, including permission for U.S. forces to fly through their airspace or establish military bases on their territory. Through a combination of Special Forces personnel on the ground cooperating with anti-Taliban forces in the north, and the extensive use of airpower, the United States–led coalition successfully overthrew the Taliban government in November. Military operations continued in an effort to catch and defeat Taliban and Al-Qaeda forces in the south of the country. Many senior Taliban and Al-Qaeda figures were captured or killed, but Osama Bin Laden himself seems to have eluded capture or death. Approximately 600 Al-Qaeda and Taliban suspects have been detained at the U.S. naval base at Guantanamo Bay, Cuba. The detention of these suspects has been very controversial, with critics charging that the U.S. is violating international law by detaining the suspects without trial or access to legal counsel. The United States has classified the detainees as unlawful combatants, and therefore not subject to the legal protection of the Geneva Conventions on the treatment of prisoners of war.

Even as the campaign in Afghanistan was being planned, the United States was also waging a less public but no less important battle to combat Al-Qaeda through global cooperation in intelligence gathering and the disruption of the group's financing system. The UN Security Council established a counterterrorism committee, and along with the UN General Assembly adopted several resolutions on combating international terrorism. The law enforcement and intelligence resources of dozens of countries were directed against Al-Qaeda, disrupting the group's capacity to communicate, travel, and raise money. In the 18 months after September 11, various financial institutions froze approximately U.S.$125 million in suspected terrorist assets.[77] Pakistan was a country of considerable importance in the effort against Al-Qaeda, due to its long common border with Afghanistan and the use of its territory by Taliban and Al-Qaeda fighters. However, the government of Pakistan was in a difficult position, as support for the Taliban regime and anti-American sentiment made cooperation with Washington deeply unpopular. In the end, the government supported Washington, but not before U.S. sanctions on Pakistan (imposed after the 1998 nuclear tests) had been lifted. The "War on Terrorism" also had an important domestic dimension around the world. In the United States, the Patriot Act was passed, increasing the power of police and intelligence agencies to arrest and detain noncitizens, and to use wiretaps and intercept e-mails. Many other countries, including Canada, also increased law enforcement powers and relaxed controls on privacy laws. The "War on Terrorism" has thus precipitated a significant civil liberties debate, with critics charging that such legal changes have infringed on the freedoms of citizens.

Has the campaign against Al-Qaeda been successful? Along with the military campaign in Afghanistan, the international diplomatic and law enforcement effort did yield some results. As many as half of the 30 key Al-Qaeda leaders and as many as 2000 confirmed Al-Qaeda fighters have been killed or arrested.[78] Several large-scale terrorist operations have been foiled, including a plot to attack several embassies in Singapore in 2002. Al-Qaeda has lost its base of operations in Afghanistan, damaging recruitment and training efforts. However, in many ways Al-Qaeda survives as perhaps a more effective and impenetrable network. The organization has been forced to become less centralized and less dependent on fixed bases and infrastructure. It has managed to maintain a communications, coordination, and financing system through the Internet and a system of clandestine individual-to-individual contacts. It has increasingly forged ties with local terrorist organizations, providing money, planning expertise, and inspiration to groups with which it may have only a loose affiliation or ideological affinity.[79] As a result, Al-Qaeda has not lost its capacity to act. Although caution must always be taken when attributing terrorism to any particular organization, Al-Qaeda is believed to have been involved, along with local terrorist groups, in the terrorist attacks in Bali in October 2002, the bombing of a hotel and the attempt to shoot down an airliner with a shoulder-launched

The aftermath in Madrid. Rescue workers remove bodies from one of the several trains bombed in the Madrid attacks on March 11, 2004. Fatalities totalled 191; there were 1800 injured. (AP Photo/Denis Doyle/CP Archive)

surface-to-air missile in Kenya in November 2002, the suicide bombings in May 2003 in Morocco, the Istanbul bombings in November 2003, and the March 2004 commuter train bombings in Madrid. These attacks show that Al-Qaeda is still capable of masterminding and executing terrorist attacks, and will be part of the international terrorist landscape for years to come.

INTERNATIONAL TERRORISM AFTER SEPTEMBER 11

One of the challenges of studying international terrorism after September 11 is to avoid an overemphasis on the United States and Al-Qaeda. The volume of media coverage dedicated to these two actors can draw our attention away from other issues and identifiable trends in international terrorism that are a cause for concern and should be part of our analysis and our search for solutions. One basic question is whether or not international terrorism is increasing in frequency. In the wake of September 11 and the extensive coverage of subsequent international terrorist incidents, it is tempting to say that the frequency of terrorist attacks has increased. However, when one takes a longer-term perspective, the opposite is true: in terms of the number of incidents of international terrorism per year, the trend is downward. International terrorist activities surged in the 1980s to a peak of 665 incidents in 1987. The number of incidents declined during the 1990s, with a high of 565 incidents in 1991 and a low of 296 incidents in 1996. In 2002, there were 199 terrorist incidents recorded.[80] Nevertheless, terrorist incidents tend to be spectacular and highly publicized; as a result, governments are compelled to respond and make discernible gains in the battle against international terrorism because of public outrage. Yet one must question whether international terrorism deserves all the attention it receives. Without diminishing the impact that terrorist activity can have on individual lives, there is some doubt as to whether international terrorism presents a significant threat to national and international security when compared with other security issues such as war, gross violations of human rights, and the spread of nuclear weapons.[81] However, there is the risk that terrorism, if unchecked, will undermine the security and stability of a society.

Another characteristic of contemporary international terrorism is the growing link between different terrorist individuals and groups. International terrorist networks exist, although estimates of their extent vary. Such networks facilitate the sharing of memberships, training facilities, weapons, information, and finance; they are part of wide webs of underground communication conduits, making individual groups less reliant on client states for sponsorship. Some analysts have argued that globalization is enhancing the terrorist threat: Audrey Kurth Cronin contends that "the current wave of international terrorism, characterized by unpredictable and unprecedented threats from nonstate actors, not only is a reaction to globalization but is facilitated by it."[82] However, others claim that globalization also provides opportunities to combat terrorism. As Kendall Hoyt and Stephen G. Brooks argue, "many of the most effective tools for dealing with the terrorist threat are themselves partly the product of globalization."[83] Another trend is the emergence of many terrorist groups that have somewhat different motivations than traditional terrorist groups. Most terrorism is motivated by a set of goals that have a material content; that is, the goals can be quantified in terms of land, political power, or independence. However, the objectives of what Walter Laqueur has called "postmodern terrorism" are not political; they are inspired by religious or cult beliefs or by racial hatred. These motives are not as amenable to conflict management efforts or negotiated settlements, and so there is considerable concern that such groups cannot be addressed by responding to root causes or by offering concessions. Perhaps most disturbing of all is the fact that these groups seem to have turned away from hijackings and the targeting of specific individuals and toward more indiscriminate killing.[84] Finally, there is growing concern that terrorist groups may increasingly have access to chemical, biological, or even nuclear weapons. This has already occurred in at least one high-profile case (see Profile 6.6). While the prospects for a terrorist attack using nuclear weapons are remote, the possibility of terrorists employing radiological or "dirty" bombs (weapons using highly radioactive substances) does exist. Chemical and biological weapons are not particularly difficult to produce, and a future attack using such weapons is considered inevitable by many in the security industry.

September 11 has led counterterrorism experts into a dangerous game of speculation as to what type of attacks terrorist groups may undertake in the future. Since September 11, terrorists have attacked nightclubs and street markets, civilian aircraft, embassy buildings, and train stations to name a few. They could attack nuclear power plants or chemical industries with potentially devastating effects. Port facilities could be attacked using bombs planted on commercial ships or small civilian craft. National transportation infrastructure such as bridges, pipelines, power cables, dams, subways, and railways are all considered vulnerable. More ominously, terrorists with chemical or biological weapons could attack water supplies, public places, or urban areas using "crop duster" aircraft intended to spray agricultural pesticides. The anthrax attacks in the United States after September 11 used the postal service to deliver anthrax spores to a range of individuals in letter-sized envelopes. It is also possible that terrorists will turn to "weapons of mass disruption" in the future, choosing to attack computer and telecommunications networks in what are sometimes called "cyber-attacks."[85] Furthermore, terrorists do not have to actually plant a bomb or conduct an attack; often the mere threat that a bomb exists or an attack is imminent can cause mass fear and disruption of transportation systems. In other words, wherever we look we are likely to see opportunities for terrorists. While such an exercise can be prudent if it leads to sound security improvements, it can also lead to an exaggerated sense of vulnerability and fear, and the expenditure of large amounts of resources to defend against an attack that may never come.

COMBATING TERRORISM: APPROACHES AND METHODS

Can international terrorism be stopped? Can a "War on Terrorism" be won? Asking this question demands some humility, for terrorism has been an enduring feature of the history of human violence. However, terrorist groups can be defeated with a combination of sound policies. First, few if any counterterrorism efforts can be successful without some effort to address root causes. To the extent that terrorism is rooted in grievances, injustices, and a desire for autonomy or independence, efforts to address such grievances or desires could reduce or eliminate terrorist activity.

PROFILE 6.6 **The Tokyo Subway Attack**

In March 1995, 12 people were killed and more than 5000 injured by a sarin nerve gas attack on several Tokyo subway lines. The attack was carried out by members of a religious cult known as Aum Shinrikyo (Supreme Truth), a well-financed organization with more than 10 000 members in Japan and some 100 000 abroad. Asahara Shoku founded the cult in 1994, and his teachings spoke of an imminent Armageddon for modern society, which he believed was corrupt. Although many more casualties have been caused by terrorist bombings and shootings around the world, the Aum Shinrikyo acts are especially disturbing. For the first time, chemical weapons have been used on a large scale in an urban terrorist act. The cult maintained front companies and laboratories that employed highly skilled technicians and graduate microbiologists to develop and produce the gas used in the subway attack. In addition, the cult was a religious organization, not a political one, and was interested in promoting a theological outcome, not one designed to advance a political agenda or extract concessions from the Japanese government. As such, its actions cannot be responsive to political change designed to eliminate the root causes of terrorism.

Of course, particularly radical or extremist individuals or groups might not be satisfied with any level of accommodation short of their objectives, and would continue to engage in acts of violence. However, these individuals and groups would be increasingly isolated from their broader community, and easier to combat with law enforcement efforts. Of course, this approach presumes that governments or societies are willing to address root causes. In many cases, governments and publics are committed to preserving the status quo, and are highly resistant to making the economic, political, or social changes required. Furthermore, in many regions of the world, poverty, despair, hatred, and other social ills are so pervasive that eliminating the terrorism that develops from such conditions would require revolutionary changes, which may be beyond the resources as well as the political will of governments.

Second, governments can employ military and/or police force against terrorist organizations or the states that sponsor their activities. Such counterterrorist operations might include the use of highly trained teams of police or military personnel in large-scale search operations or the bombing of terrorist training grounds and facilities from the air. The United States justified the bombing of Libya in April 1986 and the use of **cruise missiles** against alleged terrorist facilities in Afghanistan and Sudan in August 1998 as antiterrorist operations. The war in Afghanistan was fought with a combination of Special Forces personnel, local allies, and airpower. However, the usefulness of the military against terrorist organizations is limited. Terrorist organizations are hard to track and target because they are often small, compartmentalized into highly secretive cells, and composed of committed individuals. The prospect for infiltration or cultivating informants is also quite low. Military operations against terrorists also face tactical and political obstacles. Terrorist facilities are often located in sponsoring states, and any attack against them would have to take into account the military capability of the host state as well as the political repercussions of attacking its territory. Often, military force is a very blunt instrument: attacking terrorists or their facilities can lead to the deaths of innocent individuals. As a result, the use of military force can create new grievances and new martyrs for the terrorist cause. There is another danger in focusing on military responses to terrorism. By declaring a "War on Terrorism" the Bush administration did manage to capture a mood of sadness and anger that prevailed in the United States immediately after September 11. However, by using the language of war, and repeating the mantra that the United States was at war, the administration may also have intentionally or unintentionally militarized the campaign against terrorism. The language of war focused discussion on military responses, while reducing the importance of nonmilitary responses and the need to address the root causes of terrorism.

Third, efforts can be made to reduce the vulnerability of a country and its people to terrorist attacks. Physical security around prominent government buildings, transportation infrastructure such as airports, and public places and events can make it more difficult for terrorists to attack such targets. The security of computer networks can be improved. The increased use of police and surveillance of public places can also increase security. Immigration and refugee applicants can be screened more thoroughly, and visitors to a country can be subjected to a higher level of search and investigation. However, these measures all carry the risk of infringing on people's rights, the selective application of security measures to certain minority groups (sometimes called "racial profiling"), and the creation of obstacles to the free movement of goods and services. There is also a practical limitation on efforts to increase the physical security of a society: the scale of cross-border traffic and trade is simply immense, and security measures are at odds with the economic advantages of the free flow of goods and services. For example, after September 11 the United States faces the challenge of improving its national security against future terrorist attacks. However, the U.S. has 301 ports of entry, 340 000 border crossings, and 420 commercial airports. Inside the

United States are 103 nuclear power plants, 2800 other power plants, and 600 000 bridges. Over 1.3 million people and 14 million shipping containers enter the United States every year. Each day, 58 000 cargo shipments enter the country.[86] Against such realities the limitation of defensive security measures are all too apparent.

Fourth, governments can seek to strengthen international cooperation on counterterrorism. In order to meet the threat posed by international terrorist networks, states must design comprehensive and integrated strategy incorporating economic, political, legal, diplomatic, cultural, and military responses. Intelligence agencies must cooperate to share information and coordinate law enforcement efforts. Intelligence agencies and financial institutions must also cooperate to combat terrorist financing. States can establish bilateral agreements on extradition of terrorists for trial. For example, the political offence exception rule in extradition law allows defendants accused of terrorist acts to claim that they were engaged in political acts of conscience so that they are not subject to extradition. Bilateral agreements, such as the United States–United Kingdom extradition treaty can remove this exception from certain acts of terrorism, such as skyjacking. A number of international multilateral treaties on terrorism also exist, though many states have yet to sign them (see Profile 6.7). However, in democratic societies, strengthening domestic law to combat terrorism is a serious matter, raising the danger of excessive restriction of freedoms and a slide into **authoritarianism** in the name of combating subversion (many people felt that the Canadian federal government did just this with the War Measures Act during the FLQ crisis, described earlier).

A last point to be made about terrorism is the complex role of the media in covering terrorist events. Publicity is a major objective behind terrorist activities. Acts of terrorism bring

---

PROFILE 6.7 **International Agreements on Terrorism**

There are 12 major multilateral conventions on terrorism. In addition, there are many other instruments, treaties, and agreements between states on counterterrorism.

1963	Convention on Offences and Certain Other Acts Committed on Board Aircraft (Tokyo Convention)	1988	Convention for the Suppression of Unlawful Acts against the Safety of Maritime Navigation
1970	The Hague Convention for the Suppression of Unlawful Seizure of Aircraft (Hague Convention)	1988	Convention for the Suppression of Unlawful Acts of Violence at Airports Serving International Civil Aviation
1971	Convention for the Suppression of Unlawful Acts against the Safety of Civil Aviation (Montreal Convention)	1988	Protocol for the Suppression of Unlawful Acts against the Safety of Fixed Platforms Located on the Continental Shelf
1973	Convention on the Prevention and Punishment of Crimes against Internationally Protected Persons, Including Diplomatic Agents	1991	Convention on the Marking of Plastic Explosives for the Purpose of Detection
1979	International Convention on the Taking of Hostages (Hostages Convention)	1997	International Convention on the Suppression of Terrorist Bombings
1980	Convention on the Physical Protection of Nuclear Material (Nuclear Materials Convention)	1999	International Convention for the Suppression of the Financing of Terrorism

attention not only to the attack itself but also to the individuals and groups who carried out the act, the cause or aim they purport to achieve, and the grievances or injustices they are struggling against. Terrorism attracts the attention of the media, the public, and government officials and elected leaders. The role of the media in covering terrorist incidents is controversial. Some argue that media coverage of terrorist incidents encourages terrorism (by providing terrorists with the publicity they seek) and that such coverage lacks sophistication and a high level of informed comment. Others argue that a free media is an essential component of a free society and that media reporting on terrorism, as long as it remains within appropriate ethical and legal boundaries, should not be constrained.

INTERNATIONAL ORGANIZED CRIME

Traditionally, organized crime has been regarded as a domestic political problem for societies and governments. While this is still largely the case, criminal activity has become increasingly internationalized, and "transnational organized crime" is now considered a serious global security issue. The increased attention placed on transnational organized crime is reflected in international agreements. At the 1995 G-7 summit in Halifax, the participating states declared that organized crime represented a growing threat to the security of the G-7 countries.[87] In December 2000, the United Nations Convention against Transnational Organized Crime was established, obligating member states to cooperate on extradition, mutual legal assistance, and joint investigations. Member states are also obligated to establish domestic laws against participation in international criminal groups, money-laundering activities, corruption, and obstruction of justice. Two optional protocols to the convention cover trafficking in humans and the exploitation of women and children for sexual activities or sweatshop labour. In October 2003, the United Nations Convention against Corruption was established, aimed at eliminating the growing threat presented by criminal activity to election and political party financing, judicial neutrality, and fair government contracting. Transnational crime has been identified as an international security issue for the following reasons:

- International criminal activity has escalated in terms of monetary scale and international scope. The world's organized crime syndicates are estimated to gross U.S.$1.5 trillion a year. The retail value of the global drug trade alone has been estimated at between U.S.$400 billion annually (about 8 percent of world trade).[88] Drugs flow from production centres to virtually every region in the world.

- Organized crime has expanded into international banking, investment, finance, and business activity. The German Federal Intelligence Service has reported that economic crime is the "world's largest criminal growth area."[89] Before it was exposed, the infamous Bank of Credit and Commerce International (BCCI) served as a money-laundering and criminal finance system for organized crime. For most of its 1.4 million depositors, the BCCI was a bank like any other. The amount of money laundered by organized crime (hiding the origin of dirty money so it can be used openly) is estimated at U.S.$500 million to U.S.$3 billion a year.[90]

- Criminal organizations have become threats to governments. In Italy, the Mafia has used assassinations and bombings to intimidate the Italian government and Italian law enforcement authorities. In Colombia, drug cartels have killed judges and politicians.

- Criminal organizations can erode the social fabric of a country, undermining political authority and corrupting the economic and political leadership of states and their governments. In some cases, however, this is because criminal organizations actually improve the standard of living of rural workers or inner-city youths, whereas governments neglect them.

- In some countries, organized crime represents a threat to the conventional economy and the ability of the government to manage it. In Russia, organized crime accounts for a major portion of economic activity that is beyond government regulation and taxation. According to international crime analyst Louise Shelley, "the most lucrative element of post-Soviet transnational criminality lies in the area of large-scale fraud against government."[91]

- Worrisome indications exist that organized crime may be involved in the international sale of materials required for the production of weapons of mass destruction, in particular nuclear materials, which have appeared in small quantities for sale in Europe.

- The distinction between organized crime and terrorist and revolutionary movements is blurring as terrorist and revolutionary organizations obtain funding from the sale of drugs and as governments funnel money from illegal arms sales to revolutionary militias.

Organized crime exists in virtually all societies in all regions of the world, but the United States, Canada, Mexico, Colombia, Italy, Russia, China, and Japan harbour particularly powerful criminal organizations. Many of these organizations have been increasing their cooperation with one another across state and regional boundaries. In North America and Italy, the Mafia, or Cosa Nostra—with operations in 40 other countries—dominates organized crime. Its activities include drug trafficking, union control and corruption, loan sharking, illegal gambling, prostitution, and financial fraud. Mexican crime organizations smuggle drugs on behalf of the South American drug cartels and smuggle illegal immigrants (with the assistance of the Chinese Triads) into the United States. In Russia, the Russian *mafiya* has expanded rapidly, making inroads into North America and Europe. Its activities include slavery, theft, extortion, murder, money laundering, and poppy production (for the world heroin market). In Asia, the Six Great Triads (based largely in Hong Kong and Taiwan) form the largest and oldest criminal network in the world. They are involved in drug trafficking, arms trafficking, illegal immigration, gambling, prostitution, fraud, and product piracy. The Japanese *boryokudan,* or *yakuza* (the name used in the West for Japanese organized crime syndicates), also operate throughout Asia.

The expansion of crime into an international activity and the growing communication and cooperation among organized crime syndicates has been facilitated by the growth of global interdependence. Other contributing factors include the collapse of Communism in the Soviet Union and the growth of capitalism in China, which have removed social barriers to criminal activity in those countries. The establishment of free trade areas and customs unions (especially in North America and Europe) has facilitated the flow of criminal goods and services across borders. The weakening of state authority in many countries has eroded the capacity of police and judicial systems to combat organized crime, and, of course, many governments are quite literally supportive of, and supported by, organized crime. Criminal organizations often form alliances and agreements, designed for mutual benefit. For example, Colombian cocaine trafficking syndicates have exchanged cocaine for heroin provided by Nigerians. The Sicilian Mafia has cooperated with the Colombian drug syndicates, providing access to their distribution system in Europe in exchange for access to the Colombian distribution system in the United States to recapture the market share they had lost to Asian heroin producers.[92] Of course, these arrangements between criminal organizations are often fleeting and are based purely on self-interest; few other incentives hold such alliances together. In addition, the world of international organized crime is also one of conflict, as criminal organizations often seek to eliminate their competitors by whatever means necessary.

The line between organized crime and terrorism and guerrilla movements used to be very distinct: terrorists were motivated more by ideological objectives. In contrast, criminal organizations were interested in increasing their sales, markets, and revenues. Terrorist goals included the weakening of the state and the social and political order. Criminal organizations had an interest in economic stability so that they could pursue their business activities. However, the lines between the criminal, the terrorist, and the guerrilla are blurring. Many terrorist organizations are increasingly engaged in profit-generating criminal activity, and many criminal organizations have embarked on campaigns of politically inspired violence. Criminal and terrorist or guerrilla organizations are also engaging in cooperation. As former director of the Central Intelligence Agency James Woolsey warned, "In Latin America powerful drug groups have established *ad hoc*, mutually beneficial arrangements with terrorist groups such as the Sendero Luminoso in Peru and the Revolutionary Armed Forces of Colombia, or FARC ... insurgents are sometimes paid to provide security services for drug traffickers, they often 'tax' drug operations in areas they control, and, in some cases, are directly involved in drug cultivation."[93] Of course, one would need a fine-toothed comb indeed to discover all the connections to organized criminals and terrorists Mr. Woolsey's organization has fostered over the years!

As the operations of criminal organizations have become increasingly international, the effort to combat international crime has involved greater cooperation and coordination of effort between countries. The United States, for example, has developed a very high level of cooperation with many South American countries to assist in the effort against the drug cartels. This cooperation involves agreements on punishments and extradition, law enforcement coordination, intelligence sharing, and military cooperation. As international crime is likely only to increase, measures such as these may become increasingly common as governments seek to join forces to combat criminal organizations that possess resources greater than those of many states. Meanwhile, the demand for drugs in the United States, the real source of the Colombian cartel's wealth, continues. Until this demand is reduced, there is little hope that the drug trade can be defeated. The United States continues to wage a largely futile war on drugs in the Caribbean and South America. In 2000, the United States committed U.S.$1.3 billion to "Plan Columbia," an effort to eradicate that country's coca production. Critics charge that this military aid is undermining Colombian democracy, ignoring the social plight of Colombia's poor, and supporting paramilitary groups that have been accused of human rights violations.

CONCLUSIONS

In this chapter, we have explored some of the major issues facing international security in current global politics. Is the world a more dangerous place after the Cold War? It is true that the end of the Cold War made the world safer from the threat of global nuclear war. Another positive is that the likelihood of a great-power war remains low. However, the sad fact is that the world is significantly safer only for people living in certain parts of the world. In much of the rest of the world, there has been no respite from regional wars or the threat of the outbreak of such wars. Indeed, it is possible to speak of the world in terms of zones of peace and zones of instability. Zones of peace, such as North America and Western Europe, enjoy relative peace and freedom from the threat of war, a high level of prosperity, and high levels of economic and political cooperation. Within zones of instability, wars rage unchecked, the threat of war looms over daily life, prosperity is a distant hope, and economic and political cooperation is limited or fragile. The question is, which of these zones will widen in the future? Will more regions become increasingly stable and free of conflict, or will instability and violence spread?

We have also looked at weapons proliferation, intrastate conflict, international terrorism, and transnational organized crime. These are just some of the issues that are currently shaping the current international security field, and we will encounter others in subsequent chapters. We now turn our attention to the efforts made to prevent, control, or manage warfare and international security challenges. This effort is collectively known as conflict management.

Endnotes

1. Edward Hallett Carr, *The Twenty Years' Crisis 1919–1939: An Introduction to the Study of International Relations* (London: Macmillan, 1942), 139.
2. Joseph S. Nye Jr., "U.S. Power and Strategy After Iraq," *Foreign Affairs* 82 (July/August 2003), 60.
3. See, for example, K. Krause and M.C. Williams, "Broadening the Agenda of Security Studies? Politics and Methods," *Mershon International Studies Review* 40 (1996), 229–54; S. Smith, "The Increasing Insecurity of Security Studies," *Contemporary Security Policy* 20 (1999), 72–101; and P. Stoett, *Human and Global Security: An Exploration of Terms* (Toronto: University of Toronto Press, 2000).
4. Peter Andreas, "Redrawing the Line: Borders and Security in the 21st Century," *International Security* 28 (Fall 2003), 78. See also Christopher Coker, *Globalisation and Insecurity in the Twenty-first Century: NATO and the Management of Risk*, Adelphi Paper 345 (Oxford: Oxford University Press, 2002); and B. Buzan, O. Waever, and J. de Wilde, *Security: A New Framework for Analysis* (Boulder, CO: Lynne Rienner, 1998).
5. See M.C. Williams, "Words, Images, Enemies: Securitization and International Politics," *International Studies Quarterly* 47 (December 2003), 511–31; and T. Farrell, "Constructivist Security Studies: Portrait of a Research Program," *International Studies Review* 4 (Spring 2002), 49–72; and the ground-breaking book by David Campbell, *Writing Security: United States Foreign Policy and the Politics of Identity* (Minneapolis: University of Minneapolis Press, 1992).
6. See for example, John Keegan, *A History of Warfare* (New York: Alfred A. Knopf, 1993); and John A. Lynn, *Battle: A History of Combat and Culture* (Boulder, CO: Westview Press, 2003).
7. Jack S. Levy, *War in the Modern Great Power System, 1496–1975* (Lexington: University Press of Kentucky, 1983), 117.
8. Jack S. Levy, Thomas C. Walker, and Martin S. Edwards, "Continuity and Change in the Evolution of War," in Zeev Maoz and Azar Gat, eds., *War in a Changing World* (Ann Arbor: University of Michigan Press, 2001), 15–48.
9. See Ruth Leger Sivard, *World Military and Social Expenditures 1991* (Washington, DC: World Priorities, 1991), 20.
10. See Sivard, 20.
11. See M. Eriksson, P. Wallensteen, and M. Sollenberg, "Armed Conflict: 1989–2002," *Journal of Peace Research* 40 (2003), 593–607.
12. See Kalevi J. Holsti, *The State, War, and the State of War* (Cambridge, UK: Cambridge University Press, 1996), 22.
13. Stockholm International Peace Research Institute, *SIPRI Yearbook, 2003* (SIPRI) (Oxford: Oxford University Press, 2003), 109.
14. See G. Strada, "The Horror of Landmines," *Scientific American,* May 1996, 40.
15. See SIPRI, 304.
16. See SIPRI, 306.
17. See SIPRI, 304.
18. Quincy Wright, *A Study of War,* vol. 1 (Chicago: University of Chicago Press, 1942), 17.
19. S. Freud, *Civilization, Society, and Religion,* edited by A. Dickson, translated by J. Strachey (New York: Penguin Books, 1985), 357.
20. K. Lorenz, *On Aggression* (New York: Harcourt Brace, 1966). See also P. Shaw and Y. Wong, "Ethnic Mobilization and the Seeds of Warfare: An Evolutionary Perspective," *International Studies Quarterly* 31, no. 1 (1987), 5–32.
21. See R. Jervis, *Perception and Misperception in International Politics* (Princeton: Princeton University Press, 1976), 154; and M.G. Hermann, "Explaining Foreign Policy Behaviour Using the Personal Characteristics of Political Leaders," *International Studies Quarterly* 24 (March 1980), 8.
22. See the discussion in John Keegan, *A History of Warfare,* 86–89.

23. Kenneth Waltz, *Man, the State, and War* (New York: Columbia University Press, 1959), 232.

24. See G. Modelski, *Exploring Long Cycles* (Boulder, CO: Lynne Rienner, 1987); and W. Thompson, *On Global War: Historical-Structural Approaches to World Politics* (Columbia, SC: University of South Carolina Press, 1988).

25. See L. Freedman and E. Karsh, *The Gulf Conflict 1990–1991: Diplomacy and War in the New World Order* (Princeton: Princeton University Press, 1993), 408–09. See also Anthony H. Cordesman and Abraham Wagner, *The Gulf War* (Boulder, CO: Westview Press, 1996).

26. For an interesting prewar assessment of U.S. interests and objectives, see Philip H. Gordon, Martin Indyk and Michael E. O'Hanlon, "Getting Serious About Iraq," *Survival* 44 (Autumn 2002), 9–22. For another prewar assessment see Carl Kaysen et al., *War with Iraq: Costs, Consequences, and Alternatives* (Cambridge, MA: American Academy of Arts and Sciences, 2002).

27. For background material on the Iraq War, see Micah L. Sifry and Christopher Cerf, eds., *The Iraq War Reader: History, Documents, Opinions* (New York, Touchstone Books, 2003); and Anthony H. Cordesman, *The Iraq War* (Westport: Praeger, 2003).

28. Remarks by the President at 2002 Graduation Exercise of the United States Military Academy, West Point, New York, 1 June 2002.

29. The National Security Strategy of the United States of America, September 2002, 6, 14.

30. See Geoffrey Forden, "Intention to Deceive: Iraqi Misdirection of UN Inspectors," *Jane's Intelligence Review* 16 (March 2004), 30–39.

31. Remarks to the United Nations Security Council by Secretary of State Colin L. Powell, New York City, 5 February 2003.

32. See Anthony H. Cordesman, *The Iraq War* (Westport, CT: Praeger, 2003).

33. See Richard A. Clarke, *Against All Enemies: Inside America's War on Terror—What Really Happened* (New York: The Free Press, 2004).

34. Augustus Richard Norton, "Making War, Making Peace: The Middle East Entangles America," *Current History* 103 (January 2004), 3–7.

35. On the case for vigilant containment, see John J. Mearsheimer and Stephen M. Walt, "An Unnecessary War," *Foreign Policy* 134 (January/February 2003), 50–59.

36. Former U.K. Defence Minister Peter Kilfoyle, quoted in Nicholas Watt and Michael White, "Wrong War, Wrong Time, Wrong Enemy, Warns Labour Rebel," *The Guardian*, 19 March 2003.

37. Kenneth M. Pollack, "Spies, Lies, and Weapons: What Went Wrong," *The Atlantic Monthly*, January/February 2004, 78–92.

38. James Fallows, "Blind into Baghdad," *The Atlantic Monthly*, January/February 2004, 52–74.

39. Norton, 4.

40. For a collection of observations, see "A Special Survey: U.S. Foreign Policy, Seen from the Other Side," *Bulletin of the Atomic Scientists* 60 (March/April 2004), 18–34.

41. *A Year After Iraq War: Mistrust of America in Europe Ever Higher, Muslim Anger Persists* (Washington, DC: The Pew Research Center for the People and the Press, 2004).

42. See Daniel Byman, "Constructing a Democratic Iraq: Challenges and Opportunities," *International Security* 28 (Summer 2003), 47–78; and Alan Sorensen, "Iraq's Reluctant Nation Builders," *Current History* 102 (December 2003), 407–10. For a broad discussion of postwar issues, see "From Victory to Success: Afterwar Policy in Iraq," *Foreign Policy* 137 (July/August 2003), 50–72.

43. See, for example, Joseph S. Nye Jr., "U.S. Power and Strategy After Iraq," 60–73.

44. "Africa's Forgotten War," *The Economist*, 8 May 1999, 41.

45. M. Brecher, *Crisis in World Politics: Theory and Reality* (Oxford: Pergamon Press, 1993), 68–69, 171.

46. See Herbert K. Tillema, "Foreign Overt Military Intervention in the Nuclear Age," *Journal of Peace Research* 26 (May 1989), 179–95; and Herbert K. Tillema *Overt Military Intervention in the Cold War Era* (Columbia, SC: University of South Carolina Press, 1996).

47. This term is employed by Ted Robert Gurr, *Minorities at Risk: A Global View of Ethnopolitical Conflicts* (Washington, DC: United States Institute of Peace, 1993).

48. See M. Small and J.D. Singer, *Resort to Arms: International and Civil Wars, 1816–1980* (Beverly Hills: Sage, 1982); J.D. Singer, "Peace in the Global System: Displacement, Interregnum, or Transformation?" in C.W. Kegley Jr., ed., *The Long Postwar Peace* (New York: HarperCollins, 1991), 56–84; and P. Wallenstein and K. Axell, "Armed Conflict at the End of the Cold War, 1989–1992," *Journal of Peace Research* 30 (August 1993), 331–46.

49. Holsti, *The State, War, and the State of War*, 22.

50. D. Carment, "The International Dimensions of Ethnic Conflict," *Journal of Peace Research* 30 (May 1993), 137–50.

51. SIPRI, 109.

52. M. Esman, *Ethnic Politics* (Ithaca, NY: Cornell University Press, 1995); S. Griffiths, *Nationalism and Ethnic Conflict* (New York: Oxford University Press, 1993); J.A. Spence, "Introduction and Overview," Special Issue on Ethnicity and International Relations, *International Affairs* 72 (July 1996).

53. Gurr, *Minorities at Risk*, 3.

54. See Stuart J. Kaufman, *Modern Hatreds: The Symbolic Politics of Ethnic War* (Ithaca, NY: Cornell University Press, 2001).

55. Holsti, *The State, War, and the State of War*, 20.

56. Mats Berdal and David M. Malone, "Introduction," in Mats Berdal and David M. Malone, eds., *Greed and Grievance: Economic Agendas in Civil Wars* (Boulder, CO: Lynne Rienner, 2001), 4.

57. Berdal and Malone, 5.

58. David Keen, *The Economic Functions of Violence in Civil Wars*, Adelphi Paper 320 (Oxford: Oxford University Press, 1998), 11–12.

59. International Institute for Strategic Studies, *Strategic Survey, 2002–2003: An Evaluation and Forecast of World Affairs* (Oxford: Oxford University Press, 2003), 120–23. See also Gail Lapidus, "Contested Sovereignty: The Tragedy of Chechnya," *International Security* 23 (Summer 1998), 5–49.

60. See B. Bueno de Mesquita and W.H. Riker, "An Assessment of the Merits of Selective Proliferation," *Journal of Conflict Resolution* 26 (June 1982), 283–306; J. Mearsheimer, "The Case for a Ukrainian Nuclear Deterrent," *Foreign Affairs* 72 (Summer 1993), 50–66; and K. Waltz, "Nuclear Myths and Political Realities," *American Political Science Review* 84 (September 1990), 731–45.

61. *The Spread of Nuclear Weapons: More May Be Better*, Adelphi Paper 171 (London: International Institute for Strategic Studies, Autumn 1981), 5.

62. See L. Dunn, *Containing Nuclear Proliferation*, Adelphi Paper 263 (London: Oxford University Press, 1991); K. Kaiser, "Non-Proliferation and Nuclear Deterrence," *Survival* 31 (March/April 1989), 123–36; and S. Miller, "The Case against a Ukrainian Nuclear Deterrent," *Foreign Affairs* 72 (Summer 1993), 67–80.

63. For three models of weapons proliferation incentives, see S. Sagan, "Why Do States Build Nuclear Weapons? Three Models in Search of a Bomb," *International Security* 21 (Winter 1996/97), 54–86.

64. See Paul Kerr, "North Korea Crisis Chronology," *Arms Control Today* 33 (June 2003).

65. See R. Molander and P. Wilson, "On Dealing With the Prospect of Nuclear Chaos," *The Washington Quarterly* 17 (1994), 32; and Jon B. Wolfsthal and Tom Z. Collina, "Nuclear Terrorism and Warhead Control in Russia," *Survival* 44 (Summer 2002), 71–84.

66. Tavleen Singh, "Get Back to Basics," *India Today*, 8 June 1998.

67. See Judith Miller, Stephen Engleberg, and William Broad, *Germs: Biological Weapons and America's Secret War* (New York: Simon and Schuster, 2001), 297–98.

68. See SIPRI, 443.

69. See SIPRI, 466.

70. "The Covert Arms Trade," *The Economist*, 12 February 1994, 21.

71. Ibid.

72. Walter Laqueur, "Postmodern Terrorism," *Foreign Affairs* 75 (September/October 1996), 24–36.

73. Cindy Combs, *Terrorism in the Twenty-First Century* (Upper Saddle River, NJ: Prentice Hall, 1997), 8.

74. Paul Wilkinson, "A European Viewpoint on Terrorism," in Joseph S. Nye Jr., Yukio Satoh, and Paul Wilkinson, *Addressing the New International Terrorism: Prevention, Intervention, and Multilateral Cooperation,* Report to the Trilateral Commission (Washington, DC: The Trilateral Commission, 2003), 21.

75. Suman Gupta, *The Replication of Violence: Thoughts on International Terrorism after September 11th 2001* (London: Pluto Press, 2002), 1.

76. International Institute for Strategic Studies, *The Military Balance, 2003–2004* (London: Oxford University Press, 2003), 356.

77. Ibid., 355.

78. Ibid.

79. See Rohan Gunaratna, "Al-Qaeda Adapts to Disruption," *Jane's Intelligence Review* 16 (February 2004), 20–22.

80. See *Patterns of Global Terrorism, 2002* (Washington, DC: United States Department of State, 2003), 161. There are ongoing disputes about the methodology employed by such studies, however.

81. See J. Simon, "Misunderstanding Terrorism," *Foreign Policy* (Summer 1987), 104–20.

82. Audrey Kurth Cronin, "Behind the Curve: Globalization and International Terrorism," *International Security* 27 (Winter 2002/2003), 30.

83. Kendall Hoyt and Stephen G. Brooks, "A Double-Edged Word: Globalization and Biosecurity," *International Security* 28 (Winter 2003/2004), 124.

84. Laqueur, "Postmodern Terrorism," 25.

85. Stephen J. Lukasik, Seymour E. Goodman, and David W. Longhurst, *Protecting Critical Infrastructures Against Cyber-Attack*, Adelphi Paper 359 (Oxford: Oxford University Press, 2003).

86. *Jane's Sentinel Security Assessment: North America, 2002.* (Coulsdon, Surrey: Jane's Information Group Limited, 2002), 149.

87. Robert Chote and Peter Norman, "Leaders Zero In on Crime and Nuclear Safety," *Financial Times*, 19 June 1995, 5.

88. *Human Development Report 1999* (New York: United Nations, 1999).

89. Karl-Ludwig Guensche, "BND Warns against New Mafia Methods," *FBIS Report*, AU0507132496 Berlin Die Welt, 5 July 1996, 2.

90. Peter Lilley, *Dirty Dealing: The Untold Truth About Global Money Laundering, International Crime and Terrorism* (London: Kogan Page, 2003).

91. Louise I. Shelley, "Transnational Organized Crime: An Imminent Threat to the Nation-State?" *Journal of International Affairs* 48 (Winter 1995), 485.

92. See Shelley, "Transnational Organized Crime."

93. James Woolsey, "Global Organized Crime: Threats to U.S. and International Security," Address for the Center for Strategic and International Studies, Washington, DC, 26 September 1994, 1.

Suggested Readings

Bennis, Phyllis. *Before and After: US Foreign policy and the September 11 Crisis.* New York: Olive Branch Press, 2003.

Berdal, Mats, and David M. Malone, eds., *Greed and Grievance: Economic Agendas in Civil Wars.* Boulder, CO: Lynne Rienner, 2001.

Berdal, Mats, and Monica Serrano, eds., *Transnational Organized Crime and International Security: Business as Usual?* Boulder, CO: Lynne Rienner, 2002.

Betts, Richard K., ed. *Conflict after the Cold War: Arguments on Causes of War and Peace.* New York: Macmillan, 1994.

Buckley, Mary, and Rick Fawn. *Global Responses to Terrorism: 9/11, Afghanistan, and Beyond.* London: Routledge, 2003.

Bueno de Mesquita, Bruce. *The War Trap.* New Haven, CT: Yale University Press, 1981.

Buzan, Barry, O. Waever, and J. de Wilde. *Security: A New Framework for Analysis.* Boulder, CO: Lynne Rienner, 1998.

Cashman, Greb. *What Causes War: An Introduction to Theories of International Conflict.* New York: Lexington Books, 1993.

Chalk, Peter. *Non-Military Security and Global Order: The Impact of Extremism, Violence, and Chaos on National and International Security.* London: Macmillan, 2000.

Clarke, Richard A. *Against All Enemies: Inside America's War on Terror—What Really Happened.* New York: The Free Press, 2004.

Claude, Inis L., Jr. *Power and International Relations.* New York: Random House, 1962.

Coker, Christopher. *War in the Twentieth Century: the Impact of War on Modern Consciousness.* London: Brassey's, 1994.

Cordesman, Anthony. *The Iraq War.* Westport, CT: Praeger, 2003.

Creveld, Martin van. *Technology and War: From 2000 B.C. to the Present.* New York: Free Press, 1989.

Edwards, Adam, and Peter Gill, eds., *Transnational Organized Crime: Perspectives on Global Security*. London: Routledge, 2003.

Feffer, John, ed. *Power Trip: Unilateralism and Global Strategy after September 11*. New York: Seven Stories Press, 2003.

Freedman, Lawrence, ed. *War*. New York: Oxford University Press, 1994.

Gilpin, Robert. *War and Change in World Politics*. Cambridge, UK: Cambridge University Press, 1981.

Gupta, Suman. *The Replication of Violence: Thoughts on International Terrorism after September 11th 2001*. London: Pluto Press, 2002.

Heymann, Philip B. *Terrorism, Freedom, and Security: Winning Without War*. Cambridge, MA: MIT Press, 2003.

Holsti, K.J. *Peace and War: Armed Conflicts and International Order 1648–1989*. Cambridge, UK: Cambridge University Press, 1991.

Jones, Clive, and Caroline Kennedy-Pope, eds. *International Security in a Global Age: Securing the Twenty-first Century*. London: Frank Cass, 2000.

Kaufman, Stuart J. *Modern Hatreds: The Symbolic Politics of Ethnic War*. Ithaca, NY: Cornell University Press, 2001.

Kegley, Charles W., Jr. *International Terrorism: Characteristics, Causes, Controls*. New York: St. Martin's Press, 1994.

Maoz, Zeev, and Azar Gat, eds., *War in a Changing World*. Ann Arbor: University of Michigan Press, 2001.

Sederberg, Peter C. *Fires Within: Political Violence and Revolutionary Change*. New York: HarperCollins, 1994.

Sifry, Micah L., and Christopher Cerf, eds. *The Iraq War Reader: History, Documents, Opinions*. New York: Touchstone Books, 2003.

Vasquez, John A. *The War Puzzle*. Cambridge, UK: Cambridge University Press, 1993.

Wiseman, Geoffrey. *Concepts of Non-Provocative Defence: Ideas and Practices in International Security*. New York: Palgrave, 2002.

Wyn Jones, R. *Security, Strategy, and Critical Theory*. Boulder, CO: Lynne Rienner, 1999.

Suggested Websites

Center for Defense Information
http://www.cdi.org

DefenseLINK: United States Department of Defense
http://www.defenselink.mil

Federation of American Scientists
http://www.fas.org

International Crisis Group
http://www.crisisweb.org/home/index.cfm

International Peace Academy
http://www.ipacademy.org

International Relations and Security Network
http://www.isn.ethz.ch

Stockholm International Peace Research Institute
http://www.sipri.se

United Nations
http://www.un.org

Conflict Management in Global Politics

We are here to choose between the quick and the dead.

—Bernard Baruch, 1946[1]

RESPONDING TO THE INTERNATIONAL SECURITY AGENDA

In Chapter 6, we examined some of the key issues and challenges facing the contemporary international system from a security studies perspective. This chapter explores the instruments and tools of conflict management, including direct and indirect diplomatic interaction, arms control and disarmament, the concept of human security, the use of international organizations (IOs) and law, peacekeeping and humanitarian intervention, and sanctions. Our aim in this chapter is to evaluate what could be called the international conflict management tool kit. What instruments have been developed to control, prevent, or otherwise manage security challenges in global politics? To what extent have these instruments been useful or found wanting? Like the study of international security, the study of international conflict management has evolved with changing agendas and new challenges. As we will see, traditional conflict management instruments have been adapted to the post–Cold War setting with mixed results.

THE NATURE OF DIPLOMACY

Diplomacy is essential to any understanding of global politics in general and interstate relations in particular. Diplomacy is as old as politics, and it has survived the many changes in international relations and society from the ancient world to today.[2] Definitions of diplomacy traditionally have been confined to statecraft and the activities of professional diplomats. In this sense, diplomacy can be defined as purposeful communication between states. However, the definition of diplomacy is widening to include a variety of activities in contemporary foreign policy, which includes diplomatic activity between not only states and groups and non-state actors, but also individuals who may not be in formal positions of political power in a state apparatus. In more traditional approaches to diplomacy, the concepts of representation and communication are fundamental components of diplomatic activity. Representatives of states are acting on behalf of the government of that state, and are almost always acting under the instructions of their government. Communication protocols and formalities allow states to interact with one another (and with nonstate actors) using established and mutually acceptable procedures. While diplomacy is an everyday feature of international life, it is also the foundation of efforts to prevent, contain, and manage international conflict. Of course, diplomacy may also be quite bellicose and militaristic, and even diplomatic efforts intended to avoid war can use threats and intimidation to achieve state objectives.[3]

Public and private diplomatic affairs are highly formalized events, characterized by painstaking attention to tradition and protocol. For example, when a **head of state** makes a formal visit to a foreign country, an elaborate reception protocol demands a formal reception at the airport, a red carpet, a greeting line of dignitaries, an honour guard (dutifully inspected by the visitor), a band (playing the national anthem of the visitor), an escorted motorcade to a hotel or the seat of government, and at least one formal state dinner. While the receptions for visitors or diplomats of lesser rank are not as elaborate, they are no less established as conventions. Though many of the trappings of past diplomatic practice have been discarded, many of the key traditions, such as diplomatic immunity, linger in contemporary diplomacy. As we discussed in Chapter 5, states that have embassies in foreign countries can legitimately lay claim to that space as part of their own territory. This principle of **extraterritoriality** is a cornerstone of diplomatic tradition. According to Garret Mattingly, it evolved in the early days of the Westphalian state system, when states "found they could only communicate with one another by tolerating within themselves little islands of alien sovereignty."[4] Diplomatic protocol prevents individuals, groups, and states from clashing on issues of symbolism and prestige and maintains the image that diplomats, officials, and leaders of equivalent rank are treated as equals. Formality and protocol also reduce the chances that personalities will interfere with communication between governments, but they are not always successful. Miscommunication occurs often in global politics, sometimes with tragic results. Personalities are often a crucial influence on affairs of state. Canadians, for example, have often expressed an interest in the personal relationship between the prime minister and the president of the United States, and they have expressed anxiety when the two leaders do not get along (John Diefenbaker and John F. Kennedy) and when they seem to get along too well (Brian Mulroney and Ronald Reagan).

Say "cheese." Canadian Prime Minister Paul Martin and U.S. President George Bush meet for the first time at the Summit of the Americas at Monterrey, Mexico, in 2004. Multilateral and bilateral summits are increasingly important in global politics. (CP Photo/ Tom Hanson)

However, diplomacy has undergone some significant changes, particularly in the latter half of the 20th century. Decolonization and increased global interdependence have forced diplomatic services to adjust to larger numbers of states and a much wider variety of language and cultures. Some Canadian embassies now have more staff than the entire Canadian foreign policy establishment employed before World War II. The increasing number of states in the world has increased the relevance of multilateral diplomacy and conference diplomacy, both within and outside established institutions. In many cases, the process of diplomatic exchange and communication simply becomes more efficient if all of the states involved are represented around a single table (although this does not mean the chances of an agreement are any greater). Furthermore, the growimg complexity of the diplomatic agenda requires more and more specific technical knowledge on matters as varied as satellites to coral reef management. In most cases, the traditional diplomatic service lacks this kind of knowledge. As a result, communication and dialogue between government agencies other than foreign ministries (sometimes called "paradiplomacy") has become ever more common.[5] The character of diplomatic life has also changed. Developments in global communications have made contact between governments and their representatives abroad virtually instantaneous. Gone are the days when diplomatic pouches would outline broad policy and give a diplomat considerable leeway to make decisions.

Another change in the character of diplomacy is the expanding role of nonstate actors. Governments now maintain active links to a wide variety of groups, NGOs, firms, and individuals. In addition, businesses, NGOs, academics, and bureaucrats have greater opportunities for interaction that can have an impact on international diplomacy. Increasing the contact between different levels of society between two or more states is sometimes called *track-two diplomacy*.

As indicated in Chapter 3, foreign policy remains a relatively closed area of government activity. Nevertheless, open availability of information about international events and the heightened relevance of public opinion in many countries have made diplomacy a much more public affair, and this has many implications. The views and opinions of professional career diplomats may be rejected or ignored by political leaderships if no public support exists for such measures. Conversely, public opinion may compel leaders to act in ways that are contrary to the advice of the diplomatic service. In one sense, then, public opinion may cause the diplomacy of a state or group to be more reflective of the body of the people; however, it may lead to rash or dangerous diplomacy designed primarily to capture votes.

Finally, increasing importance is attached to summit diplomacy, the formal meeting of heads of state and government. Summit diplomacy has both its advocates and its detractors. Summits can enable leaders to establish a personal rapport and remove the frustrating constraints of the slow and bureaucratic diplomatic process. The **Camp David** accords, which brought Egyptian President Anwar el-Sadat and Israeli Prime Minister Menachem Begin together at President Jimmy Carter's official Maryland retreat, resulted in a peace agreement between two countries that had fought four wars in the past 30 years. However, summitry can lead to ill-advised decisions made by leaders without adequate consultation with experts or time for reflection. At the Yalta Conference in 1945 (discussed in Chapter 2) between Winston Churchill, Franklin Roosevelt, and Josef Stalin, Roosevelt acquiesced to an agreement that would divide Europe into spheres of influence and pave the way for Soviet domination of Eastern Europe. Summits have also been criticized as being little more than photo opportunities and cocktail parties, often leading to no substantive progress or involving only the signing of agreements worked out in advance by diplomats. Summits also attract large protest gatherings, as demonstrated during the Summit of the Americas in Quebec City in April 2001 and the G-8 Summit in Evian, France, in June 2003.

DIPLOMATIC TECHNIQUES AND CONFLICT MANAGEMENT

Throughout history, states and groups have employed a variety of diplomatic techniques to secure their objectives. These techniques can essentially be reduced to the use of threats and promises. The effectiveness of diplomacy as a conflict management instrument depends heavily on one variable: whether a set of proposals can be developed that each party prefers over reaching no agreement at all or over using violence to settle their dispute. In the absence of a set of outcomes acceptable to all sides, diplomacy will fail as a means of preventing, controlling, or managing conflict. Conflict management diplomacy is about facilitating and encouraging the development of such sets of proposals.[6] One of the ironies of diplomacy as a conflict management tool is that in periods of war or crisis, at precisely the time when effective diplomatic communication is most valuable, such communication is least frequent. Often, countries in a dispute will break off diplomatic relations, necessitating an eventual reopening of communication or the involvement of a third party. Several diplomatic techniques have been employed to facilitate conflict management efforts. These include

Signalling

States and groups use signals to communicate intent, commitment, and displeasure. Signals may be very direct, coming in the form of speeches, written statements or proclamations, or direct diplomatic contact with individual representatives of other states or groups. Statements expressing the Canadian government's opposition to the testing of nuclear weapons by India and Pakistan in 1998 and to the assassination of Hamas spiritual leader Sheik Ahmed Yassin by Israel in 2004 are examples of direct government-to-government signalling. At other times, signals may be indirect and may come in the form of deliberate symbolic actions such as official or unofficial visits, the recall of ambassadors, or displays of military power. The problem with all signals is that they can be misunderstood or misinterpreted and sometimes missed altogether. Some signals can be very circumspect. In a particularly famous example, China invited the U.S. table tennis team to visit China during an international table tennis tournament in Japan in 1971. After some deliberation, it was decided (correctly) that this was an overture by the Chinese leadership to improve relations between China and the United States. Thus, the term *Ping-Pong diplomacy* was coined.

Bargaining and Negotiation

Another technique is the use of bargaining, an attempt to reach an agreement on issues of symbolic or substantive value to all parties. Bargaining and negotiation (bargaining in a formal setting) establishes how such symbolic and substantive desires and aims will be exchanged and divided among the parties to the mutual agreement of all. Not all agreements will be equally beneficial to all sides; in fact, some agreements will be very unequal. This imbalance occurs because parties to a dispute bring different means of leverage to the bargaining or negotiation process. Leverage originates with power capabilities, and these can be employed by offering rewards; issuing threats; or appealing to sentiments of friendship, allegiance, or shared ideology or religion. When one or some parties have leverage over the others, unequal arrangements are frequently (though not always) the result.[7] Over time, several tactics for successful negotiation have emerged:

- Discourage zero-sum views of the issues.
- Establish a fair compromise to ensure a lasting settlement.
- Avoid ultimatums and posturing; encourage dialogue and debate.
- Avoid humiliating one's opponents.
- Blend rewards and threats.
- Avoid personal *ad hominem* attacks on the other party.
- Look for bridges, solutions that are acceptable to both sides but different from the positions taken at the beginning of negotiations.
- Look for nonspecific compensation, in which one side gets what it wants but gives up something that was not part of the original dispute or discussion.
- Divide the issue into separate and more manageable subjects for agreement.

Third-Party Mediation

Third parties, whether individuals, groups, organizations, or states, can be invited by the parties to assist the process of reaching a settlement. Mediation is a more common form of diplomatic conflict management than bilateral negotiations between parties.[8] Third parties can offer a number of services, which include

- Providing **good offices** (acting as a conduit for communication), a role performed on two separate occasions by U.S. Secretaries of State Henry Kissinger and James Baker in their "shuttle diplomacy" flights between Middle East capitals during negotiations; this role is a primary function of the secretary-general of the UN

- Providing a neutral site for negotiations (a role often performed by Switzerland, and specifically the city of Geneva)

- Clarifying facts and evidence (which may involve providing figures or conducting fact-finding missions)

- Acting as a mediator by becoming active in negotiations, making suggestions that might be agreeable to all sides, and breaking deadlocks when they occur

- Acting as an arbitrator (making a judgment on the dispute and establishing a fair settlement) with the consent of the parties

- Acting as an adjudicator (making a judgment with reference to international law)

Naturally, any international actor entrusted with such roles must be acceptable to all sides, be perceived as neutral with little or no agenda of its own, and be capable of performing such tasks. In the end, the parties to the conflict retain the power to decide on outcomes: despite the best efforts of a mediator, the parties to a conflict may choose to abandon mediated talks or to reject some or all of the terms of any agreement that is reached.

DIPLOMACY AS A CONFLICT MANAGEMENT INSTRUMENT

The record of diplomatic efforts to prevent, control, or manage conflicts is mixed. Certainly there have been spectacular failures, most notably in the weeks before the outbreak of World War I. Of course, when wars do break out, any diplomatic efforts to prevent them are by definition failures. However, there have been successful cases of diplomatic conflict management, and most conflicts between actors in the international system are resolved peacefully through diplomatic means. In 1987, Costa Rican President Oscar Arias designed a peace accord for Central America involving Costa Rica, El Salvador, Nicaragua, Honduras, and Guatemala. All parties agreed to eliminate restrictions on dissent, offer political amnesty to rebel movements, hold national elections, negotiate ceasefires between governments and rebel groups, deny the use of their territory to rebel groups from other countries, and cut off superpower aid to rebel groups. It was a remarkable achievement, and although never fully implemented, the Arias Plan won Oscar Arias the 1987 Nobel Peace Prize. In 2002, India and Pakistan were poised on the brink of war, with an implicit threat of nuclear hostilities hovering over the crisis. However, because of diplomatic intervention from abroad, exchanges between the two countries led to the defusing of the crisis, though not to a resolution of the underlying issues between the two states. Two of the most watched diplomatic conflict management efforts today are the Middle East peace process and the Northern Ireland peace process, and we expand briefly on these below.

DIPLOMACY AND CONFLICT MANAGEMENT IN THE MIDDLE EAST

Since the late 1940s, the key component of the Middle East peace process has been the Israeli–Palestinian conflict. Other actors such as Syria and Egypt and various armed groups in

Lebanon are also part of the conflict management equation, but a lasting peace in the Middle East is heavily dependent on an Israeli–Palestinian accommodation. At the root of the conflict is land: both Israelis and Palestinians claim the same territory, and so conflict management efforts have concentrated on issues such as control of land, Palestinian self-rule, control of Jerusalem (which both sides regard as their indivisible capital as well as a holy centre), the return of Palestinian refugees to their homes in Israel, Israeli settlements on the West Bank, economic opportunity for Palestinians, and access to water resources. For decades, this conflict resisted all efforts at diplomatic management, with the Palestine Liberation Organization (PLO) and the government of Israel using acts of terror, assassinations, military action, civil disturbance (such as the Palestinian youth uprising, or *Intifada*), and economic coercion to promote or protect their interests.

A breakthrough occurred in September 1993. Israeli and PLO officials had been meeting in secret in Oslo, Norway. With the mediation of the Norwegian government, negotiators reached agreement on a Declaration of Principles signed in Washington by Israeli Prime Minister Yitzak Rabin (who was assassinated in 1995) and Yasser Arafat on September 13, 1993. In this declaration, Israel recognized the PLO as the legitimate representative of the Palestinian people, and the PLO recognized Israel's right to exist and renounced terrorism. The declaration also included the goals of future negotiations, the most important of which was Israeli withdrawal from the Gaza Strip and the West Bank, and self-rule for Palestinians in those territories. A follow-up Interim Agreement signed in 1995 provided for the phased transfer of some land to Palestinian control, the phased withdrawal of Israeli forces from those areas, easier movement for Palestinians between Gaza and the West Bank, and greater freedom for the Palestinian economy, which is heavily dependent on Israel. In return the PLO agreed to prevent further terrorist attacks on Israel. However, the hope that this agreement might pave the way to peace has largely been dashed. While some parts of the agreement were partially implemented, disputes over outstanding issues began to erode support for the agreement on both sides. Some additional progress was made: an agreement to divide the city of Hebron was reached in 1997, and both sides renewed their commitment to peace in the Wye River Memorandum in 1998. However, the continued development of Israeli settlements in the West Bank caused consternation among Palestinians, and renewed terrorist attacks by Palestinian groups. Israel criticized the Palestinian Authority for not doing enough to stop the attacks and suspended implementation of the agreement.

On July 10, 2000, Israeli Prime Minister Ehud Barak and Yasser Arafat held a summit, with the mediation of U.S. President Bill Clinton, in an effort to break the deadlock. The talks broke up on July 25 over disagreement about the future of Jerusalem. More meetings were held in Taba in December 2000, but these also failed to resolve the key issues. Frustration with the peace process was growing. The economic hardships facing Palestinians were mounting, Israeli settlements were still being built, and terrorist attacks were still being committed. Both sides were preparing for a renewal of violence. Some Palestinian leaders began to call for an uprising to compel Israel to agree to a separate Palestinian state, while the Israeli Defence Force (IDF) prepared to crush any Palestinian uprising.[9] All that was needed was a spark, and that spark came when the Likud party leader Ariel Sharon (a man many Palestinians accused of being a war criminal), visited the Temple Mount/Haram al-Sharif, a site considered holy to both Muslims and Jews, in the fall of 2000. Palestinians were outraged that Sharon would visit a site considered holy to Muslims, while many conservative Israelis were outraged at the idea that Sharon should not be able to visit a site holy to Jews. In the wake of the visit, neither side showed any restraint: the El-Aqsa Intifada was launched in September 2000, and the IDF responded with a massive campaign to suppress the Palestinian uprising.[10] Sharon was later elected prime minister, on February 6, 2001. Suicide bombings by Palestinian militant groups

A moment of hope. The signing of the 1993 peace accords by Israeli Prime Minister Yitzhak Rabin and PLO Chairman Yasser Arafat with U.S. President Bill Clinton in the background. This agreement was achieved with the mediation assistance of Norway and the United States. (AP Photo/Ron Edmonds, File/CP Archive)

increased, while the Israeli army conducted frequent raids into Palestinian areas, killing terrorist suspects and civilians, destroying buildings and homes, and arresting terrorist suspects. By the end of that year, 300 Palestinians and 38 Israelis had been killed.

The ongoing violence once again led to international efforts to find a resolution to the conflict. The new U.S. President, George W. Bush, called for an end to the construction of Israeli settlements in the West Bank, a cessation of Palestinian attacks, and the creation of a Palestinian state. However, active U.S. economic and military support for Israel, efforts to undercut the leadership of Yasser Arafat, and muted criticisms of Israeli military action against Palestinians continued to frustrate the Palestinian leadership and most of the Arab world, and undermined the ability of the United States to break the negotiation deadlock. On separate occasions, U.S. Secretary of State Colin Powell and CIA Director George Tenet attempted to broker lasting ceasefires but were unsuccessful.[11] In February 2002 Saudi Arabia proposed a "grand bargain" that called for Israeli withdrawal to pre-1967 boundaries in exchange for full normalization of relations with all Arab states. A diluted version of the draft proposal was accepted at an Arab Summit in Beirut in March 2002. The United States signalled its support for the proposal, but Israel was less enthusiastic as the proposal called for a Palestinian capital in East Jerusalem and openly supported the El-Aqsa Intifada. Any momentum the Saudi Arabian proposal may have had died away in a renewal of suicide bombings and Israeli reprisals.[12]

The violence continued through 2002 and 2003, as suicide bombings and Israeli military actions in the West Bank and the Gaza Strip escalated. Israel attacked key Palestinian Authority installations (at one point even surrounding Yasser Arafat's compound), terrorist training facilities, and residential areas. Many towns in the West Bank were reoccupied by the Israeli army as it searched for terrorist suspects. This reassertion of Israeli control meant that

The "security fence" under construction. This section of the Israeli security fence is being built on the outskirts of Jerusalem, through the village of Abu Dis, January 2004. (AP Photo/Enric Marti/CP Archive)

by early 2003 the boundaries established by the Oslo Agreements had been practically eliminated. Moreover, in early 2002, Israel had begun construction of a "security fence" designed to close off the border between Israel and the West Bank, with five crossing points for Palestinian workers and tourists. The security fence has become another focal point in the conflict, as the wall not only cuts through communities and separates many Palestinians from their work in Israel, but also cuts into the West Bank and therefore is seen by Palestinians as an effort by Israel to annex land. The Israeli government maintains that the fence is a necessary barrier to the movement of terrorists into Israel.[13] In April 2003, yet another peace plan was unveiled. Known as the "Road Map," this plan was designed and endorsed by the United States, Russia, the EU, and the UN. It called for a comprehensive settlement of the Israeli–Palestinian dispute by 2005. In the agreement, a ceasefire would be established; the Palestinian Authority would carry out reforms; Israel would dismantle illegal settlements set up since 2001; a Palestinian state would be created, and negotiations would be conducted on final borders, the status of Jerusalem, and the right of return for Palestinian refugees. However, the "road map to nowhere" achieved little.[14] Dozens of terrorist attacks were thwarted during the supposed ceasefire, and Israel dismantled only a few of the illegal settlements.

Even as the violence has escalated, the domestic politics of Israel and the Palestinian Authority have become increasingly defined by the conflict. Israeli party politics are characterized by varying attitudes toward any peace process. While many parties support a return to the peace process, many small conservative parties show little interest in negotiation or compromise. And the complex politics of coalition governments means that to stay in power Israeli leaders must often cater to such parties to maintain a majority in parliament. In the Palestinian Authority, support for Yasser Arafat has fallen, and militant groups now often secure more popular support from the Palestinian population. While Arafat's control over more radical elements of the PLO was always in question, he has little or no control over newer and more radical Palestinian groups, who opposed the Oslo peace process and accused Arafat of corruption and incompetence in the management of Palestinian-controlled territory. It is increasingly the case that any future political settlements will have to include not only the Palestinian Authority but also other more radical Palestinian groups who direct the suicide-bombing campaigns. Given that Israel and the Palestinians, and the international community at large, have struggled to achieve a conflict management solution, the prospect of increasingly fractious internal politics in Israel and among the Palestinians is not encouraging. In the meantime, the economic situation for most Palestinians worsened dramatically as the Israeli government pursued a policy of economic and physical isolation of the West Bank and Gaza. Palestinian GDP had contracted to below 1986 levels by 2003. Between September 2000 and December 2002, the number of Palestinians living in acute poverty increased from 21 percent to 60 percent of the population. More than half the Palestinian population was dependent on food aid by mid-2003. Unemployment rates for Palestinians ranged between 30 and 50 percent from 2000 and 2003. The number of demolished homes exceeded 2500 by mid-2003.[15] These economic conditions only add to the grievances and resentment felt by Palestinians. Meanwhile, suicide bombings continue to kill civilians in Israel, with targets including shopping areas, nightclubs, and commuter buses. In 2004 Israel assassinated two Hamas leaders, and Palestinian civilians continue to be killed in Israeli military operations against Hamas and other groups the Israelis accuse of terrorism. By 2004 the death toll in the violence since the start of the El-Aqsa Intifada had exceeded 3000. The Israeli–Palestinian conflict continues to defy conflict management efforts, and illustrates the limits as well as the necessity of diplomatic solutions to armed conflicts.

DIPLOMACY AND CONFLICT MANAGEMENT IN NORTHERN IRELAND

The conflict in Northern Ireland has its origins in the Protestant English conquest of Catholic Ireland in the early 17th century. It has since become a conflict involving nationality, sovereignty, and self-determination. English dominance in Ireland was secured by William of Orange at the Battle of the Boyne in 1690. Catholic resistance and revolt through to the early 20th century (including the famous Easter Rising in 1916) increased sentiment in England for Home Rule in Ireland. Protestants opposed this idea as a recipe for absorption into the Catholic majority. After the Irish Civil War (1919–21) between the British and the Irish Republican Army (IRA) ended in a truce and the independence of Southern Ireland in 1922, sectarian violence in the North continued between Catholic Nationalists or Republicans, who wanted the six counties of Northern Ireland united with the South, and Protestant Loyalists or Unionists, who wanted Northern Ireland to remain under British rule. The period between 1922 and 1969 was relatively calm, but sectarian violence returned in what has been called the modern "time of troubles" in which more than 3200 people have been killed. The revived IRA began a campaign of violence against Protestants, and the British Army returned to Northern Ireland to restore stability. However, after the shooting of unarmed protestors in Londonderry in 1972 (known as "Bloody Sunday") and the imposition of direct rule from London, the British Army was regarded as an occupying force by most Catholics. Bombings and shootings by the IRA and extremist Protestant organizations continued through to the early 1990s. As with so many conflicts, most people and parties in Northern Ireland want a peaceful settlement, but extremist violence polarized the two sides and made compromise and reconciliation difficult. Many diplomatic efforts have been made to resolve the conflict, but they have foundered because one or more of the parties refused to negotiate or because acts of violence derailed peace initiatives.

A new round of peace talks began in 1996, under the mediation of U.S. Senator George Mitchell. Present were the Irish and British governments, and after the IRA announced a ceasefire and came to the table in 1997, all the major parties were present. Working under a deadline imposed by Mitchell, a diplomatic breakthrough occurred on April 10, 1998. The settlement was called the Belfast Agreement, but it is commonly called the Good Friday Agreement. The agreement included the following: Northern Ireland would remain a part of Great Britain as long as a majority of people wanted it; an assembly would be established in Northern Ireland for self-governance; institutions would be established to develop more cooperation between Northern Ireland and the Republic of Ireland; and the civil rights of Catholics would be established and protected. The agreement went to a referendum and passed by a large majority. Elections were held for the new assembly in June. However, violence did continue in the all too familiar forms of bombings, assassinations, and attacks on property. Tensions rose during the infamous "Orange Marches," which commemorate the Battle of the Boyne. In late 1999, the implementation of the Good Friday Agreement stalled, and the British government suspended the new assembly when the IRA refused to disarm.

Attempts to revitalize the Good Friday Agreement in 2000 and 2001 were not very successful. Both sides accused the other of noncompliance with the Agreement, and after a number of political resignations and the suspension of political institutions in Northern Ireland it seemed as if the process had failed.[16] However, in the wake of the September 11 attacks, the IRA was under increased pressure to meet its commitments to decommission its weapons and disarm.[17] The window of opportunity was lost amidst revelations that the IRA had been spying on the government. This scandal, and the very slow pace of IRA disarmament, once again led to the suspension of political institutions. In an effort to save the peace process, the British and Irish governments issued joint declarations in October 2003, calling on all sides to restore the momentum behind the Good Friday Agreement. Nevertheless, in early 2004 the peace process remained stalled, the political institutions of Northern Ireland function poorly, and the decommissioning of weapons continues to be slower than expected. While large-scale violence has not resumed, it remains a possibility if both sides do not renew their commitment to the peace process.

The cases of the Israeli–Palestinian conflict and the Northern Ireland conflict illustrate the enormity of the challenges facing diplomatic efforts to resolve violent disputes in global politics. For diplomacy to be a successful conflict management instrument, the parties to a dispute must prefer a negotiated settlement to other available alternatives (such as war or achieving no settlement at all). This is not always the case, and if one or more parties to a dispute are not interested in negotiations or bargain in bad faith or refuse to compromise on certain issues, diplomacy stands little chance of success. Even when there is a commitment from all parties to achieving a settlement, they may have difficulty controlling their own people in order to implement the results of negotiation. As a result, the outcomes of diplomatic conflict management efforts may be many and varied. Results can include an improved climate between the parties to a dispute, the establishment of a basis for further negotiation, the creation of a short-term agreement to settle an immediate problem, or the establishment of a firm basis for a lasting peace. However, results can include the creation of an agreement that becomes a point of dissatisfaction or humiliation for one of the actors or a breakdown in negotiations and the collapse of diplomatic efforts. Diplomatic outcomes will not necessarily eliminate the possibility of future disputes between the parties, but diplomatic effort is a crucial instrument for resolving conflicts in global politics. Without it, recourse to armed struggle is often the consequence.

DISARMAMENT AND ARMS CONTROL

The main assumption behind disarmament and arms control efforts is that weapons contribute to the outbreak of war, a position juxtaposed with the view that peace and stability can be attained only through balances of power or through preparation for war.[18] Advocates of disarmament and arms control argue that the frequency of war can be reduced by eliminating threatening or destabilizing weapons, preventing arms races that increase tensions and hostility and absorb financial resources, promoting mutual trust and confidence, and limiting the destructiveness of war if it does occur. In certain periods in history, the idea of disarmament and arms control has been well received. The destructiveness of World War I led to several arms control efforts. After World War II, the development of the atomic bomb and the nuclear arms race between the superpowers vastly increased the sense that something had to be done to control the development and production of these weapons. Peace movement organizations sponsored rallies, marches, and concerts dedicated to ending the arms race. Here we see non-state actors playing in what was previously a very state-centric game. In the contemporary post–Cold War period, interest has surged in existing arms control arrangements (as well as in the prospects for creating new ones) that are relevant to transnational security issues.

At this point, an important distinction must be made. Disarmament efforts seek to drastically reduce or eliminate all weapons as an important step toward the elimination of war itself. Arms control, however, aims at regulating the growth of weapons and sometimes (but not always) reducing arms levels. The aim of arms control is not the eradication of weapons or the elimination of war but the reduction in the risk of war through efforts to stabilize the status quo, build confidence between states and groups, encourage the peaceful resolution of disputes, and discourage the use of force. Therefore, "arms control is fundamentally a conservative enterprise. Disarmament seeks to overturn the status quo; arms control works to perpetuate it."[19]

Not surprisingly, few historical examples of disarmament efforts exist. Some of the more notable efforts include

- In sixth-century B.C.E. China, several states formed a disarmament league that contributed to a century of peace.

- In 1817, Great Britain and the United States signed the Rush–Bagot Treaty, which demilitarized the Canada–U.S. border and called for the dismantling of a number of military vessels on the Great Lakes, establishing the basis for what would become the world's longest undefended border.

- At the end of World War I, U.S. President Woodrow Wilson called for national disarmament to the lowest point consistent with domestic safety, a provision later watered down to disarmament to the lowest level consistent with national safety, which could mean almost anything.

- The League of Nations sponsored a World Disarmament Conference in 1932, which attempted to ban offensive weapons but foundered on the definition of which weapons were defensive and which were offensive.

- The United Nations has held a number of special sessions on disarmament since its inception in 1945.

Other examples of disarmament are forced measures (such as the restrictions placed on German armaments in the Versailles Treaty and on Japan after World War II) or are unintentional, caused by chaotic conditions within a state (such as the effect of the Iranian revolution on the Iranian armed forces, or the effect of the decline of the Russian economy on the

Russian armed forces today). In short, disarmament has a very limited historical record, although, as we will see, a new trend toward disarmament efforts may be developing.

In contrast, the historical record of arms control agreements is vast and varied. In almost all cases, arms control efforts have attempted to ban the production or deployment of a specific weapon (or a variant of a weapon) or to restrict the number of weapons a signatory is allowed to possess. For example, in the 11th century an effort was made by the Second Lateran Council to ban crossbows, and in 1868 the St. Petersburg Declaration banned explosive bullets. The 1899 and 1907 International Peace Conventions at The Hague banned a number of weapons (including poisonous gas). At the Washington Naval Conferences (1921–22), the United States, Great Britain, Japan, France, and Italy agreed to fixed ratios for the number of capital ships in their battle fleets, a production moratorium on new ones, and the scrapping of a significant number of those extant. During the Cold War, two broad types of arms control agreements existed. The most prominent of these were the bilateral agreements established by the two superpowers. In addition, several multilateral arms control agreements involving other countries were established. Some of these multilateral arrangements were directly related to the Cold War, while others were intended to have a wider, universal effect. Some arms control agreements covered a specified territory or region, while others had a global, or system-wide, scope. Many of these agreements survive to this day and form the foundation of contemporary efforts to address the transnational security issues of the post–Cold War world.

BILATERAL ARMS CONTROL AFTER THE COLD WAR

Bilateral agreements cover issues that concern two states. Compared with multilateral agreements, they tend to be easier to achieve because negotiators have to concern themselves with only one set of interests and differences. As we saw in Chapter 3, during the Cold War, superpower arms control focused on nuclear weapons and on ways to reduce the prospects for nuclear war. The signing of arms control agreements often accompanied larger efforts to improve the relationship between the United States and the Soviet Union in periods of détente. In addition, some arrangements were made in an informal manner: U.S. President Jimmy Carter and Soviet Foreign Minister Andrei Gromyko promised each other that their countries would never be the first to use nuclear weapons. This pledge was never made formal in an agreement, despite the efforts of "no first use declaration" advocates. NATO maintained the right to retaliate with nuclear weapons throughout the Cold War. Old habits are hard to break: in 1993 the government of Russia reaffirmed its right to use nuclear weapons to defend itself.

With the fall of the U.S.S.R., the Russian government did not speak for all of the nuclear weapons in the former Soviet Union. Ukraine, Belarus, and Kazakhstan now possessed weapons on their territories. After a period of intense negotiation (in particular with Ukraine, which had a powerful domestic constituency favouring the retention of nuclear weapons), all three countries signed the Lisbon Protocol to the START agreement in May 1992. This agreement obligated them to eliminate all nuclear weapons on their territories and sign the Non-Proliferation Treaty (NPT). All three countries have now done this, and in the process have joined South Africa as the only countries to dispossess themselves of nuclear weapons. In June 1992, at a summit in Washington, President Bush and President Yeltsin surprised the world by agreeing to a Joint Understanding under the START agreement that would reduce the nuclear arsenals of the superpowers by 60 percent—to 3000 warheads for Russia and 3500 warheads for the United States—by the year 2003 (later 2007). Formally signed as the START II Agreement in January 1993, the agreement is also significant in that it eliminates multiple warheads on all land-based ICBMs and restricts SLBM warheads to no more than 1750. Thus the START II Agreement has been hailed for enhancing strategic stability, by eliminating the weapons that would be most useful in a first strike by either side.

The end of the Cold War reduced the significance of bilateral arms control between the United States and Russia, but bilateral arms control agreements remain relevant for three reasons. First, such agreements between Russia and the United States remain a sign of positive diplomatic relations and mutual trust and confidence. Even though the Cold War was over, on May 24, 2002, U.S. President George W. Bush and Russian President Vladimir Putin signed the Strategic Offensive Reductions Treaty (SORT). The treaty restricts each country to possessing no more than 1700 to 2200 strategic warheads by December 31, 2012. While significant, the treaty did not address warhead destruction or reductions in nonstrategic (sometimes called "tactical") nuclear warheads. Nevertheless, if fully implemented, SORT will result in further cuts to the nuclear arsenals of the United States and Russia (see Figure 7.1 for a comparison of the number of nuclear warheads held by the United States and Russia under START and SORT). Second, bilateral arms control remains relevant in the context of securing Russia's nuclear warheads, fissile material, and nuclear weapons infrastructure. In 1991, the United States passed the Nunn–Lugar Act, otherwise known as the Cooperative Threat Reduction Program. This program, initiated with the cooperation of the Russian government, provides U.S. financial assistance to Russia for the identification, securing, and destruction of Russian nuclear and chemical weapons, as well as assists Russian nuclear scientists to find work in peaceful industries. Among other accomplishments, in the first 10 years of the program, 6212 warheads were removed from their missiles and many were dismantled and the fissile material secured.[20] Third, bilateral arms control between other sets of countries that have histories of conflict and crises can be a relevant strategy to secure regional stability and build confidence and trust. For example, nuclear arms control agreements, even of a limited nature,

Figure 7.1 Reductions in Strategic Nuclear Weapons under the START and SORT Processes

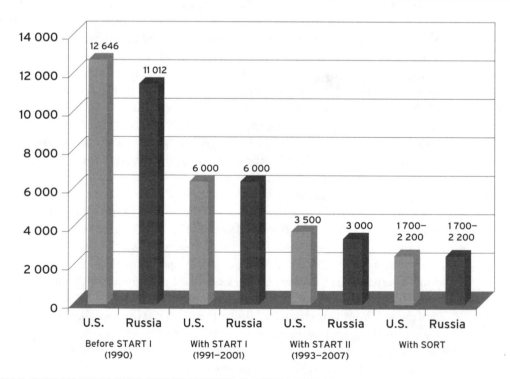

SOURCE: CENTER FOR DEFENSE INFORMATION AND FEDERATION OF AMERICAN SCIENTISTS.

between India and Pakistan will be an important component of any improvement in relations between these two countries.

MULTILATERAL ARMS CONTROL DURING AND AFTER THE COLD WAR

After the Cold War, the focus of arms control shifted away from the management and control of the nuclear arms race between the superpowers. Today, the focus of arms control is on transnational security issues, which by definition require the engagement and cooperation of a large number of countries. Some new agreements have been established to meet new threats, but for the most part older Cold War agreements have been revisited in an effort to strengthen them and adapt them to new international conditions (see Profile 7.1). In particular, interest has been renewed in Cold War multilateral agreements controlling the spread of nuclear, chemical, biological, and conventional weapons. In this section, we will examine the effort to respond to the threat of weapons proliferation using the instrument of multilateral arms control agreements.

As we discussed in Chapter 6, the proliferation of nuclear weapons is a priority in global politics. Two agreements figure prominently in the global effort to control the spread of nuclear weapons: the Non-Proliferation Treaty (NPT) and the Comprehensive Test Ban Treaty (CTBT). The NPT is the most important international treaty on the issue of nuclear proliferation. Signed in July 1968 and renewed every five years, the NPT had 187 signatories in 2003. At the April 1995 renewal conference, the NPT was extended indefinitely. The NPT binds its signatories to several provisions. Nuclear weapons states are obligated not to transfer nuclear weapons or related technology to non-nuclear weapons states. In turn, non-nuclear weapons states are obligated not to try to acquire nuclear weapons or related technology. Materials related to nuclear energy are exempt from these provisions; the NPT was designed to facilitate the spread of peaceful nuclear technology. Peaceful nuclear explosions are permitted, and all signatories pledge to work toward universal nuclear disarmament. The International Atomic Energy Agency (IAEA) is charged with verifying compliance with the NPT through constant monitoring of nuclear facilities in signatory countries and the use of on-site inspections.

The NPT has been the subject of considerable criticism. First, as an international treaty it binds only its members, and not all nuclear weapons states are signatories (e.g., Israel, Pakistan, and India). Despite the efforts of the IAEA, some non-nuclear weapons states have managed to build significant nuclear weapons development programs. Iraq possessed a sophisticated program during the 1980s, which was exposed after the end of the 1990–91 Gulf War. In 2003, IAEA inspectors discovered traces of highly enriched uranium (not needed for nuclear energy but usable in nuclear bombs) at nuclear facilities in Iran. Later that year, the IAEA director general stated that Iran had not lived up to its treaty obligations.[21] In 2004, further inspections revealed that Iran had hidden enrichment technologies from inspectors. In April 2003, North Korea had informed U.S. officials that is possessed a nuclear bomb. These examples have brought charges that the IAEA is ineffective as a **verification** and compliance mechanism as it lacks (among other things) sufficient resources and an enforcement capacity. Furthermore, the NPT is criticized for its role in encouraging the spread of nuclear energy. This role has been considered questionable in its own right, and civilian reactor programs can be the first step in acquiring a bomb. Finally, countries such as India (a recent member of the nuclear club) have argued that the NPT also obligates nuclear states to work for disarmament, and in the absence of progress on nuclear disarmament, it is hypocritical of nuclear weapons states to criticize countries such as India for developing nuclear weapons and violating a treaty they did not even sign. However, these criticisms should not obscure the fact that the NPT does maintain the norm that the spread of nuclear weapons is dangerous and should be avoided. The NPT, along with a network of agreements among suppliers of nuclear technology, does add another obstacle to keep potential nuclear weapons states from acquiring the weapons. Without the NPT, a bomb would be much easier to build and develop.[22]

	Major Multilateral Arms Control Treaties and Agreements	
PROFILE 7.1		
DATE	AGREEMENT	PRINCIPAL AIMS
1959	Antarctic Treaty	Prohibits military use of the Antarctic, including nuclear weapons testing
1963	Limited/Partial Test Ban Treaty	Prohibits testing nuclear weapons in the atmosphere, underwater, and in outer space
1967	Outer Space Treaty	Prohibits testing or stationing any weapons in space, and bans military manoeuvres in space
1967	Treaty of Tlatelolco	Creates Latin American nuclear weapons–free zone
1968 (1995)	Nuclear Non-Proliferation Treaty	Prohibits transfer of nuclear weapons and technology to non-nuclear states
1971	Seabed Treaty	Prohibits deployment of weapons of mass destruction (including nuclear weapons) beyond a 12-mile (20-kilometre) coastal limit
1972	Biological Weapons Convention	Prohibits production and stockpiling of biological weapons
1977	Environmental Modifications Convention	Bans use of technologies that can alter global weather patterns or ecology
1981	Inhumane Weapons Convention	Prohibits or restricts certain fragmentation weapons, incendiary weapons, and treacherous weapons
1985	South Pacific Nuclear Free Zone (Rarotonga Treaty)	Prohibits testing, acquisition, or deployment of nuclear weapons in the South Pacific
1986	Confidence Building and Security Building Measures and Disarmament in Europe (CDE) Agreement	Requires prior notification and on-site inspection of military exercises
1987	Missile Technology Control Regime (MTCR)	Restricts export of ballistic missiles and technology
1990	Conventional Forces in Europe (CFE) Treaty	Limits numbers of five categories of weapons in Europe (extended to former Soviet Union states in 1992)
1992	Open Skies Treaty	Permits surveillance and verification flights over signatory countries
1993	Chemical Weapons Convention	Requires all stockpiles and production facilities to be destroyed within 10 years
1993	UN Register of Conventional Arms	Calls on states to submit sale and receipt information on seven categories of conventional arms to a central registry
1996	Comprehensive Test Ban Treaty	Requires all signatories not to test nuclear weapons
1997	Global Land Mines Treaty	Requires all signatories to destroy stocks of land mines and not produce or export them

The CTBT also has a long history. Since the late 1950s, periodic efforts have been made to ban all nuclear tests. A Partial Test Ban Treaty signed in 1963 by the United States, Britain, and the U.S.S.R. (and joined by France in 1974 and China in 1980) did not include underground tests, a step that would constrain the development of new types of nuclear weapons. In the 1990s, several countries (including the United States) followed unilateral moratoriums on testing. With the signing of the CTBT on September 24, 1996, more than 90 countries committed themselves not to test nuclear weapons.[23] The CTBT had 171 signatories in 2004 (with 110 countries having ratified the treaty). The CTBT also prohibits peaceful nuclear explosions, closing an important loophole in the NPT. However, India and Pakistan, two nuclear weapons states, have refused to sign the CTBT. India has argued that the treaty provisions violate its sovereignty, and Pakistan will not sign until the security situation in South Asia changes (meaning until India signs).

The two most important mechanisms designed to address the problem of chemical and biological weapons proliferation are the Chemical Weapons Convention (CWC) and the Biological Weapons Convention (BWC). The CWC was signed in January 1993 and entered into force in April 1997. It is an ambitious and forward-looking treaty, aimed at disarmament rather than arms control. The signatories to the CWC are obligated to complete the destruction of all of their chemical weapons and production facilities within 10 years of the treaty entering into force. Signatory countries must declare whether they possess chemical weapons or manufacturing facilities and provide a precise inventory of both, along with plans for their destruction. Signatories are also obligated to declare whether they have received chemical weapons from another country or whether they have transferred them to another country. The CWC also has a complex verification system in which countries may mount challenge inspections in other countries to verify compliance. As of 2004, 182 countries had signed the CWC (162 had ratified the treaty). The United States ratified the treaty in 1997. However, once again the CWC binds only its signatories, and the ease with which chemical weapons can be manufactured has led to suspicion that clandestine chemical weapons facilities may evade the attention of the world community.

The Review Conferences of the BWC have convened periodically since the signing of the BWC (1972) and its entry into force (1975). The BWC was the first multilateral arms control effort aimed at eliminating an entire class of weapons of mass destruction. The BWC prohibits the development, production, and stockpiling of biological weapons, although it does not explicitly ban their use since the 1925 Geneva Protocol for the Prohibition of the Use in War of Asphyxiating, Poisonous, or Other Gases and of Bacteriological Weapons of Warfare had already done so. However, the BWC has been heavily criticized for lacking a verification system and allowing signatories to continue research into biological weapons and protective measures for defensive purposes. In recognition of the limitations of the BWC and the increasing threat posed by biological weapons, in 1995 an Ad Hoc Working Group of governments began discussions to strengthen the BWC. Over six years later, the working group drafted a proposed protocol to the BWC that would require signatories to declare the existence and location of treaty-relevant facilities, and put in place a system of verification inspections. However, in 2001 the United States rejected the draft protocol, arguing that it did not cover enough relevant facilities, would be applied mostly to Western states and not those states most suspected of developing biological weapons, and could be used as an instrument of industrial espionage against U.S. biotech companies. The U.S. rejection of the proposed protocol was met with a great deal of criticism and condemnation, with supporters of the treaty inside the United States and around the world dismissing the concerns of the U.S. government as unwarranted and even inaccurate. However, the U.S. rejection of the protocol effectively erased any hopes for strengthening the BWC. The signatories of the BWC continue to meet in conferences, but there has been little progress on the key issues.

For much of the Cold War, there was not a great deal of discussion of arms control proposals aimed at the problem of conventional weapons proliferation. One mechanism in place (and it is still in place) was the end-user certificate, which accompanied any shipment of weapons. The end-user certificate specified the country of final delivery and prohibited that country from diverting the weapons to any other country. This mechanism was subject to the effects of bribery (paying border officials to ignore the certificate), counterfeit certificates, and smuggling. During the Cold War, much of the effort directed toward conventional arms control was aimed at the conventional balance of forces in Europe. However, as concern over the spread of conventional weapons has increased, greater attention has been placed on establishing controls over such weapons. Some prominent examples of non-nuclear multilateral arms control efforts are the Conventional Forces in Europe (CFE) Treaty, the Missile Technology Control Regime (MTCR), and the UN Register of Conventional Arms. The CFE Treaty grew out of the Mutual and Balanced Force Reduction (MBFR) Talks, which were conducted from 1973 to 1988. The aim was to reduce the levels of conventional weapons in Europe maintained by both NATO and the Warsaw Pact. The MBFR Talks were generally unproductive, but they laid the foundation for the CFE Treaty, signed by 23 European states in November 1990. The treaty entered into force in 1991 and was extended to include the newly independent states of the former Soviet Union in 1992. The treaty classifies weapons into five broad categories of Treaty Limited Equipment (TLE) in a geographic area from the Atlantic Ocean to the Ural Mountains in Russia (the so-called Atlantic to the Urals, or ATTU, zone). All countries have allowable limits in TLE, which they cannot exceed, although in practice most countries maintain arsenals lower than they are permitted under the CFE. However, the CFE has been criticized, as countries in Europe have "cascaded" more modern armaments to other countries, which have in turn sold their old weapons on the international market.

The MTCR is an informal arrangement designed to control the spread of **ballistic missile** technology. As such, it is not a treaty, nor is it legally binding on its membership. Formed in 1987 by seven producers of ballistic missile technology, the MTCR initially covered nuclear-capable missiles and was later expanded in 1993 to include chemical-capable and biological-capable missiles as well. The MTCR now comprises 33 states. However, because the MTCR is not a treaty, compliance is voluntary. In 1993, China (which had pledged to abide by the provisions of the MTCR) was found to have transferred ballistic missile components to Pakistan. India, Pakistan, Iran, and North Korea continue to develop their ballistic missile programs, and all have received at least some international assistance in doing so. On the other hand, the MTCR has contributed to the cancellation of some ballistic missile development programs, by making it difficult to acquire certain technologies or creating a political environment that condemns such efforts. Brazil, South Korea, Taiwan, Argentina, Egypt, and South Africa have all stopped or suspended ballistic missile development efforts.

The UN arms register was created in 1991 by a UN General Assembly resolution. The register is an attempt to establish an information service to track arms shipments around the world in seven categories of weapons: tanks, armoured combat vehicles, heavy artillery, combat aircraft, attack helicopters, warships, and missiles and missile systems. Ideally, states will submit information to the register on any exports and imports of weapons. In 2002, 120 states notified the UN registry of arms transfers. It is hoped that this information will increase the transparency of arms transfers around the world and so reduce the secretive nature of arms transfers and the tensions and suspicions this secrecy can create. Critics of the registry argue that it places no real limits on the transfer of weapons and is entirely dependent on the willingness of states to provide information about their arms sales and purchases. In addition, the register can compile information only on the open arms trade; it has no effect whatsoever on the covert arms trade and may, in fact, increase it.

In addition to these mechanisms, other arms control instruments do exist, but they are unilateral, or measures agreed to by relatively small groups of states. In other words, they lack the near-universal quality of global arms control treaties. In the Western Hemisphere, 20 countries have signed the Inter-American Convention on Transparency in Conventional Weapons Acquisitions, which requires signatories to report their regional weapons sales and purchases. States can impose arms embargoes against other states, and impose arms sales codes of conduct on their domestic producers. Groups of states can agree not to transfer certain technologies to other states: for example, the 33 countries of the Wassenaar Arrangement have agreed to exchange information on certain weapons transfers to encourage the responsible transfer of weapons and related technologies. All of these mechanisms have their limitations, and the challenges facing arms control agreements in general have raised questions as to the effectiveness of arms control efforts.

CRITICS OF ARMS CONTROL

Both disarmament and arms control efforts have been subjected to heavy criticism. This criticism has varied with the nature of agreement under discussion, but several critical themes have emerged consistently over time:

- Arms control is risky and even dangerous because success depends on trusting one's opponents not to cheat.

- Because the word of one's opponents is not to be trusted, arms control compliance must be verified, a complicated and difficult task.

- Arms control agreements will be violated in times of crisis or war.

- Weapons cannot be effectively banned because the knowledge to manufacture them exists.

- Those weapons that are banned or restricted have little military utility and are not considered useful weapons.

- Arms control agreements succeed only in channelling arms competitions into weapons-system types that are not banned or restricted (the SALT limits on missile numbers led to the deployment of multiple warheads on missiles).

- Technological developments can render arms control agreements obsolete or ineffective.

- Making agreements with authoritarian governments is ill advised, because they are more apt to cheat and are able to conceal this cheating with greater effectiveness.

- Arms control agreements bind only signatories, not nonsignatories, who may proceed with arms buildups or the manufacture of certain banned weapons.

- Arms control arrangements are often violated. (There were 12 alleged uses of chemical or biological weapons between 1975 and 1981 that violated the BWC, and more than three-quarters of all nuclear tests were conducted after the Partial Test Ban Treaty went into effect.)

In response to these criticisms, advocates of disarmament and arms control maintain that states and groups have entered into arms control negotiations with deceitful purposes. States have used arms control to gain an advantage over an opponent. In some cases, states have made arms control proposals while they are ahead in the arms race. In other cases, states have sought to use arms control to permit weapons and capabilities where they have advantages and to restrict weapons and capabilities where they are at a disadvantage. At times, arms control has been used to subjugate other states. Many arms control advocates also suspect that states enter arms control arrangements as public relations exercises. Until governments around the world are committed to the idea of disarmament and arms control for the mutual long-term benefit of all, the capacity of disarmament and arms control measures to live up to their promise of a more peaceful world will be limited.

There is no doubt that the end of the Cold War created a climate that facilitated the negotiation of many far-reaching arms control agreements. In addition, agreements such as the CWC represent a significant increase in both the aims and the provisions of arms control. The trend may be toward attempts to control weapons that are seen as especially inhumane or indiscriminate. However, any optimism must be tempered by several sobering facts. First, governments continue to direct more resources toward researching and developing new weapons than to attempts to control weapons. Second, military and political leaders remain wary of disarmament and arms control as a means of strengthening their security. Trusting in the word and restraint of others remains perilous in an anarchic, self-help international system. As a result, military preparedness remains a primary instrument of state security. Third, leaders are reluctant to engage in arms control either because they want to attain a certain military capability (whether nuclear weapons or ballistic missiles) and are unwilling to commit themselves to an agreement not to acquire it, or because they possess a superiority in a certain military capability and see no reason why they should accept constraints on it. Fourth, increasingly, arms control is not a matter of East and West (as it was in the Cold War), but a matter between the North and the South, with Southern governments viewing global efforts to prevent the spread of certain weapons as discriminatory acts by the rich nations anxious to perpetuate their military superiority. Fifth, a growing number of states are becoming capable of developing and manufacturing sophisticated weapons systems, making the process of reaching an arms control agreement among a larger and larger number of states an increasingly difficult proposition. Finally, when it comes to arms control, expectation has always exceeded results. Arms control cannot be regarded as a panacea, for true international security "depends not as much on arms or arms control as on reducing as much as possible the sources of conflict in international situations and on finding effective nonviolent means of resolving the conflicts that remain."[24]

HUMAN SECURITY AND ARMS CONTROL

We introduced the concept of human security in Chapter 6, but expand on it here because much of the human security agenda is in fact a conflict management agenda. Human security is an idea that calls for a shift in thinking on security matters from the level of the state to the level of the human individual. In doing so, human security envisions placing individual security considerations first in global politics, in essence proposing a new global hierarchy of security priorities, in which the security of individuals is placed above state sovereignty and territorial integrity, particularly if a state proves unwilling or unable to provide for the human security of its population. Human security was first articulated in the UN Human Development Report in 1994. The report argued that "human security can be said to have two main aspects. It means, first, safety from such chronic threats such as hunger, disease and repression. And second, it means protection from sudden and hurtful disruptions of daily life—whether in homes, in jobs, or in communities."[25] Former Canadian Foreign Affairs Minister Lloyd Axworthy was one of the leading advocates of the human security approach. Axworthy defined human security as "security against economic deprivation, an acceptable quality of life, and a guarantee of fundamental rights … [this] requires that basic needs are met, but it also acknowledges that sustained economic development, human rights and fundamental freedoms, the rule of law, good governance, sustainable development, and social equity are as important as arms control and disarmament."[26] The human security concept did attract some governments, such as Canada and Norway, who made it a prominent component of their foreign policies. A Human Security Network was established, which currently consists of 13 states. Human security attracted many NGOs in the arms control, humanitarian, and aid communities, and governmental and NGO cooperation became a signature of the human security approach in practice, realized in such initiatives as the 1997 Treaty to Ban Landmines.

Human security has been criticized, most notably for a lack of precision. *Human security* is by nature a very vague term, a large tarp that covers a wide range of issues and topics and agendas. While this makes the term politically useful, unifying a large range of actors and causes, it is a poor guide for establishing priorities. As Roland Paris argues, "Human security is like 'sustainable development'—everyone is for it, but few people have a clear sense of what it means."[27] The vagueness and scope of the term also create contradictions: there are material and moral consequences to intervening on behalf of human security, just as there are material and moral consequences of not intervening. In Canada, the human security concept was accused of being "pinchpenny diplomacy" (diplomacy on the cheap) and "pulpit diplomacy" (preaching morality while alienating allies).[28] Nevertheless, human security did establish a role and a voice for Canada.[29] Human security was also a driving intellectual force behind a number of concrete initiatives that culminated in international treaties or agreements, most notably the Ottawa Treaty (see Profile 7.2). Other initiatives that human security can claim as policy offspring are the International Criminal Court and diplomatic initiatives on child soldiers. Efforts are underway to develop arms control agreements on cluster bombs and the proliferation of light weapons. The lasting impact of the human security concept in global politics is uncertain. Nevertheless, there is no question the concept will continue to have a place in the discourse on security, and a place in the policy initiatives of some states and NGOs. The lasting significance of human security may well be the entrenchment of the idea that security cannot, and should not, always be defined in state-centric terms. However, it is unclear if the concept can continue to be a driving force behind arms control in the absence of a significant number of states to champion the idea and act according to its principles.

INTERNATIONAL LAW AND CONTROLS ON WAR

Efforts to prevent or control war through international law have concentrated on two issues: the prohibition or outlawing of war as an instrument of policy, and the imposition of rules and regulations to establish a lawful conduct in war. Many efforts have been made to prohibit war, although many of these efforts were qualified in some way. The Hague Conventions of 1899 and 1907, for example, bound signatories to seek a peaceful resolution to their disputes before resorting to force. Presumably, if no peaceful resolution could be found, war was permissible. The Bryan Treaties of 1913–14 banned declarations of war by one state against another before an arbitration committee had met to consider the circumstances of the conflict. The Covenant of the League of Nations bound League members to renounce aggression, and the signatories to the 1928 Kellogg–Briand Pact forfeited the right to go to war (see Profile 7.3). The Charter of the UN (Article 2/4) prohibits the use or threat of force in the international system, and a 1974 General Assembly resolution banned aggression. However, none of these efforts has succeeded in achieving the real goal of banning the use of military force, war, or aggression.

Partly because of the historical record of attempts to prohibit war, much of the body of international law on war concerns its conduct. As early as 1400 B.C.E. agreements had been established concerning the treatment of prisoners, and poisoned weapons were outlawed in India in 500 B.C.E. Modern legal efforts to control war are founded on the Geneva Conventions

PROFILE 7.2 Weapons Proliferation and Human Security: The Global Land Mines Problem

The Ottawa Treaty. The signing of the Convention on the Prohibition of the Use, Stockpiling, Production and Transfer of Antipersonnel Mines and on Their Destruction, 3 December 1997. From left are International Campaign to Ban Landmines representative Jody Williams, President of the International Committee of the Red Cross Cornelio Sommaruga, UN Secretary-General Kofi Annan, Canadian Foreign Affairs Minister Lloyd Axworthy, and Canadian Prime Minister Jean Chrétien. (CP Photo)

Anti-personnel land mines (APLs) are designed to explode automatically in response to pressure or tripwires. Because they are easy to make and deploy, and are cheap (as little as $3 to $15 for simpler mines), they have become very common in intrastate wars around the world. In the mid-1990s, an estimated 60 million to 110 million land mines were buried around the world in 64 countries. More mines were laid every year, while extraction rates were low: every year UN or private de-miners took out 10 000 mines. It was estimated that extracting the mines already buried could take 1100 years at a cost of U.S.$33 billion. The human costs of land mines were horrific; land mines killed or wounded an estimated 26 000 people a year through the late 1980s and early to mid-1990s. It is estimated that there are currently 250 000 "mine amputees." Mine injuries are painful and crippling, involving costly treatment and lengthy rehabilitation. They are also an obstacle to post-hostilities recovery and development, rendering land unusable for crops or grazing and preventing safe passage on roads or trails. Mines are indiscriminate: they kill men, women, children, combatants, and noncombatants (as well as livestock), in many cases long after the war in which they were laid is over.

Land mines represent a serious threat to human security in countries such as Cambodia, Angola, and Bosnia.

Efforts to ban the stockpiling, production, and export of land mines grew in the 1990s. A UN resolution called for a moratorium on land mine exports (with then Secretary-General Boutros Boutros-Ghali giving the matter his personal attention), and NGOs such as the International Committee of the Red Cross and the International Campaign to Ban Landmines increased their pressure on governments. By 1996 Canada had begun to exert international leadership on this issue, imposing a unilateral moratorium on the production, export, and operational use of anti-personnel land mines. In 1997 Canada led a successful campaign to conclude a global anti-personnel land mine treaty, which was signed in Ottawa on December 2, 1997. The treaty bans the use, production, transfer, and stockpiling of anti-personnel mines and obligates signatories to destroy their stock of mines. The government of Canada contributes funds for mine clearance, medical treatment, rehabilitation, and artificial limbs. However, key countries did not sign the treaty, including the United States, Greece, Turkey, Russia, China, India, Pakistan, Iraq, and Iran. The 47 countries outside the treaty had a combined stockpile of over 200 million land mines in 2004. The treaty also cannot solve the problem of the mines already buried: between 15 000 and 20 000 people are killed or injured by land mines every year. Nevertheless, the treaty was a major diplomatic and arms control success and a significant breakthrough for the human security concept. In 2004, 143 countries had acceded to the treaty, and land mine use has declined. Production of land mines has dropped, de-mining efforts continue, and the number of victims per year has declined.

SOURCES: "THE UNITED NATIONS AND MINE CLEARANCE," *OVERVIEW*—JUNE 1995, UNITED NATIONS DEPARTMENT OF HUMANITARIAN AFFAIRS, INTERNATIONAL MEETING ON MINE CLEARANCE, GENEVA, 5–7 JUNE 1995; ARMS CONTROL ASSOCIATION FACT SHEET: THE OTTAWA CONVENTION: SIGNATORIES AND STATE PARTIES (WASHINGTON, DC: THE ARMS CONTROL ASSOCIATION, 2004); AND *LANDMINE MONITOR REPORT 2003: TOWARD A MINE-FREE WORLD*. INTERNATIONAL CAMPAIGN TO BAN LANDMINES (NEW YORK: HUMAN RIGHTS WATCH, 2003).

PROFILE 7.3 The Kellogg–Briand Pact

Formally known as the Treaty Providing for the Renunciation of War as an Instrument of State Policy, the Kellogg–Briand Pact was originally a treaty agreed to by the governments of the United States and France in 1927. U.S. Secretary of State Frank B. Kellogg and French Foreign Minister Aristide Briand agreed to outlaw war between their two states. The enthusiasm of the U.S. government led to an open offer to other governments to sign the treaty; by 1934, 64 states (most of the states in the world at that time) were signatories. However, the hopes of the treaty were never realized. Most signatories placed caveats on their commitment to the renunciation of war; Japan, for example, insisted on the right to wage war in self-defence, while Great Britain insisted on its right to intervene militarily in areas of the world of interest to it (meaning its colonies). The treaty contained no enforcement mechanism and was unable to respond to acts of aggression. The treaty was also signed by states that had clear expansionist or revisionist ambitions. As a result, the treaty has been derided as an example of the emptiness and futility of efforts to outlaw war.

of 1948, and the additional Protocols of 1977. This body of law, sometimes referred to as the laws of war or International Humanitarian Law (IHL), has focused on establishing rules of conduct that include distinguishing between combatants and noncombatants (civilians), the treatment of prisoners of war, establishing what is considered an indiscriminate attack, restrictions on carpet bombing, extrajudicial executions, and the establishment of war zones. International law has also focused on defining war crimes such as genocide (see Chapter 8), and on the prohibition or restriction of specific types of weapons. Modern efforts at the latter are largely derived from two special UN conferences on conventional weapons held at Lucerne in 1974 and Lugano in 1976. These conferences laid the foundation for the three protocols of the 1981 Inhumane Weapons Convention, which banned different types of weapons systems. Protocol I covers fragmentation weapons, banning the use of toxic fragments and fragments that are undetectable by X-ray. Protocol II covers treacherous weapons, prohibiting booby traps, the use of mines against civilians, the placement of mines, and the recording of minefields. Protocol III covers incendiary weapons, prohibiting attacks on the natural elements (unless they are used as cover for military movements) and the use of incendiary weapons against civilians.

Despite the letter of international law, these provisions are frequently violated. Many states and substate groups violate IHL because they are unaware of the law or they choose to violate it knowing the chances of enforcement are slim. To use the example of land mines, today many mines are manufactured out of plastic, which is difficult to detect by X-ray. Mines are also laid indiscriminately, and communal group militias or insurgency groups seldom record their locations. Few, if any, enforcement mechanisms exist to support the observation of international law in war. In fact, the efforts to build and apply such a law—the Nuremberg and Tokyo war crimes trials and the war crimes trials in Bosnia and Rwanda—have been criticized as victors' justice, imposed on the losers of a conflict by the winners (see Chapter 9 for more on this). International law also has difficulty keeping up with technological developments; many new weapons systems are not covered by international law. Nevertheless, international law on war establishes norms of conduct and seeks to ban certain weapon systems that are especially inhumane; to violate these norms is to invite international condemnation and the loss of legitimacy.

INTERNATIONAL ORGANIZATIONS AND CONFLICT MANAGEMENT

IOs perform several tasks and roles that are both directly and indirectly related to conflict management. IOs can act as a forum for debate and discussion, assisting members to become familiar with one another, reducing the chance of misunderstanding or misinterpretation, and providing an opportunity for actors to float or test proposals or ideas to gauge the initial reaction of others. In this capacity, IOs can also act as a steam valve for international conflict and crises, permitting political leaders to accuse and condemn their opponents without resorting to violence. This ability can be particularly useful when public opinion back home demands a verbal response, especially in cases where doing nothing best serves the interests of peace. Of course, governments can also be criticized for avoiding substantive action on an issue by raising it in an international forum but doing little else.

IOs can provide third-party mediation services in times of crisis or war. Because they are established actors with a permanent location and membership, they can provide physical facilities, staff, and diplomatic support for negotiations. The UN provided intermediaries that facilitated the ceasefire in the Iran–Iraq War. Other members of an IO can also encourage the parties to a dispute to come to a settlement and offer rewards and threats to that end. IOs can establish fact-finding and information missions designed to obtain more objective sources of evidence and information. In other cases, the staff or leadership of the organization itself may become involved in facilitating an agreement. In 1988, UN Secretary-General Javier Perez de Cuellar and UN diplomats helped develop the plan under which Soviet forces withdrew from Afghanistan. Finally, with the agreement of the parties to a dispute, IOs may act as arbitrators.

IOs can also provide legitimacy to the policies of a state or a group of states, and can serve to constrain unilateralism. How can the international community constrain unilateral actions? To act as a collective, IOs require the consensus of their membership (depending on the voting procedure of the organization). If states or groups want to act as a collective, with the advantages of added legitimacy that joint action provides, then some states or groups will have to compromise or alter their positions so that a common stance can be reached. Therefore, organizations can help alter outcomes in such a way as to enhance peace by inhibiting or restraining certain members from aggressive actions. For example, Canadian (and European) support for NATO is partly attributed to the constraining effect of NATO on the United States. The Iraq War proved that in some cases states will act on their own or in a group without the legitimacy provided by an IO (in this case, the UN). However, the relatively low level of international support for the United States–led war is in part attributable to the lack of a UN Security Council resolution authorizing the war.

IOs can promote peace and stability by establishing norms and principles of conduct and governance among their members. Members must often commit to the rejection of aggression and military force as means of resolving disputes. Over time, this norm of nonviolence may become so pervasive that governments and substate groups will no longer regard military force as an option in the conduct of their affairs with each other. Karl Deutsch referred to such groups of countries as "security communities," which share common values, predictability of behaviour, and mutual responsiveness (the capability and willingness to respond quickly to one another).[30] Finally, IOs seek to promote domestic values and systems of governance that are regarded as stabilizing and nonaggressive. Examples include the **Organization for Security and Co-operation in Europe (OSCE)**, which is built on the promotion of the principles of democracy and the protection of human rights, and the Organization of American States (OAS), which maintains a unit for the promotion of democracy. Of course, a realist would remind us that these organizations are nothing more than the creations of states and will act only when states agree to act. In contrast, the Neo-Marxist perspective would reject this as yet another example of Western cultural imperialism.

In recent years, emphasis has shifted toward regional multilateral organizations as conflict management instruments. The hope is that they may contribute to regional peace and security by encouraging and facilitating cooperation among their members, establishing norms for the peaceful resolution of disputes, and acting as conduits for regional efforts to manage conflict. Among the many examples of the involvement of regional organizations in conflict management efforts are the following:

- *The North Atlantic Treaty Organization (NATO).* Founded in 1949 to defend Western Europe against a Soviet attack, NATO has altered its political purpose to the maintenance of stability and has changed its military structure to respond to crises. The organization has created a number of consultative instruments to strengthen cooperation between its members and the states of the former Warsaw Pact and Soviet Union. Two prominent examples are the Partnerships for Peace (PFP) and the Euro-Atlantic Partnership Council (EAPC). NATO has achieved a higher level of political and military cooperation among its membership than virtually any other organization in the world. NATO troops enforced the Dayton Agreement in the former Yugoslavia in 1995, and NATO forces are still deployed in Bosnia. NATO launched an air war against Serbia in 1999, and maintains a security force in the troubled territory of Kosovo. NATO is also in charge of the international security presence in Afghanistan. NATO has expanded to 26 members and has an increasingly global role in world affairs.

- *The Organization of American States (OAS).* Founded in 1948, the OAS was preoccupied with the issue of the spread of Communism to Latin America during the Cold War. Initially heavily influenced by the United States, the membership took an increasingly anti–United States stand later in the Cold War, unanimously opposing the intervention in Grenada in 1983. Since the Cold War, the central task of the OAS has been the promotion of mutual security, regional economic and social development, nonintervention and sovereign equality, the peaceful settlement of disputes, and democracy and human rights. Although the OAS is linked to the Rio Treaty, a security pact among the countries of the Western Hemisphere, it has rarely been involved in security issues. An indication that this stance may be changing came with the involvement of the OAS in the termination of several insurgency conflicts in Central America in the 1990s.

- *The Organization of African Unity (OAU).* Established in 1963, the OAU was built on the concept of Pan-Africanism and the effort to encourage decolonization and economic development. Created to promote African solidarity in world affairs, the cooperation of African countries, and the defence of the sovereignty and territory of African countries, the OAU had some success in mediating conflicts. However, it has failed to address more complex interstate and intrastate disputes such as the Nigerian Civil War, the Ethiopia–Somalia War, and the civil wars in Angola and Mozambique. More recently, the OAU was unable to mediate a settlement to the communal conflict in Somalia or to the Ethiopian–Eritrean War, though a ceasefire has been reached in the latter. In the Sirte Declaration of 1999, the OAU launched the African Union, a new organization dedicated to the political, economic, and social unity and development of the continent. Another African regional organization, the **Economic Community of West African States (ECOWAS)**, dominated by Nigerian participation, has had mixed results in its efforts to manage the conflicts of West Africa.

- *The Arab League.* Formed in 1945, the Arab League was designed to promote cooperation between Arab countries on economic and social affairs, communications, culture, and health. Egypt was expelled for making peace with Israel in 1979 but was readmitted in 1987. As a mechanism for conflict management, the Arab League has not been very successful; most of its proclamations and plans have gone unheeded. It was unable to broker a resolution in the events leading up to Iraq's invasion of Kuwait and ended up authorizing its member states to cooperate with the United States–led coalition against Iraq in 1990–91. Tensions over this decision led several states to boycott the League. Subsequent disagreement over the maintenance of sanctions against Iraq kept the League divided. The League has been criticized for its failure to respond effectively to the Iraq War, and it has had little or no impact in resolving interstate or intrastate conflicts among its members.

- *The Association of Southeast Asian Nations (ASEAN).* ASEAN was formed in 1967. Formally a mechanism for regional cooperation, ASEAN has addressed a widening range of issues from trade liberalization to refugees to the drug trade. ASEAN has moved slowly into the realm of security issues. It played a significant role in ending the Vietnamese occupation of Cambodia. Today, ASEAN is the basis for regional political and security arrangements, including joint military exercises. ASEAN members are involved (often as a collective) in larger Pacific-wide cooperation initiatives, such as the Asia-Pacific Economic Cooperation (APEC) arrangement. In 1993, ASEAN expanded its security role with the creation of the ASEAN Regional Forum (ARF). However, there has been little progress on deepening security cooperation in this forum.

In part, this trend toward regionalism in conflict management is due to the troubles facing the UN (see Chapter 5). Short of money and resources, the UN has found it increasingly difficult to maintain its current obligations and programs and even harder to undertake new operations and tasks. However, the turn to regional organizations is also a function of the belief that they are more effective as conflict management instruments within their respective regions than are extraregional or universal organizations such as the UN. Indeed, the UN Charter calls explicitly for cooperation between the two levels.

Regional organizations do have advantages when addressing crises or wars within their own region. First, their members will be more familiar with local disputes and tensions and will place the conflict in the hands of locals rather than in the distant headquarters of the UN. Second, regional organizations may not be constrained by disagreements among countries at the UN. To the extent that a regional consensus exists on a response to a crisis or conflict, a local mechanism may prove more capable of a response than a divided UN Security Council (or General Assembly). Third, regional organizations, by virtue of their geographic proximity, are better able to respond quickly than the UN is, particularly if a peacekeeping or intervention force is required. In some cases, regional organizations may have better capabilities than the UN and a more streamlined political and military decision-making structure (this is certainly the case with NATO).

However, regional organizations also have some drawbacks. First, the fact that local actors are involved may lead some of these actors to pursue their own interests in the crisis or conflict. Similarly, the parties to a dispute may feel that local actors and regional organizations lack the requisite neutrality and impartiality to act as mediators or facilitators. An extraregional actor may be advantageous in such cases. Second, regional organizations are often incapable of offering sufficient rewards (such as economic aid) or acting on threatened punishments (such as economic sanctions). Most lack the economic resources and military capabilities to undertake significant action. In many cases they are unable under their respective charters to undertake such actions, and they are unable to enforce their will on states by any means other than moral appeal. Third, most regional organizations in the world do not have a high level of political or military cohesion. The members of such organizations are often deeply divided, and a meaningful consensus is often very difficult to achieve. Nonetheless, the potential certainly exists for regional organizations to play an increased role in conflict management, especially in cooperation with other organizations or extraregional actors.

FROM UNITED NATIONS PEACEKEEPING TO HUMANITARIAN INTERVENTION

From its inception, the UN was first and foremost a security institution, designed to establish peace and security in the post–World War II world. As stated in the first sentence of the Preamble to the Charter, the UN was intended to "save succeeding generations from the scourge of war."[31] The UN was designed as a collective security system, and the UN Charter committed member states to resolve their differences peacefully and refrain from the use of force.[32] However, the UN Charter also recognized the limitation of collective security as experienced by the League of Nations; under Article 51 of the Charter, UN member states retain the right of self-defence, and under Article 52, member states retain the right to engage in regional arrangements (such as alliances) to protect their security. The UN system is also built around the state as the key unit in global politics, a unit that enjoys the principle of sovereignty and freedom from interference in its domestic affairs. In matters of security, the UN Charter strikes a balance between the collective security provisions of the UN and the rights and the sovereignty of states.

The conflict management provisions of the UN are found in Chapters 6 and 7 of the UN Charter. Chapter 6, entitled "Pacific Settlement of Disputes," calls on member states to resolve their disputes through "negotiation, enquiry, mediation, conciliation, arbitration, judicial settlement, resort to regional agencies or arrangements, or other peaceful means of their own choice." The UN Security Council is able to investigate disputes to determine whether they endanger international peace and security and, in that eventuality, make recommendations for methods of resolution. Chapter 7, entitled "Action with Respect to Threats to the Peace, Breaches of the Peace, and Acts of Aggression," is the heart of the collective security function of the UN. In Article 40, the UN Security Council may call on the parties to a dispute to abide by Security Council resolutions concerning the conflict. In Article 41, the UN Security Council can then call on member states to observe measures directed at the parties to a dispute that do not involve the use of force (these are commonly sanctions in some form). Finally, if these measures prove inadequate, the Security Council can invoke Article 42, which reads

> Should the Security Council consider that measures provided
> for in Article 41 would be inadequate, it may take such action
> by air, sea, or land forces as may be necessary to maintain or
> restore international peace and security. Such actions may
> include demonstrations, blockade, and other operations by air,
> sea, or land forces of Members of the United Nations.

Chapter 7 also specifies the obligation of member states to provide forces, facilities, and transit rights for such operations.

The Cold War had a profound influence on the UN, but the most fundamental consequence was the inability of the UN to perform its collective security function because of the divergence between the veto-holding permanent members of the Security Council. Only the Korean anomaly (see Chapter 3) stands as an example of UN collective security in action during the Cold War. As a result, the most visible and significant conflict management role performed by the UN since its creation has been peacekeeping. Between 1945 and 2003, the UN created 56 peacekeeping operations (37 of them between 1990 and 2003), a remarkable achievement considering that peacekeeping is an entirely improvisational activity and is not even mentioned in the UN Charter. The origin of UN peacekeeping lies in the use of observer and truce supervision missions, a tradition drawn from the experience of the League of Nations.[33] In 1947, the UN General Assembly established an observer mission along the Greek border to ascertain whether the Greek Communists in the Greek Civil War were receiving aid from their Communist neighbours (they were). In June 1948, following the Arab–Israeli War of that year, the UN established the United Nations Truce Supervisory Organization (UNTSO) to supervise and observe the truce in Palestine. In 1949, after a UN-facilitated ceasefire ended a war between India and Pakistan, the UN established the Military Observer Group in India and Pakistan (UNMOGIP). However, the term "peacekeeping" was not coined until 1956, when the Suez Crisis prompted (under the suggestion of Canadian Secretary of State for External Affairs Lester B. Pearson) the creation of the first United Nations Emergency Force (see Profile 7.4).

These early experiences laid the foundation for UN peacekeeping during the Cold War. Over time, a set of conventions about the composition, aims, and tasks of peacekeeping operations emerged, which were for the most part consistently followed in most UN peacekeeping operations. The conventions of what came to be called "traditional" peacekeeping included

- *Impartiality.* No side should be seen as being favoured by the UN peacekeepers. Unlike Chapter 7 collective security operations, UN peacekeeping did not identify an aggressor (although an individual's acts could be condemned and blame assigned). The maintenance of this impartiality was essential if the missions of the UN were to be successfully carried out.

- *Nonhostile and lightly armed personnel.* As UN peacekeepers were not present to engage in offensive military operations and could not appear to be a coercive presence, UN peacekeepers were unarmed or lightly armed (generally with service rifles and sidearms) for self-defence only.

PROFILE 7.4 The United Nations Emergency Force

The Suez Crisis was precipitated by the nationalization of the Suez Canal by Egypt on July 26, 1956. Three months later, Israel, France, and Great Britain invaded Egypt. Israel sought to damage the Egyptian military in a pre-emptive war, while France and Great Britain were attempting to seize the canal. The invasion was widely condemned by the international community, including the United States. Under pressure from domestic opposition and from Washington, the warring parties agreed to a ceasefire on November 6–7. In previous weeks, Canada had proposed the creation of a UN force and had supplied a draft resolution and presented it to the General Assembly for approval. The creation of the United Nations Emergency Force (UNEF) satisfied many interests. France and Great Britain were spared some of the embarrassment of being forced to obey the United States; the United States achieved an end to the war without direct intervention. Canada prevented a serious rift between the United States and Great Britain; Egypt secured the canal; and Israel obtained a ceasefire after damaging the Egyptian armed forces. Launched on November 4, 1956, under a UN General Assembly resolution, the mission was mandated to secure and supervise the cessation of hostilities and facilitate the withdrawal of France, Great Britain, and Israel from Egyptian territory, and to serve as a buffer between Egyptian and Israeli forces. UNEF began to deploy after the ceasefire was in place. It reached a strength of 6000 personnel, from Brazil, Canada, Colombia, Denmark, Finland, India, Indonesia, Norway, Sweden, and Yugoslavia. UNEF I was expelled from Egypt in 1967, and another Arab–Israeli war soon followed.

- *Consent.* Respect for state sovereignty required the UN to obtain the consent of the parties to a dispute before a UN force could be dispatched. The UN presence also depended on host consent to remain in place. These first three conventions formed the foundation of the modalities of traditional UN peacekeeping and were closely interrelated.[34]

- *Keep, but don't make, the peace.* UN peacekeepers could not create the conditions for their own success; in other words, a peace had to be in place before the peacekeeping operation was deployed. Put simply, there had to be a peace to keep; UN peacekeepers could only facilitate and reinforce a larger peace process.

- *Military personnel.* UN operations were carried out primarily by individuals with military status. These individuals were trained, equipped, and organized; deployable overseas; disciplined; and under firm command and control.

- *Proper authorization.* UN peacekeepers had to be dispatched under UN authorization (or by organizations authorized to do so by the UN). In practice, this has meant the Security Council (although some early missions were authorized by the General Assembly), which also established the mandate for the mission (the legal and operational boundaries of the mission) and the rules of engagement (the legal and operational boundaries of the personnel in the mission).

- *Reliance on member states.* As the UN had no army, UN peacekeeping operations were entirely dependent on contributions of money, personnel, and equipment from member states. In practice, small states and middle powers (such as Canada) provided most of the forces, as the great powers generally lacked impartial credentials.

- *Nonterritoriality.* Peacekeeping operations did not attempt to seize or hold territory. UN peacekeepers did not occupy territory against an opponent; they patrolled a zone or line that had been negotiated by the parties to a dispute. They had no legal claim to that territory, nor did they exercise sovereignty over it.

Patrolling the Green Line. A British soldier with the United Nations Force in Cyprus walks the Green Line between the Greek and Turkish controlled parts of the island. This part of the Green Line, which runs through the Old City in Nicosia, is only three metres wide. In April 2004, Greek Cypriots rejected a UN-brokered peace plan to reunite the island. (Canadian Press STRJMC/CP Archive)

Based on these principles, the tasks of traditional UN peacekeeping included interposing between belligerents, gathering information and facts, observing ceasefire lines and reporting violations, supervising the withdrawal of belligerent forces, defusing tensions, preventing or controlling the outbreak of violence, assisting in the maintenance of order, acting as mediators and buffers between the parties to a dispute, and engaging in humanitarian tasks. For the most part, UN peacekeeping operations during the Cold War conformed to the above principles and tasks. The exception was the United Nations Operation in the Congo (ONUC), in which the UN became involved in a civil war (see Profile 7.5). While the Congo experience was sobering, UN peacekeeping missions continued to be mounted throughout the Cold War, with some missions lasting for decades. UN peacekeeping operations thus occupied a middle ground between Chapter 6 and Chapter 7 of the UN Charter, leading to their description by former UN Secretary-General Dag Hammarskjöld as "Chapter

Six-and-a-half" operations. Up to the end of 1987, 13 UN operations were underway in the world, deploying a total of 10 000 personnel. Peacekeeping had established itself as one of the most visible and respected of UN functions, and UN peacekeepers were collectively awarded the Nobel Peace Prize in 1988. Canadian troops played a prominent role in UN peacekeeping missions throughout the Cold War.

However, the character and qualities of peacekeeping operations began to change by 1990–91 for several reasons. First, intrastate conflicts dominated the international security agenda, and these conflicts were often identified as threats to international peace and security. The UN (and specifically the UN Security Council) therefore became engaged to an unprecedented degree in communal, intrastate conflicts. Second, the Security Council, freed from the constraints of the Cold War, was more capable of reaching agreements on the creation of peacekeeping forces. Third, there was much optimism that the UN would be able to perform as the instrument of international peace and security, as the drafters of the UN Charter had intended. This optimism was reflected in *An Agenda for Peace*, a document prepared in 1992 by Secretary-General Boutros Boutros-Ghali, in which he proposed to enhance the role of the UN in international peace and security:

> In these past months a conviction has grown, among nations large and small, that an opportunity has been regained to achieve the great objectives of the Charter—a United Nations capable of maintaining international peace and security, of securing justice and human rights and of promoting, in the words of the Charter, "social progress and better standards of life in larger freedom." This opportunity must not be squandered. The Organization must never again be crippled as it was in the era that has now passed.[35]

As a result, the number of peacekeeping operations mounted by the UN surged. In 1988, the UN was operating 5 missions, consisting of a total of 13 000 personnel, at a cost of U.S.$266 mil-

---

PROFILE 7.5 The Special Case of the Congo

The Congo Crisis was precipitated by the independence of the Congo from Belgium on June 30, 1960. Violent disorder spread throughout much of the country between the government and rebellious groups and regions, prompting Belgium to intervene in its former colony. The Congo appealed to the UN for help, and on July 14 the UN Security Council authorized a peacekeeping mission for the Congo. The UN force in the Congo was initially mandated to remain neutral in the conflict. However, the secession of Katanga province, the assassination of the Congolese prime minister, and the threat of a wider war prompted the UN Security Council to use more forceful measures to restore law and order, enforce a ceasefire, prevent civil war, and evacuate Belgian forces and foreign mercenaries. The force was expanded from 17 500 in 1960 to almost 20 000 by July 1961. UN forces participated in the suppression of the secessionist movement in Katanga, which eventually brought peace to the country. However, the Congo operation had damaged the peacekeeping instrument. Disputes arose between participating states about how to implement the new mandate and how much force was permissible. The Soviet Union and its allies accused the United States and Western countries of political interference in the UN mission and refused to pay for their share of mission costs. The fact that the UN had become involved in a war and in the politics of a state made many countries, both contributing states and developing states, wary of future UN peacekeeping operations. Future UN operations were usually very circumscribed, cautious, and traditional in nature.

lion. However, by 1994 the UN was operating 17 missions, with 76 500 personnel deployed, at a cost of over U.S.$3.3 billion.[36] Peacekeeping had become the preferred method of responding to the many intrastate conflicts that confronted UN member states in the early to mid-1990s.

Not only did UN missions experience a surge in frequency, the missions themselves experienced a number of qualitative changes.[37] These changes included

- *Increased size.* The size of many UN operations increased dramatically. The big three UN operations of the post–Cold War period—the United Nations Transitional Authority in Cambodia (UNTAC), the United Nations Protection Force in the Former Yugoslavia (UNPROFOR), and the second United Nations Operation in Somalia (UNOSOM II)—all deployed more than 20 000 personnel at their peak. During the Cold War, only the UN Operation in the Congo (ONUC) approached this size. Several other UN operations also deployed more than 6000 personnel, including the United Nations Confidence Restoration Operation (UNCRO), the United Nations Mission in Haiti (UNMIH), and the United Nations Assistance Mission for Rwanda (UNAMIR).

- *Deployment within states.* Most post–Cold War UN peacekeeping operations have been conducted within the borders of states. As a result, while peacekeeping personnel may still perform missions associated with traditional peacekeeping, such as supervisory and observer tasks, they are doing so not between states but between warring parties within states. Often, there is no clear boundary between the combatants, and therefore no clear "line" to be patrolled.

- *Lack of consent.* In some post–Cold War UN operations, the principle of consent has changed dramatically. UNPROFOR and UNOSOM II were both authorized under Chapter 7 of the UN Charter, and such operations are not, at least in principle, bound by the consent provision of traditional peacekeeping. In practice, both UN operations took place in areas without a central government to provide consent. In these cases, the UN sought consent from the next highest level of authority: the warring communal groups and factions themselves. However, the universal consent of all such groups was not seen as a prerequisite for deployment, as a peacekeeping force could not have its existence dependent on one local faction leader. At the local level, however, consent remained very important, as peacekeepers often could not operate successfully on a day-to-day basis without the cooperation of local leaders.

- *Operations in hostile environments.* Many post–Cold War UN peacekeeping missions were deployed in areas where there was no peace to keep. Negotiated arrangements among the warring factions were either nonexistent or fragile, and many warring factions had not given consent or were at best ambivalent about the UN's presence. UN peacekeepers have been deployed in war zones and in areas of virtual anarchy and civil disorder. As a result, UN contingents attempting to facilitate the delivery of humanitarian relief or to establish safe areas for refugees have encountered obstruction and threats and have come under armed attack both from organized communal groups and from lawless bands of armed individuals who are not under firm political control.

- *Increased use of force.* The UN has also demonstrated a greater willingness to employ force and the threat of force during peacekeeping missions, in part because of the erosion of the principle of consent. However, the UN was widely criticized (particularly in UNPROFOR and UNOSOM II) for standing by while humanitarian relief supplies were blocked, while human rights abuses were perpetrated, while cities were bombarded, and while UN personnel were obstructed and abused. In response, the UN employed a greater level of force against warring parties, and UN contingents became more heavily armed. However, this placed UN peacekeepers at risk of retaliatory attacks, led to civilian casualties, and undermined the impartiality of the UN force.

- *Proliferation of mission tasks.* The scope of UN missions has also changed. UN contingents now perform a much wider range of mission tasks. These include electoral support or management (Cambodia), judiciary and policy reform (El Salvador), refugee resettlement (Mozambique), facilitation of the delivery of humanitarian relief supplies (former Yugoslavia), disarmament of warring factions and weapons cantonment (former Yugoslavia), mine clearing and education (Cambodia), and protection of safe areas (former Yugoslavia). As a result, UN operations now include a wide variety of functional experts, such as civilian police, electoral personnel, human rights experts, and information specialists, and often involve close cooperation with aid and humanitarian relief agencies.

- *Peacebuilding and national reconstruction.* Many of the above tasks have a long-term objective: the reconstruction of a viable, stable country, including the repair of infrastructure, the creation of democratic political processes, and the entrenchment of law and civil society. This ambitious process is based on the belief that establishing ceasefires and a peace arrangement is not enough; the underlying conditions for peace must be created if a UN effort is to be successful over the long term. As Boutros-Ghali put it, "UN operations now may involve nothing less than the reconstruction of an entire society and state. This requires a comprehensive approach, over an extended period. Security is increasingly understood to involve social, economic, environmental, and cultural aspects far beyond its traditional military dimension."[38] This objective has transformed UN peacekeeping operations from almost exclusively military operations to missions coordinating a vast aid and development effort. In fact, many of the UN missions created since the mid-1990s have emphasized peacebuilding, and often with an explicit human security dimension.[39]

As a consequence of the changing nature of peacekeeping operations and the different environments in which they were operating, UN peacekeeping experienced what can only be described as a time of troubles in the post–Cold War period. Highly publicized UN failures in the former Yugoslavia, Somalia, and Rwanda revealed the mismatch between traditional peacekeeping and the intrastate communal conflicts of the post–Cold War world.

YUGOSLAVIA

The UN experience in Yugoslavia was, at best, mixed. Although the UN Protection Force (UNPROFOR) succeeded in facilitating the delivery of humanitarian relief to the civilian population, the UN failed to end hostilities in Bosnia-Herzegovina. UN personnel were the targets of intimidation and harassment, were shot at, and were taken hostage. All sides during the Bosnian war routinely defied the UN. In one incident that has become a symbol of UN futility in Bosnia, Dutch peacekeepers protecting a UN safe area around Srebrenica found themselves outgunned by the Bosnian Serbs and withdrew, leaving the Muslim inhabitants to their fate (an estimated 7000 Muslim men were subsequently massacred). It was the shifting nature of the military balance on the ground, the intervention of NATO, and the use of air strikes that prompted the signing of the Dayton Agreement in 1995. The implementation of the settlement was facilitated by the deployment of 60 000 NATO troops.

SOMALIA

The UN experience in Somalia was almost a complete failure. UNOSOM I was initially deployed to facilitate the delivery of humanitarian relief supplies. The obstruction of UN and aid agency efforts and the continued fighting in Somalia prompted the creation of the United States–led Unified Task Force (UNITAF), authorized under Chapter 7 of the UN Charter. While UNITAF was initially successful in achieving order, it became involved in a shooting war against one of Somalia's factions. Because of casualties to U.S. forces, UNITAF was deactivated and replaced by UNOSOM II. However, the failure to establish a peace settlement and the continued fighting in Somalia led to the withdrawal of UNOSOM II in March 1995. Although many lives were saved, Somalia is no closer to political stability today than it was before UN intervention.

RWANDA

The call for the creation of a UN force for Rwanda came on the heels of the Somalia imbroglio. A conflict between the Hutu government and the Tutsi-led Rwandan Patriotic Front (RPF) had been raging for decades. A peace settlement (the Arusha Accords) was signed in August 1993, and the United Nations Assistance Mission for Rwanda (UNAMIR) began deploying later that year. However, in 1994 an orchestrated genocide began in Rwanda. The UN force commander, Canadian General Roméo Dallaire, has often argued that if he had been given more troops and an appropriate mandate, he could have prevented the worst of the genocide. In fact, neither was forthcoming, and UN member states (remembering the Somalia experience) refused to acknowledge that genocide was underway and actually reduced the size of UNAMIR. By then, 500 000 people had died, and many more would die as the world watched and did nothing. An interventionary UN force, supplied by France, arrived after the bulk of the killing had taken place, and was controversial in itself, often protecting Rwandan troops from advancing rebel groups trying to stop the genocide.

The story of post–Cold War UN peacekeeping is not entirely one of failure. The UN made some progress in reinforcing peace in Cambodia (UNTAC) and Angola (UNAVEM). Mozambique (UNOMOZ) is widely regarded as a success, and the UN has made some

A sad return. Roméo Dallaire, right, with a Rwandan security guard in Kigali, 5 April 2004, the 10th anniversary of the beginning of the Rwandan genocide (see Chapter 9). Dallaire is the retired Canadian general whose UN peacekeepers had to stand by helplessly as the slaughter unfolded. Dallaire, who went into suicidal depression because of his experiences in Rwanda, was on his first visit back to the country. (AP Photo/Sayyid Azim//CP Archive)

progress in restructuring the police and the judiciary in El Salvador (ONUSAL). However, these relative successes have been obscured by the high-profile failures in Yugoslavia, Somalia, and Rwanda. In 2004, the renewal of political violence in Haiti dashed hopes that the UN peacekeeping effort in Haiti from 1993 to 2000 had brought a sustainable peace to that country. Because of these failures, the credibility of the UN as an effective conflict management instrument has been called into question. Much of the criticism has been directed at the UN itself. Former UN Assistant Secretary-General for Political Affairs Giandomenico Picco argued that "neither the post–Cold War climate nor civil wars can rightfully be blamed for the failures that have beset the United Nations since 1991. One must look to the workings of the United Nations itself."[40] Saadia Touval argued that

> It is increasingly apparent that the United Nations possesses inherent characteristics that make it incapable of effectively mediating complex international disputes. It does not serve well as an authoritative channel of communication. It has little real political leverage. Its promises and threats lack credibility. And it is incapable of pursuing coherent, flexible, and dynamic negotiations guided by an effective strategy.[41]

The UN has also been criticized for its inability to manage the peacekeeping operations it has mounted. UN peacekeeping missions have been plagued by a variety of operational problems, including poor communication with UN headquarters in New York; a shortage of long-range transportation and tactical airlift; the uneven quality of troop contributions and incompatibility of equipment; little or no capacity to gather information or intelligence; and slow reaction times, with as much as six months passing before a UN operation is ready to be deployed. A situation faced by Canadian General Lewis Mackenzie while serving with UNPROFOR in the former Yugoslavia dramatically illustrates UN shortcomings. The general, requiring a decision from UN headquarters in New York, was unable to contact anyone on the telephone because he placed his call after office hours.

While much of this criticism is justified, blaming the UN is somewhat misleading. Certainly, the organization struggled to manage the increase in peacekeeping operations, and there are bureaucratic and structural shortcomings within the UN system. However, it is member states that authorize peacekeeping missions (or refuse to do so), it is member states that provide the mandates for those operations, it is member states that provide the resources and troops and diplomatic support for those missions, and it is member states that decide whether those missions are to be renewed or increased or decreased. Often, blaming the UN is a tactic states use to evade responsibility for their actions or inactions. The capacities of the UN are largely dependent on the commitment of member states, and so the UN can hardly be held solely accountable for failures in peacekeeping. As the 1990s wore on, the increased costs and risks involved in peacekeeping made governments increasingly cautious about supporting the creation of new missions or contributing to UN peacekeeping. This caution, in turn, compromised the ability of the UN to mount successful operations. As early as 1993, Boutros Boutros-Ghali warned: "Our renaissance remains in question; demands made upon the United Nations are not being matched by the resources to do the job."[42] Peacekeeping fatigue was beginning to emerge. States were less willing to contribute money and resources to UN operations. By 2000, the UN was still operating 17 missions, but these were smaller and less ambitious efforts, deploying 38 500 personnel at a cost of US$1.8 billion. The peacekeeping surge was over, and the high hopes for the UN in the early 1990s turned into disappointment.

In the face of such problems, some attempts have been made to improve the capacity of the UN to create and deploy peacekeeping missions. The Department of Peacekeeping Operations

(DPKO) has created a 24-hour situation centre that provides UN headquarters with command, control, and communications capabilities. In 1992, the Department of Humanitarian Affairs (DHA) established a Humanitarian Early Warning System. In 1993 a Standby Arrangements program was developed to establish a roster list of forces and capabilities that contributors were willing to make available to the UN on short notice. A logistics base stockpile was established at Brindisi, Italy. Prompted by the failure in Rwanda, in 1995 Canada released a set of proposals on establishing a United Nations Rapid Reaction Capability. As a result, the UN established a rapidly deployable peacekeeping headquarters designed to react swiftly in times of need. Larger proposals have also been forwarded, including the long-standing suggestion that the UN should possess its own army. However, this idea has foundered because of opposition from most member states who fear the creation of a military instrument under UN control and because of the prohibitive costs of such a venture. In August 2000, the UN released the *Report of the Panel on UN Peacekeeping Operations*, otherwise known as the Brahimi Report. The report recommended (among other things) an extensive restructuring of the Department of Peacekeeping Operations, an improved capacity to react rapidly to crises, and an enhanced headquarters capable of better planning and coordination. It remains to be seen to what extent the recommendations of the Brahimi Report will be implemented.

UN peacekeeping is still a valuable conflict management instrument in the international system. In September 2002, the UN authorized the deployment of a traditional peacekeeping mission to the border between Ethiopia and Eritrea. Ongoing missions continue to contribute to the maintenance of peace around the world, and in future conflicts and crises the mechanism of UN peacekeeping will continue to be a conflict management option. In early 2004, the UN operated 15 missions, deploying some 49 000 personnel. Over 90 countries contributed troops, civilian police, or civilian personnel to UN operations. However, the effectiveness of peacekeeping in the future will be determined by three factors: (1) the careful consideration of the demands of a proposed mission and the mandates and capabilities required to carry it out; (2) the willingness of contributing states to offer money and resources, including troops; and (3) the willingness of the parties to a dispute to stop fighting and begin the process of building a peace. It is in the area of peacebuilding that the UN has become increasingly active. Peacebuilding, as defined by the UN Security Council, "is aimed at preventing the outbreak, the recurrence, or continuation of armed conflict and therefore encompasses a wide range of political, developmental, humanitarian, and human rights programmes and mechanisms."[43] The emergence of peacebuilding coincided with the need to develop the means to consolidate the gains of peace settlements. What point was there to deploying costly and risky UN peacekeeping missions if the underlying causes of conflict were not resolved, and there was no basis for a lasting, self-sustaining peace? By the mid-1990s, the UN peacekeeping missions were engaging in demobilization, disarmament, and reintegration of militias; refugee return; democratization; restoration or introduction of market activity; institution building; promoting dialogue and reconciliation; police and judicial reform; trauma recovery; and development assistance. Peacebuilding is thus based on the promotion of liberal values in societies torn by war or deep social conflict, and assumes that a lasting peace can be achieved through the instruments of the liberal peace formula.

However, peacebuilding has also been criticized. The premise that political and economic liberalization will lead to peace has been challenged as an attempt at "social engineering" that could in fact lead to more conflict in a society as "both democracy and capitalism encourage conflict and competition—indeed, they thrive on it."[44] Many countries in the developing world are suspicious of peacebuilding, worried that it could lead to intervention in the domestic affairs of a society. Peacebuilding also faces the same challenges as peacekeeping: if member states do not support peacebuilding efforts with diplomatic backing, funding, and adequate resources, then UN efforts to build sustainable peace in war-torn societies will be unsuccessful.[45] The sheer magnitude of the task is also significant. Peacebuilding contemplates nothing less than rebuilding a viable and sustainable country out of the ashes of war and the trauma of violence. Peacebuilding efforts must promote economic and social development, good governance and institutional reform, and social reconciliation and justice, while at the same time dealing with "spoilers" who might wish to derail the peace efforts for their own gain.[46] Perhaps this is why early assessments of peacebuilding success are not encouraging. In one study, out of 22 cases of UN missions with a prominent peacebuilding component, only 3 can be said to have achieved the goal of a self-sustaining peace. Fifteen of the cases showed no significant development toward a self-sustaining peace, as the development of democracy, institutions, civil society, and the rule of law had not taken root. Violence returned to 8 of the countries in the sample.[47] Nevertheless, peacebuilding remains critically important. Without successful peacebuilding, international military forces will have to remain in war-torn countries for a long time (as has been the case in Cyprus), and the possibility of a return to violence will threaten long-term development efforts.

HUMAN SECURITY AND HUMANITARIAN INTERVENTION

With UN peacekeeping increasingly regarded as unsuited to the challenges of major regional conflicts and gross violations of human rights, states have turned to regional organizations or "coalitions of the willing" that are unburdened by the constraints of the UN system. The interventions in Kosovo and East Timor are two examples of so-called humanitarian intervention, efforts to respond to humanitarian crises or gross violations of human rights using military force. Humanitarian intervention can, of course, be conducted through the UN (many recent peacekeeping missions could be described as humanitarian interventions), but in recent years the term has increasingly referred to efforts mounted by regional organizations or coalitions of the willing operating with UN authority (this is sometimes called "contracting out") or without UN authority. Either way, the role of the UN is diminished. In such cases, the UN no longer exerts direct control over the military mission or the political process, and in effect becomes a legitimating device for the coalitions or regional organizations that are conducting the operation through their own means and according to their own counsel.

The concept of human security has a complex and controversial relationship with the concept of humanitarian intervention. The genocide in Rwanda was a benchmark in the development of human security because of the recognition that hundreds of thousands of people were slaughtered while the international community stood by and did nothing. The lesson of Rwanda was that a relatively small military force could have conducted a humanitarian intervention that would have saved many of the lives that were lost. Of course, this would have meant intervening in the internal affairs of Rwanda, but as the human security concept suggests this is no crime if governments cannot protect the human security of their own population (or if governments were actively involved in the persecution of their own population, as was the case in Rwanda). The genocide in Rwanda prompted an effort to get the UN to grapple with the question of when violations of state sovereignty and armed interventions against states would be permissible in the cause of protecting people threatened by gross violations of human rights. However, there was limited enthusiasm for this venture in the UN, where the vast majority of states (especially those in the developing world) stood firm on the principle of sovereignty, arguing it was one of their few protections against interference from powerful states. This prompted an effort to develop a dialogue outside the UN system, which led to the **International Commission on Intervention and State Sovereignty**. This commission consisted of leading experts and practitioners, and with the support of several govern-ments the commission published its final report in December 2001. The final report was titled *The Responsibility to Protect* and argued that

a. State sovereignty implies responsibility, and the primary responsibility for the protec-tion of its people lies with the state itself.

b. Where a population is suffering serious harm, as a result of internal war, insurgency, repression or state failure, and the state in question is unwilling or unable to halt or avert it, the principle of non-intervention yields to the international responsibility to protect.[48]

The report was published after two episodes that are now considered cases of humanitarian interventions. Both cases illustrated the logic of the humanitarian intervention idea, and the controversies and moral dilemmas associated with it.

NATO AND HUMANITARIAN INTERVENTION AGAINST SERBIA

Since the creation of Yugoslavia, Kosovo has been a predominantly ethnic Albanian province of Serbia. Tensions grew between the Albanian majority, which called for greater autonomy or outright independence, and the Milosevic government in Belgrade. Violence broke out between Albanian separatists (later called the Kosovo Liberation Army, or KLA) and the Serbian police in the early 1990s. The violence intensified in 1998 and 1999 as an increasingly indiscriminate government campaign aimed at suppressing the KLA escalated into ethnic cleansing disturbingly similar to the kind witnessed in the Bosnian War. Incidents of mass murder became ever more frequent, and a serious refugee crisis developed inside and outside Kosovo. NATO threatened Serbia with air strikes unless the campaign against ethnic Albanians stopped. The Serbian government agreed to attend talks at Rambouillet, France, but refused to sign a peace agreement that would have given Kosovo considerable autonomy and provided for a future referendum on independence. Today, controversy exists as to whether Rambouillet was a good-faith effort at negotiation or a NATO ultimatum. What is clear is that it was Milosevic's last chance to avoid the use of force against Serbia. On March 24, 1999, NATO began a bombing campaign against Serbia that would last 78 days until, on June 10, the Milosevic government accepted NATO demands to withdraw its security forces from Kosovo. On June 12, NATO began deployment of Kosovo-force (K-FOR) to restore law and order, demilitarize the KLA, and assist the UN with the restoration of civilian authority.

NATO's campaign against Serbia remains controversial. Critics charge that NATO acted illegally, as no UN resolution was ever passed authorizing the air campaign (K-FOR did have UN approval). Critics also argued that not enough time or effort was given to diplomacy. The bombing campaign itself was criticized as excessive and more damaging to civilian targets than to the Serbian military. NATO had violated the rights of a sovereign state and had in effect severed Kosovo from Serbia by force. Critics also charged that NATO was being selec-tive. Why did it intervene against Serbia but not against Algeria (embroiled in a brutal civil war) or in Chechnya (under assault by Russia)? Supporters of the NATO campaign argued that Serbia had violated international law, rejected diplomatic overtures, and had engaged in ethnic cleansing, which demanded a swift reaction before more Albanians died and the region became destabilized. To do nothing, supporters argued, would allow ethnic cleansing to con-tinue and risk human rights violations on the scale of those in Bosnia. The air campaign was conducted to avoid civilian casualties as much as possible, and in any case Milosevic could have stopped the bombing by agreeing to terms far earlier. Serbia may have been a sovereign state, but by committing violations of human rights, it had given NATO countries little choice and every right to intervene. Finally, NATO could not be expected to intervene everywhere; not intervening in Algeria or Chechnya did not make intervening in Kosovo wrong. The government of Canada was confronted with the decision of whether or not to contribute to the war, and Foreign Affairs Minister Lloyd Axworthy, who was a champion of human security, grappled with the conflicting morals of intervening and killing Serbian civilians, or not intervening and allowing ethnic cleansing to continue. In the end, Canada participated in the war.

The legacy of NATO's campaign is mixed and the future of Kosovo uncertain. The bombing devastated the Serbian economy, with the lower damage estimates placed at U.S.$4 billion. Estimates of civilian deaths range from 500 deaths to the Serbian government claim of 2000. NATO is a dirty word among the Serbian people, who maintain that their country was unjustly attacked. In Kosovo, which is now a *de facto* NATO protectorate, the return of something resembling normal life and a general gratitude toward NATO must be balanced against high unemployment in a destroyed economy and Albanian violence against the Serb minority. K-FOR has struggled to provide protection for Kosovar Serbs, and some 130 000 have fled to Serbia. Ethnic tolerance is hard to find in Kosovo. At the end of 2000, the government of Slobodan Milosevic was overthrown by a popular uprising, and new elections brought Vojuslav Kostunica to power. It remains to be seen whether this new leadership will mark the beginning of a new and better future for Kosovo, even as UN war crimes inspectors exhume bodies from mass graves.[49] In 2004, a renewed outbreak of violence required the reinforcement of K-FOR personnel from nearby Bosnia, and highlighted the lack of progress toward peacebuilding and a political settlement on the issue of Kosovo's future status.

HUMANITARIAN INTERVENTION IN EAST TIMOR

East Timor was a Portuguese colony for almost 500 years. In 1975, it was invaded by Indonesia and subjected to a brutal occupation that saw at least 200 000 deaths between 1975 and 1980 alone from executions, starvation, and military operations. East Timor became a symbol of the world's failure to respond to such human rights disasters. In 1998, a leadership change in Indonesia opened the way for a UN-supervised referendum on independence. However, violence perpetrated by pro-Indonesian militias supported by the Indonesian Army required the postponement of the referendum. Finally, on August 30, 1999, an extraordinary 98 percent of registered voters went to the polls despite threats of physical violence. Almost 80 percent voted against remaining tied to Indonesia. The pro-Indonesian militias reacted with a campaign of violence and intimidation, which rapidly escalated into the pillaging of East Timor. Faced with a humanitarian crisis, an Australian-led coalition developed plans for an intervention force to restore order and protect the East Timorese people. The proposed force received UN approval on September 15, and on September 20, an Australian-led force of 8000 personnel began arriving in East Timor with the grudging consent of the Indonesian government (interestingly, Australia was one of the few states that had recognized the

Humanitarian intervention in East Timor. Australian troops assist in the withdrawal of Indonesian troops from Dili, October 1999. (AP Photo/Richard Vogel/CP Archive)

annexation as valid earlier). The force moved quickly to establish order and forced the militias out of East Timor. In February 2000 the Australian-led force withdrew and was replaced by a UN peacekeeping force. On May 20, 2002, East Timor became fully independent and changed its name to Timor-Leste, and joined the United Nations as the 191st member state.

It is difficult to find a critic of the Australian-led humanitarian intervention in East Timor because of the circumstances of the intervention, which included a clear moral purpose, UN authorization, and the consent of the Indonesian government. In this case, the circumstances were quite different from those confronted by NATO in Kosovo. However, some critics wonder why it took so long for the international community to respond to Indonesia's brutality in East Timor (which had lasted for almost 25 years). For most of that time, governments traded with Indonesia, participated in IOs with Indonesia, and held summits with Indonesian leaders (such as the now infamous APEC summit in Vancouver in 1997). It took a change in East Asia's security environment (a consequence of the end of the Cold War), a change in the Indonesian government, the collapse of the Indonesian economy in the Asian financial crisis, and another humanitarian crisis to create the conditions for the outside world to respond to one of the longest lasting human rights outrages in the world.[50]

Many welcome the idea of humanitarian intervention as a positive development because it represents a willingness to act in support of human rights and international humanitarian law and against those regimes that perpetrate atrocities against groups of people. The alternative—to stand by and do nothing or wait for sanctions to work—is simply unacceptable. The big question then becomes one of resources: humanitarian intervention (or intervention of any kind) requires globally deployable military forces, and these are in increasingly short supply and must be buttressed if humanitarian interventions are to be conducted in the future.[51] Critics argue that humanitarian intervention is seldom purely humanitarian, is selectively and inconsistently applied, and results in the deaths of innocent civilians and the destruction of civilian infrastructure. The legal, moral, and political terms of this debate are now an important issue in the study of conflict management.

ECONOMIC STATECRAFT, DEMOCRACY, AND CONFLICT MANAGEMENT

Economic instruments have also played a significant role in conflict management. One such instrument is trade; recall how the liberal perspective asserts that wars can be prevented through the promotion of economic interdependence. Another economic instrument is the use of economic sanctions. Finally, a widely held proposition in recent years suggests that democracies do not fight one another and that promoting democracy around the world can prevent war.

INTERDEPENDENCE AS A CONSTRAINT ON WAR

Liberals have long argued that growing economic ties between countries (in areas such as trade, finance, and shared production) will reduce incentives to go to war. Richard Cobden wrote that free trade would unite states, making them "equally anxious for the prosperity and happiness of both."[52] Just before the outbreak of World War I, Norman Angell argued that the increasing level of trade between countries was making war "commercially suicidal."[53] States had to choose between old power politics methods and peaceful trade. Since war was no longer profitable, states would choose the latter. Undaunted by the outbreak of World War I, Angell went on to make the same argument in the 1930s. War broke out, he argued, because state leaders failed to understand that war no longer pays; World War I only confirmed this point.

The argument that economic interdependence promotes peace has experienced a rebirth since the surge in global economic activity of the past few decades. States are mutually vulnerable to the damage war would cause. War disrupts trade, eliminates markets, compromises the joint production of goods, and complicates access to resources. Richard Rosecrance argues that states have a choice between becoming "trading states" (emphasizing wealth through commerce) or "territorial states" (emphasizing gains through territorial expansion). In the modern global economy, states will choose the former. For Rosecrance, in an interdependent world the "incentive to wage war is absent ... trading states recognize that they can do better through internal economic development sustained by a world wide market for their goods and services than by trying to conquer and assimilate large tracts of land."[54] In addition, war has become increasingly costly (especially when nuclear weapons might be involved), both in terms of the monetary costs of fighting a war and in terms of destruction. For all these reasons, as economic interdependence between countries grows, they will be less inclined to go to war because they would lose the gains and value of trade and incur the high costs of war. Put simply, interdependence promotes peace because states can do better through trade than through conquest: don't invade—trade.

The opposing (realist) view is that economic interdependence does not promote peace; in fact, it encourages war because interdependence means dependence and vulnerability. States are dependent or vulnerable if they are forced to rely on others for imports of crucial goods or resources, which could be cut off or used as political blackmail. As a result, dependent states have an incentive to go to war, to secure access to vital resources. Kenneth Waltz suggests that states in an anarchic international system will want to "control who they depend on or to lessen the extent of their dependency."[55] For their part, critical perspectives assert that economic interdependence facilitates greater exploitation and thus causes more conflict.

The historical record concerning the relationship between interdependence and war is uncertain and the subject of considerable debate. Both perspectives cite the World War I and interwar period as evidence supporting their claims. For liberals, the 1920s was a period of high interdependence, and in that period there were no wars. In the 1930s, when protectionism led to the erosion of interdependence, tensions increased and war broke out. Realists point out that before World War I the European powers had reached unprecedented levels of trade among themselves, but despite this, world war did break out. In the 1930s rising tensions and eventual war were caused by the rise of revisionist states. This debate is unlikely to be resolved in the near future; since the variables that can lead to war are so numerous, it is very difficult to isolate the impact of interdependence.

SANCTIONS AND CONFLICT MANAGEMENT

Economic sanctions are "deliberate government actions to inflict economic deprivation on a target state or society, through the limitation or cessation of customary economic relations."[56] Economic sanctions, therefore, are coercive instruments. Nevertheless, they have been employed as instruments of conflict management in the international system. Economic sanctions may take several forms, including trade boycotts, embargoes, or restrictions on financial interactions (such as access to overseas assets or international financial institutions). Sanctions may be imposed unilaterally by one state, or multilaterally, by a group of states (or by the membership of an IO). When sanctions are imposed, the sending or initiating countries might have a number of possible goals or aims:

- *Compliance:* "to force the target to alter its behaviour to conform with the initiator's preferences"
- *Subversion:* "to remove the target's leaders or overthrow the regime"
- *Deterrence:* "to dissuade the target from repeating the disputed action in the future"

- *International symbolism:* "to send messages to other members of the world community"
- *Domestic symbolism:* "to increase its domestic support or thwart international criticism of its foreign policies by acting decisively"[57]

The use of sanctions has deep historical roots. In his history of the Peloponnesian War, Thucydides describes a trade embargo put in place by Athens against Megara, a Spartan ally. Under Napoleonic domination, most of continental Europe limited grain sales to Great Britain. However, the use of sanctions increased dramatically in the 20th century. One study found that since World War I, economic sanctions have been used 120 times, with 104 of those examples occurring since World War II.[58] The increased use of economic sanctions as an instrument of policy can be explained by the attractiveness of sanctions as a policy choice. Diplomatic measures, although they may carry the weight of the displeasure of one country against another or the force of global or world opinion, tend not to have the same strength as other instruments for two reasons: (1) the leverage one can exert against a target state is limited, and (2) the sending or initiating countries incur few costs, so diplomatic measures are less credible as expressions of will or commitment. Military measures, however, are both costly and risky, although they may have a greater chance of succeeding than would diplomatic efforts. States may, therefore, find economic sanctions an attractive option because although costs are involved (the severing of some or all economic ties with the target state), they do not carry the costs of military action and have more credibility than mere diplomatic measures.

Despite the frequency of their use, the effectiveness of economic sanctions in achieving their goals has been limited at best. The consensus is that when results are measured against goals and objectives, economic sanctions usually fail and often harm the most vulnerable people in target states. One study found that between 1914 and 1989, "although sanctions were successful in 34 percent of 115 cases … success has become increasingly elusive in recent years … The success rate among [the 46] cases begun after 1973 was a little less than 26 percent."[59] Several possible explanations exist as to why the success rate of economic sanctions is so low:

- The target state is usually able to find alternative sources of supply or markets for its exports (for this reason, unilateral sanctions are frequently ineffective, and most sanction efforts are multilateral in nature).

- In target states, sanctions may provoke nationalist sentiments and a willingness to sacrifice in the name of resistance against outside interference.

- Sanctions may do the most harm to the very people they are supposed to benefit. Authoritarian rulers who care little for the economic hardships of their people will not be swayed by sanctions. The people will suffer for the actions of their leadership. As Jim Hoagland has observed: "The logic of the policy seems to be to make unarmed citizens desperate enough to rise up and throw off the brutal regimes that other powers are not willing to use the world's best armies to topple."[60]

- Sanctions are often undercut by the actions of domestic companies, the companies of other countries, or by foreign governments. The longer sanctions last, the greater the likelihood that they will erode and collapse.[61]

- The imposition of sanctions can actually increase the power of undesirable political elites in the target country, as the sanctions can be used to justify their increased control over the country, or to create a lucrative environment for black market activity. Sanctions can also create a "rally around the flag" effect that can boost the popularity of an authoritarian leader.

- Sending or initiating countries can have inflated expectations about the utility of sanctions. Economic deprivation has never been a reliable means of forcing political change; the political context is usually a more important factor in the political outcome.[62]

The success of sanctions appears to depend on several variables. First, the relationship between the state (or states) sending the sanctions and the target is very important. If the target state is less economically powerful than the sending states, or is a close trading partner of the sending states, economic sanctions will have a greater effect on the target country. Second, when sending countries impose sanctions quickly and decisively, and when sanctions do not involve significant economic hardships for sending countries, the sanctions will have greater credibility, for they reflect firm resolve and will be sustainable over time. Third, clear conditions must be established for the lifting of sanctions. In other words, it must be clear to the target country why the sanctions were imposed and what actions they must undertake to have them lifted. Furthermore, if objectives are broad and general, sanctions will not have the same chance of success as if the objectives are specific and clearly defined. Sanctions should, therefore, be imposed to give the target country an incentive to change certain specific policies rather than as a general punishment for a broad range of actions. Finally, sanctions will be more effective if an internal faction exists within the target state that supports the imposition of sanctions and can exert domestic pressure against the government using sanctions as a political argument for changing a policy; this was certainly an instrumental factor in the case of apartheid South Africa (see Profile 7.6). It is likely that sanctions will continue to be a frequently used instrument in conflict management. Compliance with stated goals is not the only objective of sanctions. They remain a valuable tool to signal disapproval and are an important alternative to the use of military force. Sanctions are also versatile as they can be used to respond to a wide variety of security concerns.

PROFILE 7.6 Sanctions

QUALIFIED SUCCESS AND THE CASE OF SOUTH AFRICA

The South African apartheid regime was a prominent human rights issue during the Cold War. Apartheid institutionalized racial separation and discrimination against the Black majority in South Africa, and to end this system sanctions were imposed on South Africa from a variety of sources. The UN imposed a voluntary arms embargo against South Africa in 1963, and this was made mandatory in 1977. Many other countries, including Canada, began to impose stronger unilateral sanctions against South Africa as well. In addition, campaigns in many countries led many corporations and social institutions (such as universities) to divest themselves of their interests and operations in South Africa. However, stiffer multilateral sanctions against South Africa could not be imposed because of the opposition of

Great Britain and the United States. Both countries argued that sanctions would hurt only the Black African majority in South Africa. Instead, the Reagan administration opted for a policy of **constructive engagement** in 1981. Critics charged that the United States was being soft on South Africa because of its importance as a source of raw minerals and its opposition to Communism in Africa. However, in 1985 Congress overrode a presidential veto and imposed harsh economic sanctions against South Africa. In 1989, F.W. de Klerk came to power in South Africa, intent on reform. He released the long-time jailed leader of the **African National Congress (ANC)**, Nelson Mandela, and opened negotiations with the ANC, which, in 1993, led to the dismantling of apartheid, to universal democracy, and to a Black majority government. Sanctions were lifted, and South Africa was no longer an isolated country.

PROFILE 7.6 Sanctions (cont'd)

Did sanctions succeed in this case? The consensus is that they played a role; the South African economy was certainly damaged by sanctions, as trade fell, debt rose, loans were not renewed, foreign investment declined, and growth rates declined. Two questions remain: How much of this economic damage was due to sanctions, and how much was due to falling world prices for gold (a key South African foreign-exchange earner)? What would have happened had a hard-line South African leader determined to resist sanctions come to power, instead of the reform-minded de Klerk? In any event, the South African example stands as a success story for sanctions.

QUALIFIED FAILURE AND THE CASE OF IRAQ

When Iraq invaded Kuwait in 1990 the international community responded with diplomatic expressions of opposition and economic sanctions. These sanctions were organized through the United Nations and included a total ban on imports and exports to and from Iraq, with the exception of humanitarian imports such as medicine and some foodstuffs. Iraq was a vulnerable target, as its main export was oil (with only two routes of egress, both easily blocked), and it was heavily dependent on food imports. The stated goal of sanctions was to compel Saddam Hussein's government to withdraw from Kuwait. It was also hoped that sanctions would promote the overthrow of Saddam Hussein. However, confidence in sanctions was never very high; therefore, the military option was developed as quickly as possible and force was eventually used to eject Iraqi forces from Kuwait.

After the end of the Gulf War, sanctions remained in place against Iraq. The goal of the sanctions was to compel Saddam Hussein to cooperate with United Nations Special Commission (UNSCOM) weapons inspectors seeking to destroy Iraq's weapons of mass destruction program. Between 1991 and 1998, UN inspectors continued their work of compiling information on Iraq's programs and destroying the weapons and weapons-related infrastructure they found, all in the face of Iraqi efforts to hide evidence and obstruct the inspectors' work. However, the sanctions became increasingly controversial. Critics charged that the sanctions were causing extensive human suffering inside Iraq due to shortages of medicine, food, and basic industrial needs. On the other hand, supporters argued that sanctions remained the only lever available (other than the use of force) to pressure Iraq to give up its weapons of mass destruction and to prevent more aggressive behaviour by the Iraqi regime. International support for the sanctions began to waver, and public protests against sanctions grew in many countries. In an effort to reduce the human impact of sanctions the UN authorized the delivery of humanitarian supplies (including food) to be paid for by authorized sales of Iraqi oil (which was otherwise under embargo by the sanctions). By August 1998, Iraq announced that it would no longer cooperate with the inspector teams, which were withdrawn in November. American and British air strikes followed, and a renewed weapons inspections program was mounted by the creation of the United Nations Monitoring, Verification, and Inspection Commission (UNMOVIC) in 2001. Meanwhile, the "food for oil" program was never successful in trying to strike a balance between sanctions and human suffering in Iraq, and it was abandoned in 2001. By then, several countries were openly calling for an end to sanctions, and the entire sanctions regime against Iraq looked close to unravelling. It is unlikely that sanctions would have worked in the case of Iraq, but ultimately we can never be sure as the debate over the 2003 Iraq War, and the subsequent invasion, ended the debate over sanctions against Iraq. However, the broader debate over sanctions continues, and the Iraq case remains a good illustration of the limitations, and potential human costs, of sanctions efforts.

A DEMOCRATIC PATH TO PEACE?

The idea that democracies are inherently peaceful forms of government is not unique to the post–Cold War era. Immanuel Kant suggested that constitutional governments and their respect for international law would be a constraint on war. However, the idea of a democratic peace took on a new significance after the Cold War. A belief prevails in most Western countries that democracies rarely, if ever, fight one another (although they do fight nondemocratic states). It follows that if you expand the number of democracies in the world, you will increase the chances of peace. This was one of the pillars of U.S. foreign policy during the Clinton Administration, which promoted the concept of "enlargement of the world's community of market democracies" as a replacement for the Cold War strategy of containment.[63] According to former U.S. President Bill Clinton, "enlargement" is in the interest of the United States because "democracies rarely wage war on one another."[64]

The argument that democracies do not fight one another is based on two assumptions. First, the domestic institutional structures of democratic states act as a constraint on war. Democracies must answer to their citizens, and the financial and human costs of war might result in a government losing the next election. In addition, there are constraints on leaders in democracies; the checks and balances that exist in parliamentary and republican systems will help prevent warlike or renegade leaders from coming to power. Authoritarian governments, in contrast, have fewer constraints, and are thus more likely to engage in aggressive or warlike behaviour. Second, the norms of democratic governance promote the peaceful resolution of disputes. Democracies are governed by the rule of law and by norms and principles that seek to establish a balance between the rights of the individual and the common good. As a result, democracies use **adjudication** and bargaining to avoid violent conflict, externalizing their internal behaviour, and so advocates of the idea of a democratic peace argue that they will be more likely to negotiate, adjudicate, and bargain when disputes arise between them. As Bruce Russett suggests, "the culture, perceptions, and practices that permit compromise and the peaceful resolution of conflicts without the threat of violence within countries come to apply across national boundaries toward other democratic countries."[65] Michael Doyle agrees, suggesting that democracies that "presume foreign republics to be also consensual, just and therefore deserving of accommodation."[66]

However, the idea of a democratic peace has been challenged. First, critics argue that institutional constraints will not necessarily prevent wars between democracies. If they did, they would prevent democracies from going to war against any kind of opponent. The fact that democracies have often gone to war (although not necessarily with other democracies) raises doubts about the salience of democratic constraints on war. Public opinion has, in fact, favoured war: American public opinion favoured war with Spain in 1898, and the publics of Europe enthusiastically welcomed war in 1914. Second, democracies have nearly gone to war with each other on numerous occasions. In one study, Christopher Layne argues that in four cases of near-war between democracies (the United States and Great Britain in the Trent Affair of 1861; the United States and Great Britain in the Venezuela Crisis of 1895–96; France and Great Britain in the Fashoda Crisis of 1898; and France and Germany in the Ruhr in 1923), war was avoided only because one side backed down due to fears that a war would end in defeat or quagmire.[67] Third, there have been very few democracies in history, and as a result there have been fewer opportunities for conflict and warfare between them. Furthermore, most states are rarely at war, so it should be no surprise that democracies are rarely at war.[68] Fourth, democracies have actually fought one another. Or have they? Here the problem is the definition of democracy. World War I saw democratic states fight one another. However, some debate exists as to whether Germany was a democracy and how democratic any of the combatants were in the realm of foreign policy decision making.[69] In another ambiguous case, the United States Civil War was a war that occurred within a democracy. Although this war has been dismissed as only a civil war, the War Between the States did have the character of an interstate conflict. In any case, why did the democratic institutions of the United States not save the country from civil war?

The debate over the idea of a democratic peace has profound policy implications. For example, should Canada support the spread of formal democracy in the hope that it will lead to a more peaceful world? Is it not possible that the effort to encourage or promote democracy will drag Canada (or other countries) into interventions and even wars in the cause of a democratic peace, thus increasing global insecurity?

CONCLUSIONS

This chapter has explored some of the conflict management instruments available to actors in global politics. As we have seen, conflict management efforts in global politics are plagued by several obstacles, most notably the problem of compliance, trust, and self-interest. Many actors sign international agreements or take on obligations but do not abide by them. Other actors refuse to engage in bilateral or multilateral conflict management efforts because they do not trust other countries to live up to their obligations. Many conflict management instruments founder because global actors do not believe it is in their best interests to pursue such a course.

Conflict management is by its very nature a cooperative enterprise, and as we have seen, cooperation in a world that is at least in part anarchic is a difficult enterprise (see the discussion on game theory in Chapter 3). As a result, conflict management tends to be a very controversial subject. Despite the less than illustrious history of conflict management, some cause for optimism remains. Emerging transnational security issues may compel international actors—especially states—to increase their efforts to establish more rigorous and effective arms control agreements in the future. Peacekeeping, by both regional organizations and the UN, continues to offer hope, and economic statecraft will also be employed by states in the name of conflict management. But can all this diplomatic activity really affect the condition of individuals in the contemporary age? Our next chapter, which examines global inequities, will address this question.

Endnotes

1. From his speech to the First Meeting of the Commission to Deal with the Problems Raised by the Discovery of Atomic Energy and Other Related Matters, Hunter College, The Bronx, New York, 14 June 1946.
2. Christer Jönsson, "Diplomacy, Bargaining, and Negotiation," in Walter Carlsnaes, Thomas Risse, and Beth A. Simmons, eds., *Handbook of International Relations* (London: Sage, 2002), 121.
3. Alexander L. George, *Forceful Persuasion: Coercive Diplomacy as an Alternative to War* (Washington, DC: United States Institute of Peace Press, 1991).
4. Garrett Mattingly, *Renaissance Diplomacy* (Baltimore: Penguin, 1964), 244.
5. See Jan Melissen, "Introduction," in Jan Melissen, ed., *Innovation in Diplomatic Practice* (London: Macmillan; New York: St. Martin's Press, 1999).
6. For a highly readable and general text on negotiation, see R. Fisher and W. Ury, *Getting to Yes: Negotiating Agreement without Giving In* (Boston: Houghton Mifflin, 1981).
7. See K. Boulding, *The Three Faces of Power* (Newbury Park, CA: Sage, 1990); and W. Habeeb, *Power and Tactics in International Negotiation: How Weak Nations Bargain with Strong Nations* (Baltimore: Johns Hopkins University Press, 1988).
8. See Jacob Berkovitch, ed., *Resolving International Conflicts: The Theory and Practice of Mediation* (Boulder, CO: Lynne Rienner, 1996).
9. Jeremy Pressman, "Visions in Collision: What Happened at Camp David and Taba?" *International Security* 28 (Fall 2003), 44–77.
10. For a study on the El-Aqsa Intifada, see Hayim Gordon, Rivca Gordon, and Shriteh Taher, *Beyond Intifada: Narratives of Freedom Fighters in the Gaza Strip* (Westport, CT: Praeger, 2003).

11. For a discussion of the U.S. role in the Middle East, see Shibley Telhami, *The Stakes: America and the Middle East* (Boulder, CO: Westview Press, 2002).

12. For a discussion of the unravelling of the peace process, see Neal Kozodoy, ed., *The Mideast Peace Process: An Autopsy* (San Francisco: Encounter Books, 2003). See also Bernard Wasserstein, *Israel and Palestine: Why They Fight and Can They Stop?* (London: Profile Books, 2003).

13. For a discussion of the issues surrounding the security fence, see Jonathan Rynold, "Israel's Fence: Can Separation Make Better Neighbors?" *Survival* 46 (Spring 2004), 55–76.

14. Rynold, 56.

15. Sara Roy, "The Palestinian State: Division and Despair," *Current History* 103 (January 2004), 31–36.

16. For an overview, see Stefan Wolff, "The Peace Process Since 1998," in Jörg Neuheiser and Stefan Wolff, eds., *Peace at Last? The Impact of the Good Friday Agreement on Northern Ireland* (New York: Beghahn Books, 2002).

17. Mari Fitzduff, *Beyond Violence: Conflict Resolution Process in Northern Ireland* (Tokyo: United Nations University Press, 2002).

18. See R. Johansen, "Swords into Plowshares: Can Fewer Arms Yield More Security?" in C. Kegley Jr., ed., *Controversies in International Relations Theory: Realism and the Neoliberal Challenge* (New York: St. Martin's Press, 1995), 224–44.

19. J. Kruzel, "Arms Control, Disarmament, and the Stability of the Postwar Era," in C. Kegley Jr., ed., *The Long Postwar Peace* (New York: HarperCollins, 1991), 249.

20. Remarks by Senator Richard G. Lugar, Chairman, Committee on Foreign Relations, at the Chemical and Biological Arms Control Institute Tenth Anniversary Symposium, 19 November 2003. (Washington, DC: Bureau of International Information Programs, U.S. Department of State, 2003).

21. International Atomic Energy Agency. "Implementation of the IAEA Safeguards Agreement in the Islamic Republic of Iran." Report by the Director General (GOV/2003/40). 6 June 2003.

22. For a discussion of the issues facing the NPT, see *Arms Control Today: Atoms for Peace Anniversary Issue* 33 (December 2003).

23. See R. Johnson, "The In-comprehensive Test Ban," *Bulletin of Atomic Scientists* 52 (November/December 1996), 30–35.

24. Kruzel, "Arms Control, Disarmament, and the Stability of the Post–Cold War Era," 268.

25. United Nations Development Programme, *Human Development Report, 1994.* (New York: Oxford University Press, 1994), 22.

26. Lloyd Axworthy, "Canada and Human Security: The Need for Leadership," *International Journal* 52 (Spring 1997), 184.

27. Roland Paris, "Human Security: Paradigm Shift or Hot Air?" *International Security* 26 (Fall 2001), 88.

28. See Richard K. Nossal, "Pinchpenny Diplomacy: The Decline of 'Good International Citizenship' in Canadian Foreign Policy," *International Journal* 54 (Winter 1998–99), 88–105; and Fen Osler Hampson and Dean Oliver, "Pulpit Diplomacy: A Critical Assessment of the Axworthy Doctrine," *International Journal* 53 (Summer 1998), 379–407.

29. Fen Osler Hampson, Norman Hillmer, and Maureen Appel Molot, eds., *The Axworthy Legacy. Canada among Nations 2001* (Oxford: Oxford University Press, 2001).

30. See K. Deutsch, *Political Community and the North Atlantic Area* (Princeton: Princeton University Press, 1957).

31. See *Charter of the United Nations and Statute of the International Court of Justice* (New York: United Nations), 1.

32. See Article 2/4, *Charter of the United Nations and Statute of the International Court of Justice*, 4.

33. For case studies of peacekeeping before the creation of the UN, see A. James, *Peacekeeping in International Politics* (New York: St. Martin's Press, 1990).

34. For more discussion of these principles and their interrelated nature, see F.T. Liu, *United Nations Peacekeeping and the Non-Use of Force*, International Peace Academy Occasional Paper Series (Boulder, CO: Lynne Rienner, 1992).

35. *An Agenda for Peace: Preventive Diplomacy, Peacemaking, and Peacekeeping* (New York: United Nations, 1992), 1–2.

36. Data from UN Department of Public Information and Global Policy Forum, http://www.globalpolicy.org/security/peacekpg/index.htm (accessed 26 June 2004).

37. For discussions of the changing nature of peacekeeping, see Indar Rikhye, *The Politics and Practice of United Nations Peacekeeping: Past, Present, and Future* (Toronto: Brown Book Company, 2000); and Oliver P. Richmond, *Maintaining Order, Making Peace* (New York: Palgrave, 2002).

38. B. Boutros-Ghali, "Beyond Peacekeeping," *New York University Journal of International Law and Politics* 25 (Fall 1992), 115.

39. See Edward Newman and Oliver P. Richmond, eds., *The United Nations and Human Security* (New York: Palgrave, 2001).

40. Giandomenico Picco, "The UN and the Use of Force: Leave the Secretary-General Out of It," *Foreign Affairs* 73 (September/October 1994), 14.

41. Saadia Touval, "Why the UN Fails," *Foreign Affairs* 73 (September/October 1994), 45.

42. Quoted in Paul Lewis, "United Nations Is Finding Its Plate Increasingly Full but Its Cupboard Is Bare," *The New York Times,* 27 September 1993, A8.

43. See United Nations Security Council, S/PRST/2001/5, 20 February 2001.

44. Roland Paris, "Peacebuilding and the Limits of Liberal Internationalism," *International Security* 22 (Fall 1997), 56.

45. See Elizabeth M. Cousens, Chetan Kumar, and Karin Wermester, *Peacebuilding as Politics: Cultivating Peace in Fragile Societies* (Boulder, CO: Lynne Rienner, 2001).

46. See Stephen John Steadman, "Spoiler Problems in Peace Processes," *International Security* 22 (Fall 1997), 5–53.

47. Allen G. Sens, "From Peacekeeping to Peacebuilding: The United Nations and the Challenge of Intrastate War," in Mark W. Zacher and Richard M. Price, eds., *The United Nations and Global Security* (New York: Palgrave Macmillan, 2004), 141–60.

48. *The Responsibility to Protect*, Report of the International Commission on Intervention and State Sovereignty (Ottawa: International Development Research Centre, 2001), xi.

49. See Barry Posen, "The War for Kosovo: Serbia's Political-Military Strategy," *International Security* 24 (Spring 2000), 3–50; William Arkin, "Smart Bombs, Dumb Targeting?" *Bulletin of the Atomic Scientists* 56 (May/June 2000), 46–54; and Adam Roberts, "NATO's Humanitarian War over Kosovo," *Survival* 4 (Autumn 1999), 102–23.

50. See James Cotton, "The Emergence of an Independent East Timor: National and Regional Challenges," *Contemporary Southeast Asia* 22 (April 2000); and James Traub, "Inventing East Timor," *Foreign Affairs* 79 (July/August 2000), 74–89.

51. Michael O'Hanlon and P.W. Singer, "The Humanitarian Transformation: Expanding Global Intervention Capacity," *Survival* 46 (Spring 2004), 77–100.

52. Richard Cobden, *The Political Writings of Richard Cobden* (London: T. Fisher Unwin, 1903), 225.

53. Norman Angell, *The Great Illusion*, 2nd ed. (New York: G.P. Putnam's Sons, 1933), 33, 59–60. Or as the late great rock artist Frank Zappa once commented, there won't be a nuclear war in our time "because there's too much real estate involved."

54. Richard Rosecrance, *The Rise of the Trading State: Commerce and Conquest in the Modern World* (New York: Basic Books, 1986), 24–25.

55. Kenneth Waltz, *Theory of International Politics* (New York: Random House, 1979).

56. D. Leyton-Brown, "Introduction," in D. Leyton-Brown, ed., *The Utility of International Economic Sanctions* (New York: St. Martin's Press, 1987), 1–4.

57. J. Lindsay, "Trade Sanctions as Policy Instruments: A Re-Examination," *International Studies Quarterly* 30 (June 1996), 153–73.

58. See G. Hufbauer, J. Schott, and K. Elliott, *Economic Sanctions Reconsidered: History and Current Policy*, 2nd ed. (Washington, DC: Institute for International Economics, 1990).

59. K. Elliot, "Sanctions: A Look at the Record," *Bulletin of the Atomic Scientists* 49 (November 19), 32–35.

60. See J. Hoagland, "Economic Sanctions Sometimes Do More Harm Than Good," *The State* 11 (November 1993), A12.

61. See Hufbauer et al., *Economic Sanctions Reconsidered*, 100–01.

62. Ibid., 94.

63. (Former U.S. National Security Advisor) Anthony Lake, "From Containment to Enlargement," United States Department of State, Bureau of Public Affairs, *Dispatch* 4, no. 39 (September 1993), 3.

64. William Clinton, "Confronting the Challenges of a Broader World," United States Department of State, Bureau of Public Affairs, *Dispatch* 4, no. 39 (September 1993), 3.

65. Bruce Russett, *Grasping the Democratic Peace: Principles for a Post–Cold War World* (Princeton: Princeton University Press, 1993), 31.
66. Michael Doyle, "Kant, Liberal Legacies and Foreign Affairs," Part One, *Philosophy and Public Affairs* 12 (Summer 1983), 205–35, 230.
67. C. Layne, "Kant or Can't: The Myth of a Democratic Peace," *International Security* 19 (Fall 1994), 5–49.
68. D. Shapiro, "The Insignificance of the Liberal Peace," *International Security* 19 (Fall 1994), 50–86.
69. Layne, "Kant or Can't," 40–44.

Suggested Readings

Anderson, M.S. *The Rise of Modern Diplomacy.* New York: Longman, 1993.

Askari, Hossein, et al. *Economic Sanctions: Examining their Philosophy and Efficacy.* Westport, CT: Praeger, 2003.

Berdal, Mats R. "Whither UN Peacekeeping?" *Adelphi Paper* 281 (October 1993).

Bundy, McGeorge, William J. Crowe, Jr., and Sidney D. Drell. *Reducing Nuclear Danger: The Road away from the Brink.* New York: Council on Foreign Relations Press, 1993.

Carment, David, and Frank P. Harvey. *Using Force to Prevent Ethnic Conflict: An Evaluation of Theory and Practice.* Westport, CT: Praeger, 2001.

Cooper, A., J. English, and R. Thakur, eds. *Enhancing Global Governance: Toward a New Diplomacy?* Tokyo: United Nations University Press, 2002.

Cousens, Elizabeth M., Chetan Kumar, and Karin Wermester. *Peacebuilding as Politics: Cultivating Peace in Fragile Societies.* Boulder, CO: Lynne Rienner, 2001.

Diehl, Paul F. *International Peacekeeping.* Baltimore: Johns Hopkins University Press, 1993.

Durch, William J. *The Evolution of UN Peacekeeping.* New York: St. Martin's Press, 1993.

Fisher, Roger, and William Ury. *Getting to Yes.* Boston: Houghton Mifflin, 1981.

Fisher, Roger, et al. *Coping With International Conflict: A Systematic Approach to Influence in International Negotiation.* Upper Saddle River, NJ: Prentice Hall, 1997.

Fitzduff, Mari. *Beyond Violence: Conflict Resolution Process in Northern Ireland.* Tokyo: United Nations University Press, 2002.

Grieves, Forest L. *Conflict and Order.* Boston: Houghton Mifflin, 1977.

Hampson, Fen Osler, Norman Hillmer, and Maureen Appel Molot, eds. *The Axworthy Legacy. Canada among Nations 2001.* Oxford: Oxford University Press, 2001.

Hufbauer, Gary Clyde, Jeffrey J. Schott, and Kimberly Ann Elliott. *Economic Sanctions Reconsidered: History and Current Policy.* 2nd ed. Washington, DC: Institute for International Economics, 1990.

James, Alan. *Peacekeeping in International Politics.* New York: St. Martin's Press, 1990.

Jensen, Lloyd. *Bargaining for National Security: The Postwar Disarmament Negotiations.* Columbia: University of South Carolina Press, 1988.

———. *Negotiating Nuclear Arms Control.* Columbia: University of South Carolina Press, 1988.

Kozodoy, Neal, ed., *The Mideast Peace Process: An Autopsy.* San Francisco: Encounter Books, 2003.

Lasswell, Harold D. *Politics: Who Gets What, When, How.* New York: Meridian, 1958.

Martin, Lisa L. *Coercive Cooperation: Explaining Multilateral Economic Sanctions.* Princeton: Princeton University Press, 1992.

Melissen, Jan, ed. *Innovation in Diplomatic Practice.* London: Macmillan; New York: St. Martin's Press, 1999.

Neuheiser, Jörg, and Stefan Wolff, eds., *Peace at Last? The Impact of the Good Friday Agreement on Northern Ireland.* New York: Beghahn Books, 2002.

Newman, Edward, and Oliver P. Richmond, eds., *The United Nations and Human Security.* New York: Palgrave, 2001.

Richmond, Oliver P. *Maintaining Order, Making Peace.* New York: Palgrave, 2002.

Ripsman, N. *Peacemaking by Democracies: The Effect of State Autonomy on the Post-World War Settlements.* University Park: Pennsylvania State University Press, 2002.

Talbott, Strobe. *Deadly Gambits.* New York: Random House, 1985.

Telhami, Shibley. *Power and Leadership in International Bargaining: The Path to the Camp David Accords.* New York: Columbia University Press, 1990.

_____. *The Stakes: America and the Middle East.* Boulder, CO: Westview Press, 2002.

Viotti, Paul R., ed. *Conflict and Arms Control.* Boulder, CO: Westview Press, 1991.

Wasserstein, Bernard. *Israel and Palestine: Why They Fight and Can They Stop?* London: Profile Books, 2003.

Weston, Burns, ed. *Toward Nuclear Disarmament and Global Security.* Boulder, CO: Westview Press, 1984.

Zacher, Mark W., and Richard M. Price, eds. *The United Nations and Global Security.* New York: Palgrave Macmillan, 2004.

Suggested Websites

Arms Control Association
http://www.armscontrol.org

Center for Defense Information
http://www.cdi.org

Federation of American Scientists
http://www.fas.org

Global Policy Forum
http://www.globalpolicy.org

Human Security Network
http://www.humansecuritynetwork.org

United Nations
http://www.un.org

CHAPTER 8

Globalization, Marginalization, and Regionalization in the World Economy

If present trends continue, economic disparities between industrial and developing nations will move from inequitable to inhuman.

—*James Gustave Speth,*
UN Development Programme Administrator[1]

INTRODUCTION: THE GLOBAL ECONOMY TODAY

Few issue-areas better reflect the convergence/divergence theme emphasized in our introductory chapter than the state of the global economy today. On the one hand, there has been substantial growth in the world economy since 1945, in terms of production of goods and services, consumption, and trade and investment. More people around the world enjoy a higher standard of living than at any time in human history. On the other hand, there has been a widening gap between rich and poor states and rich and poor peoples in the world economy since 1945. This gap in quality of life between the wealthy and the poor has never been greater. Around the world, poor states and their citizens are burdened with heavy external debt loads, environmentally unsustainable agricultural and industrial processes, and the human and social costs of extreme poverty. This divergence is a central issue in any discussion of globalization or world economic management, and it has become a focus of acrimonious world trade negotiations. Convergence in the global economy can also be found in the form of regional economic integration (especially in Europe and North America), the increase in bilateral free trade agreements between states, and the growing membership of the World Trade Organization (WTO), which in 2004 boasted 147 members. Divergence in the global economy can also be found in the persistence of trade disputes between states, the increasing division of the world into trade blocs, the imbalance in investment flows across the world, and the failure of recent world and regional trade talks to reach agreement on a wide range of issues. Meanwhile, the debate over globalization and liberal economics continues. While many economists see globalization as an inevitable process driven by market forces largely beyond political control, others see it as a self-serving ideology motivated by economic interest. Globalization has proponents and opponents, and is the most hotly contested ground in the marketplace of ideas that is the study of contemporary International Political Economy (IPE).

This chapter begins with a re-examination of the central perspectives of international political economy introduced in chapters 1 and 4. An emphasis is placed on more contemporary concerns over the role of women in the world economy and environmental considerations. Next we discuss in greater detail the conceptual challenge posed by the term *globalization*. The relationship between globalization, economic activity, and politics is illustrated through an examination of the role of multinational corporations (MNCs) in the world economy. The chapter then examines what some critics consider the main counterpoint to globalization: regionalization. Is the world economy globalizing or regionalizing? We discuss what other critics argue is the main problem with globalization: marginalization. Is the world economy bringing greater wealth to more and more people, or is it creating inequities in the distribution of wealth? We then explore whether globalization has prompted a reorientation of state and nonstate warfare. Far from bringing us into an age of the Kantian ideal of a perpetual peace fuelled by trade and commerce, or even into an age dominated by the lofty claims of democratic peace theory, globalization may well be ushering in an age of increasing conflict and violence. Finally, we reflect on the role of energy politics in IPE, particularly the politics of oil.

As this chapter's structure suggests, a lot is going on in the world economy. The many actors in the world economy (states, MNCs, NGOs, individuals) are increasingly interlinked and, on the surface, look more and more like a single (albeit rather chaotic) entity. However, much of the economic integration that has occurred has been at the regional, as opposed to truly global, level. Some analysts suggest a world of three or four trade blocs has emerged, one that might preclude the grander globalization many liberals would prefer. Other analysts remind us that poverty and relative powerlessness continue to escalate in many regions of the world, despite the creation of great wealth elsewhere. Beyond these trends, we have seen some major developments over the past few years. Financial crises have become common: Mexico, Argentina, and Russia all experienced crises in the 1990s. But the foremost of these crises was the 1997–98 Asian financial crisis, which had a ripple effect throughout the world economy. Foreign investors and currency speculators have come to play a huge role in the daily economic life of countries, and when they remove their money amid concern over its safety (as they did in the above cases) the chaos can be immediate and long lasting. Another trend is the persistence of the debt crisis. Government debt has been reduced in some cases (Canada, for example, has managed balanced budgets in recent years), but it has soared in others, especially in Asia. New research has identified another development: women of all ages have become even more integrated with the modern production process than ever before. However, this is often occurring under exploitative conditions, most notably in the infamous "sweatshops" in many developing countries that produce goods for export for MNCs or locally owned businesses. Another trend is the increasing demand for energy, especially fossil fuels. Energy production remains a central issue with geostrategic importance, and oil politics are likely to become ever more salient in the future. The attempts to manage the global economy, from the shelved **Multilateral Agreement on Investment (MAI)** to the meetings of the WTO, have met with increasing opposition from protest groups concerned with the impact of globalization on societies, cultures, the workplace, employment, and the environment. Finally, technological innovations, such as **genetically modified organisms (GMOs)**, have further complicated trade negotiations, international law, intellectual property rights, and the agenda of protest groups. In short, the global economy has become more complex than anyone could have envisioned when the principles and institutions of the world economy were established during and immediately after World War II.

FROM THEORY TO PRACTICE IN THE CONTEMPORARY GLOBAL ECONOMY

In Chapter 4, we examined the different theoretical perspectives in the study of international political economy, and noted that the structures and institutions of the global economy were based on liberal economic theory. In the contemporary context, theoretical perspectives have lost none of their importance. First, recall that realists see world politics as a struggle between states for preservation and power. In IPE, realists argue that economic nationalism (or neomercantilism) will prevail. States will cooperate in the world economy when it is in their interests to do so, but frequently they will be in conflict or competition. Governments are primarily concerned with the health and security of the nation-state itself, and economic power is simply a means to maintain or increase that power. In the contemporary world economy, realists point to the maintenance of protectionist trade barriers, the provision of subsidies and tax benefits to crucial (and politically powerful) industries and economic sectors, the disagreements between states in world and regional trade talks, and the existence of trade wars (such as the 2004 U.S.–EU dispute over steel) as evidence that the world economy is a competitive arena in which states pursue their interests. Realists argue we can expect only limited progress from world and regional trade talks and from financial institutions and trade organizations. These institutions and organizations are controlled by states, and beneath the veneer of liberal principles and rhetoric, most states most of the time will pursue their own interests first and foremost. For realists, this explains the failure to reach trade and financial agreements, the persistent gap between rich and poor countries, and the existence of trade wars.

Where the economic nationalist sees states struggling to survive or prosper in the world economy, liberals see individuals, households, and firms maximizing their opportunity to pursue mutually beneficial exchange in the global marketplace. Through comparative advantage, a world adhering to the principles of free trade will reap the benefits of the efficient use of capital and resources. The institutions of the world economy were built by states in accordance with these liberal economic principles, and through tariff reduction, nondiscrimination, national treatment, and the harmonization of regulations, a rules-based trade and financial system has emerged. This development is taken to be a positive one, for through greater cooperation and economic interdependence a wealthier and less warlike world can be built. There is considerable debate among liberals on the role of the state and regulation in the world economy. Some liberals, sometimes called "neoliberals," (or confusingly, "neoconservatives" or "neocons") argue that states should play a minimal managerial role in economic affairs. More state intervention will create only more obstacles to market activity. A typical neoliberal agenda would extract the state from as much of the economic realm as possible, and indeed many of those who espouse globalization believe state interference is but a hindrance to a more rational, less nationalist global society. Neoliberal institutionalists believe rational actors will converge in common institutions and regimes to facilitate this process. This is the heart of the liberalist version of the "global governance" literature: a postnationalist international society can emerge with deliberate cooperation and institution building, but the global marketplace should not be subject to extraordinary controls or be responsible for the redistribution of wealth. There is, however, a great deal of variation among liberals on the influence such institutions or regimes (see Chapter 5) should have. Other liberals, those in the Keynesian tradition, argue that there needs to be more intervention by states in the global economy, and especially more of an effort to manage the global economy in the interests of poor countries and poverty reduction. They argue that the world economy is being driven into disaster by the neoliberal agenda, which has captured international financial institutions and allied itself with the interests of big corporations. Today, this intraliberal debate is one of the key features of the dialogue on globalization, with authors such as Joseph Stiglitz and George Soros stimulating debate on how the principles of liberal economics should be put into practice.

The Marxist perspective is far from irrelevant in contemporary dialogues on the world economy. Marxism rejects both mercantilist and liberal diagnostics and prescriptions: these interpretations are seen as mere shadows or reflections of the real structure of economic power. The global economy is characterized by the spread of world capitalism, which is defined by a class system in which economic elites dominate and exploit the poor. This class structure has spread to global proportions and works to keep the majority of people poor while the rich few, protected by the instrument of the state system, get richer. This system is strengthened by the growth of a transnational economic elite, which includes exploitative classes in postcolonial states. Today, Marxist thought is a powerful contributor to more transformative programs for political and economic change, and remains an ideological approach that to varying degrees has a sympathetic audience in some antiglobalization movements. Not to be outdone, postmodernists argue that what is needed is a re-examination of all these theories and the principles on which they are based.

Feminist and gendered perspectives have brought a new energy to debates on global economic issues. This energy has focused on the role of women in the world economy and what this means for global economic management and the social impact of globalization. More women are participating in the formal workforce than ever. But we should keep in mind the immense importance of the informal work that women (and many men) do in the home. Ultimately, women are disproportionately engaged in the process of reproducing the labour force that drives formal production. In other words, the world economy would surely grind to a halt were it not for those who clothe, teach, and care for children. For that matter, the predominantly male workforce in many areas is also fed and clothed by women who produce most of the clothing and food consumed domestically in most developing countries.

The workforce in industrialized states has undergone significant demographic change since women began working in factories during the world wars. Many economies have shifted to a service and information orientation (see Chapter 12), and this shift has meant that more women are in positions of decision-making power. Governments have often supported or encouraged this transition with employment equity programs. From a liberal feminist perspective, then, progress has been made—though just how much progress is still a matter of considerable debate. For example, a large international sex trade, which relies primarily on female labour, is a mainstay of the contemporary global economy, and it is often animated by brutal coercion. For example, the Coalition Against Trafficking in Women estimates that 200 000 Bangladeshi women were forced to work in Pakistan in the 1990s, and that as many as 30 000 Burmese women/girls are smuggled into Thailand each year. Similar cases have been reported regarding Filipino women in Japan, Eastern European women in Mexico and the United States, Nigerian women in Italy, and many other cases elsewhere.[2]

Among academics and politicians alike, much more attention has been paid in recent times to the role of women in development. Countries such as Canada have made women central players in their development assistance programs, though with mixed results. This is part of a more general, and welcome, move away from large infrastructure projects designed to bring Western-style growth to impoverished areas and toward focusing instead on smaller-scale development that involves local communities. International agencies, such as **UNICEF**, have been involved with acquiring bank loans for women in small-business sectors in countries

Women have made great strides in terms of economic equality, but feminists argue that many problems remain. For example, large-scale production in a globalized economy often exploits women and children. The match factories of Tamil Nadu rely almost exclusively on female labour working 12-hour days for 15 rupees (less than 50 cents) per day. (AP Photo/Cindy Andrew/CP Archive)

such as Egypt and Pakistan. In many Southern states, women have organized cooperatives, income-producing businesses that range from garment production to food processing.[3] This focus on women in development is important because their labour does not always show up in economic statistics, yet without it the world economy would stop moving. Still, most of the malnourished and undereducated children in the world are female. Among the Southern regions, only in Latin America do women's literacy rates even approach those of men. In addition, there is an increasing tendency for large MNCs and emerging local businesses to employ women in countries such as Indonesia and Malaysia for assembly work in export-oriented sectors such as electronics. While this employment may appear as progress to some, freeing women from the constraints of rural life, others argue it amounts to a form of gender-discriminatory slavery, since the women work long hours and are paid very little for their efforts. Some investors and plant managers prefer female workers because they have smaller hands, greater endurance, and are less likely to organize unions.

Ecofeminists, meanwhile, argue that despite all the media attention paid to the environment, industrialized Western society still doesn't understand the link between violence against women and environmental exploitation. The world economy remains heavily dependent on the extraction of large amounts of resources, for both fuel and products. Violence against women remains a widespread phenomenon, especially in times of war, as witnessed in the former Yugoslavia in the early 1990s. Efforts have been made at numerous levels to deal with both types of exploitation. While the type of deep change ecofeminists call for is a long way off, economists are recognizing the importance of the environment as both a causal variable and an ongoing concern in their work. The most widely publicized endorsement of the importance of the environment was the 1987 report of the Bruntland Commission, titled our *Our Common Future*.[4] This was followed by the environmental focus of the United Nations Conference on Environment and Development in Rio de Janeiro in 1992. Most basically, the environmental perspective in IPE emphasizes the idea that "if economic activity is to result in sustainable forms of development, environment can no longer be regarded as a factor separate from and secondary to economic decision-making; it must be fully integrated into the economic decision-making process in government, industry, and the home."[5] Ecofeminists would argue for much deeper structural change in human-to-human and human-to-ecology relations, stressing "the link between structural violence against women and the overexploitation of the environment."[6] However, the environment is now accepted as a crucial component of the study of the global economy and IPE. Concerns over the gender dynamic in the international workforce and the environmental problems resulting from large-scale industrialization and agriculture are increasingly reflected in contemporary debates on the meaning, implications, and sustainability of globalization. We turn now to a brief discussion of this widely used, but little understood, term.

WHAT IS GLOBALIZATION?

It is such a common term today that *globalization* is often accepted, without much examination, as an inevitable trend in the world economy. But when did we begin thinking about a borderless world in which transnational forces, spurred on by technological developments (especially in the field of communications), are shrinking the globe? One might argue this has been a long-term project that commenced when humans first began communicating; some feel it will end only with the global domination of liberal democracy and capitalism. Seen this way, globalization may be the logical end of history: other stages (the city-state system, feudal Europe, the nation-state system) of global development have merely been the means to this end. Others, however, might reject such a teleological approach or see the current era as the beginning of a new history, marked by the spread of Western culture around the globe, resistance to it, and continued disparities in wealth and opportunity.[7] Some even suggest that global capitalism, driven by its own "manic logic," is creating an inhumane world based on internationalized predatory capitalism.[8]

Perhaps the most succinct definition of globalization is offered by Malcolm Waters in his short but fascinating book on the topic. As a sociologist, Waters is more interested in the relationships inherent in global shifts. He defines globalization as a "social process in which the constraints of geography on social and cultural arrangements recede and in which people become increasingly aware that they are receding."[9] Waters believes globalization has always

Can we measure globalization simply by the amount of goods and services traded from port to port? By cross-national investment flows? Or is there a deeper cultural meaning to the question? (AP Photo/Nick Ut/CP Archive)

been taking place, proceeding through the "fits and starts of various ancient imperial expansions, pillaging and trading oceanic explorations, and the spread of religious ideas." This path was interrupted by the European Middle Ages, a period of "inward-looking territorialism" but then picked up again in the 15th and 16th centuries, when the Copernican revolution convinced humanity that it occupied a globe (instead of a flat endless plain) and when European expansion took the ideas that today still shape the global economy—market-based trade, for example—to distant lands where people had previously lived in "virtually complete ignorance of each other's existence."[10]

Others, such as the renowned Canadian international political economist Robert Cox, argue that the analysis of what Cox terms the "globalization thrust" must ultimately begin with an understanding of the internationalization of production:

> The internationalizing process results when capital considers the productive resources of the world as a whole and locates elements of complex globalized production systems at points of greatest cost advantage. The critical factor is information on how most profitably to combine components in that production process ... Producing units takes advantage of abundant, cheap, and malleable labour where it is to be found, and of robotization where it is not.[11]

While Waters's explanation rests more on the spread of ideas, Cox relies more on a *materialist* explanation (stressing the political implications of economic forces). Cox also takes a Gramscian approach, suggesting the hegemonic nature of globalization's ideology reflects the preferences of the structurally advantaged.

In general, international relations theorists have very mixed reactions to the assertion that we are in a new stage of world history in the process of globalization. Realists point to the stubbornness of the institution of state sovereignty. Anyone travelling across a border and dealing with the officials stationed there to protect it realizes very quickly that borders still exist, and if anything border controls have become tighter after September 11, 2001. Although the functionalist school (see Chapter 5) believed international institutions would eventually supplant the state, they did not have the multinational corporation (MNC) in mind. Further, it would be ludicrous to argue that the UN is anywhere near becoming a world government: it is used by states when it can further their policy designs, but has limited acceptance as an autonomous authority. For their part, Marxists would reject globalization as the continuation of older forms of **imperialism**. In fact, they would be apt to wonder what all the fuss is about, since this process has been a constant feature of economic and political life since the beginning of the expansion of the ruling elite in ancient societies. The fallen socialist bloc did not stop imperialism, but merely and temporarily stalled its spread. The periphery of the world system continues to be integrated by core finance and marketplaces, feeding the voracious appetite of global capitalism.

Beyond these debates are questions about the important cultural implications of increased trade, investment flows, and telecommunications capacity, a theme to which we return in Chapter 12. In terms of globalization's cultural impact, some would no doubt argue that globalization is the modern equivalent of what development theorists earlier referred to as *modernization*. The latter term was harshly criticized because it implied that only Western states were modern and that those developing states that had failed to reach the point of mass consumption societies were "unmodern," perhaps because of geographic, cultural, or even personality traits prevalent in their societies. Thus, one might argue that the pressure to globalize, to become even further involved with the world economy and its regimes, is a destructive one that implies that non-Western societies have no choice, if they want to experience economic growth and development, other than to adopt the conventional attributes of the West: capitalism, commercial culture, secular governance, and an emphasis on the present. Opposition to this cultural set of values is of course common in many regions, and even Western states are concerned about the intrusion of external cultural influences. Canada and France frequently seek to protect culture in world trade talks, for example. For Indigenous peoples around the world, the stakes are high: the intrusion of external cultural influences may threaten their very existence. The cultural destruction of Indigenous persons (which we discuss as a human rights issue in the next chapter) was an earlier variant of the wide-scale westernization we see taking place today.

On the other hand, some would insist that the very concept of globalization, and its continual promotion by the corporate elite, belittles the strong cultural differences that exist today. One author argues that the world is still fundamentally divided into at least eight civilization groupings, the Chinese (Confucian–Taoist–Buddhist), Hindu, Islamic, Japanese (Shinton–Buddhist–Confucian), Latin American syncretist, Islamic, non-Islamic African, and Christian.[12] Does a secular vision of globalization, based on markets and investment and common values, do justice to the inherent diversity of humanity? What about the major split, presented as axiomatic by some analysts, between the Eastern and Western, or Islamic and Christian, communities? What about the differences within every nation-state, between rich and poor, between ethnic groups, between male and female? In short, can the forces of globalization overcome the realities of human diversity and environmental diversity? Perhaps **homogenization** is further off than a simplified vision of proliferate Western products and advertisements would have us believe. Examining the idea that globalization will produce some sort of global culture, Canadian author Randall White asks,

> Just what could some authentic global culture possibly be? To take just the most obvious point, how would it deal with the at once simple but highly complex fact that in the world at large today we do not all speak anything like the same language? In the face of such monumental questions … globalization ideology as a practical matter can only fall back on something that bears a close resemblance to the old imperialism that really did exist, but that the world at large now rightly regards as too repugnant for the future.[13]

What is perhaps most pernicious about the globalization idea is that it suggests some superior force is at work driving us all toward convergence along the Western model. It is common for both corporate executives and politicians to talk of globalization as if it were inevitable and as if those who do not succumb to its tide will lose out in the future. If this is true, then there is little use in even thinking about alternatives. It suggests that we must, perhaps grudgingly, accept the fact that many people will be harmed by globalization even as others gain. After all, this has been a consistent theme in the evolution of economic systems: economic change tends to harm one part of a society even though society as a whole might benefit. However, this perspective suggests that we must be prepared to tolerate suffering on a grand scale. The author of a report on the UN Human Development Index, for example, believes that a "new vision of global solidarity is needed to match the push for globalization. Without this vision and action, globalization will become a monster of gargantuan excesses and grotesque inequalities."[14] Of course, many would argue that the monster is already upon us. We soon will discuss the inequality and marginalization that have risen in recent decades. But first we examine the Holy Grail of globalization's enthusiasts, the international marketplace.

PROFILE 8.1 "Toyotism"

Some observers have suggested that an emerging global corporate culture is pervading the workplace on an unprecedented scale. Thus the idea has been proposed that we are moving from a Fordist economy, in which relatively highly paid assembly-line workers receive the benefits of a welfare state, to one in which firms have more impact on workers' lives by encouraging them to actively participate in the design of the production process, even encouraging the establishment of a corporate culture. While it is difficult to establish whether such a trend exists, the emergence and success of giant industrial producers such as Toyota, which demand more concentration and production from employees in Western states such as Canada, suggests a shift in this direction. "Toyotism" consists of several principles that are held as guiding lights for large firms; it is based on the Japanese model of industrial production. These principles include

- *Strategic management*, which demands long-term outlooks and results in policies such as low price setting to get a product off the ground

- *Just-in-time inventory systems*, which minimize inventory levels (stocks) of material at all stages of the production process because the material is delivered only when needed; this system can be a weakness in the event of transportation problems

- *Managerial decentralization*, giving workers a greater role in the design process, which is generally done in a nonunionized working environment

SOURCE: K. DOHSE, U. JURGENS, AND T. MALSCH, "FROM 'FORDISM' TO 'TOYOTISM'? THE SOCIAL ORGANIZATION OF THE JAPANESE AUTOMOBILE INDUSTRY," *POLITICS & SOCIETY* 14, NO. 2 (1985), 115–46.

THE GLOBAL MARKET: THE TRIUMPHANT INVISIBLE HAND?

The state-run economies that formed the "Second World" during the Cold War have largely collapsed. Although some states, such as China and Cuba, retain the rhetorical vestiges of socialism, they too have turned to what we might loosely label **marketization** (characterized ideally by the introduction of private property, free competition between firms, and the use of foreign capital). North Korea remains steadfastly committed to a noncapitalist path, but it is literally in shambles, with a large part of the population suffering from malnutrition and starvation. In the 1990s, the former Soviet and Eastern-bloc states were labelled "transition economies" as they strove to emulate the Western model. Many of these states are among the 10 countries that joined the decidedly capitalist European Union on May 1, 2004. Therefore, it appears as though liberal economic principles and the Western model of capitalist development has outperformed all challengers, and emerged triumphant as the superior model of social and economic organization. However, although liberalism has certainly been embedded in the structures, institutions, and practices of the world economy since 1945, it is the neoliberal or neoconservative agenda that has continued to gain strength as the prevailing orthodoxy in government philosophy since the 1980s and 1990s.[15] This orthodoxy has increasingly institutionalized the belief in the invisible hand of the market in international financial and trade organizations. Therefore, as states (particularly those in the developing world) struggle to stimulate economic growth and deal with debt loads, the trend is for international institutions and organizations to champion a set of fiscal and economic policies designed to decrease the intervention of the state in the economy in order to permit market forces to work their magic. Collectively, these policies are most commonly referred to as the Washington Consensus.

John Williamson coined the term *Washington Consensus* in 1990 to describe a set of policies designed by international financial institutions (IFIs) based in Washington to stimulate economic growth and development in Latin America. The phrase is now generally used (or as

Williamson himself has argued, misused) to describe the neoliberal approach to economic development the world over. Although Williamson's original formulation did not include many of the practices now taken to be part of the Washington Consensus formula, the term has stuck, and it has become a focal point of the globalization debate. However, to suggest a "consensus" exists on these measures is highly misleading! For anti-globalization activists and critical government officials, the phrase is taken to be synonymous with the harmful effects of neoliberal practices in the world economy. For neoliberals, it is a set of baseline policies for future economic growth in the world, especially in the developing world. The Washington Consensus formula is based on 10 policies, each of which has been vilified by critics and defended by advocates:

- *Fiscal discipline.* Governments should balance their budgets to avoid deficits (and therefore debt); without fiscal discipline, governments will overspend themselves into debt. Critics charge that this has forced governments to cut back on social welfare spending.

- *Reordering public spending priorities.* Governments should spend money on sectors of high economic return. Proponents argue that governments spend too much money on subsidies to weak industries and on big projects plagued by corruption. Critics argue that spending cuts have de-prioritized health, education, and the environment.

- *Tax reform.* Governments should lower tax rates and expand the tax base. Critics charge that this benefits the rich, while proponents argue that lower taxes will stimulate the economy and increase employment.

- *Interest rate liberalization.* Governments should relax controls over interest rates, or hand control over to a regulated central bank. Liberals argue that this removes the temptation of government to manipulate interest rates for political purposes, while critics charge that it removes the ability of governments to encourage domestic savings rates and to fight inflation and capital flight.

- *A competitive exchange rate.* Governments should allow their currencies to float on international financial markets. Liberals argue that this makes the country attractive for investment and makes exports attractive to foreign consumers. Critics argue that this leaves the country vulnerable to currency speculation and international financial crises, which can bring sharp drops in the value of people's wages and savings.

- *Trade liberalization.* Governments should lower tariffs and encourage trade. For liberals, this allows comparative advantage to work and makes more products from abroad affordable for consumers. Critics argue that this leads to the failure of domestic industries due to foreign competition and, consequently, high levels of unemployment.

- *Liberalization of **foreign direct investment**.* Governments should allow foreign investment into their country with fewer regulations and controls. This allows industries and individuals to gain access to capital. This allows foreign industries and individuals to gain control over domestic economies, say critics.

- *Privatization.* Governments should encourage the transfer of state-owned industries to private hands in order to increase competitiveness and productivity; critics argue this will create a new elite class and lead to job cuts to reduce costs and increase efficiency.

- *Deregulation.* Governments should abolish trade barriers and cumbersome restrictions on private sector activity, creating more room for entrepreneurial innovation. Critics argue that this will lead governments to abolish regulations on safety and the environment to conform to international trade rules.

- *Property rights.* Governments should promote and enforce laws encouraging the private ownership of property. For liberals, private property rights are the key to capitalist growth. For critics, this will lead only to a few possessing most of the land and industry in a country, while others will have little or no property or wealth.

The Washington Consensus formula has been imposed on developing countries by international donors such as the G-7 states, and by IFIs such as the **IMF** and the **IBRD** (World Bank), as conditions for the extension of loans or debt-relief packages. Critics (including interventionist liberals) argue that this has been done without due regard for local social, cultural, economic, geographic, or environmental conditions. Many liberals see this "conditionality" as the necessary counterpart to loan guarantees to developing countries: it makes little sense to loan money to countries that are not following sound fiscal and economic policies. However, critics argue that this means governments have been forced to adopt a set of fiscal and economic policies that may be harmful to the most vulnerable sectors of their society, and may result in lower government spending on education, health care, and general welfare. A further criticism is that none of the advanced capitalist states have followed the rules themselves: they run deficits, protect their markets, and (as a government funding scandal in Canada demonstrated in early 2004) have their own corruption problems.

Another development in the global market, and another reflection of the triumph of liberal economics, is the rise of financial markets and **currency speculation**. Daily turnover on foreign-exchange markets has grown to around U.S.$1.5 trillion, about the same as the total currency reserves of the world's central banks. In 1992, the exchange rate mechanism (ERM) of the **European monetary system** fell apart, and in 1994 the Mexican peso took a huge plunge, which led to IMF and U.S. efforts to bail out investors (mostly Americans). Similar problems surfaced in the once vibrant Asian stock markets in 1997. These events have led to fears that the power of these markets, based largely on speculative purchases and quick sales, has challenged the ability of the nation-state to control its own economic fortune. This fear has led to calls for measures to moderate these activities and generate revenue from them for international charitable projects. In fact, more than 20 years ago, economist James Tobin suggested that a tax be levied on international currency exchanges. Different analysts have suggested different figures, but the usual amount is 0.1 percent on all foreign-currency trades, which alone would raise well over $100 billion a year. A "Tobin tax," it is often argued, would limit the amount of speculation international investors engage in, and the resulting revenue could be used for international humanitarian purposes, such as paying for peacekeeping operations, or paying off the debt owed by the UN. However, it would be difficult to convince market-oriented governments that this type of intervention is justified, and, as an article in *The Economist* points out, unless every state participated, "trading would simply shift to tax-free havens. Also, financial wizards would quickly devise tax dodges: rather than trade yen for dollars, say, they might agree to swap Japanese government bonds for American Treasuries."[16] Finally, the increasing use of the **Internet** for commercial transactions would make such a taxation scheme even more difficult to implement.

Though the state still plays a major role in the economies of all countries, and especially in the industrialized North, the role of the state is decreasing in certain areas of economic management as governments attempt to maintain growth or are forced to deal with debt loads. Yet, if we have seen a triumph of the market on an almost global scale, it is not by accident. One need not accept the entire ideological thrust of Marxism to agree with critical theorists that the economic elite has a tremendous impact on the formation of government policy. This statement is as true in matters of trade as it is in domestic issues. Governments explicitly incorporate the private sector in foreign policy decision making and in domestic market production. Few countries make this incorporation as evident as does Canada: when the international trade minister travels to a foreign state he or she is accompanied by a virtual army of representatives from businesses and Crown corporations seeking to break into new markets with products and expertise. For example, "Team Canada" trips to China have resulted in the sale of Canada's CANDU nuclear reactors. This sale has generated some criticism, since (1) the federal government waived the usual environmental assessment procedure, and China does not have a strong reputation on such matters, and (2) the sale of the reactors was financed in part by the Canadian Export Development Corporation in Ottawa, meaning essentially that Canadian taxpayers have subsidized an ailing nuclear industry at home and supported a Chinese regime many find repugnant. In another example, the business delegation that accompanied then International Trade Minister Art Eggleton to Russia and Poland in October 1996 included high-level representatives from more than 50 major Canadian companies, such as Alcan Canada-Vostok, Atomic Energy of Canada, Bombardier Regional Aerospace Division, Canadian Imperial Bank of Commerce, Dreco Energy Services, McCain Foods, Molson Breweries, Northern Telecom, Nortel, the Saskatchewan Wheat Pool, and many others.[17] This begs the question of what governments should be doing in world affairs. Beyond providing the most rudimentary of national defence against invasion, should governments exist primarily as a mechanism to extend trade opportunities abroad? Or do they exist to promote and protect the quality of life, or to attain the status of a winner in the global economy? Are the concerns of development and human security being sacrificed for economic gain? At the same time, if a government is elected primarily with a mandate to create jobs, and if increased government spending is not a realistic option due to debt burdens or public opposition to tax increases or spending cuts, then perhaps a strong pro-trade foreign policy orientation is its only viable option, and one that would be supported by much of the voting public.

If the market has won over the hearts and minds of a transnational economic elite, it may not have done so among the millions of people who continue to forge their own path of development somewhere else. It would be a gross overgeneralization to argue that all that is left is **capitalism** with minimal state interference. From the quiet fields of agrarian communities around the world, to the streets of the bustling megacities, people are engaged in forming their own substate arrangements and interpersonal relationships. For example, female workers formed many cooperative ventures to produce textiles in Guatemala; women in Kenya founded the Green Belt movement, planting millions of trees to stop **desertification**; artistic communities in many Northern states formed mutually supportive networks; people rose in widespread protests to halt the privatization of water provision in Bolivia; and unique regimes in environmental management are being forged as we grapple with problems of the commons. There is much more to the global political economy than the amorphous entity we refer to as the market, and though the conventional path of socialism may well be dead, with its stench of economic failure and political repression, a new one may be emerging, one that is being cleared by the survival strategies implemented by people in both hemispheres.[18] However, there is little doubt that the marketplace, as defined by neoliberal ideology, retains a special place in the hearts and minds of those who benefit most greatly from globalization. This is best demonstrated with reference to a peculiarly 20th-century innovation with deep consequences, the multinational corporation.

THE CENTRAL ROLE OF MULTINATIONAL CORPORATIONS

Perhaps one of the most remarkable characteristics of the contemporary global economy is the expansive rise of the MNC. MNCs (also sometimes referred to as transnational corporations, or TNCs) are businesses with extensive investments or operations in more than one country. Typically, MNCs are headquartered in a home country, and own and operate affiliate businesses in other countries around the world. Larger MNCs may control large product lines and brand names, acquired through strategic corporate alliances, mergers, purchases of other companies, or hostile takeovers. Largely through the operations of MNCs, world production has become increasingly globalized, as production facilities are moved around the world and product components are increasingly manufactured and assembled in a wide variety of countries. An estimated 25 to 33 percent of world trade is intrafirm trade between the affiliates of MNCs. While some companies are major competitors, MNCs also cooperate extensively, often sharing production facilities and forming partnerships with local firms. American, European, and Japanese MNCs are generally the largest and most powerful. As early as the 1960s, the power of MNCs led to questions about the primacy of the nation-state.[19] In particular, the dominance of American multinationals has caused Canadians, Europeans, and South Americans to worry about the influence of American corporate commercialism on their cultures (in the Canadian case, a short-lived spate of Canadian nationalism arose out of these concerns).[20] MNCs are regarded either as necessary suppliers of investment and technical knowledge or as predatory entities that perpetuate the underdevelopment of poor countries. In either conception, their influence is substantial (see Profile 8.2).

The sheer size of modern MNCs is intimidating. The Ford Motor Company, for example, has operations in 30 countries and employs more than 300 000 people worldwide. Some MNCs have a large number of subsidiary corporations. For example, Yum! Brands Inc. owns A&W, All American Food, Pizza Hut, Taco Bell, Long John Silver's, and Kentucky Fried Chicken, and together operates 33 000 restaurants in 100 countries and territories, generating over U.S.$24 billion in revenues in 2002. Yum! Brands Inc. was formerly Tricon Global Restaurants, itself a spinoff from PepsiCo in 1997. Corporate mergers have accelerated the growth of some MNCs: in 2000, the French car manufacturer Renault took over Nissan; in the pharmaceutical sector Glaxco Wellcome merged with SmithKline Beecham in an effort to capitalize on the drug potential of the human genome project; and America Online merged with Time Warner, creating a company with a market value of U.S.$340 billion (although the drop in tech stocks in the latter half of 2000 reduced this figure by $140 billion). In some cases, MNCs produce goods from components that are manufactured in different countries and assembled in the market country. Sometimes, they share ownership of a subsidiary with another MNC, or with the host government, because of legal requirements or to reduce risk. These arrangements are called *joint ventures*, and many such ventures operate in the former Soviet Union and in China. In other cases, MNCs decide not to invest directly in other countries, instead choosing to establish licensing arrangements with foreign companies or governments, permitting the latter to produce products in return for a fee and share of the profits.

MNCs are extremely powerful economic entities, and their significance in the global economy has grown as world trade has expanded. In 1978, the 430 largest MNCs accounted for more than U.S.$1.8 trillion of global economic output. In 1994, the 37 largest MNCs in the world produced more than U.S.$3 trillion of goods and services, over 10 percent of world economic output.[21] Today, the operations of MNCs are responsible for approximately 20 percent of world production. It is striking that when the annual revenues of the largest MNCs in the world are compared with the annual GNP of states, more than one-third of the world's largest economic units are MNCs. Even more stark is the fact that while the UN regular budget is approximately U.S.$1.4 billion, over 30 of the largest MNCs have annual revenues over U.S.$100 billion. MNCs are also significant because of their numbers: there are over 60 000 MNCs in the world, with over 450 000 affiliates, or subsidiaries. Few countries in the world do not host an MNC or a subsidiary within their territorial boundaries. Furthermore,

MNCs have a great deal of control over the global capacity to manufacture products, sell services, and provide finance, and they are leading developers of technology and services. Most of the largest MNCs are in the manufacturing sector (Mitsubishi, General Motors), oil (Exxon, Royal Dutch/Shell Group), and electronics (IBM, AT&T). In other sectors, financial corporations such as Citigroup Inc. and Deutsche Bank are among the world's largest MNCs. In this sector, Japanese banks have dominated for years, with roughly half of the 50 largest banks in the world headquartered in Japan (where domestic laws permit them to expand into a wide variety of financial services, unlike U.S. banks, which are restricted by law to specific financial services, such as brokerage or insurance). However, recent events in Asia suggest that the era of Japanese banking prowess may be at an end. The service sector also has many large MNCs, including McDonald's and Wal-Mart, that can change the entire commercial and aesthetic landscape in the towns where they locate, often forcing small businesses into bankruptcy.

MNCs' influence can be measured by the familiarity with which we recognize the household names IBM, Hitachi, Microsoft, General Electric, Du Pont, PepsiCo, Eastman Kodak, Toyota, Mitsui, Volkswagen, Bayer, Renault, Michelin, Ciba-Geigy, Seagram, Thomson, Fiat, Philips, Unilever, and others. Billions of dollars are spent on advertising in home and foreign markets so that the products, logos, and advertising campaign themes of these corporations have become part of popular rich-world, largely Western culture. As these products are marketed around the world, they become visible reflections of Western presence, or what critics would term instruments of **cultural imperialism**.

Obviously, the role played by MNCs in the global economy is a controversial one. Some see MNCs as agents of their home states, used by states to further their own economic and even political interests in the world. Indeed, some MNCs have become deeply involved in the politics of host countries, even to the point of engineering the overthrow of governments. A

PROFILE 8.2

The Debate over MNCs: Do They Exploit Southern Countries?

YES

1. MNCs decapitalize less-developed countries (LDCs). MNCs take more money in profit out of LDCs than they invest.

2. MNCs are obstacles to social progress. The profit motive makes MNCs unresponsive or opposed to progressive political change.

3. MNCs contribute to inequality. MNCs create an elite socioeconomic class in LDCs, isolated from the poor majority.

4. MNCs discourage indigenous development. They oppose efforts by LDCs to industrialize, as this would create domestic competition.

5. MNCs create dependence. LDC economies come to depend on MNCs for investment, technology, and markets.

6. MNCs use LDCs as sources of raw materials. MNCs extract raw materials for a low price and manufacture products abroad, forcing LDCs to purchase expensive finished products.

NO

1. MNCs provide investment. MNCs invest a lot of their own money and also attract foreign investors.

2. MNCs support peaceful domestic environments. MNCs require peace to operate effectively, and therefore have an interest in long-term stability.

3. MNCs create jobs. They have an interest in a capable workforce and provide training and education.

4. MNCs promote development. MNCs help create modern infrastructure and share technology and technique, therefore creating conditions conducive to domestic growth.

5. MNCs increase fiscal resources of LDCs. MNCs create royalties and tax revenues for LDCs.

6. MNCs give LDCs access to world markets. They provide a channel to markets for products as well as markets for purchase, enabling LDCs to access the global marketplace.

famous example of this is the involvement of International Telephone and Telegraph (ITT) in the events that led to the overthrow of the Allende government in Chile in 1973. Others see MNCs as essentially benign actors, acting in the interests of their shareholders and motivated by profit, and essential to the efficient development, production, and distribution of goods and services in the global economy. Still others see MNCs as exploitative actors, preying on cheap labour markets and raw materials, and selling the resulting products at huge profit margins. For example, in the early 1990s, many Nike shoes were manufactured in Indonesia, where the typical worker was paid $1 a day in 1991 (minimum-wage legislation and labour rights are seldom enforced in Indonesia). A pair of Nike shoes can cost more than $100 in Canada. For critics of MNCs, situations like this are repeated in all economic sectors in poor countries around the world. Indeed, critics often charge that MNCs do not just take advantage of poverty, but with their limited investment in human development, lax environmental standards, and outsourcing of labour, help to create it as well. Certainly, they are major players in many people's lives today, in both the North and the South. But the causes and extent of poverty are much more complex than the dynamics of MNC activity, as our next section will demonstrate.

THE GREAT DIVIDE: THE POLITICAL ECONOMY OF THE RICH AND THE POOR

The gap between the rich and the poor peoples of the world is enormous, whether measured in terms of economic statistics or quality of life. This gap is often described in terms of a generally rich Northern Hemisphere and a generally poor Southern Hemisphere. In practice, however, there are significant exceptions to this generalization; for example, North Korea is relatively poor, while Australia is relatively rich. Nevertheless, issues surrounding poverty and development are often cast in terms of a North–South debate. Similarly, the term *Third World* is still in use, although it is in decline (see Profile 8.3). Countries are also classified along "rich" and "poor" lines, with the countries of the developed world having attained a high level of wealth through industrialization and technological development, relatively equitable levels of income distribution, and high standards of living in stable, civil societies. In contrast, countries of the "developing world" have lower levels of wealth, agricultural or subsistence economies, and inequitable income distribution in societies dominated by small elites. From this distinction has grown the term **less-developed country** (**LDC**). These supposedly polar opposites—rich and poor, North and South, modern and traditional—are, by and large, misleading caricatures.

It is important to remember that there are rich and poor in both the developed and developing worlds. Indeed, poverty is a serious problem in most of the world's leading industrialized economies, and an extravagantly wealthy upper class is often visible in most countries. Furthermore, some groups—especially minority groups and working-class women—tend be more marginalized than others from the benefits of the economy. Nevertheless, however one classifies the problem, the reality of economic inequality in the world is staggering, and for many this is the most serious global issue facing the world today. As we will see, considerable dispute exists over the most appropriate and effective means of addressing and alleviating the gap between the rich and the poor. Optimistic liberals see this gap as a natural component of uneven growth in the world economy that will even out over time, as the tide of globalization lifts even the most reluctant economies. Marxists and dependency theorists see it as a legacy of imperialism and exploitative colonial rule, which continue in a different form to this day. Postmodernists would explain it as a legacy of intellectual domination of Western approaches to politics, the marginalization of other traditions, and a reflection of racism. Feminists see it as a legacy of economic and political approaches that have marginalized women.

PROFILE 8.3 The "Third World"

Throughout this text, we have often avoided using the term *Third World* where it is usually employed. The term has been criticized as demeaning to less-developed states. However, although obvious ethnocentricity has been involved in labelling the developed capitalist states the *First World*, the term *Third World* was first used to indicate a non-American, non-Soviet path of political and economic alignment. Over time, however, it slipped into general usage as meaning the Southern states with low GNPs, and here it quickly began to make less sense, not only because there are large discrepancies in GNP figures among these states, but because, with the end of the Cold War, there is no longer a distinct Second World of Communist states. Alternative phrases have proliferated over the years, such as *developing states*, *less-developed*

states, *underdeveloped states*, the *periphery*, the *South*, the *global South*, and the *Majority World*. The broader question is not really which is appropriate, since they are all derived from political perspectives, but whether any sort of label is appropriate, given the diversity of states and peoples in the developing world. Enormous differences exist in wealth, income distribution, political systems, social structure, and economic organization. In the past, some scholars have suggested differentiating states in the developing world by creating additional categories, such as the Fourth World, the Fifth World, or the least developed of the less-developed countries (LLDCs). Nevertheless, terms such as *North–South* and *developing world* remain widely employed in diplomatic language, especially in the context of UN-sponsored forums.

If we define the South as including the majority of lower-income states, we find the Northern Hemisphere contains one-quarter of the world's people but consumes three-quarters of its goods and services, while the Southern Hemisphere contains three-quarters of the world's people but consumes only one-quarter of its goods and services. Of the U.S.$23 trillion world GDP in 1993, U.S.$18 trillion was in the "high-income economies." By 2002, world GDP had climbed to well over U.S.$32 trillion, with U.S.$26 trillion of this total in the high-income states (the United States alone accounted for U.S.$10.383 trillion of this, Japan for U.S.$3.993; Canada's GDP was U.S.$0.714).[22] The

A boy walks past a Coca-Cola sign on a destroyed wall in Kukma, India, February 2001. The United Nations Children's Fund (UNICEF) estimates that 2.5 million children below the age of 14 lost family members, homes, and schools in the January 26 earthquake that killed at least 19 000 people. While MNCs might bring employment opportunities, they cannot replace the need for a sound state infrastructure to respond to developmental needs. (AP Photo/Eugene Hoshiko/CP Archive)

UNDP *Human Development Report* of 2003 contained many striking facts about global inequity. For example, some 54 states actually have less income and net worth in 2002 than they had in 1990; more malnutrition was recorded in 21 states; infant mortality (the death rate for those under five years of age) has increased in 14 states, and primary school enrolment rates have fallen in 12 states. Further, the rate of inequality, both within and across states, has increased as well. Indeed, incomes are distributed less evenly across the globe than within even the more stratified states. One method of measuring income inequality is the Gini coefficient, or a measure that ranges between 0, indicating perfect equality, and 1, indicating complete inequality. In the 2003 UNDP *Human Development Report*, the global Gini coefficient was estimated at 0.66. The richest 5 percent of the world's people receive 114 times the income of the poorest 5 percent, while the richest 1 percent receive as much income as the poorest 57 percent. Of the world's 128 countries with at least 1 million people in 1990 (and with sufficient data), 76 countries saw per capita incomes grow between 1980 and 1998. However, 52 countries saw per capita incomes shrink.[23]

The relationship between these grim economic figures and quality of life is direct and real. While measures based on monetary shares cannot tell the whole story (some societies with very low per capita GNP rates nevertheless are successful in providing for **basic human needs**), the human dimension of these economic statistics is appalling. At the aggregate level, and at the individual level, global inequality has taken a devastating toll on the human condition in much of the world. In all, 1.3 billion people live in abject poverty, on less than U.S.$1 per day, without access to basic nutritional requirements, health care, waste disposal, or adequate housing. Put simply, the basic human needs of vast numbers of the world's population are not being met. For example, consider the following statistics:

- *Food, water, and nutrition.* Nearly 800 million people in the world do not receive enough food, and about 500 million are chronically malnourished (unable to maintain body weight). Another 1.3 billion people lack access to safe drinking water, and more than half of the world's people do not have adequate water supplies.

- *Health and health care.* Seventeen million people die every year from treatable infectious and parasitic diseases. The most common are respiratory infections (7 million deaths a year), diarrhea (4 million), tuberculosis (3 million), and malaria and hepatitis (1 to 2 million). Of the world's 18 million people infected with HIV, 90 percent live in the Southern Hemisphere. Only 30 percent of the world's doctors practise in these countries, despite the fact that 75 percent of the world's population live in these countries.

- *Children.* More than one-third of children in the South are malnourished, and the under-five mortality rate is six times higher than in the North. Every three seconds, a child dies from malnutrition-related problems (more than 1000 an hour, 30 000 a day, 10 million a year).

- *Education.* About 130 million children in the South do not attend primary school, and 275 million (approximately half of the children in the South) do not attend secondary school. One billion people in the world are illiterate.

- *Women.* Seventy percent of the people in abject poverty in the world are women. Two-thirds of illiterate people are women. In the South, maternal mortality rates are 12 times higher than in the OECD countries. Eighty percent of malnourished children are female. For women, the problems of poverty are compounded by inferior social status: female children are less valued; women face barriers in education and career prospects; and women are underrepresented politically, holding only 10 percent of seats in the world's legislative assemblies and parliaments.

The UN has developed a program of action known as the Millennium Development Goals, aimed at reducing these and other shortfalls in human well-being by 2015 (see Profile 8.4).

In light of these statistics, it might be useful to reflect on how Canada compares to the rest of the world. The UN employs a measure called the Human Development Index, which is based on achievements in basic human capabilities across states. The HDI is measured by life expectancy, educational attainment, and income (GNP per capita). In the 1999 report, Canada ranked number one in the world (as it has since 1992), though it has slipped in more recent years, finishing eighth in 2003, behind Norway, Iceland, Sweden, Australia, the Netherlands, Belgium, and the United States. (Of course, eighth out of over 190 states is still a rather posi-

PROFILE 8.4 The Millennium Summit Goals

In 2000, Secretary-General Kofi Annan hosted the Millennium Summit in New York, attended by most heads of state and other officials. He set out a series of challenges, which received a warm welcome and expressions of support from the gathered politicians. However, despite the earnest desire to curb the ill effects of poverty, it would be foolish to suggest we are anywhere near the accomplishment of these goals. Can the global economy possibly achieve these goals without significant or perhaps radical change?

FREEDOM FROM WANT: *THE MILLENNIUM DEVELOPMENT GOALS*

- *Eradicate extreme hunger and poverty.* Target for 2015: Halve the proportion of the world's people (currently 22 percent) whose income is less than one dollar a day and those who suffer from hunger.

- *Achieve universal primary education.* Target for 2015: Ensure that all boys and girls complete primary school.

- *Promote gender equality and empower women.* Target for 2015: Eliminate gender disparities in primary and secondary education.

- *Reduce child mortality.* Target for 2015: Reduce by two-thirds the mortality rate of children under the age of five.

- *Improve maternal health.* Target for 2015: Reduce by three-quarters the number of women dying in childbirth.

- *Combat HIV/AIDS, malaria, and other diseases.* Target for 2015: Halt, and begin to reverse, the spread of HIV/AIDS, malaria, and other diseases, providing at least 95 percent of young people with access to HIV-prevention services.

- *Ensure environmental sustainability.* Target for 2015: Integrate principles of sustainable development, improve drinking water, improve conditions of slum dwellers.

- *Develop a global partnership for development.* This would involve governments, IOs, civil society, and the private sector

tive assessment of the quality of life in Canada!) These high rankings do not mean that Canada does not face problems associated with poverty, homelessness, or the economic and political marginalization of certain groups in society. Nevertheless, it should give Canadians pause to consider what ethical obligations they might have to work to alleviate global inequalities.

INTERNATIONAL RESPONSES TO GLOBAL INEQUITY AND POVERTY: TOO LITTLE, TOO LATE?

Before discussing contemporary multilateral efforts to ease the plight of the poor, some background is in order. In Chapter 2 we examined how the European empires expanded around the world and how non-European empires also expanded and conquered territories abroad, imposing alien systems of economic and political organization. Many of the problems that beset the Southern states have their origins in the nature of this colonial rule. As we have seen, these empires began to collapse after World War II, and many states gained their political independence. However, the end of colonial rule left most of these former colonies woefully unprepared to govern their political, economic, or social affairs. Although some colonies were better prepared for independence than others, in general the colonies lacked individuals trained or involved in the administration of independent government. Furthermore, the arbitrary nature of colonial borders left many new independent states with complex mixtures of ethnicities, languages, religions, and clans, many of which had historical animosities. The effort to build nationalism around loyalty to the state, as opposed to loyalty to ethnicity or clan, was never very successful, as we saw in our discussion of ethnic conflict in Chapter 6. Finally, a postcolonial dependence lingered: Southern states needed Northern capital, while Northern states continued to exploit Southern natural resources and labour. The legacy of imperialism had left the former colonies with the illusion of political freedom but the reality

Canadians and others who buy coffee on a daily basis might want to consider the plight of Segundo Espinosa, 6.
Here he lies on the bare board of his bed in squalid living quarters for coffee workers and their families in Los Milagros, Nicaragua, August 2001. His family was one of the few that were not driven off the coffee plantation when others were fired the previous November due to a dramatic drop in international coffee prices. Daily wages on the plantation are $1.48 for men, $1.11 for women and 55 cents for children (all figures in U.S. dollars). (AP Photo/ John Moore/CP Archive)

of economic subjugation, which in turn left them vulnerable to political interference and domination. Concern over the North–South split increased during the 1960s and 1970s, and became a major issue at the UN (where it is still an issue today). Southern states were now stuck in a cycle of underdevelopment, one that they felt was perpetuated by the investment activities of large corporations, the accumulation of external debt to the North, and the unequal trading arrangement of the world economy. Liberals counter that many of these states have followed poor economic practices and have corrupt leaders and economic elites more interested in personal enrichment than the welfare of their people. Under such circumstances, states cannot be expected to develop.

Efforts to change the place of poorer countries in the world began at the Bandung Conference in 1955, a meeting of 25 Asian and African states that condemned colonialism. In 1964 a group of developing states in the UN formed the **Group of 77 (G-77)**, which called for the development of favourable terms of trade for developing countries in GATT. The G-77 did succeed in creating the pressure behind a **Generalized System of Preferences (GSP)**, an arrangement whereby rich states would permit certain products from the developing world to enter their economies on favourable terms (i.e., lower tariff barriers). But this concession was not the decisive or major step the developing world sought. In 1974, the G-77 called for the establishment of a **New International Economic Order (NIEO)** that would give Southern states a better position in the world trading system. Many developing states had evolved into what economists have referred to as "one-commodity countries." Some examples include Bolivia (natural gas), Colombia (coffee), Venezuela (petroleum), Botswana (diamonds), Niger (uranium), Zaire (copper), and Fiji (sugar). The price of such items is susceptible to sudden and dramatic shifts in demand, and if the price drops, the country suffers. The NIEO called for commodity agreements that would free states highly dependent on a few products from suffering the effects of wild price fluctuations. It also called for an increase in economic aid from Northern states; debt relief by forgiving or postponing repayment; the provision of preferential treatment for exports from developing countries; transfers of appropriate technology to the

South; and greater Southern influence on the boards of the main financial institutions, such as the IMF and World Bank Group. These demands, and others associated with the NIEO movement, called for heavy state intervention in the global economy, thus contradicting the principles of free trade on which the GATT trade system was slowly evolving. Despite a modest effort to bolster developing countries' trade through the European Economic Community in 1975 in the **Lomé Convention** (which currently covers trade with over 70 **African, Caribbean and Pacific [ACP] states**), the overall thrust of the NIEO plan was so antimarket and demanding from the North's perspective that it never had a serious chance of being implemented. Today, the G-77 countries (which now number more than 120) continue to press for changes to the international trading system, but their profile is no longer what it once was.

As efforts to decisively change the global trading system foundered and foreign direct investment proved insufficient, the developing world increasingly relied on financial aid for development. This aid came from three primary sources: loans from the World Bank Group and the IMF, private capital markets, and Official Development Assistance. Today, the World Bank Group includes the International Bank for Reconstruction and Development (IBRD), the **International Development Association (IDA)**, the **International Finance Corporation (IFC)**, and the Multilateral Investment Guarantee Agency (MIGA), and the International Centre for Settlement of Investment Disputes. Together, the Group extended U.S.$23 billion in financial assistance in 2003. The money in the bank comes from governments (which pay according to a quota) and from borrowing on private financial markets. Loans are extended by a vote, with countries that contribute most to the funds of the Group having increased voting weight. As a result, the United States has disproportionate influence, and the rich countries dominate the voting. The IBRD approves only hard loans, that is, loans that have a good prospect for obtaining returns (repayment with interest). The IFC acts as a bridge between the developing world and private investors and financial institutions, while the IDA assists the world's poorest countries in obtaining soft loans, with easier terms of repayment and lower rates of interest. The International Monetary Fund has become a crisis lender to governments in immediate need of funds to balance their payments or compensate for a drop in commodity prices. In 2004, the IMF had outstanding loans of U.S.$107 billion to 87 different countries.

The institutions of the World Bank Group and the IMF have received considerable criticism. Critics charge that the world's richest countries control these institutions (through **weighted voting**), and as a result the institutions lend based not on the need of the developing world but in the interests of capital lenders. The terms of the loans of the World Bank are little better than those from private institutions, and the amount of money dispensed by the Group has never been sufficient to make a decisive difference in the position of the developing world. Finally, the World Bank Group and especially the IMF are criticized for imposing extensive and often harsh conditions for loans, conditions that critics argue are based on the flawed formula of the Washington Consensus. The **structural adjustment programs (SAPs)** recommended by the IMF and World Bank demand reductions in public spending (which hurt the poor the most) and a focus on trade liberalization and the exportation of natural resources, which harm the environment and curtail more diverse economic development. These measures can increase hardship in developing states and often create political instability.[24] Critics charge that the basic aim of SAPs "is to pry open further the markets of dependent, export-oriented economies, forcing them to compete at a disadvantage with TNCs and industrialized economies."[25] Liberals argue that this is simply not the case. Conditionality on Bank or IMF loans is put in place to ensure that the money is used properly and in accordance with sound economic practices. Otherwise, liberals argue, the money would be wasted on inefficient government-run industries, or due to corruption would not reach the people who need it most.

Through the IFC or through private negotiations, governments in the developing world also obtain finance from private lending institutions, primarily the major international banks. In the late 1960s and through the 1970s, private banks extended massive loans to the developing world. They were more than willing to offload heavy investments from the oil-exporting Arab states, but in the process flooded developing states with short-term infusions of often mismanaged cash. Many of the projects built with these loans failed to yield the expected economic returns, and by the late 1970s and early 1980s, many Southern states were facing massive debt crises. Defaults on interest charges began to occur, and many loans were extended or simply written off. As a result, today private lending institutions are very careful about lending money to the developing world, compounding the capital shortage in poor countries, and paying off the debt has dominated domestic policy decisions. Indeed, many poverty activists have long argued that debt relief is a vital first step to help Southern states escape the vicious cycle of repayment; in 2004, total external debt was U.S.$2.3 trillion, and roughly 6.5 percent of developing states' gross national income went to servicing debt.[26]

Yet many of the Southern states that are in great debt, such as Brazil, Argentina, and Nigeria, remain strong regional military powers, spending valuable resources on military equipment often supplied through the Northern states. Meanwhile, a vague promise made by the United States in 1999 to lessen the debt of the developing world has yet to be realized.

The third primary source of finance is Official Development Assistance (ODA), which consists of government grants or loans specifically intended for economic development. ODA is extended on a bilateral basis or a multilateral basis (through an international organization). Although the countries of the North agreed in 1970 (and again in 1992) to maintain ODA targets of 0.7 percent of GNP, they have fallen far short of that goal. The United States was the world's leader in ODA transfers in dollars in 2002, with a total of U.S.$13.3 billion, followed by Japan (U.S.$9.3 billion). Based on percentage of GDP, the leading ODA donors in the world in 2002 were Denmark (0.96 percent), Norway (0.89 percent), and Sweden (0.83 percent). In 2002, Canada's ODA totalled U.S.$2 billion, at 0.28 percent of GDP, and the figure has hovered in that area since, far short of the 0.7 percent target. The country with the poorest performance in terms of percentage of GDP is the United States, which contributed only 0.13 percent in 2002.[27] The problem with ODA is that because the lenders are governments, the cause of development is often lost in political considerations. For example, most U.S. ODA goes to a very few allies: Israel, Egypt, Turkey, and Jordan. The largest recipients of total ODA in 2002 were China and India. While poverty is a serious problem in these two countries, China has sent a man into space and India has developed a large nuclear weapons program. Are these countries that need aid?

The future of foreign aid itself is another topic worthy of discussion here. During the Cold War, development assistance was often an unashamedly political device. Both the United States and the Soviet Union were interested in acquiring what we may term *client states*. Those siding with the West would embrace capitalism and foreign investment; those siding with the East would reject this path and pursue close ties with the U.S.S.R. However, with the utter collapse of the Eastern bloc, development assistance has lost its strategic rationale. What remains, many critics argue, is insufficient for the purpose of meeting basic human needs around the world at a time when the fiscal crisis experienced by many Northern states has significantly curtailed their propensity to engage in North–South financial transfers. Furthermore, the political pressure to divert aid to the struggling states of the former Soviet bloc became an important factor in reducing the availability of funds for other parts of the world in the 1990s.[28]

In the Northern states, the provision of foreign aid has become an industry itself, involving government agencies, NGOs, and individual researchers and on-site workers contracted by those institutions, including the large UN network. Most aid is **tied aid**: recipients must use the funds to buy the donor's services. Other conditions, for example, on governance and liberalization measures, may apply as well. It remains to be seen whether development aid can, in the long run, provide the solutions to the more pressing problems facing many Southern states. One can argue, with a great deal of certainty, that aid often has a beneficial impact, particularly when it goes to health-related programs such as disease prevention and sanitation improvement. However, many analysts regard aid as a mistake, since it can increase dependency on Northern states. And in times of increased fiscal constraint in the North, it would seem to be very dangerous to rely on Northern beneficence.

Further, leaders from developing countries complain of the reverse transfer of technology, or *brain drain*, that has often occurred. Developed countries and MNCs have been reluctant to establish research and development and other facilities that employ and train local skilled labour, but they are often willing to take the brightest and hardest working and train them in the North. One study suggested that, between 1960 and 1976, more than 300 000 people migrated from developing countries to work as engineers, scientists, physicians, surgeons, and other technical workers in the United States, Canada, and the United Kingdom alone (see Chapter 11).[29] The loss of these highly skilled workers makes it even more difficult to develop indigenous technological capabilities. This increases the dependence of Southern states on the North, and there is no indication that the trend is reversing. Indeed many AIDS activists complain bitterly that qualified doctors and nurses are being drained into states such as Canada, when they are badly needed at home to help with the pandemic.

Alternatives do exist to the formal economies largely controlled or regulated by states. Indeed, the real growth area in Latin America may well be in the informal sector, characterized by low-paying jobs that offer no form of formal social protection but are often supported by networks of family and friends. We have already mentioned the tremendous amount of domestic work, usually performed by women, that offers little monetary compensation but can provide for family needs through local agriculture or barter. Similarly, small communities work to support each other without the help of formal state and international institutions, and we should not overlook this. Up to 60 percent of the African urban workforce is employed in the informal sector, and up to 53 percent in Latin America was in the 1980s (understandably, it is difficult to obtain accurate statistics on this!).[30] We must also recognize the fact that transnational organized criminal activity will generate employment as well (see Chapter 6), ranging from illicit drug production to prostitution to weapons smuggling. Although Northern states want to deal with these human security issues, which often threaten their own countries, there is reluctance to engage in the kind of sweeping economic reform and development programs that would encourage people to seek livelihood in the formal, rather than informal or black market, economy. For example, in Afghanistan, it is far more lucrative for farmers to grow poppies for drug production than to grow legitimate food crops, and many farmers have their lives and the lives of their families threatened if they do not grow poppies. In a similar situation, what choice would you make? To change this situation will require a combination of economic development, access to markets for legitimate products, security for people against threats, and a significant drop in demand for goods such as drugs and services such as prostitution. Small initiatives will make a difference for some people in the poor parts of the world, but not for all. We turn now to a discussion of the management of global trade, assumed by many to be conducted largely for the benefit of Western states.

"MANAGING" GLOBAL TRADE LIBERALIZATION

As we saw in Chapter 4, the push toward freer trade continued through the successive negotiation rounds of the General Agreement on Tariffs and Trade (GATT), culminating with the conclusion of the Uruguay Round in 1994. The Uruguay Round agreed to establish a new international organization to manage world trade, and in 1995 the World Trade Organization (WTO) was created. As mentioned in Chapter 4, the authors of the Bretton Woods system had originally envisioned the establishment of an International Trade Organization (ITO) that would have the same legal status as the IBRD and IMF and contribute to the development of a free trade–based global economy. It was not until the creation of the WTO that this goal was realized. The WTO is an international organization headquartered in Geneva, staffed by a modest secretariat of 601 people. The significance of the WTO is in its membership (147 countries in 2004) and the fact that it inherits all of the results of the GATT negotiation rounds. In effect, the WTO replaces GATT, and therefore the organization is built on the principles of liberal trade theory: comparative advantage, tariff reduction, nondiscrimination, national treatment, and regulatory harmonization. The WTO is the central forum for world trade negotiations, and WTO agreements reflect the ability of the 147 member states to reach agreement on trade liberalization. Biannual ministerial meetings are supposed to dictate WTO direction, and this ministerial council has subsidiary working bodies to administer WTO agreements in specialized areas of trade such as goods, services, the environment, and intellectual property. Countries accused of unfair trading practices must answer to the council, and other states are legally permitted to impose countervailing sanctions and to receive whatever compensation the WTO panel judges deem appropriate (see Profile 8.5). This dispute management system is a significant development, since GATT outcomes were often ignored. However, this process does give rise to complaints (in particular by economic nationalists) that the WTO represents the subordination of national sovereignty to an international organization without accountability to the citizens of individual states.

The WTO is entering a crucial phase in its short history. The current round of trade negotiations launched in November 2001, known as the Doha Round, have proven acrimonious and divisive. In September 2003 the Cancun meetings of the WTO collapsed without an agreement on the specifics of the Doha Round agenda. The future of the Doha Round, which was rather optimistically expected to be complete by the end of 2004, was plunged into uncertainty. In essence, countries could not agree on how to implement the Doha Round's ambitious agenda, which envisioned, among other things, a number of measures designed to improve the economic situation of poor countries. First, the agenda called for the elimination of agricultural subsidies in rich countries, which make the agricultural exports of poor countries uncompetitive. This is no small matter: government subsidies given to farmers in the OECD countries have averaged U.S.$300 billion per year for the last 15 years, undercutting foreign producers who cannot hope to compete against such massive support. Second, the reduction of tariffs on farm goods would allow developing states' agricultural products to enter the rich countries' markets at a lower price to the consumer. Third, the elimination of agricultural export subsidies by rich states would make developing states' products more competitive the world over. Fourth, the reduction in industrial tariffs on certain products (especially textiles) would stimulate industrialization and economic growth in poor countries as their products could get better access to rich markets. The Doha agenda also promised liberalization in the trade of services, and would have established new global rules on the four "Singapore Issues" raised at an earlier WTO meeting: competition, investment, government procurement, and trade facilitation.

What went wrong? Put simply, countries in both North and South were unwilling to make the concessions and politically difficult sacrifices necessary to reach agreement at Cancun. The EU refused to eliminate export subsidies. India argued that it had not agreed to discuss new rules on the Singapore Issues. Japan refused to contemplate reductions in its tariffs on rice. A group of states led by China, Brazil, and India insisted on deep cuts to agricultural subsidies and liberalization of farm trade by rich countries. Other countries, especially in Africa, were less enthusi-

PROFILE 8.5 The WTO and Canada: Good News, Bad News

Decisions made by the WTO will help some governments achieve their goals while hampering others. It will become increasingly difficult to promote free trade in some products and yet remain protectionist with others. Compare the two accounts below for an idea of how the WTO will sometimes give but sometimes take away.

CANADA AND THE JAPAN LIQUOR TAX CASE

In October 1996, the WTO Appellate Body requested that Japan change its liquor tax regime to remove barriers to imports of a wide variety of distilled liquor products (ranging from whisky to gin). In Japan, imported distilled liquor is taxed at significantly higher rates than competing Japanese distilled spirits such as *shochu*. Canadian, European, and American distillers want to sell their products in Japan at what they consider fair prices. This was the first Appellate Body ruling involving Canada and was the second complaint involving Japanese barriers to imported liquor. (In 1987 a panel under GATT upheld a complaint by the European Commission that Japan's liquor tax law gave a competitive advantage to Japanese distilled liquor. Although Japan changed its law, *shochu* continued to receive preferential tax rates.) Under WTO rules, the Appellate Body report must be adopted within 30 days of being circulated to WTO members. Japan would then have 30 days to notify the WTO Dispute Settlement Body of its plans for implementing the report's recommendation. "I am very pleased with this ruling, a first for Canada," said Art Eggleton, Canada's international trade minister at the time. "It will end a long-standing dispute, and we expect that it will lead to higher Canadian exports to the Japanese distilled liquor market. I urge Japan to carry out the ruling quickly." Japan did not carry out the

ruling quickly, but began lowering taxes and tariffs on imported liquor in 1998.

CANADA AND THE MAGAZINE CASE

In January 1997, a WTO panel ruled that the Canadian government's efforts to support the Canadian magazine industry violated world trade rules, finding that Ottawa was at fault for preventing the sale of magazines containing mostly U.S. editorial content. The case was filed by the Office of the U.S. Trade Representative at the Geneva-based WTO and followed a prolonged effort by Time Warner Inc. to establish an edition of *Sports Illustrated* magazine in Canada. The decision was regarded as a serious blow to Canadian government efforts to protect the cultural sector from Americanization. The decision by a WTO panel rejected Ottawa's attempts to prevent *Sports Illustrated* from publishing a Canadian edition with mostly U.S. editorial content. However, this was only part of the ruling, since the three-member panel also struck down key policies that supported the entire Canadian magazine industry and protected it from all-out competition, including preferential postal rates, a tariff restriction, and an up to 80 percent tax on split-run magazines. "We lost," said a Canadian governmental official. Canada now faced a choice of either implementing the WTO ruling or allowing Washington to establish trade barriers against Canadian products equivalent to protectionist measures directed against U.S. magazines. Although the Canadian government vowed to fight the ruling, in 1999 the two governments announced an agreement improving the access of U.S. publications to the Canadian market.

SOURCES: (LIQUOR LAWS) DEPARTMENT OF FOREIGN AFFAIRS AND INTERNATIONAL TRADE, NEWS RELEASE, 4 OCTOBER 1996; (MAGAZINES) D. FAGAN AND L. EGGERTSON, "CANADA LOSES MAGAZINE CASE," *THE GLOBE AND MAIL*, 17 JANUARY 1997, A1.

astic about liberalizing farm trade, as they believed this would threaten the preferential access they already enjoyed with Europe. Other African countries wanted to see the United States eliminate its cotton subsidies, which amount to U.S.$3 billion a year, making the United States the world's biggest exporter of cotton and the source of low world prices for that commodity. The United States showed no willingness to budge on this issue, perhaps because the chairman of the Senate Agriculture Committee in the U.S. Congress is an ally of U.S. cotton farmers. In the end, the talks concluded amid acrimonious rhetoric from some states and intransigence by most. Some representatives from some states were pleased: Tanzania's delegate was "very happy" that the talks had failed. Others, such as the tearful trade minister of Bangladesh, remarked that "This was the worst thing we poor countries could have done to ourselves."[31]

The future of the WTO is now in question. The difficulty of achieving progress in larger multilateral economic organizations is in doubt. The opposition to globalized liberalization is widespread, as evidenced by the differences at Cancun and the "Battle in Seattle," which disrupted the WTO General Meeting in Seattle in 1999 (see Profile 8.6). Many people—from environmentalists to trade unionists—resent the idea that global trade negotiations and a disconnected body in Geneva can make decisions that have such a large impact on national development issues. Similar opposition, spread through the Internet, was discernible during the failed OECD negotiations for the establishment of the Multilateral Agreement on Investment (MAI), which would have taken the basic principles of trade agreements such as NAFTA and internationalized them, protecting international investors from government interference.[32] Beyond this, there are practical limitations to a global trading system. Protectionism still exists, though it may in some cases be disguised. Trade disputes are frequent in the international system. Examples include the serious split between the United States and the EU on agricultural subsidies; the efforts of Southern states seeking greater access to Northern markets; the debate over genetically modified organisms and other health and environmental issues; and the debate over enforcing intellectual property rights. As a result of the slow process characteristic of world trade talks in GATT and now in the WTO, states have created a number of regional organizations to manage trade liberalization. These regional trade agreements have terms of trade that are preferential to the terms of trade found in the WTO, because they can be negotiated between a smaller number of more like-minded countries. This has raised the possibility that the future of trade liberalization rests not in the global arena through the WTO, but in various regions through regional trade agreements.

Much of the free trade debate and dialogue in the world is, in fact, oriented toward regional trade agreements. These agreements are sometimes called *preferential trade agreements*, because they represent regions, or zones, of preferred terms of trade among participating countries. In Europe, a process of economic integration has been underway since the 1950s. In 1957, the European Economic Community (EEC) created a **customs union** covering all products among its members. In 1967, The EC marked the successful elimination of most of the remaining impediments to the free flow of goods, labour, and capital across the borders of member states. In 1993, the EC became the European Union (EU) after the **Maastricht Treaty** was ratified. The EU enlarged to a total of 25 member states as of May 1, 2004. Under the terms of the Maastricht Treaty, member states have developed a monetary union, which has already resulted in the establishment, and partial implementation, of a common currency, the **euro**.

The process of integration in Europe has provoked protest over the loss of state control over national economies, social institutions, and culture. These concerns continue to plague the operation of the EU and the ability of governments to reach common policies on controversial issues. In particular, efforts to coordinate political and military policy through the EU have not been particularly successful. Nevertheless, the EU is the most highly integrated and institutionally developed of the world's trading areas, leading some to argue that the EU will soon become a supranational organization, perhaps even a "United States of Europe." In reality, the EU is far from this since member countries remain politically sovereign, although they have agreed to share decision-making responsibility and place some of the authority to make decisions in the hands of the EU. This strategy is sometimes called *pooled sovereignty*. The economic power of the EU (centred on the economic strength of a united Germany) is felt throughout Europe, and it acts as a centre of gravity for economic activity across the continent.

PROFILE 8.6 **The Battle in Seattle**

A group of Seattle police officers stand in a cloud of smoke near WTO protesters in downtown Seattle, 30 November 1999. Demonstrators temporarily succeeded in delaying the opening session of the WTO. This scene resembles a war zone, or police state, more than a liberal democracy. Is the conflict over trade liberalization leading to further divides in domestic as well as international social structures? (AP Photo/Beth Keiser/CP Archive)

Civil disobedience is a time-honoured method of expressing one's opposition to government policies. An estimated 40 000 people took to the streets in Seattle in 1999 to register their opposition to the WTO as a regulatory body. Their main concern, although they had an impressive variety of concerns overall, was that the WTO was being granted too much power—the ability to make key decisions affecting people's health, environment, employment, and other issues. For many, the WTO represented the dark side of globalization. The sheer number of protestors surprised local authorities, and when a small minority became violent, the police responded with arrests and tear gas. Inside the WTO meetings, the ministers of member states were unable to reach a consensus on the issues that divided them. The meeting broke up with little in the way of substantive agreements. The protestors had made their point, and the governments of the world could not make the WTO meetings a success, possibly because of the increased public awareness brought about by the debate over globalization. Similar, though less violent, protests were mounted during the IMF annual meeting in Washington in April 2000 and the Summit of the Americas in Quebec City in April 2001. Seattle, Washington, and Quebec City are likely just the beginning of a global campaign of protest against the institutions promoting globalization.

The present EU, however, has moved beyond efforts at economic integration and toward monetary union as well. Other EU members have tired of relying principally on the German economy and its central bank, the Bundesbank, which tends to raise interest rates quickly whenever inflation becomes a possibility.[33] As of 2004, the euro is common currency in Belgium, Germany, Greece, Spain, France, Ireland, Italy, Luxembourg, the Netherlands, Austria, Portugal, and Finland. In other words, the euro is the currency in all EU states except the United Kingdom, Denmark, Sweden, and the new member states. The 10 new member states that joined the EU on May 1, 2004—Czech Republic, Estonia, Cyprus, Latvia, Lithuania, Hungary, Malta, Poland, Slovenia, and Slovakia—will join the euro area once they have fulfilled the necessary conditions. This movement toward monetary union is a huge step, but one unlikely to be repeated elsewhere. For example, it would be difficult to imagine the Federal Reserve of the United States and the Bank of Canada allowing some other agency to determine monetary policy for both states, though it is obvious that American monetary policy has a tremendous impact on the Canadian economy. However, the rise of the euro's value raises the prospect that it could eventually replace the United States dollar as the preferred currency of international trade.

Germany felt it imperative that states earn the right to use the euro, and the 1992 Maastricht Treaty stipulated key attributes that states must have to be allowed to participate in the new regime. For example, they must limit their government deficit to 3 percent of gross domestic product (GDP). They must ensure that their national debt does not exceed 60 percent of GDP; they must avoid currency devaluations for two years before the onset of the euro; and, not surprisingly, they must keep their inflation rate within 1.5 percentage points of the average rate of the three EU members with the lowest inflation. These are tough standards for most European states, especially those with less stable economies, such as Spain and Portugal. These standards have also alienated citizens in countries such as France and Ireland that only narrowly accepted the **Maastricht Treaty** in the first place. These standards may be even harder to meet for the new members. Germany seeks to reduce the role currently played by the national veto, relying instead on majority votes to enact changes. Britain strongly disagrees, insisting on its right to maintain the veto system. On serious matters of foreign policy, such as defence, common front or not, it is highly unlikely the veto will be abolished.

However, the biggest question IR scholars ask about the evolution of the European Union concerns its long-term effect on the institution of state sovereignty. As seen in Chapter 2, the right to make decisions regarding the national economy, as well as the right to have an independent currency, has been viewed as fundamental to sovereignty. The new EU threatens this, since states are gradually giving increasing responsibility to a supranational institution and have largely adopted the euro.[34] Also of great interest is the European Court of Justice ruling that a member state can be sued for damages for failure to honour EU law. The case involved Spanish fishing companies that had set up shop in the United Kingdom to avoid the quota assigned to Spain. The British denied 84 Spanish fishing companies the right to fish from the United Kingdom. Britain may be obliged to pay the companies roughly U.S.$45.8 million in compensation for lost potential income. The court set three conditions for determining whether an individual or a company is justified in taking a member state to court: when "the government violates rights conferred on individuals; does so in a 'sufficiently serious' manner; and when the victim can show clearly that damages occurred as a result of the state's action."[35]

United for currency. Moments after the official launch of the single European currency, the euro, finance ministers raise their arms for a group picture at the Council of the European Union in Brussels, 31 December 1998. From left to right are Germany's Economics Minister Werner Mueller, French Finance Minister Dominique Strauss-Kahn, Luxembourg's Prime and Finance Minister Jean-Claude Juncker, and EU Finance Commissioner Yves-Thibault de Silguy. At bottom right is Austrian Finance Minister and Council President Rudolf Edlinger. Person at bottom left is unidentified. (AP Photo/Yves Logghe/CP Archive)

Whether or not the euro comes into effect across the expanded EU, the changes that have characterized European integration have set landmarks in the transition of world politics from a state power focus to a transnational economic focus. Genuine concerns exist about the viability of the project, but no one can deny that despite centuries of animosity among the great powers of Europe, there is a higher level of policy coordination, trust, and communication and travel than ever. However, we should be very careful about using the EU as a prototype for future regionalism. In fact, it is a common criticism of the neo-functionalist school that it uses European investigation as an embryonic standard that simply is not exportable elsewhere. Europe has a very high standard of living (though there are differences within the region, which the EU is supposed to attempt to rectify); it has global connections in both trade and diplomacy; and it has had the military protection of the United States. Clearly, the EU should be considered a unique situation, and other free trade agreements, such as NAFTA, are not intended to introduce the same level of economic and political integration (though NAFTA's more vocal Canadian critics argue it will ultimately have this effect).

At the same time, we can argue that there is a noticeable trend toward regional integration in trade and investment and the creation of political mechanisms to facilitate this (see Profile 8.7). Under the Free Trade of the Americas (FTAA) negotiations, we could well have a free trade area from Alaska to Argentina before 2010. The Pacific states could become more closely integrated by that time, with Japan and China vying as regional leaders and states belonging to the **Association of Southeast Asian Nations (ASEAN)** forming a bloc. And Europe's integration, both economic and political, will probably continue. These integrations present a potential tri-regional model of the future world economy: the Americas, Europe (with Eastern Europe, Russia, and Africa connected, though unlikely to be made prosperous), and Asia, with increased cooperation between these regions.

Such a model contrasts in style and ultimately in purpose with the more global approach encouraged by the WTO. Those liberals who argue that peace follows commerce might be concerned that dividing the world into three large trade zones will encourage a tripolar mentality that could even lead to military conflict as the interests of the three areas begin to be incompatible. Liberals would also point out that a world largely managed by three regional blocs would in effect exclude most poor countries. The success of the WTO is therefore regarded as crucial, for the alternative is the greater isolation of the developing world from the rich world. Others, especially those from the Marxist tradition, contend that each area will be a political empire of the dominant power and its capitalist classes. Thus, imperialism continues in a highly integrated fashion, and imperial powers inevitably come into conflict as resources grow scarce and expansionism becomes the driving norm (this was, partially, Lenin's explanation of World War I).

Some of globalization's proponents, however, might argue that regional integration is just a step along the road to a harmonized global economy. It occurs simultaneously as the world economy develops as well; the two processes reinforce rather than challenge each other. And, as regional organizations form, the political machinery of multilateralism is created. Though it has become almost habitual among students of international political economy to refer to the European Union as the primary example of regional neo-functionalism, other situations exist in which states are engaging. A famous example, of course, is the North American Free Trade Agreement (NAFTA), which includes Canada, the United States, and Mexico, and may soon include several Latin American countries as well. The Canada–U.S. Free Trade Agreement was signed in January 1989, between the two countries that exchange more goods and services than any other two in the world. This bilateral arrangement was expanded in 1992 with the addition of Mexico. NAFTA provides for the increased flow of goods and services across the borders of these states, especially in agriculture, automobile products, and clothing and textiles. The agreement was not without considerable controversy. There were

PROFILE 8.7 The Canada–Chile Free Trade Agreement

Countries continue to sign bilateral free trade agreements, as well as multilateral agreements. Rather quietly, the governments of Canada and Chile signed a free trade agreement, which is not part of NAFTA, in 1996, and it became operational in 1998. The agreement's key features, from the Canadian standpoint, are as follows:

• Immediate duty-free access for 75 percent of Canadian exports, and the elimination of Chile's 11 percent import **duty** on almost all remaining industrial and resource-based goods over five years

• Much better access for a range of agricultural goods (for example, tariffs for durum wheat, which represents 35 percent of exports in this sector, were immediately eliminated)

• Significant new protection for Canadian investments in Chile, including an agreement to automatically grant Canadian investors the benefits of any future liberalization, and an

undertaking to negotiate a bilateral double taxation agreement

• The creation of a Free Trade Commission and a secretariat to ensure the timely and effective resolution of disputes

• Side agreements on environment and labour, the first agreements of this nature ever signed by the government of Chile

Should Chile grant even better access for certain agricultural products in a future trade agreement with the **Mercosur** countries (Argentina, Brazil, Paraguay, and Uruguay), Canada will automatically have similar access for milling wheat, wheat flour, and oilseed products. However, this agreement is not nearly as extensive as NAFTA: for example, it does not include chapters on energy, financial services, or intellectual property or deal with sensitive sanitary and phytosanitary measures affecting agricultural trade.

SOURCE: GOVERNMENT OF CANADA, NEWS RELEASE, NO. 211, 18 NOVEMBER 1996.

many concerns in Canada that NAFTA was a threat to Canadian sovereignty and culture and that NAFTA might threaten safety regulations and environmental protection in Canada, as well as social programs such as health care. (Such concerns continue today.) Others were concerned that jobs would leave Canada and head to Mexico, where salaries are lower. Advocates of NAFTA responded that Canadian sovereignty, social programs, and standards were protected under NAFTA. (And these advocates point out today that there is little or no evidence to suggest that NAFTA has led to job losses in Canada.) Similar concerns about jobs were voiced in the United States, while in Mexico some expressed fears about becoming an economic colony of the United States.

Two side agreements accompanied NAFTA, one on labour and one on the environment. These were made largely to counter opposition on the grounds that NAFTA would promote the degradation of labour standards, wages, and the environment. The environmental agreement created the Commission for Environmental Cooperation (or CEC, headquartered in Montreal), and it has filtered funding to many NGOs that have developed projects related to sustainable development. Examples include a project by the Air and Waste Management Association (Ottawa) to advance air quality in Hamilton, Ontario, and Monterrey, Mexico; the development of nonwood forest products in Oaxaca, Mexico; and water quality-monitoring project for Colonia residents in El Paso County/Valle de Juarez. However, critics charge that NAFTA, by encouraging investment along the U.S.–Mexican border, is designed primarily to keep Mexicans there (and not migrating northward) and will inevitably result in a lessening of environmental protection in the already heavily polluted region. The CEC has been criticized as an ineffective watchdog, having no real power to force any of the states to improve environmental standards.

"We're not shy about congratulating ourselves." A decade after the United States, Canada, and Mexico signed the North American Free Trade Agreement, former Mexican President Carlos Salinas de Gortari, left, former U.S. President George H.W. Bush, centre, and former Canadian Prime Minister Brian Mulroney, right, gather for a conference on NAFTA at the Woodrow Wilson International Center for Scholars in Washington, 9 December 2002. The three leaders who forged the agreement marked the 10th anniversary of NAFTA's signing in a joint appearance where they reminisced on its beginnings and accomplishments. (AP Photo/J. Scott Applewhite/CP Archive)

In Asia, Japan is the regional leader, although the rise of China as an economic power may pose a long-term threat to that distinction. In Asia, however, regionalism is far less defined and far less institutionalized. In part, this difference is due to the tradition of bilateral economic diplomacy in Asia, as well as fear of Japanese political hegemony (with the memory of World War II still fresh in people's memories). Nevertheless, some regional arrangements have taken shape, most notably ASEAN, established in 1967 to promote economic, political, and social cooperation among its members. ASEAN now comprises 10 countries.

Perhaps the most visible development in the world economy in the past few decades has been the emergence of the Pacific Rim as a major trading area. The Asia-Pacific Economic Cooperation forum (APEC) was founded in 1989 and currently involves 18 countries that touch the Pacific Rim, states as diverse as Australia, Brunei, Canada, Indonesia, South Korea, Japan, Malaysia, China, Thailand, New Zealand, the Philippines, Singapore, Mexico, Hong Kong, Taiwan, Chile, the United States, and Papua New Guinea. At its third ministerial meeting in Seoul, Korea, the Seoul Declaration stated four common objectives: to sustain growth and development of the region, to enhance positive gains resulting from increased trade, to further develop and strengthen the multilateral trading system, and to reduce barriers to trade in goods and services among participants. In total, members of APEC account for 40 percent of the world's population and half of the world's economic production.

The organization hopes to go beyond trade matters to facilitate technological cooperation and cultural awareness. In 1993, at Bill Clinton's suggestion, the conference met with official heads of state in attendance; this brought the leaders of China, Taiwan, and Hong Kong together for the first time (although this did not change the PRC/Taiwan/Hong Kong relationship: Taiwan continues to be denied state status by the Chinese, and Hong Kong became Chinese territory in 1997). In the longer term, analysts foresee the formation of a PAFTA (Pacific Area Free Trade Agreement) that would tie Asian, North American, and South American states together, though such an arrangement remains speculative at present. The 1997 APEC meeting took place in Vancouver, and it was dominated by concerns over economic instability in some key Asian states and, outside the conference, concerns with human rights violations, by both dictatorial states such as Indonesia and by the Royal Canadian Mounted Police, who used pepper spray on protesters (with or without the prime minister's blessing).

1997 was a tumultuous year for many of the Asian economies as the Asian financial crisis engulfed the region. Many explanations are available for the currency crisis, and we can hardly approach doing them justice here. Some blame the overextension of Japanese and other local banks; some blame the decision to make several key currencies (previously pegged to the U.S. dollar) convertible, attracting foreign currency speculation; others blame the herd-like mentality of investors, who panic when they see trouble and thus caused huge capital outflow from the region. The "crony capitalism" that characterized some of the economies is often cited as well: since politicians have had such a strong personal involvement in the economy, corruption was rampant. After China devalued the yuan (its currency) in 1996, there was a glut of exports in the inter-Asian market. The Japanese economy was in the midst of a prolonged slowdown. Prices for real estate were artificially high, and the amount of lending had become reckless, both driven by speculation over future profits that would never materialize. The crisis began in Thailand, as it became evident that huge mega-projects in the country would not yield a return on the investment provided to build them. The Thai economy began to tumble as foreign investors pulled their money out of the country. Nervous investors also withdrew their money from the region as a whole, and the "contagion" quickly spread to Indonesia, Malaysia, and the Philippines. As these economies began to fall, the rest of the world hoped Japan or the United States would step in to bail them out, much as the United States had done with Mexico in 1995. They did not, and although the IMF provided massive loan guarantees, they were insufficient to compensate for the enormous volume of capital drawn out of the region by investors (over U.S.$100 billion). The crisis affected economies as far away as South Korea, Japan, Russia, and Brazil. Political institutions in Asia were affected as well: Thailand pursued a new constitution and there were changes in government in Indonesia and South Korea. Countries were forced to sell off domestic industries and, as usual, the poor were hit hardest of all, with little support following massive layoffs and the drop in the value of their currencies. Asian economic elites moved their money to safer locations, such as the United States and Western Europe.

Will these economic regions coalesce into antagonistic trade blocs? Many fear that political and economic friction between countries, as well as pressure from disaffected publics, will promote protectionism and provoke trade wars between regions. Economic regionalism will turn into political regionalism, and the world will become Balkanized and divided in a scenario not dissimilar to the interwar experience. Others are more optimistic, arguing that economic regions are beginning to overlap in their membership and that virtually all countries have a stake in the continued health of the global economy.

While it is impossible to forecast the long-term outlook of the world economy, we can say that both the trend toward regional integration and the broader trend toward globalization will continue in the near future. Barring a major military confrontation, which is always a possibility, trade among nations will probably increase as economic growth continues, which will please most liberals, some economic nationalists, few environmentalists, and even fewer Neo-Marxists. Ironically, one of the more widely hailed benefits of international commerce—the idea that with increased trade comes increased mutual vulnerability and understanding, and thus the reduced likelihood of warfare—is often challenged by those who argue globalization is simply redirecting conflicts between states into the realm of economics. We turn to a discussion of this perspective now.

FUTURE WARS FOR ECONOMIC POWER?

An intimate link between economics and conflict has always existed. Throughout history, economic concerns or incentives have sparked the outbreak of wars or have influenced the conduct of military campaigns. Through war, states and empires could acquire territory, natural resources, population, and industrial capacity. During war, economic targets have often been a priority. In the ancient period, wells were poisoned and land rendered unsuitable for agriculture (usually by salting the soil). In the modern period, economic blockades and embargoes have been imposed on some states, such as Germany during World War I. In total wars, states have engaged in the strategic bombing of manufacturing and energy infrastructure to cripple the war effort and weaken the civilian morale of the target nation. Historically, the most powerful countries have possessed the largest and most powerful economies, in part because this wealth has underwritten the development of powerful military capabilities. However, as we discussed in Chapter 4, the importance of economic power has also been the source of economic competition between states. Even when they are not at war in a military sense, states are engaged in a struggle for economic power. In the contemporary international system, concern exists that this historical pattern is reappearing and that we are heading into a future characterized by an intense economic competition between states (in effect, a global economic war) and the possibility that economic competition and economic disputes could escalate into political and military rivalries and possibly even military wars.

After the military confrontation of the Cold War, there was a short-lived perception that military power had declined in utility and importance. Instead, economic power was viewed as the key index of power in the world, and actors in the international system (especially states) now increasingly regard the health of their economies as a security issue. As a result, economics is becoming the primary arena of competition and conflict between states. As Robert A. Isaac argues, "Although the Cold War has ended, the primacy of insecurity—of the infinite striving for security—has not. Where military security prevails, such as in most of the industrialized democracies, there has merely been a shift in the form of insecurity to the economic or psychological realms, as nations seek to increase economic competitiveness and to reduce unemployment."[36] In this view, the ability of a country to provide a high quality of life to its citizens is a motivating factor in the aim for economic security.

However, Edward Luttwak has suggested that we are entering a world in which states will compete with each other in the economic realm solely to achieve economic power (see Profile 8.8). As Luttwak argues,

> In traditional world politics, the goals are to secure and extend the physical control of territory, and to gain diplomatic influence over foreign governments. The corresponding geoeconomic goal is not the highest possible standard of living for a country's population but rather the conquest or protection of desirable roles in the world economy. Who will develop the next generation of jet airliners, computers, bio-technology products, advanced materials, financial services, and all other high value output in industries large and small? Will the designers, technologists, managers, and financiers be Americans, Europeans, or East Asians?[37]

In other words, states will continue to battle one another not for territory or resources, or for religious, political, or ideological reasons, but for economic supremacy. At stake is nothing less than the future power position of all states in the system. Long-term (perhaps permanent) winners and losers will emerge from this economic war. For the winning states, the spoils of victory will include industrial supremacy, technology and information leadership, and the economic capacity to sustain a modern military. The losing states will face the problems created by reduced fiscal resources: reduced economic growth and a smaller economic pie; permanent relegation to the ranks of the resource extraction, branch plant, or cash crop economies; second-rate technology and information systems; and a lack of the economic means to escape a cycle of poverty.

PROFILE 8.8 Survival of the Smartest: Geoeconomic Warfare

Many realists predict a return to economic nationalism in the future world economy. In particular, Edward Luttwak makes the following arguments:

- Geoeconomics is spreading and becoming the dominant phenomenon in the central arena of world affairs, but not all states are equally inclined or equally capable of participating in the new struggle.

- Small but well-educated countries can be much more successful in geoeconomics than they could ever be in world politics, where size always counts and may alone be decisive.

- States will tend to act geoeconomically simply because of what they are: territorially defined entities designed precisely to outdo each other on the world scene.

- When there is no strategic confrontation at the centre of world affairs that can absorb the adversarial feeling of the nations, those ill feelings may be diverted into the nation's economic relations.

- The emerging geoeconomic struggle for high-technology industrial supremacy among Americans, Europeans, and Japanese is eroding their old alliance solidarity. Increased geoeconomic activity will characterize their economic relationship, as opposed to free-trade economics.

SOURCE: EDWARD LUTTWAK, "THE COMING GLOBAL WAR FOR ECONOMIC POWER," *THE INTERNATIONAL ECONOMY* 7 (SEPTEMBER/OCTOBER 1993), 20. REPRINTED WITH PERMISSION.

The economic war between states is, therefore, cast in zero-sum terms; that is, gains for one side are seen as a loss for the other. This view is different from liberal perspectives on global economic cooperation in which both sides should benefit (and usually do). Indeed, predictions of future economic wars are informed by realist views of international relations. Realists would argue that states are concerned with relative economic gains because their economies are the foundation of their power. As Michael Mastanduno argues, "Even if nation-states do not fear for their physical survival, they worry that a decrease in their power capabilities relative to those in other nation-states will compromise their political autonomy, expose them to the influence attempts of others, or lessen their ability to prevail in political disputes with allies and adversaries."[38] As a result, states will compete for economic advantage, seeking not only absolute gains but also relative gains in their favour, to prevent other countries from surpassing their own economic power (and therefore their position in world affairs).[39]

Luttwak contends that just as in war, offensive weapons will dominate in the new global struggle for economic power. Luttwak envisions a new mercantile world, with states using unilateral actions to alter the balance of trade in key economic sectors (those sectors identified as desirable). The weapons in this economic competition will be the instruments used by governments and their self-interested bureaucracies to encourage economic development in certain sectors. These instruments include a combination of incentives and trade barriers. Incentives include the following:

- *Research and development programs to encourage the development of certain economic sectors.* For example, the governments of Japan and the United States (as well as the EU) have established programs to develop new computer and computer-related technologies. In 1990, the United States launched a project to develop a more efficient battery for electric cars. The project was funded by the government and all three major U.S. automobile manufacturers and is aimed, Luttwak argues, at the Japanese auto industry.

- *Subsidies to certain industries.* Governments may also promote certain industries through financial assistance. Luttwak cites Airbus Industrie (a European consortium that produces passenger aircraft in direct competition with U.S. manufacturers such as Boeing) as an example of how governments can offer direct financial support to certain economic sectors. States can also offer subsidies in the form of preferred national treatment, such as government purchase of products on favourable terms. The Japanese government, for example, purchased Japanese computers to assist the development of Japan's computer industry, then in direct competition with the U.S. industry, which is led by IBM.

- *Export assistance to domestic firms to encourage foreign sales.* Governments have also used loans (at low rates of interest) to encourage the purchase of their domestic products. Most exporting countries have export banks that offer loans and credit to finance exports. Purchasers from abroad can secure credit to purchase products at rates lower than they would find in their own countries or in other countries. Of course, if a sale is considered particularly lucrative, governments may compete for that sale by competitively lowering the interest rates offered by their export banks. Luttwak calls this "predatory finance."[40]

States will employ these instruments in an attempt to encourage exports to other countries, acquiring market share abroad, and thus ensuring the health of certain favoured sectors (such as high technology). At the same time, states will erect trade barriers to certain products coming from abroad, to limit the market share foreign firms can acquire in their own domestic economies. Such barriers may take the form of tariffs, customs duties, or regulations on product standards.

Because of the severity of the stakes involved in the struggle for economic power in the future, states will find themselves in an increasingly cutthroat competition for economic development, a competition that could compromise the political relationship between them. This compromise raises the question of whether economic disputes will spill over into political and even military disputes in the future. The Cold War tended to reduce the intensity of economic disputes between countries in the interests of maintaining unity in the face of the mutual threat. Japan, the United States, and Germany may have been economic competitors, but they were security partners. The Cold War is now over, and the concern is that trade disputes could escalate as states retaliate against one another by imposing tariffs, duties, or other barriers to trade. Not only would this have a damaging effect on the global economy (and on the economies of the states themselves) but it also would lead to rising political tensions. If this tension should occur between the major trading states in the future, it would represent the breakdown of the political partnership of the Cold War era. Economic rivals might be increasingly perceived as political and even military rivals, ushering in a new era of political and military competition. Arguably, the split over the invasion of Iraq in 2003 was compounded by increasing rivalry between the United States and Europe on a number of political and economic issues.

Obviously, Luttwak is no liberal. He assumes economic conflict will predominate over economic cooperation. He assumes that states will not be willing to sacrifice some material economic interests for the sake of greater overall gains from trade and collaboration. Luttwak also assumes that international economic conflict management instruments (in the form of institutions) will be unable to stop self-interested defections from beginning a slide to a new mercantile world. Of course, Luttwak is correct when he points to the existence of economic disputes and competition in the global economy. However, these disputes have yet to compromise the basic cooperative character of most international economic activity. Liberals would argue that the trend toward interdependence, globalization of trade and finance, and the development of institutions of economic management all suggest that cooperation, rather than conflict, is the future for the global economy. In contrast, Marxists would argue that the current economic system is exploitative and predatory; the axis of conflict in the global economy will not be between states, it will be between rich and poor; and cooperation will not be based on the enlightened self-interest of states, but on the interests of transnational elites. But they would agree that competition over resources would be a defining characteristic of the world economy. Arguably, the most important resources are those that provide the energy needed for production and consumption.

THE POLITICAL ECONOMY OF ENERGY PRODUCTION AND CONSUMPTION

The world economy is powered by a vast infrastructure of energy production, distribution, and consumption; without it, the wheels of the global economy simply would not turn. The primary sources of industrial energy today remain oil (at 38 to 42 percent) and coal (at slightly over 30 percent), though natural gas use is rising quickly and makes up almost one-quarter of world energy production. It is clear that fossil fuels are by far the largest energy sources in the present context. Though hydroelectricity and nuclear power remain in use, large dams are notorious for creating environmental damage, and nuclear power has proven highly expensive and sometimes dangerous (see Profile 8.9). We should note also that citizens in North America consume far more energy resources per capita than all but a very few countries in the world.[41] Consumption is also very high in Western Europe, Japan, and Australia. Some of this consumption is due to the cold winter climates in some of these places, but it also reflects highly consumptive lifestyles. By comparison, citizens in South Asia and Africa consume very little energy. Europe and Japan are far more efficient in their use of energy than North America. The Western states are net importers of energy, and the Middle East, with its high levels of oil deposits, is the greatest net exporter of energy, though others, such as Laos, are net exporters of hydropower as well.

Oil remains synonymous with power and wealth. It is relatively cheap (if environmentally dangerous) to transport; it provides exporters, including Russia, Mexico, Venezuela, Canada and Nigeria, but especially the Persian Gulf states (Kuwait, Saudi Arabia, Iran, the United Arab Emirates, Qatar, Bahrain, Oman, and Iraq), with hard currency. To ensure a steady supply of oil from the Middle East, the area was colonized by the Europeans early in this century and inundated with American MNCs after that. As we saw in Chapter 4, OPEC's oil price increases brought on worldwide confusion and **recession** in the early 1970s and 1980s. Though the George H.W. Bush Administration in the United States and the UN Security Council emphasized the importance of protecting Kuwait's sovereignty, it is quite clear that dependence on Middle Eastern oil was an important contributory factor in causing the West to go to war against Iraq in 1991. Oil was also a factor (though not the only factor) in the decision to invade Iraq in 2003.

As Hanns Maull writes, the two chief concerns regarding the control of oil are price stability and access:

> Price stability does not necessarily mean stable prices; it implies only that prices move smoothly, without drastic jumps, roughly in line with world inflation and towards the cost of alternative sources of energy. Access is defined as the availability of supplies in sufficient quantities over time without major disturbances.[42]

The chairman of Exxon, one of the world's largest oil multinationals, once complained that predicting oil prices was much like "trying to paint the wings of an airplane in flight."[43] When

PROFILE 8.9 Fuel in Nuclear Arms?

Nuclear power remains the most expensive and often-criticized form of power production. The costs are so high that it would be impossible to maintain nuclear power without significant government subsidies. It has a very limited future in most countries, and, though Japan and France maintain active and expanding nuclear programs, problems exist there as well. In 1994, Ontario Hydro and Atomic Energy of Canada Limited began to study a proposal to process surplus U.S. weapons-grade plutonium from leftover Cold War stockpiles and turn it into fuel for Canada's nuclear power plants. Canada's reactors currently run on uranium, but a facility to be built in the United States would produce mixed oxide fuel, a mixture of plutonium and uranium that can be used in CANDU reactors. After being used in this manner, the plutonium would be in a form difficult to use in the construction of nuclear weapons. In 1996, the government of Canada endorsed this proposal in principle. However, by 2003 no final decision on the project had been made. This proposal puts opponents of nuclear energy, most of whom were also vocal opponents of the Cold War nuclear weapons buildup, in a somewhat awkward position, since the project would represent a Canadian contribution to disarmament but would also legitimize nuclear power and leave Canada with additional nuclear wastes to deal with. For members of the peace and disarmament movement who oppose nuclear power, it is a tough ethical choice.

SOURCE: M. MITTELSTAEDT, "HYDRO, AECL BID TO PROCESS PLUTONIUM," *THE GLOBE AND MAIL*, 19 JULY 1996, A3.

OPEC was founded in 1960, the price of oil was determined by that of Saudi Arabian light, a medium-density oil used as a standard for crude-oil prices until 1980. The price then was about U.S.$2 per barrel. An Arab oil embargo after the Middle East war of 1973 caused widespread panic buying, and OPEC was able to raise the price of crude to $11.50 a barrel by 1974. By January 1980, after the Iranian revolution induced further panic buying, Saudi Arabian light was selling for as much as $36 a barrel. These prices not only contributed greatly to the recession of that time but also forced Western states to focus on alternative sources (such as North Sea oil) and conservation. The current benchmark oil is in fact North Sea Brent Blend, which has varied markedly over the past few years with price fluctuations related to the Gulf War, oil gluts, Iraq's partial re-emergence on the world market, high demand from the United States for heating oil, and rising energy demand worldwide. World crude oil demand rose in the 1990s by nearly 12 percent, driving world prices for crude oil to nearly $40 a barrel in late 2000, a price that resurfaced in mid-2004. Approximately 40 percent of that crude oil comes from the OPEC countries.

According to estimates published in *The Economist*, by 2010 the industrialized Northern states will consume less than half of the world's energy; the former Soviet bloc will consume one-sixth, and developing countries (the South) will consume 40 percent of the world's energy. The World Energy Council suggests that by 2020, more than 90 million barrels of oil will be consumed daily and that coal output will almost double to 7 billion tonnes. So, too, will natural gas demand double, reaching 4 trillion cubic metres. This huge increase in energy demand will result from the increasing industrialization of the Latin American and, especially, Asian regions.[44] China, the world's sixth-biggest oil producer (ahead of Venezuela), became a net oil importer at the end of 1993. It will probably have to rely heavily on the Middle East for its supply, further complicating the geopolitical situation there, and on the prospect of oil deposits in the heavily contested South China Sea. Ultimately, many analysts believe that a global conversion toward alternative fuel sources must take place, and in particular to the renewable resources such as wind, geothermal, and solar power that many environmentalists

Electric refugees: pedestrians leaving Manhattan flood New York's 59th St. Bridge to Queens, 14 August 2003, after a power blackout crippled the city. The outage, which affected everything from mobile phones to traffic lights, occurred across much of the northeastern United States and Ontario. (AP Photo/Tina Fineberg/CP Archive)

have advocated for decades. This conversion is especially important for developing countries: in India, for example, 2 million small power plants are turning cow dung into electric power and cooking fuel.[45] However, we should be very cautious about assuming that this transition can take place on a truly global scale. Though their benefits are real, these technologies are still expensive propositions and are in no position to replace oil or coal. Natural gas may be the stepping-stone toward renewable energy sources; compared with other fossil fuels, it is clean and still relatively cheap. It releases less carbon when burned, contains little sulphur (responsible for acid rain), and, if the technology is right, releases fewer nitrogen oxides as well. Environmentalists argue that natural gas is a poor substitute for more renewable energy, and charge that states are structurally favourable to big oil, coal, and nuclear power provision. Meanwhile, the blackout in eastern North America in the summer of 2003 certainly forced many North Americans to reconsider the implications of large electric grids.

Optimistically, the push for increased efficiency by environmentalists and managerial elites alike will force states such as China and the United States to mitigate the potential excesses of development and further explore renewable energy sources. Technological improvements and even lifestyle changes in the West have, in some cases, reduced energy consumption, though overall it continues to rise. Most states have an avenue toward energy self-sufficiency; Canada has huge oil and natural gas reserves, for example. But the current pace of industrialization around the world and the uncertainties associated with oil prices make it difficult to suggest that the more advanced industrialized states have achieved any form of everlasting energy security; one might argue that their dependence (and resulting vulnerability to both supply disruption and the effects of climate change) has increased.

CONCLUSIONS

This chapter has reinforced the central paradox of global politics. On the one hand, the global economy displays a trend toward *convergence* in the form of increased trade between countries and peoples, increased levels of global and regional economic cooperation and management, and growing financial interdependence and levels of transactions across state borders. On the other hand, one can also identify trends of *divergence,* in the form of the regionalization of the global economy, the persistence of economic nationalism, and the widening gap between the rich and poor peoples of the world. All the key variables discussed above, as well as many others, will affect the development of the world economy after 2005. We should also keep in mind that the other topics discussed in this text, such as resource scarcity, overpopulation, international organization and law, and even military spending, will affect economic outcomes (according to the Stockholm International Peace Research Institute, American military spending alone was U.S.$260 billion in 1998; it rose to U.S.$336 billion in 2002, and is expected to exceed U.S.$400 billion in 2004).[46] The different strands of world politics are so closely woven that it is often impossible to tear them apart. If the world economy stays on its present course, we can predict more overall economic growth, but with occasional turmoil similar to the Asian financial crisis, increased consumption and waste, and increased disparities between rich and poor. This growth will result in more prosperity for some states, and these states will be forced to take ever more stringent security measures to protect their accumulated wealth. But this economic growth will be uneven, and will result in both a continuation of the cycle of poverty for billions and the degradation of the environment, both locally and globally.

It is difficult to imagine how all these ongoing concerns will affect the study of IPE itself. During the 1980s it seemed as though the postmodernist account was gaining considerable currency within the discipline, but this is less clear now as analysts return to their roots— whether liberal or mercantilist—and as many of them have become captivated by the globalization debate. Of course, all this is interrelated (much of the literature critical of globalization has postmodernist leanings, for example), and the introduction in this chapter of a distinct environmental perspective further suggests that the field is evolving and expanding as we face the problems of the 21st century. What does seem common is that although increased trade is widely forecasted, and this should result in unprecedented levels of global economic activity, specialists in IPE are increasingly wary about the easy claims of a simplistic faith in globalization. They are concerned with the disparities in wealth that are forming with the new economic order, and the long-term human consequences of those disparities.

In conclusion, although we may marvel at the dramatic surge in trade and financial flows around the world, this affluence is utterly alien to most of the people on this planet. The global economy is exceedingly complex and involves many different actors, and level of wealth and quality of life vary tremendously across states and within them, so simplification is a perilous exercise. The socioeconomic character of the world is one of profound division between rich and poor, and the ideology of globalization cannot gloss over this fundamental fact. This division leads to questions about social justice and equality, questions that have been on the IPE and IR agendas for some time but that have often been overlooked because of a primary focus on interstate warfare and trade. We turn to the issues of social justice and equality in the next chapter, which examines the complex interplay between human rights and global politics.

Endnotes

1. Quoted in *The Globe and Mail,* 17 July 1996, A10.

2. United Nations, *The World's Women 2000: Trends and Statistics* (New York: UN Publications, 2000), 158. See also K. Kempadoo, *Global Sex Workers: Rights, Resistance and Redefinition* (London: Routledge, 1998).

3. See J. Bystydzienski, ed., *Women Transforming Politics: Worldwide Strategies for Empowerment* (Bloomington: Indiana University Press, 1992).

4. The World Commission on Environment and Development, *Our Common Future* (Oxford: Oxford University Press, 1987). In fact, an entire subfield, referred to as *ecological economics*, has emerged in recent decades.

5. J. MacNeil, P. Winsemius, and Taizo Yakushiji, *Beyond Interdependence: The Meshing of the World's Economy and the Earth's Ecology* (Oxford: Oxford University Press, 1992), 32.

6. Vandana Shiva, *Staying Alive: Women, Ecology, and Development in India* (New Delhi: Kali for Women, 1988); and for a critical analysis, see Janet Biehl, *Finding Our Way: Rethinking Ecofeminist Politics* (Montreal: Black Rose Books, 1991). See also W. Sachs, ed., *Global Ecology: A New Arena of Political Conflict?* (London: Zed Books, 1993).

7. For an expanded treatment of this section, see P. Stoett, *Human and Global Security: An Exploration of Terms* (Toronto: University of Toronto Press, 1999), 97–118.

8. W. Greider, *One World, Ready or Not: The Manic Logic of Global Capitalism* (New York: Simon and Schuster, 1997); J. Gélinas, *Juggernaut Politics: Understanding Predatory Globalization* (London: Zed Books, 2003); and J. Petras and H. Veltmeyer, *System in Crisis: The Dynamics of Free Market Capitalism* (London: Zed Books, 2003).

9. M. Waters, *Globalization* (London: Routledge, 1995), 3.

10. Ibid., 4.

11. R. Cox, "The Global Political Economy and Social Choice," in D. Drache and M. Gertler, eds., *The New Era of Global Competition: State Policy and Market Power* (Montreal/Kingston: McGill-Queen's University Press, 1991), 335–49, 336.

12. V. Kavolis, "Contemporary Moral Cultures and 'the Return of the Sacred,'" *Sociological Analysis* 49, no. 3 (1988), 203–16.

13. R. White, *Global Spin: Probing the Civilization Debate* (Toronto: Dundurn, 1995), 127. See also A. Linklater, "Globalization and the Transformation of Political Community," in J. Baylis and S. Smith, eds., *The Globalization of World Politics: An Introduction to International Relations*, 2nd ed. (Oxford: Oxford University Press, 2001), 617–34.

14. Richard Jolly, quoted in J. Stackhouse, "Canada Is the Best, UN Reports," *The Globe and Mail,* 17 July 1996, A10.

15. This is rather confusing, since international relations scholars use the terms *liberal, neoliberal,* or even *neoliberal institutionalism* differently. To add to the confusion, in many states, such as Canada and Great Britain, it has been the Conservative parties that initially implemented the neoliberal economic agenda (no one ever said political science would be a straightforward endeavour).

16. "Floating the Tobin Tax," *The Economist,* 13 July 1996, 84.

17. Canada, Department of Foreign Affairs and International Trade, "Eggleton Travels to Poland and Russia to Promote Trade and Investment," news release, 9 October 1996. In early 1997 "Team Canada" visited South Korea, despite a serious labour dispute in that country.

18. See, for example, J. Goodman, *Protest and Globalisation: Prospects for Transnational Solidarity* (Annandale: Pluto Press, 2002).

19. R. Vernon, *Sovereignty at Bay: The Multinational Spread of U.S. Enterprises* (New York: Basic, 1971); R. Barnet and R. Muller, *Global Reach: The Power of Multinational Corporations* (New York: Simon and Schuster, 1974).

20. See, for example, K. Levitt, *Silent Surrender: The Multinational Corporation in Canada* (Toronto: Macmillan, 1970).

21. See John M. Stopford, John H. Dunning, and Klaus O. Haberich, *The World Directory of Multinational Enterprises* (New York: Facts on File, 1980), xxv; United States Central Intelligence Agency, *The World Factbook 1994,* (Washington, DC: U.S. Government Printing Office, 1995); and *Fortune,* 7 August 1995, F1–F10.

22. UNDP, *Human Development Report, 1996* (New York: Oxford University Press, 1996), 2; World Bank figures obtained from WB Indicators Database, http://www.worldbank.org/data/databytopic/GDP.pdf (accessed 24 April 2004).

23. *Figures are from the UNDP's Human Development Report, 2003*, http://hdr.undp.org/reports/global/2003/pdf/hdr03_complete.pdf (accessed 24 April 2004).

24. See T. Lairson and D. Skidmore, *International Political Economy* (Fort Worth: Harcourt Brace, 1993), 65–66; S. George, *The Debt Boomerang* (Boulder, CO: Westview Press, 1992); and Gélinas, *Juggernaut Politics*, 63.

25. S. George, *A Fate Worse Than Debt* (Harmondsworth: Penguin, 1988).

26. World Bank Group, http://devdata.worldbank.org/external (accessed 23 April 2004).

27. Data from OECD DAC Statistical Tables, 2003, http://www.oecd.org/document/11/0,2340,en_2825_495602_1894347_1_1_1_1,00.html (accessed 26 May 2004).

28. See Jeanne Kirk Laux, "From South to East? Financing the Transition in Central and Eastern Europe," in M. Appel Molot and H. von Riekhoff, eds., *A Part of the Peace: Canada among Nations 1994* (Ottawa: Carleton University Press, 1994), 172–94.

29. UNCTAD Secretariat, *Technology: Development Aspects of the Reverse Transfer of Technology*, Report of the Secretariat (New York: United Nations, 1979), para. 6.

30. ILO, *World Labour Report 1995* (Geneva, 1993).

31. "Special Report: The Doha Round," *The Economist*, 20 September 2003, 26–28.

32. There is a Canadian connection here, since the Council of Canadians, an antiglobalization coalition, was the organization that initially circulated a copy of the proposed MAI over the Internet in April 1997. See T. Clark and M. Barlow, *MAI: The Multilateral Agreement on Investment and the Threat to Canadian Sovereignty* (Toronto: Stoddart, 1997), 21–22.

33. One of the reasons some EU members were fond of the more flexible euro concept is that the Bundesbank has had such a strong anti-inflationary agenda that it has resulted in a "single-minded fixation on price stability [that] has left Europe facing a long-term crisis of joblessness." James Laxer, "Germans Are Creating a Monetary Quagmire," *Toronto Star*, 21 July 1996, F3.

34. See David Long, "Europe after Maastricht," in Appel Molot and von Riekhoff, eds., *A Part of the Peace*, 131–53.

35. B. Coleman, "EU Court Backs Damage Claims," *Wall Street Journal*, 6 March 1996, 1.

36. Robert A. Isaac, *Managing World Economic Change: International Political Economy*, 2nd ed. (Englewood Cliffs, NJ: Prentice Hall, 1995), 30.

37. Edward Luttwak, "The Coming Global War for Economic Power," *International Economy* 7 (September/October 1993), 20.

38. Michael Mastanduno, "Do Relative Gains Matter? America's Response to Japanese Industrial Policy," *International Security* 16 (Summer 1991), 78.

39. Joseph M. Grieco, "Anarchy and the Limits of Cooperation: A Realist Critique of the Newest Liberal Institutionalism," in Charles W. Kegley Jr., ed., *Controversies in International Relations Theory: Realism and the Neoliberal Challenge* (New York: St. Martin's Press, 1995), 151–71.

40. Luttwak, "The Coming Global War for Economic Power," 20.

41. See "Energy Consumption: Consumption per Capita," Energy and Resources database, World Resources Institute, http://earthtrends.wri.org/ (accessed 27 June 2004); and recent Human Development Index Reports.

42. "The Control of Oil," *International Journal* 36, no. 2 (1981), 273–93.

43. Quoted in *The Globe and Mail*, 15 March 1994.

44. Survey, *The Economist*, 18 June 1994, 1–6.

45. P. Sampat, *World Watch* (November/December 1995), 21–23.

46. See Stockholm International Peace Research Institute, *SIPRI Yearbook, 1999* (Oxford: Oxford University Press, 1999); and same, *SIPRI Yearbook, 2003* (Oxford: Oxford University Press, 2003). Estimates for 2003 and 2004 are even more astronomical.

Suggested Readings

Adriaansen, W., and J. Waardensburg, eds. *A Dual World Economy*. Groningen: Wolters-Noordhoff, 1989.

Afshar, H. *Women, Development and Survival in the Third World*. New York: Feminist Press, 1991.

Barber, B. "Jihad vs. McWorld." *Atlantic*, March 1992, 53–63.

Baylis, J., and S. Smith, eds. *The Globalization of World Politics: An Introduction to International Relations*. 2nd ed. Oxford: Oxford University Press, 2001.

Boas, Morton, and Desmond McNeill, eds. *Global Institutions and Development: Framing the World?* London and New York: Routledge, 2004.

Cameron, D., and F. Houle, eds. *Canada and the New International Division of Labour.* Ottawa: University of Ottawa Press, 1985.

Chase-Dunn, C. *Global Formation: The Structures of the World Economy.* Cambridge, MA: Basil Blackwell, 1991.

Cohen, M.G. *Free Trade and the Future of Women's Work: Manufacturing and Service Industries.* Toronto: Garamond, 1987.

Conklin D., and T. Courchene, eds. *Canadian Trade at a Crossroads: Options for New International Agreements.* Toronto: Ontario Economic Council, 1985.

Croucher, Sheila L. *Globalization and Belonging: The Politics of Identity in a Changing World.* Lanham, MD, and Rowman and Littlefield, 2004.

Dolfsma, Wilfred, and and Charlie Dannreuther. *Globalisation, Social Capital and Inequality: Contested Concepts, Contested Experiences.* Cheltenham, UK, and Northhampton, MA: Edward Elgar, 2003.

Drache, D., and M. Gertler, eds. *The New Era of Global Competition: State Policy and Market Power.* Montreal/Kingston: McGill-Queen's University Press, 1991.

Eaton, Heather. *Ecofeminism and Globalization: Exploring Culture and Religion.* Lanham, MD: Rowman and Littlefield, 2003.

Garten, J. "Lessons for the Next Financial Crisis." *Foreign Affairs* 78, no. 2 (1999), 76–92.

Fisher, W., and T. Ponniah, eds. *Another World Is Possible: Popular Alternatives to Globalization at the World Social Forum.* Black Point, Nova Scotia: Fernwood, 2004.

Flusty, Steven. *De-Coca-colonization: Making the Globe from the Inside Out.* New York and London: Routledge, 2004.

Gill, S., ed. *Gramsci, Historical Materialism and International Relations.* Cambridge, UK: Cambridge University Press, 1993.

Haggard, S., and R. Kaufman, eds. *The Politics of Economic Adjustment: International Constraints, Distributive Conflicts, and the State.* Princeton: Princeton University Press, 1992.

Head, Ivan. *On the Hinge of History: The Mutual Vulnerability of South and North.* Toronto: University of Toronto Press, 1991.

Held, D. *Democracy and the Global Order.* Stanford, CA: Stanford University Press, 1995.

Hettne, B., A. Inotai, and O. Sunkel, eds. *Globalization and the New Regionalism.* Toronto: Macmillan, 1999.

Holm, H.-H., and G. Sorensen, eds. *Whose World Order? Uneven Globalization and the End of the Cold War.* Boulder, CO: Westview Press, 1995.

Hülsemeyer, Axel. *Globalization in the Twenty-first Century: Convergence or Divergence?* Houndmills, UK, and New York: Palgrave Macmillan, 2003.

Jackson, K., ed. *The Asian Contagion: The Causes and Consequences of a Financial Crisis.* Boulder, CO: Westview Press, 1999.

Jomo, K.S., ed. *Tigers in Trouble: Financial Governance, Liberalisation and the Crisis in East Asia.* London: Zed Books, 1998.

Jones, K. *Who's Afraid of the WTO?* Oxford: Oxford University Press, 2004.

Kardam, N. *Bringing Women In: Women's Issues in International Development Programs.* Boulder, CO: Lynne Rienner, 1990.

Larson, Thomas D., and David Skidmore. *International Political Economy: The Struggle for Power and Wealth.* Belmont, CA: Thomson/Wadsworth, 2003.

Lele, J., and W. Tettey, eds. *Asia: Who Pays for Growth? Women, Environment and Popular Movements.* Aldershot, UK: Dartmouth, 1996.

Lieber, R. "Oil and Power after the Gulf War." *International Security* 17, no. 1 (1992), 155–76.

Lopez, G., et al. "The Global Tide." *Bulletin of the Atomic Scientists* (July/August 1995), 33–39.

Magdoff, H. *Imperialism Without Colonies.* New York: Monthly Review Press, 2004.

Massiah, J., ed. *Women in Developing Economies: Making Visible the Invisible.* New York: Berg, 1992.

Mittelman, J., ed. *Globalization: Critical Reflections.* Boulder, CO: Lynne Rienner, 1997.

Naisbitt, J. *Global Paradox: The Bigger the World Economy, the More Powerful Its Smallest Players.* New York: Avon, 1994.

Nef, J. *Human Security and Mutual Vulnerability: An Exploration into the Global Political Economy of Development and Underdevelopment.* Ottawa: International Development Research Centre, 1995.

O'Brien, Robert. *Global Political Economy: Evolution and Dynamics.* New York: Palgrave Macmillan, 2004.

Paehlke, R. *Democracy's Dilemma: Environment, Social Equity, and the Global Economy.* Cambridge, MA: MIT Press, 2003.

Pattullo, P. *Last Resorts: The Cost of Tourism in the Caribbean.* 2nd ed. New York: New International, 2004.

Redclift, M. *Sustainable Development: Exploring the Contradictions.* London: Methuen, 1987.

Reich, R. *The Work of Nations.* New York: Alfred Knopf, 1991.

Ritzer, G. *The McDonaldization of Society.* Thousand Oaks: Pine Forge, 1993.

Sassen, S. *Losing Control? Sovereignty in an Age of Globalization.* New York: Columbia University Press, 1996.

Soros, G. "The Capitalist Threat." *Atlantic Monthly,* February 1997, 45–58.

Steans, Jill. *Gender and International Relations: An Introduction.* New Brunswick, NJ: Rutgers University Press, 1998.

Stiglitz, J. *Globalization and Its Discontents.* New York: W.W. Norton and Co., 2002.

Sylvester, Christine. *Feminist International Relations: An Unfinished Journey.* Cambridge, UK: Cambridge University Press, 2002

Tchantouridze, Lasha. *Globalism and Regionalism: The Evolving International System.* Winnipeg: The University of Manitoba, 2002.

Tsoukis, Christopher. *Aspects of Globalization: Macroeconomic and Capital Market Linkages in the Integrated World Economy.* Boston and London: Kluwer Academic Publishers, 2004.

Wade, R. "National Power, Coercive Liberalism, and 'Global' Finance." In *International Politics: Enduring Concepts and Contemporary Issues,* edited by R. Art and R. Jervis, 482–98. New York: Longman, 2000.

Williamson, J., and P. Kuczynski, eds. *After the Washington Consensus: Restarting Growth and Reform in Latin America.* Washington, DC: Institute for International Economics, 2003.

Suggested Websites

APEC
http://www.apec.org

Europa@Internet
http://www.uv.es/cde/euinternet

European Union
http://www.europa.eu.int

International Chamber of Commerce
http://www.iccwbo.org

Link to Women's Studies/Women's Issues WWW Sites
http://research.umbc.edu/~korenman/wmst/links.html

Nasdaq Stock Market
http://www.nasdaq.com

New Left Review
http://www.newleftreview.net

Oneworld.Net
http://www.oneworld.net

Virtual Library on International Development
http://w3.acdi-cida.gc.ca/virtual.nsf/pages/index_e.htm

World Trade Organization
http://www.wto.org

CHAPTER 9

Human Rights: Global Unity and Division

No one shall be subjected to torture or to cruel, inhuman or degrading treatment or punishment.

—*Universal Declaration of Human Rights, 1948, Article 5*

There is little evidence to suggest that mankind has advanced much beyond [the] level of jungle morality.

—*Robert Gilpin[1]*

INTRODUCTION: CAN WE INSTITUTIONALIZE ETHICS ON A WORLD SCALE?

The theme of human security, adopted as a guiding principle for Canadian foreign policy, reflects a growing awareness of human rights in the post–Cold War world. The question remains, however, whether this theme can exceed rhetoric and become a truly influential standard for policy making. Though humanitarian and human rights law, as introduced in previous chapters, is more developed than ever, it still faces serious challenges: the privileged position of states over individuals; the continued resort to force by both state and nonstate actors; the impact of globalization on developmental rights; and growing concerns over the approach to civil liberties during efforts to curb terrorism. This chapter will reflect on human rights issues from a global politics perspective, grounded in the belief that human rights continue to exert influence on the security, economic, and sustainable development agenda. Human rights issues also contribute to both convergence and divergence in global politics.

In March 1995 the world lamented the passing of a Canadian author who, though virtually unknown outside diplomatic circles, helped pen what may be the most important single document recognized by the global community, the Universal Declaration of Human Rights. Professor John Peter Humphrey was the founder and first director of the United Nations Human Rights Division, a post he held for 20 years; he also founded the Canadian Human Rights Foundation and the Canadian branch of Amnesty International, a nongovernmental organization dedicated to protecting citizens from state human rights abuses. However, Humphrey will be most widely remembered for the Declaration,[2] but not because the Declaration has become the standard by which all governments run their countries. On the contrary, most observers consider it a largely symbolic work, albeit one of great significance; as a declaration, it does not carry the status of international law attributed to a convention or treaty. This is but one example of the general frustration with international law encountered by those who would aspire to produce a more standardized world order or human rights regime. Some wonder whether law can even be said to exist if there is no formal, coercive mechanism to enforce it. Indeed, if we need reliably effective enforcement machinery to establish law, we do not have international law. Though states will often engage in punitive measures to attempt to enforce trade agreements, or to sanction gross violations of human rights such as the institutionalization of apartheid by the former South African government, it is another thing entirely to speak of a systematic law that is applied even-handedly across the globe.

Others, however, argue that the absence of an enforcer does not imply that law, in a less strict sense, does not exist. One might argue that, outside the confines of a domestic legal system, a law that relies on force alone for its legitimacy is bound to be short lived and is often more tyrannical than helpful. International law is a system in which consent-granting state leaders choose to participate not because they have to—though no one would deny the fact that some pressure does exist—but because they believe that it will ultimately benefit them. This is perhaps the ultimate example of enlightened self-interest in action. The Roman and British empires spread law throughout many lands, but it was the law of an empire, not of consensual states. When Hugo Grotius published his *De jure belli ac pacis* (*On the Law of War and Peace*) in 1625, he was writing in an age when the dominant European colonial powers were defining international law for the rest of the world (see Chapter 5). The periods of decolonization that followed, ending most recently in the 1970s, have changed that perception.

Formal state sovereignty, and its protection in documents such as the UN Charter, ensures that international law is not something imposed by Romans or Europeans but is something that has gained the acceptance of self-determining members of the international community. It may be argued, then, that the participation of states in international legal arrangements reflects an even stronger incentive to comply than if that system of law were coercive or imposed. One of the problems with this perspective, however, is that in many areas of international law, including questions about human rights, the people who are threatened by abuses are not those who control the government in power or who have consented to participate in international rights regimes. The people who are threatened by abuses are the citizens of those states, and the principle of territorial sovereignty does not distinguish between democratically elected leaders and tyrants. Another problem is that conceptions of human rights vary, on both philosophical and political grounds. This variation raises the tricky question of whether the international community has an obligation, or for that matter the ability, to institutionalize conceptions of justice, law, and human rights on an international level. However, recent movements toward individual accountability under international law, such as the development of the International Criminal Court, suggest we may be moving toward a system characterized by both state voluntarism and a potentially viable effort to hold state leaders responsible for the more egregious crimes against humanity. We expand on these questions below when we discuss human rights law more specifically. For now we will examine the essential divisions of opinion on human rights.

As we noted above, serious philosophical differences of opinion exist regarding human rights. The first debate concerns the subject matter and its definition: do we focus on the political rights of the individual or the socioeconomic rights of the collective? The tension between the two has been the source of considerable political controversy in global politics and a mainstay of heated debate. A second debate revolves around the question of whether human rights is a relative or a universal concept. Some charge that the prevalent approach to human rights is an imposed Western idea, and that civilizations, societies, peoples, and groups have different conceptions of the term. Others argue that basic human rights are universal for

PROFILE 9.1	International Days and Weeks Declared by the United Nations

Note that most of the days and weeks declared by the UN celebrate some sort of human rights–related issue. But does all this celebration really advance these causes?

March 8	International Women's Day	First Monday of October	World Habitat Day
March 21	International Day for the Elimination of Racial Discrimination	October 9	World Post Day
		October 16	World Food Day
March 21–28	Week of Solidarity with the Peoples Struggling against Racism and Racial Discrimination	October 17	International Day for the Eradication of Poverty
March 22	World Water Day	October 24	United Nations Day
March 23	World Meteorological Day	October 24–30	Disarmament Week
April 7	World Health Day	November 6	Day for Preventing the Exploitation of the Environment in War and Armed Conflict
May 3	World Press Freedom Day		
May 15	International Day of Families	Week of November 11	International Week of Science and Peace
May 17	World Telecommunications Day	November 20	Universal Children's Day
May 31	World No-Tobacco Day	November 20	Africa Industrialization Day
June 4	International Day of Innocent Children Victims of Aggression	November 29	International Day of Solidarity with the Palestinian People
June 5	World Environment Day	December 1	World AIDS Day
June 26	International Day against Drug Abuse and Illicit Trafficking	December 3	International Day of Disabled Persons
July 11	World Population Day	December 5	International Volunteer Day for Economic and Social Development
September 8	International Literacy Day		
Third Tuesday of September	International Day of Peace	December 10	Human Rights Day
October 1	International Day of Older Persons		

all peoples. A third debate concerns the usefulness and effectiveness of international laws on human rights. Each theoretical perspective on global politics that we have introduced in this book regards the issue of human rights very differently.

INDIVIDUAL VERSUS COLLECTIVE CONCEPTIONS OF HUMAN RIGHTS

During the Cold War it became standard for the two opposing camps to each present their vision of human rights as morally defensible and worthy of emulation. The West insisted that the individual is the most important component of any political system, and that an individual's rights must be protected from encroachment by the state. The Soviet Union naturally rejected this definition of human rights, arguing that collective rights, or those of entire populations, had to come first. The Communist parties of the East rejected the right to private property, long taken as a fundamental right in the West. They also rejected the right to practise religion freely, which remains a highly contested right in some societies today where a single religion is instituted as that of the nation-state, such as in Iran. Even in Western states, repetitious references to God and country raise concerns about protecting religious diversity and tolerance.

Naturally, we are engaging in what some might consider *excessive dichotomization* here. Clearly, every society needs some sort of balance between the individual and collective conceptions of rights, such as the right to individual liberties and the right to be free from life-threatening poverty. Individual rights can be superseded in the most liberal states by the need to protect collective rights; for example, in many parts of the United States, where individual liberties are fairly well protected, the state can still kill people who are found guilty of treason or other crimes. Sometimes, the logic of group rights can lead to divisive debate. For example, the Universal Declaration of Human Rights states that "the family is the natural and fundamental group unit of society and is entitled to protection by society and the State" (Article 16/3). This statement remains open to interpretation but can be used to challenge the legitimacy of same-sex marriage. In Canada, there are various competing conceptions of which should take precedence, the individual or groups such as francophones in Quebec or First Nations peoples. This philosophical dispute is also at the root of international disputes over human rights and systems of governance. States such as Malaysia have argued that Western notions of individual liberty are fine, but they should not be imposed on non-Western states that emphasize collective rights. Human rights groups such as Amnesty International argue that there are some things all individuals should be protected from, including repression and **torture** at the hands of the state. This helps form the basic argument that in international law, *jus cogens* (preemptory norms that override all treaties or agreements), universally agreed standards, and protections from the more extreme violations of human rights, exist. This leads however to our next topic: beyond the right to life itself, whose norms, or belief systems, should receive universal protection?

RELATIVISM VERSUS UNIVERSALISM IN HUMAN RIGHTS

In the African country of Ghana, a few isolated communities still practise an ancient Ewe custom. The custom holds that for serious crimes against the community such as murder, rape, or theft, "the spirits can be appeased only by the enslavement of young [female] virgins from the offender's family in the shrines of traditional priests." This enslavement of girls as young as 12 includes the expectation that the girls will participate in sexual acts with the priests. Many Ghanaians are campaigning against the practice, which is said to have enslaved "as many as 10 000 girls." But in the Ghanaian coastal village of Tefle, the village men insist they have the right to practise what they consider to be a vital custom.[3] This is an extreme case; others, such as child labour, invoke similar feelings of horror among Westerners accustomed to a different set of principles. However, many Africans and South Americans consider the Western tradition of putting older citizens into retirement facilities instead of keeping them at home with extended families to be equally barbaric, and the lack of care for the homeless in major urban centres is viewed with similar disdain. So we realize that there are cultural differences between different societies, as there have always been. The question is whether some practices, often claimed as integral to those cultures, should be universally condemned.

As suggested above, we have to ask also whether it is even appropriate to condemn some states for human rights violations: what gives anyone, or another state, the right to make such pronouncements? Some reject the premise of a universal moral order, arguing that norms and principles are subject to a specific time and place. In other words, what is morally acceptable today may not be tomorrow; this is certainly the case with some widespread institutions, such as that of slavery in the Americas. It has been suggested that as we progress toward a more civilized world order, we are redefining certain types of behaviour as illegitimate. As described in Chapter 5, the institutionalization of this process of redefinition has been specifically referred to as the social construction of *global prohibition regimes*: they are guided by norms that "strictly circumscribe the conditions under which states can participate in and authorize these activities and proscribe all involvement by nonstate actors."[4] Once we have made some sort of collective decision regarding the immorality of an act or even a sociopolitical system, such as apartheid in South Africa, or state repression in Burma, then we should make an attempt to universalize this decision and spread it around the world, through education or outright coercion.

To many, this sounds rather confusing, for while it may have the most progressive of foundations (such as outlawing slavery, for example), it also implies that the majority (or perhaps merely the strong) has the moral right (or even duty) to impose its will on others. Is this much different from what the imperial powers did during the dark years of colonial administration? Does this simply replace the old political and economic dominance of the West with a new form of cultural imperialism?[5] This term usually refers to the imposition of one society's values on another, through either the force of law (as in direct colonialism) or the less overt manipulation of minds through the media (television, radio, newspapers, or even the Internet). However, when it comes to standards of international law and human rights in particular, the promotion of Western values with aid policies designed to award liberal democratization are equally suspect, as are rhetoric-laden UN resolutions, which can be seen as the soft law of cultural imperialism.

The idea behind cultural relativism is that ethical values (ostensibly the root cause of governments' human rights policies) vary from place to place and over time. As R.J. Vincent writes, this means "that moral claims derive from, and are enmeshed in, a cultural context which is itself the source of their validity."[6] In other words, beyond condemning the most brutal of practices such as slavery and torture (and even these are subject to relativist definitions), it is intrinsically unfair to criticize the ethical positions of others, since they arise out of the specific conditions faced by them at the time. Japan has always had a strong dependency on seafood, for example; perhaps we should not be surprised or outraged that some Japanese still sell whale meat in restaurants in Tokyo and elsewhere. Amsterdam's "red light" district, where prostitution is on open and legal display, would appear distinctly unethical in many other areas of the world. While the United States often condemns states for engaging in repressive policies, many point to the increasing use of the death penalty and the disproportionately high incarceration of minorities in that country as an indication of regressive public ethics. The role of women has changed rapidly in Western societies (see Chapter 8), but does this imply that all states should adopt similar legal provisions for women's rights? Since no states are without human rights problems and controversies, it may not be just cultural imperialism to force one's own values onto the international stage; it may be nakedly hypocritical as well.

Even the more obvious cases can become complicated with a close look. For example, the right to food is often used as an example of a universal human right.[7] However, we must ask whether people have a simple right to adequate amounts of food, or even equitable amounts of food within their own societies (few, if any, states would pass that test). We might argue that the right to environmental security should be universally applicable, that is, that all people should be able to live in a local environment free from profound ecological threats. However, any attempt to ensure this right would not only challenge sovereignty as an institution but also in many cases require the redistribution of resources within societies. At the same time, cultural relativism can become a cloak behind which abusers of basic rights can hide, and we should not let it stop us from analyzing touchy issues. Or, in the words of the distinguished scholar Fred Halliday,

> While an awareness of relativity and difference is essential to an
> explanation of how and why systems of domination originate
> and are maintained, such a recognition need not necessarily

lead, out of a misplaced anthropological generosity, to denying
that forms of oppression do exist and recur in a wide range of
societies and historical contexts.[8]

A yet broader issue concerns whether questions of ethics and morality should even be part
of the study of international relations.[9] If state sovereignty is sacrosanct, states really have no
right to comment on what goes on in other states in the first place. If this were the case, the
ethical responsibilities of government leaders would not extend beyond the borders of their
own countries.[10] Since the most fundamental principle of international law is state sovereignty, international law reinforces, rather than challenges, this perspective. However, leaving
questions of permanence aside, states are almost invariably involved in each other's domestic
economies; they often share transnational cultural understandings; and much migration has
occurred in the past two centuries. All of this leads us to suggest that, whether they like it or
not, government leaders do bear some measure of ethical responsibility for what occurs outside their borders and for what their citizens do outside them as well. While this responsibility
has always pertained to the actions of soldiers, it includes the actions of civilians. For example,
the Canadian government has joined several other states to make it possible to prosecute
Canadians who purchase sex with children when abroad. Similarly, activists have campaigned
for MNCs to adopt ethical guidelines, or codes of conduct, when operating in low-income
regions. When a government provides low-cost insurance for firms investing in conflict zones,
it is making an ethical decision on the implications of investing there. In fact, most questions
related to foreign policy, as well as our own individual policies when we interact with the
world, involve the realization and implementation of ethical standards, even if we don't habitually agonize over our choices.

As Sidney Bailey and Sam Daws write, "from a moral point of view, human rights are about
the behaviour of individuals. From a legal point of view, human rights are about the responsibilities of governments."[11] Until roughly the mid- to late 19th century, human rights concerns were regarded as within the domestic jurisdiction of rulers. Campaigns to abolish the
slave trade and to provide humanitarian care for wounded soldiers helped break this confine-
ment, although the principle of non-intervention maintains its prominent place in the UN
Charter today. The human rights field has expanded considerably in scope since the end of
World War II, the cataclysmic event that so horrified the world that the international community began to gradually accept the notion that international law could play a role in
avoiding future holocausts (see "Genocide and War Crimes" on page 342). Where the human
rights issue-area departs most noticeably from conventional international legal matters, however, is that it forces us to look beyond the usual tradition that defines international law as law
for, and by, states. Even in the World Court, states are still recognized as the sole actors in
international law. This distinction becomes increasingly difficult to maintain as global human
rights conventions, agreements, and movements flourish, since human rights are ultimately
about people and not about the relatively abstract conceptions we call states.

In recent decades, human rights issues have become increasingly prominent concerns for governments, international organizations, and publics. Why has this happened? In the first place,
awareness has increased. Global communications, travel, and print and television media have
made us more aware of what goes on in other countries. States are no longer as capable of controlling information flows across their borders as they once were, though many argue media
images are still controlled by elites. Economic interdependence and global communications have
provided governments, groups, and individuals with the means to act to promote human rights,
through mechanisms such as trade restrictions, boycotts, and public information campaigns and
protests. For example, consumer boycotts of multinational corporations (MNCs) have had some

PROFILE 9.2 Recent Nobel Peace Prize Winners

Shirin Ebadi, winner of the Nobel Peace Prize, right, holds up the hand of Narges Mohammadi, wife of Taqi Rahmani, a prominent jailed political activist, during a gathering at the Amir Kabir University in Tehran, Iran, 29 October 2003. In her most biting criticism of the ruling hard-line Islamic establishment yet, Ebadi said she owes the award to Cyrus the Great, king of ancient Persia, and to Iran's writers and intellectuals in jail. (AP Photo/Vahid Salemi/CP Archive)

Former U.S. President Jimmy Carter right, waves alongside Cuban President Fidel Castro at the airport in Havana, Cuba, 17 May 2002. Carter wrapped up a historic visit after seeking to bring Cuba and the United States closer by challenging both countries to change after more than four decades of enmity. (AP Photo/Gregory Bull/CP Archive)

The Nobel Peace Prize has often been awarded to outstanding members of the human rights community; the assumption is that true peace is impossible without freedom and dignity for all. In 2003, Shirin Ebadi of Iran won the esteemed prize for her work on women's rights and democracy in Iran. She was born in Tehran in 1947, and served as the president of the city court of Tehran, as one of the first female judges in Iran, in the 1970s. After the 1979 revolution, she was forced to resign. She now works as a lawyer and teaches at the University of Tehran; as an activist and researcher she has lobbied for increased rights for refugees, women, and children. She represents a movement called Reformed Islam, and argues for a new interpretation of Islamic law that is in harmony with vital human rights such as democracy, equality before the law, religious freedom, and freedom of speech. She uses Islam as her starting point to promote peaceful solutions, and promotes new thinking on Islamic terms. She has displayed great personal courage as a lawyer defending individuals and groups who have fallen victim to a powerful political and legal system that is legitimized through what many consider an inhumane interpretation of Islam. Ebadi has shown her willingness and ability to cooperate with representatives of secular as well as religious views.

Critics charge that she received the prize precisely because her views are in line with Western critiques of Iranian theocracy, but this overlooks her commitment to Islam and personal achievements.

In contrast, the Nobel Peace Prize winner of 2002 was well known around the world: former U.S. President (1976–80) Jimmy Carter. Carter has long been active since his defeat by Ronald Reagan in undertaking various peace diplomacy missions, with mixed results; in 2004 he was involved in efforts to calm the Haitian crisis. However, one could as plausibly argue that his Peace Prize reflected the international communities' respect for his work in the human rights field. Founded in 1981, the Carter Center is an Atlanta-based organization devoted to global peace and social justice. Carter has travelled around the globe monitoring elections, promoting human rights, and providing health care and food to the world's poor; the Carter Center is also involved in providing low-cost housing to the poor in the United States. There is always some controversy about the Nobel Peace Prize; some critics felt that a former U.S. president was not a sound choice, given that state's mixed record on promoting human rights abroad. Most, however, felt the Norwegian Nobel Committee got it right this time, rewarding a stalwart defender of rights for the poor and a reliable voice for calm.

success, as many consumers resist buying products produced by victims of repression. Consumer awareness campaigns directed at Heineken, Carlsberg, British Home Stores, and Liz Claiborne compelled those MNCs to leave Burma. Campaigns have also been mounted against Royal Dutch/Shell for its operations in Nigeria, Total and Unocal in Burma, Nike in Indonesia, Disney in Haiti, and Zenith and General Motors for gender discrimination in Mexico.[12]

The growth of human rights groups has also given interested individuals the opportunity to devote more time and effort to the cause of human rights. Such nongovernmental organizations (NGOs) include Amnesty International, Human Rights Watch, the International League for Human Rights, and the International Commission of Jurists. As we discussed in Chapter 5, these NGOs work to create awareness and persuade governments to act on human rights issues. As a result, governments are no longer regarded as the primary means of advancing human rights. In fact, governments are increasingly regarded as serious obstacles to progress. Yet they remain an essential piece of the puzzle.

HUMAN RIGHTS AND GOVERNMENTS

Governments are a factor in human rights issues on three levels. First, human rights are a factor in foreign policy decision making. Many governments have participated in efforts to build international law and international regimes to promote them, and they have responded to human rights abuses with diplomatic protests and economic sanctions (such as those directed against apartheid South Africa and against China after the June 1989 Tiananmen Square massacre in which the Chinese military crushed a pro-democracy protest). Other governments have also taken steps to improve human rights in their own societies by prosecuting abusive officials and exposing the stark legacies of their past. For example, the Truth and Reconciliation Commission in South Africa undertook an investigation that implicated top-level officials in the former South African government in the apartheid-era state violence. The Guatemalan government

acknowledged past abuses and purged the military and the police of the worst human rights offenders. The government of South Korea has convicted two former presidents for their role in a 1980 massacre of civilians by the South Korean military. The newly formed government of Iraq intends to prosecute Saddam Hussein and his surviving leadership with crimes against the Iraqi people.

Second, governments have displayed inconsistency and a lack of commitment on human rights issues. In particular, governments around the world (including the government of Canada; see Profile 9.3) appear consistently willing to subordinate human rights concerns to their desire for trade and investment opportunities. Governments have defended this approach by arguing that trade, investment, and interdependence will generate social change in countries with human rights problems

Standing up for liberty. In this now famous photograph, an anti-government protester stands in front of advancing tanks in Beijing's Tiananmen Square on June 5, 1989, at the height of the pro-democracy protests. Deng Xiaoping is believed to have given the final orders for the military suppression of the 1989 Tiananmen Square pro-democracy protests, which claimed hundreds, perhaps thousands, of lives. Though China has partially liberalized its economy, the Communist Party continues to hold an iron grip on political representation, has actively repressed spiritual groups such as the Falun Gong, and continues its tyranny over Tibet. (AP Photo/Jeff Widener/CP Archive)

PROFILE 9.3 Talisman and Sudan

President and Chief Executive Officer of Talisman Energy Jim Buckee gestures as he responds to a reporter's question following the company's annual general meeting in Calgary, 6 May 2003. Talisman Energy Inc. reported a jump in first-quarter profits to $573 million after booking a big gain on the sale of its Sudan oil interests and also announced it will fast-track development of a new oil discovery in Malaysia. (CP Picture Archive/Adrian Wyld)]

TALISMAN AND SUDAN

The concept of human security was put to an interesting test in the recent dispute over a Canadian oil firm's investment and operations in the North African state of Sudan. Civil war has raged in that country for almost 50 years, and reports of mass displacement and military attacks continue in 2004. The northern Arab-dominated National Islamic Front government has been fighting the Christian and animist southern region in a brutal confrontation that has killed some 1.5 million southerners and has seen the use of food as a weapon, concentration camps, and reports of southern villagers being taken into slavery by northern militias. (Western Christian groups have engaged in so-called redemption programs, literally buying back slaves from their oppressors, but this has been criticized as well since it drives up the price of slaves.)

In October 1998 Talisman Energy acquired Arakis Energy for C$200 million. This gave Talisman a 25 percent share in the Greater Nile Oil Project, a consortium with China and Malaysia. In southern Sudan, huge oil fields are being drilled and a major pipeline to Port Sudan is planned. The project employs 2000 Sudanese, and more than 100 Canadians have helped train them. However, the southern rebels, in particular the Sudan People's Liberation Army, consider this collaboration with the northern government an affront to their territorial sovereignty and have declared such installations legitimate military targets. As a result the Sudanese government, which takes a share of the revenue generated by the oil extraction, employed military forces to protect the Canadian workers and installations.

Critics charged that a Canadian firm was helping to fund a genocidal war. In response, the Canadian government sent African expert John Harker to investigate the situation, and his report was largely condemnatory. In early 2000 the Canadian government decided that no sanctions would be imposed against Talisman but that the company should be encouraged to carefully monitor the situation and perhaps create a trust fund to help southerners after the conflict is over. Human rights activists, who argue that the conflict will not end as long as the Sudanese government is funded by oil revenues, expressed dismay at this decision. The decision also angered the United States, which has imposed tough sanctions (with some notable exceptions) on Sudan because of suspected terrorist connections. Should the Canadian government have taken steps to force Talisman out of Sudan, or is business just business? Finally, in response to shareholder concerns over human rights abuses, and an American threat to delist the company from the New York Stock Exchange, Talisman agreed in March 2003 to sell its 25 percent stake in Sudan's Greater Nile Oil Project to an Indian state-owned oil company called ONGC Videsh. Indeed, Talisman profited from the sale! The episode heightened awareness of the potential impact of foreign investment, and raised questions about the human costs of promoting "business as usual."

SOURCES: A. NIKIFORUK, "OIL PATCH PARIAH," *CANADIAN BUSINESS*, 10 DECEMBER 2000, 69; *HUMAN SECURITY IN SUDAN: REPORT OF A CANADIAN ASSESSMENT MISSION PREPARED FOR THE MINISTER OF FOREIGN AFFAIRS*, OTTAWA, JANUARY 2000; S. THORNE, "CANADA CONSIDERS MORE MEASURES TO ENCOURAGE PEACE IN SUDAN," CANADIAN PRESS, 15 FEBRUARY 2000.

and that interdependence will create leverage that can later be used to promote human rights. This "constructive engagement" approach has angered critics, who charge that it amounts to a façade of a human rights policy rather than any genuine commitment.[13] Governments also tend to exert human rights pressure on poor states while not doing the same with economically attractive states, and great powers have often continued to provide Official Development Assistance (ODA) and even military aid to some abusive regimes. Governments have also obstructed efforts to reveal the involvement of their own officials in human rights abuses. The U.S. government, for example, has been reluctant to release documents related to the activities of the Central Intelligence Agency (CIA) in Haiti, Honduras, and Guatemala, obstructing the human rights investigations in progress in those countries.

Third, governments often fail to act on human rights abuses, and many continue to perpetrate abuses at home. Governments were slow to react to the human rights abuses in the former Yugoslavia and to the genocide in Rwanda. Governments in Angola and Cambodia have extended amnesty to human rights abusers. The Japanese government remains unwilling to formally compensate for the treatment of the 200 000 "comfort women" used as sex slaves for the Japanese military in World War II. Many other countries are struggling with political opposition to the investigation of human rights abuses, and some governments attempt to intimidate human rights advocates, harassing many, imprisoning some, and killing others.[14] The record of governments in human rights issues is, therefore, rather poor; although governments can be important agents of progress, all too often they are obstacles, or the very source of the problem. This fact complicates related diplomatic initiatives. For example, at least two highly murderous regimes have had nonpermanent seats on the Security Council (Cambodia, then called Kampuchea, in the mid-1970s; and Rwanda in 1994) even while massive campaigns of genocide were carried out back home.

HUMAN RIGHTS AND THE UN SYSTEM

In June 1993, the UN-sponsored World Conference on Human Rights in Vienna declared that "the promotion and protection of all human rights is a legitimate concern of the international community."[15] Similar sentiments had been expressed at previous UN conferences and forums. Yet such declarations conflict with the principle of sovereignty enshrined in the UN Charter. As Stephen Marks has observed, "Human rights in the United Nations has been, to a large extent, the story of tension between the principle that the United Nations cannot intervene in the domestic affairs of states and the principle that states must act with the United Nations to realize fully all rights."[16]

While the UN Charter does call explicitly for international cooperation on economic, social, cultural, and humanitarian matters, and the promotion of human rights and fundamental freedoms (Articles 4 and 55, respectively), it is the Universal Declaration of Human Rights, adopted by the General Assembly in 1948, that has the most impact on legal thinking regarding the obligations of states toward their citizens. More than 60 other human rights instruments have been adopted by the General Assembly since 1948, including the International Covenant on Civil and Political Rights and the International Convenant on Economic, Social and Cultural Rights. The two international convenants and the Universal Declaraton of Human Rights are collectively known as the International Bill of Rights. Despite considerable dissension, the UN-sponsored World Conference on Human Rights in Vienna (the first in a quarter-century) concluded with a commitment to the idea of universal human rights, and established the post of a UN High Commissioner for Human Rights. The high commissioner helps coordinate the work of the 53-member Commission on Human Rights (a subsidiary body of ECOSOC), and in 2004 a well-respected Canadian jurist, Louise Arbour, was appointed to this demanding post.

PROFILE 9.4 Selected UN Human Rights Instruments

Note: After each convention appears the year it was opened for signature and the year it entered into force.

GENERAL HUMAN RIGHTS

International Covenant on Civil and Political Rights, 1966, 1976

Optional Protocol to the International Covenant on Civil and Political Rights, 1966, 1976

International Covenant on Economic, Social and Cultural Rights, 1966, 1976

UN World Conference on Human Rights: Vienna Declaration, 1993

RACIAL DISCRIMINATION

International Convention on the Elimination of All Forms of Racial Discrimination, 1965, 1969

International Convention on the Suppression and Punishment of the Crime of Apartheid, 1973, 1976

International Convention against Apartheid in Sports, 1985

RIGHTS OF WOMEN

Convention on the Political Rights of Women, 1952, 1954

Convention on the Nationality of Married Women, 1957, 1958

Convention on Consent to Marriage, Minimum Age for Marriage and Registration of Marriages, 1962, 1964

Convention on the Elimination of All Forms of Discrimination against Women, 1979, 1981

SLAVERY AND RELATED MATTERS

Convention for the Suppression of the Traffic in Persons and of the Exploitation of the Prostitution of Others, 1949, 1951

Slavery Convention of 1926, as amended in 1953, 1953, 1955

Protocol Amending the 1926 Slavery Convention, 1953, 1955

Supplementary Convention on the Abolition of Slavery, the Slave Trade, and Institutions and Practices Similar to Slavery, 1956, 1957

REFUGEES AND STATELESS PERSONS

Convention on the Reduction of Statelessness, 1949, 1951

Convention relating to the Status of Refugees, 1951, 1954

Convention relating to the Status of Stateless Persons, 1954, 1960

Protocol relating to the Status of Refugees, 1966, 1967

OTHER

Convention on the Prevention and Punishment of the Crime of Genocide, 1948, 1951

Convention on the International Right of Correction, 1952, 1962

Convention on the Non-Applicability of Statutory Limitations to War Crimes and Crimes against Humanity, 1968, 1970

Convention against Torture and Other Cruel, Inhuman or Degrading Treatment or Punishment, 1984, 1987

Convention on the Rights of the Child, 1989

International Convention on the Protection of the Rights of All Migrant Workers and Members of Their Families, 1990

Draft Declaration on the Rights of Indigenous Peoples, 1992

In addition, many other bodies in the UN address human rights issues. These include the Committee on the Elimination of Racial Discrimination, the Commission on the Status of Women and the Committee on the Elimination of Discrimination against Women, the High Commissioner for Refugees, the High Commissioner for National Minorities, the International Labour Organization, and the Crime Prevention and Criminal Justice Division in Vienna.

HUMAN RIGHTS AND REGIONAL ORGANIZATIONS

In addition to efforts to promote human rights through the UN, regional IGOs have also made similar efforts, though with varying degrees of commitment and concrete results. In Europe, the foundation for the large body of human rights legislation and institutions is the 1953 European Convention for the Protection of Human Rights and Fundamental Freedoms, drafted to prevent a recurrence of the Nazi crimes against humanity. Two institutions in Europe have built on the principles of the European Convention. The **Council of Europe** maintains the European Court, which, among other cases, has heard charges against the British government alleging that the laws enacted to suppress the Irish Republican Army (IRA) violated the human rights provisions of the European Convention. The Organization for Security and Co-operation in Europe (OSCE), established in 1994 as a replacement for the Conference on Security and Cooperation in Europe (CSCE), was built on the principles of the Helsinki Final Act of 1975, which provided for the protection of human rights by all signatory governments across Europe (including the U.S.S.R.) and North America (including Canada and the United States). In 1990, the Charter of Paris committed members to observe the human rights provisions of the CSCE Final Act (and any subsequent amendment) and proclaimed human rights as a "legitimate concern" of all signatory governments. The OSCE mounts periodic fact-finding missions to investigate human rights concerns. In addition, much of the European Convention on Human Rights is reflected in the local laws of several EU member states, the most recent being that of Britain.

The Organization of American States (OAS) Charter of 1948 has a Declaration of the Rights and Duties of Man, and in 1978 the American Convention on Human Rights (with an Inter-American Court of Human Rights) came into force. In Africa, the 1981 African Charter on Human and Peoples' Rights (the Banjul Charter) was adopted by the OAU. In Asia, the Association of Southeast Asian Nations (ASEAN) possesses a human rights commission, and the Asia-Pacific Economic Cooperation (APEC) forum possesses a Human Resources Development Working Group. However, while most of these regional human rights efforts are staffed by dedicated and hard-working personnel, and while many of them perform important roles and tasks on a variety of human rights issues, all of them suffer from the problems of limited financial and human resources and the intransigence (and sometimes the resistance) of member governments.

CONTEMPORARY HUMAN RIGHTS ISSUES

Before looking at specific examples of human rights issues, we should mention the difficulty involved in choosing such examples. As space constrains us from embarking on anything approaching a comprehensive survey, we have chosen several issues that have had a high public profile in the press in recent years. Although this selection is of course arbitrary, we hope we have covered issues of concern to most contemporary students and encourage you to look elsewhere for information on other pertinent topics, such as freedom of speech, the right to food and education, and gay and lesbian rights. In addition, we have not included a discussion of the refugee crisis (which many consider the most pressing and perhaps challenging human rights issue of our time) in this chapter because we deal with it at length in Chapter 11 on population and population movements. We deal with reproductive rights in that chapter as well.

ETHICS AND CONSTRAINTS ON WAR

We include a discussion of the ethical reasoning behind war efforts because war is, at heart, a human rights issue. If war is justified, then killing individual human beings to win one may be justified, and this justification is subject to all the dilemmas inherent in the universal/particular split mentioned above. Have we established a universal code of ethics that tells us when national leaders should declare war on other states, thus risking the lives of their own citizens as well as endangering those of others? The relationship between war and ethics has been a complex one.[17] Most of the world's ethical systems (heavily influenced by religion) deplore the act of killing as a general principle. And yet virtually all ethical systems establish sets of conditions under which such killing is justified or permissible. Ethicists, theologians, and philosophers have established the foundations for the ethical rejection of international violence and war, while at the same time their arguments have been used to support or justify international violence and wars; for example, in the name of national liberation or humanitarian intervention.

There is also the sentiment that war is a distinct human activity in which ethics have no place. *Inter arma silent leges*: "in times of war the law is silent." Despite this ethical debate, moral condemnation of the ethics of war tends to be *utilitarian* in nature; that is, the benefits and costs of any act must be judged in moral and ethical terms. As a result, war can be justified in certain cases, such as resisting and punishing aggression, although such wars must still be fought in accordance with certain ethical principles. The problem with utilitarian approaches is that states and groups will manipulate ethical principles to sanction the use of violence, at which point utilitarian ethics may erode into apologies or justifications for the very worst acts of war. *Absolutist* ethics, however, maintain that nothing can justify a certain act, which forms the foundation of the beliefs of pacifists, who maintain that international violence and war are never justified, no matter what the circumstances. The problem with absolutist ethics is that a refusal to use violence or go to war may permit the most horrible acts to take place; inaction itself can be morally bankrupt.

Those who advocate a "just war" doctrine attempt to constrain warfare by establishing the conditions under which it is just to enter into a war and by establishing what level of violence is considered acceptable in the prosecution of that war. This hinges on the distinction between **jus ad bellum** (the justice of a war) and **jus in bello** (the justness of the manner in which a war is fought). In his writing on *jus ad bellum*, Michael Walzer argues that only aggression can justify war, and that wars fought in self-defence are just.[18] The aggressor, once defeated, is to be punished, for punishment will deter future aggression. In society, we punish criminals to deter criminal violence; internationally, aggression is punished to prevent future aggression. From this basic principle are drawn the criteria by which just wars are measured:

- A just war is a war of last resort; all other means of resolution must be explored.
- A just war must be authorized by a legitimate authority, either the state or an international organization.
- A just war must be waged for a just cause, not for aggression or a desire for vengeance.
- A just war must have a good chance of successfully achieving a desirable outcome, and wars fought for good causes that are ultimately hopeless are not justifiable.
- A just war must end in a peace that is preferable to the situation before the outbreak of war.

Jus in bello maintains that a war may also be just or unjust in the manner in which it is fought. A war may have just origins, but it cannot be fought unjustly. Two measures determine the just conduct of a war:

1. A just war must be fought in ways consistent with the principle of proportionality. The potential positives deriving from military activity (such as a bombing campaign) must outweigh the negatives of destruction and death. Military methods must also be limited to the level of violence required to achieve the mission at hand, and any risk to civilians must be proportionate to the military value of the target.

2. A just war must discriminate—combatants and noncombatants must be treated differently. Civilians cannot be the intentional targets of military operations, and civilian casualties must be minimized when this is possible.

Just war doctrine thus argues that wars should be limited and that the conduct of war is (and should be) governed by rules of behaviour and conduct. It is important to remember that in practice few wars meet all of these criteria, and so debates about the justness of a war generally revolve around examples of when certain principles might have been violated or argue to what extent a war can be considered just.

Nuclear weapons, and in particular nuclear deterrence, pose a challenge to ethical constraints on war. During the Cold War, most secular and religious ethicists agreed that nuclear weapons are by their very nature indiscriminate and disproportionate, and so nuclear war was generally regarded as inherently unjust. However, nuclear deterrence, the deployment of nuclear weapons in an effort to deter their use, was more controversial. Is it legitimate or just to threaten an action that would be immoral or unjust if it were carried out? The legitimacy of nuclear deterrence was justified on the grounds that it is necessary to avoid a greater evil (aggression by an enemy or subjugation of the free world at the hands of totalitarianism). However, many argued that the arms race invalidated the moral basis of deterrence as a temporary measure; nuclear deterrence was endangering peace, not contributing to it. So, for example, the United Methodist Council of Bishops argued that "the moral case for nuclear deterrence, even as an interim ethic, has been undermined by unrelenting arms escalation. Deterrence no longer serves, if it ever did, as a strategy that facilitates disarmament. Deterrence must no longer receive the churches' blessing."[19] Although the prominence of this issue has receded somewhat, the ethical status of nuclear weapons remains a subject of intense debate, particularly in the context of proliferation and post–Cold War efforts to ban nuclear weapons.

Critics of just war doctrine charge that since the judges of whether a war is just tend to be the very states, governments, or peoples engaged in the violence, a natural tendency exists to frame whatever one side does in good or just terms and to frame everything the opposition does in bad or unjust terms. Nevertheless, to reject just war doctrine outright would be to invite the separation of morality and war. Furthermore, opposition to war is generally founded on judgments of what is considered just. Opposition to the Vietnam War in the United States was largely built on the view of many that the war was unjust, both in terms of its conduct and its origins. Before the Gulf War, extensive efforts were made by governments to convince public opinion that the cause was just; this has proven rather more difficult during and after the U.S.–Coalition invasion of Iraq in 2003. While many people were willing to accept the war in Afghanistan as a just response to the terror attacks of 9-11, the proffered causes for the Iraqi operation—that Saddam Hussein was a viable threat to Western states, capable of developing and using weapons of mass destruction in the near future—were rejected by many as either the consequence of a trigger-happy Bush Administration or, worse, deliberate misinformation. To the extent that support for a war is a function of the extent to which it is just, the criteria of just war doctrine would seem to have some value.

GENOCIDE AND WAR CRIMES

Few words are as connotative as *genocide*. That the term refers to mass murder is common knowledge; less well known but equally important, it refers to mass murder perpetrated by a state or a nonstate actor against a specific group of people.[20] This definition is important not only because it recognizes a form of collective rights (freedom from discriminatory murder), but also because it implies that the state—traditionally the guarantor of citizens' rights—can at times become the worst enemy of the people. The Convention on the Prevention and Punishment of the Crime of Genocide (1948) grew out of the recognition of three types of crimes during warfare: crimes against humanity, crimes against peace, and war crimes.

After World War II, trials were held in which the losers—Germany and Japan—were judged by the victors. At the most famous of these trials, the **war crimes trials** in Nuremberg held from 1945 to 1949 (the Tokyo war crimes trials are less well known), **crimes against humanity** were considered to be murder, extermination, enslavement, deportation, imprisonment, torture, rape, or persecutions on political, racial, or religious grounds committed against any civilian population (including one's own). The term was first introduced in the London Agreement of August 8, 1945 (issued by the United States, the U.S.S.R., Great Britain, and France). **Crimes against peace** included planning, preparing, initiating, or waging a war of aggression and participating in a common plan or conspiracy for the accomplishment of war crimes. Nazi aggression was considered a crime against peace, though its chief architect, Adolf Hitler, had killed himself before the bitter end of the struggle in Berlin, thus escaping trial. **War crimes** were considered murder, ill treatment or deportation to slave labour, killing of hostages, and plunder and wanton destruction with no military necessity.

Obviously some measure of overlap exists in these crimes, but they are considered important legal precedents. Polish jurist Raphael Lemkin coined the word *genocide* during the implementation of Hitler's "final solution." Lemkin had a wide awareness of the atrocities being waged across Europe largely on racial grounds and affecting one ethnic group in particular, the European Jewish community. Thus, he introduced a new term "to denote an old practice in its modern development," derived from the Greek word for race or people, *genos*, and the Latin *caedere* (cide), which means to kill.[21] The Holocaust is still widely considered the ultimate example of genocide. Estimates vary, but at least 6 million Jews—and many others, including Gypsies, prisoners of war, and German "undesirables," such as people with disabilities and homosexuals—were killed.[22] Due to the massive numbers involved, and the administrative efficiency of such systematic murder, the Holocaust remains a singular event in history, but many examples of genocide exist, such as the murder of millions of Armenians by the Ottoman Turks during World War I.

Two events in the 1990s brought the term *genocide* and the mechanism of the war crimes trial back into public view (and others, such as the continuation of hostilities in Sudan, keep it there). The first was the outbreak of war in the former Yugoslavia (see discussion in Chapter 6) and the "ethnic cleansing" (see Profile 9.5), concentration camps, mass murders, and rape that characterized the conflict. The second was the outbreak of the carnage in Rwanda in the spring and summer of 1994. This orchestrated campaign of genocide shocked the Western world with images of dismemberment, displacement, starvation, and bloated corpses floating down the Kagera River entering Uganda and Lake Victoria. As a result of just two months of intense violence, UN officials estimated the death toll of unarmed civilians in Rwanda at over 500 000.[23] State-employed Hutu militia men are thought responsible for much of the killing, which began after Hutu President Juvenal Habyarimana was killed in a rocket attack on his plane. Rwanda has been plagued with violence, before and after its achievement of independence from Belgian rule in 1962; indeed, it was a massacre of Tutsis in 1959 that originally created an exiled Tutsi community in Uganda, remnants of which returned to Rwanda in an unsuccessful invasion in 1990 and again in 1994 with the currently governing Rwanda Patriotic Front. But nothing in known African history has equalled the recent bloodbath in terms of its scope and, as chilling, the speed with which events took shape.[24] The repercussions of these events spread through the African Great Lakes region in 1996 and 1997, in the form of massive refugee flows and the fall of the long-time president of Zaire, Mobutu Sese Seko, and an escalation in the subsequently established Democratic Republic of the Congo, where millions have died as a result of civil war as well.

PROFILE 9.5 — Ethnic Cleansing: A Question of Definition?

A term that gained much popularity during the war in the former Yugoslavia is *ethnic cleansing*. The term is often used freely without consideration of its meaning. Professor John McGarry has looked into this troubling question in considerable detail. In a paper presented to the Canadian Political Science Association, he writes, "The methods used in ethnic cleansing campaigns are both direct and indirect. Direct methods involve coercive physical expulsions where victim groups are forced onto various types of conveyance and transported or shipped into exile ... Direct expulsions may follow from a unilateral decision by the expelling authorities, as was the case in regions of Croatia and Bosnia in the early to mid-1990s, or they may result from bilateral 'exchange' agreements, where neighbouring states agree to swap their ethnic minorities for compatriots living in other countries. Such agreements were reached between Greece and Bulgaria and between Greece and Turkey just after the first world war, and between Hungary and Czechoslovakia just after the second world war.

"Indirect methods of ethnic cleansing are designed to induce emigration or flight ... Before they proceeded to direct physical expulsions after the Anschluss with Austria in 1938, Nazi authorities openly sought to induce emigration through an array of repressive legislation, particularly the Nuremberg laws of 1935. These laws were supplemented by pogroms such as that which occurred during Kristallnacht [9–10 November 1938: "The night of broken glass"] and they resulted in the migration of 150 000 of Germany's Jewish population ... Zionist settlers in early twentieth-century Palestine sought to induce the emigration of Palestinians by purchasing land from landlords and excluding Palestinian labour from it ... In the former Yugoslavia, a panoply of different tactics have been employed to induce flight, including the murder or expulsion of elites, mass-killings, psychological warfare, rape, artillery onslaughts on urban areas, use of snipers, commando raids, and destruction of the physical infrastructure on which urban life depends (electricity, heating plants, kiosks selling newspapers, TV and radio transmitters, communal bakeries).

"What this means is that ethnic cleansing can take place even if there are no formal authorised steps to expel minorities. Public officials ... have obvious reasons for refraining from direct methods when indirect ones will do ... Whether expulsions are direct or indirect, perpetrators often claim that the expelled left 'voluntarily' or that they fled fighting rather than being expelled ... On the other hand, minorities which oppose policies unacceptable to them may claim that these policies are designed to force them out, even if such a claim seems implausible. The extent to which these rival assertions are true is often difficult to discover ... Assiduous research, however, can go some way towards destroying myths and establishing what actually happened. There are also two major questions which can be asked to help ascertain if expulsion has taken place: Was there an 'expulsion discourse' in the dominant community before the minority's flight/expulsion? And are the refugees allowed to return home after the fighting has stopped?"

SOURCE: JOHN McGARRY, "ETHNIC CLEANSING: FORCED EXPULSION AS A METHOD OF ETHNIC CONFLICT REGULATION," PAPER PRESENTED TO THE ANNUAL MEETING OF THE CANADIAN POLITICAL SCIENCE ASSOCIATION, BROCK UNIVERSITY, ST. CATHARINES, ON, JUNE 2, 1996, 2–3, 42. REPRINTED BY PERMISSION OF THE AUTHOR. SEE ALSO A. BELL-FIALKOFF, "A BRIEF HISTORY OF ETHNIC CLEANSING," *FOREIGN AFFAIRS* 72 (1993), 110–21; AND A.M. DE ZAYAS, *A TERRIBLE REVENGE: THE ETHNIC CLEANSING OF THE EAST EUROPEAN GERMANS, 1944–1950* (NEW YORK: ST. MARTIN'S PRESS, 1994). REPRINTED WITH PERMISSION.

In 1993, the UN Security Council created the International Tribunal for the Prosecution of Persons Responsible for Serious Violations of International Humanitarian Law in the Territory of the Former Yugoslavia since 1991 (known as the ICTFY, or International Criminal Tribunal for the Former Yugoslavia), and in 1995 the Dayton Agreement called for the respective sides to the conflict to cooperate with the tribunal (this has been less than forthcoming, however). After the fall of Slobodan Milosevic's regime in 2000, he has himself been put on trial at The Hague, though health problems have considerably delayed this high-profile trial. In 1994, the

A place of death. A Christian figure stands between human skulls, August 2003 at the Ntarama church in Nyamata (south of Kigali) where up to 5000 people were killed during the 1994 Rwanda genocide, which claimed the lives of approximately 800 000 Tutsis and moderate Hutus. (AP Photo/Karel Prinsloo/CP Archive)

Security Council created the International Criminal Tribunal for Rwanda (ICTR). This tribunal operates in Arusha, Tanzania, though it has tried only a tiny fraction of those responsible for the genocide: the governmental elite. The others captured by the Rwandan Patriotic Front in 1994 have certainly suffered a worse fate, as some 80 000 were crammed into a prison system built for 13 000. Many of them were children at the time and are now fully grown men and still imprisoned awaiting trial in 2004 (though efforts to utilize a village justice system in its place, wherein prisoners can return home if their home communities elect to forgive them, show some remarkable progress at this stage). The objective of both of these tribunals is to bring the perpetrators of war crimes, crimes against humanity, and genocide to justice. The progress of the tribunals has been slowed by financial problems, the active opposition of those who fear exposure and retribution, and an inability to physically apprehend many of those charged. Nevertheless, the tribunals have been active and have secured convictions (see Profile 9.6). The international community, especially the United States, saw both tribunals as an effort to compensate for the relatively lacklustre response to the carnage that occurred in the Balkans and Rwanda. The establishment of a permanent International Criminal Court (discussed below) is related to the ICTFY and ICTR's efforts.

On a broader scale, one might argue that the term *genocide* can be used to describe the manifestations of structural violence as well.[25] Murder, including state murder, takes many forms: the deliberate starvation of entire communities and the use of food as a weapon in general; the lack of clean water supplies in the slums of major cities; the destruction of East Timor by the Indonesian military, or of Tibet by the Chinese, or of parts of Indochina by the Americans, or of political opponents of various Soviet regimes; or the drainage of marshes in southern Iraq. All these cases involve mass death inflicted with obvious intent. By such an expanded definition, war itself could be seen as an inherently genocidal project. Cultural destruction that has a physical component, commonly called *ethnocide*, is a type of genocide, the destruction of the indigenous peoples in the Americas after 1492 being a prime example; similarly, the construction of large-scale dams that displace millions of people, the Himalayan deforestation that has caused floods, and other forms of ecocide (see Chapter 10) could be termed genocidal when death results. Most lawyers and scholars reject this expanded conception of the term, with good reasons, but we shouldn't be immune to the large-scale death and destruction that results from conflict and change that has not been labelled genocide according to the 1948 Convention.

The advent of the nuclear age takes us further toward an alternative and expanded perspective on genocide. It can be argued that nuclear deterrence, based on the threat of mass annihilation, was based on the threat of implementing the ultimate genocidal policy. Of course, one might argue that the threat of nuclear war introduced a new concept to the lexicon, that of omnicide. However, since nuclear strategy was predicated on the destruction of a specific enemy, omnicide was not contemplated (though it did not take a considerably bright individual to predict it would result). It is this element of intention, or even incitement, that can lead to the labelling of the nuclear arms race as genocidal. If, as UN officials have insisted, we can consider the Rwandan slaughter an instance of genocide because, for example, a Hutu official had given a speech in 1992 in which he "explicitly called on Hutus to kill Tutsis and dump their bodies in the rivers,"[26] then what can we make of a system of national defence that called on thousands of soldiers to take part, if necessary, in the complete annihilation of hun-

PROFILE 9.6   The Canadian Global Human Rights Commissioner

Former UN war crimes Chief Prosecutor Louise Arbour holds a news conference in Pristina, Kosovo, in this 13 July 1999 photo. The UN General Assembly on February 25, 2004, approved the appointment of Louise Arbour as UN High Commissioner for Human Rights. (AP Photo/ Visar Kryeziu/CP Archive)

In 1992 the Security Council of the UN created a Commission of Experts to investigate and report on "the evidence of grave breaches of the Geneva Conventions and other violations of humanitarian law in the territory of the former Yugoslavia" (Res. 780, 1992). After the taking of an interim report, which clearly indicated that mass murder had taken place, the Security Council established an international tribunal for the prosecution of individuals responsible (UN Doc. S/Res/808, 1993). In March 1996 Canadian Justice Louise Arbour was appointed chief prosecutor for the International Criminal Tribunals for the former Yugoslavia and Rwanda. She was previously a member of the Court of Appeals for Ontario. The term of chief prosecutor runs four years and is renewable after that; Arbour left for the Supreme Court of Canada in September 1999 and was replaced by Carla Del Ponte of Switzerland. In early 2004, Arbour was appointed UN High Commissioner for Human Rights. This may well be her greatest challenge yet, since the international community remains fundamentally divided on many key human rights issues.

dreds of millions of civilians? Or does international, as opposed to civil, war justify such technique? While The Hague Convention[27] merely states that the "right of belligerents to adopt means of injuring the enemy is not unlimited," it is certainly difficult to argue that the use of hydrogen bombs would be limited in any real manner.[28]

FEMALE GENITAL MUTILATION

One of the more complex human rights issues involves the practice commonly called *female genital mutilation*, which is also often called *female castration, circumcision,* or *genital cutting.* It refers to the practice in many Islamic countries of removing or altering parts of the female genitalia at a certain age as a rite of passage. As you can tell, even the question of which name we assign to this practice is highly controversial, for each carries a strong connotation regarding the legitimacy of the act. Two forms of genital mutilation remain prevalent among certain segments of African women: *infibulation,* the severing of the clitoris and labia while the two sides of the vulva are sutured (tied together); and *clitoridectomy,* the partial or complete removal of the clitoris or the removal of both the clitoris and the labia minora. Either procedure comes under severe criticism from many quarters, while it is defended as a cultural priority in others. Several Western states, such as Canada and the United States, have made it illegal for doctors to perform the procedure. This law is not insignificant, since large numbers of recently arrived African women live in both states. No strong opposition to the practice exists at the international level, though UN agencies such as the World Health Organization generally oppose it.

The medical case against female genital mutilation is a very strong one: it can result in excessive bleeding, infection, and even death when improperly performed; and the after-effects include the risk of childbirth complications and of developing obstetric fistulae—holes between the vagina and the bladder, the rectum, or both. Beyond this, however, it represents to many women an act of oppression because it involves removing part or the entire clitoris and thus denies women a basic form of sexual pleasure.[29] Thus, the issue has become a rallying cry for the feminist movement in general. Other Islamic customs, such as *purdah,* have come under intense criticism by Western feminists in particular, but genital mutilation remains the most widely condemned. The international implications of this condemnation can be seen in Canadian refugee policy, which has periodically adopted the inclusion of women fleeing persecution based on discrimination against their sex as a valid reason to seek asylum. However, most women who undergo the procedure are quite young and are unable to leave their native countries on their own.

Howard French, in an article written for *The New York Times* that explores the issue within the context of the question of cultural relativity, writes about a small group of women in Sierra Leone who are working to ban the practice. One of the group's leaders argues that stopping the practice must be done in as culturally sensitive a manner as possible. For example, genital cutting was traditionally the culmination of a months-long retreat, known as *Bondo,* to mark the passage into womanhood, when older women would share their wisdom with the young. As the years passed, the retreat withered into an increasingly shorter ceremony and was finally represented almost solely by the cutting. Trying to restore the full value of *Bondo* might lead to a greater acceptance of the idea that the circumcision is part of a larger process and may eventually be discarded for hygienic reasons. For many, of course, this approach is far too timid. However, stronger appeals can lead to almost immediate condemnation by religious groups; for example, when a Freetown newspaper published a series of articles critical of the custom, "it became the target of a hostile protest movement by a group of women sworn to defend the rite."[30]

As an issue that forces us to examine the universal/relativist, as well as the gender-related discussions above, female genital mutilation, circumcision, or genital cutting will continue to outrage many communities. However, those who are campaigning to stop it are in a difficult bind: the harder they work, especially when they manage to publicly question or challenge the legitimacy of the practice, the more the protraditional forces will be inspired to resist change. Governments will have to seriously consider this matter when directing development assistance toward health programs abroad, and when determining their own operational definition of refugee status.

HEALTH AS A HUMAN RIGHT: HIV/AIDS

It is often argued that one of the most fundamental human rights is access to decent health care. This issue forces the divide between those willing to accept the need for societies to redistribute resources and those who reject this need. In the case of HIV/AIDS (see Chapter 11), questions of equal access to health care have come to represent severe human rights questions because many of the anti–retro virus drugs that can mitigate the effects of the disease are still not widely available, especially in sub-Sarahan Africa where millions suffer and hundreds die each day from AIDS, despite the relatively low death rates in the West, where such drugs are widely obtainable. Efforts to force pharmaceutical companies to dispense the drugs at cheaper cost met with resistance, but declarations by states such as Brazil and South Africa that they would proceed, despite international patent laws, with their own generic versions of the drugs, have gradually shifted Western perceptions on the matter.

Beyond this particular North–South dispute, there are other human rights issues associated with the spread of deadly disease. AIDS victims, in particular, are often subject to ostracization (this is doubly tragic for women who have acquired HIV/AIDS after being raped, which is not uncommon in Rwanda and elsewhere). Many of the fundamental human rights of people living with HIV/AIDS, such as the right to nondiscrimination, equal protection and equality before the law, privacy, liberty of movement, work, equal access to education, housing, health care, social security, assistance and welfare, are often violated based on their known or presumed HIV/AIDS status. It can also be argued that people living without access to decent health care and related education are more susceptible to acquire the disease in the first place; this would include those caught in the global sex industry, where worker protection is all too often the last of concerns. Other serious health concerns, such as malaria, malnutrition, amputation (common in areas, such as Angola and Cambodia, where landmines were used extensively during conflicts), and psychological problems, severely hamper the human development of millions—indeed, billions—of people today. Is the achievement of freedom from these problems to be seen as an essential human right, or a privilege obtainable by only a few?

TORTURE

The word *torture* is derived from the Latin word *torquere*, which means "to twist." As a means to ensure the compliance of the people to a ruler's wishes, torture is as old as governance itself. When we mention torture, we are referring essentially to acts committed by governments, though it is clear that nongovernmental forces in wars and even terrorist and resistance groups resort to it as well. Torture is an old and tested technique that can be employed to get people to confess to just about anything, whether or not they have committed the act in question. Historians write of the unspeakable brutality inflicted by Ivan the Terrible and the Spanish Inquisition burnings, both during the 1500s. Torture was an accepted form of public punishment during the early development of the European penal systems, and it was employed as a device to facilitate slavery and colonialism.

The 1789 French Declaration of the Rights of Man forbade torture "forever"; the U.S. Bill of Rights forbade "cruel and unusual punishment." As incarceration in prisons began to

PROFILE 9.7 Stephen Lewis, Tireless and Eloquent

Stephen Lewis, left, speaks at a press conference at the United Nations, 1 June 2001, after he was named the Special Envoy of the Secretary-General for HIV/AIDS in Africa. Deputy Secretary-General Louise Frechette, also a Canadian, looks on at right. (AP Photo/Stephen Chernin/CP Archive)

Canadian Stephen Lewis is currently the UN Secretary-General's Special Envoy for HIV/AIDS in Africa. Lewis previously served as Deputy Executive Director of the United Nations Children's Fund (UNICEF) from 1995 to 1999, former Canadian Ambassador to the United Nations, and leader of the New Democratic Party of Ontario. Five key objectives for the global anti-AIDS campaign include preventing the epidemic's further spread, reducing mother-to-child HIV transmission, providing care and treatment to all, delivering scientific breakthroughs, and protecting the vulnerable, especially orphans. Lewis has been a tireless campaigner, employing his well-known eloquence, and celebrities such as Oprah Winfrey and U2's Bono, to chide the Northern states to do more for Africa's 11 to 14 million AIDS orphans, and to provide affordable, life-saving drugs to the poor. *Maclean's* chose him as Canadian of the Year in 2003:

At the beginning of 2003, frustrated and disheartened by Western nations' willingness to ignore the crisis and commit "mass murder by compla-

cency" while they devoted billions to ousting Saddam Hussein, Lewis agonized over whether he could continue. But he decided to turn his despair and anger to advantage, and push all the harder. "I'm still at the end of my rope because I find myself not handling things well when I travel. I get too distraught, too quickly," says Lewis. "But what is my emotional disarray compared to the hell that is happening? I'm in a great rage now, as I understand how many lives we have lost. But I don't want to leave until I see the breakthrough" ...

At home, he has started the Stephen Lewis Foundation (www.stephenlewisfoundation.org), devoted to providing small-scale funding to communities dealing with the ravages of AIDS. In nine months, it has raised close to $900,000, mostly from individual donations. In Namibia, the money will pay for funerals and coffins; in Kenya, for home care for the dying; in Zambia for a prevention program. Lewis says he has been humbled and revitalized by the outpouring of support. "If our governments were one-tenth as generous as average Canadians, the problem would be solved," he says. "Truthfully, when I see what we can accomplish with money on the ground, it's the only time in my life I have wished I was Bill Gates."

replace torture as the chief means of punishing criminals (though many would equate imprisonment with torture as well), it became a less acceptable means of enforcing law and order. During World War II, however, torture came back into vogue—particularly as a device frequently employed by the Nazi Gestapo—and has remained so ever since. The Soviet state under Stalin was renowned for its ability to punish dissidents with psychological torture; but it would be difficult, if not impossible, to find a society where some form of state-sanctioned torture has not occurred at some time.

Torture continues to be employed as a means of extracting knowledge from political participants around the world. It involves the deliberate infliction of pain for this end, and torture is often administered by people who have been specially trained as torturers. This distinction is important. The act takes place as a means to something else, be it the suppression of popular dissent or the acquisition of information deemed important by government bureaucrats. Though some individuals involved in its application are no doubt sadistic themselves, they are merely employees in a larger project. This definition helps us distinguish torture in the political sense from that in the criminal sense. Obviously, however, the very definition of torture leaves a great deal open to interpretation. Though the international community has signed many agreements[31] that make the use of torture by governments against the convention of international law, the principle of nonintervention requires that states avoid interfering in the domestic affairs of other states.[32] During the Cold War, many dictatorial or military regimes practised torture, and this was largely ignored for the sake of maintaining alliances (both Western and Eastern). Several Latin American regimes, for example, most notably that of Pinochet in Chile in the 1970s, were infamous for their human rights abuses and torture techniques, and we should note the complicity of the superpowers themselves in many of these cases. In the post–Cold War era, when the old bloc system can no longer be used to justify the toleration of such excesses, some Western governments are moving toward making the receipt of donor assistance contingent on the pursuit of democratic institutions, which would (one might hope) by definition preclude torture. However, critics have pointed out that the "War on Terrorism" itself is employing torture in various forms, including the American incarceration of so-called unlawful combatants at Guantanamo Bay, and the well-publicized mistreatment of some of the prisoners in Iraq.

Nongovernmental organizations such as Amnesty International and Helsinki Watch monitor human rights abuses, including the practice of torture. Several medical institutions have also been established around the world to deal exclusively with helping victims recover from the physical and psychological damage sustained by torture experiences. The very issue of torture is embarrassing to governments that have been involved in its application. Surely we can achieve a universal condemnation here! If we live in a world where torture is accepted, then we are truly in a dark age. What is needed is the vigilant casting of light on such practices where they exist, a subject we will return to below when we discuss the special role played by NGOs in the human rights issue-area.

CHILD LABOUR

As mentioned earlier in this chapter, the international community has condemned slavery for some time, beginning with the major European powers at the Congress of Vienna in 1815. By 1880 more than 50 bilateral treaties on the subject were concluded. At the Brussels Conference in 1890, an antislavery act was signed and later ratified by 18 states. This act instituted a number of mutually agreed measures to suppress the slave trade both in Africa and on the high seas, including the right of high seas visits and searches, the confiscation of ships engaged in the trade, and the punishment of their masters and crew. Though slavery is still reported in some parts of the world, such as in the Sudan in Africa, it is generally considered to be outdated.

However, some would argue that the international community has done much less, and should do much more, to suppress another form of economic activity that many feel is the modern-day equivalent to slavery: the use of child labour. It is impossible to provide accurate estimates of the number of children working in the world because of disputes over what constitutes exploitative labour and because many countries refuse to participate in surveys. The

Malova, left, and her sister Bharti sit together on the road near Saundatti in Southern India on their way to be initiated as *devadasis*, young girls dedicated to a Hindu goddess. In modern times the religious trappings have all but disappeared, and the *devadasi* system has become a network for recruiting child prostitutes in India. (AP Photo/Sherwin Crasto/CP Archive)

United Nations Children's Fund (UNICEF) estimates that the number of children working in exploitative conditions in the world is in the hundreds of millions.[33]

In itself, child labour is nothing new; one might argue that it is only Western notions of adolescence that make the phenomenon recognizable. In other words, before we had anything resembling high school, teenagers simply worked in the fields and factories. It is, therefore, a Western notion of industrial progress that helps us see child labour as abhorrent. However, in some cases we might argue further that there is an absolute abhorrence involved, since it is not unusual to find children as young as six toiling away at repetitive and physically demanding jobs in Africa, Asia, and South America. Though it is unfair to generalize, the conditions of children at work around the world are often appalling. In Malaysia, children work up to 17-hour days on rubber plantations enduring insect and snakebites. In Tanzania and Kenya, they pick coffee, inhaling pesticides. In Portugal, children as young as 12 work on construction sites. In Morocco, they sew carpets for export. In the United States, children are exploited in sweatshops. Many children end up working to pay off their parents' debts, and their opportunities for education and an escape from the cycle of poverty are virtually nonexistent. Many young female workers (and some young male workers as well) must also often endure the additional burden of sexual abuse, including the sexually transmitted diseases associated with prostitution.

The products of child labour, many of which are in the textile industry and include clothing and rugs, often end up for sale in North America and Europe. In Bangladesh, textile and clothing exports to the United States have doubled since 1990. As a result of American pressure, some 30 000 children were removed from the country's textile industry between 1993 and 1995. However, one problem that Western governments will have an even harder time addressing is that many of these children do not end up in school (indeed, many of them are from regions where school is a luxury for the privileged few) but end up on the street, engaging in begging and prostitution to make a living. As an *Economist* editorial suggested, corporate codes of conduct regarding child labour may not end it at all, but "merely shift it to shadier areas of the economy that are far harder to police."[34]

Foreign investors are often criticized for exploiting local labour, which usually includes child labour. In response, Levi Strauss provides schooling for child workers in its suppliers' plants in Bangladesh. This raises yet another ethical dilemma, since one can argue the company is merely reinforcing dependence on it and reaping profits in the process. However, without this schooling, what type of future would the children have?

The question of child labour poses one of the harshest challenges to the concept of universal human rights and the Canadian government's use of the term *human security*. Although it may be possible for people in the West to look on child labour as an awful thing, that is because we can afford to. Generally, people in developing states do not force children to work

PROFILE 9.8 Canada and Child Labour

Prompted by child rights activists, Western governments are starting to speak loudly about the continued problem of child labour. Canada has joined this international chorus. In 1996, the Canadian government made a contribution of $700 000 to the ILO's International Program for the Elimination of Child Labour. In August 1996 in Stockholm, then–Minister of Foreign Affairs Lloyd Axworthy, Senator Landon Pearson, and the Honourable Hedy Fry attended the World Congress against the Commercial Sexual Exploitation of Children, along with 700 representatives from 119 countries, more than 100 participants from other international organizations, 500 NGOs and youth delegates, and 500 media representatives. On April 18, 1996, Bill C-27 was tabled, proposing amendments to the Criminal Code to allow for the prosecution of Canadian citizens and permanent residents who engage in commercial sexual activities with minors while abroad—a practice commonly known as "sex tourism."

SOURCE: LLOYD AXWORTHY, CANADIAN MINISTER OF FOREIGN AFFAIRS, ADDRESS BEFORE THE PARLIAMENTARY SUB-COMMITTEE ON SUSTAINABLE HUMAN DEVELOPMENT OF THE STANDING COMMITTEE ON FOREIGN AFFAIRS AND INTERNATIONAL TRADE, OTTAWA, 2 OCTOBER 1996.

because they derive pleasure from it (sadly, there are exceptions to this, both in the North and South); rather, they do so because they have to ensure the survival of a family. The economic conditions of the underprivileged seem to be worsening, not improving, as time moves on and markets become increasingly global (see Chapter 11). It is difficult to conceive of an end to child labour in light of this fact. Consider the remarks of a mother (a sweeper and latrine cleaner) from India:

> Nearly all our girls work as sweepers. Why should I waste my time and money on sending my daughter to school where she will learn nothing of use? … So why not put my girl to work so that she will learn something about our profession? My elder girl who is fifteen years old will be married soon. Her mother-in-law will put her to cleaning latrines somewhere. Too much schooling will only give girls big ideas, and then they will be beaten up by their husbands or abused by their in-laws.[35]

The split is pronounced between the North and South on the general issue of labour standards. The United States and some other Western countries have expressed a desire to use the World Trade Organization to fight child labour, unfair (i.e., too low) wages, "union-busting," and other practices that they argue may give other countries an unfair advantage in a world moving toward free trade. Southern politicians and economic representatives argue that this effort is really just old protectionism in new clothing. The International Labour Organization, a UN Special Agency, has for years tried to implement a universal code of conduct regarding conditions of employment, but it is up against opposition in the South and North. Consumers everywhere can investigate the origin of their products and refuse to purchase those made with child labour, but without simultaneous advances in poverty eradication it is of limited use.

SELF-DETERMINATION

To give a more rounded assessment of the concept of collective rights, we turn now to a discussion of the principle of self-determination. Self-determination can be defined variously as the right of all peoples to choose their own government or the right of all peoples to independence and sovereign statehood. As we will see, this issue-area presents all sorts of headaches for national leaders and cuts to the root of the problems inherent in maintaining a status quo international system while attempting to institutionalize ethics on a global scale.

In 1996, the Nobel Peace Prize was awarded to Bishop Carlos Belo and Jose Ramos Horta of East Timor. They had both worked to restore the right of self-determination to the people of East Timor, which has been occupied by Indonesia for more than two decades. This dedication shows how strong the ethic of self-determination remains today, even if it is still unrecognized in many parts of the world. Woodrow Wilson emphasized the right to self-determination in his famous "Fourteen Points" speech following World War I. It was, and still is in many parts of the world, seen as the principle that would guide the way out of colonial domination. States such as the United States were born of revolution and war; states such as Canada found their way gradually, eventually achieving the self-determination necessary to become recognized (in the Canadian case, in the League of Nations) as a sovereign state. More recently, the dissolution of the Soviet empire can be seen also as the achievement of self-determination by the peoples of the former U.S.S.R. and the former Warsaw Pact countries. Some of them, like the Czechs and Slovaks, decided to split even further. Others, such as the Chechens, have become military targets of Moscow instead. Recently, the East Timorese elected to establish full independence, finally ending years of brutal rule by Indonesia; after protracted and intense conflict, a UN-sponsored Australian peacekeeping team entered the country to try to maintain order despite the opposition of some elements of the Indonesian military (see Chapter 7), and the Timorese have finally obtained independence.

The concept of self-determination remains so difficult, however, because of the collective nature of the right. It begs the further question of just who has the right to self-determination (see Profile 9.9). In the Canadian case, two groups, First Nations peoples and Quebec separatists, argue that they should have the right to self-determination; some of them demand a sovereign state of their own. Even the seemingly monolithic United States has separatist movements emerging in idyllic Hawaii (see Profile 9.10), Puerto Rico, and Texas. The problem is much more acute in areas such as the former Yugoslavia, where pronouncements of sovereignty (and their recognition by the international community) have given rise to ethnic conflict and cleansing. One can argue that the right to self-determination, while acting as a vehicle toward freedom for colonized peoples in the past, invariably creates conflict within states.

PROFILE 9.9 A Voice for the Unheeded?

Arvol Looking Horse, a leader of the North Dakota Sioux community called Lakota Nation, is searching for a way to gain international recognition for his culture and religion. He is not alone. In Hawaii, Mililani Trask is seeking a forum where the voice of an Indigenous nation calling itself *Ka Lahui Hawai'i* can be heard. The Crimean Tatars, the Albanians in Greece, and the Ogoni of Nigeria knock fruitlessly on the doors of the United Nations and its agencies, perennially frustrated, asking for a hearing. "Even when the debate was specifically about their situations, there was no provision in the UN for these people to address the gathering," said Michael van Walt, who helped these groups—and others—come together in 1991 to create a forum for the unheard. He drew on his experience as a legal adviser to the Dalai Lama and to nationalist groups in the Baltic States before the collapse of the Soviet Union gave them back their independence. Ten years later, the Unrepresented Nations and Peoples Organisation (UNPO) has more than 50 members, from Abkhazia to Zanzibar; 4 supporting members that recently moved up to UN membership—Armenia, Estonia, Latvia, and Georgia; and 17 applicants. The organization supports only nonviolent campaigns and works to defuse tensions, not heighten them.

PROFILE 9.10 Hawaiian Sovereignty?

We usually think of Hawaii as only a popular and expensive tourist destination, but an independence movement there has gained strength over the years. Dozens of pro-sovereignty organizations have appeared, and in 1993 the state legislature passed several laws and resolutions acknowledging sovereignty as a long-term goal. An article in the *Boston Globe* explained the roots of the movement:

> In 1920, 20 years after the islands were annexed as a territory and 39 years before statehood, the U.S. Congress passed legislation to which many historians trace the situation today. The Hawaiian Home Act carved out 203 500 of the island's 4.1 million acres—including some of the least productive and poorly situated land—for use by natives. Most of the remaining land was held by private interests or placed under state control, while the U.S. military signed 99-year leases, at $1 each, for several large, strategically located parcels of land. The Indigenous people, known in their language as *kanaka maoli* and defined as those with at least 50 percent Hawaiian blood, have since experienced many of the same difficulties many native peoples face: lower income, higher-than-average alcoholism rates and health problems, and resentment over their "colonization." Their fight for independence continues in 2004, including campaigns by the Hawaii Nation to educate American tourists, who are often blissfully ignorant of the fact that Hawaii is in effect an occupied territory.

HUMAN RIGHTS AND THE SPECIAL ROLE OF NGOS

By now you are no doubt aware that one of the trickiest aspects of human rights work is that the perpetrators of crimes are so often the same people or institutions that are supposed to uphold and enforce them—in other words, the state itself. For this reason, many people argue that it is short-sighted to trust governments, and that nongovernmental organizations, without formal ties to governments, can do a better job of providing information about and evidence of human rights violations. For example, many NGOs have participated in the work of the War Crimes Commission of Experts in the former Yugoslavia, including Amnesty International, the International Committee of the Red Cross, Physicians for Human Rights, Médecins Sans Frontières, Helsinki Watch, the International League of Human Rights, the Union for Peace and Humanitarian Aid to Bosnia and Herzegovina, the International Criminal Police Association, the National Alliance of Women's Organizations, and the International Centre for Criminal Law Reform.[36]

The most prominent NGO involved in the human rights issue-area is Amnesty International, which was started in London in 1961 as a campaign by several lawyers and writers. Peter Berenson drew attention to the campaign with an article in London's *Observer Weekend Review*, in which he suggested that the revulsion we often feel regarding human rights violations could be put to good use: "If these feelings of disgust all over the world could be united into common action, something effective could be done."[37] Amnesty now has more than 1 million members, subscribers, and donors in more than 150 countries, and it seeks to publicize the plight of people who are held as political prisoners around the world. Other groups, such as Americas Watch, Asia Watch, and Africa Watch, monitor human rights adherence by governments, including their foreign policy activities. Church groups are often involved as well, especially in Latin America. The International Committee of the Red Cross is also a prominent player in the human rights issue-area.

PROFILE 9.11 A Human Rights Advocate: Aung San Suu Kyi

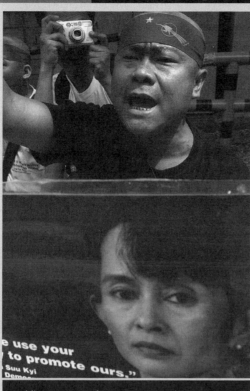

Holding a poster of Myanmar's pro-democracy leader Aung San Suu Kyi, a Myanmar worker shouts a slogan during a rally in front of Myanmar's embassy in Seoul, Korea, 3 June 2003. Dozens of protesters demanded the release of Suu Kyi, who was detained May 30. (AP Photo/ /Choe Young-soo, Yonhap/CP Archive)

Myanmar is a small Southeast Asian state, known as Burma before a military coup in 1988. Today the State Law and Order Restoration Council, or SLORC, is known as one of the most oppressive governments on earth, severely curtailing freedom of expression and movement and accused of using the forced labour of its citizens. It has actively suppressed opposition with military means. In this context, Aung San Suu Kyi, daughter of Aung San, the founder of the Anti-Fascist People's Freedom League, has arisen as the key representative of a democratic voice. She has also been consigned to house arrest and had her movements curtailed. However, she was the winner of the Nobel Peace Prize in 1991, and her status as an international figure has restrained the SLORC from more violent methods of limiting her influence. Aung San Suu Kyi's father was killed in 1947, after leading the struggle for Burmese independence, and she lived in India with her mother and attended Oxford University in England in the late 1960s and 1970s before returning to Burma for the last open multiparty elections there in 1990. Her party won the elections but the SLORC refused to recognize the results. She has never left Burma since and refuses to cease her condemnation of the regime. Sadly, her husband, Michael Aris, died of prostate cancer in London in March 1999, and she was unable to see him. He was denied entry to Burma, and she feared that if she were to go to him, she would not be allowed back in the country to resume her struggle. Thus are the hardships those committed to such demanding causes must endure. On-and-off "house arrests" have become routine events for this activist, and as late as 2004 there is uncertainty about her immediate fate.

NGOs use a wide variety of strategies[38] to call attention to their efforts. They campaign in local settings, exhort members to participate in letter-writing campaigns to pressure public officials to reverse certain decisions, and occasionally participate in protests that result in media coverage as well. Information technology, discussed at greater length in Chapter 12, offers newfound opportunities also. In Thailand, people have referred to the "cellular phone revolution" in which students protesting against the government were joined by relatively affluent Thais with modern phones and fax machines. Protestors used mobile phones to keep in touch after an army crackdown in 1992.[39] During and after the infamous Tiananmen Square massacre of 1989, the Chinese government made a concerted effort to control the flow of information in and out of China. Police monitored incoming faxes, but students were able to use electronic mail on the Internet for some time before authorities detected this and began shutting down computers as well. Indeed, a quick Internet search under the phrase "human rights" will produce a bewildering variety of NGO-sponsored websites and media reports.

The increased participation of women in international affairs is obvious, especially if one looks at the proliferation of women's groups active in the transnational context.[40] Though many feminists argue that women have yet to influence the real citadels of power in a meaningful way, the UN has always paid some attention to the gender question. In 1946, the 45-member Commission on the Status of Women was established to collect data on women's rights and make recommendations. It had an immediate impact as the Declaration of Human Rights was being drafted; the original text, borrowing ideas from the American Declaration of Independence, had begun, "All men are brothers …"; the Commission on the Status of Women objected to this sexist language and the draft was amended to read, "All human beings are created free and equal in dignity and rights."[41] It was Eleanor Roosevelt, widow of American President Franklin Roosevelt, who played a key role in the writing and passing of the Declaration itself.

In the 1970s ECOSOC (the UN's Economic and Social Council) created the International Research and Training Institute for the Advancement of Women (INSTRAW). As well, the UN Development Fund for Women (UNIFEM), part of the UN Development Programme, was established in 1976 to provide direct support to women's projects. In 1979 the General Assembly passed the Convention on the Elimination of All Forms of Discrimination against Women (CEDAW), and 23 experts were appointed to oversee that convention's implementation. In 1985, the UN Division for the Advancement of Women was set up following the important outcome of a conference in Nairobi, Kenya, a document called *The Forward Looking Strategies for the Advancement of Women to the Year 2000*. The UN Fourth World Conference on Women was held in Beijing in September 1995. The UN has an active Commission on the Status of Women, a 45-member intergovernmental body that meets annually in New York and prepares reports for ECOSOC. On March 8, 1993, International Women's Day, the Commission on Human Rights adopted by consensus a resolution aimed at integrating the rights of women into UN human rights mechanisms; in December of that year, the UN adopted a Declaration on the Elimination of Violence against Women.

It is obvious that NGOs, including women's groups, will continue to develop their role in the human rights issue-area. They form part of an expanding and increasingly influential network. However, it is unrealistic to assume that such organizations can battle the very real power of states that continue to grossly violate their citizens' rights; that takes concerted international efforts as well as change from within. The fall of apartheid in South Africa is a brilliant example of how that combination can succeed, but the continuation of poverty and violence there is indicative of the long road ahead.

THE QUESTION OF JUSTICE

Many of the issue-areas discussed above lend themselves to a discussion of preventive measures. Although it may be impossible to avoid child labour without eradicating poverty or to stop genital female mutilation without a radical change in cultural perspective, it can be argued that crimes against humanity, such as genocide and torture, can be avoided by pursuing what domestic legal experts and judges call the power of deterrence. In other words, if state and military leaders have reason to fear retribution, be it through domestic or international means, they may refrain from excessive atrocities. This was the initial idea behind the Nuremberg war crimes trials, discussed above, and it is one of the main justifications for the two international criminal courts described above, as well as the new International Criminal Court.

Both of the extant courts have received mixed reviews. The International Criminal Tribunal for the Former Yugoslavia has more than 1000 staff members from more than 75 countries, and an annual budget of more than U.S.$90 million. It has indicted 94 individuals for various war crimes, including grave breaches of the 1949 Geneva Conventions, violations of the laws or customs of war, genocide, crimes against humanity, and sexual offences. Several individuals have been found guilty, but of course they have the right to appeal and have done so. Similarly, the International Criminal Tribunal for Rwanda has become a fairly major operation; more than 40 Rwandans have been arrested to stand trial, including the former prime minister as well as all senior military leaders and high-ranking government officials, several of whom have been convicted for genocide and crimes against humanity. While fairly widespread support for both courts exists, they face many problems regarding acquisition of both the indicted and evidence; they are often viewed as partial courts, where guilty verdicts are inevitable (and thus they are equated with Nuremberg, largely viewed as a "victor's court"). Maintaining adequate funding is an ongoing concern as well; these are but temporary institutions (though proceedings will no doubt drag on well into the latter half of this decade). The need for a more permanent tribunal was central to many NGO and state demands in the mid-1990s.

States and NGOs met in Rome in 1998 to hammer out a treaty to establish an International Criminal Court (ICC), based partly on the ICTY and ICTR experience but also as an effort to deter future acts of state genocide and torture. The resulting Rome Statute was ratified on July 1, 2002, when the required 60 **ratifications** were obtained. Canada ratified the Rome Statute in July 2000, but several key states, including Russia and China, refused to sign. The United States initially refused to sign, did so in December 2000, and rescinded its participation on May 6, 2003. The ICC will focus only on the most egregious crimes, such as genocide, crimes against humanity, war crimes, and aggression (when an agreeable definition of the term is found).[42] Many disputes influenced the adoption of the statute: the permanent members of the Security Council insisted that the Council had ultimate control over the Court, while others wanted a strongly independent chief prosecutor's office. During negotiations, the Americans expressed three main reservations, which determined their decision not to ratify. First, the United States feared the ICC would be an untamed animal, with unchecked prosecutorial power, despite the statute's built-in principle of complementarity (ensuring that the ICC is the court of last resort). Second, the United States feared that the ICC's pledge to be apolitical would undermine the influence and integrity of the Security Council. Finally, the United States claimed that the ICC threatens American sovereignty. Thus, the United States tried to persuade states to enter impunity agreements that would prevent

Newly elected International Criminal Court President Philippe Kirsch of Canada addresses the Court flanked by the Court's vice presidents—Akua Kuenyehia of Ghana, left, and Elizabeth Odio Benito of Costa Rica—during the inaugural session of the International Criminal Court in The Hague, 11 March 2003. The Court will have jurisdiction to punish war crimes, including genocide, in any country that has ratified the statute, if that country has refused to prosecute suspects itself. Nonparty states can ask the Court to intervene, as can the UN Security Council. (AP Photo/Dusan Vranic/CP Archive)

A premature celebration. Relatives of dissidents who disappeared after being arrested under the former dictatorship of General Augusto Pinochet hold portraits of their loved ones as they celebrate outside the Supreme Court building in Santiago, Chile, 8 August 2000. The Supreme Court stripped Pinochet's immunity, clearing the way for the former dictator to be tried on human rights charges. However, his continued "health problems" have kept the legal system from conducting the trial. (AP Photo/Eduardo Di Baia/CP Archive)

U.S. nationals accused of genocide, crimes against humanity, or war crimes from being surrendered to the ICC. Prior to ratification, Rome Statute proponents argued that such a court (though it is restrained by prospective power) is long overdue.

The claim that the ICTY and ICTR are inherently unfair suggests that a greater level of impartiality is needed for a truly international criminal court, one that can try cases regardless of location. The ICC takes us beyond the capabilities of the ICJ, which can deal only with states and not individuals. In a significant step, the statute does recognize sexual offences as crimes against humanity, including forced pregnancy and sexual slavery. But until the other three permanent members of the Security Council sign on, the court will have limited impact on the ground; and, one might argue, it does little to overcome the concern that there are two sets of international law, one for the powerful and another for the rest. (Although France and the United Kingdom have signed on, they retain what is in effect a veto over the ICC's powers of prosecution action via their Security Council positions.)

Another means to achieve justice is unilateral action, and the case of General Augusto Pinochet of Chile provides a promising, but cautionary, tale. Pinochet assumed control of Chile in a brutal coup in 1973 (the former leader, socialist Salvador Allende, was killed; thousands of opponents were jailed and tortured, many of them disappearing altogether during Pinochet's lengthy rule). Chileans rejected his bid to be installed as president-for-life in 1988, but for the plebiscite on this to take place, an agreement was reached that he would be retained as head of the army and that criminal charges would not be laid against members of his regime. While in London for back surgery in October 1998 he was arrested by British authorities, who planned to extradite him to Spain. The Spanish wanted to charge him with various crimes (in the end these were reduced to the charge of torture) against Spanish nationals during his reign. The international community was quite divided over this issue since it is highly irregular to detain a former head of state who can claim diplomatic immunity. Eventually, British authorities (the Home Secretary), concerned with Pinochet's failing health, decided he had the right to return to Chile, where he may face charges brought on by his own country. However, his health seems to fail whenever such a prospect looms.

At any rate, this was an interesting development because it involved a former head of state. Other developments suggest such people will not be immune from prosecution in the future, with or without an ICC. A judicial investigation has been initiated in Senegal, at the request of a coalition of human rights groups, against the former President of Chad, Hissein Habré, for alleged crimes under international law, including torture, committed during his 1982 to 1990 rule. And Slobodan Milosevic, former president of the Federal Republic of Yugoslavia, is under an international indictment for crimes committed in the former Yugoslavia. However, it could be a chaotic situation if every head of state is brought to justice for crimes committed during his or her rule; few would be exempt, depending on one's definition of crimes. The dif-

Seeking truth and opening wounds. Of the Truth and Reconciliation process, Chair of the TRC Anglican Archbishop Desmond Tutu wrote in the final report that people "risked opening wounds that were perhaps in the process of healing." (AP Photo/Sasa Kralj/CP Archive)

ficult task of moving on—in Chile's case, difficult indeed, as thousands of relatives and friends of present-day Chileans suffered under Pinochet's iron-fisted rule, or in the case of Cambodia, where over 1 million citizens were murdered by the infamous **Khmer Rouge** in the late 1970s—remains.

Another path suggests that South Africa's Truth and Reconciliation Commission (TRC)[43] is a superior way to mend the pain of the past while bringing the negative into the open. This is a hard sell in many places, however, and it is dependent on the willingness of both past oppressors and victims (who may prefer to try to forget and move on) to expose themselves to the community at large, as well as the questionable process of granting amnesty to those who partici-pate. The Commission includes three committees. The Human Rights Violations Committee investigated human rights abuses that took place between 1960 and 1994, established the identity of and located the victims, and referred them to the Reparation and Rehabilitation Committee. A President's Fund, funded by Parliament and private contributions, was established to pay urgent interim reparation to victims in terms of the regulations prescribed by President Nelson Mandela. Finally, and most controversially, the Amnesty Committee considered applications for amnesty from those accused of human rights violations. Applicants could apply for amnesty for any act, omission, or offence associated with a political objective committed between March 1, 1960, and December 6, 1993 (the cutoff date was later extended to May 11, 1994). Archbishop Desmond Tutu chaired the Commission, lending his considerable moral weight to the proceedings. Between early 1996 and mid-1998, the commission heard more than 20 000 people give evidence, including members of the ruling ANC party who had resorted to violence during the struggle against apartheid.

This process was, no doubt, constructive for many. Although one might have a hard time equating appeals for amnesty with repentance, and most of the major administrators of apartheid never appeared before the commission (they do not believe they did anything wrong), it was a progressive step to air old animosities and, importantly, cases in which blacks had engaged in abuse were given equal footing. Even Mandela's own party, the ANC (African National Congress), tried to block the final Report's publication in 1998, concerned about allegations of ANC atrocities committed outside South Africa. At the same time, such a public step could unleash a swell of demands for compensation the state cannot possibly provide, and it might inflame an already volatile country. It was certainly a risk, though in South Africa's case it appears to have been worth it. Whether this could be a means used elsewhere, however, is uncertain. For example, it will be difficult for Indonesia to come to terms with the legacy of the Suharto dictatorship, even if his family is forced to pay back some of the hundreds of millions of dollars he effectively stole from the country, since the old political machinery is still largely in place in Indonesia. Cambodia's promise to hold a similar truth committee has been criticized as too little, too late by many; and the projected trial of Saddam Hussein in Iraq, should it even occur, will undoubtedly be rejected as "victor's justice" by many in the Arab world—as Milosevic's trial at The Hague is seen by many Serbians.

The call for justice and reconciliation will continue to ring out as long as gross human rights violations take place. Students of international relations will remain interested in how the international system responds to human rights violations, and how, in turn, these responses will shape the international human rights context.

CONCLUSIONS

The end of the Cold War has shaken the East–West foundation of the human rights discourse. Although the split between two competing conceptions of human rights (those that protect the individual and those that seek to protect the collective) remains a strong one, governments no longer have the Cold War to blame for ignoring gross human rights violations. One might argue that the current debate centres on the legitimacy of a universal approach that seeks common ethical themes we can apply across the globe against a relativist conception of rights that argues each state has its own right to make its own domestic laws and apply them as each deems necessary. As we have seen, human rights as an issue-area covers a diverse range of topics, but they all point toward the difficulty of applying any sort of universal barometer of human well-being at the global level.

We also examined the important role played by NGOs and women in the evolution of an international human rights regime. While NGOs are still relatively powerless compared with the states they seek to monitor, they can publicize cases that may otherwise remain hidden from the international community. Likewise, while the feminist movement has not altered the fundamental discrepancy in power between men and women, women have made considerable progress in popularizing their causes in international forums such as the United Nations. What remains to be seen, however, is whether this progress can be sustained as the economic forces of globalization take precedence in government thinking. We discussed the two opposing policy responses to countries that clearly violate human rights. Though little concrete evidence exists that such states can be forced to change their ways in the short run, the experience of South Africa suggests a sustained drive by the international community—in this case, a sustained rejection of the legitimacy of the policy of apartheid—can make a difference.

We looked also at various efforts to affect postatrocity justice, including international criminal tribunals and courts, unilateral prosecution, and truth and reconciliation commissions. We should note also, however, that many analysts and activists argue that real justice must involve economic factors as well: that the world is still divided between the very affluent, the middle class, and the very poor, and that the international system encourages rather than presents an obstacle to this trend. Further, human rights are of little benefit without a survivable environment in which to enjoy them. We turn to the theme of environmental security in global politics in the next chapter, the beginning of the third, and final, section of this text.

Endnotes

1. *War and Change in World Politics* (Cambridge, UK: Cambridge University Press, 1981), 224.
2. For J.P. Humphrey's obituary, see *The Globe and Mail,* 16 March 1995, A20. Interestingly, Humphrey was not originally credited with writing the Declaration: "French human-rights activist Rene Cassin, who claimed authorship of the declaration, was honoured with a Nobel Peace Prize in 1968. Yet when researchers pored over Prof. Humphrey's papers at the McGill library [in Montreal], they discovered the original copy in his handwriting."
3. H. French, "Africa's Culture War: Old Customs, New Values," *The New York Times,* 2 February 1997, E1.
4. E. Nadelmann, "Global Prohibition Regimes: The Evolution of Norms in International Society," *International Organization* 44, no. 4 (1990), 481–526.
5. Note, however, that it can be argued that racist conceptions of universal morality delayed the spread of a universalized conception of human rights. Asbjorn Eide reminds us that "there was a long debate in Spanish

theological and philosophical discourse on whether the Indians had a soul. This was also the period in which the theories of racism were gaining ground in Europe. From the simplest efforts at classification of human groups by Kant, Linneaus, and Buffon, to full-fledged racist ideologies like that of Gobineau (mid-1850s), these were obstacles to the evolution of universal human rights, as distinct from the Western 'natural rights' which for a long time was limited to the male Caucasian." See "Linking Human Rights and Development: Aspects of the Norwegian Debate," in I. Brecher, ed., *Human Rights, Development and Foreign Policy: Canadian Perspectives* (Halifax: Institute for Research on Public Policy, 1988), 5–30, 27n6.

6. R.J. Vincent, *Human Rights and International Relations* (Cambridge, UK: Cambridge University Press, 1986).

7. See K. Tomasevski, ed., *The Right to Food: Guide through Applicable International Law* (Dordrecht: Martinus Nijhoff, 1987).

8. *Rethinking International Relations* (Vancouver: UBC Press, 1994), 167.

9. See R. Niebuhr, *Moral Man and Immoral Society* (New York: Scribner's, 1947); and T. Nardin, *Law, Morality, and the Relations of States* (Princeton: Princeton University Press, 1983).

10. Thus the title of Stanley Hoffmann's important book, *Duties Beyond Borders* (Syracuse: Syracuse University Press, 1981).

11. Sidney Bailey and Sam Daws, *The United Nations: A Concise Political Guide*, 3rd ed. (London: Macmillan, 1995), 87.

12. *Human Rights Watch World Report 1997* (New York: Human Rights Watch, 1996), xxi.

13. Ibid., xiii.

14. Ibid., xxvi.

15. World Conference on Human Rights, *Vienna Declaration and Programme of Action*, Part I, Para. 4.

16. Stephen P. Marks, "Social and Humanitarian Issues," in *A Global Agenda: Issues before the 51st General Assembly of the United Nations* (Lanham, MD: Rowman and Littlefield, 1996), 173.

17. For an important early treatment of this subject, see Q. Wright, "The Outlawry of War and the Law of War," *American Journal of International Law* 47 (1953), 365–76.

18. Michael Walzer, *Just and Unjust Wars*, 2nd ed. (New York: Basic Books, 1992).

19. See United Methodist Council of Bishops, *In Defense of Creation: The Nuclear Crisis and a Just Peace* (Nashville, TN: Graded Press, 1986).

20. Article II of the Genocide Convention defines genocide as "any of the following acts committed with intent to destroy, in whole or in part, a national, ethnical, racial, or religious group, such as (a) Killing members of the group; (b) Causing serious bodily or mental harm to members of the group; (c) Deliberately inflicting on the group conditions of life calculated to bring about its physical destruction in whole or in part; (d) Imposing measures intended to prevent births within the group; (e) Forcibly transferring children of the group to another group." The last two are clearly related to the policies employed by the Nazi regime regarding forced sterilization and a program to transfer Aryan-looking children into Aryan families.

21. See his landmark *Axis Rule in Occupied Europe* (Washington, DC: Carnegie Endowment, 1944), 79.

22. R. Hilberg, *The Destruction of the European Jews* (New York: Holmes and Meier, 1983); see also H. Fein, *Accounting for Genocide: National Response and Jewish Victimization during the Holocaust* (New York: Free Press, 1979).

23. A United Nations report by three African jurists concluded that the killings were part of a larger plan aimed at exterminating the Tutsis; they also noted that "some reliable estimates put the number of victims at close to one million, but the world is unlikely ever to know the exact figure." *The Globe and Mail,* 3 December 1994, A13. Most experts accept 800 000 as the most likely figure now.

24. See, for example, A. Destexhe, "The Third Genocide," *Foreign Policy* 97 (Winter, 1994–95), 3–17; and A. Des Forges, *Leave None to Tell the Story: Genocide in Rwanda* (New York: Human Rights Watch, 1999). The entire Congo region (formerly known as Zaire) has erupted into violent conflict in the years following the 1994 genocide, and the neighbouring state of Burundi has an equally distressing political past and may be on the verge of similar chaos.

25. See P.J. Stoett, "This Age of Genocide: Conceptual and Institutional Implications," *International Journal* 50, no. 3 (1995), 594–618.

26. *The Globe and Mail,* 3 December 1994, A13.

27. Article 22 of the regulations annexed to The Hague Convention of 1907.

28. To quote two international legal experts: "In light of the multifarious effects of hydrogen-bombs, and particularly the area of devastation from 'fall-out' with its unpredictable genetic effects, it could not be said

that a belligerent in resorting to thermo-nuclear weapons was adopting a means of injuring the enemy which was 'limited' in any sense of the word." N. Singh and E. McWhinney, *Nuclear Weapons and Contemporary International Law*, 2nd ed. (Dordrecht: Martinus Nijhoff, 1989), 115–16.

29. See A. Walker and P. Parmar, *Warrior Marks: Female Genital Mutilation and the Sexual Blinding of Women* (New York: Harcourt Brace, 1993).

30. French, "Africa's Culture War."

31. The most important of which are the Universal Declaration of Human Rights and the Convention against Torture and Other Cruel, Inhuman or Degrading Treatment or Punishment.

32. Note also that if torture takes place during war, it is considered a crime against humanity.

33. United Nations Children's Fund, *The State of the World's Children 1997* (Oxford: Oxford University Press, 1997), 26.

34. "Child Labour: Consciences and Consequences," reprinted in *The Globe and Mail*, 5 June 1995, A17.

35. Neera Burra, *Born to Work: Child Labour in India* (Delhi: Oxford University Press, 1995), 211.

36. As well, four Canadians participated in a team of 11 women lawyers, sponsored by the Dutch government, who went to the former Yugoslavia to interview victims of sexual assault and collect evidence for the related military tribunals. See also B. Allen, *Rape Warfare: The Hidden Genocide in Bosnia-Herzegovina and Croatia* (Minneapolis: University of Minnesota Press, 1996).

37. P. Berenson, "The Forgotten Prisoners," *Observer Weekend Review*, 28 May 1961, 21.

38. See, for example, V.P. Nanda, J. Scarritt, and G. Shepherd, eds., *Global Human Rights: Public Policies, Comparative Measures, and NGO Strategies* (Boulder, CO: Westview, 1981).

39. See P. Shenon, "Mobile Phones Primed, Affluent Thais Join Fray," *The New York Times*, 20 May 1992, A10.

40. See S. Shreir, ed., *Women's Movements of the World: An International Directory and Reference Guide* (Essex: Longman, 1988).

41. Bailey and Daws, 90.

42. For text of the treaty, see the UN website at http://www.un.org/law/icc. As of July 17, 2000, the following states had ratified: Belgium, Belize, Canada, Fiji, France, Ghana, Iceland, Italy, Norway, San Marino, Senegal, Tajikistan, Trinidad and Tobago, and Venezuela. For slightly outdated but comprehensive treatments of the state of international criminal law, see S. Ratner and J. Abrams, *Accountability for Human Rights Atrocities in International Law: Beyond the Nuremburg Legacy*, 2nd ed. (Oxford: Oxford University Press, 2001); and A. Cassese, *International Criminal Law* (Oxford: Oxford University Press, 2003).

43. The commission has its own website: http://doj.gov.za/trc/index.html

Suggested Readings

Andrews, J. *International Protection of Human Rights*. New York: Facts on File, 1987.

Arendt, H. *Eichmann in Jerusalem: A Report of the Banality of Evil*. New York: Viking, 1963.

Bauer, J., and D. Bell, eds. *The East Asian Challenge for Human Rights*. Cambridge, UK: Cambridge University Press, 1999.

Beigbeder, Y. *Judging War Criminals: The Politics of International Justice*. New York: St. Martin's Press, 1999.

Brecher, I., ed. *Human Rights, Development and Foreign Policy: Canadian Perspectives*. Halifax: Institute for Research on Public Policy, 1989.

Cassese, A. *International Criminal Law*. Oxford: Oxford University Press, 2003.

Charlesworth, H., C. Chinkin, and S. Wright. "Feminist Approaches to International Law." *American Journal of International Law* 85 (October–November, 1991), 613–45.

Donnelly, J., and R. Howard, eds. *International Handbook of Human Rights*. New York: Greenwood, 1987.

Falk, R., S. Kim, and S. Mendlovitz, eds. *The United Nations and a Just World Order*. Boulder, CO: Westview, 1991.

Forsythe, D. *The Internationalization of Human Rights*. Lexington, MA: D.C. Heath, 1991.

Gutman, R., and D. Rieff, eds. *Crimes of War: What the Public Should Know.* New York: Norton, 1999.

Hannum, H. *Autonomy, Sovereignty, and Self-Determination: The Accommodation of Conflicting Rights.* Philadelphia: University of Pennsylvania Press, 1990.

Horowitz, I. *Genocide: State Power and Mass Murder.* New Brunswick, NJ: Transaction Books, 1976.

Howard, R., and J. Donnelly. "Human Dignity, Human Rights, and Political Regimes." *American Political Science Review* 80, no. 3 (1986), 801–18.

James, A. *Sovereign Statehood: The Basis of International Society.* London: Allen and Unwin, 1986.

Johnson, J.T. *Can Modern War Be Just?* New Haven: Yale University Press, 1984.

Kratochwil, F. *Rules, Norms, and Decisions: On the Conditions of Practical and Legal Reasoning in International Relations and Domestic Affairs.* New York: Cambridge University Press, 1989.

Kuper, L. *Genocide.* New Haven: Yale University Press, 1981.

Lemkin, R. *Axis Rule in Occupied Europe.* Washington, DC: Carnegie Endowment, 1944.

Margolian, H. *Conduct Unbecoming: The Story of the Murder of Canadian Prisoners of War in Normandy.* Toronto: University of Toronto Press, 1998.

Matas, D. "Prosecution in Canada for Crimes against Humanity." *New York Law School Journal of International and Comparative Law* 11 (1991), 347–55.

Matthews, R.O., and C. Pratt. *Human Rights in Canadian Foreign Policy.* Montreal/Kingston: McGill-Queen's University Press, 1988.

McCormick, J., and N. Mitchell. "Human Rights and Foreign Assistance: An Update." *Social Science Quarterly* 70 (1989), 969–79.

Meron, T. "The Case for War Crimes Trials in Yugoslavia." *Foreign Affairs* 72, no. 3 (1993), 122–35.

Nowak, Manfred. *Introduction to the International Human Rights Regime.* Herndon, VA: Brill Academic Publishers Martinus Nijhoff, 2003.

Orend, B. *Human Rights: Concept and Context.* Toronto: Broadview Press, 2002.

Ratner, S., and J. Abrams. *Accountability for Human Rights Atrocities in International Law: Beyond the Nuremburg Legacy.* Oxford: Oxford University Press, 1997.

Robertson, A. *Human Rights in the World: An Introduction to the International Protection of Human Rights.* New York: St. Martin's Press, 1982.

Robertson, D. *A Dictionary of Human Rights*, 2nd ed. London: Europa, 2003.

Rosas, A. "State Sovereignty and Human Rights: Toward a Global Constitutional Project." *Political Studies* 43 (1995), 61–78.

Rotberg, R., and D. Thompson, *Truth versus Justice: The Morality of Truth Commissions* (Princeton: Princeton University Press, 2000).

Schabas, W. *Genocide in International Law: The Crimes of Crimes.* Cambridge, UK: Cambridge University Press, 2000.

Schmitz, G., and V. Berry. *Human Rights: Canadian Policy toward Developing Countries.* Ottawa: North-South Institute, 1988.

Scott, C. "Indigenous Self-Determination and Decolonization of the International Imagination: A Plea." *Human Rights Quarterly* 18, no. 4 (1996).

Sheperd, O.W., and V.P. Nanda, eds. *Human Rights and Third World Development.* Westport: Greenwood, 1985.

Shue, H. *Basic Rights: Subsistence, Affluence, and U.S. Foreign Policy.* Princeton: Princeton University Press, 1980.

Steiner, H., and P. Alston. *International Human Rights in Context: Law, Politics, Morals.* Oxford: Oxford University Press, 1996.

Sullivan, M. *Measuring Global Values.* New York: Greenwood, 1991.

Tomasevski, K. *Development Aid and Human Rights.* London: Printer, 1988.

United States Department of State. *Country Reports on Human Rights Practices.* Washington, DC: various years.

Van den Berghe, P., ed. *State Violence and Ethnicity.* Niwot, CO: The University Press of Colorado, 1990.

Weiss, T., and L. Minear. "Do International Ethics Matter?: Humanitarian Politics and the Sudan." *Ethics and International Affairs* 5 (1991), 197–214.

Woodiwiss, Anthony. *Making Human Rights Work Globally.* London and Portland, OR; Glasshouse, 2003.

Zappala, S. *Human Rights in International Criminal Proceedings.* Oxford: Oxford University Press, 2003.

Suggested Websites

Amnesty International
  http://www.amnesty.org

The Carter Center
  http://www.cartercenter.org

Child Sex Tourism Fact Sheet
  http://www.voyage.gc.ca/main/pubs/child_fact-en.asp

Hawaii Nation
  http://www.hawaii-nation.org

Human Rights Internet
  http://www.hri.ca/index.aspx

Human Rights Watch
  http://www.hrw.org

Human Rights Web
  http://www.hrweb.org

International Centre for Human Rights and Democratic Development
  http://www.ichrdd.ca/splash.html

Montreal Institute for Genocide and Human Rights Studies (MIGS)
  http://migs.concordia.ca

Notre Dame Law School
  http://www.nd.edu/~ndlaw

Research Guide to Human Rights
  http://www2.spfo.unibo.it/spolfo/HRLAW.htm

Senator Landon Pearson's Website
  http://www.sen.parl.gc.ca/lpearson

Women, Law, and Development International
  http://www.wld.org

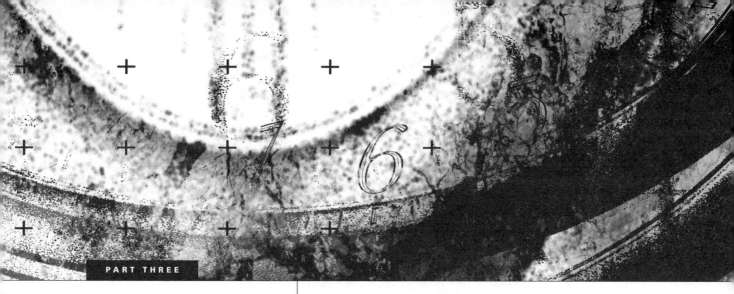

PART THREE

Directions

In this final section, we will look forward. All the themes discussed here are familiar ones, including environmental degradation and conflict, population growth, migration and dislocation, the impact of technology on global politics, and future directions in theoretical thinking and various issue-areas. However, in this section we explore what the future may hold for these themes and elaborate on the scholarly and policy challenges they pose in the 21st century. Although the prognostications can at times be bleak, the fact that the human race has survived so far offers some comfort; and, as we discussed in preceding chapters, the chances of cooperation and positive movement are always as high as conflict and despair. However, as usual, sharply contrasting perspectives exist on just what progress in global politics entails, and what directions we will (or should) take.

CHAPTER 10

Global Ecopolitics: Learning the Limits

The whole point of being a doomsayer is to agitate the world into proving you wrong or into doing something about it if you are right.

—Les Kaufman[1]

It is time to understand "the environment" for what it is: the national security issue of the twenty-first century.

—Morton Kaplan[2]

INTRODUCTION: CAN WE SUSTAIN OURSELVES?

The earth has endured centuries of human population growth, agricultural development, resource extraction, landscape-ravaging wars, and industrial pollution. Now, we often find ourselves asking whether it can continue to do so without irreversibly harmful ecological consequences. As we watch the polar ice caps melt at unusually fast rates, the Amazon jungle continue to burn, and the oceans emptied of fish by industrial harvesting, we must begin to wonder if we can manage, despite all the divisions and conflicts between states and peoples that have plagued global politics, to cooperate to prevent the great biospheric collapse feared by many environmentalists. Or have we moved into this millennium under such a dark ecological shadow that there is no way toward sunlight? The concern is immediate. The most common cause of species extinction is not hunting, poaching, or the direct consumption of toxic chemicals. Species extinction is caused primarily by the destruction of habitat. Viewed from a distance, one might conclude that human society has been committing collective suicide over the past century with an unrelenting assault on its own habitat, the **biosphere**. Though some believe in the almost unlimited nature of the earth's resources and the innate ability of humankind to adapt, many see the current situation as reflective of human folly and greed. The symptoms of the environmental stresses placed on the earth range from the global, such as the depletion of the ozone layer and global warming, to the local, such as the erosion of soil that has been overworked in small African communities and the collapse of the cod fishery off Newfoundland.

Every region on earth faces environmental problems. Though Western environmentalists have long been lamenting the effects of industrial excess in North America, Europe, and Japan, it has become quite clear that environmental problems in Eastern Europe and the former Soviet Union are approaching catastrophic levels. This fact is reflected by the serious health threats faced by citizens of the industrialized former Soviet bloc, a legacy of centralized economic industrialization.[3] Forced industrialization in Eastern Europe and the former Soviet Union took place at the expense of that region's environment. The implications of this pollution are local and international. Poor waste-disposal practices and industrial emissions are causing human health problems across Russia, Ukraine, and Kazakhstan. Carbon emissions from outdated energy plants and automobile engines contribute to both global warming and regional deforestation in Western Europe. Another immediate danger is the decrepit state of outdated nuclear reactors in Eastern Europe. With the Chernobyl disaster still in recent memory, it is obvious that greater technical assistance is needed if further catastrophe is to be avoided. This assistance will come mainly from a frightened Western Europe.

But the problems facing Eastern Europe and the former Soviet Union are only one example of the magnitude of the looming environmental challenges we face in other regions throughout the international system. Asia, with its unprecedented economic growth, is putting new and disturbing strains on the environment. As China and India industrialize and increase their consumption of energy, the pollution their large populations will create (even if their per capita pollution rates remain below Western levels) will compound an already serious local environmental degradation problem. India and China are expected to be among the major contributors to global warming in the next 10 to 20 years. In Africa, farmers already are suffering from the increasing severity and duration of droughts and desertification. As global warming continues, these trends are expected to accelerate, placing more stresses on populations that are already vulnerable to food shortages. In North America, old-growth temperate rainforests are threatened by logging and climate change. Despite the efforts of activists who are willing to go to jail to protect old-growth forests, which are often cut down for short-term profit, the political imperatives of jobs and logging community survival make long-term solutions difficult to reach. In South America and Asia, rainforest areas and their **biodiversity** are threatened by slash-and-burn agriculture, cattle industries, population pressure, and the need to pay off foreign debts. All of these environmental concerns need to be viewed in the context of future demands for resources. The world supports well over 6 billion people today, and the population of the planet is expected to reach 8 billion by 2025. As a result, the demand for natural resources will continue to rise, and the aggregate environmental impact of industrial and agricultural activity will increase each day.

What impact will these environmental issues have on the conduct of global politics? Realists argue that the environment—defined primarily as utilizable resources—will be an increasing source of conflict in the future. Environmental degradation will not alter the nature of world politics, but will lead to increased conflict and wars between states and peoples in environmentally stressed regions. Resource wars over oil, water, arable land, and strategic materials are increasingly likely. The environment is also likely to become a more prominent feature of power politics. For example, China and India may have increased bargaining power in a world frightened of the global environmental impact of mass industrialization in either of those highly populated states, and these countries will use this to obtain leverage in future negotiations on pollution treaties, energy agreements, and trade talks. On the other hand, liberals emphasize the potential for increased cooperation on environmental issues. For liberals, a complex and growing network of international institutions and regimes is evolving, which will give us the capacity to deal with environmental problems while the world economy continues to grow. Furthermore, states have shown a willingness to reach agreements on water management, pollution controls, offshore mineral exploration, fishing disputes, and a wide variety of other issues, without resorting to military force. Meanwhile, Marxists tend to see

Industrialization and environmental destruction: till death do they part? A spectacular column of smoke and fire rises beside the derrick as the first oil and gas is flared at Imperial Oil's Leduc No. 1 on February 13, 1947, in Alberta, Canada. The initial daily production was about 1000 barrels. Almost 60 years later, we are as addicted to oil as ever. (CP Photo/CP Archive)

deforestation and soil degradation as part of the process of capitalist exploitation in the periphery. Ultimately, there can be no final answer to environmental problems until the exploitative elites that dominate the capitalist system are overthrown and capitalism is itself replaced. An ecofeminist perspective would largely concur, and would link the destruction of habitat with the institution of patriarchy. Postmodern and constructivist thought examines how the environment is framed or presented as an issue, concluding that most perspectives are fitting the environment within the established belief systems of positivist theories. As a result, new thinking might not be forthcoming. While most efforts to link ecological thought with theory have been pursued in the critical theory camp, the environment is now such a prominent concern that all perspectives at least acknowledge it and are attempting to conceptualize how the environment will affect global politics in the future.

One important point of debate surrounding the treatment of environmental issues in global politics is whether the environment can or should be considered as a new or separate issue. For example, constructivist theorists (and many environmental activists) doubt whether environmental problems should be treated as international security problems. Of course, national security must include concern for the environment, but there is considerable reluctance by both military strategists and environmentalists to include each other in their circles. Daniel Deudney (himself a critic of linking security and environment) writes that if "the Pentagon had been put in charge of negotiating an ozone-layer protocol, we might still be stockpiling chlorofluorocarbons as a bargaining chip."[4] Furthermore, the language of security usually casts issues in terms of threats from identifiable sources, and implies intent to harm or cause damage to people or the institutions of a state. But when it comes to the environment, who is the threat, and what is their intent? However, since war has a tremendous impact on the environment and conflict over resources can itself be a cause of war, environmental security will be a part of the study of global politics for some time to come. We return to this theme toward the end of this chapter, but suffice it to say that long-term ecological issues have indeed become serious security concerns today.

In this chapter, we introduce some prominent environmental problems and the ecopolitics that surround them. Ecopolitics is where ecological concerns meet political theory and action. We address the more specific issue of overpopulation and the movement of peoples, as well as the spread of infectious diseases, in Chapter 11. Here, we will focus on how environmental problems are a source of both convergence and divergence in global politics. On the one hand, states, NGOs, and individuals have cooperated in response to environmental concerns in unprecedented ways. On the other hand, environmental degradation has contributed to the collapse of states and societies, refugee and migration flows, and exacerbated clashes over access to resources.

PROBLEMS OF THE COMMONS

Global environmental problems are often characterized as problems of the commons, or more technically, international common pool resources. According to Wilfred Beckerman, this "refers to situations in which nobody can be excluded from the use of an asset—such as common grazing land, or fishing grounds, or the atmosphere [but] one person's use of the asset reduces the amount available to other potential users' unrestricted use of the asset and can easily lead to over-use, so that only if some voluntary or enforcement mechanism is introduced can the supply be matched to the demand."[5] One example of an international common pool resource is the moon. Clearly, the moon does not belong to a single state, single individual, or group of people. The Americans may have landed there first, and they may even have hit a golf ball there, but no state can lay claim to territorial ownership. A 1967 treaty, the Treaty on Principles Governing the Activities of States in the Exploration and Use of Outer Space, Including the Moon and Other Celestial Bodies, obligates signatories not to indulge in military activities on the moon. However, most resources are rather more accessible than the moon. The essential economic problem is that everyone has an incentive to conserve the commons together but an incentive individually to exploit them. This becomes a political problem when cooperation is necessary to balance these counterincentives. Or, as Stephen Krasner puts it, "the basic challenge for states is to overcome market failure, the situation in which individual rational self-interested policies produce outcomes that leave each state worse off than it might otherwise have been."[6] The added dimension of environmental degradation demands we move beyond asking simply how states can share resources to asking how they can simultaneously conserve or preserve them.

Solutions to typical problems of the commons are rather elusive. Many have argued that the privatization of land or other resources will increase the sense of environmental responsibility or stewardship by rights holders. This proposition is debatable enough in a domestic context, but is even less clear when it comes to the international arena, where privatization is akin to territorialization. The 1982 Convention on the Law of the Sea (LOSC) designated new 200-nautical-mile (approximately 370-kilometre) exclusive economic zones (EEZ) in which coastal states would have not only resource rights but also inherent environmental responsibilities. The hope was that inside the 200-mile limit, increased coastal authority by individual states would lead to better management. Instead, "coastal countries such as Canada and the United States displaced overseas fleets from Europe and Japan with new programs and subsidies to build up their domestic fleets [then] scooped up cod and salmon on both coasts with alarming speed, and disastrous results."[7] Therefore, relying on the responsibility or stewardship of rights holders (be they individuals or states) may not be the best approach to protecting the environment. Furthermore, the entire principle of private property and legal ownership of resources is far from universal, and some peoples, such as indigenous groups, would reject this as an imperialistic act.

Further, some areas of the commons, such as the open seas and atmosphere, are simply not amenable to the expansion of national territories. The United Nations Convention on the Law of the Sea took nine years to negotiate (1973–82). One hundred fifty-nine states and other entities signed the Convention. In November 1993, Guyana became the 60th state to deposit its instrument of ratification with the United Nations, and the Law of the Sea officially became effective in November 1994. However, the United States was unwilling to sign the treaty owing to what the Reagan administration perceived as its anti–free enterprise character. The Law of the Sea established an International Seabed Authority that would facilitate the sharing of deep-sea resources, particularly any derived from deep-sea mining, among all states. This notion of sharing proceeds from resource extraction was opposed in the United States (and some other Western states), which argued that such revenue sharing would undermine the profitability of deep-sea mining. As a result, many Western states have signed the Law of the Sea but have not ratified it. Canada did not ratify the Law of the Sea until November 2003.

One of the central ecopolitical questions that concerns scholars is how dealing with the commons affects national sovereignty, the core principle of the UN Charter. Does the rise of transboundary pollution problems justify infringements on the sovereignty of states, as it does in cases of extreme international security concerns and genocide? Does the need to regulate the commons, or at least to avoid the tragedy of the commons, demand a pooling of sovereignty in certain issue-areas? Has the creation of institutions designed to mitigate environmental damage threatened the long-term future of the nation-state as predicted by the older functionalist school (see Chapter 5)? It is quite clear, in the legal sense, that the principle of sovereignty remains sacrosanct. In 1962, the UN General Assembly adopted a resolution that referred to the "inalienable right" of all states to freely "dispose of their natural wealth and resources."[8] Malaysia made particular reference to this precept during the forestry negotiations leading up to the UN Conference on Environment and Development (UNCED) in 1992. This is a common North–South sticking point as Southern state elites claim that any global environmental agenda infringes on their national sovereignty. Principle 2 of the Rio Declaration

PROFILE 10.1 The Asian Brown Cloud

In early 1999 scientists were startled to discover a brown haze covering most of the South and Southeast Asian regions, as well as large swaths of the Indian Ocean—a haze covering approximately 10 million km². This was at first attributed to forest fires (most deliberately set to clear brush for agriculture), but it is now believed to be the consequence of a mixture of pollutants, including fossil fuel combustion. According to the United Nations Environment Programme (UNEP), "Simulations with global climate models indicate that the haze could have major impacts on the monsoon circulation, regional rainfall patterns and vertical temperature profile of the atmosphere."

One of the most interesting things about the haze, which in 2004 has been identified as drifting into the Middle East as well, is that it is probably misnamed. One atmospheric scientist at the Scripps Institution of Oceanography at the University of California, Veerabhadran

Ramanathan, said the major contributors to this worldwide circle of pollution were Los Angeles, Delhi, Bombay, Beijing, and Cairo: "Pollution in the eastern United States can go in four or five days to Europe and in a week it goes from Europe to South Asia. This is fast transport which converts a local problem into a regional and global problem," the Indian scientist said. Ramanathan said he suspected the effect of the shroud of pollution across the globe would be to dry the planet.

The brown cloud demonstrates both the problems of scientific inquiry into such large-scale problems and the urgent need to protect the commons.

SOURCES: UNEP/EARTHSCAN, *GLOBAL ENVIRONMENT OUTLOOK 3: PAST, PRESENT AND FUTURE PERSPECTIVES* (LONDON, 2002), 222; A. HAMMOND, "SCIENTIST SAYS 'ASIAN BROWN CLOUD' THREATENS GULF," ENVIRONMENTAL NEWS NETWORK, 25 FEBRUARY 2004, http://www.enn.com/news/2004-02-25/ s_13447.asp (ACCESSED 26 MAY 2004).

(one result of the negotiations at UNCED) asserts that "states have the sovereign right to exploit their own resources pursuant to their own environmental and developmental policies."

There is also the question of cost distribution or who should pay for international efforts to save the commons. On issues such as ozone-layer depletion and global warming, there is a large divide between the developed and the developing world on burden sharing. Some agreements, such as the Montreal Protocol to the ozone-layer agreement and the Convention on Global Warming, have set important precedents regarding cost sharing and the question of sovereignty. R.E. Benedick concludes, "As a consequence of the ozone issue, the richer nations for the first time acknowledged a responsibility to help developing countries to implement needed environmental policies without sacrificing aspirations for improved standards of living."[9] Similar concerns clouded the negotiations for a biodiversity treaty: "even before the negotiation began, there was a history of disagreement about the allocation of the economic benefits and technological advances derived from Southern biodiversity."[10] Principle Seven of the Rio Declaration makes note of the "different contributions to global degradation" and resulting "common but differentiated responsibilities." The basic argument is that since the South has suffered from the northern states' indulgence in industrialization and colonialism, and because most of the pollution and environmental damage has been caused by industrialized states to this point, future environmental and resource-sharing agreements must be based on differentiated responsibility.

The political difficulty faced by efforts to respond to global or regional environmental problems is a familiar one. Environmental problems are by definition transboundary in character, but the state (the primary political means of responding to political problems) is a territorially defined and sovereign entity. Can a world of sovereign states reach appropriate and effective agreements on environmental issues that by definition are nonterritorial, and require the cooperation of virtually all states to succeed? In some cases, the answer is yes: one of the more fascinating cases of the management of the commons is that of Antarctica, which demonstrates that such cooperation can in fact be achieved.

ANTARCTICA

Antarctica is an important place. To naturalists, this fact is obvious. Antarctica is not, contrary to popular perception, barren of life; its waters contain a diversified ecosystem and what is known as the "fastest ocean food chain." It is in essence the world's largest wildlife sanctuary, home to 100 million birds and six species of seals. Fifteen species of whales, toothed and baleen, summer there. The global scientific value of this place, where the lowest thermometer reading ever was recorded (−89.6°C, in 1983 at the U.S.S.R.'s Vostok Research Station in East Antarctica), is increasing. Antarctica offers a "window on the sky," especially for observation of the hole in the ozone layer since 1985. Antarctica also offers a "window on the past," for as Lee Kimball writes, "exhuming trapped air in ice cores at depths of more than 2000 metres, halfway down to bedrock, scientists have found a priceless record of some 150 000 years of atmospheric and climate change."[11] Perhaps most important, Antarctica's environment provides us with a planetary early warning system regarding global warming.

The Antarctic Treaty, which was in many ways a landmark event, was signed in 1959. Though several nations have laid (and maintain) claim to specific parts of Antarctica, they all agreed to adhere to a common management scheme. Both of the Cold War superpowers signed, and Antarctica became the world's first nuclear-free zone. Antarctica has maintained its nonmilitarized status since. The treaty provides on-site verification measures on research conducted in the region, and it opened the door for nonclaimant nations to establish research

A lonely penguin appears in Antarctica during the Southern Hemisphere's summer season, 1997. Experts say that global warming is affecting Antarctica and among other things is causing penguin colonies to dwindle in the areas closer to the sea as the birds are migrating toward the inland territories, where temperatures remain lower. (AP Photo stf/Rodrigo Jana/CP Archive)

facilities on the continent. Canada participates in the **Antarctic Treaty System (ATS)** as a nonconsultative party (i.e., it has no voting rights in ATS meetings but can attend as an observer). The ATS involves other management regimes, such as the **Convention on the Conservation of Antarctic Marine Living Resources (CCAMLR)**, well known for its ecosystem approach to resource management. The Antarctic marine ecosystem is protected as a whole, not according to strictly delineated territorial lines. Living resources can be harvested only if ecological relationships are unchanged, if ecological changes are potentially reversible within two to three decades, and if harvesting does not interfere with the recovery of depleted populations. However, as Lee Kimball laments, the burden of proof that excessive damage *is* being done lies with CCAMLR's Scientific Committee. Kimball and others feel that the harvesters should have to prove that excessive damage will *not* be done.

Other than the treaty and CCAMLR, the third pillar of the ATS was to be the Convention on the Regulation of Antarctic Mineral Resource Activities (CRAMRA). This agreement was highly controversial since it articulated the possibility of managed mining for exploration and, eventually, exploitation in Antarctica. Many parties objected to the very idea, claiming even limited mining would destroy the fragile Antarctic ecosystem. However, CRAMRA was never established since Australia and France (both consultative parties) refused to sign. On October 4, 1991, in Madrid, the Protocol on Environmental Protection to the Antarctic Treaty was signed. Antarctica was designated a natural reserve, all mineral resources activities were prohibited for at least 50 years, and regulations were extended to cover tourist activity. A group of annexes provide for a comprehensive protection regime, including an environmental impact assessment guideline, the conservation of fauna and flora, waste disposal and management, and the prevention of marine pollution.[12]

Antarctica came onto the UN agenda in 1983, ostensibly because the world community decided to deal with the UN Convention on the Law of the Sea negotiations (UNCLOS) before this second commons problem was tackled. The consultative parties were not fond of what they perceived to be their adequate management system receiving such scrutiny and, with the exception of the issue of South African participation in the ATS (denounced by the UN General Assembly), refused to participate. For example, they did not vote on the General Assembly resolution (44/124B-1989) that called for the establishment of an Antarctic world park. This resolution was very important, since it dispelled fears that nonsignatories were demanding access to decision-making on Antarctica simply because they wanted access to possible resource extraction opportunities in the future. The resolution also challenged the 24 consultative parties' right to exclusive decision-making status on what many felt was indeed part of the **global commons**, not the domain of a select group of states who were capable of conducting scientific research there.

So the protocol mentioned above could be seen in this light: it is an attempt to contain calls for a world park without world management, or common ownership, and it is an attempt to preserve the exclusivity of the ATS and deny the UN system an acquisition that many policy planners think is too much like world government for their comfort. Reactions to this awkward middle ground are mixed. By adopting the moratorium, consultative parties have made it clear that, at least for now, they have temporarily—and 50 years is an extremely long time in world politics—discarded the promise of exploitation of the continent. This decision is a practical and symbolic victory for some, but others are still convinced that Antarctica should be legally recognized, within the UN framework, as part of the global commons. After all, 50 years is not a long time in the history of the planet.

Is the Antarctic a model or a unique case? A great deal of sensible cynicism exists concerning the ATS and not just because it has not evolved into the universal-membership body some hoped it would. Though it is a symbol of peace and cooperation, Antarctica never offered an especially alluring military advantage to anyone. It is difficult to argue that the ATS represents an unusual instance of economic restraint when it is not, as far as we know, worth exploiting in economic terms. No huge mineral deposits have been found. Oil is suspected but not confirmed, and we gave up on the idea of towing icebergs north for fresh water some time ago. In other words, skeptics argue, Antarctica remains so pristine because it is, in conventional terms, worthless. No doubt a grain of truth lies in this realistic appraisal, but it should not belittle the significance of Antarctic cooperation or dampen enthusiasm for the future of Antarctica, which remains, despite the recent protocol, vulnerable to the advances of the industrial world. For a "worthless" chunk of ice, many people have spent a lot of time in intense negotiations over its future. It is not as easy, however, to deal with other problems of the commons, such as climate change and global warming.

CLIMATE CHANGE AND GLOBAL WARMING

Beyond nuclear Armageddon, the biggest long-term threat to humanity may well emanate from the prospect of major disturbances to the earth's climate. Our heavy reliance on the burning of fossil fuels (coal, oil, and natural gas) releases billions of tonnes of carbon dioxide into the atmosphere each year, and deforestation from slash-and-burn agriculture, cement production, and other activities add millions more. The ozone layer has been affected by industrial chemicals that stay in the atmosphere for more than a century. Global warming could bring catastrophic results: the ice caps could melt and sea levels would rise and flood highly populated coastal zones; agriculture could dwindle in what are now productive areas; and the tropics could become uninhabitable, forcing millions to flee as environmental refugees. Coral reefs are threatened by rising ocean temperatures, and migratory birds are harmed as well. Indeed entire species of biota may be forced to move to cooler climes, altering local ecosystems and shifting agricultural patterns. Unusual warming could also shift the distribution and seasonal appearance of vector-borne diseases such as malaria, dengue fever, and schistosomiasis. Many concerned observers argue that these effects are already occurring and cannot be dismissed as alarmist projections.

We have seen a major increase in the level of attention politicians have afforded the broad issue of climate change, and most of this attention has been spent on global warming and ozone-layer depletion. Though the talk of politicians is often viewed as cheap, we knew global warming was being taken seriously because those most prudent of institutions, insurance companies, became worried about its effects. At international talks in Geneva in July 1996, 57 European insurance firms urged national delegates to hold a climate change conference to reduce carbon emissions.[13] Four years earlier, A Framework Convention on Climate Change had been signed at the UNCED in Rio, committing the signatory states to reductions in their emissions of greenhouse gases, most notably carbon dioxide. However, by 1996 little progress had been made on implementing the Framework Convention, as signatory states proved unwilling to undertake the politically difficult task of establishing domestic laws on fuel consumption and emissions controls. As a result, calls for another treaty and substantive progress on controlling emissions grew louder, and not just from the insurance industry. By this time, most scientists and a growing number of NGOs called for a renewed international effort to combat global warming. As a result, at a conference of the Rio signatories in Kyoto, Japan, in December 1997, states committed themselves to more strict emissions controls. The exact formula was different for each state: Canada pledged to reduce emissions to 94 percent of the 1990 level by 2010. However, Canada has made little progress toward this goal, as implementation is complicated by the objections of several provincial governments. In fact, Canada ratified the Kyoto Accord only in late 2002. Overall, Kyoto calls for signatory states to cut their emissions of greenhouse gases to levels averaging just over 5 percent below 1990 emissions levels.

Almost immediately, states began to contemplate ways to reduce the economic (and political) pain that would be caused by any implementation of the rules and regulations required to lower state emissions of greenhouse gases. Some suggested a system of emissions trading. Countries that successfully reduced their emissions below their Kyoto targets could sell their "surplus" emissions as "credits" to countries that had failed to meet their own targets! Other countries suggested that they should receive "carbon sink" credits. Because trees absorb carbon dioxide, countries with a lot of forest cover, and countries that planted and preserved forests, should receive carbon sink credits for doing so. These credits would then be applied to their Kyoto emissions cuts targets, thus reducing the actual need to cut emissions. Not surprisingly, Canada (a country with a lot of trees) found this approach rather appealing. Clearly, both of these measures would allow large industrialized states to avoid the economic pain of implementing emission cuts. However, another Conference of the Parties to the UN Framework Convention on Climate Change in fall 2000 at The Hague failed to achieve a unified approach to these proposals. A shadow still remains over the entire Rio framework, for two vital states, the United States and Russia, have not ratified the protocol as of September 2004. The United States, under the G.W. Bush administration, argues that Southern states must make solid commitments to emissions cuts as well. This is not an outrageous argument, as India and China in particular will be leading emitters of greenhouse gases in the near future. However, the Bush administration is also reluctant to accept both the science of global warming and the domestic economic costs of implementing emissions cuts. In the Canadian case, the federal government representatives who went to Kyoto made a promise they could not possibly keep. In Canada's federal system, the provinces are responsible for natural resources, and some of them, such as heavily industrialized Ontario or coal- and oil-producing Alberta, do not intend to accept the economic consequences of emissions cuts on their own. In the end, the attempt to address the problem of global warming reminds us of the challenges of achieving cooperation among states. A structural explanation for state behaviour would suggest that the competitive nature of the world economy will limit states' willingness to sacrifice economic growth for the sake of future generations unless they are sure that all states will comply. Global warming negotiations are thus a gigantic game of prisoner's dilemma. Others would argue that the major producers of fossil fuel emissions are simply too powerful and too reluctant to change.

Even as the future of Kyoto remains in doubt with the refusal of the United States to ratify, very little debate remains about the validity of the claim that the earth is warming because of excessive industrial pollution and activity. No one doubts the logic of the greenhouse effect: the buildup of greenhouse gases in the earth's atmosphere is preventing more and more heat absorbed from the sun from escaping back into space. Carbon dioxide accounts for about half of the greenhouse effect; methane, nitrous oxide, ozone, and chlorofluorocarbons make up the rest. As global temperatures are generally increasing and more of these gases are being released into the atmosphere by modern society, it stands to reason that a correlation exists. Nonetheless, some argue that nature is still the chief cause of fluctuations in global climate patterns. For example, in 1991, Mount Pinatubo in the Philippines erupted, spilling some 22 million tonnes of sulphur dioxide into the stratosphere, affecting weather patterns around the world. Others feel it is premature to conclude that the warming trend will continue or argue that its implications are unclear and that acting to solve the problem would cause undue economic harm. For example, one of the chief causes of global warming is deforestation, since burning trees releases carbon and dead trees cannot absorb carbon. However, stopping the destruction of the rain forest is rather difficult when those burning it down are doing so to survive. Therefore, there is a direct link between global warming and the development challenge identified in Chapter 8. Meanwhile, the average American car is believed to release its own weight in carbon into the atmosphere every year, an especially harmful situation as Sport Utility Vehicles clutter the roadways.[14]

The Intergovernmental Panel on Climate Change (IPCC), which was instrumental in getting climate change on the global agenda, concludes that the CO_2 concentration in the atmosphere was about 370 parts per million in 2001, a 30 percent increase since 1750. And the problem is expected to get much worse: carbon dioxide emissions are expected to increase between 1997 and 2020 from 6175 million metric tonnes to 10 009 million metric tonnes per year.[15] Even if scientific consensus is reached on this issue, we still face a daunting ethical proposition because of the scope of the problem in spatial and temporal terms. As two Worldwatch analysts indicate, the question of global climate change is unprecedented in its "geographical breadth and multigenerational time frame—challenging societies to work cooperatively to protect distant populations as well as those yet unborn."[16] The result is a very complex multilateral bargaining situation, one that opens many doors to confusion. The UN Environment Programme is working with the World Meteorological Organization (WMO) to measure changes in climate (as are thousands of other nationally based scientific institutions around the world), and the UN-sponsored IPCC will continue to produce reports (see the section on the role of science in global ecopolitics in this chapter). But unless the major emitters (including the United States, the EU, Russia, China, Brazil, and India) can be convinced to take concrete steps toward reducing emissions, adopting renewable energy sources, and refraining from promoting fossil fuel technology elsewhere, the warming process can only continue. We may find ourselves in the position of working mainly to adapt to the changes to come, rather than trying to avoid them. In this adaptation, states will seek their own advantage, elites will protect themselves, and the poor will suffer the most.

The other major problem related to climate change is that of ozone-layer depletion. Volatile chemicals known as **chlorofluorocarbons (CFCs)** used in refrigeration, industrial production, and aerosol cans have damaged the stratospheric ozone layer, which protects us from ultraviolet radiation from the sun. CFCs, along with carbon and other so-called greenhouse gases, prevent infrared radiation from escaping the earth's atmosphere. The result is not only increased global warming potential but also increased rates of skin cancer and eye problems and adverse agricultural effects. Ultimately, entire ecosystems and immune systems could be disrupted if the ozone hole increases in size. For example, marine biologists fear the immune systems of whales are being affected by increased ultraviolet ray exposure. Ozone cannot be replaced by any known technology, and the ozone produced by burning fossil fuels does not replace stratospheric ozone but pollutes the lower atmosphere. In September 2000 the Antarctic ozone hole was more than 28 million square kilometres in size.

Unlike the global warming issue, which has generated much debate but relatively little firm commitment on the part of industrial states, the problem of ozone-layer depletion has been met with sound action. Once a certain measure of scientific consensus was reached regarding its origin, ozone-layer depletion generated a quick international response through a series of conferences that culminated with the signing of the famous Montreal Protocol in 1987 (Montreal has become an important centre for international organizations dealing with environmental problems; see Profile 10.2.). The United States banned the use of CFCs in aerosol cans in the early 1980s. By 1990, 93 states had agreed to halt CFC production altogether by 2000, and by then some $1.1 billion had been dispersed through a Multilateral Fund to provide technical assistance to Southern states to help them develop acceptable substitutes. China and India had refused to sign the Vienna Convention for the Protection of the Ozone Layer unless this help was included. By 1992, most industrial states had agreed to unilaterally phase out CFC use by 1995, and the UNEP reports in 2003 that by 2000 the total consumption of ozone-depleting substances had been reduced by 85 percent, a trend in continuation in 2004.[17]

The increase in governmental regulation to prohibit the sale of Freon, a major ozone-depleting substance used predominately in the air conditioning units of older cars, has been so marked that a black market in the product is flourishing. In the United States, small-scale smugglers have been caught bringing thousands of kilograms of Freon from Mexico (the latter has delayed the prohibition of Freon). As reported in *The New York Times*, the street price for a 30-pound (14-kilogram) cylinder of Freon more than doubled between 1995 and 1996 to more than $500. Thomas A. Watts-Fitzgerald is the American attorney who has coordinated an investigation into the matter named Operation Cool Breeze. He calculates that buying cocaine, converting it to crack, and selling it brings a 4:1 profit ratio, while buying a canister of Freon in another country for $42 and selling it in the United States for $550 produces a 13:1 profit ratio.[18] Despite the rise of such regulatory problems, the costs of reducing CFC use are much lower than those of reducing greenhouse gas emissions in general. One might argue that the Montreal Protocol, a fairly demanding document reached in a relatively short time, was successful because remarkable scientific consensus existed regarding the causes of ozone depletion,

PROFILE 10.2 The Montreal Connection

Montreal is world renowned for its old-world charm, cosmopolitanism, and summer jazz festival. However, given its location next to the heavily polluted St. Lawrence River, few would expect Montreal to become a magnet for international organizations dealing with environmental problems. Yet, with the support of the federal government (no doubt influenced by continued fears over separatism), Montreal has attracted a great deal of expertise and officialdom to the area. In fact, one can take a cursory glance at the extent of multilateral action on environmental issues with a survey of the bodies that have located there. The following organizations are already located in Montreal:

- The Secretariat of the Multilateral Fund of the Montreal Ozone Protocol

- The North American Commission for Environmental Cooperation (a North American Free Trade Agreement institution)

- The Secretariat of the United Nations Convention on Biological Diversity

- The Montreal office of the World Conservation Union

- The Network of Expertise for the Global Environment

- The International Secretariat for Water

Montreal lost a bid for the Desertification Secretariat, which was located in Bonn, Germany.

as did genuine international fear of the consequences. However, this type of cohesion of knowledge and expectation has yet to be reached in many other areas related to the environment.

Global warming and ozone-layer depletion both raise the question of who should pay for the damage that industrial society has unleashed on the world. Northern states have contributed the most to the problem, but they cannot solve it alone, and the newly industrialized countries such as Brazil, India, and China will make similar pollution contributions in the near future. Ultimately, this is a problem of the commons, and we must reach multilateral agreements, which are in turn enforced by governments, to deal with them. It is far from certain we can do so in a competitive world economy.

DEFORESTATION AND LAND DEGRADATION

Another serious global problem is the impact of human activity on the world's land surface, in particular the removal of the world's forests and the decreasing availability of arable land. Deforestation has become an increasingly popular and public issue in the past decade. While tropical rain forest depletion has gathered the most attention, it is important to remember that temperate rain forest depletion is as serious a problem; in fact, many of the world's temperate rain forests in Europe have already vanished, and depletion rates in Canada, the United States, and Russia are very high. This fact is a source of friction in international efforts to curb deforestation. Developing countries see these efforts as inimical to their own economic development. From their perspective, the industrialized countries, having exploited much of their own forests, are now trying to prevent the developing countries from exploiting their own. However, tropical rain forest depletion is especially severe; every year, an area the size of Belgium is cleared of rain forest, often by slash-and-burn methods. In Brazil's Amazon Basin, more than 11 percent of the jungle has been destroyed since 1975 (an area the size of Morocco), and deforestation continues at even higher rates. In June 2003, the deforestation rate in Brazil's Amazon increased by 40 percent in that year. According to Environmental News Network, figures released by the Brazilian environment ministry showed "deforestation in the Amazon jumped to 9840 square miles last year—the highest since 1995—from 7010 square miles in 2001."[19] Tropical rain forest is also being depleted in Indonesia, Colombia, Thailand, and the Philippines. In Haiti, more than 90 percent of the country's rain forest has disappeared. In the 1980s alone, the world lost about 8 percent of its tropical forests; the net loss of forest area in the 1990s was 2.4 percent.[20] Rain forest depletion occurs for many reasons, including a local desire for pastureland, cropland, fuel, and lucrative foreign markets for hardwood.

Up in smoke. Indians of the Xingu Reservation in the central Brazilian state of Mato Grosso walk among charred trees. According to news reports, fires in that state alone burned more than 150 000 hectares and killed at least 400 head of cattle in August 1998. Fires earlier in the year in the Amazon jungle burned an area the size of Belgium. (AP Photo/Agencia Estado, Humberto Paradera/CP Archive)

Another tragedy of rain forest depletion is the impossibility of full regeneration. Old-growth timber areas (in both tropical and temperate zones) possess ecosystems and biodiversity developed over thousands of years. Although they cover less than 10 percent of the earth's surface, it is estimated that tropical forest ecosystems may contain up to 90 percent of all species. Replanted or second-growth regions never achieve this level of biodiversity.[21] In addition, because in many cases forests are cleared for pastureland or cropland, the delicate soil is often exhausted after a few years. As a result, the forest cannot regenerate because the land cannot support it. Deforestation has several global environmental implications. The loss of trees reduces the capacity of the earth to produce oxygen and absorb carbon dioxide, which in turn contributes to climate change. Rainfall patterns are affected, and soil erosion increases because of a lack of root structures, contributing to life-taking floods in states such as Bangladesh.

In addition to loss of forest cover, land and soil degradation is a serious environmental problem. At the Johannesburg Earth Summit in 2002, soil degradation was estimated to affect some *2 billion* hectares worldwide, and about two-thirds of the world's agricultural land. This degradation is once again caused by human activity: deforestation, overgrazing, and agricultural mismanagement. In severe cases, soil degradation can result in desertification and complete loss of land productivity, a condition that affects 5 to 6 million hectares of land every year.[22] Because it takes thousands of years to form a few centimetres of topsoil, this problem has severe implications for the world's food supply (see Chapter 13). Further, poorly designed irrigation systems can cause salinization, waterlogging, and other problems, and the use of pesticides and herbicides, a major interest of MNCs involved in agri-business, can cause many long-term problems for both ecology and human health. Others worry that the introduction of GMOs and new biotechnology will further homogenize crops, lowering food security in the long run and harming poor farmers who are forced to buy biotech products.

Taken together, deforestation and land degradation represent a serious assault on the earth's land mass. A UN Convention to Combat Desertification was signed after the Rio Summit of 1992, and there are two major international initiatives to govern world forestry, the international Tropical Timber Organization of 1983 and the Tropical Forestry Action Plan, launched in 1985 (later renamed the National Forestry Action Programme). But none of these agreements have significantly slowed these problems. In the meantime, as our next section indicates, we are fundamentally changing the evolutionary path of the world's species, altering some, and finishing others altogether.

PROFILE 10.3 The Causes of Land Degradation

Note: Causes are listed in order of magnitude of impact, according to estimates by the Food and Agriculture Organization (FAO) report *Our Land Our Future* (Rome: FAO, 1996).

1. *Overgrazing*: Over 20 percent of pasture and rangelands have been damaged, most severely in Africa and Asia

2. *Deforestation*: Large-scale logging, clearance for farming, and urban use

3. *Agricultural mismanagement*: Water erosion, soil salinization, waterlogging

4. *Fuelwood consumption*: Wood remains a primary energy source in the southern hemisphere

5. *Industry and urbanization*: Road construction, mining and industrial development, suburban developments

SOURCE: COMPILED FROM THE UNEP *GLOBAL ENVIRONMENT OUTLOOK 3* (LONDON: EARTHSCAN, 2002), 64. REPRINTED WITH PERMISSION.

SPECIES IMPOVERISHMENT

The physical division of the earth into nation-states is contrary to the flow of nature, and this becomes most apparent when we consider the fate of migratory mammals that do not recognize borders and have their paths disrupted by such constructions. This issue begs a broader question: are the many species of animals and plants that are currently endangered part of the commons, regardless of where they live? From an ecological viewpoint, the crisis presented by dwindling whale and tiger populations and current attempts to save them is really one of biodiversity, or, put more emphatically, what M. Brock Fenton and others term *species impoverishment*.[23] Though there is nothing unnatural and certainly nothing new about extinction, the 20th century in particular saw more extinctions in the wild world than ever before. The fear of many specialists during the height of whaling was that the great whales were facing the same fate as the now extinct dodo, and they were facing that fate not because of any natural catastrophe but because of human misunderstanding or, worse, greed. The same fear underlies attempts to save what is left of the tropical rain forests today.

Scientists are still debating the causes of the late Cretaceous extinction, in which the large dinosaurs were rendered extinct, about 65 million years ago. This is a question partly of effect, for as David Jablonski notes in a fascinating essay on the topic, the late Cretaceous extinction is a very complex phenomenon: "Tropical marine groups were more severely affected than temperate or polar ones; open-ocean plankton and larger swimmers, such as the mosasaurs, were affected more than bottom dwellers; and large land dwellers more affected than small ones, even though some larger forms survived as well."[24] Whatever caused this extinction, it did not kill off all the species on earth at the time, nor did it even come close to doing so. This is the key difference: it was, by any account, not preventable with human effort (humans weren't around). Humans are believed to be at least partially responsible for the large extinction of land animals in the Pleistocene period. The development of agriculture so fundamentally changed the human–nature relationship that we have been able to affect a myriad of ecosystems, even the biosphere, with our economic activities.

The human tendency to overhunt constitutes a principal threat to biodiversity today. Columbus discovered the Caribbean monk seal, the single tropical pinniped, in what was called the New World. It has not been seen since 1922. The Steller's sea cow was spotted by a Russian hunting expedition in 1741 in the Aleutians; it was regarded as extinct by the late 18th century. More recently, we have witnessed massive fish extinctions—more than 200 species—from Lake Victoria in Africa. These extinctions had many causes, including overfishing, pollution, and the introduction of alien species, such as the Nile perch. Les Kaufman has referred to Lake Victoria as the "Hiroshima of the biological apocalypse."[25] Canadian and European commercial fishers know all too well the economic effects of the rapid reduction of fish species such as cod, turbot, and Pacific salmon, and the significant role played by overfishing.

The reduction of species populations will, of course, have a severe impact on their reproductive health. While this may increase the chances of survival for some, since there is less competition for limited resources, it may lessen the chances of survival for the group as a whole. An important element here is the gene pool, which itself must be sufficiently diverse for healthy populations to thrive: "Gene pools are being converted into gene puddles vulnerable to evaporation in an ecological and evolutionary sense."[26] The loss of genetic diversity may well be the most serious long-term threat to our environment. As James Scarff notes,

> [the] elimination of a species reduces the genetic capacity of the ecosystem to respond to perturbations or long-term changes in the environment. Such a loss may also initiate irreversible ecological adjustments which destabilize the

ecosystem leading to further extinctions. Economically, the extinction of a species represents the permanent loss of a renewable resource of unknown value [as well as] potential uses for medicine, scientific research, human food, education, and recreation.[27]

The international community has taken steps to limit the degradation of wildlife species. There are numerous fisheries agreements and institutions in place, such as the Northwest Atlantic Fisheries Organization (discussed below) and the International Whaling Commission. Early organizations included the International Council for Bird Preservation (1909) and the International Congress for the Protection of Nature (1913). As early as 1886 a Treaty Concerning the Regulation of Salmon Fishing in the Rhine River Basin was signed by Germany, Luxembourg, the Netherlands, and Switzerland. The first international agreement to conserve a marine mammal was in all likelihood the Fur Seal Convention of 1911, signed by Japan, Russia, Great Britain (for pre-independence Canada), and the United States.

Another groundbreaking agreement was the U.S.–Great Britain Migratory Birds Convention, signed in 1916. In the contemporary setting, what Robert Boardman has called the "linchpin of the system"[28] of international conservationist organizations is the **IUCN–The World Conservation Union (IUCN)**, originally formed in 1948 as the International Union for the Protection of Nature (IUPN) in conjunction with the United Nations Educational, Scientific and Cultural Organization (UNESCO). IUCN is a unique umbrella organization that covers intergovernmental and transnational conservation activity, often working laterally with a plethora of other organizations—both state multilateral and nongovernmental in composition—that have achieved global significance. The **Convention on International Trade in**

Orangutans Oyoi, nine months, left, and Martisen, three months, are carried by a caretaker at Nyaru Menteng Orangutan Refuge in Central Kalimantan province, Indonesia, 2 March 2001. With their natural habitat shrinking at an alarming rate due to logging, urban expansion, and forest fires, orangutans and other wildlife on the Island of Borneo are finding themselves the first casualties. (AP Photo/Charles Dharapak/CP Archive)

Endangered Species of Wild Fauna and Flora (CITES) is often heralded as a diplomatic success; it has resulted in the controversial international ivory trade ban of 1989 (partially lifted in 1997 to allow a one-time sale of stockpiled ivory from three southern African states to Japan). But CITES is torn between Northern states demanding complete protection of species and Southern states wanting to trade in animal parts as part of a broader conservation strategy. The role of opposing NGOs lobbying CITES delegations is interesting as well, as they compete to have their world-views accepted by state delegates.

The Biodiversity Treaty, signed in Rio de Janeiro in 1992, further committed states to preserving biodiversity and committed the North to paying the South for use of genetic material found in the latter. The treaty, signed by more than 160 countries in 1992 (the United States signed after Bill Clinton's election later that year, but has not ratified the treaty), went into effect in 1993. Delegates from all the signatories form a conference of parties, which meets every year to review progress made toward the three central thrusts of the treaty: the conservation of biodiversity, the sustainable use of biological resources, and the equitable sharing of the benefits arising from such use. A Biosafety Protocol for the Convention on Biological Diversity (CBD) was negotiated in 2000.

However, one can argue that all these treaties are meaningless if the broader problem, the preservation of habitat, is not addressed, and that task requires much more than the regulation of fishing fleets or the ban of alligator-skin purses or the confiscation of exotic plants at borders. It requires creating the conditions in which humankind no longer has the perceived need to destroy natural habitat. Despite encouraging conservation programs around the world, we are a long way from environmental sustainability, and scientists are raising the question of whether or not we should begin cloning endangered species to ensure the continuation of their gene pools.

PROTECTING THE GLOBAL ENVIRONMENT: FROM STOCKHOLM TO RIO TO JOHANNESBURG

When it comes to the environmental impact of the role played by the major development players in the UN system, many analysts are highly critical. In particular, the International Bank for Reconstruction and Development (IBRD or World Bank) and the International Monetary Fund (IMF) have come under fire for promoting large-scale industrialization and structural adjustment programs that encourage the depletion of natural resources for export.[29] We should note, however, that the World Bank and others are slowly beginning to take environmental questions seriously, and initiatives such as the Global Environmental Facility, administered by the World Bank, United Nations Environment Programme (UNEP), and UN Development Programme (UNDP) are contributing to the development of environmental technology (see Profile 10.4 for Canada's environmental commitments).

In 1972 the United Nations sponsored the Conference on the Human Environment (UNCHE) in Stockholm, where the UN Environment Programme was created. UNEP is not an institution or a specialized agency of the UN, such as the World Health Organization. Rather, it is made up of all the activities undertaken within the UN system that deal with the environment. It has a governing council with 58 nations, elected by the General Assembly for a three-year term. It meets every two years and in special sessions whenever necessary. It has a secretariat, based in Nairobi, Kenya; a voluntary Environment Fund; and the Environment Coordination Board (ECB), which attempts to coordinate all the UN bodies involved in environmental areas. The ECB is chaired by UNEP's executive director, who in the latter half of the 1990s was a Canadian, Elizabeth Dowdeswell. One of UNEP's most important tasks was to aid in the setup of UNCED, held in Rio de Janeiro, Brazil, in June 1992, under the leadership of another Canadian, Maurice Strong. UNCED was the largest diplomatic summit ever,

| | PROFILE 10.4 | **Canada's Major International Environmental Commitments** |

1909	Treaty between the United States and Great Britain Relating to Boundary Waters
1916	Convention between the United States and United Kingdom for the Protection of Migratory Birds in Canada and the United States
1946	International Convention for the Regulation of Whaling (Canada withdrew in 1982)
1963	Treaty Banning Nuclear Weapons Tests in the Atmosphere, in Outer Space, and under Water
1971	Convention on Wetlands of International Importance
1972	Canada–U.S. Great Lakes Water Quality Agreement Stockholm Declaration on the Environment
	London Convention on the Prevention of Marine Pollution by Dumping of Wastes and Other Matter
	Convention Concerning the Protection of World Cultural and Natural Heritage
1973	Convention on International Trade in Endangered Species of Wild Fauna and Flora
1978	Protocol on the International Convention for the Prevention of Pollution from Ships
1979	Convention on Long-Range Transboundary Air Pollution (LRTAP)
1982	UN Convention on the Law of the Sea (ratified 2003)
1985	Vienna Convention on the Protection of the Ozone Layer (reduction of sulphur emissions or their transboundary fluxes by at least 30 percent)
	Canada–U.S. Agreement Concerning Pacific Salmon

1986	Canada–U.S. Agreement on the Transboundary Movement of Hazardous Waste
1987	Montreal Protocol on Substances That Deplete the Ozone Layer
1989	Basel Convention on the Control of Transboundary Movements of Hazardous Wastes and Their Disposal
1991	Canada–U.S. Air Quality Agreement
	NO_x Protocol to the 1979 LRTAP Convention/Declaration on the Protection of the Arctic Environment
1992	UN Framework Convention on Climate Change
	Convention on Biological Diversity
	Agenda 21
	"Rio Declaration"
	Statement of Guiding Principles on Forests
1993	North American Agreement on Environmental Co-operation
1994	International Tropical Timber Agreement
	Protocol to LRTAP on Sulphur Emission Reductions
1995	UN Agreement on Straddling Fish Stocks and Highly Migratory Fish Stocks)
1996	Comprehensive Nuclear Test Ban Treaty
1997	Kyoto Protocol on Climate Change (ratified 2002)
	Canada–Chile Agreement on Environmental Co-operation
2000	Biosafety Protocol for Biodiversity Convention (signed but not ratified)

and it generated a great deal of press coverage around the world. Several outcomes of UNCED deserve mention here. One was the establishment of a UN Commission on Sustainable Development (CSD), which would meet regularly and follow up on the conclusions of UNCED, including a major five-year review in 1997. Second, an agreed text for forestry conservation emerged, amounting to little more than a statement of principles. UNCED produced the Rio Declaration, which was to have been a more all-embracing "Earth Charter," and which we discussed in our section on the commons; the Framework Convention on Climate

Change, mentioned earlier in this chapter; and Agenda 21, a comprehensive action plan on various aspects of future environmental protection. Since it suggests practical policy initiatives, Agenda 21 is really the core UNCED achievement. It did not, however, obtain stringent financial commitments from the Northern states to pay for it.

Ten years after UNCED, in the late summer of 2002, delegates reconvened in a follow-up conference in Johannesburg, South Africa, labelled the World Summit on Sustainable Development. At Johannesburg, delegates were assigned the task of evaluating the successes of Agenda 21, as well developing new standards for its effective implementation, and focusing the world's attention toward emergent challenges, including improving people's lives (this followed on the heels of the Millennium Summit commitments mentioned in Chapter 8). Participants of Johannesburg emphasized that the protection of global resources depends on the cooperation of all sectors of society. In addition to governments, there was active participation at the Summit by representatives from business and industry, children and youth, farmers, indigenous peoples, local authorities, NGOs, scientific and technological communities, women, and workers and trade unions. These represent the Major Groups identified in Agenda 21. Of particular interest was the movement to ensure that the summit was conducted in an environmentally responsible way. Thus, the "Greening the WSSD" initiative was established to ensure that the thousands of delegates that descended on Johannesburg generated minimal waste. However, there were little concrete results from this follow-up conference, which took place when September 11–related security issues were dominating the international agenda. Unlike UNCED, many heads of state did not even attend.

However, this is not necessarily an indication that ecopolitics have been shoved aside in the 21st century. Indeed, it would be impossible for politicians to completely ignore environmental considerations today, since they impact so directly on their constituents' lives. Many ecopolitical issues may seem rather distant, involving things such as the global commons, but many are quite local in character, and involve close neighbours.

TRANSBORDER ENVIRONMENTAL ISSUES

Transborder pollution flows from one country into another, through rivers, streams, lakes, air, and even underground. Since power differentials usually exist between neighbouring states—one is often more industrialized or has a geographic advantage, such as being upstream—realists argue that transborder pollution will be the cause of future violent conflict. However, many states—Canada and the United States, with the **International Joint Commission (IJC),** are often used as an example—co-manage their mutual frontiers on an ongoing basis. Even so, the potential for conflict exists: Canada and the United States argued for years over the effects of **acid rain** that came to Canada from industrial regions in the United States and continue to dispute the co-management of the Pacific salmon stock, the prospects of drilling for oil in the Arctic Wildlife Refuge in Alaska, and other points of contention.

In the past several decades, growing public awareness of the detrimental effect of pollution has come to underscore a variety of measures at the national and international levels to stem the tide of pollution as societies continued to industrialize, and to industrialize agriculture, releasing previously unknown chemicals into defenseless ecosystems.[30] Atmospheric nuclear tests in the 1950s created radioactive fallout that travelled thousands of kilometres, raising public concern over the discovery of cesium-137, strontium 90, carbon 14, and various isotopes of plutonium in the environment.[31] This concern helped push the United States toward signing the Partial Test Ban Treaty, which limited future nuclear testing to underground facilities.

Perhaps the most famous case of transborder pollution resulted from an accident at the Chernobyl nuclear reactor in Ukraine in April 1986 (at the time, Ukraine was still part of the

Aftermath of ecological calamity. Workers who constructed the cement sarcophagus covering Chernobyl's reactor in 1986 pose with a banner reading: "We will fulfill the government's order!" next to the uncompleted construction. Thousands of workers who took part in the cleanup of Chernobyl have died from the after-effects suffered during the work, according to information from the Union-Chernobyl-Ukraine, and their children have suffered severe health problems, including thyroid cancer, congenital birth deformities, and leukemia. The area remains cordoned today. (AP Photo/Volodymyr Repik/CP Archive)

Soviet Union; it is now an independent state). A meltdown in a reactor unit caused an explosion and fire that spread airborne radioactivity as far away as Italy and Sweden. Soviet leaders made matters worse by initially shrouding the event in secrecy, not even informing neighbouring states of incoming radioactivity. In Scandinavia, nomadic Laplanders were severely affected as their reindeer herds ate toxic grass. Leaks of radioactive inert gases and iodine from a reactor near St. Petersburg in the 1990s have accentuated the fear that more Chernobyls are waiting to happen. Throughout the Cold War, Eastern Europe had served as a captive market for the Soviet nuclear industry, and Soviet-designed reactors (located in Czechoslovakia, Hungary, Bulgaria, and Eastern Germany) did not always include sufficient emergency core cooling systems or containment vessels. Since the unprecedented nuclear disaster at Chernobyl, a new customary norm has emerged in international law: states have an obligation to inform bordering states if a disaster with such far-reaching consequences has occurred.

Other transborder pollution problems have resulted from industrialization. Several regional agreements aim at reducing acid precipitation (acid rain), which damages trees; for example, in 1988, 24 European states signed a treaty to limit nitrogen oxide emissions to 1988 levels by 1995, and Canada and the United States have a bilateral agreement that was the result of many years of protracted bargaining.[32] However, without funding for effective scrubbers for smokestacks for industries burning lignite (a highly sulphurous coal), acid rain will continue to be a major problem, particularly in Eastern Europe.

Yet another transborder environmental issue is the circulation of pesticides, an issue that illustrates the complexity of both modern science and the world economy. For example, in 1990 U.S. manufacturers exported more than 24 million kilograms of pesticides such as DDT, dieldrin, toxaphene, endrin, ethyl parathion, and other compounds that were banned, restricted, or unregistered for use in the United States. Most of these were shipped to Southern states, such as Argentina, Colombia, Ecuador, and the Philippines, though a significant amount went to Belgium, Japan, and the Netherlands. An agreement on persistent organic pollutants has been signed that should limit this trade. Nevertheless, in his excellent study of pesticide regulation, John Wargo draws attention to the difficulty of regulating such international commerce in products that are highly hazardous to both human and ecosystem health:

> An active ingredient produced in the United States may be shipped to Switzerland where it is combined with other ingredients and shipped to Egypt. In Egypt, it might be applied as an insecticide to cotton. Cottonseeds may then be harvested and sold to a commodity broker in Israel, who then sells them

to a manufacturer of cottonseed oil in Italy. The Italian firm
may then sell the oil, perhaps mixed with other oil from seeds
grown in Guatemala with the help of another pesticide, to an
American food processing company.[33]

Another local and regional environmental issue is access to fresh water. Though recent events, such as flooding in India, Bangladesh, and Mozambique, suggest that the problem of water is one of overabundance, the longer-term issue will no doubt be scarcity. Only about 3 percent of the world's water is fresh, and much of that is frozen in the Arctic icecaps. In effect, less than 1 percent of the world's water is easily accessible fresh water. Global water use doubles every 21 years, and water use now exceeds sustainable consumption limits. Astoundingly, about 1.1 billion people, or 18 percent of the world's population, lack access to safe drinking water, and 2.5 billion are without proper sanitation.[34]

Aquifers (underground water supplies) in many of the world's regions are running dry or becoming contaminated with seawater. Many major rivers are mere streams when they reach the coast due to diversion of water for irrigation. The demand for fresh water comes from agriculture (66 percent of the total consumption), industry (25 percent), and human consumption (9 percent). In some regions, the increased rate of water use has had dramatic consequences. A stark example can be found in the Aral Sea region of Central Asia. During Soviet rule, massive quantities of water were diverted from the river systems feeding the Aral Sea to irrigate a huge agricultural project. The flow of water to the Aral Sea slowed to a trickle, and as a result the Sea has now shrunk by one-half. Not only has this devastated the local fishing industry, but the dry sea salt is swept up by winds into dust storms, which deposit salt over a wide area, poisoning land and people.[35] The reduced flow of water in the tributary rivers of the shrinking Sea has

---

PROFILE 10.5 Canada's Freshwater Supply

Canada has a large supply of fresh water, and this is expected to be a growing issue in its relations with the United States. In both Canada and the United States, water demand continues to increase, making successful management all the more important in the future. According to a recent report, Canadians rank "a dismal 28th out of 29 OECD nations in water consumption per capita, with only Americans consuming more water. The amount of water consumed in Canada has increased by 25.7%" between 1980 and 2001.

Other factors to consider:

- Between 1972 and 1991, Canada's water usage increased from 24 billion cubic metres per year to over 45 billion cubic metres per year—a rise of more than 80 percent; in the same period, population increased only 3 percent.

- Freshwater lakes, rivers, and underground aquifers hold only 3.5 percent of the world's water. By comparison, saltwater oceans and seas contain 95.1 percent of the world's water supply.

- Canada has about 9 percent of the world's fresh renewable water supply, compared with 18 percent for Brazil, 9 percent for China, and 8 percent for the United States.

- The Great Lakes constitute one of the largest systems of freshwater reservoirs on earth, with 18 percent of the world's fresh surface water.

- About 7.6 percent of Canada is covered by fresh water in lakes and rivers—755 165 square kilometres. To this can be added 195 059 square kilometres of perennial snow and ice.

There is increasing pressure on provincial governments to begin bulk water exports to the increasingly dry United States, but this is a highly sensitive subject to Canadians. One can reasonably expect this pressure to increase, however.

SOURCES: D. BOYD, *CANADA VS. THE OECD: AN ENVIRONMENTAL COMPARISON* (UNIVERSITY OF VICTORIA, 2001); ENVIRONMENT CANADA, http://www.ec.gc.ca/water (ACCESSED 26 MAY 2004).

been a cause of concern for the newly independent states of the former Soviet Union though they have established an intergovernmental commission for water coordination.

In fact, a new term has been coined to refer to conflicts over water resources: *hydropolitics*.[36] Water conflict has been an acute problem in areas with arid climates, such as northern Africa and the Middle East (see Profile 10.6). As water consumption increases alongside population and economic growth, the quest for sources of fresh water becomes more dramatic and has already been the cause of conflict between several states. There are 261 river basins shared by two or more states, including the Nile, Jordan, Euphrates, Amazon, Mekong, Rhine, Ganges, Indu, Colorado, and others. They are all potential sources of both conflict and cooperation. As we discussed at the outset of this chapter, water scarcity will not automatically lead to protracted and perhaps violent future conflict. Some argue that shared resources can bring out the best in states, promoting their ability to cooperate when they must to achieve mutual benefits. Thomas Homer-Dixon argues that, though there are historical examples of wars caused by the quest for nonrenewable resources (such as oil and minerals), "the story is different for renewables like cropland, forests, fish and fresh water. It is hard to find clear historical or contemporary examples of major wars motivated mainly by scarcities of renewables."[37] This analytic caution is certainly warranted, but it does not really contradict the claim that conflicts over resources are potential causes of international and civil warfare, as well as factors in long-range

---

PROFILE 10.6 — ## Water and Interstate Conflict in North Africa and the Middle East?

THE NILE

The Nile River is one of the most famous and historic rivers of the world. It is also a river of tremendous regional economic importance. The Nile is the primary source of water for both human consumption and agriculture in Northeast Africa, in particular Egypt and the Sudan. In fact, almost all of Egypt's water is drawn from the Nile. However, almost all of the source water of the Nile originates outside Egypt, in the seven countries that straddle the Nile River Basin: Sudan, Ethiopia, Kenya, Rwanda, Burundi, Tanzania, and Zaire. The exploitation of water resources in these countries would reduce the flow of water to the Nile and to Egypt. To the Egyptian government, this is a major security concern, prompting former Egyptian president Anwar Sadat and former Foreign Minister Boutros Boutros-Ghali to warn that conflict over water might result in Egypt going to war. In 1999, the Nile Basin Initiative was signed, and there are hopes that this can help manage the situation as well as promote development in the region.

THE JORDAN RIVER BASIN

The Jordan River Basin is a valley in the central Middle East that collects most of the rainwater that falls on the region. Syria, Lebanon, Israel, Jordan, and the West Bank are heavily dependent on the Jordan Basin for their water supplies, and since the creation of Israel in 1948 access to this water supply has been a factor in the Arab–Israeli conflict. In fact, approximately 40 percent of Israel's groundwater originates in the territories occupied by Israel in 1967. Water demands in Israel are rising as the population increases, and this has resulted in an increased dependence on water drawn from the Jordan Basin. Israel has also drawn water from groundwater aquifers, which are becoming saline from overuse. Israel runs a *water deficit*, drawing out more water than nature replaces. Water has become a crucial point of discussion and dispute between Israel and the Palestinian people (who have had their access to water restricted by the Israeli government), as well as between Israel and neighbouring Arab states. Conflict over water could easily spark a wider conflagration in a region already beset with conflicts and high levels of tension, and resource sharing must be part of any future peace negotiations.

SOURCE: MIRIAM R. LOWI, *WATER AND POWER: THE POLITICS OF A SCARCE RESOURCE IN THE JORDAN RIVER BASIN* (CAMBRIDGE, UK: CAMBRIDGE UNIVERSITY PRESS, 1993).

geostrategic thinking (and trade policy, as water-rich states such as Canada contemplate bulk water exports). Water is not the only resource that might spark future conflicts, but given the increasing consumption and decreasing availability of this vital resource, water may become as much a factor in war between states as oil and strategic minerals have been in the past.

While thirsts for essential resources such as oil and water are obvious potential causes of conflict in the modern age, states have also come into conflict over other resources, including those found in the commons. Managing international fisheries has often proven to be one of the more complex diplomatic tasks. The so-called cod wars between Iceland and Britain in the 1960s and 1970s provide a historical example of potential conflict over dwindling resources, but Canadians have a more recent example on which to reflect: a dispute over straddling turbot stocks off the coast of Newfoundland, which quickly assumed international proportions. The case involved the Spanish fishing fleet and an uncharacteristically assertive Canadian government. The Spanish Basques were fishing off the coast of Newfoundland as early as 1530, though they called it *Terranova* then. By the 1580s, French Basque ships were returning from the area loaded with cod and, eventually, whale oil. In 1994, the multilateral Northwest Atlantic Fisheries Organization (NAFO) had set limits on the total allowable catch of Greenland halibut (or turbot), allocating national quotas for this resource. The European Union, pressured by Spain and Portugal, rejected the quotas as unfair.

Canada imposed a unilateral moratorium, concerned with the depleting turbot stocks, and eventually seized the Spanish fishing vessel *Estai*, claiming that the trawler was not only violating the quota rules but also using illegal fish nets in the process. Since the vessel was on the high seas, Canada was, in effect, breaking international law. Canada's seizure of the Spanish trawler led to international tension, because Canada's international legal jurisdiction stops after the 200-nautical-mile (370-kilometre) limit imposed by the exclusive economic zone (EEZ) provision of the Law of the Sea. Thus, the fishery dilemma quickly became a foreign policy problem. Eventually, Canada passed legislation that would make it legal (in the domestic context, if not in the international) to physically stop ships from fishing near the exclusive economic zone.[38] A subsequent international agreement on straddling stocks was hammered out in New York, giving coastal states the right to inspect ships fishing near such areas. The lesson here is that Canada had to break international law to make it.

In 1997, Canada became embroiled in another fisheries dispute, this time off the West Coast of Canada. The dispute broke out between Canada and the United States over Pacific salmon quotas and the failure of efforts to negotiate a new Pacific salmon treaty. Tensions escalated between the governments of British Columbia and Alaska, Washington state, and Oregon. At one point, Canadian fishers surrounded an Alaskan ferry in anger. The fishing season ended with no resolution of the dispute. Dwindling stocks of fish on both coasts may lead to increasingly intense disputes in the future. However, it is unlikely that this conflict will lead

Seized ship: a victory for conservation, or piracy? Onlookers watch the Spanish trawler *Estai* arrive at St. John's on March 12, 1995. A Canadian fisheries patrol vessel fired the first salvo in what became the Great Turbot War between Canada and the European Union. (CP Picture Archive/Fred Chartrand)

to a violent confrontation between Canada and the United States, although violence between individuals remains a possibility.

ENVIRONMENTAL DEGRADATION AND MILITARY CONFLICT: AN ONGOING CIRCLE

Environmental degradation has been increasingly regarded as a security issue in the study of international relations. However, as we noted earlier the conceptualization of the environment as a security problem is not without its detractors. Skeptics argue that it is inappropriate to characterize environmental issues as security issues because the environment is not an enemy and environmental issues cannot be addressed through traditional military means. Others argue that little hard evidence exists to support the link between environmental degradation and conflict and war.[39] However, we would argue that there is often a vicious circle at play when it comes to military conflict and the environment. War can cause severe environmental destruction, which contributes to resource scarcity, which in turn contributes to structural conditions conducive to conflict and more war. We will deal with each turn of the circle in this section.

On November 5, 2003, the UN declared that each November 6 would be recognized as the International Day for Preventing the Exploitation of the Environment in War and Conflict. While it may seem self-evident, the fact that war is bad for the environment is often overlooked. The environment can be harmed incidentally, a function of strategic necessity or negligence; it can be harmed deliberately, as a strategy in itself often referred to as ecocide; and it can be harmed in the course of military preparation, not only in terms of munitions/weapons testing, but also in terms of the atmospheric pollution, chemical spills, and radioactive waste emitted by the military-industrial complex.[40] Invariably, military strategy and tactics, offensive and defensive, involve a good deal of environmental assault and modification. As early as 2400 B.C.E., Entemenar—the ruler of Sumer—modified the land by constructing a canal that diverted water from the Tigris to the Euphrates watershed, which ceased Sumer's dependence on the Kingdom of Umma. As Fred Roots has pointed out, the groundwater rose with this construction, which caused rapid salinization, impoverishing Umma. Eventually, however, Sumer suffered as well, as its own overirrigated desert soils were leached. Roots concludes that by 2200 B.C.E., "mighty Sumer was easy prey for upstart Babylon, which had less wealth and poorer technology but a clean environmental base." On a further note, Roots cites the most famous Biblical example of environmental modification for military purposes, the parting of the Red Sea by Moses: "The mechanism by which Moses accomplished this rapid environmental modification is not clear to ordinary mortals today, but presumably he did it all by triggering tectonic movements. Certainly the geological structure and accumulated crustal stress in the Red Sea graben makes this a good potential location ... if God is on your side."[41]

An incomplete list of major ecologically disruptive wars stretches back to the Persian–Scythian War of 512 B.C.E. (as the Scythians retreated they hindered Persian pursuit with a scorched-earth policy, a theme found frequently over the long years of military history). The Peloponnesian War (431–404 B.C.E.), made famous by Thucydides, saw the annually repeated destruction of Athenian grain crops by the Spartans. At the end of the Third Punic War, the Roman victors polluted the farmland around Carthage with salt. Genghis Khan, leading the Mongols through Asia and Eastern Europe, killed all unappropriated livestock and destroyed irrigation works located along the Tigris River in Mesopotamia. The Dutch flooded their own land to keep away French troops in the Franco-Dutch War of 1672–78. Destruction of agricultural land, intended to starve rebellious states into the Union, was routine policy during the last years of the American Civil War. The Chinese used scorched-earth tactics to put down the Taiping Rebellion (1850–64). The Portuguese used herbicides to destroy crops during the Angolan War of Independence (1961–75). Water and water-related facilities have often been targeted in times of war. In the ancient period, wells were poisoned to deny water to the enemy, a practice that continued for centuries. In the 20th century, hydroelectric dams were targets during World War II and the Korean War. Irrigation systems in North Vietnam were bombed by the United States during the Vietnam War, and Syria and Israel had violent clashes over water in the mid-1960s. In the Gulf War, Kuwaiti desalination plants were destroyed by Iraq, while coalition bombing largely destroyed Iraq's water supply system, both in 1991 and in 2003.

In North America and Europe, concerns with the environmental impact of war first became pronounced in the 1960s. It became apparent that, with the advent of nuclear weapons, it was now possible for military conflict to destroy most of the biosphere. Perhaps the most widely read account of such Armageddon-like forecasting was Carl Sagan's discussion in *Foreign Affairs* of the possible climatic catastrophe—nuclear winter—that would follow even small-scale nuclear war. An earlier book by Jonathan Schell received a popular reaction, and public awareness of the ill effects of nuclear testing (including the discovery of iodine in breast milk) was partly responsible for the eventual acceptance of the Partial Test Ban Treaty in 1963.[42]

The end of the Cold War and the deliberate burning of an estimated 500 million barrels of oil in Kuwait after the Gulf War of 1990–91 provoked a shift from an understandable nuclear preoccupation to concerns over how conventional warfare has harmed ecosystems and caused related population displacements in various regions of the world. However, the extensive damage caused by what was arguably the largest single assault on an ecosystem, that inflicted on Indochina's forests by American armed forces during the Vietnam War, provided investigative focus in the early 1970s. Localized ecosystem destruction, intended to flush out enemy forces in high-cover areas such as forests, marshes or grasslands, and to deprive them of food supply, is best achieved by a narrow range of special-purpose weapons, especially chemical herbicides such as the infamous Agent Orange (2,4-D and 2,4,5-T), Agent White (2,4-D and Picloram), and Agent Blue (Cucodylic Acid). In addition to the landscape alteration wrought by the infamous Rome plough (which tore up entire fields to destroy farming capability), more than 17 000 square kilometres of South Vietnam were damaged by herbicides, and over 1500 square kilometres of ecologically sensitive mangrove forest was completely destroyed. This campaign generated understandable moral outrage in the United States itself, and while some 10 000 affected U.S. veterans won $180

Toxic conflict. A U.S. soldier from the 1st Marine Expeditionary Force stands guard at a burning oil well at the Rumeila Oil fields in Iraq, 23 March 2003. Several oil wells were set ablaze by retreating Iraqi troops in the Rumeila area, the second largest offshore oil field in the country, near the Kuwaiti border. (AP Photo/Ian Waldie/Pool/CP Archive)

million in damages in a civil suit against Dow, Monsanto, and other manufacturers, the Vietnamese have never been compensated.[43] The Vietnam War coincided with a growing domestic environmentalist movement in the United States, and was probably the first military campaign that was heavily criticized in some quarters for its environmental impact. Richard Falk wrote in 1973: "surely it is no exaggeration to consider the forests and plantations treated by Agent Orange as an Auschwitz for environmental values, certainly not from the perspective of such a distinct environmental species as the mangrove tree or nipa palm." In the recent military intervention in Serbia (1999), NATO bombing "destroyed fertilizer plants and oil refineries located on the tributary of the Danube river, resulting in fires and the release of petroleum byproducts and other carcinogens into the water. Additional bombs … released large amounts of PCBs and liquid mercury into other Danube tributaries, posing severe danger to human life."[44]

Despite a treaty designed to curb the deliberate damage of the environment during warfare in 1977 (the Convention on the Prohibition of Military or Any Other Hostile Use of Environmental Modification Techniques, or ENMOD), it is clear that ecocide continues to be employed in war. In Colombia, the so-called War on Drugs has seen widespread spraying of "broad spectrum herbicides in ecologically fragile areas. In a single two-week period in 2000, approximately 25,000 hectares were fumigated from the air with a glyphosate-based chemical agent." Is this spraying meant simply to stop narcotics production, or is it an instrument of war against rebels? In Mexico, Zapatista rebels have "denounced what they consider to be hostile environmental modification aimed at stopping their insurgency. According to villagers in Zapatista regions, the government's massive spraying of pesticides to control the Mediterranean fruit fly has deliberately hit food crops, ruining them. The villagers say the spraying is a thinly disguised attempt to destroy the food security of farming communities suspected of harbouring rebel sympathizers. The Mexican government of Ernesto Zedillo, while admitting that the Army played a role in fruit fly control, insisted that spraying was purely for phytosanitary reasons." The same communities suspect local forest fires could be deliberately set as well, a theme repeated by the Yanomami in the Brazilian Amazon, and indigenous peoples in Kalimantan, Indonesia.[45]

The use of such techniques has long-term consequences. The German Army first used liquid chlorine (which inflames the lungs, causing those exposed to drown in their own exudation) near Ypres, Belgium, in April 1915. In June 1916, the Allies first used the even deadlier phosgene during the famous Battle of the Somme. According to Robert Harris and Jeremy Paxman, "Long after the initial bombardment had occurred, an area which had been contaminated by mustard gas was liable to remain dangerous. The liquid formed pools in shell craters … It polluted water. In cold weather it froze like water and stayed in the soil: mustard used in the winter of 1917 poisoned men in the spring of 1918 when the ground thawed."[46] Landmines destroy people and arable land long after they are planted as well. Similarly, areas near many of the nuclear weapons production plants in the United States and Russia are contaminated by various chemical hazards and radiation, and Canada continues to lament the chemical residue left by the long-abandoned Cold War Distant Early Warning System in the North. Today, we are more likely to worry about whether there will be a long-lasting health impact from depleted uranium (DU) projectiles fired by U.S. tanks and planes to penetrate Iraqi and Serbian armour. We can safely predict that there will be similar instances and long-term problems in the future so long as states do not take the ENMOD convention seriously. Military research projects involving even more ambitious environmental modification techniques, such as cloud seeding and other forms of weather modification, have been ongoing. Research in even more exotic fields, such as nanotechnology and the ionosphere, will also have military applications.

However, our circle does not end here. Military violence and political instability can lead to increased environmental scarcity and, thus, enhance the prospects for more military conflict. The hypothesis that environmental degradation is a cause of conflict in the international system is built on the logic of scarcity. Both renewable and nonrenewable resources are finite in quantity. As the population of the planet increases, and as industrialization and consumption continue to grow and spread, the scarcity of resources will become increasingly acute for three main reasons:

1. Human activity will increasingly consume more resources, degrading the quality and availability of resources.

2. Population growth will increase the number of people making demands on a shrinking resource pie.

3. Resources will not be distributed equally, and the concentration of resources in a small segment of the population will decrease the availability of that resource to the rest of the population.

As available resources deteriorate or are depleted, competition for access to these resources will increase. Conflict and war over resources will be the inevitable result. Indeed, some would argue that this process has already begun. A major Canadian-led international research project on environmental scarcity and violent conflict reached the following conclusion:

> Scarcities of renewable resources will increase sharply. The total area of high quality agricultural land will drop, as will the extent of forests and the number of species they sustain. Coming generations will also see the widespread depletion and degradation of aquifers, rivers, and other water resources; the decline of many fisheries; and perhaps significant climate change … environmental scarcities are already contributing to violent conflicts in many areas of the world. These conflicts are probably the early signs of an upsurge of violence in the coming decades that will be induced or aggravated by scarcity.[47]

A number of different environmental issues have been cited as causes of existing or future conflicts:

- The degradation and loss of arable land, with consequent implications for crop and livestock production.

- The destruction of forests and consequent loss of forestry-related employment, revenue, topsoil, and species diversity.

- The depletion and degradation of fresh water supplies.

- The depletion of strategic minerals, including oil.

- The overexploitation and consequent depletion of fisheries resources.

An illustration of the link between environmental degradation, resource scarcity, and political upheaval and violence can be found in the plight of Haiti. A combination of population growth, land shortages, and corrupt leadership bent on expropriating available wealth has left Haiti the poorest country in the Western hemisphere. Haiti's forests have virtually disappeared, cut down to create more land for cultivation. Poor Haitians move up the mountainsides, clearing more forests and exhausting the land. The loss of the forest contributes to soil erosion, which has rendered almost half of the countryside unsuitable for farming. This, coupled with population growth, has led to a fall in per capita incomes. People have migrated to the cities, especially Port-au-Prince, a teeming city dominated by enormous slums. Many others have fled Haiti as refugees. Political instability and civil strife have characterized recent Haitian politics as the rich political classes use increasing levels of force and repression to maintain their control over the country. In 1986 the "Baby Doc" Duvalier regime collapsed, and international intervention restored civilian rule. Political instability in Haiti in the early 1990s resulted in the creation of a UN peacekeeping mission that helped to restore order, but the environmental and economic problems of the country were never resolved. In 2004 violence erupted as President Aristide was pushed from power. The UN has returned to Haiti again, and order is likely to be restored. However, the severity of environmental degradation in the country raises doubts about the prospects for long-term economic and political stability.

In Brazil, fears persist that the unequal distribution of land and wealth could create domestic instability and increasingly violent conflict in the future. Although Brazil ranked ninth in the world in gross domestic product in 1996, the distribution of wealth in Brazil is highly unequal. In fact, the poorest 40 percent of the Brazilian population receives only 7 percent of total income. Land distribution is even more unequal, with less than 1 percent of all landowners controlling almost half of Brazil's privately held land. As a result, Brazil has some 12 million landless peasants while more than 180 million hectares of farmable land lie unused. Many of these peasants have migrated to the cities, feeding Brazil's expanding urban slums. Lack of housing, jobs, and access to government services, as well as extreme poverty, have contributed to a soaring crime rate. Recently, there has been a move to return to the land, in the form of squatting and occupying unused tracts of land. This has brought the landless peasants and the Landless Workers' Movement, the organization that represents them, into conflict with local landowners and the police. This confrontation has not always been peaceful: more than 1700 people have been killed in the past decade. More radical organizations committed to armed struggle have grown rapidly. Unless meaningful land reform is enacted over the opposition of the politically powerful landowning class, a violent conflict over land distribution may be in Brazil's near future.

As discussed in chapters 6 and 8, many would argue that access to oil was a major factor in the 2003 invasion of Iraq. But there are many other, less well-known examples. The dispute over the Spratly and Paracel Islands in the South China Sea carries the potential for interstate conflict over the right to exploit oil and mineral deposits on the seabed. The Spratly Islands are a group of 500 small islands situated in the South China Sea. Six states lay claim to some or all of the Spratly Islands or their territorial waters: Brunei, China, Malaysia, the Philippines, Taiwan, and Vietnam (see Chapter 6). Although most of the islands are mere outcroppings of rock or coral, they possess strategic value for three reasons: they are located in the middle of an important international sea lane, their territorial waters are rich in fish stocks, and their seabeds contain oil and mineral deposits. The Spratly Islands dispute has had a violent dimension, particularly between Vietnam and China. These two countries have clashed over some of the islands in 1974, 1982, 1988, and 1992. Most countries that lay claim to some or all of the islands maintain military garrisons on selected islands, and all maintain an air force and naval presence in and around the islands. Despite calls for a regional conference on the future of the islands, and the opening of talks between China and Vietnam, the Spratly Islands remain a subject of intense interstate dispute. There are concerns that this dispute, and many others with similar profiles, could result in armed conflict at any time.

The violence–environmental degradation circle can be broken only when states and civil society cooperate to stem both military conflict and resource scarcity. The prognosis does not look good, but this is no excuse for admitting defeat. Many activists have devoted their lives to the cause of environmental protection, some with controversial results. We briefly examine the increasingly important role of such activists below.

NONGOVERNMENTAL ACTORS AND THE ENVIRONMENT IN GLOBAL POLITICS

Little doubt remains that the environment has become an important foreign policy issue for most governments. For example, Canada has an official ambassador for the environment, John Fraser, who attends multilateral conferences such as the September 1995 meeting in Geneva that amended the Basel Convention to prohibit the sale of toxic wastes from OECD countries to Southern ones for final disposal or recycling; currently he is chairman of the Pacific Fisheries Resource Conservation Council. The current Ambassador for the Environment is Gilbert Parent, who chaired the Canadian National Secretariat Round Table Consultations and the Aboriginal and Industry Consultations in preparation for the World Summit on Sustainable Development. He was a member of Canada's delegation to the WSSD in Johannesburg and serves as a member of the International Advisory Board to the American Council on Renewable Energy. However, despite such governmental actors, and the plethora of intergovernmental organizations active today, it would be impossible to approach a thorough treatment of global ecopolitics without reference to the nongovernmental actors that have converged to participate in this field. In fact, many would claim that NGOs have been the principal instigators all along, the ones that forced states to take environmental concerns seriously in the first place.

A member of Greenpeace, seen through the mouth of a giant cob of corn, scales a building to hoist a banner protesting a conference on genetically modified foods on January 24, 2000, in Montreal. Many environmental groups are fond of public displays to draw attention to their causes, while others labour in virtual anonymity to try to affect change "within the system." (CP Photo/ Paul Chiasson)

NGOs are active in many areas with clear international implications. For example, an NGO that has seen recent success in stemming the tide of large-scale infrastructure development is the International Rivers Network, based in Berkeley, California. It led a successful coalition that lobbied strongly against the World Bank's financing of a Nepalese hydropower project and participated in an earlier effort to stop the Bank's funding of India's notorious $3.5 billion Narmada Dam. The World Bank's financing of large dams dropped from an average of 18 a year between 1980 and 1985 to only 6 a year between 1986 and 1993.[48] Perhaps most symbolically, the Bank is staying away from the Three Gorges Dam on China's Yangtze River, which will involve the resettling of more than 1 million people. Meanwhile, a Paris-based professional IGO, the International Commission on Large Dams, has a more positive attitude toward dam construction. As some 843 large dams are under construction around the world, this body not only supports

PROFILE 10.7

Examples of Activism: Option Consumers and the Seikatsu Club

Option Consumers is a Montreal-based consumer group. In a February 3, 2004, report called "The State of Food Safety in Quebec," Option Consumers made recommendations to protect Quebecers from what they considered to be the perils of genetically modified foods (see our discussion on GMOs below). The organization advocated precaution, accountability, increased access to information, and the imposition of rigorous biological and environmental standards. Option Consumers is part of a coalition of Canadian consumer and environmental groups dedicated to the imposition of mandatory labelling rules for genetically modified foods. This task proves difficult because the Consumers Association of Canada (CAC), the federal government, and the food industry are all in favour of voluntary labelling—basically an honour system for food companies to disclose whether their products contain genetically modified products.

In Japan, meanwhile, the Seikatsu Club is a consumer group involving some 170 000 households throughout Japan. It was founded by women in the early 1970s in reaction to

Minamata disease, the fish-borne mercury poisoning that causes neurological disease, paralysis, and death. Recognizing the negative impacts of pesticides and other agricultural chemicals on health and the environment, the club uses its purchasing power to promote the development of organic and ecological farming. After the Chernobyl nuclear accident, the club created the Radiation Disaster Network, which monitored radioactive substances in food imported in Europe. The Seikatsu Club is one of 13 000 consumer groups in Japan that are advancing Japan's self-sufficiency in food and leading a nationwide movement to reform consumer habits and lifestyles. The objectives of the Seikatsu Club are to learn how to govern society through self-management, to rebuild local societies, and to create locally based economies with cooperative systems of welfare, health, education, and culture.

SOURCES: http://www.option-consommateurs.org (ACCESSED 27 MAY 2004); D. GOLDIN ROSENBERG, "INITIATIVES IN FEMINISM, ENVIRONMENTALISM AND ACTION," *ALTERNATIVES: PERSPECTIVES ON SOCIETY, TECHNOLOGY AND ENVIRONMENT* 21 (1995), 20–21.

the general idea that hydroelectric power is the cleanest and most efficient of energy sources but also is willing to help in its development. Obviously these two groups are at opposite ends of the spectrum and receive their funding from quite different sources!

The confrontation between environmental groups and large multinational corporations is usually covered in the media. A little-known but important exception is the longest-running civil suit in British legal history, involving McDonald's, the American hamburger giant, and two unemployed environmentalists. The two belonged to London Greenpeace when it distributed a leaflet in the mid-1980s called "What's Wrong with McDonald's: Everything They Don't Want You to Know." McDonald's sued for libel but may have been sorry it did, since the two alleged libel-mongers have forced the company to defend itself in court. For example, the court has heard evidence that McDonald's paid people to infiltrate London Greenpeace. A nutrition expert employed by McDonald's itself testified that "it is 'very reasonable' to tell the public that 'a diet high in fat, sugar, animal products and salt and low in fibre, vitamins and minerals is linked with cancer of the breast and bowel and heart disease.' That was one of the very allegations in the pamphlet against which McDonald's is complaining."[49] Today, one of the biggest confrontations is between activists and large food processors over GMOs, a controversy we return to below in our discussion of the role of science.

NGOs have often assumed a watchdog role, reporting on the activities of MNCs and states for the general public; they also influence government policy at the national level. For example, Greenpeace members are included in the official American delegation to the International Whaling Commission, where the United States has consistently opposed lifting the global

Protecting the seals? Police officers stand guard as protesters lie in the road outside the Canadian High Commission, Grosvenor Square, London, 16 April 2004, where they are venting their feelings against the country's seal cull. A total of 200 000 seals were taken. (AP Photo/Edmond Terakopian/PA/CP Archive)

moratorium on commercial whaling now in place (controversially, it insists Alaskan Inuit and First Nations peoples should have the right to whale, but not Japanese or Norwegian coastal fishermen). NGOs also influence the operations of multilateral forums, contributing to CITES and World Conservation Union meetings and their outcomes. At times, they are criticized for insisting on a Western environmentalist ethic, even in local situations where people are more attuned to living on the land than most NGO members have ever been, and for focusing on a few key issues, ones that can aid in fundraising appeals. No doubt, this is a cause of some friction, as the debate over the Canadian seal hunt suggests. Groups such as the International Fund for Animal Welfare strongly oppose the hunt, which in 2004 was allocated a quota of 350 000 seals. Sealers argue they are engaging in a vital aspect of their livelihood in economically depressed regions, and that urban environmentalists neither understand nor care about them. Though taking baby whitecoat seals is banned, harp seals over two weeks old can be killed, which enrages those who campaign tirelessly against this hunt. Seal products remain banned in the United States and they find only limited acceptance in most of Western Europe, but new markets have emerged in Russia, Ukraine and Poland. The best way to influence the Canadian government on such issues, it is often suggested, is by campaigning abroad so as to embarrass it.

THE ROLE OF SCIENCE IN GLOBAL ECOPOLITICS

The current debate over the safety of genetically modified organisms (GMOs) has drawn attention to the role of scientific certainty, or perhaps more precisely, the lack of scientific certainty facing decision makers. **Genetic engineering** refers to a variety of techniques aimed at deliberately changing the genetic makeup of a cell or organism. Scientists have been able to modify the genes of many crops, including tobacco, tomatoes, corn, squash, potatoes, and cotton. Some genetically engineered crops, such as the FlavrSavr tomato (which is designed to stay fresher longer), are on the market in the United States. The tomato is FDA (Food and Drug Administration—U.S.A.) approved, but critics have argued that the long-term effects on health are unknown. Further, they argue that the cross-pollination effect from farms using genetically modified seeds is unknown. Some plants have been modified to be resistant to weed killers, insects, viruses, or fungi. Corn plants have been genetically modified to help farmers rid their fields of weeds without destroying the crop.

Researchers can also genetically engineer many food animals, including fish, cows, goats, sheep, and pigs. For some animals, scientists can combine genetic engineering with cloning to produce many identical, genetically modified animals. Such animals can be used for research into human health issues and even for organ transplants. Again, critics are concerned about the ethical implications of modifying nature and about possible accidents. And of course cloning is a major concern, not only because numerous experiments have been successfully (though with mixed results) carried out, but because the act of cloning human beings, with all this implies for human rights issues, is not far off, though most states have banned direct research. The powerful biotechnology industry, most of it located in the United States and Japan, wants the Europeans and others to open their markets to GMOs, while the EU, reflecting public opinion, is reluctant to do so. The industry argues that such technology improves farming techniques and will, in the long term, provide more food for more people, but concerns remain about the tendency of the industry to force farmers to use its products and the lack of labelling specifying GMO products in supermarkets. Organizations such as Greenpeace have made an anti-GMO stance part of their platform. The Biosafety Protocol of the CBD dealt with the issue to some degree, but it remains a contested trade, public health, and ethical issue.

The global warming debate is another prime example of the role of science in global ecopolitics. Although acceptance of the fact that the earth is currently warming and that the greenhouse effect facilitates this is widespread, less certainty exists over whether this will have the effects some have predicted (see above) and over who exactly is to blame. On September 10, 1995, *The New York Times*, on the front page of its widely read Sunday edition, announced: "Experts Confirm Human Role in Global Warming." This was a highly publicized acknowledgment that the global warming issue—once characterized by a great deal of scientific uncertainty and, therefore, difficult to deal with politically—is becoming less of an uncertain phenomenon. Indeed, from a political perspective, the series of conclusions published by the Intergovernmental Panel on Climate Change could be a vital step toward achieving the type of collective action such global problems demand, confirming what many political analysts have suggested: science is playing an increasingly large role in galvanizing political action, even at the international level. This point is well made in *An Agenda of Science for Environment and Development into the 21st Century*, which is the published summary of a conference held in Vienna in November 1991. The conference, ASCEND 21, which featured presentations by specialists in many interrelated fields such as population, energy, marine and coastal systems, biodiversity, and public awareness, aimed to provide a contribution to the Agenda 21 UNCED process but also made the case for the importance of integrating the social and natural sciences as we strive for necessarily complex solutions to frustratingly complex problems.[50] There is a fine line between the necessary use of science to protect human and ecological health, and the adoption of a technocratic approach to governance that would place inordinate power in the hands of "scientific experts," many of them employed by large corporations with their own commercial interests.

Richard Elliot Benedick, who was a member of the American delegation to negotiations over the ozone protection regime, writes in his book *Ozone Diplomacy*,

> Politicians must resist a tendency to lend too much credence to self-serving economic interests that demand scientific certainty, maintain that dangers are remote and unlikely, and insist that the costs of changing their ways are astronomical. The signatories at Montreal knowingly imposed substantial short-run economic dislocations even though the evidence was incomplete; the prudence of their decision was demonstrated when the scientific models turned out to have underestimated the effects of CFCs on ozone.[51]

What emerges from much of the scientific community is an emphasis on adopting the so-called precautionary principle in environmental management. The principle, which is endorsed in the consensually based Rio Declaration (Principle 15) of 1992, Agenda 21 (Chapter 17, para. 17.2), the United Nations Framework on Climate Change (1992), the Convention on Biological Diversity (1992), and the Montreal Protocol on Substances That Deplete the Ozone Layer (1987), insists that governments have an obligation to prevent environmental degradation, and that, in the absence of scientific certainty regarding the future impact of human activity, we should err on the side of caution and resist undertaking threatening actions.[52] Today, the precautionary principle seems more logical a path to take than ever.

CONCLUSIONS

The need for a shift toward sustainable development and human security gets a lot of airplay from governments today, even in the age of the "War on Terrorism." But does it amount to much? For example, the most recent Canadian foreign policy statement, *Canada in the World*, makes repeated reference to sustainable development, including a pledge to "ensure that Canadian foreign policy promotes sustainable development globally through the careful and responsible balancing of trade, development and environmental considerations."[53] The environment, along with basic human needs, women in development, infrastructure services, human rights, democracy and good governance, and private sector development, remains a priority for development assistance. However, the vast majority of Canadian development projects abroad are in the form of tied aid, which obliges the recipient to spend aid money on Canadian products or expertise. There is also the matter of selective assistance: beyond emergency aid situations, Ottawa is primarily interested in developing the newly emerging markets in Asia and Eastern Europe and in selling CANDU nuclear reactors abroad.

Two industrial accidents with ecological consequences raise further questions. The more infamous of the pair occurred in southern Spain on April 24, 1998, when 4 billion litres of toxic waste spilled from a tailings dam at a Canadian-owned zinc mine. Hundreds of acres of farmland were stained by the sudden flood, and the company involved, Toronto's Boliden Limited, has refused to accept full responsibility. The other accident occurred when a truck carrying sodium cyanide up the Tien Shan mountain range crashed in Kyrgyzstan in 1998. It was a Canadian-owned gold-mining firm, Cameco, that was running the mine and, again, the company refused to pay compensation to those affected (some dispute exists as to the extent of damages in both cases). The cyanide fell into the Barskaun River, which supplies a local town with drinking water and eventually runs into Lake Issyk-Kul. Such incidents serve to remind us it is not just diplomatic activity that is required to ensure sustainable development. We must all do our part, whether we are running companies or simply buying products here at home. And there is always the need to urge governments to keep the issues front and centre as well. Although it would be wonderful to conclude that environmental diplomacy reflects a global consciousness that is transforming old notions of parochial interests, it would also be premature at best. As time passes and it becomes increasingly apparent that the larger common threats such as global warming, ocean pollution, and biodiversity reduction have direct impacts on all states, then we might see substantive shifts in foreign policy perspectives.

In this chapter, we've discussed the problems of the commons, including global warming and ozone-layer depletion; transborder pollution; resource conflicts; and the impact of military activity. All these problems are interrelated and require concerted international action to meet the challenges they pose. We have also discussed the important roles of science and NGOs. We return to the theme of human security in the next chapter, where we discuss overpopulation, urbanization, and refugee movements. The conclusion of this chapter is that global ecopolitics is here to stay, not only as a valid and challenging subfield of the study of international relations, but as a vital academic discipline, complete with a growing theoretical foundation, in its own right.

Endnotes

1. "Why the Ark Is Sinking," in L. Kaufman and K. Mallory, eds., *The Last Extinction*, 2nd ed. (Cambridge, MA: MIT Press, 1993), 1–46, 12.

2. "The Coming Anarchy," *Atlantic Monthly* (February 1994), 58.

3. See M. Feshbach and A. Friendly, *Ecocide in the USSR: Health and Nature under Siege* (New York: Basic Books, 1992); and more recently, L. Andonova, *Transnational Politics of the Environment: The EU and Environmental Policy in Central and Eastern Europe* (Cambridge, MA: MIT Press, 2003).

4. "The Mirage of Eco-War: The Weak Relationship among Global Environmental Change, National Security and Interstate Violence," in I. Rowlands and M. Greene, eds., *Global Environmental Change and International Relations* (London: Macmillan, 1992), 169–91, 178. See also P. Stoett, "The Environmental Enlightenment: Security Analysis Meets Ecology," *Coexistence* 31 (1994), 127–46.

5. "Global Warming and International Action: An Economic Perspective," in A. Hurrell and B. Kingsbury, eds., *The International Politics of the Environment* (Oxford: Clarendon Press, 1992), 253–89.

6. "Sovereignty, Regimes, and Human Rights," in V. Rittberger, ed., *Regime Theory and International Relations* (Oxford: Clarendon Press, 1993), 139–67. See also P.M. Wijkman, "Managing the Global Commons," *International Organization* 36, no. 3 (1982), 511–36; S. Buck, *The Global Commons: An Introduction* (Washington, DC: Island Press, 1998); E. Ostrom, *Governing the Commons: The Evolution of Institutions for Collective Action* (Cambridge, UK: Cambridge University Press, 1990).

7. M. M'Gonigle and D. Babicki, "The Turbot's Last Stand?" *The Globe and Mail*, 21 July 1995, A19.

8. General Assembly Resolution 1803 (XVII), 14 December 1962. See N. Schrijver, *Sovereignty over Natural Resources: Balancing Rights and Duties* (Cambridge, UK: Cambridge University Press, 1997).

9. *Ozone Diplomacy: New Directions in Safeguarding the Planet* (Cambridge MA: Harvard University Press, 1991), 207. See also R.R. White, "Environmental Management and National Sovereignty: Some Issues from Senegal," *International Journal* 45 (Winter 1990), 106–37.

10. T. Brenton, *The Greening of Machiavelli: The Evolution of International Environmental Politics* (London: Earthscan, 1994), 202.

11. Lee Kimball, *Southern Exposure: Deciding Antarctica's Future* (Washington, DC: World Resources Institute, 1991).

12. For the complete text, see *Antarctic Journal of the United States* [Natural Science Foundation], 26, no. 4 (December 1991). See also O. S. Stokke and D. Vidas, eds., *Governing the Antarctic: The Effectiveness and Legitimacy of the Antarctic Treaty System* (Cambridge, UK: Cambridge University Press, 1996).

13. The Swiss Reinsurance Co. even has a full-time climate-change adviser. P. Knox, "Weather Talk Becoming Urgent," *The Globe and Mail*, 27 July 1996, A1.

14. B. McKibben, "Reflections: The End of Nature," *The New Yorker*, 11 September 1989, 47–48.

15. Michael T. Klare, "Resource Competition and World Politics in the Twenty-First Century," *Current History* 99 (December 2000), 407.

16. C. Flavin and O. Tinali, *Climate of Hope: New Strategies for Stabilizing the World's Atmosphere*, Worldwatch Paper 130 (Washington, DC: Worldwatch Institute, 1996). See also I. Rowlands, *The Politics of Global Atmospheric Change* (Manchester: Manchester University Press, 1995); and M. Paterson, *Global Warming and Global Politics* (London: Routledge, 1996).

17. UNEP, "Report of the Twelfth Meeting of the Parties to the Montreal Protocol," UNEP Ozone Secretariat, http://www.unep.org/ozone/12mop-9.shtml (accessed 27 May 2004).

18. C. Goldberg, "A Chilling Change in the Contraband Being Confiscated at Border Crossings," *The New York Times*, 10 November 1996, 15.

19. See Axel Bugge, "Amazon destruction jumps; environmentalists are shocked," Environmental News Network, http://www.enn.com/news/2003-06-27/s_5841.asp (accessed 27 May 2004).

20. See UN Food and Agricultural Organization, *Forest Resources Assessment 1990: Tropical Countries*, Forestry Paper 112 (Rome: UN FAO, 1993); and UNEP's *Global Environmental Outlook 2003*, 92.

21. See United Nations Department of Public Information, "Press Release of the Secretary-General's Report on Implementing Agenda 21," Johannesburg Summit 2002, http://www.johannesburgsummit.org/html/media_info/pressreleases_factsheets/ press_summary_sg_report2801.pdf (accessed 27 May 2004).

22. United Nations Environment Programme, *Global Environment Outlook 1* (New York: Oxford University Press, 1997), 235.

23. M.B. Fenton, "Species Impoverishment," in J. Leith, R. Price, and J. Spencer, eds., *Planet Earth: Problems and Prospects* (Montreal/Kingston: McGill-Queen's University Press, 1995), 83–110. See also P. Ehrlich and A. Ehrlich, *Extinction* (New York: Wiley, 1986); N. Eldredge, *The Miner's Canary: Unravelling the Mysteries of Extinction* (New York: Prentice Hall, 1991); and P. Colinvaux, *Why Big Fierce Animals Are Rare: An Ecologist's Perspective* (Princeton: Princeton University Press, 1978).

24. David Jablonski, "Mass Extinctions: New Answers, New Questions," in L. Kaufman and K. Mallory, eds., *The Last Extinction*, 2nd ed. (Cambridge, MA: MIT Press, 1993), 47–68, 52.

25. "Why the Ark Is Sinking," in L. Kaufman and K. Mallory, eds., *The Last Extinction*, 2nd ed. (Cambridge, MA: MIT Press, 1993), 1–46, 43. See also Kaufman's "Catastrophic Change in Species-Rich Freshwater Ecosystems: The Lessons of Lake Victoria," *Bioscience* 42, no. 11 (1992), 846–58; and Y. Baskin, "Africa's Troubled Waters: Fish Introductions and a Changing Physical Profile Muddy Lake Victoria's Future," *Bioscience* 42, no. 7 (1992), 476–81.

26. T. Foose, "Riders of the Last Ark: The Role of Captive Breeding in Conservation Strategies," in L. Kaufman and K. Mallory, eds., *The Last Extinction*, 149–78.

27. "Ethical Issues in Whale and Small Cetacean Management," *Environmental Ethics* 2, no. 3 (1980), 241–80, 244 n., 14.

28. Robert Boardman, *International Organization and the Conservation of Nature* (Bloomington: Indiana University Press, 1981).

29. See, for example, B. Rich, *Mortgaging the Earth: The World Bank, Environmental Impoverishment and the Crisis of Development* (London: Earthscan, 1994).

30. An important contribution to this awareness was the famous text by Rachel Carson, *Silent Spring* (Boston: Houghton Mifflin, 1962).

31. See Catherine Caufield, *Multiple Exposures: Chronicles of the Radiation Age* (London: Secker and Warburg, 1989).

32. See Don Munton and Geoffrey Castle, "Reducing Acid Rain, 1980s," in Don Munton and J. Kirton, eds., *Canadian Foreign Policy: Selected Cases* (Scarborough: Prentice Hall, 1992), 367–80. Critics charge that the G.W. Bush Administration has been slowly dismantling the Clean Air Act of 1972, thus harming this bilateral agreement as well.

33. J. Wargo, *Our Children's Toxic Legacy: How Science and Law Fail to Protect Us from Pesticides* (New Haven: Yale University Press, 1996), 281.

34. See United Nations Department of Public Informaton, "Johannesburg Summit Secretary-General Calls for Global Action on Water Issues," Johannesburg Summit 2002, http://www.johannesburgsummit.org/html/media_info/pressrelease_prep2/ global_action_water_2103.pdf (accessed 27 May 2004). Water-related diseases include malaria, severe diarrhea, intestinal worms, trachoma (which causes blindness), cholera, and schistosomiasis.

35. See William S. Ellis, "A Soviet Sea Lies Dying," *National Geographic* (February 1990), 73–93.

36. See L. Ohlsson, ed., *Hydropolitics: Conflicts over Water as a Development Constraint* (London: Zed, 1995). See also M. Lowi, *Water and Power: The Politics of a Scarce Resource in the Jordan River Basin* (Cambridge: Cambridge University Press, 1993); and for a discussion of the Danube, see E. Benvenisti, "Domestic Politics and International Resources: What Role for International Law?" in M. Byers, ed., *The Role of Law in International Politics* (Oxford: Oxford University Press, 2001), 109–30.

37. Thomas Homer-Dixon, "The Myth of Global Water Wars," *The Globe and Mail,* 9 November 1995, A23. He adds that the alarmist concern with inevitable water wars "distracts the public's attention from the real results of water scarcity. Shortages reduce food production, aggravate poverty and disease, spur large migrations and undermine a state's moral authority and capacity to govern. Over time, these stresses can tear apart a poor society's social fabric, causing chronic popular unrest and violence."

38. P. Koring, "Canada to Block Fish 'Pirates,'" *The Globe and Mail,* 12 January 1994, A1, A2. Canadian Fisheries Minister Brian Tobin, who made this announcement during a meeting with EC Fisheries Commissioner Yannis Paleokrassas, told reporters: "It's an act of conservation; nobody could call it an act of war. We're out to declare enough is enough when it comes to the desecration of cod stocks by nations that operate outside

of any civilized norms." For a succinct analysis of the Canada–Spain "fish war," see Andrew Cooper, *Canadian Foreign Policy: Old Habits, New Directions* (Scarborough: Prentice Hall Allyn and Bacon, 1997), 142–72.

39. See, for example, Marc S. Levy, "Is the Environment a National Security Issue?" *International Security* 20 (Fall 1995), 35–62, and Astri Suhrke, "Environmental Change, Migration, and Conflict: A Lethal Feedback Dynamic?" in C. Crocker, F. Osler Hampson, and P. Aall, eds., *Managing Global Chaos: Sources of and Responses to International Conflict* (Washington, DC: United States Institute of Peace Press, 1996), 113–27.

40. See William Thomas, *Scorched Earth: The Military's Assault on the Environment* (Philadelphia: New Society Publishers, 1995); Niles Gleditsch, "Armed Conflict and the Environment" in Paul F. Diehl and Nils Petter Gleditsch, eds., *Environmental Conflict* (Boulder, CO: Westview Press, 2001) 251–72; and Susan Lanier-Graham, *The Ecology of War: Environmental Impacts of Weaponry and Warfare* (New York: Walker and Company, 1993).

41. E.F. Roots, "International Agreements to Prohibit or Control Modification of the Environment for Military Purposes: An Historical Overview and Comments on Current Issues," in Bruno Schiefer, ed., *Verifying Obligations Respecting Arms Control and the Environment: A Post Gulf War Assessment* (University of Saskatchewan, 1992), 13–34, 13.

42. Carl Sagan, "Nuclear War and Climatic Catastrophe: Some Policy Implications," *Foreign Affairs* 62 (Winter 1983/84), 257–92; Jonathan Schell, *The Fate of the Earth* (New York: Knopf, 1982).

43. See P. Robinson, *The Effects of Weapons on Ecosystems*, (Toronto: Pergamon for UNEP, 1979), 15; A. Westing, ed., *Herbicides in War* (London: Taylor and Francis, 1984). For a fascinating legal and sociological discussion of the reactions of American Vietnam veterans to Agent Orange, see J. Jacobs and D. McNamara, "Vietnam Veterans and the Agent Orange Controversy," *Armed Forces and Society* 13, no. 1 (1986), 57–80; and F. Wilcox, *Waiting for an Army to Die: The Tragedy of Agent Orange* (New York: Random House, 1983).

44. Falk, "Environmental Warfare and Ecocide: Facts, Appraisal, and Proposals," *Bulletin of Peace Proposals* 4, no. 1 (1973), 84; E. DeSombre, *The Global Environment and World Politics: International Relations for the 21st Century*. (London: Continuum, 2002), 46.

45. All quotes from S. Pimiento Chamorro and E. Hammond, "Addressing Environmental Modification in Post–Cold War Conflict," paper presented to the Civil Society Conference to Review ENMOD and Related Agreements on Hostile Modification of the Environment, Amsterdam, May 2001, The Sunshine Project, http://www.edmonds-institute.org/pimiento.html (accessed 30 May 2004).

46. Robert Harris and Jeremy Paxman, *A Higher Form of Killing: The Secret Story of Gas and Germ Warfare* (London: Chatto and Windus, 1982), 27. This is a fascinating book for anyone interested in the evolution of chemical and biological weapons.

47. Thomas F. Homer-Dixon, "Environmental Scarcities and Violent Conflict: Evidence from Cases," *International Security* 19 (Summer 1994); see also his *Environment, Scarcity, and Violence* (Princeton: Princeton University Press, 1999).

48. Eduardo Lachica, "U.S. Turns Back on Big Dams," *The Globe and Mail,* 14 March 1996, A16.

49. Tom Utley, "McDonald's vs. Greenpeace," *Kitchener Record,* 29 June 1996, A13.

50. J. Dooge et al., eds., *An Agenda of Science for Environment and Development into the 21st Century* (Cambridge: Cambridge University Press, 1992).

51. *Ozone Diplomacy: New Directions in Safeguarding the Planet* (Cambridge, MA: Harvard University Press, 1991), 204–05.

52. D. Freestone, "The Precautionary Principle," in R. Churchill and D. Freestone, eds., *International Law and Global Climate Change* (London: Graham and Trotham, 1991), 21–39.

53. *Canada in the World.* (Ottawa: CIDA Information Services, 1995), 36–37.

Suggested Readings

Andonova, L. *Transnational Politics of the Environment: The EU and Environmental Policy in Central and Eastern Europe.* MIT Press, 2003.

Attfield, Robin. *Environmental Ethics: An Overview for the Twenty-First Century.* Cambridge, UK; Malden, MA: Polity Press, 2003.

Boyden, S. *BioHistory: The Interplay between Human Society and the Biosphere, Past and Present.* Paris: UNESCO, 1992.

Brown, N. "Climate, Ecology and International Security." *Survival* 31 (1989), 519–32.

Caldwell, L.K. *International Environmental Policy: Emergence and Dimensions.* Durham, NC: Duke University Press, 1990.

Canadian Centre for Policy Alternatives. *An Action Plan for Kyoto.* Alternative Federal Budget 2003, Technical Paper #2, 27 January 2003.

Choucri, N., ed. *Global Accord: Environmental Challenges and International Responses.* Cambridge, MA: MIT Press, 1993.

Dalby, S. "Ecopolitical Discourse: 'Environmental Security' and Political Geography." *Progress in Human Geography* 16, no. 4 (1992), 503–22.

Dauvergne, P. *Shadows in the Forest: Japan and the Politics of Timber in Southeast Asia.* Cambridge, MA: MIT Press, 1997.

DeSombre, E. *Domestic Sources of International Environmental Policy: Industry, Environmentalists, and U.S. Power.* Cambridge, MA: MIT Press, 2000.

Diamond, I., and G. Orenstein, eds. *Reweaving the World: The Emergence of Ecofeminism.* San Francisco: Sierra Club, 1990.

Haas, P., R. Keohane, and M. Levy, eds. *Institutions for the Earth.* Boston: MIT Press, 1993.

Huang, M. "The Anti-Nuclear Power Movement in Taiwan: Claiming the Right to a Clean Environment." In J. Bauer and D. Bell, eds., *The East Asian Challenge for Human Rights.* Cambridge: Cambridge University Press, 1999, 313–35.

Hurrell, A., and B. Kingsbury, eds. *The International Politics of the Environment.* Oxford: Clarendon Press, 1992.

Jasanoff, S., and M. Martello, eds. *Earthly Politics: Local and Global in Environmental Governance.* Cambridge: MIT Press, 2004.

Keohane, R., and M. Levy, eds. *Institutions for Environmental Aid: Pitfalls and Promise.* Cambridge, MA: MIT Press, 1996.

Litfin, K. *Ozone Discourses: Science and Politics in Global Environmental Cooperation.* New York: Columbia University Press, 1994.

MacDonald, D., and H. Smith. "Promises Made, Promises Broken: Questioning Canada's Commitments to Climate Change." *International Journal* LV, no. 1 (1999), 107–24.

Mann, J., D. Tarantola, and T. Netter, eds. *AIDS in the World 1992.* Cambridge, MA: Harvard University Press, 1992.

Meadows, D.H., et al. *The Limits to Growth.* New York: Universe Books, 1972.

———. *Beyond the Limits: Global Collapse or a Sustainable Future.* London: Earthscan, 1992.

Middleton, Neil. *Rio Plus Ten: Politics, Poverty and the Environment.* London; Sterling, VA: Pluto Press, 2003.

Mies, M., and V. Shiva. *Ecofeminism.* Halifax: Fernwood Publications, 1993.

Minger, T., ed. *Greenhouse Glasnost: The Crisis of Global Warming.* New York: Ecco Press/Institute for Resource Management, 1990.

Mitchell, Ronald B. 1994. *Intentional Oil Pollution at Sea: Environmental Policy and Treaty Compliance.* Cambridge, MA: MIT Press.

Mol, A. *Globalization and Environmental Reform: The Ecological Modernization of the Global Economy.* Cambridge: MIT Press, 2003.

Munton, D. "Dependence and Interdependence in Transboundary Environmental Relations." *International Journal* 36 (1981), 139–84.

Myers, N. "Environment and Security." *Foreign Policy* 74 (1989), 23–41.

Nanda, V.D. *International Environmental Law and Policy.* New York: Transnational, 1995.

Porter, G., and J. Welsh Brown. *Global Environmental Politics.* Boulder, CO: Westview, 1991.

Price-Smith, A. *The Health of Nations: Infectious Disease, Environmental Change, and Their Effects on National Security and Development.* Cambridge: MIT Press, 2001.

Renner, Michael. *Fighting for Survival: Environmental Decline, Social Conflict, and the New Age of Insecurity.* New York: Norton, 1996.

Rodriguez, Maria Guadelupe Moog. *Global Environmentalism and Local Politics: Transnational Advocacy Networks in Brazil, Ecuador and India.* Albany, NY: State University of NY Press, 2004.

Sayer, Jeffery and Campbell, Bruce. *The Science of Sustainable Development: Local Livelihoods and the Global Environment.* Cambridge, UK; New York: Cambridge University Press, 2004.

Shiva, V., et al. *Biodiversity: Social and Ecological Perspectives.* London: Zed, 1991.

Smith, R. "New Problems for Old: The Institution of Capitalist Economic and Environmental Irrationality in China." *Democracy and Nature* 5, no. 2 (1999), 249–74.

Tickell, C. "The World after the Summit Meeting at Rio." *Washington Quarterly* 16 (1993), 75–82.

Westing, A. *Global Resources and International Conflict: Environmental Factors in Strategic Policy and Action.* Oxford: Oxford University Press, 1986.

Wapner, P. *Environmental Activism and World Civic Politics.* Albany: SUNY Press, 1996.

Young, O., ed. *The Effectiveness of International Environmental Regimes: Causal Connections and Behavioral Mechanisms.* Cambridge, MA: MIT Press, 1999.

Suggested Websites

Climate Action Network Europe
http://www.climnet.org

Energy and Environment Links
http://zebu.uoregon.edu/energy.html

EnviroLink
http://www.envirolink.org

Global Environmental Facility
http://www.gefweb.org

GreenNet
http://www.gn.apc.org

The Panos Institute
http://www.panos.sn

TRAFFIC North America
http://www.traffic.org/about/in_field_tna.html

UNEP
http://www.unep.ch

CHAPTER 11

Population Growth and Movement

To couple the concept of freedom to breed with the belief that everyone born has an equal right to the commons is to lock the world into a tragic course of action.

—Garrett Hardin[1]

The existence of refugees is a symptom of the disappearance of economic and political liberalism. The basic real solution of the refugee problem, real or potential, is necessarily therefore related to the solution of the great problems of economic and political adjustment in the contemporary world.

—Sir John Hope Simpson, 1938[2]

INTRODUCTION: THE OVERPOPULATION DEBATE

Two of the most obvious global trends in the immediate future will be continued population growth and population movements, and both have serious implications for human health and national security. This chapter will examine the debate over whether overpopulation is as important an issue as is often claimed. We will further examine **urbanization** and women's rights in the context of the overpopulation debate. In addition, we discuss trends in migration and government responses, and the spread of infectious diseases, such as **HIV/AIDS** and **SARS**. We then look at the questions associated with the plight of refugees and internally displaced persons: the people fleeing persecution and disaster number in the millions.

Sometime in 2001, the population of Canada exceeded 31 million. At the end of the last Ice Age, when people began migrating to the area we now know as the Americas, the entire earth probably supported fewer than 10 million people. By 1930, there were 2 billion of us; by 1972, 3.85 billion; by 1995, 6 billion; by 2004, close to 7 billion; barring some large-scale calamity such as nuclear war, there could be well over 8 billion before the year 2025. After accounting for deaths, we are adding almost 80 million people a year to the planet. It is not uncommon to hear estimates of a global population of well over 10 billion by 2050. Demographers liken population growth rates to large cargo ships: one can stop the engines, but it will be some time before the boat stops, even if we reverse them. Because so many women are of childbearing age, even if they all had but one child, the population would still increase dramatically since the newborns would be alive at the same time as their parents and grandparents.

This population growth comes at a time when a major food crisis may be looming on the horizon. During the 1960s and 1970s, the so-called green revolution increased crop yields through the use of irrigation, pesticides, and fertilizer. This is a less viable option today, when almost all prime arable land has been put to use and the excessive use of pesticides has often caused more problems than it has solved. The promise of GMOs (see Chapter 10) remains politically and scientifically contentious. Though enough food is available to feed everyone now, and malnutrition and undernourishment are largely a consequence of inadequate distribution, this may not be the case when we have 12 billion people to feed. Current trends indicate that the distribution of food continues to be uneven, creating some areas of overindulgence and others of severe malnutrition.

The so-called **demographic transition** that characterized European development involved the decline of both death and birth rates as industrialization created advanced medical technology and people became less likely to raise large families. High infant mortality rates encourage parents to have more children since their survival is less certain. Demographers expected this pattern to repeat itself elsewhere, but this clearly has not been the case for many Southern states, where population continues to rise. Though death rates have dropped in many places, birth rates stay high and populations continue to grow at 2.5, 3.0, and 3.5 percent or higher per year. Most growth takes place in the South: "Less developed countries recorded fertility at 3.1 children per woman over the period 1995–2000, while developed countries recorded fertility at 1.57 children per woman over the same period—well below the replacement level of 2.1 children per woman." (Life expectancy was 63 years in the former, 75 in the latter.)[3] Several states now have, or will soon have, more than 100 million inhabitants (see Profile 11.1).

In China and India, each with more than 1 billion citizens, it is doubtful any sort of transition can stem massive population increases, and many argue that China's one-child policy, while a threat to individual liberty (and to the lives of consequently unwanted children—usually female), was a necessary step that should be followed elsewhere. The idea of a population bomb was popularized in the 1970s by writers such as Paul and Anne Ehrlich, who argued that massive increases in population threatened not just the standard of living of people around the globe, but human life itself.[4] In what has become a classic piece of **neo-Malthusian** literature, "The Tragedy of the Commons," professor of human ecology Garret Hardin argued that we simply cannot afford to allow population increases and that to ensure our future collective survival, even the freedom to reproduce must be limited.[5]

Of course, many dismiss this as an extreme position; some argue population growth will level off with economic prosperity or with famine and disease. State control of reproduction is certainly viewed as an infringement on civil liberties in most regions, and contradicts the conventions espoused by most religions. Indeed population rates have been slowing dramatically in some states, such as Germany and Russia, and it is more likely for states such as Canada and the United States to worry about caring for an aging population than a young one (the so-called population pyramid is top-heavy in the North, bottom-heavy in the South). Others suggest that high populations themselves are not to blame for the environmental problems we face, but rather that the consumption patterns of citizens in the relatively affluent states are unsustainable. According to a classic formula developed in the 1960s, the environmental impacts of population size, affluence (i.e., consumption), and technology are interrelated.[6] This formula suggests that, while absolute increases in population do put added strains

PROFILE 11.1 The 20 Most Populous States, 2002

Note: As with all statistics, we must be cautious about accepting population figures; they are in essence estimates, based on government census (which often miss the homeless and those living in remote rural areas) and, in many cases, on past growth rates; calculations based on population losses from war, pandemics, and natural disasters; and other factors.

1. China 1 280 975 000	11. Mexico 100 921 000
2. India 1 048 279 000	12. Germany 82 495 000
3. United States 288 369 000	13. Vietnam 80 525 000
4. Indonesia 211 716 000	14. Philippines 79 944 000
5. Brazil 174 485 000	15. Turkey 69 626 000
6. Pakistan 144 902 000	16. Ethiopia 67 335 000
7. Russian Federation 144 071 000	17. Egypt, Arab Republic 66 372 000
8. Bangladesh 135 684 000	18. Iran, Islamic Republic 65 540 000
9. Nigeria 132 785 000	19. Thailand 61 613 000
10. Japan 127 144 000	20. France 59 442 000

SOURCE: WORLD BANK GROUP DEVELOPMENT INDICATORS DATABASE, JULY 2003. http://www.worldbank.org/data/databytopic/POP.pdf (ACCESSED 10 APRIL 2004).

on ecosystems, what that population consumes (and how it does so) is just as important. However, while the Northern states have clearly contributed more to global warming and other industry-related problems than the Southern ones, the most rapid population growth, by far, has been in the South. So the question of whether population growth itself is the culprit of all our problems may be misleading; one cannot ignore the substantial environmental and consumption impact that millions more people have each year. It should be clear, then, that both the North and the South have an important role to play in decreasing the negative effects of population growth, but there is the additional ethical question of whether governments are right to impose birth control on their populations.

China's one-child policy has been the most controversial in this regard. Renamed the Population and Family Planning Law in 2002, it in fact limits reproduction to one child for each couple in the cities, and two for those who live in rural areas and whose first child is a girl. Families of ethnic minorities are allowed to have two or three children. This demonstrates some sensitivity to the problems of gendercide and ethnocide the original policy entailed. The government claims that the 12-year policy has led to 300 million fewer births to the world's biggest population, which is now at 1.3 billion, and has vowed to carry on the policy to achieve its goal of controlling the population at the 1.6 billion level by 2050. Inducements to comply include charging fees for services for second children that were free for the first and rewarding single-child couples with promotions at work and free university education for the child. Abortions are strongly encouraged in the advent of a second pregnancy. In some cases, this policy has resulted in **infanticide**: since baby boys are more highly valued than girls, couples intent on having a son may resort to murder should a girl be produced. Similarly, families in India, China, and elsewhere have used prenatal amniocentesis and ultrasound scanning to discover the sex of fetuses, and then aborted the females.[7] During the 1970s, China's fertility rate fell from 6 children per woman to about 2.5. Despite this drop, most people would agree that China still has a tremendous overpopulation problem. However, the ethical questions remain and will become only more pronounced as governments and international aid agencies struggle with continued population growth.

While a UN Conference on Population and Development in Cairo in 1994 did produce a plan to prevent world population from exceeding 7.2 billion people by 2015, it remains to be seen whether states will actually commit the resources this entails. Ultimately, it is up to individual governments to stem poverty and provide family-planning possibilities; the record so far is not encouraging. Two of the more visible outcomes of the population explosion are urbanization and the demand for family-planning policies in crowded states.

URBANIZATION

One of the most pronounced effects of population growth and movement is urbanization.[8] The city has often been viewed as a primary indicator of "modernity"; urbanization followed industrialization, which meant that **gross national product (GNP)** was increasing and society was advancing toward the Western ideal. Cities came to symbolize a certain notion of progress, but do Bangkok's steel and glass high-rises offer positive proof of Thailand's economic miracle? Or do they merely put a glittering face on the detrimental effects of rapid development? For proletarian migrants, is the quality of life in burgeoning Mexico City an improvement over life in rural Mexico? Has urban life in North American cities improved for the majority of their inhabitants in the age of globalization?

A universal problem: a row of blue-tarpaulin shacks are seen along Tokyo's Sumida River, 6 November 2002. Though small and strangely tidy, urban slums have long existed side by side with Japan's economic miracle. But for perhaps the first time since the widespread destitution immediately after World War II, homelessness is a problem Japan is now finding hard to ignore. (AP Photo/ Katsumi Kasahara/CP Archive)

The pure logic behind the quest for the city is clear. Big cities with high population densities reduce the *unit costs of infrastructure*: it becomes cheaper to supply essential services (such as water, electricity, and education) to people if they live closer together. Employment opportunities, and the image of a better life, attract migratory labour. Companies are more likely to invest in cities, where both labour pools and urban middle-class markets are easily accessible. And since all this activity is highly concentrated, it can be regulated by government and, to the extent possible under a market economy, urban planning can facilitate a more humane, less alienating centre of human life.

Throwing the environmental question into this equation presents a profound challenge to such logic. If cities produce more pollution than can be safely managed, if traffic congestion not only creates smog but also actually impedes transportation, if neighbouring land is degraded because of waste disposal needs and excessive demands on natural resources, and if most rural–urban migrants end up in unsanitary and politically marginalized shantytowns, is urbanization really a step in the right developmental direction? Increasingly, Northern and Southern analysts of sustainable development cast rapid urbanization in a negative light. This view is tied, of course, to population growth. Most dramatically, the spectre of rising **megacities**, great centres of sprawl, chaos, and pollution, looms over projected images of the Southern hemisphere's future. In 1975,

PROFILE 11.2 Megacities

Generally, *megacities* are defined as those with more than 10 million inhabitants. In 1950, the 2 largest cities were London and New York. By 2015, it is estimated that there will be more than 30 megacities. Below we list the world's megacities in 1975, in 2000, then estimates, based on UN projections, of the largest in 2015.

Note: It is very difficult to compare estimates of city size, since different surveys include different areas as part of city centres. For example, if we exclude the suburban areas around Los Angeles or Tokyo, their numbers would be considerably reduced. Also, however, the homeless often go uncounted. Finally, cities can have an incentive to exaggerate their numbers for purposes of obtaining funding. So figures can be high or low.

All numbers below are in millions. For example, 19.8 = 19 800 000

TABLE 1: MEGACITIES, 1975	TABLE 2: MEGACITIES, 2000	TABLE 3: PROJECTED MEGACITIES, 2015
Tokyo 19.8	Tokyo 26.4	Tokyo 26.4
New York 15.9	Mexico City 18.1	Mumbai 26.1
Shanghai 11.4	Mumbai 18.1	Lagos 23.2
Mexico City 11.2	São Paulo 17.8	Dhaka 21.1
São Paulo 10	Shanghai 17	São Paulo 20.4
	New York 16.6	Karachi 19.2
	Lagos 13.4	Mexico City 19.2
	Los Angeles 13.1	New York 17.4
	Kolkata 12.9	Jakarta 17.3
	Buenos Aires 12.6	Kolkata 17.3
	Dhaka 12.3	Delhi 16.8
	Karachi 11.8	Metro Manila 14.8
	Delhi 11.7	Shanghai 14.6
	Jakarta 11	Los Angeles 14.1
	Osaka 11	Buenos Aires 14.1
	Metro Manila 10.9	Cairo 13.8
	Beijing 10.8	Istanbul 12.5
	Rio de Janeiro 10.6	Beijing 12.3
	Cairo 10.6	Rio de Janeiro 11.9
		Osaka 11.0
		Tianjin 10.7
		Hyderabad 10.5
		Bangkok 10.1

SOURCE: UNFPA, STATE OF THE WORLD POPULATION 2001, http://www.unfpa.org/swp/2001/english/tables (ACCESSED 30 JUNE 2004). REPRINTED WITH PERMISSION.

1.5 million people lived in cities; by 1995, 2.6 billion, and by 2000, 2.9 billion. Put another way, in 1950, 30 percent of people lived in urban centres; by 2000 47 percent did, and projections suggest 60 percent will by 2030.

It is hardly questionable that the combination of urbanization, poverty, poor services, and lax regulations can have disastrous environmental effects. Katmandu, Nepal, a city designed for some 40 000 occupants, now has more than 710 000, and the famous Katmandu Valley is covered by a blue haze of pollution from cars, wood fires, kilns, and construction, which forces pedestrians and cyclists to wear cloth masks (a scene common in Mexico City as well). The rapid urbanization of Bhopal, India, was what made the 1984 industrial accident in that city so disastrous in terms of human casualties, as leaked gas from a Union Carbide pesticide plant descended on the sleeping occupants of a nearby shantytown. Only 2 percent of Bangkok is connected to city sewers. Violence is common in many urban centres throughout the world, as are illicit forms of economic activity; schooling is relatively inadequate, and there are fewer social opportunities for restless youth. In Kibera, Kenya, the biggest slum in Africa, where population density can exceed 80 000 per square kilometre (without sanitation or electricity systems) the government has been bulldozing shantytown dwellers' shacks into the ground,

PROFILE 11.3 An Emerging Global Megacity System?

Here is an interesting scenario: as globalization reduces the importance of the nation-state, the megacity replaces it as the primary means of expressing political power and conducting global interaction. The trend toward the megacity is evident in Ontario, where the provincial government amalgamated the different districts of Toronto into one big administration, and in Montreal, where the same thing happened in 2003 (neither effort was without controversy). Business today is conducted largely between cities, not countries. Likewise, travel is from metropolis to metropolis. As cities increase in size and wealth, devouring more of the countryside around them, the megacity may become the most important political unit. This is not without some historical precedent: in the period 800 to 322 B.C.E., a Greek city-state system flourished. The population of the cities varied: larger states such as Syracuse, Acragas, and Athens had around 50 000 citizens, while smaller cities, such as Siris and Thourioi in Sicily, had but several thousand.* Eventually, Athens formed a far-reaching empire that kept other cities under domination; this move was opposed by Sparta and other cities in the Peloponnesian League. War between the two alliances broke out in 431 B.C.E., and the entire system fell to Philip of Macedonia later that century. Might we see a world where dominant cities such as New York, London, and Tokyo battle it out for commercial and cultural supremacy? While this is an interesting scenario, most states retain tight control over borders in the post–September 11 era, and large cities are especially vulnerable to terrorist attack. This suggests that if megacities are to rise as the new centres of political power, they will have to usurp the traditional, jealously guarded security role played by the national state apparatus first, which is unlikely.

*See K. Holsti, *International Politics: A Framework for Analysis*, 7th ed. (Englewood Cliffs, NJ: Prentice Hall, 1995), 36; he also cites K. Freeman, *Greek City States* (London: Methuen, 1948). See also G. Modelski, *World Cities: –3000 to 2000* (Washington, DC: Faros, 2003); and P. King and P. Taylor, eds., *World Cities in a World-System* (Cambridge, UK: Cambridge University Press, 1995).

leaving them homeless. The sorry list goes on and on: infrastructure unable to meet city demands; unequal access to the infrastructure that is available; and lack of precautions against the environmental risks, both natural and industrial, that face certain segments of city populations.[9] Rural populations, meanwhile, must play the role of provider to the large city, not only servicing it with food, wood, textile resources, and other commodities, but also absorbing the pollution and waste that is expelled.

However, none of this guarantees that megacities must become dark dystopias in the future. Many cities are coping well with growth, adopting cleaner environmental standards and recycling programs that lower the total waste burden, pursuing urban agriculture, attracting tourists with their historical importance while protecting cherished monuments, and diversifying their economic activities to avoid the traps inherent in dependent development. Large cities are centres of commerce and culture, and they continue to play a leading role in defining the nation-state (and, for that matter, globalization itself). The dangers are that growth will spiral out of anyone's control, that those marginalized within large cities will continue to suffer, that urban bias will lead to the further neglect and exploitation of the rural countryside. As always, human societies encounter tremendously difficult choices when facing the immediate future.

WOMEN'S RIGHTS AND BIRTH CONTROL

If we do accept the proposition that overpopulation is a real and urgent problem, we must ask next what we can do about it and what ethical implications will be raised. Birth control has been the technological cause of reduced fertility in the industrialized North, combining with higher education levels and higher standards of living to reduce reproductive rates. In the

South, irreversible female sterilization is often the most common form of birth control. Concerns are mounting about the health impact of new birth control technologies, such as a drug called quinacrine, which is in fact an antimalarial drug that causes scar tissue if placed directly in the womb. The scarring causes the fallopian tubes to become permanently blocked. Quinacrine also damages DNA in bacteria, so experts worry it might cause cancer in women. It was banned in India in 1998, but is apparently still in use in West Bengal, Chile, the Philippines, Venezuela, Vietnam, and elsewhere.[10]

Beyond immediate health concerns, many raise questions regarding the ethical appropriateness of encouraging women—largely rural, uneducated women in underdeveloped states—to submit themselves to birth control measures. A common complaint is that the population issue, when it gets into the hands of government leaders and international bureaucrats at the UN and elsewhere, becomes a quantified issue or a numbers game. Groups such as the International Planned Parenthood Federation promote birth control as a means toward greater societal stability but thus deflect attention from women's sexuality and reproductive freedom.[11] The abortion issue is even more divisive, since many religious representatives refuse to deal with policies that they think legitimize abortion-on-demand. During the Reagan and Bush administrations, the United States refused to fund Planned Parenthood programs because of their acceptance of abortion, a policy reinstated immediately after G.W. Bush took office. Yet the health impacts of unsafe abortion practices pose a major threat to women in many regions today.

Others argue that instead of focusing on reducing sheer numbers, policies designed to limit population increases should concentrate on infant mortality and women's health. The lack of access to health care is a primary factor here. A study released by the **World Health Organization (WHO)** and UNICEF estimated that 585 000 women die from pregnancy-related causes each year, with almost all these deaths (99 percent) occurring in low-income states.[12] In the developing countries, complications associated with pregnancy are often the leading causes of death among women of childbearing age; a high death rate is also associated with the process of sterilization. By the mid-1990s, an African woman faced a 1 in 21 chance of dying as a result of pregnancy; the risk for a North American woman is 1 in 6366.[13] Developing states are further burdened with the growing transference of diseases such as HIV/AIDS to newborns.

We should also consider the words of Mahbub ul Haq, a special advisor to the administrator of the UN Development Programme (UNDP). While he was the minister of planning and finance in Pakistan (1982–88) he worked hard, aided by a **USAID** grant, to "saturate the villages with condoms." Nonetheless, "it was my greatest policy disaster. Despite the campaign, the population growth rate actually went up, from 3 to 3.1 percent. What went wrong? The answer is that female literacy in the villages was only 6 percent. Without investing in educating women, it was naïve to expect investment in condoms to yield any effective results. If I had to do it all over again, I would put almost all that money into boosting female literacy."[14] These are hard-learned lessons, and there simply isn't enough development funding to afford many more of them. Of course, birth control is the responsibility of men as well. Millions of men have undergone vasectomies in the past two decades, and medical advances may make it possible for men to take a birth control pill themselves. Failing this, the good old-fashioned condom is a safe and reliable way to avoid unwanted pregnancy and to protect partners from sexually transmitted diseases.

We now turn to one of the more pronounced effects of a heavily populated world: the rise in mobility of people in the form of both migrants and refugees. One of the primary stimulants to migration has always been employment opportunity, so we begin with a brief look at the contemporary context.

EMPLOYMENT AND MIGRATION

People have always been on the move, for the purpose of escape, enrichment, or just plain adventure. As Sidney Klein has demonstrated, mass migrations "go back millions of years," long before the advent of the modern nation-state.[15] To name just a few examples, early movements in Mesopotamia of Assyrians and Hittites, and of Indo-Europeans into India, date back to 2000 B.C.E. The people who developed Greek civilization filtered down through the Balkan peninsula to the shores of the Aegean Sea about 1900 B.C.E., undermining the older Cretan civilization, and around 1150 B.C.E. other Greek-speaking tribes invaded from the North. The Greeks would go on to form the city-states, such as Athens and Sparta, which many historians view as the beginning of the international system (see Chapter 2).

Many generations later, the industrializing states of Europe used the emigration of tens of millions of Europeans to head off a looming overpopulation problem in the 19th and early 20th centuries; they encouraged immigration in the post–World War II period to provide the labourers needed for reconstruction. In fact, Europe's burgeoning cities would have suffered from unprecedented overpopulation between 1840 and 1940 were it not for the migration of almost 60 million people from Europe to countries such as the United States, Russia, Argentina, Canada, Brazil, and Australia. The great European exodus was caused by a combination of push and pull factors. Politically, the age of individual liberalism meant that people were for the first time literally free to move. Europeans were pushed out of Europe by rises in population and scarcity of work; in an extreme case, millions fled the famine in Ireland in 1846. As usual, technological advances played a decisive role as well. The steamship made it easier, and cheaper, to cross the sea (an experience enjoyed previously only by the very rich or by sailors). Railroads were instrumental in distributing people to and from ports. Some people were fleeing from political persecution, such as the many Russian and Polish Jews who entered the United States before World War I. On the pull side, many of the receiving states actively campaigned to attract Europeans as valuable labourers and farmers (exceptions to this pattern were Australia and New Zealand, which discouraged the importation of cheap labour). Migrant labourers would prove to be a valuable source of remittances back home, and this transfer of funds continues today.

For the vast majority of people, work is not an option: it is necessary for survival. While socialist states accepted the premise that providing work is the responsibility of the state, market-based economies struggle with this question. As discussed in Chapter 4, one of the most important functions of government during the Keynesian era was to provide employment for citizens of states hit by temporary depression or recession. Several shifts in employment patterns can be noted in the industrialized states. Technological development, particularly the rise of microelectronics, has certainly reduced the need for manual labour; this leads to what we call *structural unemployment*, as opposed to unemployment caused simply by the standard growth–recession cycle. Also, many countries are moving toward smaller and more flexible production units, subcontracting and outsourcing work, and using temporary or part-time hiring. These systems allow for rapid adjustment to market conditions and reduce the need to pay employees long-term benefits.

Perhaps most importantly, MNCs are increasingly able and likely to use cheaper labour in the Southern Hemisphere to produce their goods. **Capital mobility**, the increase in communications and transportation capability, and the ability to parcel out components of the work process have produced downward pressure on wages, suggesting that the standard of living, measured in real terms, is decreasing in many states, such as Canada and Britain. Most unemployment rates in the industrialized states habitually hover between 8 and 12 percent. However, unemployment levels will always fluctuate, and one might argue that a new workforce will gradually adapt to the new technology. This adaptation itself will generate employment as information technology educators train people. But this scenario may be a bit rosy and may neglect other factors. For example, former Communist states must deal with massive unemployment alongside privatization. Not only were many companies in these nations too quickly privatized but they now must compete in world markets with much more efficient and experienced Western firms. It is estimated that, from 1990 to 1992, unemployment in former Eastern bloc countries and the former U.S.S.R. rose from 100 000 to more than 4 million (14 percent in Poland, 11 percent in Hungary), and real wages have been declining as well. These rates were even higher by 2001, and unemployment continued to top 15 percent in eastern Germany as well.[16] Strikes are common as workers, fed up with terrible conditions and pay, seek to improve their condition. Even the military personnel so coveted during the height of the Cold War are reportedly undernourished and often go without pay, risking their lives in what are often inadequate safety conditions (epitomized by the sunken submarine *Kursk* in the summer of 2000). Yet, if they leave the army, they are sure to swell the ranks of the unemployed (the release of Iraqi soldiers after the occupation of Iraq in 2003 demonstrated this problem vividly). In short, the crisis of unemployment will surely be one of the toughest and most troubling issues on the agenda of the international community in 2005 and beyond.

It is difficult to imagine the large impact transformations in prevalent technology will continue to have on the global economy. Changes in technology result in changes in the way goods are produced and the manner in which people are—or are not—employed to produce them. Often, people are replaced by machines through **automation** in the form of **robotics**. Of course, this phenomenon is not new, but the new automation is much more omnipresent, and entire factories run by only a few humans and the robots they service will be commonplace in the future.[17] Japan leads in the field of industrial automation, with some two-thirds of the world's robots currently "employed" there. The problem with automation, as India's great political and spiritual leader Mohandas Gandhi and others lamented many years ago, is that it displaces traditional workers. While some might view this as a sign of progress since it relieves humans from tedious work, it is a severe unemployment crisis to others (especially to those displaced) and will cause further problems in the future. A globalized economy means that capital, more mobile than ever, will seek out rewarding returns wherever they can be found. If cheap labour is available, then it will suffice; however, cheap labour may be difficult to find in the future if highly specialized production lines continue to dominate production.

Economists have long considered migration (the crossing of borders for temporary or permanent stay) the result of push–pull factors. Unemployment, low wages, environmental deterioration, warfare, and other negatives push migrants (or, in more extreme cases, refugees), while the promise of employment, higher wages, education for children, and other positive expectations pull them into big cities and across borders. Employment has always been the central concern for economists dealing with migration and, until recently, it may be argued that migration was largely considered an employment-related phenomenon. The world's labour force is projected to grow by almost 1 billion during the next two decades, mostly in developing countries hard-pressed to generate anywhere near an adequate number of jobs. Already, the human traffic within countries like China is startling; states will have to grapple with the question of what to do about this movement when borders are involved. Despite the rhetoric of proponents of globalization, borders are a real and determinative factor today.

WHAT WOULD A TRULY BORDERLESS WORLD LOOK LIKE?

If the world had no sovereign nation-states and no borders that protected them from others, then there would be little political constraint on people's movements. Doubtless, other constraints would limit human movement. Access to transportation would be a key factor, as it has been throughout the ages. However, it is possible to travel long distances, by plane, ship, or train, with modest financial means. Another constraint would be family ties and cultural affinity, perhaps most importantly the link between people and the land on which they were born and raised. Another constraint on movement is a rather difficult thing to measure: contentment. If people are relatively satisfied with the standard of living they enjoy, they will not see a need to pick up and move on. The Europeans who flooded the United States and Canada in the late 19th century were leaving in search of a better life, just as many migrants from developing states are doing today when they move northward, sometimes under illegal and perilous conditions. In a world divided between rich and poor, there is more pressure than ever for northward migration, and were it not for the immigration controls afforded by borders, the flow would presumably be much greater. In 1989, the UN estimated that some 50 million people, or 1 percent of the world's population, lived in countries other than their country of origin, and the World Bank estimated the number of international migrants of all kinds at 100 million. By 2002, this estimate had increased to an astounding 175 million people living in countries other than their country of origin.[18]

According to a simple economic model, labour follows capital. In other words, a truly borderless world would mean that people would flock to sources of employment, wherever they might be. As the world economy becomes increasingly integrated, however, the centres of financial power and industrial production would become heavily overcrowded, and it would be increasingly difficult to sustain them. We see this domestically with the process of urbanization, discussed above, but this could occur at a global level as well, as entire areas, megacities, and even states attract labour. We do not, however, live in a borderless world (despite what some of the more assertive advocates of globalization have been telling us). In fact, the migration and refugee issue-area reinforces the concept of the state system based on territory and sovereignty, for much of the world lives behind relatively closed borders, and states are increasingly protecting their own citizens before admitting others.

The tragic toll of illegal migration: Italian police officers carry one of five bodies found in a truck at Mirabella, near Avellino, southern Italy, 31 August 2002. Five people believed to be Kurdish migrants were found dead in the back of a truck that had travelled through Bulgaria and Greece before reaching Italy, police and news reports said. (AP Photo/Tano Pecoraro/CP Archive)

Indeed, many argue that increased population pressure and migration, far from encouraging convergence, will exacerbate divergence in the world system as states, jealously protecting their borders from foreign intrusion, take even more desperate measures to control migrants. This is especially the case in the post–September 11 climate. This fact is most evident in the **immigration** control issue-area. Trade liberalization encourages capital mobility, but there has not been a commensurate opening of borders to labour migration. If anything, the opposite has occurred as Northern governments increase

PROFILE 11.4 Migrants and Refugees: What Is the Difference?

Generally speaking, the difference between migrants and refugees is that the former leave their country voluntarily, while the latter are forced to do so. However, the distinction between voluntary and involuntary migration, while important, is also necessarily fuzzy. Not all involuntary migrants would be considered refugees by the international convention on that topic. Anthony Richmond* prefers the terms *proactive* and *reactive* migration. We should note also the existence of another category of migrants who are usually labelled *nondocumented* (also known as illegal aliens). According to the Program of Action of the International Conference on Population and Development (ICPD), documented migrants are "those who satisfy all the legal requirements to enter, stay and, if applicable, hold employment in the country of destination." See also Profile 11.7 on Civil War refugees and Canada.

*See his *Global Apartheid: Refugees, Racism, and the New World Order* (Oxford: Oxford University Press, 1994).

entry requirements and attempt to lure only those migrants who can clearly afford to pay their own way or possess the means to invest in the economy. Nowhere is this as acute as in Western Europe, where the fall of the Soviet Union and Eastern bloc states has led to **emigration**, both to and from the former Soviet Union and elsewhere (see Profile 11.5); while labour mobility is incomparably fluid within the EU, it is another thing to get into the EU from the outside. The war in Yugoslavia, meanwhile, demonstrated the potential for forced migration to take place in the post–Cold War era. We need not stop at Europe, however, for a look at the contemporary **refugee** crisis. Recent mass movements of refugees have occurred in South America, Africa, and Asia, and we return to this ongoing human drama later in this chapter. Needless to say, a truly borderless world would look quite different from the one we see today or will see in the near future.

It is also important to understand that ethnicity and population movements are often closely connected. Two terms that are frequently used to reflect this are *irredenta* and *diaspora*. Irredenta are "territorially based minorities contiguous to a state controlled by their co-ethnics," people who often call for the right to self-determination.[19] Hitler used Germans living abroad to encourage acceptance of his expansionist foreign policy. A Malay–Muslim majority inhabits Thailand's four Southern provinces, though Malaysia and Thailand have maintained fairly good relations over the last few decades. Irredenta are created by shifts in political geography—the movement of borders induced by occupation or annexation, for example. Diaspora, however, are created by migration; they are groups of people who live outside their area of ethnic origin. Many diasporas have been very influential because of their cosmopolitan orientation, diverse language skills, and commercial contacts. Examples include Jews and Greeks in the Ottoman Empire, Germans in Tsarist Russia, and Chinese in many Asian states, including Thailand and Malaysia. Other diaspora are linked more directly to population movements induced by the opportunity of working abroad, such as Algerians and Senegalese in France, Jamaicans and Pakistanis in Great Britain, and Mexicans and Filipinos in the United States. These groups often become permanent citizens, and, as in the case of the American Cuban community, they can be quite vocal in political terms.

In the early 1920s the United States began to impose quota restrictions on the number of immigrants it would accept, and since then Northern states have gradually adopted policies aimed at constricting, not encouraging, emigration. Yet migration today takes place all over the world, with heavy South–North and East–West patterns. Migrant workers bring skills that are often employed in host countries because others refuse to do the work, and this generates large remittances that are sent home. Some states are highly dependent on receiving these

PROFILE 11.5 Mass Migration and the Former Soviet Union

Few areas have experienced the type of turmoil brought on by the dissolution of the Soviet Union in the late 1980s. One of the more pronounced effects of this political transformation has been a huge exodus of ethnic groups across the region. Since 1989, more than 9 million people have left their homes because of ethnic tension or environmental disasters. This figure means that 1 of every 30 residents of the former Soviet Union has migrated! Many of them were Russians moving back into Russia from former republics such as Ukraine, Latvia, and Belarus. They had originally moved as part of Moscow's efforts to "Russify" outlying areas, but after the fall of the Soviet Union they felt relatively unsafe outside Russia. In other cases it is clear that people were forced to migrate: some 3.6 million refugees have fled from the Armenia–Azerbaijan war and the fighting in Chechnya in the mid-1990s alone. Many of the migrants were trying to return to ancestral homelands after their previous forced evacuation during the Stalin era. Slavs have been moving from the five new states of Central Asia—Turkmenistan, Uzbekistan, Kazakhstan, Tajikistan, and Kyrgyzstan. The severe environmental decay of the Aral Sea in Central Asia, radiation in the Semipalatinsk nuclear testing range, and the infamous Chernobyl meltdown (see Chapter 10) have also forced citizens to move themselves and their belongings to other areas. Given the economic crises Russia has faced, many educated and highly skilled people have sought employment elsewhere, leading to a severe "brain drain" crisis. For example, "Jews made up disproportionate shares of the country's engineers, physicians, scientific personnel, teachers, and production and technical managers. Of Jewish emigrants from Russia, 21 percent have a college education against 13.3 percent for the country as a whole. Of those leaving for Israel, 30 percent have a higher education, of those to the United States, 42 percent." (Heleniak, cited below). Beyond this, a very disturbing trend has emerged involving the emigration of Russian women who are being trafficked in the global sex industry: some estimate as many as 50 000 women have left the country under these circumstances since 1990.

Concerns continue about a resumption of the old Russian nationalism of the past, perhaps abetted by the introduction of post–Soviet Communists into power in Moscow. Further, Western Europe in particular is concerned with the possibility that many of the forced migrants will eventually find their way into Western Europe, where living conditions continue to be a good deal better. So we see that political, economic, and social factors are all involved in this international dilemma.

SOURCES: SEE R. EVANS, "MASS INTERNAL MIGRATIONS UNSETTLE FORMER SOVIET STATES," *THE GLOBE AND MAIL*, 23 MAY 1996; AND T. HELENIAK, "MIGRATION DILEMMAS HAUNT POST-SOVIET RUSSIA," MIGRATION INFORMATION SOURCE OF THE MIGRATION POLICY INSTITUTE, http:// www.migrationinformation.org/Profiles/display.cfm?ID=62 (ACCESSED 28 APRIL 2004).

remittances, as they are a chief source of foreign exchange; the largest remittance recipient countries are India, Mexico, the Philippines, China, Turkey, and Egypt. As migrant workers establish themselves in new countries, they may become citizens or permanent residents and bring the rest of their families over with them. Thus, migration acts to provide labour pools in receiving countries, while it relieves unemployment in sending countries. This is the theory, at any rate: in some cases, migration increases social and economic problems in host countries, while it drains sending countries of valuable human resources, including health specialists and engineers.

Another issue related to migration is the spread of disease. Again, this is an old story, since migrants have brought their diseases, and immune systems, with them since the days of early trading in the Middle East. When the Europeans began to migrate to the Americas, the result was the death of millions of Indigenous inhabitants who were exposed to European germs. The problem remains serious today, especially in light of HIV/AIDS. We discuss infectious disease in the next section.

THE MICROENVIRONMENT AND POPULATION MOVEMENT: THE SPREAD OF INFECTIOUS DISEASE

One of the most dangerous elements of population movement is that people can carry diseases with them when travelling even great distances. Epidemics are restricted to geographic and temporal boundaries; pandemics, on the other hand (such as malaria, tuberculosis, and HIV/AIDS) know no such boundaries. We live in an age of pandemics, but human security has always faced its most prevalent and enduring threat from microorganisms. The bubonic plague, or Black Death, first struck Europe in 1348 and wiped out entire towns and villages. The plague bacillus was carried by the rats that infested the overcrowded, unsanitary towns. Between the hundreds of thousands of fatalities caused by the plague and those caused by the Hundred Years' War between England and France (1337–1453), the European population did not recover until the 1500s. After the expansion of European civilization into colonized areas such as the Americas, Indigenous peoples around the world suffered from the sudden introduction of foreign microbes; this is often considered a genocidal event as some of the diseases were deliberately spread. The historical record aside, some experts argue that the problem is getting worse, not better, despite the advancement of science. The rapid spread of the HIV/AIDS virus and highly publicized events such as the outbreak of the pneumonic plague in Surat, India, in 1994, and the Ebola virus in Zaire in 1995 have alerted various authors to the importance of infectious disease, and the understandable panic they can cause among both local and distant populations.[20]

The discovery of mad cow disease in a single Canadian-born cow residing in the United States set off a national agricultural panic in 2003. Bovine spongiform encephalopathy (BSE), also known as mad cow disease, is a fatal disease that causes progressive neurological degeneration in cattle. Similar to BSE, Creutzfeldt-Jakob disease (CJD) is a rare disease that occurs in humans. In 1996, following outbreaks of BSE among British cattle, scientists found a possible link between BSE and a new variant of CJD (vCJD). Millions of cattle were slaughtered in Britain; millions of chickens, mostly in Asia but also in British Columbia, have been slaughtered over concerns with the spread of Avian Flu in 2003–04. But these pathogens have had relatively little impact on human populations due to such precautionary measures (they might prompt us to rethink our dependence on large-scale meat production, but that is another issue). Another quite modern pathogen is the West Nile virus. West Nile is a mosquito-borne virus that can cause a range of illnesses, such as acute encephalitis (inflammation of the brain), or meningitis (inflammation of the membranes and fluid surrounding the brain and spinal cord). Birds are the main reservoir of the virus: when a mosquito bites an infected bird, the mosquito can spread the virus by biting another bird or another animal, such as a human. West Nile was first located in 1937 in Uganda. Later it was found in Asia, Europe, and the Middle East; it was not until 1999 that it was discovered in New York. Preventive measures include using insect repellent and reporting dead birds to local health workers. Though it has had limited impact in terms of taking human life, West Nile is another indication of the perils of modern travel, since the pathogen was probably delivered by way of transported infected mammals or people.

Much more dramatic was the rise of Severe Acute Respiratory Syndrome (SARS), a deadly form of pneumonia that emerged from China in November 2002, most likely linked to the practice of eating the masked palm civet and the raccoon dog in certain regions of that country. The World Health Organization issued a global alert in March 2003, warning travellers to avoid certain regions, including Toronto, where SARS was most prevalent. SARS has all the characteristics of a pandemic disease: it is easily spread, transmitted by coughing or sneezing at close range, and it is lethal—though infected persons can survive if the disease is detected in time. The virus can also spread when a person touches a surface or object conta-

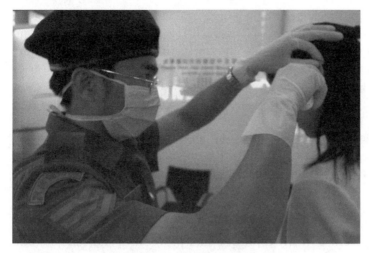

On the front line: a health worker at Hong Kong International Airport checks the temperature of a departing passenger during the city's SARS outbreak, 20 May 2003. Hong Kong saw a dramatic drop in tourist and business arrivals, which prompted the city's flagship airline to cancel numerous inbound and outbound flights. (CP Photo/Adrian Brown)

minated with infectious droplets and then touches his or her mouth, nose, or eyes; it is particularly dangerous for health care workers because of their increased likelihood of exposure. During the outbreak of 2003, at least 8098 people worldwide became sick, and some 774 died, 38 in Canada.[21] The outbreak provoked a closer look at how health care infrastructures can respond to sudden outbreaks.

Though there are many infectious diseases spread by mosquitoes, food, drinking water, and other vectors, some diseases are spread by direct human contact, and this is often exacerbated by international travel. For example, a major cause of HIV/AIDS in sub-Saharan Africa is prostitution centred on the trucking routes of the region; another is the of impact military personnel having unprotected sex (or, in worst cases, engaging in rape) when stationed abroad. Similarly, many intravenous drug users who contract the disease do so when living as transients in large urban centres, such as Amsterdam and Vancouver. The fact that the earliest genetic traces of HIV proto-DNA was taken from a male who died in Zaire in 1954 is testament to how rapidly this pathogen has spread to almost all regions of the earth. It has been nothing short of relentless. Though it is impossible to give an accurate figure, an estimated 40 million people were living with HIV/AIDS in 2003, and as many as 3 million died as a result in that year alone. In the countries most affected, such as Zimbabwe, Botswana, Namibia, Zambia, Swaziland, and South Africa, 18 to 26 percent of the population has contracted AIDS/HIV. According to these estimates, 5 million new infections occurred in 2003, with over 3 million of them in sub-Saharan Africa.[22]

AIDS stands for *acquired immune deficiency syndrome* and it is caused by HIV, the human immunodeficiency virus. HIV and AIDS have no known cure or vaccine, though anti-retro viral drugs are effective in mitigating its worst effects. Our immune systems fight off infections, and AIDS destroys this capacity. Thus, people with AIDS are highly susceptible to other sicknesses as well, such as the common cold. HIV-positive people will have antibodies to HIV, which can be discovered with a simple blood test. A positive HIV test result does not mean someone has AIDS or will necessarily develop it in the future, however. The most common prescription for avoiding HIV is to refrain from engaging in unprotected sex and from sharing intravenous needles. Intrauterine devices (IUDs), oral contraceptives, male and female sterilization, and natural family-planning methods such as rhythm and withdrawal provide no protection against sexually transmitted diseases (STDs). HIV/AIDS is reaching epidemic proportions in areas of Africa (where two-thirds of all HIV/AIDS victims live) and Asia (where the sex industry has proliferated in the past few decades). In Africa, more than 13 million people have already died of AIDS, 2 million in 1999 alone. In addition to the suffering AIDS has brought to Africa, the economies of some countries are already being affected. By 2015, the economies of countries such as Zambia and Zimbabwe are expected to fall by 25 percent. However, there are current concerns that the disease is rapidly progressing in Eastern Europe and Russia, and even in some of the states where it was considered largely under control there are fears that infection rates are slowly beginning to rise again. The struggle to distribute urgently needed antiretro viral drugs continues, as states such as Brazil and South Africa begin to dispense generic drugs to their citizens. Gradually, Northern pharmaceutical firms are being persuaded to either abandon patent protection laws and allow generics to be distributed, or to lower significantly the cost of their drugs for easier distribution elsewhere (see our profile on Canadian Stephen Lewis in Chapter 9). But this has been too little, too late for millions of people.

No doubt there are a plethora of diseases and serious health issues affecting sub-Sarahan Africans: malaria, hepatitis B, micronutrient malnutrition, iodine and vitamin-A deficiency, syphilis, gonorrhea, genital herpes, and other sexually transmitted diseases, to name but a few. But HIV/AIDS is so prevalent, and so deadly, that it is actually transforming the social profile of entire societies, resulting in an unprecedented number of orphans, and a continuous crisis in the public sector. More broadly, it can be argued that such infectious diseases are threatening the state's capacity to govern in many countries. In a provocative and careful study, Andrew Price-Smith concludes that "since increasing disease prevalence destroys or debilitates national populations and compromises both productivity and governance, infectious disease may be correctly seen as both a direct and an indirect threat to the national security of seriously affected states," and it can also "compromise the ability of transitional states (e.g., Russia and South Africa) to consolidate democratic and effective systems of governance."[23] It also results in the social isolation of the infected, and entire states, such as Haiti, have become known for its prevalence. Though a great deal can be done with improved health care and education, we can be sure that HIV/AIDS and other pandemics will continue to spread as long as people are able to travel.

Dennis Pirages argues four major transformations are underway that "seem to be strengthening the microbes' hands." Rapid population growth and urbanization lead to situations conducive to the rapid spread of disease, especially in the teeming megacities of the South, where adequate health care is seemingly beyond reach for the majority of citizens, and in areas where overpopulation has led to mass movements. Many of the refugees fleeing violence in Rwanda in 1994 died from cholera in the resulting overcrowded refugee camps. Population pressure is forcing people to inhabit previously wild areas, and this has had two consequences: new inhabitants are bringing new diseases into these areas, harming the Indigenous people and wildlife; and the newcomers themselves are exposed to new diseases, which are then spread into the general population. Pirages writes also of changes in human behaviour, such as the so-called sexual revolution of the late 1960s and 1970s in the United States and the global spread in the use of drugs, which facilitated the spread of disease. Cramped prison conditions, which help spread tuberculosis, result from policy shifts and increases in crime often linked to poverty. Third, the environment itself is changing in a way that makes it more difficult to control the spread of disease. Sudden or gradual climate change may give a temporary advantage to resident microbes. For example, Pirages suggests that a fatal outbreak of hantavirus in the desert Southwest of the United States may have been triggered by sudden rainstorms that increased population growth among the virus-carrying rodents. In each summer since 1999, the West Nile virus has surfaced in mosquitoes in New York, prompting massive pesticide sprays in the city; is this related to global warming? Finally, Pirages refers to technological innovations that have increased, rather than decreased, the ability of microbes to travel, such as the invention of the airplane: "Aircraft cabins are an excellent place for a rendezvous with cosmopolitan world-traveling viruses and bacteria."[24] A virus that causes hemorrhagic fever is said to have found its way to Baltimore from Seoul by way of wharf rats that made the journey in cargo ships. These viruses seem to understand what many global politics analysts do as well: a truly interdependent and interconnected world economy presents as much opportunity as it does danger.

PROTECTING MIGRANT WORKERS[25]

Migrant workers often end up in vulnerable positions and are perceived as needing additional, international protection. However, this is a very touchy area, since it falls within the jurisdiction of individual states to govern their own domestic labour laws. Previous work by the International Labour Organization (ILO) helped form the basis for what is arguably the most important UN General Assembly resolution dealing with migrant labour, the International Convention on the Protection of the Rights of All Migrant Workers and Members of Their Families. This is a comprehensive document that, at present, has escaped ratification by the majority of UN states, including Canada. It requests governments to pursue nondiscriminatory practices regarding migrant employees, including undocumented migrants, and their families. It is, in essence, an attempt to guarantee migrant workers the same rights that are already enshrined in the Universal Declaration of Human Rights (1948) and the subsequent International Covenants on Human Rights. For example, Article 10 states that "No migrant worker or member of his or her family shall be held in slavery or servitude"; Article 12 calls for their right to "freedom of thought, conscience and religion," including the right to "ensure the religious and moral education of their children in conformity with their own convictions"; and Article 18 gives migrants "the right to equality with nationals of the State concerned before the courts and tribunals."

At a much more visible level, the UN Conference on Population and Development at Cairo (1994) was precedent setting in that it included migration on its agenda. The most significant outcome was the establishment of the Program of Action of the International Conference on Population and Development (ICPD). Canada pushed strongly to include migration on the ICPD agenda. Chapters IX and X of the ICPD Program of Action discuss contemporary migration pressures, assuming a broad scope on the topic, including the role of development, documented and undocumented migrants, refugees, asylum seekers, and displaced persons. The program suggests that the North–South gap in wealth be reduced; that migrants' remittances be facilitated and channelled into productive investment in developing states; that discriminatory practices that harm migrants, including current outbreaks of racism and **xenophobia** (a fear or hatred of others not in one's social or ethnic group), be stopped; that family reunification of migrants be promoted; that the exploitation of undocumented migrants be prevented; and, related to the latter, that international trafficking in migrants (especially for the purpose of prostitution) be prevented. As with all such sweeping statements, most of this is a lot easier said than done.

Another multilateral effort to aid migrants has been the work of the **International Organization for Migration (IOM)**. The IOM has assisted in many efforts to help refugees but also helps migrants settle in new areas and acquire needed job skills. By 1976 the IOM had permanent offices in Indonesia, Malaysia, Singapore, and Thailand. In the 1980s the IOM became increasingly involved in migration and refugee assistance in Latin America and in 1991 was entrusted by the UN Disaster Relief Coordinator to organize the **repatriation** of foreigners stranded in the Gulf region after Iraq's invasion of Kuwait; this amounted to some 200 000 repatriations.[26] The IOM has also been involved extensively with the U.S.–Haitian refugee situation, helping with the interview process of boat people in Port-au-Prince (the in-country refugee processing system); Miami (facilitating domestic transportation for approved refugees); and also in Kingston, Guantanamo, and the Turks and Caicos Islands. The IOM prepares case files, coordinates interviews with American immigration officers, arranges for departure assistance, and aids resettlement in the United States for approved refugees.[27] More controversially, the IOM has become involved in the repatriation process as well. The IOM is often criticized for promising more than it can deliver on the policy side of the issue, and since it is dependent on receiving states for funding, it is often accused of being an organization that merely fulfills the wishes of the United States and others.

Many regional multilateral organizations have put migration somewhere on the agenda, if not front and centre. For example, the G-7 states (Canada, Japan, Italy, France, the United Kingdom, the United States, and Germany), which hold annual summits and lesser-publicized ministerial-level meetings to discuss economic coordination, often deal with migration issues; however, migration has yet to become a big-ticket item, despite the fact that it is obviously intrinsic to the often-discussed question of unemployment. The OECD surveys migration trends as well, and the EU has a variety of mechanisms designed to both facilitate labour movement within the Union and limit migration into it.

Canada has been participating in the Intergovernmental Consultations on Asylum, Refugee, and Migration Policies in Europe, North America, and Australia (commonly referred to as either the IGC or the Informal Consultations) based, with its own small secretariat, in Geneva. At present, 15 governments take part in the consultations, which began in 1985, and generate documentation on issues such as temporary protection, asylum procedures, trafficking in illegal aliens, and unaccompanied minors. The **UN High Commissioner for Refugees (UNHCR)** and IOM both participate in the process, though it has a rather closed-door image. Since the consultations are among countries of destination only, they have been criticized for what one analyst believes is a self-protective focus on "removals, prevention of asylum-seeking, and individuals seeking asylum in order to avoid asylum shopping."[28] However, we should not exaggerate the IGC's ability to realize its goal, since most states—including Canada—remain reluctant to lose their ability to be flexible on asylum, refugee, or migration policies.

REFUGEES

> "Everyone has the right to seek and enjoy in other countries
> asylum from persecution."[29]

Refugees are created when people facing persecution flee their circumstances, individually or in groups, or are forcibly expelled from their home state. Though we usually envision the former when we think of refugees, we should also keep in mind that mass expulsions have been common forms of policy throughout history: some 15 million Africans were forced overseas into slavery before 1850 and massive forced movements were notable before, during, and after World War II.[30] During the Cold War, the West often considered refugee movements to be political priorities; however, they now receive a less urgent response and though many states such as Canada have maintained fairly liberal refugee acceptance policies, international refugee assistance is clearly underfunded.

It is, of course, extremely difficult to measure the number of refugees worldwide, especially if one seeks to include people who have been displaced within their home state. When G.J. van Heuven Goedhart was appointed the first UN High Commissioner for Refugees in 1951, there were 1.25 million refugees. In 1976, with Sadruddin Aga Khan as High Commissioner, there were 2.8 million recognized refugees; by 1980, almost 8.5 million. In 1992, by contrast, there were almost 18 million. Though this figure had dropped to 10.4 million by 2002, the total number of "persons of concern to the UNHCR," including refugees (approximately half),

Dislocation in wartime. An unidentified woman carries a boy injured when local ethnic Albanians threw stones at a camp where Gypsies had taken refuge in the village of Obilicevo, near Pristina, in the Yugoslav province of Kosovo. About 900 Gypsies, fearing attacks from ethnic Albanians who accused them of collaborating with Serbs, left the town of Kosovo Polje and came to the camp in Obilicevo. (AP Photo/Amel Emric/CP Archive)

asylum seekers, those being repatriated to their homelands, internally displaced persons, and others was estimated at 20 556 700 in January 2003. Of these, 9 378 900 were in Asia, 4 593 200 in Africa, 4 403 900 in Europe, and the rest in North America, Latin America and the Caribbean, and Oceania.[31] The largest sources of refugees are, not surprisingly, from states where prolonged and severe conflict has occurred (see Profile 11.6). However, many asylum seekers come from areas where minorities are persecuted as well, even in the absence of civil or international war. Along with the unprecedented increase in refugee numbers in the early 1990s, a much more complex understanding of refugee and migration issues evolved. While political refugees were once regarded as "the tragic product of an incompatible juxtaposition, whether of faction, class, religion, ideology, or nationality,"[32] other factors such as development, overpopulation, and the environment play major roles today, necessitating even more complex models. Just as important, we need to look at multilateral efforts to deal with refugee flows, efforts that are aimed not only at mitigating the human suffering of refugees but also at protecting the states into which they flow.

REFUGEE FLOWS AND ECOPOLITICAL VIOLENCE

Environmental degradation and resource scarcity increase demands on government finances and services. For example, shortages of water require expensive dams or new irrigation systems. The loss of rural incomes from environmental degradation provokes migration to cities, increasing demands for transport, energy, water, sanitation, food, and health care. As economic activity is affected by environmental degradation, government revenues decline, reducing the ability of governments to maintain services and order. As Thomas Homer-Dixon argues, "A widening gap between state capacity and demands on the state, along with the misguided economic interventions such a gap often provokes, aggravates popular and elite grievances, increases rivalry between elite factions, and erodes a state's legitimacy."[33] As a result, conflict between communal groups within a state, or conflict between governments and disaffected communal groups, will intensify as competition to control resources and wealth grows. In many cases, political elites will hoard whatever surplus wealth is produced, and use it to maintain their power and their privileged lifestyles. The rest of the population will struggle for what share of the resource pie is left, or they will seek to overthrow the political elites. The overall result is the erosion and collapse of social order, and the disintegration of the state as different factions and groups do battle over a shrinking economic base, often

PROFILE 11.6 Where the Refugees and Asylum Seekers Are

TABLE 1: ORIGIN OF MAJOR REFUGEE POPULATIONS IN 2003

Afghanistan: 2 136 000, most in Pakistan and Iran

Sudan: 606 200, most in Uganda, Ethiopia, D.R. Congo, Kenya

Burundi: 531 600, most in Tanzania and D.R. Congo

D.R. Congo: 453 400, most in Tanzania, Congo, Zambia

Palestine: 427 900, administered by the UNRWA

Somalia: 402 200, most in Kenya, Yemen, Ethiopia, United Kingdom

Iraq: 368 500, most in Iran, Germany, Netherlands, Sweden

Vietnam: 363 200, most in China, United States, Germany

Liberia: 353 300, most in Guinea, Côte d'Ivoire, Sierra Leone

Angola: 329 600, most in Zambia, D.R. Congo, Namibia

TABLE 2: MAJOR REFUGEE MOVEMENTS, 2003

112 200 from Sudan, into Chad, Uganda, Kenya, and Ethopia

86 800 from Liberia, into Sierra Leone, Guinea, Côte d'Ivoire, and Ghana

30 000 from D.R. Congo, into Burundi, Tanzania, Zambia

22 200 from Côte d'Ivoire, into Liberia and Guinea

14 800 from Somalia, into Yemen and Kenya

13 000 from Central African Republic, into Chad

8 100 from Burundi, into Tanzania, Zambia, Rwanda

TABLE 3: ASYLUM APPLICATIONS SUBMITTED IN INDUSTRIALIZED COUNTRIES

United Kingdom: 61 100, mostly from Iraq, Zimbabwe, Afghanistan, Somalia, China

United States: 60 700, mostly from China, Mexico, Colombia, Haiti, Indonesia

France: 59 800, mostly from Turkey, D.R. Congo, Russian Fed., Algeria, China

Germany: 50 600, mostly from Iraq, Turkey, Serbia-Montenegro, Russia, China

Austria: 32 400, mostly from Serbia-Montenegro, Iraq, Afghanistan, Turkey, Russian Fed.

Canada: 31 900, mostly from Pakistan, Colombia, Mexico, China, Costa Rica

Sweden: 33 000, mostly from Serbia-Montenegro, Iraq, Bosnia-Herzegovina, Somalia, Stateless

SOURCE: *REFUGEES BY NUMBERS*, 2004 EDITION (GENEVA: UNHCR, 2004). USED WITH PERMISSION.

destroying what little in the way of resources, facilities, or livelihoods remained to them. This condition of near anarchy exacerbates environmental degradation and economic deprivation. Where there is no government or system of order, there are no regulations or laws governing the use of natural resources. Conservation and preservation become impossible. In the worst cases, these factors can converge into a horrific blend of violent conflict, crime, poverty, disease, and starvation and malnutrition. All of this occurs in those areas of the world least equipped to respond to such crises or to manage them effectively (see Profile 11.6).

In the face of such conditions, a natural reaction of people is to flee to escape the violence of war or the hardships of economic deprivation. Environmentally induced conflicts can thus create large refugee movements, migrations of peoples that move to new locations within a country or from one country to another. These migrations have been identified as another source of potential conflict, for refugee movements create tensions and disputes in the regions or countries that receive them. As Nazli Choucri has argued, "The masses of forcefully uprooted persons … might become a key element in the lethal feedback dynamic between environmental degradation and violent conflict."[34] Refugee movements can create or spread conflict because the influx of a large number of refugees can alter land availability and distribution patterns, disturb economic relations, alter the political and social climate, and upset the local ecological balance. This can provoke communal conflicts between migrant peoples and the peoples in the receiving region. This is true of international refugees (those who cross state borders) and internally displaced refugees (those who flee from one area of a country to another). In the Canadian study on environmental degradation and violent conflict discussed in Chapter 10, Homer-Dixon argued that "there is substantial evidence to support the hypothesis that environmental scarcity causes large population movement, which in turn causes group identity conflicts."[35] Similarly, Nazli Choucri claimed that "environmental degradation forces people to move, sometimes across borders, and most assuredly to impinge on and ultimately challenge [host] populations."[36]

However, because migrations and the effects they produce are influenced by a wide variety of factors, the link between environmental refugees and the spread of conflict is not an automatic one. In fact, according to Astri Suhrke, conflict will occur "only under conditions of zero-sum interaction—whether actual or perceived. The alternative is a value-added model, where migrants are incorporated into the host society without collective strife, typically by providing needed labour and skills. Nor does ethnic differentiation between host population(s) and newcomers necessarily make the incorporation process conflictual."[37] There are also constraints on the capacity of refugees to create conflict. Refugee populations may be isolated in refugee encampments in relatively remote regions. They may be too weak or disorganized to be regarded as a threat. In many cases, refugee movements that are regarded as a threat have the support of a neighbouring state, and therefore the refugees are seen as an instrument of foreign interference. Nonetheless, there are many examples of environmentally induced refugee movements provoking political and social upheaval and violence. Refugee flows from Bangladesh into Northeast India (arising largely from population growth and land scarcity) have provoked communal conflict between migrant and Indigenous peoples. In Assam, the Lalung peoples have reacted angrily and sometimes violently against the Muslim Bengali migrants, whom they accuse of appropriating scarce farmland. In Tripura, Tripuris conducted an eight-year insurgency over access to land, which was in short supply due to a massive influx of refugees from Bangladesh. Efforts by the Indian government to return dispossessed land and stop the flow of migration have met with mixed success in the face of continued environmental stresses on land resources in the region.

More generally, it is quite logical to assume that increasing environmental degradation will lead to more people being forced to move for survival reasons. At present, the Convention of Refugees would not automatically qualify them as refugees, and many would argue this is unfair, since the ecological destruction forcing their departure is so often caused by elements beyond their control, such as drought, the construction of large dams, and the industrialization of agriculture. Global warming, which could raise sea levels and flood hundreds of millions out of coastal zones, and submerge entire island states, is perhaps the biggest threat here. As things are, however, one must be fleeing abject political persecution and cross a border to either qualify as a refugee or seek asylum. It is unlikely this will change in the future, as industrialized states fear it would open the doors to hundreds of thousands of asylum seekers to include categories such as economic migrants and environmental refugees in the official definition. We turn now to a brief discussion of the international refugee regime.

MULTILATERAL RESPONSES TO REFUGEE CRISES: EFFORTS AND DILEMMAS

Usually, asylum seekers will arrive at an airport, or cross a border, by themselves or with their family. They can apply for asylum with local authorities, and the process of refugee determination will begin. They will be assisted by a lawyer, UNHCR representatives, or others who can support their claim, while the refugee determination board involved will face the difficult task of determining whether or not the applicant would suffer unacceptable persecution if returned home.

However, this is not the only scenario, and in many cases, especially where conflict has forced people to flee, refugee arrivals number in the tens of thousands, making the asylum process both impossible and unnecessary. At the international level, the UNHCR remains the principal organization whose mandate is to aid and assist refugees. The UNHCR is constantly employed today in all the major regions of the globe. While its primary mandate relates to caring for those Convention refugees who cross borders, it is increasingly dealing with internally displaced persons as well—but can do so only when requested by the Security Council, General Assembly, or host country. The UNHCR budget, which is derived from voluntary contributions (largely from states but also from nongovernmental organizations and individuals), is divided into funding for general programs (basic projects for refugee aid and durable solutions, the most important of which is repatriation) and special programs, which include responses to sudden emergencies such as the outflow of more than 1 million Rwandans from that troubled state in 1994. As the UNCHR was designed to solve what was in 1945 considered a temporary problem—the relocation of people displaced by World War II in Europe—it was not created as a permanent agency; as such, it needs to have its mandate renewed every five years, and to beg states and private donors for funding on a continual basis.

Several other UN bodies are involved in refugee protection and assistance. Most notably, the United Nations Relief Works Administration (UNRWA), another voluntary, contribution-based international organization, was established in 1949 to deal with the refugees generated by the first Arab–Israeli War, and its operations have expanded to include health care and education provision. It had more than 4.1 million people registered in 2004, located in Jordan, Syria, Lebanon, the West Bank, and the Gaza Strip.[38] The UNRWA, with more than 18 000 Palestinian employees, is the single largest operating program within the UN system. Despite the political uncertainty in the region, it "carries on a thankless task, criticized for not doing more while financial contributors grow restive in support of a relief operation that has no end in sight."[39] A Canadian-led international committee, termed the *Refugee Working Group*, has toured Jordanian refugee camps for Palestinians, with an aim toward incorporating the refugee question into the broader Middle East peace process. However, Israeli governments have been reluctant to put the right of Palestinian refugee return on the bargaining table (see Chapter 7).

There is a long tradition of humanitarian aid organizations predating World War II, but most of the extant organizations today can trace their roots directly to that epic confrontation. The UN Relief and Rehabilitation Administration (UNRRA) was established by the Allies in 1943 to follow them into liberated areas at the close of World War II to provide immediate relief to victims of the war, including concentration camp survivors. The UN International Children's Emergency Fund (UNICEF) was established in 1946, and in 1953 moved into longer-term programs beyond Europe and Asia. UNICEF delivers aid to drought- and war-stricken regions and works with WHO to help meet the nutritional requirements of refugee children. WHO is also involved with assessing the nutritional requirements of refugee populations; for example, in 1988 an international conference, Nutrition in Times of Disaster, met at WHO's headquarters in Geneva. More broadly, the UNHCR works in conjunction with the World Food Programme in many cases of unexpected refugee flows.

The UNHCR also consults with some 300 NGOs that play roles in relief operations. In 1993, more than one-quarter of the UNHCR budget went to NGOs. However, what is arguably the most significant partner is in fact an intergovernmental organization, the International Committee of the Red Cross (ICRC; in Islamic countries, the International Committee of the Red Crescent). Its history dates back to 1859, and it was charged in 1864 with overseeing the implementation of the first Geneva Convention. In 2003 the ICRC had

PROFILE 11.7 Civil War Refugees

In 1996, Canada issued new guidelines that reduce the confusion over who can be admitted as a refugee during a civil war. The chair of the Immigration and Refugee Board, Nurjehan Mawani, said these guidelines reflect what many board members were already doing, as well as the precedents set by the Federal Court of Appeal. People fleeing civil war are judged by the risk of persecution they face. Individuals do not have to be personally singled out. If they are members of a large, persecuted group, they are considered refugees under the United Nations refugee convention, which includes persecution based on race, religion, nationality, or membership in a social group. Civilians caught in indiscriminate shelling or looting are not considered refugees unless they are members of an ethnic or religious group that is a target. However, they must show that they cannot flee to another part of their home country or that another group cannot protect them. Of course, they must also make it to Canada somehow, not an easy feat for someone with no income trapped in a war zone. It is far more likely that the UNHCR and other multilateral organizations will be the relevant interventional body in most cases where war is involved, and Canada's financial contributions to them are as important as its own refugee policies.

SOURCE: LILA SARICK, "GUIDE ON CIVIL-WAR REFUGEES ISSUED," *THE GLOBE AND MAIL*, 8 MARCH 1996, A7.

offices in 169 locations, and a considerable portion of its operations involve refugee assistance. Examples of heavy ICRC involvement include El Salvador and Nicaragua, Sudan, Angola, Mozambique, Uganda and Somalia, Afghanistan, Pakistan, the Thai/Cambodian border, and the territories occupied by Israel. ICRC represents displaced civilians to governments and armed movements; actively protects them through its ability to achieve legal access (occasionally denied) to refugee and internment camps; provides medical, food, and material assistance; and runs the Tracing Agency, which seeks to reunite displaced and separated families.[40]

The ICRC and UNHCR have some overlap in their mandates, but a general division of labour has evolved: the ICRC assumes primary responsibility for persons displaced within a country during wartime, while the UNHCR has exclusive responsibility for refugees in countries of temporary or first asylum. This distinction, however, is not permanent, as was evidenced with the ill-fated Safe Haven plan in Bosnia-Herzegovina, when the UNHCR was used to protect and feed internal displaced persons. In an African case, a UN pullout left the ICRC to service genuine cross-border refugees as well.[41] Though it might appear as if these two agencies overlap considerably, it is essential that each exist independent of the other. The Red Cross is involved with warfare-related situations exclusively, while the UNHCR is not. The Red Cross operates independently from the UN system (although it has observer status in the General Assembly), while the UNHCR does not. The Red Cross is willing to go where the UNHCR is not, and the UNHCR does things the Red Cross cannot. Both are desperately needed today; unfortunately, both are entirely dependent on the voluntary contributions of states and individuals for funding, which is habitually meagre.

Meanwhile, humanitarian relief organizations find themselves in terrible on-ground dilemmas. Should they accept the military protection of forces active in the area, including international intervention forces, and thus risk losing the perception that they are impartial? Without this protection they are in effect intriguing targets for kidnapping and theft; with it they may be seen as enemies by at least one side of the conflict. Should they cooperate extensively with occupying powers, such as the coalition forces in Iraq? Should they aid refugees who are clearly violent criminals? The latter question surfaced most markedly after hundreds of thousands of Hutus fled the Rwandan Patriotic Front in 1994; many of them had participated in the genocide there before crossing into Zaire, and even used the camps as recruitment grounds for raising a possible retaliatory force. This ultimately caused some groups, such as *Médecins Sans Frontières* (Doctors Without Borders), to pull out of the camps, even though there were thousands of innocent women and children in dire need of medical assistance there.[42] It can also be argued that aid agencies contribute to structural violence, merely by seeking a return to "normalcy" in crisis situations. For example, Mark Duffield argues that the problem with helping the displaced Sudanese is not the rush to cope with emergency situations, or complicity in perpetuating the civil war in Sudan, but rather the fact that efforts to obtain peace can result in the continuation of prior relations of exploitation and, by extension, genocidal policies not directly linked to the civil war effort. As he puts it, "goal-oriented humanitarianism in the transition zone can be argued to have reinforced those everyday relations that denote 'peace.' In other words, aid agencies have strengthened and tacitly supported those economic and political relations of desocialisation, subordination and exploitation that constitute normal life. In the transition zone, since the Dinka are enmeshed in such relations, aid policy has been complicit in their oppression."[43] Similarly, the UNWRA could be accused of perpetuating the status quo in Israeli–Palestinian relations. However—and here is the hard part—these concerns must be weighed against the cost of nonintervention in immediate human suffering, lack of education for youth, chronic long-term malnutrition, and other problems.

Other NGOs play important roles in emergency humanitarian assistance as well. Notably, the Save the Children Fund has played a key role in many refugee relief situations (more than half the world's refugees are children) in places as diverse as Russia, Hungary, Korea, Algeria, Jordan, Gaza and the West Bank, Cambodia, Laos, Central America, Iraq, Rwanda, Zaire, Nepal, and Bangladesh. The Save the Children Fund was founded in 1919 by a British schoolteacher named Eglantyne Jebb, who would draft the Declaration of the Rights of the Child in 1923, adopted by the League of Nations in 1923 and, much later, redrafted as the 1989 UN Convention on the Rights of the Child. In 1979 various national units came together under the umbrella of the Geneva-based International Save the Children Alliance (ISCA), which now has 25 members.[44]

On a global level, the refugee situation is particularly acute. If the world community, and especially the primary donor states, wants the UNHCR to deal with emergency refugee flows, then it will have to increase funding for this highly strained organization. For example, Canada currently funds overseas emergency refugee assistance through the International Humanitarian Assistance (IHA) budget of the **Canadian International Development Agency (CIDA)**; this amounts to less than 3 percent of the IHA budget, and CIDA's overall funding level could be decreasing in the next few years.[45] As for the idea that giving aid to refugees will foster dependence and corrupt the initiative of refugees themselves, this has been widely disputed by scholars such as David Keen.[46] What matters is the way in which emergency aid is delivered: though it is a highly demanding policy, agencies and governments must struggle to preserve human dignity and cultural uniqueness as far as possible. Sometimes, this is just a matter of conducting sound preliminary research. But in times of severe crisis, it is difficult to prepare for the unexpected. More than ever, diligent observation of political developments, including armed conflicts and social unrest, government and rebel-group aggression and persecution, and environmental impact assessment are vital tools in the fight against harm.

THE INTERNALLY DISPLACED

As indicated above, social and environmental problems, including poverty, resource scarcity, and warfare, can induce large-scale refugee movements. However, most displaced people do not cross national borders. There are millions of "involuntary migrants" who are victims of political violence and environmental degradation yet who are not officially considered refugees because they do not step, sail, drive, or fly over an imaginary line that distinguishes one state from another. With notable exception, their plight is still considered purely one of domestic policy. Rural–urban migration; population displacement caused by large-scale development projects, deforestation, and soil degradation; and even forced expulsions between regions within states are still considered the domestic affairs of sovereign states, and although outside funding agencies can certainly wield influence in directing governments away from these processes, stopping them altogether is not a distinct possibility under the present circumstances. It is important to stress that such movements are often quite orchestrated, and not the byproduct of natural disasters beyond the control of governments. Whether the consequence of ethnic cleansing, industrialization, ecocide, or inadequate responses to disasters that marginalize certain sectors of society, such population movements are both human rights dilemmas for the international community and major sources of destabilization for national and local governments alike.[47]

The government of Indonesia has orchestrated one of the largest internal movements of people in history. In an effort to reduce overcrowding on the main Indonesian island of Java, some 6 million people have been moved to outlying islands such as Sumatra, Kalimantan, Sulawesi, and Irian Jaya. Most of those resettled work in agriculture and many now actually own their own land. Lately, the migrants have found work in other areas, such as rubber and coffee plantations, fishponds, and seaweed processing plants. However, despite reforestation projects in Eastern Kalimantan, environmentalists complain about the widespread deforestation caused by this mass migration to formerly remote areas, and many of the migrants are living in dire poverty in their new locations. Violence has frequently erupted between the newcomers and previous inhabitants (though this can be attributed to larger patterns of sectarian violence in the region.) Nonetheless, the program continues, as Jakarta, the main city on Java, continues to grow. It is estimated that the metropolis will have well over 17 million citizens by 2015 (see Profile 11.2).[48]

Two types of internal displacees exist: those who have fled warfare or extreme environmental degradation, and those who have been moved by their governments for the purposes of economic development. In either case, it is still a matter of considerable debate whether the UNHCR or any other body should be permitted to interfere in the internal affairs of a state to help internally displaced people.[49] When Russian forces caused people to flee the war zone in Chechnya, Russia asked the UNHCR to assist in the care of the internally displaced. However, this request was an exception to the rule. There are, possibly, hundreds of thousands of internally displaced people in Burma, for example, and the UNHCR has no ability to aid them. There are millions in Sudan and Colombia with little or no assistance available either. More generally, millions of internally displaced people in the next few decades will have a difficult time integrating with the rest of the societies in which they live. This difficulty will in turn increase outward, cross-border migratory pressure as well.

GENDER, THE SEX TRADE, AND TRAFFICKING IN MIGRANTS

Within the subfield of migration studies, several other issue-areas are receiving increasing attention. The question of gender is foremost among them. Women migrants and refugees face a unique set of obstacles as they resettle in new countries.[50] They are often the victims of outright repression in their home states, and, in fact, several states—Canada among them—have gone so far as to accept such women as legitimate Convention refugees.[51] This applies particularly to women who have fled states where they have legitimate fear that they will be punished for avoiding traditions such as female genital mutilation (see Chapter 9). More generally, however, women migrants face special challenges when moving to new areas where they

Born and raised in a refugee camp. Two unidentified Vietnamese girls peer out from a barbed wire fence in the Sikhiu refugee camp in Nakorn Ratchasima, northeast of Bangkok, Thailand, 19 February 1997, shortly before they were repatriated to Vietnam, ending Thailand's decades-long role as a sanctuary for tens of thousands. Women and girls face special problems in the context of humanitarian assistance operations. (AP Photo/The Nation, Kittinun Rodsupan/CP Archive)

may have a more difficult time than men obtaining employment that can adequately support them and their children. Single women, particularly, and unaccompanied minors are certainly vulnerable to harm, especially sexual abuse, in refugee camps. Many children have lived their entire lives in what were supposed to be temporary refugee camps and consequently received little if any formal education.

As the result of destitution or outright coercion, many women and children migrants become involved in the international sex-trade industry (see Profile 11.8). This represents not only a shameful aspect of the failure to provide basic human rights to those affected but also increases the health risks associated with such work. Most notably, of course, the spread of HIV/AIDS, which is virtually uncontrollable in many regions of the world today, is undeniably accelerated by prostitution, which often assumes the form of a global operation, complete with resorts attracting men from North America, Europe, and Asia. The international community has often dealt with this issue; even the long-defunct League of Nations had a Committee on the Abolition of White Slavery (terminology largely discarded today) and preceding that there was an international Agreement for the Suppression of the White Slave Traffic and related conventions in 1904 and 1910, respectively. It is impossible, therefore, to argue that this issue is too new to deal with. Yet we need more global attention to stop or at least limit this flagrant form of exploitation, as well as domestic legislation discouraging the practice.[52] However, until this issue becomes more prominent and is addressed with more energy, little will be done, as some governments are accomplices in the growth of the sex industry.

The illegal trafficking in migrants is of growing concern worldwide, despite measures such as the Convention on the Rights of the Child, which asserts, "State parties shall take measures to combat the illicit transfer and non-return of children abroad."[53] A recent seminar sponsored by the IOM on the trafficking of migrants concluded that it was part of a much broader

PROFILE 11.8 **Transnational Prostitution: A Resolution**

A large traffic in women and children for the purpose of prostitution remains, according to a recent resolution adopted by the United Nations General Assembly. In it, the UN condemned the illicit and clandestine movement of persons across national and international borders, largely from developing countries and some countries with economies in transition, with the end goal of forcing women and children into sexually or economically oppressive and exploitative situa-tions, for the profit of recruiters, traffickers, and crime syndicates, as well as into other illegal activities related to trafficking, such as forced domestic labour, false marriages, clandestine employment, and false adoption. What is neces-sary, however, is a full-frontal attack on the demand side of this equation: without an eager market, sex traders would have no incentive to engage in their activities.

SOURCE: UN RESOLUTION A/RES/49/166, 24 FEBRUARY 1995.

pattern of transnational criminal activity and could be dealt with only as an element of an internally coordinated strategy to eliminate that sector.[54] However, this is much easier said than done for a wide variety of reasons that space limitations do not permit us to explore here, such as government corruption, coercive techniques by traffickers, the stimulus of poverty, demand for cheap labour and prostitution, and many other factors. In addition, there is the question of the rights of illegal migrants, which is a particularly visible issue in the United States. The Migrant Worker's Convention outlined above would apply to these people as well, and this explains some of the overwhelming reluctance among industrialized states to even sign the agreement.

Discrimination against migrants, especially female migrants, takes many forms around the globe.[55] It might be argued that one of the greatest difficulties involves encouraging govern-ments to accept the idea that all migrants, be they permanent (settlers), temporary contract workers, temporary professional transients, clandestine or illegal workers, asylum seekers, or genuine refugees as defined by the 1951 Convention, are entitled to the same rights. This is simply not an acceptable formula; it would imply, for example, that temporary workers and even illegal migrants would have the right to vote and receive the same social services as reg-ular tax-paying citizens. And yet their contributions to society certainly imply they deserve no less than the full protection of the law.

CONCLUSIONS

This chapter has covered many topics, but we should stress how interrelated they are, in theory and practice. While avoiding simplistic linear explanations, it can be plausibly argued that population growth leads to increased population movement, massive urbanization, and drains on natural resources. This movement, in turn, increases threats to human health and political stability. In both population control measures and questions about the protection of refugees, North–South splits as well as gender issues are evident. This comes at a time when migration policies among the industrialized Northern states have, by and large, emphasized the closure of borders.[56] Overall, one might argue that we have seen a shift in how the world community views the migration issue-area. This evolution has taken us from what was once viewed primarily as a labour-related question to what is today seen primarily as a popula-tion—or, more specifically, overpopulation—question. However, in the post–September 11 climate, refugee policies will be even more cumbersome for people fleeing conflicts in Arab states in search of asylum in Europe or North America. The fear of pathogenic contamination is also quite noticeable, and will no doubt increase as the HIV/AIDS pandemic and SARS-like incidents continue to surprise us.

Even if the neoclassical framework for development and trade liberalization is effective in stimulating markets, this will not necessarily stop migratory pressure. Georges Tapinos notes this with regard to NAFTA: its initial success might absorb some of the surplus of Mexican labour resulting from industrialization and a decrease in agricultural subsidies, "but the majority will seek employment in the United States. It is a straightforward illustration of the fact that [trade and investment] liberalization between countries with significant differences in size, endowments, and production patterns cannot in the short run simultaneously achieve two objectives: an increase in the standard of living, and a decrease in the propensity to emigrate."[57] Globalization hardly seems the solution to the crises generated by population growth and movement; indeed, overconsumption of resources and skilled workers by the North is part of the problem, not the solution.

It may be true that members of affluent societies are capable of travelling the globe as never before, but this is the post–Cold War era. The East–West dynamic has largely been replaced with concerns not about political refugees who can make a splash in the newspapers when they defect from the Soviet Union but about displaced Russians seeking employment in Western Europe, or people fleeing civil war in the former Yugoslavia or in Burundi to seek haven in neighbouring states, or Haitians trying desperately to cross ocean space in decrepit boats to Florida only to be intercepted at sea and, eventually, returned. While there is little doubt that the age of capital mobility is upon us, we are far from a world in which people travel as freely across borders.

In this chapter we have examined issues related to the large population increases experienced in the 20th century, including the question of responsibility for promoting sustainable development, urbanization, birth control, and voluntary and involuntary population movements. There can be little doubt that the increase in population puts additional strain on the natural ecosystems on which we all ultimately depend, and that overconsumption in both the North and South exacerbate the environmental problems discussed in Chapter 10. If high populations are a reflection of poverty, so are large population movements. In this chapter, we discussed the push–pull factors involved in migration and then looked at the contemporary refugee crisis, with an emphasis on multilateral responses. Ultimately, however, individual governments will have to cope with both migratory and refugee pressures and the larger problem of internal displacement. Finally, we concluded that rising population levels are encouraging closed borders in the North, thus exposing a rather large hole in the convergence thesis outlined in Chapter 1.

From a global perspective, the problem may well be too large for any one or combination of international organizations to handle, and bilateral initiatives will be needed along with open immigration policies and long-term aid. However, this seems less likely as Northern governments continue to experience the crunch of financial realism, which has finally started to seriously shape fiscal policies and external aid budgets. Xenophobia remains a factor in immigration policy and fears of developing countries' population increases provoke it. The South's current condition is at least partly the result of the North's historic exploitation of it, yet the North is in a decreasingly viable position to contribute to long-term solutions. The situation is further exacerbated by post–September 11 border controls.

The global population will continue to rise, especially in the Southern hemisphere, in the future. This increase will occur despite tragic pandemics, such as the spread of the AIDS virus in Asia and Africa. The realistic question is not whether things will be moving in this direction but how we will cope with unprecedented numbers of people, millions of whom will be on the move. In the midst of all this humanity, can compassion survive?

Endnotes

1. Garrett Hardin, "The Tragedy of the Commons," *Science* 162 (December 1968), 1243–48.

2. John Hope Simpson, *Refugees: Preliminary Report of a Survey* (London: Chatham House, 1938), 193.

3. UNEP, *Global Environment Outlook 3* (London: Earthscan, 2002), 33. For a standard essay on the demographic transition theory, see H. Frederiksen, "Feedbacks in Economic and Demographic Transition," *Science* 166 (1969), 837–47.

4. See *The Population Explosion* (New York: Simon and Schuster, 1990).

5. Hardin, "The Tragedy of the Commons."

6. This formula is usually expressed as follows: I = PAT: impact is equal to population size, multiplied by per capita consumption (affluence), in turn multiplied by a measure of the damage done by the technologies chosen to supply each unit of consumption.

7. Amniocentesis uses a sample of amniotic fluid from a pregnant woman's uterus to diagnose possible genetic defects and reveals the gender of the fetus in the process. See N. Kristof, "Peasants of China Discover New Way to Weed Out Girls," *The New York Times*, 21 July 1993, A1. It was the main cause, the critics alleged, of the high ratio of 117 boys born to every 100 girls in China, compared to the world average of 106:100.

8. Parts of this section are taken from P.J. Stoett, "Cities: To Love or to Loathe?" a review article based on J. Kasarda and A. Parnell, ed., *Third World Cities: Problems, Policies, and Prospects* (London: Sage, 1993); and J. Hardoy, D. Mitlin, and D. Satterthwaite, *Environmental Problems in Third World Cities* (London: Earthscan, 1992), which appeared in *Environmental Politics* 3, no. 2 (1994), 339–42.

9. See Kasarda and Parnell, *Third World Cities*; Hardoy, Mitlin, and Satterthwaite, *Environmental Problems*; and P. Gizewski and T. Homer-Dixon, "Urban Growth and Violence: Will the Future Resemble the Past?" *Project on Environment, Population and Security* (Toronto: AAAS and University College, University of Toronto, 1995); on Kibera see J. Vasagar, "Residents Left Scrambling as Kenya Clears Shantytowns," *The Globe and Mail*, 23 April 2004, A12. Forcible eviction of slum-dwellers is fast becoming an old tradition in Africa and elsewhere; even during the 1992 Earth Summit there were reports that police in Rio de Janeiro rounded up thousands of street children and shipped them out of town for the purpose of appearances. The problem of course is that forced evictions simply displace the problem somewhere else and are human rights violations.

10. See R. Biswas, "Banned Drug Still Used on Women," *India Tribune*, 25 January 2004, http://www.tribuneindia.com/2004/20040125/herworld.htm#2 (accessed 30 May 2004).

11. See B. Hartmann, *Reproductive Rights and Wrongs: The Global Politics of Population Control and Contraceptive Choice* (New York: Harper and Row, 1987). For an excellent essay dealing with the transnational alliances and networks that have evolved related to population control issues, see B. Crane, "International Population Institutions: Adaptation to a Changing World Order," in P. Haas, R. Keohane, and M. Levy, eds., *Institutions for the Earth: Sources of Effective International Environmental Protection* (Cambridge, MA: MIT Press, 1994), 351–96.

12. "Maternity: Greater Peril?" *Populi: The UNFPA Magazine* 23, no. 1 (1996), 4–5.

13. *Our Planet* 6, no. 3 (1994), 11.

14. "Hard Lessons in Population Planning," *Our Planet* 6, no. 3 (1994), 32.

15. *The Economics of Mass Migration in the Twentieth Century* (New York: Paragon House, 1987). See also Stephen Castles and Mark Miller, *The Age of Migration: International Population Movements in the Modern World* (New York: Guilford, 1993).

16. See J. Rohozińska, "News from Poland" *Central Europe Review* 3, no. 5 (February 2001), http://www.ce-review.org/01/5/polandnews5.html (accessed 28 May 2004).

17. Note that the linguistic root of the word "robot" is in fact the Czech word for serf, *robotnik*. See P.B. Scott, *The Robotics Revolution* (New York: Oxford University Press, 1982), 10.

18. L. Hossie, "Migration Increases as Search for Good Life Grows," *The Globe and Mail*, 22 June 1993, A10; 2000 estimate from http://www.un.org/esa/population/publications/ittmig2002/press-release-eng.htm (accessed 28 May 2004). Of course, these figures are highly imprecise, given the large numbers of illegal immigrants that escape governmental detection. According to Statistics Canada's census, in 1991, 16.7 percent of the Canadian population was foreign-born; in 2001 the figure had risen to 18.8 percent. Between 1995 and 2000, Canada accepted 720 000 immigrants; the main countries of origin in 2000 were China (excluding Taiwan, but including Hong Kong), India, Pakistan, and the Philippines. See Citizenship and Immigration Canada's annual reports, http://www.cic.gc.ca/english/pub/#reference (accessed 28 May 2004).

19. M. Esman, "Ethnic Pluralism and International Relations," *Canadian Review of Studies in Nationalism* 17, no. 1–2 (1990), 83–93.

20. Two popular books are R. Preston, *The Hot Zone* (New York: Random House, 1994), and L. Garrett, *The Coming Plague: Newly Emerging Diseases in a World Out of Balance* (New York: Farrar, Straus, and Giroux, 1994). See also F. Cartwright, *Disease and History* (New York: Thomas Crowell, 1972), and W. McNeill, *Plagues and Peoples* (London: Doubleday, 1976); and especially A. Cosby, *Ecological Imperialism* (Cambridge, UK: Cambridge University Press, 1994).

21. See "SARS death toll rises to 38 in Toronto," CBC News, http://www.cbc.ca/stories/2003/06/22/sars_030622 (accessed 28 May 2004). Though the disease was well-contained after its initial period, there are reports that it has resurfaced in China in April 2004.

22. UNAIDS/WHO estimates from their joint report, "AIDS Epidemic Update" (Geneva, 2003).

23. *The Health of Nations: Infectious Disease, Environmental Change, and Their Effects on National Security and Development* (Cambridge, MA: MIT Press, 2002), 172. Price-Smith also presents an excellent chapter on how climate change can increase the range of pathogens, a topic we discuss in Chapter 10.

24. Dennis Pirages, "Microsecurity: Disease Organism and Human Well-Being," *Environmental Change and Security Project Report* (The Woodrow Wilson Center), 2 (1996), 9–14, 10; see also L. Garret, "The Return of Infectious Disease," *Foreign Affairs* 75, no. 1 (1996), 66–79.

25. Parts of this section are taken from P.J. Stoett, "International Mechanisms for Addressing Migration," *Canadian Foreign Policy* 4, no. 1 (1996), 111–38.

26. For a concise history of the IOM and discussion, see R. Appleyard, *International Migration: Challenge for the Nineties* (IOM: Geneva, 1991).

27. *IOM News* 7 (1994), 2.

28. Nazare Albuguerque-Abell, "The Safe Third Country Concept: Deflection in Europe and Its Implications for Canada," *Refuge* 14, no. 9 (1995), 1–7, 5.

29. Universal Declaration of Human Rights, 1948, Article 14.

30. The postwar expulsion of millions of Germans from various regions following the Potsdam Treaty is particularly notable, though it is often ignored in popular histories of the war. See Alfred-Maurice de Zayas, "International Law and Mass Population Transfers," *Harvard International Law Journal* 16, no. 2 (1975), 207–58.

31. *Refugees by Numbers* (Geneva: UNHCR, 2003). Note that these figures cannot reflect the large number of internally displaced people for whom the UNHCR can do nothing.

32. E. Buehrig, *The United Nations and the Palestinian Refugees: A Study in Nonterritorial Administration* (Bloomington: Indiana University Press, 1971), 3.

33. T. Homer-Dixon, "Evidence from Cases," International Security 19, no. 1 (1994) 5–40, For a good case study see C. Kahl, "Population Growth, Environmental Degradation, and State-Sponsored Violence: The Case of Kenya, 1991–93," *International Security* 23, no. 2 (1998), 80–119.

34. Nazli Choucri, "Environment, Development, and International Assistance: Crucial Linkages," in Sheryl J. Brown and Kimber M. Schraub, eds., *Resolving Third World Conflict: Challenges for a New Era* (Washington, DC: United States Institute of Peace Press, 1992), 101.

35. Homer-Dixon, "Environmental Scarcities and Violent Conflict," 20.

36. Choucri, "Environment, Development, and International Assistance," 101. See also N. Myers, *Ultimate Security* (New York: Norton, 1993).

37. Astri Suhrke, "Environmental Change, Migration, and Conflict: A Lethal Feedback Dynamic?" in Chester A. Crocker, Fen Osler Hampson, and Pamela Aall, eds., *Managing Global Chaos: Sources of and Responses to International Conflict* (Washington, DC: United States Institute of Peace Press, 1996), 116. There is a voluminous literature on environmental refugees; see, for example, A. Nash, "Environmental Refugees: Consequences of Policies from a Western Perspective," *Discrete Dynamics in Nature and Society* 3 (1999), 227–38.

38. Palestinian refugees in Israel were initially under the care of the UNRWA, but Israel assumed that responsibility in 1952. See Alexander Bligh, "From UNRWA to Israel: The 1952 Transfer of Responsibilities for Refugees in Israel," *Refuge* 14, no. 6 (1994), 7–10, 24; and "Switzerland and UNRWA to Host Major Conference on Humanitarian Assistance to Palestine Refugees, UNRWA, http://www.un.org/unrwa/news/releases/pr-2004/hqg-0404.pdf (accessed 30 May 2004).

39. Robert Riggs and Jack Plano, *The United Nations: International Organization and World Politics* (Belmont, CA: Wadsworth, 1994), 230.

40. F. Maurice and J. de Courten, "ICRC Activities for Refugees and Displaced Civilians," *International Review of the Red Cross* 280 (1991), 9–21.

41. This occurred in northwest Somalia, in 1990–91, where the ICRC extended its operations in aid of Ethiopian refugees after the World Food Programme and UNHCR suspended their activities for security reasons. The ICRC also found itself without proper military protection in Bosnia during the civil war there.

42. On this heart-wrenching decision, and others, see MSF staffer Fiona Terry's book, *Condemned to Repeat? The Paradox of Humanitarian Action* (Ithaca: Cornell University Press, 2002); on the Rwandan genocide, see P. Gourevitch, *We Wish to Inform You That Tomorrow We Will Be Killed with Our Families: Stories from Rwanda* (New York: Farrar Straus and Giroux, 1998).

43. M. Duffield, *Global Governance and the New Wars: The Merging of Development and Security* (London: Zed Books, 2001), 205.

44. For an excellent essay on the Save the Children Fund in Britain and its constant interaction with the UNHCR, World Food Programme, and other UN bodies, see A. Penrose and J. Seaman, "The Save the Children Fund and Nutrition for Refugees," in P. Willetts, ed., *"The Conscience of the World": The Influence of Non-Governmental Organizations in the UN System* (Washington, DC: Brookings, 1996), 241–69.

45. See M. Hart, "Canadian Overseas Assistance for Refugees," in H. Adelman, ed., *Refugee Policy: Canada and the United States* (Toronto: York Lanes, 1991).

46. D. Keen, *Refugees: Rationing the Right to Life* (London: Zed Books, 1992), 55.

47. See R. Cohen, *Human Rights Protection for Internally Displaced Persons* (Washington, DC: RPG, 1991); and F. Deng, *Protecting the Dispossessed: A Challenge for the International Community* (New York: Brookings, 1993).

48. S. Mydans, "Indonesia Resettles People to Relieve Crowding on Java," *The New York Times,* 25 August 1996, 4. For a report on a similar situation in Thailand, see D. Hubbel and N. Rajesh, "Not Seeing the People for the Forest: Thailand's Program of Reforestation by Forced Eviction," *Refuge* 12, no. 1 (1992), 20–21.

49. See R. Plender, "The Legal Basis of International Jurisdiction to Act with Regard to the Internally Displaced," *International Journal of Refugee Law* 6, no. 3 (1994), 345–61.

50. See S. Martin, *Refugee Women* (Oxford: Lexington Books, 2004).

51. See N. Spencer-Nimmons, "Canada's Response to the Issue of Refugee Women: The Women at Risk Program," *Refuge* 14, no. 7 (1994), 13–18. We should note also the role played by the Canadian Working Group for Refugee Women, a subgroup of the NGO-based Canadian Council for Refugees.

52. In 1996 Canada joined Sweden, Norway, Denmark, France, Belgium, Germany, Australia, the United States, Finland, Iceland, and New Zealand in passing legislation making it possible to charge citizens abroad who purchase sex from minors. J. Sallot, "Canada Targets Overseas Child Sex," *The Globe and Mail,* 4 April 1996, A4.

53. UN Resolution A/RES/44/25, 20 November 1989, Article 11.

54. "International Response to Trafficking in Migrants and the Safeguarding of Migrant Rights," *International Migration* 32, no. 4 (1994), 593–603. On the surge of this trade from the former Soviet bloc, see Victor Malarek, *The Natashas: The New Global Sex Trade* (Toronto: Viking 2003).

55. The question of discrimination against migrants seeking employment came home to Canadians recently as it was suggested that non-White Canadians were having a difficult time finding overseas jobs teaching English. "Asian Schools Avoid Non-White Canadians," *The Globe and Mail,* 28 March 1996, A1. For an interesting recent treatment of seasonal migrant workers in Canada, see T. Basok, *Tortillas and Tomatoes: Transmigrant Mexican Harvesters in Canada* (Montreal: McGill-Queen's University Press, 2002).

56. For a survey, see D. Kubat, *The Politics of Migration Policies: Settlement and Integration, the First World into the 1990s* (New York: Center for Migration Studies, 1993).

57. "International Migration and Development," *Population Bulletin of the UN* 36 (1994), 1–18, 12.

Suggested Readings

Appleyard, Reginald. *International Migration: Challenge for the Nineties.* Geneva: IOM, 1991.

Bemak, Fred. *Counseling Refugees: A Psychological Approach to Innovative Multicultural Interventions.* Westport, CT; London: Greenwood Press, 2003.

Benny, Morris. *The Palestinian Refugee Problem Revisited,* 2nd ed. Cambridge, UK; New York: Cambridge University Press, 2004.

Castles, S., and M. Miller. *The Age of Migration: International Population Movements in the Modern World.* New York: Guilford, 1993.

Cook, R. "International Human Rights and Women's Reproductive Rights." *Studies in Family Planning* 24 (1993), 73–86.

Cornelius, W., et al. *Controlling Immigration: A Global Perspective.* Stanford: Stanford University Press, 1994.

Cunliffe, A. "The Refugee Crisis: A Study of the United Nations High Commission for Refugees." *Political Studies* 43 (1995), 278–90.

Davies, J. *Displaced Peoples and Refugee Studies: A Resource Guide.* Refugee Studies Programme, Oxford University. London: Hans Zell, 1990.

Dirks, G. "International Migration in the 1990s: Causes and Consequences." *International Journal* 48, no. 2 (1993), 191–214.

Ferris, E. *Beyond Borders: Refugees, Migrants and Human Rights in the Post–Cold War Era.* Geneva: WCC Publications, 1993.

Fontenau, G. "The Rights of Migrants, Refugees or Asylum Seekers under International Law." *International Migration Quarterly* 30 (1992), 57–68.

Forbes Martin, S. *Refugee Women.* London: Zed Books, 1991.

Ghimire, K. "Refugees and Deforestation." *International Migration* 32, no. 4 (1994), 561–70.

Gurtov, M. "Open Borders: A Global Humanist Approach to the Refugee Crisis." *World Development* 19, no. 5 (1991), 485–96.

Hakovirta, H. "The Global Refugee Problem: A Model and Its Application." *International Political Science Review* 14, no. 1 (1993), 35–57.

Hartmann, B. *Reproductive Rights and Wrongs: Global Politics of Population Control and Contraceptive Choices.* New York: Harper and Row, 1987.

King, R., ed. *Mass Migration in Europe: The Legacy and the Future.* London: Belhaven Press, 1993.

Klein, S. *The Economics of Mass Migration in the Twentieth Century.* New York: Paragon House, 1987.

Kritz, M., et al. *International Migration Systems: A Global Approach.* Oxford: Clarendon Press, 1992.

Lemay, M., ed. *The Gatekeepers: Comparative Immigration Policy.* New York: Praeger, 1989.

Loescher, G. *Beyond Charity: International Cooperation and the Global Refugee Crisis.* New York: Oxford University Press, 1993.

Macionis, John J. and Parillo, Vincent N. *Cities and Urban Life,* 3rd ed. Upper Saddle River, NJ: Pearson Education, 2003.

Magotte, J. *Disposable People? The Plight of Refugees.* New York: Orbis, 1992.

Martin, Susan Forbes. *Refugee Women.* Lanham, MD; Oxford: Lexington Books, 2004.

Maurice, F., and J. de Courten. "ICRC Activities for Refugees and Displaced Civilians." *International Review of the Red Cross* 280 (1991), 9–21.

Nash, A., ed. *Human Rights and the Protection of Refugees under International Law.* Halifax: Institute for Research on Public Policy, 1988.

Nathwani, Niraj. *Rethinking Refugee Law.* The Hague; London; New York: Martinus Nijhoff Press, 2003.

Ogata, Sadako. "The UN Response to the Growing Refugee Crisis." *Japan Review of International Affairs* 7, no. 3 (1993), 202–15.

Rogers, R. "The Future of Refugee Flows and Policies." *International Migration Review* 36, no. 4 (1992), 1112–43.

Rystad, G., ed. *The Uprooted: Forced Migration as an International Problem in the Post-War Era.* Lund: Lund University Press, 1990.

Sassen, S. *Globalization and Its Discontents: Essays on the New Mobility of People and Money.* New York: The New Press, 1998.

Solomon, Daniel. *Global City Blues.* Washington, DC; London: Island Press, 2003.

Straubhaar, T. "Migration Pressure." *International Migration* 31, no. 1 (1993), 5–32.

Suhrke, A. "A Crisis Diminished: Refugees in the Developing World." *International Journal* 48. no. 2 (1993), 215–39.

Troper, H. "Canada's Immigration Policy Since 1945." *International Journal* 48, no. 2 (1993), 255–81.

Uvin, Peter. 1998. *Aiding Violence: The Development Enterprise in Rwanda.* New York: Kumarian, 1998.

Weiner, M. *International Migration and Security.* Boulder, CO: Westview, 1993.

Wheeler, Nicholas. *Saving Strangers: Humanitarian Intervention in International Society.* Oxford: Oxford University Press, 2000.

Zacher, M. "Epidemiological Surveillance: International Cooperation to Monitor Infectious Diseases," in I. Kaul et al., eds., *Global Public Goods.* Oxford: Oxford University Press, 1999.

Zayas, A. "International Law and Mass Population Transfers." *Harvard International Law Journal* 16, no. 2 (1975), 207–58.

Zolberg, J. "Un reflet du monde: les migrations internationales en perspective historique." *Revu Études Internationales* 24, no. 1 (1993), 17–29.

Suggested Websites

HungerWeb
http://nutrition.tufts.edu/academic/hungerweb

International Committee of the Red Cross
http://www.icrc.org/eng

Médecins Sans Frontières
http://www.msf.org

The Population Council
http://www.popcouncil.org

Refugees International
http://www.refugeesinternational.org

United Nations High Commissioner for Reguees
http://www.unhcr.ch/cgi-bin/texis/vtx/home

World Food Programme
http://www.wfp.org

CHAPTER 12

Global Politics and the Information Age

Technology is now, for better or for worse, the principal driving force behind the ongoing rapid economic, social, and political change. Like any irrepressible force, the new technology can bestow on us undreamed of benefits but also inflict irreparable damage.

—*Wassily Leontief, economist*[1]

INTRODUCTION: GLOBAL POLITICS AND SOCIAL REVOLUTIONS

The development of human society is often conceptualized in terms of stages or revolutions. Each stage represents a significant leap forward in human development, which lays down the foundation for successive revolutions. In each of these forward leaps, a close relationship exists between technological developments and the evolution of political, economic, and social organizations. For example, the **agricultural revolution** greatly increased food production in 18th-century Europe through a combination of mechanical innovations, cropping techniques, and changes in landholding practices. The **Industrial Revolution** represented a shift from agrarian-based economic activity to manufacturing, which profoundly altered the character of society. The very concept of work was changed, and the social relations that sustained manufacturing became the subject of historians such as Karl Marx and authors such as Charles Dickens. The **green revolution**, stimulated by the mechanization of agriculture and the development of new fertilizers, pesticides, and seeds, has had a global impact in the form of increased food production as well as concerns over the safety of chemicals in the food supply.

Others have explored the phenomenon of human development in terms of waves stimulated by technical advances. In the 1920s, Russian economist Nikolai Kondratieff identified waves in the world economy approximately 50 to 60 years long. Each cycle was characterized by a surge in economic growth and productivity. In 1939, economist Joseph Schumpeter explained these waves in terms of clusters of technical inventions, innovations (the development of new techniques and products from these inventions), and diffusion (the spread of these techniques and products around the world). Each wave of inventions, innovations, and diffusion stimulates a surge in economic activity, after which economic growth slows as all the potential from new inventions is realized. Schumpeter characterized these waves as "creative gales of destruction" because they would sweep old industries aside and replace them with new ones. Following Schumpeter's reasoning, four such waves have been identified:

1. The 1780s to 1840s, driven by the steam engine and innovations in textiles and iron

2. The 1840s to 1890s and the era of the railway

3. The 1890s to 1930s, driven by electric power, chemical technologies, and improved steels

4. The 1930s to 1980s, driven by the automobile and petroleum energy[2]

The development of the computer began discussions of another potential revolution or wave in the evolution of human society. In 1980, Alvin Toffler's book *The Third Wave* argued that the transition from an agricultural society (the first wave) to an industrial society (the second wave) was being followed by a transition to an information society (the third wave).[3] In the same year, a study on the impact of computers argued that "the computer is not the only technological innovation of recent years, but it does constitute the common factor that speeds the development of all others. Above all ... it will alter the entire nervous system of social organization."[4] Today, we do not have to stretch our imaginations to argue that the computer and the information revolution constitute another wave in social development. We have accepted this information revolution as fact. This new information age is built on the advances in microelectronics that have vastly increased the processing power of computers while reducing cost and bulk. Improvements in storage capacity and retrieval have led to an explosion in the gathering, storing, processing, and analysis of information, which has become increasingly vital to political and economic activity. The development of improved communications technologies and the creation of many different international communications channels or "networks" have allowed computers and their users to transmit or disseminate information around the world. Information and data management is now the fastest-growing area of economic activity, prompting suggestions that the industrialized world is heading into a postindustrial and increasingly globalized society where new applications of information technology (IT) could change the face of societies and global politics.

The information age is therefore taken to have a number of interrelated components. Technical innovations in processing and networking are stimulating social change. Information technologies are transforming economic activity and economic relationships, creating a "new economy." The nature of political practices, community and civil society, and governance are transforming. Old institutions, especially the state, are in decline or are changing to adjust to new interests, concerns, and opportunities brought about by largely unfettered communication and social mobilization. However, as we shall see, there are good reasons not to exaggerate the potential impact of the information age on global politics. As Christopher May argues, "... these changes are not as profound as they are often presented."[5] As realists would remind us, continuities in world politics have spanned one or more of the social revolutions in human history. We should, therefore, see continuity as well as change in the years ahead. Similarly, critical theorists would ask just how far technological changes can go towards re-ordering hierarchical societies and the international system.

THE COMPUTER AND THE INFORMATION REVOLUTION

If any form of technological change has had a profound impact on the lives of millions of people in recent times, it is the advent of the personal computer (PC). The evolution of the modern computer began in 1946 with the development of the **ENIAC** (Electronic Numerical Integrator and Calculator), widely regarded as the first electronic computer. Initially designed

Fifty years of progress. Jan Van der Spiegel holds a microprocessor (the black dot at the lower right corner of the square pad in his hand) in front of about one-tenth of the 30 000-kilogram original Electronic Numerical Integrator and Computer (ENIAC), the world's first general-purpose electronic computer, on the 50th anniversary of the machine's construction, 31 January 1996. Professor Van der Spiegel's chip has about one-twentieth the computing power of ENIAC, which was operational on February 14, 1946. (AP Photo/George Widman/CP Archive)

to calculate the trajectories of artillery shells, ENIAC was a remarkable accomplishment for its time. It could execute 5000 arithmetic calculations per second. It was also 3 metres high, 30 metres long, and weighed more than 30 000 kilograms! ENIAC used 18 000 vacuum tubes and consumed 150 000 watts of power. With the invention of the transistor in 1947, computer design was liberated from the limitation of the vacuum tube. Through the 1950s and 1960s, large centralized mainframe computers dominated the computer industry, and International Business Machines (IBM) became a dominant MNC in the 1970s. The combining of many miniature transistors on a single silicon chip (the integrated circuit) in 1959 and the development of the microprocessor (in essence a computer on a silicon chip) in 1971 profoundly altered the computer industry. Microchips rapidly became increasingly powerful. The 486 microprocessor, used in the early 1990s, could execute 54 000 000 instructions per second, weighed only a few grams, and used less than two watts of electricity. Intel's Pentium microprocessors can execute more than 200 000 000 instructions per second. The speed of microprocessors now doubles every 18 months, in a formula known as Moore's Law. The fact that this type of speed exists is amazing enough, but what is revolutionary, in political terms, is that so many people have access to it.

These advances in miniaturization, processing power, and cost effectiveness made the PC practically and economically viable, placing unprecedented processing power in the hands of individuals. The first PCs were introduced in 1975, and today's generation of personal computers are many times more powerful than the mainframe computers of the mid-1970s. With the development of the PC, the number of computers in the world began to grow rapidly. In 1971, there were approximately 50 000 computers in the world. In 1981, there were approximately 4 million. By 2002, there were at least 587 million PCs in use globally, and the pace of this growth is accelerating.[6] The computer industry has also become increasingly important to the global economy. By 1985, the output of the global electronics industry equalled the output of the world automobile industry and exceeded the output of the world steel industry.[7] Today, there are few industries or economic sectors that do not employ computers in some aspect of their operations. However, the development of computers—their increased miniaturization and cost effectiveness, and increases in processing speed—was only one part of the computer revolution. We are now entering a new stage in the evolution of the computer: the development of networks. As the 2001 Human Development Report argued, "Today's technological transformations are intertwined with another transformation—globalization—and together they are creating a new paradigm: the network age."[8]

In one sense, the idea of networks is not new. In 1833 the invention of Morse Code (by Samuel Morse) ushered in the development of the telegraph in 1837, and telegraph lines soon extended across continents. In 1876, the telephone was invented by Alexander Graham Bell, and television demonstrators were being shown as early as in the 1920s. Both inventions went on to become linked to vast networks of cables and transmission receivers around the globe. However, the networking of computers has brought a new age of communications. Coupled with advances in communications technologies, users increasingly are linking their computers with others to facilitate business, communication, financial transactions, and access to information. While the most famous of these networks is the Internet, a wide variety of other computer networks exist, such as local area networks (LANs) and wide area networks (WANs), which facilitate links between the computers of a specified group of people (such as corporate employees, bank branches, or network games players).

For those of us living in the industrialized world, the computer and information revolutions have had an enormous impact on our daily lives. Most of the alarm clocks that awaken us in the morning are operated by a microprocessor. Our kitchen appliances (which may have already begun to make our breakfast or morning beverage before we wake up) are also operated by microprocessors. The television and stereo are increasingly complex electronic devices, as is the telephone. Further, microprocessors are important contributors to the design and manufacturing of these household items. The thermostats in our homes, the electricity grids from which we draw our power, and the transportation networks we use all employ microprocessors to some extent. Many of us also use home computers for household finances, taxes, and record keeping, as well as correspondence, recreation, and education. Increasing numbers of people telecommute by working at home and sending their work to the office or to their clients by computer network. Increasingly, we can shop, bank, and earn a living using our home computers. We have increasing access to a wide range of products and investment opportunities. As individuals, most of us are highly reliant on technology and the energy that runs it, and increasingly connected to the world economy and global communications networks.

THE INFORMATION AGE AND GLOBAL COMMUNICATIONS NETWORKS

Today, the vast majority of people in the industrialized world (and increasing numbers of people in the developing world) have access to unprecedented communications links, including telephone, fax, e-mail, the Internet, television, and international radio services. People are able to communicate and exchange more information more frequently and at less cost than ever before. Much of this communication and information transfer is personal or general in nature. However, much of it is specialized, intended for experts in some scientific or commercial field. The growth of transnational communications, and the challenges and opportunities it poses for individuals, organizations, and governments, is a major issue in global politics. In the past, the speed of communication was essentially equivalent to the speed of transportation. With the exception of very basic signalling using flags or smoke, messages could travel only as fast as the messenger carrying them. In practice, this meant the use of human, animal, or mechanical transport. While some of these communications methods were relatively swift and effective (such as the pony express system of Imperial China and the use of carrier pigeons), it could take days, weeks, months, or even years to transmit messages or news. In the 18th century, a trip around the world took several years by sailing ship. Today, jet aircraft can fly around the world in less than a day carrying large parcels and other mail items. Bulk cargo ships are far faster than the merchant sailing ships of just 200 years ago. Trucks can haul large amounts of freight over expansive road networks.

However, the remarkable advances have been in the area of electronic communications. As recently as 100 years ago, the idea of virtually instantaneous global communication would have been dismissed as an unrealistic dream. Today, it is a commonplace reality for an increasing number of people around the world. The scope of transnational communication flows is remarkable. From the development of the telegraph to modern satellite communications in the 1990s, technology has improved to enable millions of people to communicate on a near-simultaneous basis with each other using telephones or computer messages.[9] For

You've come a long way, baby. Martin Cooper, chairman and CEO of ArrayComm, holds a Motorola DynaTAC, a 1973 prototype of the first handheld cellular telephone in San Francisco in this April 2, 2003, photo. (AP Photo/ Eric Risberg/CP Archive)

example, international phone traffic has increased dramatically. The use of international telephone calls (measured in terms of minutes) jumped from 38 billion minutes in 1991 to an estimated 135 billion minutes in 2002.[10] In 1960, a transatlantic telephone cable could carry 138 conversations. Today's fibre-optic cables are a fraction of the size and are capable of carrying 1.5 million conversations. In 1980, a copper wire phone line could transfer data at a rate of approximately one page per second. Today, an optical fibre the width of a human hair can carry the equivalent of 90 000 volumes of an encyclopedia per second.[11] The use of telephone satellite communications has facilitated this entire process. Of particular importance is the Intelsat network, which had its first satellite in orbit in 1964 and now has 27 satellites in operation (after the purchase of the satellites of Loral Space and Communications Corporation in March 2004). This network has increased the carrying capacity of global telephone links. With Intelsat in operation, international phone traffic has been freed from undersea or underground cables linking continents and cities. Moreover, the cost of this communication has decreased dramatically. The cost of a three-minute telephone call between New York and London fell from U.S.$244.65 in 1930, to U.S.$31.58 in 1970, to U.S.$3.32 in 1990, to 35 cents in 1998 (in 1990 dollars).[12] Sending an e-mail message from Calgary to Paris costs no more than sending an identical message from Calgary to Edmonton. Because of these developments, it is possible to speak of a communications revolution and the consequent "death of distance" made possible by the computer and the proliferation of networks around the world.

Another trend is clearly identifiable: the increasing use of wireless communications networks. With some exceptions, most communications in the 20th century required a hard link of some kind, usually in the form of a copper-based or fibre-optic cable. Increasingly, communications are wireless, using radio waves to transmit messages and data through the air (or space). Such technologies include cellular phones and satellite receivers and dishes, which enable people to communicate from remote areas or receive television broadcasts even when no physical link is available. Advances in wireless technology have been swift. The first-generation wireless phone was introduced in 1981 and was the size of a small suitcase! In 1991, second-generation wireless phones were hand held and offered messaging services. In 2001, third-generation wireless phones began to offer multimedia and networking capacities in a small handset. There has been an explosion in the use of mobile or cellular phones: in 1991 there were 16 million mobile phone subscribers, a number that had ballooned to an estimated 1.1 billion in 2002.[13] Wireless Internet access is now increasingly common, and new generations of wireless technologies are in development, promising faster access speeds and information services in virtually all products including automobiles, medical bracelets, and wearable devices. We have only just entered the age of the "wireless" revolution.

Perhaps the most significant global communications network that exploded into public awareness is the Internet. The Internet is an international network connecting thousands of independent computer networks through a common set of standards and protocols. The Internet can be conceptualized as a web of linked computers with no centralized focal point or *node*. No central computer *runs* the Internet; rather, it is a system of linked computers, which exist in a nonhierarchical arrangement. Individual computer users can access these linked computers, thus providing people with access to the entire network. The Internet's power and potential is derived from its ability to link different types of computers, software, operating systems, and independent networks through a common protocol called TCP/IP. Technical differences between computers and networks do not matter as long as they can communicate using this protocol.

The Internet originally developed out of a military communications project in the 1960s. The United States Department of Defense Advanced Research Projects Agency Network (ARPAnet) was established to ensure that communications between political and military leaders could be maintained even in the event of a nuclear attack. Because the structure of ARPAnet was decentralized, if some sections of the network were destroyed or disabled, the network would still function. ARPAnet was transferred to the National Science Foundation, which renamed the network NSFnet. NSFnet was expanded to universities and government agencies in the 1980s and then turned over to private companies. The beginning of the explosion in Internet use occurred in the late 1980s, as more powerful computers emerged and the World Wide Web (WWW) was created. The WWW software, created by Tim Berners-Lee at the European Particle Physics Laboratory (CERN) in Switzerland in 1989, established the common user protocols for addresses, languages, file transfers, and browsers. The Web facilitated the use of the Internet through easier-to-use interface software (first introduced with Mosaic in 1993), thus enabling anyone with a computer, a modem, a browser, and the requisite interest to use the Internet. The growth of the Internet has been spectacular. The International Telecommunication Union estimates that Internet use increased from 4.4 million users in 1991 to approximately 620 million in 2002.[14] The number of Internet hosts (those computers with a direct connection to the Internet) increased from 100 000 in 1988, and 36 million in 1998, to over 157 million in 2002. Internet use was expected to expand to 965 million in 2005.[15]

Some feel the long-term impact of transnational communications networks will be to bring humanity closer together, in a global village or cyberworld where national borders become irrelevant and a global awareness of a shared human identity and destiny will take shape. In other words, the Internet could be one of the most important instruments of *convergence* in human history. However, enthusiasm over the Internet and transnational communications networks in general must be tempered with some sobering realities. While the Internet promises enormous potential for business, personal communication, and access to information, the use of the Internet is dominated by the industrialized world (in particular, the United States). Approximately 80 percent of Internet users live in the industrialized world, and the vast majority of people on earth have little or no access to the Internet, even if they have heard of it. In fact, much of the world's population has never made a telephone call. Furthermore, like television programming, the quality of the websites on the Internet varies widely. Some sites are reputable and of high quality; others are virtually useless and contain false or misleading information. The Internet offers a forum to any individual or group that can construct a website (including hate groups), which demands a careful critical perspective when viewing information on the World Wide Web. One of the fastest growing sectors on the Internet is erotica and pornography, raising or renewing questions about censorship and access control and denial by governments, groups, or individuals.

While Web advocates cite the Internet's capacity to promote democracy, diversity, and the free flow of information, all information can be manipulated and controlled. Many governments manage their citizens' access to the Internet (see Profile 12.1). Despite great diversity, it can be argued that the Northern, upper-income world dominates the content on the Internet. English is the language of almost 80 percent of Internet websites. The content of the Internet is heavily corporate, and money matters in terms of vying for viewers (a familiar phenomenon to advertising executives and political campaign managers). This leaves little space for political dissent or protest, as Gregory J. Walters points out: "The Internet has been almost completely incorporated into the corporate media and communications system, and the political left has been relegated to the margins of cyberspace."[16] The Internet also raises issues related to privacy (including the security of financial and medical information) and copyright (witness the debate over Napster MP3 software). Computer piracy and hacking raise concerns about the security of computer systems and the challenges of responding to this problem in a world of governments with different legal systems.

THE INFORMATION AGE AND THE WORLD ECONOMY

The global economy is being transformed by the technological developments of the information age. In the workplace, the impact of the computer and information revolution has been dramatic. Computers and communications technologies have increased individual productivity, and have proliferated in the workplace. By 1991, companies were spending more money on computer and communications equipment than on industrial, mining, farming, and con-

---

PROFILE 12.1 China and the Internet

China is a good example of a country that is attempting to embrace communications technology while exercising political control over information content. As part of a government plan in place since the early 1990s, China has been developing its communications infrastructure, installing telephone lines at a rate of 2 million per month in 2000. Internet use has increased from 50 000 users in 1995 to 9 million in 1999, to 59 million in 2002. However, the Chinese government continues to impose tight controls on the free flow of information, fearing the consequences for the country's political system. As the late Chinese leader Deng Xiaoping once said, "When you open the window, the flies come in." The Ministry of Information Industry controls Internet traffic entering the country, blocking Western news websites such as the BBC as well as the websites of human rights organizations and Chinese dissident groups. However, users in China can bypass government controls that block access to certain domain names by finding a proxy server that provides a link to Western news websites under a different domain name. The difficulty is finding such proxy servers. E-mail is one way of providing such information to Chinese Internet users, but the Chinese government employs 30 000 people to scan e-mails entering and leaving China for this kind of information. Prison sentences have been handed out to Chinese citizens who violate domestic laws on the dissemination of information and protest material over the Internet. The answer has been to build networks within China, connected to networks outside China, that seek to promote open access to information for Chinese citizens. That is, for those who care: most Chinese Internet users seem interested in many of the same things as non-Chinese users, such as games, chat forums, and sending personal e-mail. As China becomes more connected to the world economy, and as the economic importance of information flows increases, the interaction will become a fascinating case study of the clash between the power of the state and the forces of an electronic borderless world.

SOURCE: CLARK BOYD, "BYPASSING CHINA'S NET FIREWALL," BBC NEWS, 10 MARCH 2004, UK EDITION, http://news.bbc.co.uk/1/hi/technology/3548035.stm (ACCESSED 31 MAY 2004).

struction equipment combined.[17] Businesses use computers for communications, data storage and retrieval, business administration, payroll, record keeping, and budgeting. Banking and financial industries are almost entirely dependent on computers and communications links. Manufacturing industries use computers to design new products, operate their production facilities, manage inventories, track shipments, and distribute raw materials, supplies, and parts. Medical sciences use computers and microprocessors in medical instruments and tools, diagnostic aids, and record keeping. The architecture, fashion, and graphic design fields make wide use of computers. Increasingly, education at all levels employs computers in some capacity.

The computer and information revolution has done more than increase individual productivity or alter individual work habits and tools; it has affected the very nature of work in modern industrialized societies as a whole. A massive shift in employment patterns away from agriculture and manufacturing took place in the 20th century. In the United States in the early 1800s, more than 70 percent of workers were engaged in agriculture. Today, agriculture accounts for only some 3 percent of the workforce. In the early 1900s, some 35 percent of U.S. workers were engaged in manufacturing industries. By the mid 1990s, manufacturing industries accounted for less than 25 percent of the workforce. A similar pattern can be found in Canada, despite continued reliance on the natural resource sector. In the 1950s the majority of workers in the industrialized world were involved in manufacturing or transporting material goods. It has been estimated that by the year 2010, no industrialized country will have more than one-tenth of its workforce in these traditional manufacturing sectors.[18] As Charles Leadbeater observed (perhaps with some exaggeration): "These days most people in most advanced economies produce nothing that can be weighed: communications, software, advertising, financial services. They trade, write, design, talk, spin and create: rarely do they make anything."[19] By 1996 the OECD concluded that there was a clear trend in affluent countries toward an economy in which more than half of the labour force was engaged in the production, distribution, and use of information.[20] High-technology manufacturing now accounts for 25 percent of all manufacturing output in these countries, and knowledge-based services are growing even faster, accounting for 8 out of 10 new jobs.[21] All this leads some analysts and futurologists to suggest that we are heading toward a postindustrial economy.

The idea of a postindustrial society sounds futuristic, but to a certain degree it has already arrived in advanced capitalist states such as Canada and Japan, where the service sector is as important as the manufacturing sector, and where the production of information is as important as the manufacture of products. Further, some **futurologists** argue that, just as the industrial society needed an infrastructure of railroads, bridges, and highways, the postindustrial society will be built on the computer and computer networks. Daniel F. Burton predicts the emergence of a "networked economy, an economy in which computing and communications converge to create an electronic marketplace that is utterly dependent on powerful information networks." According to Burton, a new international regime will replace the bipolar Cold War order:

> [This regime] will not be the cold peace of mercantilism that was pioneered by Japan and other Asian nations during the 1980s. Nor will it consist of the different brands of regionalism that have proliferated in Europe, the Pacific, and the Americas in recent years. Instead, the new international order will be built around the brave new worldwide web of computers and communications.[22]

In many ways, the information age has transformed international economic activity.[23] Most money is stored and exchanged in electronic form. Physical cash now makes up a small portion of most countries' money supplies, and increasingly direct deposit and credit and debit cards dominate commercial transactions. Major credit cards such as Visa and American Express are accepted worldwide, it is possible to withdraw local currency from an ATM machine connected to a global network such as Plus or Interac, and direct deposit of pay-cheques and electronic bill payments are the norm. As we saw in chapters 4 and 8, international trade and financial agreements paved the way for huge sums of money to cross borders, change hands, and be exchanged from one currency to another, often instantaneously. This was done over a growing international financial system of institutions and banks, all linked by communications networks and common information protocols. This has had a profound impact on government policy: with so much money in motion, currency controls became increasingly irrelevant, and most governments have abandoned them. Central banks struggle to defend currencies under pressure, so great is the volume of international currency flows. Individual or corporate investors and fund managers can move money in and out of markets with great speed, complicating governmental responses to domestic and international economic crises.

The Internet and the Web have precipitated an enormous increase in electronic commerce (or e-commerce). In effect, the Internet has removed personal travel from the process of purchasing goods and services. E-commerce also widens the range of choice for consumers, who can now roam across the world in search of products, including those that are restricted or banned in their own countries. While still dependent on traditional mail and courier services for the physical delivery of the product, consumers need not go to the local shopping mall: the global shopping mall has come to them. Corporations have had to adjust to e-commerce, and some have had more success than others. Online ticket purchases have hurt travel agencies, full-service stockbrokers have lost business to online trading companies, and bookstores (both local and chain companies) have lost business to online ordering. Virtually all companies, especially banks and software firms, have moved at least some of their services online. The growth in e-commerce is a challenge to governments, mindful of tax implications and the need for regulation to combat fraud, protect privacy, defend intellectual property rights, and ensure the security of financial information on the web. State regulatory policy governing financial and commercial transactions is very difficult to enforce in a world of global electronic commerce. Even international standards are hard to enforce: counterfeit brand-name products and pirated CDs produced illegally in China and other countries have become an international diplomatic issue. For now, most governments have taken a hands-off approach to e-commerce, hoping that self-regulation will work: the increased complexity of international finance and commerce is ushering in a new age of Web-based regulatory watchdogs, consumer advocacy groups, and codes of conduct.

However, many argue that this postindustrial society will not be one of promise but of increased dislocation, unemployment, and economic hardship for many, if not most, people. Unemployment and stagnant or falling wages and household incomes are growing concerns in most industrialized economies. Commentators speak of the "jobless recovery" from the recession of the early 1990s in which unemployment levels remain unacceptably high despite economic growth and expanding global trade. The cause, many allege, is the computer and information revolution, coupled with the growing globalization of the world economy. Increases in telecommunications, trade, and financial flows have increased international competition, prompting firms to downsize (the technical term for firing employees) and facilitating their efforts to shift production to low-wage countries. As a result, unemployment (and the social problems associated with it) is on the rise. In addition, those jobs that are created will be insufficient in number to replace the jobs lost, and many of them will be low-paying service sector jobs with poor benefits and low job security (sometimes called "McJobs"). Globalization and technological change have driven employers and workers farther apart in many sectors of the economy: as profits rise and wages fall, the bulk of income and revenues will go to a few individuals, widening the gap between rich and poor. These conditions have led Ethan B. Kapstein to argue the following:

> The global economy is leaving millions of disaffected workers in its train. Inequality, unemployment, and endemic poverty have become its handmaidens. Rapid technological change and heightening international competition are fraying the job markets of the major industrialized countries. At the same time, systemic pressures are curtailing every government's ability to respond with new spending. Just when working people most need the nation-state as a buffer from the world economy, it is abandoning them.[24]

Christopher May has argued that the basic divisions in society have remained despite the allegedly transformed nature of the new economy. Basic questions like who knows what, who possesses value, and who works for whom, continue to define the workplace and the economy. Employment policies are still controlled by managers, and intellectual property rights have extended ownership into the realms of information and knowledge.[25]

Alternatively, many argue that these fears are alarmist and that protesters are the equivalent of modern-day Luddites, a reference to the British workers of the early 19th century who smashed the machines that threatened their jobs. Advocates of the computer and information revolution argue that predictions that machines will cause unemployment and social dislocation have been common. In the 1930s, automation of manufacturing was blamed for increases in unemployment, and in the 1940s, others predicted that computers would throw massive numbers of individuals into enforced idleness. Today, robotics, computers and their networks, and information-based sectors are being blamed for job losses. Defenders of the new technologies argue that society benefits from technological innovation. Despite the increasing pace of technological change, and indeed because of it, employment, incomes, and living standards have risen steadily. Because computers and information systems enhance productivity, advocates maintain, they will increase real incomes, from either higher wages or lower prices. This increases the purchasing power of the average consumer, which stimulates other sectors of the economy. With respect to unemployment, innovation does not mean painful labour market adjustments will not occur, especially in the short term when we will see a pronounced shifting of the job market. The key is that these positions are in new industries rather than in traditional employment sectors. This debate is likely to continue, for it is an inescapable fact that many workers in various sectors are feeling less secure in their jobs, that unemployment remains high, and that there is general dissatisfaction with economic performance in the industrialized countries. Whether the computer and information revolution is blamed (justly or unjustly), responding to these conditions presents a major challenge to the economic and fiscal policies of the developed world, which could continue to pursue the opportunities of the information age while seeking to protect their societies against the worst of the economic dislocation globalization might bring.

However, for developing countries the information age presents an enormous challenge. The relationship between technology and development in the world economy is a complex one. There is no escaping the reality of technology in development efforts, since information is now a "basic resource needed for technico-economic activity, on a par with matter and energy."[26] The danger is that if appropriate methods are not followed, some countries will prosper, while those marginalized from evolving levels of access to information technology will become only poorer. Manuel Castells has argued that a new international division of labour has formed, and is "constructed around four different positions in the information/global economy: the producers of high value, based on information labour; the producers of high volume, based on low cost labour; the producers of raw materials, based on natural endowments; and the redundant producers, reduced to devalued labour."[27] Educational disparities are also a critical variable when development emphasizes technology. Certainly, the technology aspects of development are inseparable from the human: the next generation of complex technology will increase wealth and opportunity for those with access to education. We must keep in mind, however, that we live in a world where, despite years of literacy programs, more than 850 million adults still cannot read or write and more than 325 million children of primary and secondary school age are out of school.[28] The technology itself is unevenly distributed, both across countries and within countries. Seoul, the capital of South Korea, has as much bandwidth (the amount of data that can be transferred in a fixed amount of time) as all of Latin America. The entire continent of Africa, in turn, has less bandwidth than São Paulo, Brazil. Bangalore, India, is a world-class centre in India's thriving high-tech sector, but in Bangalore there are approximately 28 telephones for every 1000 people, and electricity consumption is half of that in China.[29] Can this divide be bridged? Technology and innovative methods may promise an answer: in Bangladesh, a bank issued micro-loans for the purchase of mobile phones to women, who then charged a cost for its shared use. This gave inexpensive phone access to millions of people.[30] Rather than view new technology as a

High hopes not met. Professor Vijay Chandru of the Indian Institute of Science, left, displays the motherboard of the Simputer as Vinay Deshpande, CEO of Encore software, shows the Simputer prototype, 21 May 2001, in Bangalore, India. The cheap, handheld computer promised to deliver technology to the developing world's poor when it was introduced, but the investors and customer commitments needed to get the Simputer to a large market at an affordable price of $200 have not emerged. (AP Photo/Namas Bhojani/CP Archive)

panacea, we should see it as a potential source of liberation from poverty and hardship if properly managed. If improperly managed, or not managed at all, technology will contribute to increased economic disparity.

How does the information age affect the future of environmental politics? One might argue that the infrastructure of the information revolution makes fewer demands on resources and pollutes less. Ships, trucks, railways, and cars require a large amount of raw materials and energy to produce and keep in operation. Furthermore, these products are the source of serious pollution problems. Work in the information age has the potential to reduce the consumption of resources and traffic congestion (through telecommuting and banking or shopping online). However, countries are already confronting serious waste disposal problems with respect to old computer products. The world economy still needs to transport enormous quantities of resources and products, often across very long distances. And all of this technology has greatly increased the demand for electricity, which in itself has serious environmental consequences, especially in an age where renewable energy sources are largely ignored. Increased use of computers has not led to a paperless office; in fact, paper consumption increased from 170 million tonnes a year in 1980 to 298 million tonnes in 1997.[31] In short, the information age does not promise a transformation in the environmental degradation caused by human economic activity.

THE DISSEMINATION OF TECHNOLOGY, INFORMATION, AND IDEAS

The computer revolution and the creation of expanding communications channels have led to an explosion in the availability of information. The volume of information available to us is extraordinary. Technology facilitates the creation, processing, accumulation, storage, and management of information on an unprecedented scale. Equally important is the decline in the cost of transmitting information. In 1970, the cost of transmitting a trillion bits of information across North America was U.S.$150,000; in 2001, the cost had fallen to 12 cents![32] Desktop, laptop, and handheld computers can now process vast amounts of information and data and create spreadsheets, charts, and multimedia presentations. Single CD/DVD and digital recording devices can store volumes of books and images and music selections. Modern libraries are increasingly electronic, storing a growing amount of their information holdings in digital form and offering computerized access to their databases and to the databases of other libraries. Traditional media sources such as newspapers, magazines, and television programming all have online resources and archives that allow us to access a wide variety of news items, technical information, images, and music. Governments can receive information on domestic political events and international political events within minutes.

Over the longer term, we can expect the availability and dissemination of ideas to have a dramatic effect on the nature of scientific discovery and on innovation. Science can be a lonely enterprise; the image of the lone scientist toiling in a lab into the late hours of the night is an accurate one. However, scientific discovery is also a collaborative enterprise. Scientists often seek out other scientists for assistance or advice. The process of scientific verification and review demands that experiments and discoveries be replicated and evaluated by scientific peer groups. The collaborative aspects of scientific discovery can thus be facilitated and accelerated by communications technology and the dissemination of information within **epistemic communities** of individuals dedicated to the common pursuit of ideas and objectives, regardless of their location or country of residence. In the past, innovations disseminated slowly, spreading only as fast as messages and people could travel. As a result, news of discoveries or innovations took a long time to come to the attention of those who could make use of them. In the television series *Connections*, host James Burke suggested that technological change was largely the result of inventors taking older discoveries, adding an innovation of their own, and applying it to the problem with which they were concerned. The result was a new way of doing things, inspired by the borrowing and adaptation of other ideas. Today, the availability and dissemination of information allows would-be innovators to access a vast reservoir of information and ideas from around the world. New ideas and innovations appear almost daily, and those who are interested in certain scientific or technical pursuits can easily access the information they are interested in or need. The potential for scientific and technical progress is therefore extraordinary.

However, the dissemination of scientific discovery and innovation is not always regarded as a good thing. In fact, many scientific discoveries and innovations are kept secret. The belief that national security may be put at risk is one rationale for preventing the spread of information. Another may be the commercial potential of the discovery and the desire to profit from it. Of course, there is an increasing trend toward using information networks for **industrial espionage** to steal information and data. This type of theft raises a number of questions about the security of personal information in an information age. Information about our financial situation, medical history, family records, and backgrounds increasingly resides in computers in electronic form. Access to them is possible. This is a growing problem for the privacy of the individual. There are similar concerns over the controversial introduction of "electronic voting" in the United States and elsewhere.

In short, the dissemination of technology and ideas will continue to affect the global economy and the workplace. As James Rosenau argues, technology has "profoundly altered the scale on which human affairs take place, allowing people to do more things in less time and with wider repercussions than could have been imagined in earlier eras."[33] At the same time, technological advances and their economic implications will be jealously guarded in a world still full of competitive states.

FROM EVENT TO LIVING ROOM: THE GLOBAL MEDIA AND HOW THEY WORK

The media (especially radio, television, and Internet) are rightfully accorded a special significance in the study of global politics. In part, this is because media technologies have spread throughout the world, and there are more people listening and watching than ever before. While this is important, it is only part of the story. Radio and television networks and their affiliates (or subsidiary stations) have access to an increasingly wide variety of news items. In the 1990s, satellite news services began to expand dramatically, and forged links with virtually all satellite and cable service providers around the world. The televised 24-hour coverage of the fall of Communism in Eastern Europe, the collapse of the Soviet Union, and the 1990–91 Gulf War ushered in a new media age. German social theorist Jürgen Habermas suggested that "through the electronic media, these events were brought instantaneously before a ubiquitous public sphere. In the context of the French Revolution, Kant made reference to the reactions of a participatory public. At that time, he identified the phenomenon of a world public sphere, which today is becoming political reality for the first time in a cosmopolitan matrix of communication."[34] As a result, we increasingly refer to a *global media* that delivers information, sounds, and images from political events, wars, natural disasters, and cultural and sporting events to a global audience. Because of this, global media have had a notable impact on the knowledge and attitudes of individuals, as well as on the policies of governments (see profiles 12.1 and 12.2).

However, we must be cautious when we proclaim that an age of global media is upon us. Perhaps it is more accurate to say that the *potential* for a global media is upon us, because the reality is that most programming in any given spot in the world is overwhelmingly local in its coverage. In his survey of evening news shows in different regions around the world, Graham Chapman concluded that "local interests" predominated, with a few major stories travelling across the world.[35] In the United States between 1983 and 1998 international news content in newspapers dropped by 10 percent—to just 2 percent of total coverage—and international television news coverage in 1995 accounted for only 13.5 percent of total television coverage.[36] The reason for this decline is in the economics of the media industry: local stories sell and are cheaper to produce, while international stories generally do not sell and are expensive to produce. When major events happen, media industries can mobilize rapidly, even sending their anchors to cover dramatic events—such as the fall of the Berlin Wall or the beginning of war against Iraq—from the scene. However, once the drama ends, and intensive or "special extended coverage" packages are no longer securing viewers, the old pattern of emphasis on local news returns. As Ted Magder suggests, "We may live in a world of globalization, but we do not yet live in the age of global news *per se*, either in the sense that audiences the world over pay attention to the same international stories on an everyday basis or even in the sense that audiences get more global (or foreign) news than in the past."[37]

The same can be said of other regions. In the Arab world, the media environment has been turned upside down by a private satellite news channel, Al-Jazeera (which roughly translates as "the Peninsula"). Al-Jazeera began broadcasting in 1996 and operates out of Qatar.[38] The station has established itself in the Arab world as an alternative to highly censored state-owned television networks and has stimulated a growing number of private broadcasting stations in the Middle East. Al-Jazeera has gained attention in the West for its broadcast of tapes by Al-Qaeda and Osama Bin Laden, but in the Arab world it is better known for its critical coverage of many Arab governments, as well as its coverage of the Israeli–Palestinian conflict and the wars in the region (particularly in Afghanistan and Iraq). This coverage is unabashedly critical of Israel and the United States. While U.S. media coverage of the invasion and occupation of Iraq, with its embedded journalists, was criticized for its failure to present a range of opinion and show the bloody consequences of the conflict, the United States accused Al-Jazeera of showing little other than civilian casualites, while providing little information on the course of the conflict or the stated U.S. reasons for fighting. In 2001, Al-Jazeera launched an Internet version of its news service, first in Arabic and then in English, which has increased the popularity of the network. It is clear that Al-Jazeera has altered the landscape of news coverage in the Arab world, but viewership outside of that world is rather small. It is also clear that Al-Jazeera and the new generation of private broadcasters in the Arab world have a narrow margin for critical commentary; governments are still capable of exerting a great deal of control over private broadcasting in the region. Nevertheless, Al-Jazeera and other stations like it can increasingly be viewed through satellite networks, perhaps representing a new age in global media diversity, and a new age of global media competition and political debate over the interpretation and framing of events.

There is also a growing critical reflection on the role of the media that calls into question the existence of a new global media age. Some suggest that during the fall of the Berlin Wall, the collapse of the U.S.S.R., and the 1990–91 Gulf War the media (and the public that watched it) were mere spectators, and not actors or agents or participants in the events. And yet the demand was for more such coverage: audiences now expect it and the media has to deliver.[39] On the other hand, concerns that the media are manipulated by economic or political elites have also grown since the 1989–91 period. The Vietnam War was a watershed for the news media: one of the turning points of the war was CBS news anchor Walter Cronkite's televised statements declaring the war a bloody stalemate in which victory was impossible. Coverage of the war brought the brutalities of the conflict to televisions in the United States, and this coverage was a major reason for the change in American public opinion. This first "living room

Making Al-Jazeera famous. In this television image broadcast on April 15, 2002, by Arab satellite station Al-Jazeera, Osama Bin Laden, right, listens as his top deputy, Ayman al-Zawahiri, speaks at an undisclosed location. (AP Photo/Al-Jazeera/APTN/CP Archive)

war" prompted a change in the relationship between the military and the media; in the 1989–90 invasion of Panama and the 1990–91 Gulf War the media were tightly grouped into reporter "pools" and provided information in a controlled environment by way of daily news briefings from the U.S. military. Gone were the violent images, dead bodies, and expressions of disgust and discouragement by soldiers: instead, coverage was sanitized, bloodless, and homogenous. In the 2003 invasion of Iraq, the media were permitted to use so-called embedded reporters, who were assigned to U.S. units and whose coverage was censored. However, media coverage after the war did show disturbing photographs of U.S. soldiers abusing Iraqi prisoners. The relationship between the military and news media has become so proximate that Daya Kishan Thissu and Des Freedman observe that "military and media networks have converged to the point where they are now virtually indistinguishable ... media constitute the spaces in which wars are fought and are the main ways through which populations (or audiences) experience war."[40] In this media age, then, the trend may not be toward greater understanding and participation, but toward passive, uncritical absorption of managed information.

The global media can disseminate information and ideas in a variety of different forms, including newspapers and magazines (print media), films, radio, television, and the Internet. The information and ideas carried by the media can in turn influence the ideas, attitudes, beliefs, and decisions of those who have access to it. The power of the media is enormous, for they are the source of much of the information that people receive about the world in which they live, and what we know of the world is for the most part what we hear or see or read. If we are not exposed to certain information or events, we generally remain unaware of them. As a result, what is reported and what is not is crucially important. In the past, newspapers, magazines, radio, and movie theatre newsreels (short news presentations shown before a feature film) were the dominant forms of media. Today, the media with the greatest political impact are radio, television, and the Internet. First pioneered as a mass propaganda device by Joseph Goebbels and the Nazi Party of Germany in the 1930s, radio remains a powerful media source largely because it is easily accessible. There are more than 2 billion radios in the world, and in countries where illiteracy rates are high the radio is the primary source of information and news about national or international events. International short-wave radio broadcasts, such as Voice of America (VOA), the British Broadcasting Corporation (BBC) World Service, and Radio Canada International, reach into the remotest regions of the world to bring news items, political perspectives, and entertainment to those with short-wave receivers. Radio was also used extensively to deliver hate speeches in preparation for the genocide committed against the Tutsis in Rwanda in 1994.

However, television is even more politically powerful, largely because of the impact that images can have on human emotions and reactions. Television brings a sense of immediacy, or presence, that other forms of media do not possess. There are over 800 million television sets in the world, and an increasing range of channels is available to most consumers. As James Rosenau has argued, "Access to television has become sufficiently global in scope that it must be regarded as a change of [fundamental] proportions."[41] Cable channels and satellite television channels continue to proliferate, and in North America, some viewers have more than 100 channels to choose from. Like radio, television also has networks devoted to international broadcasting. The U.S.-based Cable News Network (CNN) and the British-based International Television Network (ITN) are the most prominent examples. CNN ushered in the age of the 24-hour news station in 1980, as a component of Turner Broadcasting System Inc.[42] Today, the CNN Newsgroup (now owned by Time Warner) comprises 11 U.S.-based services and provides service to 200 different countries and territories through over 900 affiliates with 1 billion potential viewers. Even the steadfastly anti-Castro American government has permitted CNN to set up shop in Cuba.

The gathering of news information, still images, and digital video is all facilitated by modern media technology and communications networks. All global media outlets and many national companies employ foreign correspondents around the world, but if one is not immediately available, a local reporter or his or her video footage will be used instead. The proliferation of privately owned video cameras has allowed many networks and reporters to gain

---

PROFILE 12.2 The Web and Different Perspectives on World Events

One has to be careful with the World Wide Web, because anyone can publish almost anything on it. However, it does provide an alternative to mainstream media. For example, when Peruvian soldiers stormed the Japanese embassy in Lima in April 1997, killing all the members of the Movimiento Revolucionario Tupac Amaru (MRTA) who were holding dignitaries hostage, mainstream media coverage focused on the military action and not the reasons for the occupation in the first place: namely, that Peru is one of the worst violators of human rights, and the rebels were at least partly protesting this, as well as the entrenched and extreme disparities of wealth in Peruvian society. The MRTA, however, maintains a website to publicize its side of the conflict. The perspectives and information on the site were obviously tilted toward the MRTA's interpretation, but it was as believable an account as that offered by the government. Amnesty International also maintained a website on the conflict, in which it condemned both Peru for human rights abuses and the MRTA for terrorist activities. Today's researchers have the capacity (and, we would argue, the responsibility) to go beyond "official" interpretations of events.

SOURCE: JACK KAPICA'S "CYBERIA" COLUMN, *THE GLOBE AND MAIL*, 2 MAY 1997.

unprecedented access to visual records of events. These videos, taken by citizens, have often provided much of the visual content of certain television reports, such as the attacks on the World Trade Center in New York on September 11. Coverage of events is hastily transmitted to the network headquarters by satellite and becomes part of the daily volume of news items that are available for dissemination to national networks or to regional and local network affiliates. Often, national or other television networks will use reports, video, and interviews from other networks. As a result, it is not uncommon for Canadian viewers watching the Canadian Broadcasting Corporation (CBC) to see reports filed by reporters working for CNN, ITN, BBC, or American networks such as CBS, ABC, or NBC. Live reports can be carried over satellite and broadcast in real time around the world. Frequently, scheduled broadcasts will be interrupted to give viewers information on a news item that may have occurred only a few minutes earlier on the other side of the world.

Often, when a major story breaks, virtually every network in the world will be covering it, and coverage of this event will become part of every local municipal news broadcast. In this case, a story might become the global news "issue of the day," broadcast by networks in countries around the world (often using the same video images). This process has raised concerns about the gathering and dissemination of media reports, and the homogenization of the global media. Another concern is the concentration of international media in a shrinking number of large corporations. In the 1980s, the global media was concentrated in perhaps 50 corporations. Today, some 20 companies dominate the global gathering, processing, and dissemination of programming. For example, Associated Press (AP) and Reuters are two of the biggest distributors of audio-visual coverage of news events. Time Warner is an example of the extraordinary concentration of media services in large corporations. In 2004, Time Warner companies included America Online, Inc.; Time Warner Book Group; Time, Inc.; Time Warner Cable; Home Box Office (HBO); New Line Cinema; Turner Broadcasting System; and Warner Bros. Entertainment.

These patterns are of particular concern to developing countries. The rich industrialized world's domination of the global media and information content on the airwaves and the Internet raises concerns about the ability of the developing world to have its voice heard, its concerns expressed, and its cultures and values protected. Developing countries see the rich world's domination of the information age as another factor perpetuating dependence. Of course, some of these concerns are shared by certain industrialized countries (especially France and Canada) worried about the intrusion of American cultural products into their own societies. In the 1980s, several leaders from the Southern hemisphere called for the adoption of a New World Information and Communication Order (NWICO) that would establish limits on the domination of the media and information networks and create space for the voices of the South. This effort never overcame opposition from rich countries, but the struggle continues in the form of disputes over cultural protection and control of local independent media establishments around the world.

THE MEDIA AND POLITICAL DECISION MAKING

The media can play a critical role in the formulation of the foreign policies of governments. International events and government priorities will largely determine the foreign policy agenda. International events can compel governments to react, while governments may have particular foreign policy goals they want to achieve while in office. However, as we discussed in Chapter 3, governments are not entirely free to do whatever they want in the foreign policy realm. The agenda facing governments may be influenced by a wide variety of domestic factors. One of these factors is public opinion, which can be profoundly affected by the media, especially television. As global media continues to become increasingly pervasive, we can expect this question to grow in relevance in the study of global politics. The media can affect foreign policy decision making in a number of different ways.

Agenda Setting

The items on any government's foreign policy agenda are those that are considered important enough to demand government attention. The global media (and the domestic national media) play a role in this process by bringing issues to the attention of the public. This is not done in any purposeful manner; news is seldom intentionally manipulated by radio or television networks themselves. However, in the process of reporting on certain issues (and not reporting on others) the media influence the agenda confronting decision makers, and in so doing create a dilemma. As Stig Hjarvard argues, "Under special circumstances, the power of such globalized public opinion poses a severe problem for even the mightiest of nations, because public opinion demands political action that either contradicts national policies or outstrips the diplomatic, economic, or military power of the nations involved."[43] Hjarvard cites the example of the massacre of pro-democracy protestors in China at Tiananmen Square in 1989: the world expressed outrage, but what could be done beyond the sanctions that were levelled against China? The media may also structure agendas by influencing perceptions of which issues should have a higher priority than others, because very few issues that are raised in the media can be ignored by governments. If an issue is a public issue, then it becomes an issue for elected officials, who, after all, must be sensitive to the concerns of their constituents. In Canada and in other parliamentary democratic systems, an issue can be raised in the legislature, at a press conference, or at a public meeting. Elected officials are required to respond in an informed manner, with some explanation of how the government might respond to the issue. As a result, issues brought to the foreign policy agenda by the media become relevant to unelected officials as well. Bureaucracies and bureaucrats pay close attention to media reports, for they know that members of the legislature and ministers must respond to these issues, and will turn to the bureaucracy for advice and assistance in preparing responses. All of this depends on public awareness: if the media makes an issue a public issue, governments are likely to respond, as they did to the famine in Ethiopia and the war in Somalia. In the absence of this awareness, governments have less incentive to respond.

Shaping Perceptions

Just as the media can bring issues to public attention, the media can also influence public perceptions of these issues. Media (especially television) can transmit sounds, images, or narrative that engender a strong emotional reaction in the public. Pictures of famine victims, human rights abuses, brutality, and human suffering can create strong pressures on governments to *do something* to alleviate or stop these injustices. In many cases, the media story may blame certain individuals or groups for these injustices and highlight a possible course of action or a possible target for government policy. As a result, not only is the public made aware of the issue but also the media story may influence public perceptions of what ought to be done. This can create policy-making problems, for if governments and those advising them feel that this public perception of what ought to be done is unfeasible or even dangerous, they will be reluctant to act. Alternatively, governments may find another course of action more appropriate and face the task of selling this policy to a public that may have different perceptions of the issue.

The media can also provide the public with a sense of how their own individual feelings about an issue are shared (or not shared) by society. Media coverage of mass protests, rallies, and marches can provide a perception of what the rest of society feels is important. And because many people, from news commentators to protestors to foreign policy experts, have their opinions on what ought to be done solicited and broadcast to the public, the government must respond to the various proposals for action put forward from a wide variety of individuals (see Profile 12.3). Social constructivists would emphasize this perception-building role.

Influencing Decision Makers

The media can often have a direct impact on decision makers themselves. Elected and unelected government officials (including prime ministers and presidents) watch television, listen to the radio, and read newspapers. As a result, they can be directly affected by media stories and media portrayals of the issues. For world leaders, as for publics, news items from global television networks such as CNN or ITN are often the first indication that an event has occurred, and the first source of information on breaking events. Government officials will also monitor media coverage of their own actions and responses to see how their own policies are played out in the media and what reactions those policies are receiving from the public.

Embarrassing Government

The ability of the media to discover and reveal events around the world often forces governments to face the consequences of their actions in the international realm. It is increasingly difficult for governments to hide or ignore unfavourable news or politically problematic issues. If governments make mistakes, or make what in retrospect are poor decisions, they will quite likely have to respond to critical reports and investigations in the media. On other occasions, current government policies may be subject to criticism. As a result, governments and politicians often find themselves faced with embarrassing (and potentially politically damaging) inquiries into why the government is pursuing its course of action. For example, the efforts of the Liberal government under Jean Chrétien to expand Canadian trade in Asia through the "Team Canada" missions met with criticism from human rights organizations that the government was not doing enough to promote human rights in Asia. This criticism was accompanied by stories and images of poorly paid workers toiling for long hours under terrible working conditions.

Some might conclude that the power of the media is decisive as a determinant in foreign policy decision making, but this is inaccurate. After all, even if the agenda is at least in part set by media reports, in practice governments have a lot of flexibility over how they might actu-

---

Domestic Politics, Canadian Foreign Policy, and Haiti

In February 1996 the Chrétien government adopted a vigorous (and very public) foreign policy toward Haiti. In part, this foreign policy activism was due to a by-election in the Montreal riding of Papineau-St-Michel. The riding had a high concentration of Haitian voters, and the Liberal candidate, Pierre Pettigrew, could expect to receive strong support from this constituency if Canada was pursuing a strong foreign policy toward Haiti. Before the by-election, Canada was involved in the UN peacekeeping mission in Haiti; in addi-

tion, Pettigrew (not yet a member of the House of Commons) flew to Port-au-Prince to attend the inauguration of President René Préval. There, Pettigrew announced a Canadian government donation of C$700 000 to UNICEF for use in Haiti. Pettigrew won the by-election over Bloc Québécois candidate Daniel Turp. In 2004, continued violence in Haiti led to the overthrow of the Aristides governments, and Canada again responded with a commitment to peace and stability efforts, largely supported by Montreal's Haitian community.

ally respond to an issue. When public pressure encourages governments to do something, it seldom specifies what that something should be. Agenda setting is not policy setting. Although media stories may influence the public's perceptions of what their government ought to do, only rarely is public opinion unified on an issue. The fact that public opinion is often split or undecided allows governments considerable room to manoeuvre when making decisions. As for the media affecting government leaders and key officials directly, while this can happen, they are also surrounded by advisers and experts armed with secret intelligence or information, wider historical perspectives, and policy experience. This group enables decision makers to draw on more sources of information and ideas than those presented on television. And while it is harder for governments to escape the consequences of poor decisions, the unintended consequences of their decisions, or even criminal or unethical decisions, the media also provide governments with an unprecedented capacity to explain and defend their actions or even to apologize and acknowledge mistakes.

THE INFORMATION AGE AND GLOBAL POLITICS: THE EROSION OF THE STATE?

The information age may be the final blow to the supremacy of the state in international relations, finishing off the steady erosion in the power of the state brought on by developments in weapons technology and the globalization of the world economy. States have increasingly lost their capacity to secure their territory and populations from attack and have increasingly lost their once dominant grip on their own national economies. Now, the information age promises the flow of ideas, transactions, and communications across the world, virtually unaffected by states and governments. The state is now losing its capacity to control or influence the flow of information within and across its borders, and over what its citizens see, hear, and think. Individuals, groups, and organizations are in increasing contact, creating new communications networks, channels for ideas and debate, business and financial links, and "virtual communities."

Many governments, including the government of Canada, now make little or no effort to directly control this flow of information (though they will make efforts to manipulate it). This is particularly true of those governments in politically open societies. The struggle over the interpretation and portrayal of ideas and events goes on daily. Domestic critics of government use their unprecedented access to information to criticize the government and its policies in the media. The most open of governments still keep much of their foreign and defence policy affairs (and many other areas as well) behind a veil of secrecy, which the media and citizens' groups often try to penetrate. Governments must continually grapple with issues related to the material content of information flows, as citizens' groups call for the ban or regulation of material they consider immoral or misleading.

Governments must also contend with the power of images. In Russia, television coverage of the conflict in Chechnya contributed to growing public sentiment against the war. Somalia is a classic case of the power of images to influence policy. Images of starving people trapped in an intrastate war precipitated outrage and a large U.S. and UN humanitarian intervention effort to stop the war and bring assistance to the population. However, a few months later 18 U.S. soldiers were killed and their bodies were dragged through the streets of the Somali capital of Mogadishu. The images of this act precipitated outrage in the U.S. public, and the United States withdrew from Somalia shortly thereafter. It remains to be seen what impact future images of violence or suffering in the Middle East or Iraq or anywhere else in the world will have on the policy of governments. Meanwhile, terrorist groups attempt to use Internet-broadcast images of beheadings to frighten opponents, though this may just as well backfire and stiffen resolve. One thing is certain: access to, and control of, the media is a principal strategic issue in modern conflicts.

For many governments, the free flow of information represents a threat to the power, and even the survival, of the regime. Ideas and information, particularly if they expose lies, abuses, or the controversial nature of ideological claims, can be politically powerful. During the Cold War, the Soviet Union and Eastern Europe jammed foreign radio broadcasts (especially Radio Free Europe, the Voice of America, the BBC World Service, and Radio Liberty) and foreign television broadcasts. Telephone links to the outside world were tightly controlled and monitored; as late as 1987, the Soviet Union possessed only 16 international long-distance telephone circuits.[44] Newspapers were heavily controlled and censored. Photocopy machines were not available to the public. Underground literature (called *Samizdat*) was replicated by hand, on typewriter, and passed from person to person. Today, countries such as North Korea, Sudan, Iran, and Myanmar impose draconian restrictions on information flows within and across their borders. And as we have seen, some countries such as China are attempting to restrict access to the Internet. Western governments have not escaped criticism about the control of the media either.[45]

Despite such efforts, information and communications technologies can be powerful instruments of dissent, even in countries with highly authoritarian political systems. Audio and videotapes have played instrumental roles in the toppling of governments. In the years before the Iranian revolution, audiotapes recorded by the Ayatollah Khomeini in France and smuggled into Iran played a decisive role in the undermining of the Shah's regime and the enormous popularity of Khomeini on his return from exile. In the Philippines, the dictatorship of Ferdinand Marcos fell in part due to the circulation of videotapes showing the assassination of the Philippine opposition leader, Benigno Aquino. Telephone, fax, and computer networks have also played a role in political dissent. During and after the Tiananmen Square protests of 1989, protestors and sympathizers abroad made extensive use of fax machines and e-mail to gather and disseminate information on events at Tiananmen. The Chinese government was forced to respond by placing controls on access to fax machines and supervising incoming messages. In Thailand, protestors against the military government used telephone and fax lines to communicate and coordinate their efforts. When the government employed force to suppress the protests, cutting phone lines and shooting at the demonstrators, the opposition remained in communication using cellular telephones. In Serbia, street demonstrations broke out in protest of the government's cancellation of local election results in 1997. The protesters employed a radio station to combat government domination of the media. When this was shut down, the protestors communicated with each other and the outside world using the Internet. As Isabel Vincent observes, "It used to be that guerrilla fighters lugged AK-47s and sent battlefield news in rolled-up scraps of paper, faithfully carried by couriers through treacherous jungles and mountain passes. Today's revolutionary carries a laptop, and plugs into the Net."[46]

THE INFORMATION AGE AND THE POWER OF THE STATE: A WORLD DIVIDED?

However, governments can also harness the power offered by the computer revolution and the information age. Does this new era of technology-induced freedom from state controls exist primarily in the minds of those who foresee a technological, transboundary world? Is the computer, information, and communications revolution overrated as an agent of change in global politics? After all, information has always been an important element of state power, and computers and communications technologies permit states to access, store, and use information as never before. States employ this information to their advantage in a number of ways. In their interactions with one another and with nonstate actors, information (or "intelligence") has always been a vital dimension of diplomacy and war. Negotiation, bargaining, and conflict management efforts are facilitated by virtually instantaneous communication and the increasing capability of states to gather information independently. The telephone has become a central tool of contemporary diplomacy; leaders and officials of states often communicate with each other simply by picking up the phone. States also employ information as an instrument of state power, by disseminating information into the international system in the form of radio broadcasts, information services, and statements in the media. Governments may also spread **disinformation** in a deliberate attempt to mislead other governments (or their own populations). The ability of computers to store and retrieve information offers governments an unprecedented capability to watch over the lives of citizens and keep files on suspected subversive elements. These technologies may, therefore, increase, rather than decrease, the power of the state with respect to the individual.

This raises the issue of information power. It is quite likely that in the future the states that are world leaders in computer development, information production, and communications technology will be the most powerful states in the international system. Just as past technical innovations increased the power of certain societies or states, the information age will increase the power of those states best able to develop and harness the potential of these new technologies. Many observers argue that the country best placed to increase its power and exert leadership in the information age remains the United States:

> Knowledge, more than ever before, is power. The one country that can best lead the information revolution will be more powerful than any other. For the foreseeable future, that country is the United States. America has apparent strength in military power and economic production. Yet its most subtle

PROFILE 12.4 Hacktivism at the University of Toronto

On the campus of the University of Toronto is a facility known as the Citizen Lab. Established in 2001 through the efforts of Professor Ron Diebert, the lab engages in what Dr. Diebert calls "hacktivism," a combination of traditional computer hacking and social and political activism. Dr. Diebert believes that understanding how technology works and what is behind it is essential to a liberal, democratic society: "Citizens can't just accept technology at face value. They need to open the lid, so to speak, understand how it works, beneath the surface." By bringing together a diverse group of students from computer science through political science, Dr. Diebert wanted to encourage the creation of a group of technically adept activists. The heart of the Citizen Lab activities is the OpenNet Initiative, targeted at countries that attempt to block access to the World Wide Web. Hacktivists at the lab attempt to identify what methods

governments use to block access to certain websites. The lab also develops technologies to help citizens in these countries circumvent government controls. An interesting dilemma for the Citizen Lab is to deal with governments that say they censor Web access for the purpose of preserving culture and heritage. Hacktivists at the lab try to balance their beliefs in the freedom of access to information with a respect for the desire of sovereign states to preserve their culture. And how do target countries feel about the activities of the Citizen Lab? "Some authoritarian regimes obviously don't like what we're doing," says Diebert. "But I feel we're working in support of broader principles of human rights, so I don't mind the controversy. Sometimes it helps."

SOURCE: CLARK BOYD, "'NET NINJAS' TAKE ON WEB CENSORSHIP," BBC NEWS, 18 APRIL 2004, WORLD EDITION, http://news.bbc.co.uk/go/pr/fr=/=/2/hi/technology/3632757.stm (ACCESSED 18 APRIL 2004).

comparative advantage is its ability to collect, process, act upon, and disseminate information, an edge that will almost certainly grow over the next decade.[47]

Power in the information age will not be dependent on natural endowments of population or resources or geographic position, although these will still have relevance. Instead, power will depend on technological leadership, on political, economic, and social flexibility, and on education.

The potential for a widening global disparity between states and peoples who can experience and benefit from the information age and those who will not has raised the question of whether we are heading into a world divided between the information and technology haves and have-nots, the info-rich and the info-poor. The proponents of the convergence theme point to the expanded capacity of humankind to communicate as a primary factor in the shrinking of the world. There can be no doubt that the advances made in communications technology, from the invention of the sail to the telephone to the Internet, have resulted in both qualitative and quantitative shifts in the way we communicate with others. However, critics argue that the advent of computer technology has not provided equitable access to the information age. In fact, the computer revolution has exacerbated differentials in the standard of living, and the future prospects, of the world's people. In short, the new technology imposes a two-tier infrastructure on the world economy, in which those with education and access to it have large advantages over those who do not. Optimists argue that these differences will be overcome as the technology spreads; that in the end we will all be better off for it. Pessimists argue that the spread of the technology will be limited to those who can afford it and have the economies to sustain it, and that the mass of the people in the world will be unable to take advantage of the information age.

A GLOBAL CULTURE?

The relationship between transnational communications networks and culture is a growing topic in the study of global politics. Dramatic statements have been made on the impact of the information age in the industrialized world. Bill Gates, for example, argues that a "... global interactive network will transform our culture as dramatically as Gutenberg's press did in the middle ages."[48] Of course, it is not so much the network that will have this impact but the content the network is carrying. Today, the global impact of such networks on cultures worldwide is beginning to be understood. As with so many aspects of the information age, there are encouraging as well as discouraging dimensions to this issue. Transnational communications technologies and the global media are shrinking the planet. Individuals around the world can watch the same news reports, listen to the same music, watch the same sporting events, see the same movies, eat the same food, and be exposed to advertising for the same consumer products. As a result, a global culture may be taking form. To be sure, this global culture exists only in a very embryonic form today, if it exists at all. And even if it does develop, the larger part of the population of the planet will not share in this experience. However, we may be witnessing the beginning of a form of cultural integration or homogenization, borne on the pathways opened by transnational communications technologies and the information revolution.

Sociologists interested in technology have introduced a convergence theory that is not unlike the idea of convergence as we have used it in this book. According to this theory, "the opportunities and demands presented by modern technology promote the convergence of all societies toward a single set of social patterns and individual behaviours."[49] In other words, the adoption of Western technology and science will lead to the establishment of political institutions and cultural environments similar to those in the advanced European and

American worlds. Thus, globalization will inevitably be realized through technological standardization. As a theory, however, this leaves some room for healthy speculation. One might point to the spread of capitalism as the source of this convergence instead of to the technology employed. Obvious cases exist where distaste for Western society has led to an assertion of anti-Western political change, such as the Iranian revolution that ushered into power the late Ayatollah Khomeini. In the more general sense, one can argue that culture does not necessarily converge simply because of technological similarities. There are distinct patterns of social interaction within different societies despite a high rate of technological convergence. Japan, the United States, and Germany all have adopted industrial technology yet remain quite different in terms of cultural attributes. Though many would argue with this, we can even point to significant cultural differences between countries as similar in technological circumstances as the United States and Canada.

Television programming, movies, and music have become increasingly globalized. Audiences around the world can watch television programming—particularly in the form of drama series—from other countries. These programs can reveal the nature of life in other countries and other societies, and as a result television can be a powerful educational tool. However, television can also distort the perception of life in other countries; exported Western soap operas have created the impression among many people in other societies that all North Americans and Europeans are rich. Children and family programming is also increasingly globalized, as suggested by the international success of the *Mighty Morphin Power Rangers* (dubbed into English from the original Japanese) and the Canadian television series *Degrassi Junior High*. Movies are also distributed internationally, as are music recordings. Quality cinema is shown at international film festivals (such as the famous Cannes Film Festival). Classical musicians and conductors move routinely across national borders. In the genres of rock, jazz, and blues, tours are often international in scope. Some varieties of music are explicitly international in inspiration, and are sometimes referred to as "world music."

Sporting events have also become internationalized. The Olympic Games and the World Cup (to name only two) are now major international events, watched by hundreds of millions of people. Virtually all athletic and sporting pursuits have some version of a world championship, whether it is in figure skating, ice hockey, or car racing. Many prominent sports teams, such as the New York Yankees and Manchester United, have international followings. Frequently, sporting figures will become international celebrities, famous throughout the world and connected to the global advertising capacities of major multinationals such as Nike or Adidas. Sports can create a sense of human community, and some suggest that sporting events can be a force for peace, unifying peoples in a shared activity. Of course, sports can bring out intense state or even ethnic nationalism, as people cheer for *their* national team or competitor. Sporting events can also take on a political dimension. For example, witness the intense rivalry of the Canada–Soviet Union hockey confrontations, and the undertones of some football matches during the World Cup. However, sports bring people (both participants and spectators) together, and the increasing trend toward international competitions, visiting tours of sport teams, and exchanges and trips in youth sports is another example of the blurring of national boundaries.

The wide availability of food and consumer items from other countries (made possible by global trade) also has contributed to the globalization of culture. Many food and consumer products are indistinguishable from the culture that produced them: when one thinks of sushi, one thinks of Japan; when one thinks of Mercedes, one thinks of Germany. In addition, advertising has a powerful cultural dimension, as advertising increasingly links products and the multinational corporations that produce them with music, images, and international celebrities. Icons of certain cultures have spread dramatically, and some are approaching the

McDonald's in the United Arab Emirates, 2004. Almost all of the world's brands are present in Dubai, which will have the largest shopping mall in the world in 2005. Is this a meeting of cultures, or an imposition? (© Amar Abd Rabbo/ABACA Press 2004. All rights reserved.)

status of global icons, such as the Golden Arches and Ronald McDonald of the American fast-food chain. However, advertising also carries certain cultural values and messages, and can encourage Western-style consumerism and materialism, to the detriment of local businesses and traditions, and sometimes the very health of the local population.

Finally, the language barrier—one of the last barriers to the spread of culture and international communication—may be on the verge of being overcome (see Profile 12.5). Computer software that can translate text from one language to another is now available, as are programs that will translate website pages and allow Internet users to expand their searches to foreign-language websites. The communications revolution and the information age may be accelerating another remarkable global trend: the increasing dominance of English. Already, 80 percent of all information stored on computers is in English. English is the language of the Internet, and is growing rapidly as the international language of communication. By 2007, according to one estimate, there will be more people who speak English as a second language than there are people who speak it as a first language.[50] English dominates the scientific and intellectual communities, and English-language training is in extremely high demand around the world. As Daniel F. Burton argues, "These technologies will further loosen culture from its geographic moorings, thereby contributing to the creation of a free-floating cosmopolitan class that is not restricted by national identity."[51]

However, considerable concern remains around the world that this global culture may in fact be less of a fusion, or integration, of cultures from around the world than the spread—or, worse, imposition—of Western culture and especially American culture. Instead of a global culture emerging, some would argue, we are witnessing cultural imperialism. The global culture is dominated by the English language, the U.S. film and television industries, American and Western media networks, and advertising for Western-style consumption. Hollywood, for example, dominates global cinema and the television programming industry; it supplies

PROFILE 12.5 Toward Unicode?

How can people who speak different languages communicate on the Internet? A North American consortium has developed a universal digital code, named Unicode, that may overcome this obstacle. Computers operate on binary bits: combinations of zeros and ones. For example, ASCII (the American Standard Code for Information Interchange) represents each character by a sequence of seven zeros or ones; but only 128 possible sequences exist, so it is a limited translator. Non-English speaking countries have their own codes, with their own limitations. The developers of Unicode circumvent this by using a sequence of 16 zeros and ones, producing 65 536 different combinations. Thus, any language can have its own sequence for each character in that language. Translating software is also becoming more popular and advanced, and should be widespread in the future. E-mail will present some problems because, as A. Pollack reports, "the informal word usage and unusual punctuations that are common ... could further confuse an electronic translator." However, the gist of a message could come through, and efforts are being made to facilitate "translation of messages in transit so that e-mail sent in English, for example, could arrive at the other end in French."

SOURCE: A. POLLACK, "CYBERSPACE'S WAR OF WORDS," *THE GLOBE AND MAIL*, 10 AUGUST 1995, A10.

80 percent of the world's demand for films and 70 percent of the world's demand for television shows. By the mid-1990s, Hollywood was making more than half its money abroad.[52] While some other national film industries are growing in size and significance (most notably the huge production capacities of the Indian film industry, popularly known as "Bollywood") these tend to serve a highly local or specific audience. The vast majority of Internet users are Americans (54 percent of all Internet users in 2000). In 2000, 79 percent of all Internet users resided in the industrialized countries.[53] This dominance, in turn, may give the United States an important lead in soft power. However, it may also lead to a global cultural backlash, with populations increasingly rejecting foreign influences. This rejection is likely to be selective: even as some influences are opposed others will be accepted.

THE FUTURE OF WAR IN THE INFORMATION AGE: A REVOLUTION IN MILITARY AFFAIRS?

So far in this chapter we have explored how the rapid pace of technological change has affected (and perhaps even transformed) the global political economy, information flows, and financial markets, global cultural politics, the media, and the state. This rapid technological change has also dramatically increased the capacities of modern weapons and the efficiency of military communications and information systems. Indeed, many observers of military affairs argue that we are witnessing a profound transformation in the effectiveness of military forces. This argument is based on a particular interpretation of military history, which argues that the development of military capabilities has not progressed in a steady, evolutionary fashion. Instead, increases in military capabilities have been characterized by sudden surges, or revolutions, in the effectiveness of weapons and military technique. These surges originate from technological, organizational, and larger social and economic innovations in certain countries. It can hardly be surprising that against the backdrop of the computer and information revolution, declarations have been made that we are experiencing a parallel military revolution. For example, Alvin and Heidi Toffler wrote that "as we transition from brute-force to brain-force economies, we also necessarily invent what can only be called 'brain-force-war.'"[54] This transition is now called the **Revolution in Military Affairs (RMA)**.

An RMA is the relatively swift onset of a qualitative transformation in the effectiveness of military technologies that fundamentally alters the conduct of military operations and the nature of the strategic environment. One key concept that distinguishes changes in military technologies, doctrines, and organizations (which are not rare) from revolutionary developments (which are rare) is *discontinuity*. That is, revolutions are characterized by transformations in the nature of the conduct of military operations such that previous technologies and techniques are rendered obsolete. Early RMAs have been associated with gunpowder, the rise of the national citizen armies of the Napoleonic period, and the Blitzkrieg warfare of World War II (see Chapter 2). It is worth emphasizing that technological developments are not sufficient indicators of military revolutions, although weapons developments are almost always central to any revolution that has ever been identified. Military revolutions are also based on organizational innovation and are grounded in larger economic, social, and political changes that impact on military capabilities.

What are the components of the current RMA? Advocates of this concept point to the following:

- A decrease in the relationship between distance and accuracy, made possible by modern electronics. Precision-guided munitions are now capable of hitting targets over long distances with a high probability of success (though not as high as is often advertised by weapons manufacturers and governments);

- The increased capacity of some weapons systems to act autonomously from human operators. These military versions of robots promise a transition from current semi-autonomous warfare (a human fires the weapon, which guides itself to the target) to fully autonomous warfare (the weapons system decides when and where to fire based on its programming);

- The development of stealth technology, which renders some weapons systems extremely hard to detect by conventional radars;

- An increase in the capability to conduct surveillance and reconnaissance over the battlefield through the employment of remotely piloted vehicles, satellites, and signal-intelligence equipment;

- An increase in the capacity to store, analyze, and disseminate information in real time (no time delay) through communications and battle management systems, thus reducing the "fog of war";

- An increased capacity to fight at night and in all weather conditions with minimal degradation of effectiveness;

- An increased ability to engage in offensive information warfare to disrupt the opponent's military and civilian communications and thus influence the political and psychological dimensions of the conflict;

- The increased use of space;

- The development of doctrine and training and leadership skills assisted by realistic simulations; and

- The potential to reduce civilian casualties and *collateral damage* associated with the use of military force.

As noted above, developing technologies also promise new methods of conducting information warfare, and managing the public relations and imagery of wars and interventions. In this sense, future wars will take place not only between combatants and their weapons systems, but also in the arena of public perception and opinion, the media, and in information and misinformation efforts mounted by governments, groups, and individuals.[55]

Computers and networks at war. The communications warfare officer at work in the Operations Room on board the British naval vessel HMS *Ocean* in the Persian Gulf.

Not surprisingly, the leading proponent of the RMA concept is the United States.[56] Advocates of the RMA in the U.S. military and government argue that America is best placed to take advantage of the current RMA, and the development of doctrinal concepts from the Air-Land Battle of the late 1980s to the transformation agenda of U.S. Defense Secretary Donald Rumsfeld have been based on the RMA concept. The objective is to ensure that the U.S. armed forces remain preeminent on the battlefield in the 21st century—a key element, realists would say, of maintaining U.S. hegemony, although not all would argue that this can be sustained without being selective.[57] Some U.S. allies (including Canada) are expected to try to remain as interoperable as possible with the U.S. military to ensure that their forces can cooperate effectively on the battlefield (a major issue in allied or coalition operations). However, few if any countries have the resources to implement RMA techniques and weapons with the enthusiasm displayed by the United States. Still, as we discussed in Chapter 6, as weapons technologies continue to diffuse through the international system, more countries are acquiring more modern weapons. These may not always be the most modern weapons, but they are far more capable and destructive than previous generations of hardware and software. As a result, we can expect future interstate wars involving industrialized, information-age states to be fought with progressively more sophisticated technologies.

Considerable controversy is associated with the RMA.[58] Some security studies experts doubt that RMAs even exist, disputing the notion of historical discontinuities in the development of warfare.[59] Others point out that it is essentially an American enterprise and is, therefore, motivated more by the U.S. military and its corporate suppliers than by any sense of security requirements. Still others argue that the RMA is relevant to U.S. military requirements, but the danger is that the United States will move so far ahead of the rest of the world (including its key allies) in military capabilities that it will be less disposed toward multilateralism and more disposed toward unilateralism in the military realm. Why would the United States invite other countries to participate in multilateral military efforts when only a few countries can provide significant military contributions? The short answer is that America will still value its allies because coalitions will still impart a moral weight, or legitimacy, to U.S. actions. However, if most countries are contributing forces to U.S.-led efforts for purely symbolic purposes, and these military forces are not capable of meaningful military operations, what political influence or voice can these countries expect to have on U.S. policy? This is a particular concern in Canada, where the Canadian government has always tried to encourage the United States to pursue multilateral solutions to problems.

There is also the question of the effectiveness of the new technologies. For every measure there is a countermeasure, and even the most sophisticated weapons can be defeated using relatively simple techniques. Doubts exist as to whether RMA capabilities will be effective in forest or jungle terrain. During the bombing of Serbia, the Serbian military made wide use of decoys, which proved effective against many high-technology weapons. In other cases, controversies may erupt concerning the use of certain weapons. This has occurred with respect to the alleged health effects of depleted uranium munitions in the Gulf War and in the former Yugoslavia, and in the use of area-denial munitions and cluster bombs, some of which may fail to explode and thus represent a threat to civilians. Finally, some question the relevance of the RMA in an era where major war may be increasingly rare or even obsolete.[60] RMA capabilities will not enhance the ability of military forces to conduct peacekeeping missions or low-intensity conflicts, which are precisely the kind of operations militaries have been most frequently asked to perform. Certainly, the struggles of the U.S. and coalition forces to maintain order and fight insurgents in Iraq through late 2003 and 2004 exemplify the limitations of RMA technologies and doctrines in such operations.

This last point raises the question of whether the RMA is an effort to prepare for the wrong kind of war, and therefore we should not pay an undue amount of attention to it. The vast majority of recent and current wars are fought not with the high-technology weapons and techniques of the 21st century but with the low-technology weapons and techniques of the 20th. As we discussed in Chapter 6, almost all these wars have been fought between communal groups at the substate level. The character of war in the future is therefore likely to be bifurcated between two styles. First, wars or interventions involving advanced industrialized states will feature modern weapons systems, highly trained professional personnel, and the organizational techniques characteristic of information age societies. The Iraq War is certainly a model for this kind of warfare. Second, other wars (likely far more numerous) will feature armed groups using light weapons and the techniques of 20th-century warfare or insurgency conflicts. The war in the former Yugoslavia and the war in Liberia are examples of this kind of warfare. Interventions to stop such wars, or efforts to use peacekeeping forces to control them, will demand a capacity to met this kind of combatant when the high-technology innovations of the RMA will be of little, or marginal, utility.

MISSILE DEFENCE

The idea of missile defence—the ability to shoot down ballistic missiles in flight—began to make a comeback in the 1990s. As we saw in Chapter 3, the idea of missile defences had been shelved during the Cold War (and essentially banned in the 1972 Antiballistic Missile Treaty) in the interests of maintaining the stability of deterrence and Mutual Assured Destruction. However, during the 1990s concern over the proliferation of ballistic missiles to a wider group of countries, and the possibility that such missiles could be equipped with nuclear, chemical, or biological warheads, prompted several governments to revisit the idea. Some European governments have expressed an interest in missile defence research, and the government of Japan has openly contemplated deploying a missile defence system, having conducted research for a number of years. However, the country most energetically pursuing missile defences has been the United States. During the Clinton Administration, a research program was already underway. In 1998 a Commission to Assess the Ballistic Missile Threat to the United States warned that America could be threatened by ballistic missile attack from Iraq, Iran, or North Korea within 5 to 10 years of any decision by these states to acquire such a capability.[61] The Commission—chaired by Donald Rumsfeld—was widely criticized for being alarmist, but the threat of ballistic missile attack from a "rogue state" was considered serious enough to warrant enhanced research. There was another argument for building a missile defence system: if a rogue state could threaten the U.S. homeland with ballistic missiles and weapons of mass destruction warheads, then the United States might be deterred from pressuring that state politically or attacking it militarily. In effect, a ballistic missile system would make it possible for the United States to remain engaged or to become engaged in certain hotspots around the world while remaining invulnerable to retaliation from a ballistic missile.

On December 17, 2002, President G.W. Bush announced that the United States would develop and deploy a ballistic missile defence system by 2004–05. A few days earlier, the Bush administration had announced its intention to withdraw from the ABM Treaty. Construction on the system began shortly thereafter. The ballistic missile defence system will employ ground-based missile interceptors carrying hit-to-kill warheads. Any incoming ballistic missile warhead would be detected and tracked by radar stations in North America, Greenland, and the U.K. The ballistic missile system would launch interceptors at the incoming warhead in the hopes of hitting it and destroying it. The Bush Administration planned to have 20 interceptors deployed by 2004–05, with 16 at Fort Greely in Alaska and 4 more at Vandenberg Air Force Base in California. Follow-up plans are already in place for sea-based interceptors and an increase in the number of ground-based interceptors, perhaps to 100.

The U.S. deployment of a ballistic missile system is very controversial.[62] First, many critics argue that the system simply does not work. Testing of system components has been plagued with problems and failures, and the integrity of the testing program itself has been called into question. The technical challenge demanded of a successful intercept of an incoming warhead is considerable: both the interceptor warhead and the incoming ballistic missile warhead will be travelling at speeds in excess of that of a bullet out of the barrel of a gun. And so, the system must literally be capable of "hitting a bullet with a bullet." Second, critics argue that the system is too expensive in relation to its expected utility. In 2004 alone, the Bush Administration spent approximately U.S.$9 billion on missile defence, but this figure will increase dramatically if the system is expanded.[63] Critics argue that deterrence through punishment remains the best way of preventing attacks on North America. Third, critics argue that the ballistic missile threat is rather low, and there are many other, cheaper ways of attacking the United States, as the September 11 attacks proved. Finally, critics argue that the United States has abrogated the 1972 ABM Treaty (inflicting a setback to the international arms control regime) and damaged its relationship with Russia and China (both governments had expressed opposition to the system).[64] However, advocates of the system argue that one cannot take chances and trust dictatorial regimes to be deterred and not to attack. If deterrence were to fail, there would be nothing between a rogue state missile and hundreds of thousands, perhaps millions, of American lives. Advocates of missile defence argue that defensive systems will improve with time as technology advances, and the costs are affordable given the magnitude of the risk (the cost of the program in 2004 will represent only about 2.5 percent of the U.S. defence budget for that year). As for other ways of attacking the United States, the ballistic missile system will not defend America from those threats, but then it is not designed to. Other measures will be put in place to defend the United States against other possible attacks. Meanwhile, other states are forced to respond to the plan, invoking domestic political debate. During the Canadian 2004 election campaign, the militarization of space became one of the few foreign policy issues on the agenda; the current Liberal government seems to be undecided, but will have to adopt a related policy soon.

CONCLUSIONS

Where will the computer revolution, the communications revolution, and the information age take us? Innovation is difficult to predict; new discoveries may open up completely new areas of human endeavour, much as the development of the computer has. The question for observers of international relations is how these innovations will affect the interaction of states, groups, and individuals. As we have seen, the impact up to now has been profound. The consensus is that the information age will accelerate the erosion of the state and enhance global interdependence. A new era of global communication promises improved international understanding and the establishment of new patterns of human interaction across state boundaries. However, the information age may also enhance the power of some states in the international system and serve to make us all more vulnerable to both observation and crime. The pervasiveness of certain cultures and perspectives on computer networks and in the global media may lead to a cultural backlash against transnational communication. We must not forget that the majority of people on this planet are untouched by the information age. What does it promise these people? The information age may be a force of convergence for many in the international system, but it is also a force of divergence, as so many past revolutions in human history have been.

Endnotes

1. Quoted in Charles W. Kegley Jr., and Eugene R. Wittkopf, *World Politics: Trend and Transformation,* 5th ed. (New York: St. Martin's Press, 1995), 554.

2. See J. Goldstein, *Long Cycles: Prosperity and War in the Modern Age* (New Haven: Yale University Press, 1988); and C. Freeman, "Diffusion, the Spread of New Technology to Firms, Sectors, and Nations," in A. Heertje, ed., *Innovation, Technology, and Finance* (New York: Basil Blackwell, 1988), 38–70.

3. Alvin Toffler, *The Third Wave* (New York: Morrow, 1980).

4. S. Nora and A. Minc, *The Computerization of Society* (Cambridge, MA: MIT Press, 1980), 3.

5. Christopher May, *The Information Society: A Skeptical View* (Malden, MA: Blackwell, 2002).

6. For recent data see International Telecommunications Union, World Telecommunications Indicators Database, http://www.itu.int/ITU-D/ict/statistics (accessed 30 May 2004).

7. M. Castels and L. D'Andrea Tyson, "High Technology Choices Ahead: Restructuring Interdependence," in J. Sewell and S. Tucker, eds., *Growth, Exports, and Jobs in a Changing World* (New Brunswick, NJ: Transaction Press, 1988), 57.

8. United Nations Development Programme. *Human Development Report 2001.* (Oxford: Oxford University Press, 2001), 27.

9. See I. de Sola Pool, in Eli M. Noam, ed., *Technologies without Boundaries: On Telecommunications in a Global Age* (Cambridge, MA: Harvard University Press, 1990).

10. International Telecommunications Union World Telecommunications Indicators Database, http://www.itu.int/ITU-D/ict/statistics (accessed 30 May 2004).

11. Alex Lightman and William Rojas, *Brave New Unwired World: The Digital Big Bang and the Infinite Internet* (New York, John Wiley and Sons, 2002), 9.

12. See *Global Economic Prospects and the Developing Countries* (Washington, DC: World Bank, 1992), and *Human Development Report 1999* (New York: United Nations, 2000).

13. International Telecommunications Union, World Telecommunications Indicators Database, http://www.itu.int/ITU-D/ict/statistics (accessed 30 May 2004).

14. International Telecommunications Union, *World Telecommunications Indicators Database*, http://www.itu.int/ITU-D/ict/statistics/at_glance/Internet02.pdf (accessed 30 May 2004).

15. The Economist, *The World in 2004* (London: The Economist Newspaper Limited, 2003), 95.

16. Gregory J. Walters, *Human Rights in an Information Age: A Philosophical Analysis* (Toronto: University of Toronto Press, 2001), 5.

17. See Price Pritchett, *The Employee Handbook of New Work Habits for a Radically Changing World* (Dallas: Pritchett and Associates, 1996), 4.

18. P. Drucker, *Post-Capitalist Society* (New York: Harper Business, 1993), 40.

19. C. Leadbeater, *Living on Thin Air: The New Economy* (London: Viking, 1999), 18.

20. Dominique Foray and Bengt-Ålce Lundvall, "The Knowledge-Based Economy: From the Economics of Knowledge to the Learning Economy," *Employment and Growth in the Knowledge-Based Economy*. OECD Documents (Paris: Organisation for Economic Cooperation and Development, 1996), 16.

21. P. Woodall, "The World Economy," *The Economist*, 26 September 1996, 43.

22. Daniel Burton, Jr., "The Brave New Wired World," *Foreign Policy* 106 (Spring 1997), 23–24.

23. For a review of the impact of information technologies, see James N. Rosenau and J. P. Singh, eds., *Information Technologies and Global Politics: The Changing Scope of Power and Governance* (New York: State University of New York Press, 2002).

24. Ethan B. Kapstein, "Workers and the World Economy," *Foreign Affairs* 75 (May/June 1996), 16.

25. Christopher May, *The Information Society: A Skeptical View* (Malden, MA: Blackwell, 2002).

26. J. Salomon and A. Lebeau, *Mirages of Development: Science and Technology for the Third Worlds* (Boulder CO; London: Lynne Rienner, 1993), 86. See also Paul Kennedy's *Preparing for the Twentieth Century* (New York: Random House, 1993).

27. Manuel Castells, *The Information Age, Volume 1: The Rise of the Network Society* (Oxford: Blackwell, 1996), 147.

28. This according to the *Human Development Report 2001* (New York: Oxford University Press, 1992), 9.

29. *Human Development Report 2001* (New York: Oxford University Press, 1992), 3.

30. Alex Lightman and William Rojas, *Brave New Unwired World*, xii.

31. Michael T. Klare, "Resource Competition and World Politics in the Twenty-First Century," *Current History* 99 (December 2000), 406.

32. *Human Development Report 2001* (New York: Oxford University Press, 1992), 30.

33. J. Rosenau, *Turbulence in World Politics* (Princeton: Princeton University Press, 1990), 17.

34. J. Habermas, *Between Facts and Norms: Contributions to a Discourse Theory of Law and Democracy* (Cambridge, UK: Polity Press and Blackwell Publishers, 1996), 514.

35. G. Chapman, "TV: The World Next Door?" *Intermedia* 20 (1992), 30–33.

36. See D. Shaw, "Foreign News Shrinks in Era of Globalization," *Los Angeles Times*, 27 September 2001, A20; and K. Lang and G.E. Lang, "How Americans View the World: Media Images and Public Knowledge," in H. Tumber, ed., *Media Power, Professionals, and Policies* (London: Routledge, 2000).

37. Ted Magder, "Watching What We Say: Global Communication in a Time of Fear," in Daya Kishan Thissu and Des Freedman, eds., *War and the Media: Reporting Conflict 24/7* (London: Sage, 2003), 33.

38. See Noureddine Miladi, "Mapping the Al-Jazeera Phenomenon," in Daya Kishan Thissu and Des Freedman, eds., *War and the Media*, 149–160.

39. European Broadcast Union, *Actors or Spectators? The Media Look Back on their Role in the Gulf War* (Geneva: European Broadcast Union, 1991), 4–5.

40. See Daya Kishan Thissu and Des Freedman, "Introduction," in Daya Kishan Thissu and Des Freedman, eds., *War and the Media*, 7.

41. *Turbulence in World Politics: A Theory of Change and Continuity* (Princeton, NJ: Princeton University Press, 1990), 339–43.

42. For a discussion of CNN's development see Don Flournoy, "Coverage, Competition, and Credibility: The CNN International Standard," in Tony Silvia, ed., *Global News: Perspectives on the Information Age* (Ames, Iowa: Iowa State University Press, 2001), 15–44.

43. Stig Hjarvard, "News Media and the Globalization of the Public Sphere," in Stig Hjarvard, ed., *News in a Globalized Society* (Goteborg: Nordicom, 2001), 18.

44. A. Ramirez, "Dial Direct to Moscow and Beyond," *The New York Times*, 20 May 1992, D1.

45. Some argue that the media in advanced capitalist states are just as manipulative and that there is a connection between the owners of the media and pro–status quo forces in government. The most famous proponent of

this view is Noam Chomsky; see for example Noam Chomsky, *Media Control: The Spectacular Achievements of Propaganda* (New York: Seven Stories Press, 1997).

46. Isabel Vincent, "Rebel Dispatches Find Home on Net," *The Globe and Mail,* 11 June 1996, A1.

47. J. Nye Jr., and W. Owens, "America's Information Edge," *Foreign Affairs* 75 (March/April 1996), 20.

48. Bill Gates, *The Road Ahead.* 2nd ed. (London: Penguin Books, 1995), 9.

49. R. Volti, *Society and Technological Change,* 2nd ed. (New York: St. Martin's Press, 1992), 235.

50. "Language and Electronics: The Coming Global Tongue," *The Economist,* 21 December 1997, 76.

51. Burton, "The Brave New Wired World," 36.

52. "Star Wars," *The Economist,* 22 March 1997, 15.

53. *Human Development Report 2001,* 40.

54. A. Toffler and H. Toffler, *War and Anti-War: Survival at the Dawn of the 21st Century* (Boston: Little, Brown and Company, 1993), 10–11. See also R. Preston and S. Wise, *Men in Arms: A History of Warfare and Its Interrelationships with Western Society,* 4th ed. (New York: Holt, Rinehart, and Winston, 1979).

55. Michael Ignatieff, *Virtual War* (Toronto: Penguin Books of Canada, 2000).

56. See Richard O. Hundley, *Past Revolutions, Future Transformations: What Can the History of Revolutions in Military Affairs Tell Us about Transforming the U.S. Military?* (Santa Monica, CA: Rand, 1999).

57. For a cautious note see Barry R. Posen, "Command of the Commons: The Military Foundations of US Hegemony," *International Security* 28 (Summer 2003), 5–47.

58. For a discussion of the many issues surrounding the RMA see Thierry Gongora and Harald von Riekhoff, eds., *Toward a Revolution in Military Affairs? Defence and Security at the Dawn of the Twenty-first Century* (Westport, CT: Greenwood Press, 2000).

59. See Philip L. Ritcheson, "The Future of Military Affairs: Revolution or Evolution?" *Strategic Review* 24 (Spring 1996), 31–40.

60. Michael Mandelbaum, "Is Major War Obsolete?" *Survival* (Winter 1998/99), 20–38.

61. *Executive Summary of the Report of the Commission to Assess the Ballistic Missile Threat to the United States,* 15 July 1998, 1.

62. For a brief review of ballistic missile defences in context see Scott D. Sagan and Kenneth N. Waltz, *The Spread of Nuclear Weapons: A Debate Renewed* (New York: Norton, 2003).

63. *Strategic Survey 2002/2003* (Oxford: Oxford University Press, 2003), 37.

64. Charles L. Glaser and Steve Fetter, "National Missile Defense and the Future of U.S. Nuclear Weapons Policy," *International Security* 26 (Summer 2001), 40–92.

Suggested Readings

Alleyne, M. I*nternational Power and International Communication.* Toronto: Macmillan, 1995.

Allison, J., ed., *Technology, Development, and Democracy: International Conflict and Cooperation in the Information Age.* Albany: State University of New York Press, 2002.

Baldwin, T., D. McVoy, and C. Steinfeld. *Convergence: Integrating Media, Information, and Communication.* Thousand Oaks, CA: Sage Publications, 1996.

Castells, M. *The Rise of Network Society.* Cambridge, MA: Blackwell Publishers, 1996.

Connor, E. *The Global Political Economy of Communication: Hegemony, Telecommunications and the Information Economy.* New York: St. Martin's Press, 1994.

Downing, J., Ali Mohammadi, and A. Sreberny-Mohammadi. *Questioning the Media: A Critical Introduction.* Thousand Oaks, CA: Sage Publications, 1996.

Drucker, P. *Post-Capitalist Society.* New York: HarperBusiness, 1993.

Dutton, W., ed. *Information and Communications Technologies: Visions and Realities.* New York: Oxford University Press, 1996.

Frederick, H. *Global Communication and International Relations.* Belmont, CA: Wadsworth, 1993.

Hajnal, P., ed. *Civil Society in the Information Age.* Burlington, VT: Ashgate, 2002.

Hall, W. *Stray Voltage: War in the Information Age.* Annapolis, MD: Naval Institute Press, 2003.

Hamelink, C. *The Politics of World Communication.* Thousand Oaks, CA: Sage Publications, 1994.

Haywood, T. *Info-Rich and Info-Poor: Access and Exchange in the Global Information Society.* New Jersey: Bowker-Saur, 1995.

Hess, S. and M. Kalb, eds. *The Media and the War on Terrorism.* Washington, DC: Brookings Institution Press, 2003.

Hjarvard, S., ed. *News in a Globalized Society.* Göteborg, Sweden: Nordicom, 2001.

Krasner, S. "Global Communications and National Power: Life on the Pareto Frontier." *World Politics* 43 (1991), 336–66.

Kuypers, J. *Press Bias and Politics: How the Media Frame Controversial Issues.* Westport, CT: Praeger, 2002.

Latham, R., ed. *Bombs and Bandwidth: The Emerging Relationship between Information Technology and Security.* New York: New Press, 2003.

Leadbeater, C. *Living on Thin Air: The New Economy.* London: Viking, 1999.

Lightman, A. and W. Rojas, *Brave New Unwired World: The Digital Big Bang and the Infinite Internet.* New York: John Wiley and Sons, 2002.

Martin, W. *The Global Information Society.* Brookfield, VT: Gower, 1995.

May, C. *The Information Society: A Skeptical View.* Malden, MA: Blackwell, 2002.

Medina, A. "Canada's Information Edge." *Canadian Foreign Policy* 4, no. 2 (1996), 71–87.

Menzies, H. *The Information Highway and the New Economy.* Toronto: Between the Lines, 1996.

Muszynski, L., and D. Wolfe. "New Technology and Training: Lessons from Abroad." *Canadian Public Policy* 15 (1989), 245–64.

Pirages, D. *Global Technopolitics: The International Politics of Technology and Resources.* Pacific Grove, CA: Brooks Cole, 1989.

Pool, Ithiel de Sola. *Technologies without Boundaries: Telecommunications in a Global Age.* Cambridge, MA: Harvard University Press, 1990.

Robinson, P. *Deceit, Delusion, and Detection.* Thousand Oak, CA: Sage Publications, 1996.

Rosenau, J., and J. P. Singh, eds. *Information Technologies and Global Politics: The Changing Scope of Power and Governance.* New York: State University of New York Press, 2002.

Rozell, M., ed. *Media Power, Media Politics.* Lanham: Rowman and Littlefield, 2003.

Said, E. *Covering Islam: How the Media and Experts Determine How We See the Rest of the World.* Rev. ed. New York: Vintage, 1997.

Schenk, D. *Data Smog: Surviving the Information Glut.* New York: HarperCollins, 1997.

Smith, A. *The Geopolitics of Information: How Western Culture Dominates the World.* New York: Oxford University Press, 1980.

Thissu, D., and D. Freedman, eds. *War and the Media: Reporting Conflict 24/7.* London: Sage, 2003.

Walters, G. *Human Rights in an Information Age: A Philosophical Analysis.* Toronto: University of Toronto Press, 2001.

Webster, F., ed. *Culture and Politics in the Information Age: A New Politics?* New York: Routledge, 2001.

Suggested Websites

The Center for War, Peace, and the News Media
http://www.nyu.edu/cwpnm

Freedominfo.org
http://www.freedominfo.org

International Telecommunication Union
http://www.itu.int/home/index.html

Organisation for Economic Co-operation and Development
http://www.oecd.org/home

Wired News
http://www.wired.com

World Bank Group
http://www.worldbank.org

CHAPTER 13

New Directions in Theory and Practice

Pessimism over the future of the world comes from a confusion between civilization and security. In the immediate future there will be less security than in the immediate past, less stability. But, on the whole, the great ages have been unstable ages.

—*A. North Whitehead[1]*

Society wills and acts collectively, as the output of systems (including lawmaking systems) which aggregate the willing and acting of individual human beings. But the intervention of those systems creates a new mindworld, a new form of human reality, a new form of human world. The public mind is society's private mind. The public mind of international society is the private mind of the human species.

—*Philip Allott[2]*

Every nation, in every region, now has a decision to make. Either you are with us, or you are with the terrorists.

—*George W. Bush[3]*

INTRODUCTION: AN AGENDA FOR THE IMMEDIATE AND LONG-TERM FUTURES

This chapter will serve three functions simultaneously. First, we will revisit the central theoretical perspectives outlined in Chapter 1 and referred to throughout the text, and reflect on what guiding questions and research avenues might dominate the field of IR in the immediate future. While social constructivism certainly rose in prominence during the 1990s and early 2000s, we suggest that the "War on Terrorism" and other factors will refocus attention on the strengths and weaknesses of traditional approaches, while further highlighting the contributions of critical theories. Second, we will revisit the core subject matter of the discipline of IR, as it is presented in the chapters of this book. Moving from power politics to ecopolitics, we will reflect on some of the trends that are evident and some of the directions that policies might take in the future. As we shall see, our themes of convergence and divergence are likely to be evident in the years ahead. This will create inescapable foreign policy dilemmas for state officials, transnational activists, citizens, and academics and students. Third, this chapter is a conclusion to our journey through the study of global politics. By looking ahead to the directions that international relations might take, we seek to anticipate some of the challenges that lie before us. Can we meet these challenges in a way that promises a better future for us all?

We begin the chapter by exploring the future relevance of the issues raised in Part One of the book. How will IR theory evolve in the future, and what will be the forces driving theoretical innovation? What new ideas might emerge that will help us understand the world in which we live? We then turn to the power politics theme that was so central to our historical overview of major events and transitions from early civilizations to the Cold War. Though we are clearly in a new era, an old question remains: what distribution of power is emerging in our world? And more specifically, what will be the future role of American power in the world, especially in the context of the "War on Terrorism"? Is another tectonic plate about to shift in global politics? In Part Two of the book, we examined the challenges of international security, conflict management, and globalization. While we explored the possible origins of future wars throughout the text, is it possible that future wars will, in essence, be wars between "civilizations," and not states? Will humanitarian interventions in support of human security and human rights become increasingly common, with or without United Nations approval? In the age of globalization, what are the key issues facing the future of the global economy? In the realm of international organizations and international law, as we shall see, the future will present many new challenges to these instruments of global governance, dialogue, and cooperation. In Part Three, we examined the environment, population and health issues, and the information age. Can multilateralism succeed in meeting these challenges?

Three things seem certain at this point. All of these themes are not with us just today; they have always been with us (though the actors and implications have changed significantly), and always will be (barring a cataclysmic event such as a global epidemic, a large-scale nuclear war, or a meteor impact). Even if the state system as we know it were to crumble under the weight of globalization, we would still debate the distribution of power, the friction between ethnicities, the goals of equality and sustainable development, and other ageless themes. Second, despite the theoretical reflexivity discussed above, we will tend to see these issues through our self-adopted and learned lenses, whether that entails a structural realist, liberalist, critical theory, or some other perspective. Denying this is futile, but being imprisoned by it is not necessary either. Readers should strive to apply other ways of thinking, even those that evoke intellectual discomfort, some of which we hope you have acquired through this textbook. Third, though there will be many puzzling, complex, and even some indecipherable developments in IR theory, we can be certain that the dynamic relationship between events and theoretical innovation will continue, as long as people are genuinely interested in not only understanding their world, but also forging a new one.

REVISITING THEORY

As this text has illustrated, metatheoretical discourse—debate about theory—is important. Theory provides us with a framework for looking at the world, with structures for organizing and prioritizing the bewildering array of issues and events that constitute global politics. Despite the claim that certain perspectives (such as realism and liberalism) have had their moments of hegemonic or paradigmatic domination in the field, a more global view suggests that this has never been the case: there never has been a universally accepted theoretical wisdom on the nature and dynamics of global politics. This is why so much disagreement exists on the issues covered in this book. We have introduced several contending perspectives, such as idealism, realism, liberalism, Neo-Marxism, feminism, and constructivism, among others. However, there is considerable overlap between many of them. One can be a realist with Marxist leanings; in fact, recent interpretations of the foundational work of E.H. Carr suggested this was his persuasion.[4] One can be a structural realist based in a world systems theory of global evolution, as the Argentinean author Carlos Escude's idea of peripheral realist foreign policy suggests.[5] While most feminists would reject a realist interpretation, many of them are quite willing to accept a liberal or Marxist one.[6] Regime theory is fairly strongly rooted in liberal suppositions about cooperation under conditions of self-interest, but there have been efforts to critically analyze the normative basis of regimes as well.[7] Geopolitical theory can be analyzed from an environmentalist perspective.[8] Practical foreign policy questions, such as the wisdom of humanitarian intervention, are being revisited by trained philosophers of different persuasions.[9] Indeed, distinctions between theoretical perspectives are not hard boundaries, and theoretical innovation and flexibility is, arguably, much more common today than ever.

It may make more sense to speak of an epistemological division in the discipline, that is, a division predicated on thinking about the nature of knowledge itself, rather than a division based on essentialist ideologies or theoretical perspectives. In other words, debates between constructivists and positivists might have as much to tell us as disputes between the trifecta of realism, liberalism, and critical theory.[10] Methodological issues are still very much part of the study of global politics. The discipline has been through several periods of self-examination in the past, pushing methodology in new directions. The study of IR has moved from an historical discipline based on the analysis of leaders and military strategy to one fixated on the Cold War dyad and resulting game theoretic constructions. It has moved from a behaviouralist period, where quantification of data and rational choice assumptions regarding human nature led to elaborate efforts to model human behaviour at the international level, to a discipline concerned with the validity of its own prevalent assumptions and their impact upon the real world. Social constructivism, as developed by Alexander Wendt and others, is often seen as an effort to bridge the divide between rationalist approaches (neo-realism, neo-liberalism) and "reflectivist" approaches (postmodernism, some feminist theory, normative theory, critical theory, and historical sociology).[11]

While the split between positivists and postpositivists is still defining the work of many scholars in the field, it can be argued that both sides of this divide are more willing to listen to the other, and this is a good thing, since they both offer so much. On the one hand, the need for empirical data gathering is undeniable, and testing various hypotheses in the laboratory of distant and recent history gives us clues about patterns of behaviour, though we should always be cautious about using this to predict the future. On the other hand, the values and aspirations that guide the actors in global politics did not emerge from a vacuum; they are the product of social norm construction and the ebb and flow of events, which are interpreted according to the intellectual prisms (some would use the word *prisons*) from which we see the world. Finally, there is a place for *normative theory* in global politics, defined by Chris Brown as "that body of work which addresses the moral dimensions of international relations and the wider questions of meaning and interpretation generated by the discipline … the ethical nature of the relations between communities/states, whether [it is] focused on violence and war, or the new(er) agenda, which mixes these traditional concerns with the modern demand for international distributive justice."[12] Ethics are the topic of legitimate study in IR, even amongst those who favor Machiavelli over Kant. It is our hope that future scholars in the discipline will approach global politics with a favourable attitude toward the many possibilities of synthesis and cross-pollination this vast field has developed over the past 100 years.

In the future we can expect even greater diversity among students and scholars of global politics, as the interdisciplinary nature of the field continues to expand and sophisticated contributions increase from analysts around the world. Of course, to some degree this is already the case. Global politics as a discipline is itself globalizing. Some might argue that we have no right to call global politics a discipline because of the breadth and scope of the subject matter, but we respectfully disagree. The study of the big issues facing us all cannot be properly achieved without an interdisciplinary approach that offers a large forum for the voices and concerns that must be heard. While it is clear that most IR textbooks emanate from either the United States or the United Kingdom (and, to a lesser degree, France), there are many notable exceptions and these exceptions will increasingly become the rule. This has happened before in the study of global politics: dependency theory originated in Latin America, and many development models were conceptualized in Africa. Much of the political economy and ecofeminist literature comes from India, reflecting the postcolonial experiences in South Asia. In the future, we can expect more ideas and theoretical innovations to spread through the discipline from region to region, country to country, and scholar to scholar. The tendency for social science literature originating in the former Eastern bloc to be little more than state propaganda is eroding, and one can hope for this to occur in China as well with time. An exposure to outside ideas is gradually translating into new ideas about global politics from previously silent sources. It is our hope that the decline in the Euro-centric character of the discipline will not only permit indigenous views to develop and become part of traditional dialogues and debates, but also expose Western scholars to alternative views.[13] Conferences in the Southern hemisphere, Internet communications, and a wider audience of the curious and dedicated intellects from around the earth will further enrich the discipline in the years to come, unless we revert to fixed ideological lines and the suppression of alternative views, as was seen on both sides at various times during the Cold War. It is unlikely that the "War on Terrorism"—no matter how drastic it becomes, and no matter how firmly it becomes enmeshed with various nationalisms and unhelpful patriotic rhetoric—will dampen this spirit. On the contrary, it should give rise to thought-provoking treatments of the causes of terrorism, the use of state power, and new modes of conflict management. Further, continued concern with environmental degradation will engender more theoretical construction on issues of the commons, regime building, and the links between ecology, gender, violence, and cooperation.

Another reason we expect IR theory to become more dynamic is because more people than ever are aware of its importance. While there will always be limitations to the breadth of the discipline—for example, there are only so many jobs at universities and think-tanks for professionals to pursue such questions as part of their occupations—the interest in global politics is widespread, and though this is certainly the most interdisciplinary of trades, many people engaged in other academic disciplines now realize that global politics is a vital component of self and collective identification, economic prosperity and marginalization, environmental management, and migratory pressures. In short, global politics cannot be ignored. It has become a tired cliché to suggest that for many North Americans September 11 brought world politics home, but it is certainly the case. Europeans, engaged in their ambitious and controversial project of political integration, are also forging new self-identities in the process. Protest movements around the globe, many in areas that we would never have heard of a few decades ago, are spawning fresh insights with their lessons learned, their strategies to seek solidarity elsewhere with other transnational actors. Diasporas continue their struggles in their adopted societies, spreading awareness of far-off conflicts. Globalization can be viewed as a point of contention and division, but even here we have seen that there is considerable overlap amongst proponents and opponents.

While all of this diversification and widespread interest is a positive thing for IR theory, we would also suggest that the traditional questions raised by IR theory are alive and well. There are reliable continuities in global politics, age-old debates to which, it would seem, we are destined to repeatedly return. This text has suggested that we live in a world characterized by two forces: convergence and divergence. The simplistic question is, which is the stronger? The answer, it seems, is neither: the two phenomena seem to exist side by side in the international system. We see convergence in the increasing interdependence between states; in the growth of IGOs and NGOs; in the awareness and action devoted to transnational issues such as the environment; and in the increase in contact, travel, and transactions between the peoples of the world. However, we see divergence in the continued conflict between states; in the disintegration of some states; in ethnic conflict; in the increasing gap between rich and poor; and in the split between the technological haves and have-nots. At this point, identifying a dominant trend is impossible, although it is clear that for some convergence is the reality in their lives, while for others divergence is the more powerful influence. In Canada, we are very privileged in many ways, but we are not immune from these forces. Even as globalization links us to the world of trade, travel, and telecommunications, it stimulates national debates about our economic future and our culture. The enduring national unity debate is a reminder that we are not immune from the forces of divergence. Nor are we immune from broader conflicts between the United States and its proclaimed enemies. Indeed, the question of American dominance in world affairs is necessarily of primary importance to all states today, but this is nothing new: states were often forced to make a choice of allegiance during the Cold War as well.

The central questions asked by IR theory will continue to frame the debate to come: Is it still reasonable to view the world from a state-centric perspective? Are theories of grand evolutionary changes valid when explaining history, and if so where do they suggest we are heading? What types of subconscious learning processes are at work in the perpetuation of conflict, domination, and resistance? Is the spread of liberal democracy of inherent value, not only in terms of human development and freedom, but also in terms of the promotion of peace? Or is this simply another face on an old process, the structural growth of capital accumulation, accompanied by cultural imperialism? Perhaps the most basic question remains: when will we stop killing each other? These, and many more, theoretical questions will remain salient to the people of this century.

A CHANGING DISTRIBUTION OF POWER?

In chapters 2 and 3 we observed that changes in what realists call the *distribution of power* are an eternal feature of global politics. Historically, the rise and decline of civilizations, societies, states, and empires is accompanied by shifts in the patterns of interaction between these actors. These shifts in patterns of interaction can take a number of forms: threat perceptions might change as some states increase in power and others decline; balances in power will be destabilized; new alliances may form and old ones will weaken or disintegrate; patterns of diplomacy and trade will reflect new markets and new centres of growth and innovation; and some political units will fragment (like the Austro-Hungarian Empire) and others will amalgamate (the 13 American colonies) or be absorbed (Bavaria). Because shifts in the distribution of power can so profoundly alter the shape of IR and the security and foreign policy strategies of states, trends in relative power distribution are watched very closely. Of course, there is considerable debate about the interpretation of trends, and whether they will in fact have the impact that some prognosticators suggest. For example, in the early 1960s there were predictions that 20 states would possess nuclear weapons by the 1970s: today, eight (perhaps nine) states actually have them. A further complication is that trends can be exaggerated for political purposes, to gain attention or a share of resources such as workers and money. For example, advocates of ballistic missile defence in the United States have been accused of exaggerating the ballistic missile threat to North America in order to secure substantial funding for a missile defence system.

As we look to the future through the interpretive lens of realism and political history, what trends may impact on global politics? Perhaps the most significant question is the future of China. China's economy has been growing swiftly for over two decades, rising in the international GNP rankings. Remarkably, many economists feel that China's economy can continue to grow at 7 percent or higher for at least several more years; some suggest that China could become the world's largest economy in the next 20 years. If a national economy is the basis of national power, then China's emergence could challenge the current power status quo in global politics. As a classical realist author, Hans Morgenthau, argued: "The policy of the status quo aims at the maintenance of the distribution of power as it exists at a particular moment in history." Any "reversal of power relations" will be opposed.[14] Does the projected rise of China threaten the international balance of power? An ongoing debate is raging between those who argue that China is a rising revisionist state that will seek to remake the international system in the future. Economic power is the basis of military power, and a stronger China will exert itself regionally and globally to protect and promote its interests. As Richard K. Betts argued: "Should we want China to get rich or not? For realists, the answer should be no, since a rich China would over-turn any balance of power."[15] However, other analysts dispute the notion that China represents this kind of threat. China's leadership is focused on internal development; China faces serious environmental, labour, social, and unity problems; and China has joined a large number of international institutions and become further integrated into the global trade regime by joining the WTO. As Alastair Iain Johnston concludes, "… it is not clear that describing China as a revisionist or non-status-quo state is accurate at this moment in history."[16] Nor is there any guarantee that China will in fact reach a position of global economic prominence. It is worth pointing out that some analysts predicted growing tension between the United States and the rising economy of Japan in the 1990s.[17] However, these concerns faded when it became clear that the Japanese economy could not challenge the U.S. economy for dominance. If China also falls short of challenging the United States as the world's preeminent economic power, then fears of a destabilizing global power shift may not be realized.

The rise of China is not the only point of debate that arises from trends in the distribution of power. Russia's economic and political situation continues to cause concern. The Russian economy has not performed well, hindered by insufficient economic reforms, the decay of infrastructure, an uncertain legal environment, and widespread corruption. The state of democratic governance in Russia is uncertain, raising the possibility that the country could slide into autocratic rule. Russia is also beset with a host of environmental and social problems. The result is a country that causes concern not because of its growing power, but because of its growing weakness. Japan may not be able to retain its status as the world's third largest economy. That distinction may fall to India, a growing power in a troubled region. However, India has significant challenges with respect to poverty, resource availability, and internal stability. It also faces a regional environment that features tensions with Pakistan, China, and the ongoing troubles of Sri Lanka and Central Asia. European countries are projected to experience moderate economic growth, and some speculate that the EU may become a counterbalance to the United States, as the economies of the expanding EU (which include Germany, the U.K., France, Italy, and Spain, among others) combined exceed the size of the American economy. The problem with this projection is the high level of disagreement and disunion on foreign and security policy matters within Europe itself. While France is likely to continue to seek opportunities to develop an independent European role in the world, its successes are likely to be few and far between. The other countries that ranked in the top 15 in GDP in 2003—Brazil, South Korea, Canada, and Mexico—are not expected to increase in power to the point that they become new entrants to the great power order. The power politics of the future are thus likely to be relatively stable, characterized by a dominant United States, a rising but cautious China, a declining Russia and Japan, a prosperous but still divided Europe, and rising regional powers such as India and Brazil.

However, there are potential impact events or discontinuities that could affect such predictions of stability. Serious political upheaval in the Middle East, including a wider war or revolution, could create a lethal mix of regional war and international intervention that could compromise global peace and security. Further terrorist attacks in the United States and around the world could precipitate international discord on fighting terrorism. A global pandemic of HIV/AIDS, or a virulent strain of influenza, SARS, or Avian Flu could cause a global health disaster with enormous social and economic consequences. A large state—such as Indonesia, Iran, Nigeria, or Pakistan, to name a few—could disintegrate, creating a widening zone of instability that would threaten regional economies and other countries. A dramatic growth in antiglobalization sentiment among peoples and state leaders could threaten the structures and institutions of the world economy, leading to a rise in protectionism and a decline in global trade. As we saw in chapters 2 and 3, unforeseen events from war to disease to stock market crashes have had a habit of shattering the prevailing political order of the time. However, whatever form or shape the international distribution of power may take in the future, and whether or not that future is a stable or unstable one, power politics are likely to endure in some way.

THE FUTURE OF THE AMERICAN EMPIRE

In Chapter 4, we explored the concept of hegemony, hegemonic decline, and the debate over the decline of U.S. power. In many ways, these issues are more salient today than ever before, and we can expect debates about the role of America in the world to be a persistent theme in global politics in the future because the implications of these debates are so enormous. A growing number of people of varying ideological persuasions now feel comfortable referring to the "American Empire" as a fact of our time. However, the fate of that empire will be decisive in determining the character of global politics. Are the days of American Empire numbered? For some, such as Barry Posen, the answer is no: "Unipolarity and U.S. hegemony will likely be around for some time," he argues.[18] However, this does not mean that the United States can sustain its position indefinitely. Posen argues that the United States can maintain its preeminence, but only if it maintains a disciplined approach to foreign policy. Others argue that the United States is in decline, and that the recent spate of international activities, from the "War on Terrorism" to the war in Iraq, has damaged U.S. power. Many would not view this as a bad thing, arguing that an American empire, while assuming the façade of stability provision, in fact causes significant cultural and political disruptions in the periphery, and that its insatiable appetite for expansion and resources breeds resentment and even counterhegemonic violence.

There is certainly inconclusive evidence of decline. First, the campaigns against Al-Qaeda, the wars in Afghanistan and Iraq, and the controversial security provisions mounted at home, are plunging the United States deeper into debt and damaging the long-term health of its economy. The United States is U.S.$3 trillion in debt, and it is adding to that debt at a fantastic rate, a result of very high levels of government spending (much of it on defence) and the tax cuts implemented by the G.W. Bush Administration. Obviously, there are only two ways to make up the difference between spending and revenues while avoiding high inflation rates, and that is through borrowing or raising taxes (a politically difficult task in the United States). However, at some point the debts will have to be paid, and budgets balanced. All the while, the money spent on defence and military adventure abroad is money not being invested in infrastructure upgrades, health care, education, and scientific innovation at home. Even though the U.S. economy is large and its private scientific and research base is enormous, the diversion of some government funds away from long-term economic development is worrisome to many U.S. commentators.

Second, American legitimacy and credibility have been weakened. This is significant; according to hegemonic stability theory, a hegemon's status and preeminence depends on some loyalty from willing followers. If a hegemon provides public goods and establishes norms and rules for the governance of the system, much of the power derived from such privilege rests on the willingness of most states to accept these norms and rules. This is in essence the test of legitimacy in global politics (one faced by international institutions and law as well). However, some commentators suggest that the invasion and occupation of Iraq has damaged this vital aspect of American power. For example, G. John Ikenberry has argued that

> It is hard to think of another instance in American diplomatic history where a strategic wrong turn has done so much damage to the country's international position—its prestige, credibility, security partnerships and goodwill of other countries—in so short a time, with so little to show for it. A single-minded American campaign against terrorism and rogue states in which countries are either 'with us or against us' and bullied into support is not leadership but a geostrategic wrecking ball that will destroy America's own half-century old international architecture.[19]

Even erstwhile defenders of American power and righteousness are concerned about the implications of the anti-American backlash on U.S. power. In particular, the divide between America and Europe is troubling for those who have long regarded the strategic and political partnership of America and Europe as a bulwark of global peace and stability. In his reflection on the transatlantic divide, Robert Kagan observed that "… it is precisely the question of legitimacy that divides Americans and Europeans today—not the legitimacy of each other's political institutions, perhaps, but the legitimacy of their respective visions of world order. More to the point, for the first time since World War II, a majority of Europeans has come to doubt the legitimacy of U.S. global leadership."[20] Others have been far more biting in their criticism of the Bush Administration, not out of anti-American spite or a rejection of America's core values, but because they feel those very values are being betrayed.[21] A similar public discourse emerged during the war in Vietnam in the 1970s, and given the hundreds of Americans killed in Iraq (over 850 soldiers by June 2004) some commentators are raising the spectre of Vietnam, in which some 60 000 Americans, and over 1 million North and South Vietnamese, perished.

Third, others have suggested that U.S. foreign policy has overemphasized hard power, at the expense of an underappreciated American resource: soft power. Joseph Nye is the leading proponent of this view. For Nye, "This soft power—getting others to want the outcomes you want—co-opts people rather than coerces them. Soft power rests on the ability to shape the preferences of others."[22] Nye goes on to argue that "winning the peace is harder than winning a war, and soft power is essential to winning the peace. Yet the way we went to war in Iraq proved to be as costly for our soft power as it was a stunning victory for our hard power."[23] In the future, will American governments be more aware of the relationship between power, economics, and legitimacy? Will they recognize the significance of soft power and the importance of balancing the use of the military instrument within a larger political and diplomatic context? Will they recognize the value of multilateral action, and the fact that the United States has been uniquely fortunate since the end of World War II to face an environment in which most of the great powers of the world are its allies?

Of course, it will take more than American initiative to restore its legitimacy among its allies and its soft power around the world. America's allies must be willing to accept U.S. leadership or, at least, compromise with it, rather than seek to obstruct it. However, this may not be the reaction of other key states. States could form a grand alliance to counterbalance the United States, an alliance that could involve Russia, China, India, and France. Alternatively, states could form or strengthen regional trade and political organizations to undermine or reduce the influence of global institutions such as the WTO and the IMF. Transatlantic relations between Europe and the United States could break down over trade and political and security issues. If this happens, U.S. power will have to exert itself in a less favourable international environment than it has in the past. On the other hand, it is likely that the United States and its allies will reach accommodations more often than not. Shared interests and shared values will bring America and other countries together in cooperative efforts that may rebuild trust and confidence (see Profile 13.1). As for U.S. decline, a note of caution is warranted. The decline of the Roman Empire is sometimes recorded as beginning with the end of

---

PROFILE 13.1 Canadian Security after September 11

In Canada, the attacks of September 11 created a new set of concerns surrounding an old problem. Successive Canadian governments have faced the challenge of how to engage in political, economic, and security cooperation with the United States while still maintaining Canadian sovereignty and foreign policy independence. Even prior to September 11, U.S. officials were looking with unease at the famously undefended Canada–U.S. border as a possible route for terrorists to enter the United States. After September 11, they began looking at border security with much greater concern, and sought policy changes by the Canadian government to strengthen controls over airport security, immigration, and border management.

The Canadian government was in a difficult position. On the one hand, there were legitimate security concerns shared by both countries that required increased security cooperation. On the other hand, initial talk in the United States of "harmonizing" national regulations and building a "perimeter" around the border of North America made many Canadians very nervous. Fearing unilateral U.S. action that could have damaged Canada's access to U.S. markets, the Canadian government did increase the resources spent on a variety of security measures and entered into a new border management agreement with the United States. The U.S. government also created the Office of Homeland Security (now the Department of Homeland Security), and established a new military command known as "Northern Command" responsible for North America. Canada's engagement and relationship with these new organizations is as yet uncertain, but they will continue to raise questions about Canada's relationship with the United States in a post–September 11 world. While there was very little vocal objection to Canada's participation in the war in Afghanistan (though a "friendly-fire" incident, in which several Canadians were killed by errant American bombing, threatened this), by the summer of 2002, with little opposition left in Afghanistan, many were beginning to question the necessity of continued troop presence there. More pronounced was Canadian official opposition to the invasion of Iraq in 2003. The Canadian debate that ensued ran along familiar lines, with one political party urging the Canadian government to commit troops to show solidarity with the United States (and to guarantee a role in participating in the spoils of war, rebuilding contracts) and others opposed because of a lack of Canadian national interest and/or an ethical stance against what was considered by many an unjust war. A major review of Canadian security concerns is now underway, but is unlikely to chart a new course away from Canada's most important political and economic partner.

the Antonine Emperors in 180 C.E. The Vandals sacked Rome 275 years later. Decline, it would seem, is a slow process.

FUTURE WARS BETWEEN CIVILIZATIONS?

In a famous and controversial article published in the influential journal *Foreign Affairs* in 1993, Harvard professor Samuel Huntington argued that the primary source of conflict in the future would not be ideology, economics, or nationalism. Rather, future wars would occur between the world's civilizations. As Huntington argued, "Nation states will remain the most powerful actors in world affairs, but the principal conflicts of global politics will occur between nations and groups of different civilizations. The clash of civilizations will dominate world politics. The fault lines between civilizations will be the battle lines of the future."[24] As we discussed in Chapter 2, conflict between civilizations was a fixture of human history before the development of the modern Westphalian state system. Huntington suggests that with the state (and state nationalism) eroding and the great ideological battles over, we are returning to an era characterized by conflict between civilizations. He defines a civilization in the following manner: "A civilization is a cultural entity. Villages, regions, ethnic groups, nationalities, religious groups, all have distinct cultures at different levels of cultural heterogeneity ... Arabs, Chinese, and Westerners, however, are not part of any broader cultural entity. They constitute civilizations. A civilization is thus the highest cultural grouping of people and the broadest level of cultural identity people have short of that which distinguishes humans from other species."[25] Huntington argues that there are eight major civilizations in the world: Western, Confucian, Japanese, Islamic, Hindu, Slavic-Orthodox, Latin American, and African. Many recent and current conflicts in the contemporary international system are taking place along these fault lines, in places such as the former Yugoslavia, Azerbaijan, Armenia and Georgia, the Horn of Africa, Russia and Chechnya, India and Pakistan, and India and China. Huntington predicts that the conflicts of the future will increasingly take place along the fault lines where these civilizations meet.

Huntington offers several explanations as to why inter-civilization disputes are growing and will become the basis for most future conflicts:

- Civilizations are more basic than the state, for our self-identities owe less to the state than to the civilization to which we belong. Civilizations are differentiated by history, religion, language, culture, and tradition. Differences among civilizations are, therefore, fundamental and very enduring. As a result, differences among civilizations have generated the longest and most violent conflicts and will do so increasingly in the future.

- Increasing global interdependence, interaction, and contact between peoples of different civilizations, rather than contributing to understanding and accommodation, is making more people aware of differences between them. Interdependence and globalization are contributing to civilization consciousness among the peoples of the world.

- Economic and social change around the world is altering the relationship between individuals and traditional social institutions. In particular, the state is in decline and religion is replacing it. The revival of religion around the world means a world increasingly united around the religious heritages of civilizations rather than the nationalist heritage of nation-states.

- The spread and power of Western civilization is provoking a counterreaction in other civilizations. Civilization consciousness is in part a reaction to the encroachment of Western culture and values on traditional belief systems. An anti-Western return to civilization roots is underway around the world, from Asianization in Japan to the Hinduization of India to the re-Islamization of the Middle East and the Russianization of Russia.

- Civilization differences are less subject to change or flexible adaptation. Negotiations, compromises, and resolution of disputes that have a civilizational aspect are more difficult to achieve.

- Economic patterns are assuming civilizational forms and shapes. The development of trade blocks (see Chapter 8) will add another element to the growing cohesion of civilizations and the divisions among them. Civilization links will become more important factors in the creation of economic zones of activity, with peoples of shared heritage more disposed toward doing business with each other than they are with peoples of other civilizations.

Ultimately, Huntington argues, civilization identity is becoming increasingly important as an influence on the perceptions of peoples around the world. This influence will create an "us versus them" mentality, which will drive inter-civilization differences on a whole range of international issues, from human rights, immigration, trade and commerce to the environment.

Huntington argues that the global spread of Western culture and power is already provoking a backlash against the West. The future may be one of "the West against the rest." This argument (as Huntington himself points out) is not an original one. Kishore Mahbubani has argued that the central axis of conflict in the world in the future will be between Western civilization and the non-Western civilizations of the world.[26] This conflict will take two forms: on the one hand there will be a struggle for military, economic, and institutional power. On the other hand, there will be a struggle over culture. The response of the non-Western world in this struggle will continue to be varied. Some non-Western states will adopt a policy of isolation, in effect sealing off their societies and economies from the West. Other states will join the West and adopt Western values and institutions, including democracy, law, and human rights. The difficulty with this course of action is that it involves the import of value systems that are very different from those shared by the majority (or a significant portion) of the population. This may create social and political unrest between those who want to westernize and those who want to protect the history and culture of the society. A final option is to acquire military and economic power to resist the West and to make common cause with other non-Western peoples in this effort. The reaction of the West will also be crucial. In the long term, Huntington argues that the West must recognize that the dominance of Western civilization around the world is ending and that other civilizations will begin to re-exert their place and influence on global politics. The West, along with all of the world's civilizations, will have to develop an increased understanding of the philosophical and religious differences between them. There will be no universal civilization but a world of civilizations.

Huntington's thesis has stirred considerable debate, and the attacks of September 11, 2001, and the subsequent "War on Terrorism" launched by the G.W. Bush Administration have added more fuel to the controversy surrounding the clash of civilizations thesis. The attacks and subsequent response have been cast as a civilization clash: the attacks were carried out by militant Islamic fundamentalists preaching hatred against the West in general and the United States in particular. Walter Laqueur argues that the motive of Islamic fundamentalist terrorism does not originate with poverty or repression, but the desire to destroy Western civilization.[27] Furthermore, the "War on Terrorism" has focused on Islamic and Arab peoples, with racial profiling now a serious problem. In addition, for the most part it was Western countries that launched the wars in Afghanistan and Iraq. Of course, the divisive rhetoric emerging from extremists on both sides of the dispute add fuel to this fire.

However, there are serious limitations to this thesis. Huntington's critics argue that the boundary between civilizations is far from distinct and that conflict within a civilization—that is, intra-civilization conflict—may be more common than clashes between civilizations. The future will thus be characterized as much by (for example) wars within the Muslim world and wars within the Christian world than wars between the Muslim and Christian civilizations. Others stress that states are a far more decisive force than Huntington suggests. Instead of civilizations motivating the actions of states, it is more accurate to say that states dominate civilizations and cultures. Huntington has also been criticized for overestimating the role played by culture in the world. Most peoples and governments are motivated not by cultural concerns but by concerns over economic growth. The world is characterized not by the triumph of religious and culturally oriented governments, but by the failure of such governments. The West remains a source of attraction for non-Western peoples, in particular the young, the poor, and the oppressed. Many people today would identity themselves with neither state nor culture, reflecting cosmopolitan values centred on universal concerns such as ecology or human rights. Huntington's thesis is based on such broad generalizations that it is often decried as poor social science, closer to rhetorical incitement than serious analysis. However, it remains a serious point of discussion in the debate about the origins of the wars of the future in general and the "War on Terrorism" in particular.

THE FUTURE OF HUMAN SECURITY AND HUMANITARIAN INTERVENTION

Our preceding discussion has focused on the international distribution of power, American empire, and the clash of civilizations, all themes underwritten by the threat of large-scale warfare. However, as we have seen in this text, most of the violent warfare of the latter half of the previous century occurred at the intrastate level, and much human suffering took place at the hand of the state. Outside the sporadic cases of "spontaneous communal violence,"[28] most instances of mass killing have been cases of "death by government."[29] We would have to visit the realm of fantasy to assume there will not be large-scale atrocities committed in the future. They are committed, arguably, on a daily basis. The question that faces IOs is whether, and when, and how, to intervene. We have examined many case studies throughout this text, giving rise to some key questions regarding humanitarian intervention. How do we draw the line between intervention for the sake of protecting human rights, and intervention that is a thinly veiled effort to assert state interests, such as geopolitical dominance in a certain region? How do we ensure that the impact of intervention does not create a worse situation for those we are attempting to aid?

One need not be a hard-core realist to accept the proposition that state policies will, by and large, reflect the self-perceived national interests of those who make key foreign policy decisions. Though this may change with time, interests are a vital component of international commitments, and we would be wrong to assert that we can expect states to contribute valuable resources and, more importantly, potential lives, to humanitarian missions if there was nothing at stake. This is why the problem of "selective intervention" will always be with us. Humanitarian interventions will tend to be mounted in contingencies where both interests and values are engaged. Interventions will be less likely to occur when interests are not engaged to the same extent. This explains why NATO intervened in Bosnia and Kosovo, but did not in Albania and Algeria. Some have suggested that this is why the UN needs its own army, an independent military force that could be called into action at the UN's request. Of course, even if such a UN army existed (and it is highly unlikely that it will in the near future) it would be called into action only under Chapter 7 of the UN Charter—in other words, when all of the permanent five members agreed it was either necessary or did not challenge their interests. Even in cases when humanitarian motives were a significant factor in a decision to use military force—such as the NATO air war against Serbia in 1999—interests were engaged, in particular the desire to prevent the conflict from re-igniting a wider war and a consensus that Slobodan Milosevic had to be removed from power. However, not everyone was convinced of the sincerity of the humanitarian motive: critics saw it as yet another expression of NATO power, and another effort to generate increased military spending in the United States and elsewhere.[30] In other cases, humanitarian rationales can be virtually absent: justifying the wars in Afghanistan and Iraq as humanitarian interventions requires a great stretch of the imagination. These wars were motivated by interests, and while humanitarian rationales may have been a small part of the motivation, or were used to obtain political support, it is highly unlikely either of these wars would have been mounted on humanitarian grounds alone.

And yet, there are cases where the humanitarian argument is certainly a strong one. In Somalia in 1992 a drought and a murderous war between clan factions precipitated starvation and human suffering on a large scale. As we saw in Chapter 7, states responded with a troubled and ultimately unsuccessful intervention that was primarily based on humanitarian impulses. However, in Rwanda, where chaos and genocidal violence created a bloody inferno, an intervention would certainly have been warranted. It would also have been warranted as a response to subsequent violence in the Democratic Republic of the Congo. And yet, as we have seen, no operation was mounted in either case. In the future, humanitarian interventions will

---

PROFILE 13.2 A Case for Humanitarian Intervention? The LRA

Unfortunately, there are all too many examples of large-scale atrocities being perpetrated today. The international community must struggle with the question of when to intervene, and how. Ten years after the Rwandan genocide, we are arguably no closer to consensus on this most delicate of issues. One case where a strong argument can be made concerns the Lord's Resistance Army (LRA), led by Joseph Kony, a self-proclaimed messiah who wants to establish his kingdom of God on earth. The LRA operates mostly in Northern Uganda, attacking from bases in Sudan; it has been alleged that the Sudanese government has aided it in the past. Uganda and Sudan had for years exchanged accusations of backing each other's rebels until they struck a deal in March 2002 allowing Ugandan forces to pursue the LRA into Sudan. Most notoriously, the LRA has abducted thousands of boys and girls and terrorized them into slavery as soldiers and concubines: more than 6000 were abducted in 1998 alone. More than 500 000 people have been displaced in Northern Uganda due to the fighting there between the LRA and government troops. The attacks on sleeping villages have involved slaughter and abduction on a large scale and are a constant source of fear and anxiety in towns such as Kitgum, where 48 people were hacked to death on July 25, 2002. The Ugandan army has failed in the last 16 years to either negotiate a peace or militarily subdue LRA: despite some success in early 2004, renewed massacres occurred in February.

While it is clear that the LRA is embedded in a complex civil war in Northern Uganda involving different ethnic groups, the central government, and perhaps still the Sudanese government in Khartoum, this complexity alone does not explain the inability to stop the LRA. One reason humanitarian intervention would be difficult is that the LRA is so enmeshed in the countryside. Another is that in order to stop them, killing hundreds of child soldiers might be inescapable. Yet, a well-trained and well-equipped force would be able to decisively eliminate Kony and his top aides if the international community gave this high priority. As always, the dangers and morals of intervention must be weighed against the dangers and morals of failing to intervene.

SOURCES: GLOBALSECURITY.ORG, http://www.globalsecurity.org/military/world/para/lra.htm (ACCESSED 30 MAY 2004); AND BBC NEWS, http://news.bbc.co.uk/1/hi/world/africa/2982818.stm (ACCESSED 30 MAY 2004).

be mounted, but they will not always be where and when they are needed (see Profile 13.2). The more likely model will be great power engagement, such as the United States in Colombia, or Russia in Georgia, where interests are engaged. The UN will then be called upon to clean up the mess or to take over when the dirty work of military action is over. Alternatively, postconflict security could be provided by private security companies, which are increasingly prominent actors in global politics (see Profile 13.3). There are, of course, notable exceptions to this, as our discussion of the recent liberation of East Timor indicated. More frequently, however, intervention reflects state leaders' perceptions of opportunity or opportunity costs. India's interventions in West Pakistan (now Bangladesh) and Sri Lanka, Tanzania's invasion of Uganda (overthrowing the notorious Idi Amin), the Vietnamese invasion of Cambodia (stopping the murderous Khmer Rouge regime), and Nigeria's engagement in West Africa are all examples of interventions in which local powers perceived interests as well as opportunities. Although it may be argued that all of these actions (most of which occurred outside the parameters of UN diplomacy) had positive effects, we cannot expect interests to be separated from the humanitarian intervention equation; interests will remain an important part of any decision to intervene or not to intervene in humanitarian crises. Further, the immensely complex and expensive process of nation building in postconflict contexts remains at best an experi-

PROFILE 13.3 The Return of the Mercenary?

Observers have noticed a strong trend in recent military and peacekeeping operations: the employment of private military companies (PMCs). While the mercenary is an age-old fixture in global politics, these were less organized and, incidentally, less profitable troops that would go and fight for the highest bidder, be it a king in medieval times or a government in a colonized state in the last century. The trend now is toward large corporations providing "security services," which can entail everything from armed guard protection to actual fighting forces; they are usually hired by governments to bolster regular troops. The terrible atrocities in Iraq perpetrated upon four such men in April 2004 demonstrated the danger involved in such an occupation. Others worry about the lack of accountability of these forces, which are not subject to the usual constraints imposed by the Geneva Conventions. For example, one firm operating in Bosnia was implicated in running a prostitution ring, yet there were no criminal proceedings. On the other hand, PMCs may be effective units in situations where governments and international organizations are simply unwilling to intervene and put a stop to civil clashes, or to seek and destroy rebel groups engaged in gross human rights violations (see Profile 13.2).

One thing is certain: this is now big business, with major firms from the U.K., United States, South Africa, and elsewhere engaged in hundreds of operations worldwide. In April 2004, the United States government advertised a contract, to be worth U.S.$100 million, to guard the so-called Green Zone in Baghdad. In all, it is estimated that there are more than 20 000 employees of PMCs in Iraq alone. Global Risk Strategies has 1500 private guards in Iraq; the Steele Foundation has 500. Erinys employs about 14 000 Iraqis. Another company, Special Operations Consulting-Security Management Group, "has recruited Iraqi informants who provide intelligence that helps the company assess threats." In other words, they are engaging in highly sensitive intelligence operations as well; the line between the private sector and the state sector is increasingly blurred in military operations. Meanwhile, none of this should surprise us, as there has been a shift toward privatized security for several decades: there are more private armed security guards in the United States or Africa than there are policemen, and, even more controversially, many prisons are run as for-profit enterprises.

SOURCE: M. BARSTOW, "SECURITY COMPANIES: SHADOW SOLDIERS IN IRAQ," *THE NEW YORK TIMES*, 19 APRIL 2004, A1.

mental process that can be seen as a cross between humanitarian assistance and cultural imposition; it can be no substitute for local institution-building and recovery.

Therefore, the need for conflict prevention through the pursuit of human rights—including minority rights and sustainable development—is paramount in the quest for a more humanitarian world. In other words, the best way to avoid the need for humanitarian intervention, and the debates that surround it, is to avoid the need to intervene in the first place. This is yet another "easier said than done" prospect, but one worth pursuing for the sake of those who have perished and those who might perish in the future.

GLOBALIZATION AND THE FUTURE OF THE WORLD ECONOMY

Our discussion of the global economy in chapters 4 and 8, and to some extent in Chapter 12, focused on several key themes. First, globalization is a contested concept, an ideologically charged magnet that attracts some while repelling others. The neoliberal agenda, represented in the formula of the Washington Consensus (see Chapter 8), suggests that the global freedom of capital and reduction of state intervention is essential to foster economic growth and the improvement of living standards worldwide. International financiers, MNCs, trade negotiators, lawyers, and media pundits are the intelligentsia of this movement. Keynsian or interventionist liberals are skeptical, arguing that markets require management and regulation if equitable distributions of wealth and social development are to be achieved. This may require a far more extensive level of political coordination than currently seems plausible. As George Soros has suggested: "To stabilize and regulate a truly global economy, we need some global system of political decision making. In short, we need a global society to support our global economy."[31] However, other scholars, such as Neo-Gramscian Stephen Gill, see the agents of the global economy representing an emerging system of global economic governance ("disciplinary neoliberalism") based on a quasi-constitutional framework for the reconstitution of the legal rights, prerogatives, and freedom of movement for capital on a world scale ("new constitutionalism").[32] Where Soros envisions benevolent political control over the invisible hand of the market, Gill envisions a system designed to promote the interests of capital first and foremost. This debate is unlikely to diminish in the future, for globalization will continue to engage the passions of a wide audience.

As our previous discussions of globalization have indicated, there is little new about the theme of economic and political expansion in world history, from ancient empires to Western colonization to contemporary markets. What is new is the scale of today's global marketplace, and the presence of actors with previously unimaginable influence, such as the communications industry (see Chapter 12). On the other hand, there is a greater awareness than ever that globalization has its winners and losers, and that the losers are not expected to complain along the way, but to conform to the imperatives of global capital and thus enter the cherished realm of the winners—at some point in the future. For Edward Luttwak, the ability of states to meet the challenges of privatization, deregulation, and globalization—what he referred to as "turbo-capitalism"—would determine their capacity to be winners in the new economy.[33] There are at least three viable directions from which we can see and expect more opposition to globalization in general and the harsh competitive implications of it in particular. There are those who feel their entire cultural identity is threatened by Westernization, and that nothing is more important than the defence of a way of life. Indeed, some would explain militant fundamentalism amongst the world's religions as evidence of this defensive reaction. There are those who are forcibly removed from their homelands, relocated because they are literally in the way of "progress." Like the millions dislocated before them by colonization, industrial revolution, Stalinism in the Soviet Union, and countless other examples, they will form solidarity groups and resist, perhaps resorting to violence. Finally, there are many who reject globalization, or globalization in its simplified, "predatory capitalism" version, on ethical grounds. They ask why the marketplace (dominated by those with structural advantages) should be accepted as the best determinant of values, norms, and social priorities, when we have so many other sources of legitimacy on which to draw.

One trend in particular animates both proponents and opponents of globalization, and will continue to be a central point of ideological divergence: the privatization of the commons and the deregulation of public control over private commercial and industrial activity. This represents the continuation of a trend that began when capitalism took over as the dominant mode of production in Europe and eventually spread around the world. The acceptance of a culturally significant definition of private property was in direct conflict with many social norms in Asia, Africa, North and South America, for most of the past millennium. The process of appropriation of the commons for the pursuit of private and corporate gain remains the defining feature of global capitalism; it permeates every area of life, from resources, land, water, and the provision of previously public services to less tangible aspects of modern life, such as intellectual property rights, gene patents, and even the right to pollute. Water, in particular, will be the focus of great debate, as neoliberals argue that privatization will lead to more efficiency, while critics charge that this amounts to an appropriation of what was once considered one of the most basic human rights: access to water as a precondition for survival.[34] The biopolitics of the future will involve furious debates, in both national and multilateral forums, about the intersection between the ethics of genetic manipulation and the profit factor in their development and dissemination. And we are even seeing the privatization of security provision, not just in terms of the outsourcing of military operations to private firms, but the profit-based development of new prisons in the United States and elsewhere.

The debate over development will continue as well. Most scholars and activists engaged in the development issues of our time have largely forsaken "modernization" theory as a form of cultural imperialism, and dismissed the once-hegemonic belief that large-scale infrastructure development (dams, pipelines, highways, railroads) was the precondition for economic and political development. However, this model of development remains popular with donor states and most recipient states. This is due to a persistent belief in some circles that modernization through infrastructure development is the best path to development, and because this model of development creates opportunities for donor state corporations to secure large contracts with developing countries. Many recipient states also pursue the industrial and infrastructure model of development because industrialization is seen as synonymous with growth and economic power. Neo-Marxists would remind us of another explanation: elites in developing countries are looking after their interests above all else, and large industrial and infrastructure projects promise wealth and power for those that control them. It is likely that the infrastructure model of development will persist, and it would be inaccurate to dismiss it entirely: a very real problem in many developing countries is a lack of serviceable infrastructure. However, in the future we can expect development projects to take more of a local and community-based focus. This will place a greater emphasis on environmental sustainability, women in development, and micro-credit arrangements consisting of small loans to individuals to start their own businesses.[35] Nevertheless, we will still witness a cultural divide between those societies that have largely accepted privatization and capitalism as the dominant mode of development, and those that either reject this model or are determined to fashion it in their own way. The latter approach (local adaptation and development) would seem to hold the most promise. Ultimately, the stark dichotomy between market and socialized life is a false one. Societies around the world have thrived on marketplace interactions, and even the most industrialized states maintain the provision of certain public goods. The broader question is, what type of synthesis between public and private property rights will emerge in the long term? The answer can be determined only by the continued interaction of various societies and participants in this great debate.

Finally, the future of the global economy itself is in question. The stalled Doha Round of the WTO talks (revived in the summer of 2004), the persistence of trade disputes, and the rising tide of opposition to economic integration in most parts of the world raise doubts as to whether increased progress on world trade liberalization is possible. Has globalization, economic interdependence, the implementation of liberal economic principles in the structure of the world economy and the institutions that govern it reached the pinnacle of what is politically possible? For most liberal observers of International Political Economy (IPE), protectionism is likely to be the key issue in the management of the world economy in the future. The concern is that rising protectionist sentiment in governments and populations around the world will precipitate a new era of protectionism, reducing trade levels, stifling the international flow of capital, and leading to a world economic downturn that will lead to greater economic hardship for people around the world. Faced with the inability to make progress in the WTO, states will turn instead to regional multilateral agreements to secure markets and access to resources, or to networks of bilateral trade agreements with select partners. The result will be an increasingly fragmented world economy, with little or no capacity for the global governance Soros and many others suggest is necessary if the global economy is to be managed effectively. For liberals, the fragmentation of world economic patterns and the rise in protectionism will lead to a world that is less prosperous, less respectful of individual liberties, and less peaceful in the future.

HUMAN RIGHTS AND INTERNATIONAL LAW

We have yet to establish an international human rights order. Some would argue that this is long overdue, while others would claim that this may not be a bad thing, for any truly universal order could reflect only a process of assimilation or coercion. What is more disturbing, of course, is the unseemly level of hypocrisy that is evident in the realm of human rights: the grand pronouncements of state representatives seem to fall easily to the floor as abuses continue on a daily basis. Whether it is the treatment of indigenous peoples in Canada and Australia, the incarceration without due process of thousands of Muslim men after September 11 in the United States, the denial of the right to education to women in many states, the passive acceptance of the international trade in human beings, or hundreds of other controversial practices, no region is immune from questions about the impact of domestic and foreign policy on human rights, both in peacetime and in wartime.

Further, for all the lofty talk about the primacy of international law, the need to establish some sort of universal set of guidelines for the interaction between states, and the need to promote adherence to the founding principles of the United Nations, a world governed by law remains a hope, not a reality. While many states obey most international laws at least some of the time, they break those laws when it is in their interests to do so. Imagine, for example, telling a police officer that you were speeding down the highway because you had decided that following the law was not in your best interests that day! Imagine that most drivers on the road that day felt the same way and drove accordingly! There is no global culture of implicit acceptance of international law as the arbiter in disputes, and of course there is no police officer to enforce the law. Yet a world governed by law would promise much. For example, the American response to September 11 has been a heavily militarized one. While it quickly became apparent that the United States would interpret the attacks as an assault not only on America but also on the free world and civilization itself, others such as Mary Robinson, then the UN High Commissioner for Human Rights, suggested that it would be better to view the September 11 attacks as a crime against humanity. This would encourage a response to terrorism based not on statist reflexes and outright military power, but on a more liberal international effort to establish the rule of international law, strengthen the UN, coordinate law enforcement and intelligence-gathering institutions, increase financial regulation, use international courts, and lower the disparity between rich and poor. The turn to an excessively militarized strategy in the "War on Terrorism" may be viewed as a significant lost opportunity to strengthen international stability and order.[36] Whether or not this would have been politically palatable in the United States is, however, another matter.

Yet we have seen several developments that might well give rise to a new stage in the evolution of human rights and humanitarian law. South Africa's Truth and Reconciliation Commission represents a bold, if troubled, effort to permit a traumatized society to come to terms with its past. The establishment of the International Criminal Court, based loosely on the ad hoc tribunals for the former Yugoslavia and Rwanda, puts unprecedented emphasis on the accountability of individuals under international criminal law; the next few years should demonstrate whether the international community will take this court seriously. Given the historical record, it is likely that the court will be used only to prosecute individuals who have committed crimes against humanity in peripheral states, members of defeated military regimes, and the like. But the potential is there for a much more robust and lasting effort to take such criminals to task, including such often ignored crimes as rape as an instrument of war, ethnic cleansing, and genocide. Various ad hoc courts in places such as Sierra Leone, Cambodia, and Iraq, beset with their own unique difficulties, will further contribute to ending the culture of impunity.

For international law, the prospects are as exciting as they are daunting. Globalization is accompanied by the legal property rights regime that reflects Western institutions and corporate law, so there will no doubt be great opportunities for private international lawyers. International public law is also attracting increasing numbers of bright and ambitious students. The International Court of Justice will be used for its dual purpose: to hear cases based on disputes between states, in its role as arbitrator, and to pass judgment on questions of advisory opinion, such as the construction of the so-called security fence by Israel. These judgments do not, surely, change the behaviour of states, but they do focus attention on the issues, and suggest that the real role for international law is not as an ordering device with definitive powers, but as an instrument of legitimacy and moral suasion with limited but real influence in global politics.[37]

HUMAN HEALTH, THE ENVIRONMENT, AND MULTILATERALISM

Chapters 8 and 10 both indicated that we have some major choices ahead of us regarding the future health of the planet. Our dependence on fossil fuels for energy is affecting the climate, contributing to conflict, and limiting the options for future generations. The immense byproduct of industrialization and urban concentration, the sheer waste involved in the productive and consumptive processes of this era, is difficult to fathom. The oceans and their resources are threatened by overfishing and pollution, freshwater is becoming increasingly precious, and agriculturally viable land is decreasing. The use of chemicals in agriculture do as much harm as good and further marginalize traditional farmers while economies dependent on mono-cropping (raising very few crops for export) risk the prospect of falling prices and the long-term impact of land erosion. Deforestation is a consequence of population pressure, and expanding agricultural, forestry, and mining industries, but at a cost to biodiversity and the livelihood and rights of indigenous peoples and other local populations.

In short, the price tag of globalization (if we may simplify that term to an admittedly absurd level), is not only enormous, it is unevenly shared. The need for multilateral coordination to cope with these consequences is obvious. All liberals, and even many realists, would agree. However, critical theorists remind us that the very multilateral institutions being constructed to "manage" such issues are products of the very states that have encouraged this type of development for many decades. Thus they argue transnational solidarity with those most affected is also necessary. And we can expect the marginalized and disadvantaged to join in alliances in order to fight what they perceive as their unjust treatment by the international community (see Profile 13.4). Despite the seemingly insurmountable obstacles to change, there is hope for the future. More and more people are becoming aware of the environment; environmentally friendly practices, products, and industries are gaining in size and popularity; and most societies and traditions have some sort of stewardship principle, which suggests present generations have an ethical obligation to look ahead and consider the impact of their actions on the yet unborn. Taken together, this may manifest itself in a slow but steady movement toward the adoption of more sustainable practices and the increased universality of concepts such as the precautionary principle discussed in the conclusion of Chapter 10.

Beyond the ecological harm caused by industrialization, militarization, agribusiness, and consumption, there are many threats to human health related to the human population itself. Though the worst predictions of a "population bomb" expected a few decades ago have not come to pass, we are nonetheless living in a world with over 6 billion people, and the figure continues to rise, adding to migratory pressures and the negative aspects of mass, rapid urbanization. It is a falsehood, however, to blame these problems on population growth itself as a variable, since human behaviour is at the core of the aggregate impact of human populations. Again, there is a need for multilateral assistance, market access, and freedom from repression and corruption in order to improve the conditions of life for the millions of undernourished and marginalized people. However, the preference of most developed states is the often-criticized Washington Consensus approach outlined in Chapter 8.

We can foresee an even larger role for the informal sector, in the future as people are forced to rely less on the state and legal economic activity and more on their own survival strategies within a context of human insecurity. We can also foresee increased tensions within many countries in both the developing and developed worlds over the privatization and deregulation of everything from public space to water rights to health care. States intent on pursuing this course will face growing opposition and increasingly fractious domestic politics, while others will resort to oppressive measures, which will in turn threaten their own fragile legitimacy. And yet, this scenario too can be avoided if governments and international institutions turn away from an ideological fixation on market liberalization and boundless privatization toward a more balanced approach. There are signs this may already be happening: the Washington Consensus formula itself is under revision, and the IMF and the World Bank, among others, are increasingly cognizant of the social and environmental impact of economic policies. Perhaps the future will be characterized by a new consensus on achieving a harmony between the market and social and environmental sustainability. Critical theorists would contend that part of the problem has been the tendency to resort to blueprints, ready-made models that are supposed to apply everywhere, regardless of circumstances. This needs to change, not only because of large differences in culture, history, structural power, and other variables, but also because development and environmental management and population issues are not static, but are fluid: priorities often change over even short periods of time.

PROFILE 13.4 The Alliance of Small Island States

If trends in global warming continue, sea levels will rise (because water expands while heated, though the melting of the polar ice caps will make a smaller contribution as well). While this poses a serious threat to many heavily populated coastal areas, for some states the threat is even greater: they could be submerged entirely by rising ocean levels. Well aware of this, 43 small island states— 20 percent of the UN's total membership, and 5 percent of the world's population—have formed a coalition to achieve a greater collective voice in the struggle against global warming. The group has not established a formal charter, budget, or secretariat, and the available resources for this coopera-tive effort are strikingly limited. Yet in this fight for survival, links have been forged between people living in such diverse regions as the African coast, the Caribbean, the Indian and Pacific oceans, the Mediterranean, and the South China Sea. The coalition's current chairman is Ambassador (to the UN) Jagdish Koonjul of Mauritius. In the long term, however, these islanders must also face the very real possibility that they may have to evacuate their beloved homes, and this is so because of industrial activity that took place with very little if any benefit to them.

MEMBERS OF THE AOSIS

Antigua and Barbuda	Niue
Bahamas	Palau
Barbados	Papua New Guinea
Belize	Samoa
Cape Verde	São Tomé and Príncipe
Comoros	Seychelles
Cook Islands	Singapore
Cuba	Solomon Islands
Cyprus	St. Kitts and Nevis
Dominica	St. Lucia
Federated States of Micronesia	St. Vincent and the Grenadines
Fiji	Suriname
Grenada	Tonga
Guinea-Bissau	Trinidad and Tobago
Guyana	Tuvalu
Haiti	Vanuatu
Jamaica	
Kiribati	**OBSERVERS**
Maldives	American Samoa
Malta	Netherlands Antilles
Marshall Islands	Guam
Mauritius	U.S. Virgin Islands
Nauru	

SOURCE: AOSIS MEMBERS AND OBSERVERS, SMALL ISALAND DEVELOPING STATES NETWORK, http://www.sidsnet.org/aosis/members.html (ACCESSED 30 MAY 2004).

One of the more visible elements of fluidity is the fact that, as we have seen, people are on the move in our world. They are seeking employment, fleeing terror, searching for better con-ditions of life. There are no easy solutions to the problems this causes, no easy culprits to blame. While refugee crises are common events today, and borders are being tightened after September 11, we cannot afford to overlook the even larger issues of internally displaced peo-ples, refugee camps that have become permanent holding grounds, and the gender violence that so often accompanies destitution and homelessness. Institutions such as the UNHCR and International Committee of the Red Cross remain extremely underfunded, and their workers are often put in precarious situations. In short, the helpers need help. Those who advocate a fortress mentality in today's global economy may succeed in creating xenophobia and distrust, but they cannot seriously argue the garrison approach is a realistic option in the long run. For a time, it may serve the interests of national elites and frightened populations who are fairly well insulated by their wealth, security forces, and ideological convictions. But what good is life—even a good life—lived behind fences and military forces when anxiety is building, threats are encroaching, and short-sighted blindness to empathy and compassion has made a world of enemies?

Another threat to human security that has made numerous appearances in this text is the modern pandemic. HIV/AIDS has killed an estimated 20 million people in the last three decades. As is the case with the uncountable deaths the world has witnessed due to malnutrition and easily preventable diseases, many HIV/AIDS victims in the poor parts of the world will die young because the medical services required to help them are absent or in short supply. This is indisputably harming the prospects of future generations as well. In 1999, for example, some 860 000 sub-Saharan African primary school children lost their teachers to AIDS.[38] While there has been some progress made toward achieving the Millennium goals outlined in Chapter 8, there is an urgent need to accelerate such action, and once again the costs of delay are as debilitating as they are heart-wrenching. All the wireless networks we create, and renewable energy advances we pursue, and peace negotiations we conduct, will be in vain if the international community does not address these fundamental threats to human security. Every year billions of dollars are spent on military production, on combating the epidemic of obesity in high-income states, and on the production of goods and services that are simply not needed. Can the will and a way be found to devote the mere fraction of these resources that would be necessary to mitigate the intolerable harm done by disease and marginalization around the world?

The population of the planet will continue to increase. However, population growth rates have slowed in many areas, in some cases due to tragic circumstances, but in most due to active family-planning measures and changing perspectives on the utility and challenges of having several children. But we will face new demographic challenges in the future. In areas devastated with pandemics, especially in the HIV/AIDS context, states will have to cope with an unprecedented number of orphans and single-parent families. Areas affected with rampant violence will struggle with accompanying physical and psychological health problems, as well as the legacy of environmental destruction, land mines, and the need to overcome the past. And another health crisis is quickly looming: the economic impact of aging populations in both high-income Western states and many poorer non-Western states. This "greying" of society will have a profound impact on the workforce, perhaps stimulating relaxed migration policies and redefinitions of health itself.[39]

CONCLUSION: ON THE THEME OF INEVITABILITY

Many of the topics we have covered in this book elicit despair. As we warned in the introduction, the complexity of global politics is overwhelming, and the challenges seem insurmountable. Global structures and processes are driven by forces beyond our individual control. Much of the ideological fixations of the past and present, from the recourse to violent conflict throughout history to the tide of globalization, seem as inevitable as changes in the weather. Yet change is the result of human actions, decisions, nondecisions, fear, courage, and other inherently intangible factors. We are all actors on the global stage, and we cannot absent ourselves from the judgments of history; in this light, we all have an obligation to be as informed as possible.

This would, we think, include the need to reflect upon history itself. To even attempt to understand the global politics of the present and future, we need a firm grounding in the past. This grounding will of necessity be formed within our own perspectives on the world, shaped by our experiences and what we have learned through socialization and intellectual inquiry. Yet sensitivity to the past is vital. For example, the word *crusade* has a strong connotation for many people because it evokes an era when Christian forces strove to force their world-view on others, including Muslims and Jews. George W. Bush's initial use of the term after September 11 was quickly rescinded, but it spoke volumes about the general historical ignorance that threatens to make the "clash of civilizations" thesis become an all-consuming reality. This does not in any way justify the use of terrorism, but implies that responses to terrorism, and all of the challenges we will face in the future, need to be cautious and grounded in a sound knowledge and sensitivity to the contemporary implications of history.

The changing nature of global politics suggests that the nature of the global economy, the future of the state, environmental degradation, and the widening gulf between rich and poor countries and peoples may produce tensions that could lead to increased interstate and intrastate violence and war in the 21st century. Increasing our understanding of these dynamic and interrelated factors, and thus our ability to prevent episodic violent conflict, remains the principal task of students of IR today. We have suggested further, however, that threats to planetary and human security are just as important in this day and age, and that the extreme divisions between the wealthy and the marginalized are themselves a source of instability. Further, while there are strengths and weaknesses to all the theoretical perspectives introduced in this text, new and exciting syntheses are emerging, and the normative questions about the ethical implications of our actions are as important as (indeed, they are inseparable from) the analytical models and theorems designed to enhance our explanatory prowess.

It is our hope that this textbook has provided you with a foundation for understanding the world in which we live, and that your interest in global politics will not end here. This is only the beginning of a lifelong attentiveness to the challenges we will all face in the future. Again, it is tempting to look back at the collective experience of global politics and sigh, resigned to the depressing state of human relations and the immense problems involved in achieving international cooperation on the vital issues we face today and will face tomorrow. Yet our perspective must change in spite of (and indeed because of) what appears to be the increasing parochialism of humanity. Given the continuing threats we collectively face—from poverty to terrorism, from war to planetary environmental degradation—it is clear that decision makers and citizens alike must think as globally as possible. The construction of the international equivalent of gated communities, built on ultimately unsustainable foundations, is no long-term answer. States and peoples cannot deal with the increasingly transnational global agenda in a unilateral or isolationist fashion. Our very survival will depend on our capacity for cooperation. States with extensive multilateral ties, such as Canada, have a vital role to play. But more to the point, we all do. The first step toward solving such problems is learning about them, and we hope this text has provided a challenging introduction to, as well as encouraged further exploration of, the complex world of global politics.

Endnotes

1. *Science and the Modern World* (New York: New American Library, 1953), 208.
2. "The Concept of International Law," in M. Byers, ed., *The Role of Law in International Politics* (Oxford: Oxford University Press, 2001), 69–89, 70.
3. Speech to a Joint Session of Congress, Washington, DC, 20 September 2001.

4. See the excellent introduction by Michael Cox to the most recent edition of Carr's classic, *The Twenty Years' Crisis 1919 to 1939: An Introduction to the Study of International Relations* (London: Palgrave, 2001); and M. Cox, ed., *E.H. Carr: A Critical Reappraisal* (London: Palgrave Macmillan, 2000); and R. Falk, "The Critical Realist Tradition and the Demystification of Power," in S. Gill and J. Mittleman, eds., *Innovation and Transformation in International Studies* (Cambridge, UK: Cambridge University Press, 1997).

5. See C. Escude, *Foreign Policy Theory in Menem's Argentina* (Gainesville: University of Florida Press, 1997).

6. See J. Ann Tickner, "Identity in International Relations Theory: Feminist Perspectives," in Y. Lapid and F. Kratochwil, eds., *The Return of Culture and Identity in IR Theory* (Boulder, CO: Lynne Rienner, 1997), 147–62; and C. Enloe, *The Morning After: Sexual Politics at the End of the Cold War* (Berkeley: California University Press, 1993).

7. See O. Young, "Rights, Rules, and Resources in World Affairs," in same, ed., *Global Governance: Drawing Insights from the Environmental Experience* (Cambridge, MA: MIT Press, 1997), 1–23; and A. Hasenclever, P. Mayer, and V. Rittbeuger, "Integrating Theories of International Regimes," *Review of International Studies*, 26, no. 1 (2000), 3–33.

8. See D. Deudney, "Bringing Nature Back In: Geopolitical Theory from the Greeks to the Global Era," in D. Deudney and R. Matthew, eds., *Contested Grounds: Security and Conflict in the New Environmental Politics* (Albany: SUNY Press, 1999), 25–57. See also E. Laferrière and P. Stoett, *IR Theory and Ecological Thought: Toward a Synthesis* (London: Routledge, 1999).

9. See A. Jokic, ed., *Humanitarian Intervention: Moral and Philosophical Issues* (Toronto: Broadview Press, 2003).

10. This is not to argue, however, that the familiar trichotomy is not inherently useful, or cannot be used to great effect. See, for example, M. Doyle, *Ways of War and Peace: Realism, Liberalism, and Socialism* (New York: W.W. Norton, 1997).

11. This explanation is offered by Steve Smith, "Reflectivist and Constructivist Approaches to International Theory," in Steve Smith and J. Baylis, eds., *The Globalization of World Politics: An Introduction to International Relations*, 2nd ed. (Oxford: Oxford University Press, 2001), 224–49.

12. C. Brown, *International Relations Theory: New Normative Approaches* (Hemel Hempstead: Harvester Wheatsheaf, 1992), 3–4. For an example of normative analysis see R. Irwin, ed., *Ethics and Security in Canadian Foreign Policy* (Vancouver: UBC Press, 2001). Environmental issues have raised the further question of intergenerational ethics: see E.B. Weiss, "Intergenerational Equity: Toward an International Legal Framework," in N. Choucri, ed., *Global Accord: Environmental Challenges and International Responses* (Cambridge, MA: MIT Press, 1993).

13. This is also important for understanding the past and could be a key contribution of the constructivist approach. As N. Inayatullah and D. Blaney write, a "commitment to a constructivist IR theory requires ... a comparative and historical analysis of how cultures conceptualise others." "Knowing Encounters: Beyond Parochialism in IR Theory," in Y. Lapid and F. Kratochwil, eds., *The Return of Culture and Identity in IR Theory* (Boulder, CO: Lynne Rienner, 1997), 65–84, 82.

14. H. J. Morgenthau, *Politics Among Nations: The Struggle for Power and Peace*, 5th ed. (New York: Alfred A. Knopf, 1978), 46.

15. R.K. Betts, "Wealth, Power, and Instability: East Asia and the United States after the Cold War," *International Security* 18 (Winter 1993/94), 55.

16. A. I. Johnston, "Is China a Status Quo Power?," *International Security* 27 (Spring 2003), 6.

17. G. Friedman and M. Lebard, *The Coming War with Japan* (New York: St. Martin's Press, 1991).

18. B. Posen, "Command of the Commons: The Military Foundations of U.S. Hegemony," *International Security* 28 (Summer 2003), 6.

19. G. John Ikenberry, "The End of the Neo-Conservative Moment," *Survival* 46 (Spring 2004), 7. Note that this was written before the prisoner abuse scandal emerged from Bahgdad, which seriously undermined any claim to ethical superiority.

20. Robert Kagan, "America's Crisis of Legitimacy," *Foreign Affairs* 83 (March/April 2004), 65.

21. George Soros, *The Bubble of American Supremacy: Correcting the Misuse of American Power* (New York: Public Affairs, 2004).

22. Joseph S. Nye Jr., *Soft Power: The Means to Success in World Politics* (New York: Public Affairs, 2004), 5.

23. Ibid., xii.

24. Samuel P. Huntington, "The Clash of Civilizations?" *Foreign Affairs* 72, no. 3 (Summer 1993), 22.

25. Ibid., 23–24.

26. Kishore Mahbubani, "The West and the Rest," *The National Interest* (Summer 1992), 3–13.

27. Walter Laqueur, *No End to War: Terrorism in the Twenty-First Century* (New York: Continuum, 2003).

28. K. Holsti, "From Khartoum to Quebec: Internationalism and Nationalism Within the Multi-Community State," in K. Goldmann, U. Hannerz, and C. Westin, eds., *Nationalism and Internationalism in the Post-Cold War Era* (London: Routledge), 143–69, 169.

29. R. Rummel, *Death by Government* (New Brunswick, NJ: Transaction Books, 1994).

30. For a controversial treatment see Diana Johnstone, *Fool's Crusade: Yugoslavia, NATO and Western Delusions* (New York: Monthly Review Press, 2002).

31. G. Soros, *The Crisis of Global Capitalism: Open Society Endangered* (New York: Public Affairs, 1998), xxix.

32. S. Gill, "New Constitutionalism, Democratisation and Global Political Economy," in *Pacifica Review* 10, no. 1 (1998).

33. E. Luttwak, *Turbo-Capitalism: Winners and Losers in the Global Economy* (New York: HarperCollins, 1999); see also his "Power Relations in the New Economy," *Survival* 44 (Summer 2002), 7–17.

34. See in particular M. de Villiers, *Water* (Toronto: Stoddart, 2000); and M. Barlow and T. Clarke, *Blue Gold: The Battle against Corporate Theft of the World's Water* (Toronto: Stoddart, 2002), from whom we steal this lovely quote by Michael Parfit (p. xi): "Watersheds come in families; nested levels of intimacy. On the grandest scale the hydrologic web is like all humanity—Serbs, Russians, Koyukon Indians, Amish, the billion lives in the People's Republic of China—it's broadly troubled, but it's hard to know how to help. As you work upstream toward home, you're more closely related. The big river is like your nation, a little out of hand. The lake is your cousin. The creek is your sister. The pond is her child. And, for better or worse, in sickness and in health, you're married to your kitchen sink."

35. See H. Weber, *The Politics of Microcredit: Global Governance and Poverty Reduction* (London: Pluto, 2001).

36. See D. Archibugi and I. Young, "Envisioning A Global Rule of Law," in J. Sterba, ed., *Terrorism and International Justice* (Oxford: Oxford University Press, 2003), 158–70.

37. For a collection of sophisticated discussions on international law, see M. Byers, ed., *The Role of Law in International Politics* (Oxford: Oxford University Press, 2001).

38. M. Carballo, J. Cilloniz, and S. Braunschweig, "HIV/AIDS and Security," International Centre for Migration and Health Report (Geneva, 2002).

39. See S. Raymond, "Foreign Assistance in an Aging World," *Foreign Affairs* (March/April 2003), 91–105.

Suggested Readings

Achcar, G. *The Clash of Barbarisms: September 11 and the Making of the New World Disorder.* New York: Monthly Review Press, 2004.

Barnett, M. "What is the Future of Humanitarianism?" *Global Governance* 9, no. 3 (2003), 179–98.

Betts, R., ed. *Conflict After the Cold War: Arguments on Causes of War and Peace,* 2nd ed. New York: Longman, 2002.

Behnke, A. "Ten Years After: The State of the Art of Regime Theory." *Cooperation and Conflict* 30, no. 2 (1995), 179–97.

Brysk, A., ed. *Globalization and Human Rights.* Berkeley: University of California Press, 2002.

Campbell, D. *National Deconstruction: Violence, Identity and Justice in Bosnia.* Minneapolis: University of Minnesota Press, 1998.

Chomsky, N. *9-11.* New York: Seven Stories Press, 2001.

Cilliers, J., and P. Mason, eds. *Peace, Profit or Plunder? The Privatisation of Security in War-Torn African Societies.* Pretoria: Institute for Security Studies, Pretoria, 1999.

Cooper, A., J. English, and R. Thakur. *Enhancing Global Governance: Towards a New Diplomacy?* Tokyo: United Nations University, 2002.

Cox, R. and T. Sinclair. *Approaches to World Order.* New York: Cambridge University Press, 1996.

Dewitt, D., D. Haglund, and J. Kirton, eds. *Building a New Global Order: Emerging Trends in International Security.* Toronto: Oxford University Press, 1993.

Doyle, M. *Ways of War and Peace: Realism, Liberalism, Socialism.* New York: Norton, 1997.

Falk, R., S. Kim, and S. Mendlovitz, eds. *The United Nations and a Just World Order.* Boulder, CO: Westview, 1991.

Frost, M. *Ethics in International Relations: A Constitutive Theory.* Cambridge, UK: Cambridge University Press, 1996.

Fry, G., and J. O'Hagen, eds. *Contending Images of World Politics.* Basingstoke: Macmillan, 2000.

Gordon, N., and B. Wood. "Canada and the Reshaping of the United Nations." *International Journal* 47 (1992), 479–503.

Hastedt, G., ed. *One World, Many Voices: Global Perspectives on Political Issues.* Englewood Cliffs, NJ: Prentice Hall, 1991.

Harding, J. *After Iraq: War, Imperlialism and Democracy.* Black Point, Nova Scotia: Fernwood, 2004.

Henkin, A., ed. *Honouring Human Rights: From Peace to Justice.* Washington, DC: Aspen Institute, 1998.

Hobson, J.M. *The State and International Relations.* Cambridge, UK: Cambridge University Press, 2000.

Holzgrefe, J., and R. Keohane, eds. *Humanitarian Intervention: Ethical, Legal, and Political Dilemmas.* Cambridge, UK: Cambridge University Press, 2003.

Jones, R. *Critical Theory and World Politics.* Boulder, CO: Lynne Rienner, 2000.

Kaldor, Mary. *New and Old Wars: Organized Violence in a Global Era.* Stanford, CA: Stanford University Press, 1999.

Keck, M., and K. Sikkink, *Activists beyond Borders: Transnational Advocacy Networks in International Politics.* Ithaca: Cornell University Press, 1998.

Mahajan, R. *The New Crusade: America's War on Terrorism.* New York: Monthly Review Press, 2002.

Modelski, George. "Is World Politics Evolutionary Learning?" *International Organization* (Winter 1990), 1–24.

Newman, E. "Humanitarian Intervention: Legality and Legitimacy." *The International Journal of Human Rights* 6, no. 4 (2002), 108–30.

Nossal, Kim Richard. *The Politics of Canadian Foreign Policy.* 3rd ed. Scarborough, ON: Prentice Hall, 1997.

Ougaard, M., and R. Higgot, eds. *The Global Polity.* London: Routledge, 2001.

Pettman, J. *Worlding Women: A Feminist International Politics.* St. Leonards, Australia: Allen and Unwin, 1996.

Ritter, S. *Endgame.* New York: Simon and Schuster, 1999.

Roberts, A. "A New Age in International Relations?" *International Affairs* 67 (July 1991), 506–25.

Rochester, J.M. *Waiting for the Millennium: The United Nations and the Future of the World Order.* Columbia, SC: University of South Carolina Press, 1993.

Scholte, J. *Globalization: A Critical Introduction.* Basingstoke: Macmillan, 2000.

Singer, P. *One World: The Ethics of Globalization.* New Haven: Yale University Press, 2002.

Smith, S., K. Booth, and M. Zalewski, eds. *International Theory: Positivism and Beyond.* Cambridge, UK: Cambridge University Press, 1996.

Sterba, J. *Terrorism and International Justice.* Oxford: Oxford University Press, 2003.

Toffler, A. *Power Shift: Knowledge, Wealth, and Violence at the Edge of the 21st Century.* Toronto: Bantam, 1990.

Wheeler, N. *Saving Strangers: Humanitarian Intervention in International Society.* Oxford: Oxford University Press, 2000.

White, R. *North, South, and the Environmental Crisis.* Toronto: University of Toronto Press, 1993.

Vines, A. "Mercenaries and the Privatisation of Security in Africa in the 1990s." *The Privatisation of Security in Africa.* Edited by G. Mills and J. Stemlau. Johannesburg: The South African Institute of International Affairs, 1999, 47–80.

Suggested Websites

DefenseLink: United States Department of Defense
http://www.defenselink.mil

The Evolutionary World Politics Homepage
http://faculty.washington.edu/modelski

Global Policy Forum on Humanitarian Intervention
http://www.globalpolicy.org/empire/humanint

Institute for the Advanced Study of Information Warfare
http://www.psycom.net/iwar.1.html

International Communication and Negotiation Simulations (ICONS) Project
http://www.icons.umd.edu/pls/staff/about

IR Theory Colloquium
http://globetrotter.berkeley.edu/irforum

The IR Theory Knowledge Base
http://www.irtheory.com/know.htm

Project Ploughshares
http://www.ploughshares.ca

ZNet
http://www.zmag.org/ZNET.htm

Glossary

This glossary contains very brief descriptions of important terms used in the textbook. The glossary has been compiled using a number of sources, including the "Historical Glossary" found in Hans J. Morgenthau, *Politics among Nations: The Struggle for Power and Peace,* brief ed., revised by K. Thompson (New York: McGraw-Hill, 1993); Cathal Nolan's *The Longman Guide to World Affairs* (White Plains, NY: Longman, 1995); and our own general knowledge. We gratefully acknowledge the suggestions of an anonymous reviewer of an earlier draft of this manuscript as well.

ABM   Antiballistic missile, designed to intercept and destroy incoming ballistic missiles. The development and deployment of ABMs has been restricted by the 1972 ABM Treaty.

Absolute advantage   Adam Smith's principle that free trade will benefit all states because they will specialize in those goods they produce most efficiently and trade with other states for those goods they do not produce efficiently. The result is a more efficient use of resources, more goods for consumption, and the political benefits of increased cooperation.

Absolute gains   When all members of a set or sample of countries or other actors experience an increase in capacity (such as economic wealth).

Absolute poverty   The condition of being unable to meet basic subsistence needs of food, clothing, and shelter.

Acid rain   Sulphur dioxide and nitrogen oxide combined with precipitation; caused by industry, automobiles, and power plants. Harms forests and acidifies lakes.

Acquired immune deficiency syndrome (AIDS)   A fatal disease that destroys the body's immune system; spread mainly through sexual contact or injection with infected blood.

Adjudication   Deciding a legal issue through the courts or some other third party that can make a binding decision.

Advisory opinion   An ICJ (International Court of Justice) nonbinding legal opinion for the UN or a specialized agency.

African, Caribbean and Pacific (ACP) states   Fifty-eight states associated with the European Union.

African National Congress (ANC)   South African political party, founded in 1912, that for years opposed apartheid but is now governing that state. Its leader, Nelson Mandela, was released from prison in 1990 and served as South Africa's first president.

Agricultural revolution   Large-scale shifts in prevailing food production methods that have an impact on the whole of society.

Alexander the Great (Alexander III)   356–323 B.C.E. King of Macedon, 336–323 B.C.E. Conquered Thrace, Illyria, and Egypt; invaded Persia and northern India; virtual leader of Mediterranean centre of civilization.

Alliance cohesion   The degree to which alliance members hold common goals and coordinate policy.

Alliances   Groups of actors who pool their resources for a common cause, usually in relation to national defence.

American Civil War   1861–65. War between the United States of America (Union) and the secessionist Southern Confederate States of America (Confederacy). The war ended the dream of an independent South and ended slavery.

Anarchy   In its most basic form, the absence of central government. A prominent part of the realist perspective's ontology. More generally, it refers to lawlessness.

Angell, Norman   1874–1967. Famous British pacifist who wrote *The Great Illusion,* 1910. Somewhere between an idealist and a liberal.

Antarctic Treaty System (ATS)   A set of negotiated agreements based on the Antarctic Treaty, signed in 1959 by 12 so-called consultative parties with claims on and able to demonstrate a substantial scientific interest in Antarctica. Established the area as a demilitarized zone; various subsequent agreements have been added on conservation and environmental protection.

Anticipatory compliance   A phenomenon in governmental or nongovernmental organizations in which junior officials, trying to anticipate what their superiors want to hear, will omit or de-emphasize information that contrasts with the views of senior officials and leaders.

Anti-Semitism   Prejudice, discrimination, or persecution against Jewish people.

Apartheid   Racial separation policy in South Africa until the early 1990s.

Appeasement   An attempt to satisfy a potential aggressor by making territorial or other concessions to that potential aggressor. This technique failed to satisfy Adolf Hitler.

Arab League   Founded in March 1945, a voluntary association of 22 Arab states.

Armistice   A general term for a negotiated peace, but most often used to describe the end of World War I.

Arms control   Any diplomatic effort designed to regulate levels or types of arms (bilaterally or multi-laterally, with conventional or nuclear arms).

Asian Development Bank   A multilateral bank similar to the World Bank with a regional focus; head-quarters established in 1966 in Manila, Philippines.

Association of Southeast Asian Nations (ASEAN)   Formed by the Bangkok Declaration 1967; includes Indonesia, Malaysia, the Philippines, Singapore, Thailand, Brunei, Myanmar, and Laos.

Atlantic Charter   Statement of general principles, signed by Roosevelt and Churchill in August 1941, related to postwar order, including principles of national self-determination, opposition to aggression, disarmament, and equal access to trade and raw materials.

Atomic bomb   A weapon based on the rapid splitting of fissionable materials, thereby inducing an explosion with deadly blast, heat, and radiation impact; a nuclear weapon.

Authoritarianism   Political system in which individual freedom is subordinate to the power of the state, concentrated in one leader or group that is not accountable to the people.

Automation   The replacement of human workers with machines. See **robotics**.

Balance of payments   The net flow of money into, and out of, a state. Encompasses trade, tourist expenditures, sales of services, foreign aid, debt payments, profits, etc.

Balance of power   A term used to describe a contemporary or historical system (regional or global) in which no one state has the power to dominate all the others.

Balance of trade   The relationship between exports and imports.

Ballistic missile   A missile using a ballistic guidance system influenced by gravity and friction and employing no thrust after its initial boost phase. Some missiles travel 300 metres; others can travel halfway around the world.

Basic human needs   Adequate food intake (calories, vitamins, protein, minerals, etc.), disease-free and toxin-free drinking water, minimum clothing and shelter, literacy, sanitation, health care, employment, and dignity.

Bay of Pigs   Part of the Cuban coastline where in 1961 a group of Cuban refugees staged a failed invasion under American auspices.

Beggar-thy-neighbour policies   Attempts to alter a trade balance by devaluing currency and raising barriers to imports.

Berlin Wall   Constructed in 1961 by East Germany, the Berlin Wall encircled West Berlin, a part of the city controlled by the Western allies during the Cold War. Erected to prevent people from fleeing East Germany into the West, the wall was a symbol of East–West division until it was dismantled in 1989 as the Cold War ended.

Biodiversity   Greatly varied flora and fauna in a habitat; is under threat in many areas of the world.

Biosphere   Life and living processes at or near the earth's surface, extending from the oceans' floors and the lithosphere to about 75 kilometres into the atmosphere.

Bipolarity   Global political system with two competing poles of great power, such as during the United States–U.S.S.R. Cold War era.

Bipolycentrism   A distribution of power in which there are two main poles of power as well as a number of other less powerful, but still significant, power centres.

Bolsheviks   Members of the radical minority in the Russian Social Democratic Party (1903–17), led by Vladimir Lenin. Carried out the Communist revolution of 1917.

Bounded rationality   The argument that rational-actor decisions are seldom made under ideal conditions due to time constraints, incomplete information, and limited individual capacity.

Boycott   The refusal of a country to import goods and services from another country; done for punitive reasons.

Bretton Woods system   The post–World War II international monetary order, named after the 1944 conference held at Bretton Woods, New Hampshire. Main institutions in the system were the IMF, IBRD, and GATT.

Bureaucratic politics model   An approach to the study of foreign policy that focuses on bargaining and compromises among governmental organizations and agencies pursuing their own interests.

Camp David   A mountain retreat for the U.S. president in Maryland and site of the famous Camp David accords, signed in 1978 by President Anwar el-Sadat of Egypt and Prime Minister Menachem Begin of Israel.

Canadian International Development Agency (CIDA) Agency of the Canadian government responsible for planning and implementing Canada's development programs.

Capitalism An economic system based on the private ownership of property and commercial enterprise, competition for profits, and limited government interference in the marketplace.

Capital mobility Ability of international investors to invest in foreign countries with minimal constraints.

Cartel An international agreement among producers of a commodity that attempts to control the production and pricing of that commodity. See **Organization of the Petroleum Exporting Countries**.

Catherine the Great (Catherine II) 1729–96. Tsarina of Russia, 1762–96. Expanded and strengthened the Russian Empire, chiefly at the expense of Turkey.

Chlorofluorocarbons (CFCs) Gaseous compounds found in aerosols, refrigeration chemicals, and in the manufacture of plastics; thought to be largely responsible for ozone-layer depletion.

Churchill, Winston 1874–1965. British prime minister (1940–45, 1951–55), naval officer, and author.

Classical liberals Liberals such as Adam Smith and David Ricardo who established the principles of modern liberal economic theory, based on free trade and minimal government interference in the operation of the market.

Client states States highly dependent on great powers for military or economic aid.

Cold War Hostility between the United States and the U.S.S.R. in the bipolar era (roughly 1947–90).

Collective defence An effort by two or more states to defend their territory or their interests against a common threat or enemy. Collective defence arrangements are generally called alliances.

Collective security Mutual multilateral consent to an agreement that declares that aggression by one state on any other is an attack on the whole; the primary security mechanism created by the UN Charter.

Commonwealth Voluntary association of former dominions, colonies, and other overseas territories of Britain. Forty-nine states belong; annual meeting of heads of state generates some attention.

Commonwealth of Independent States (CIS) Arrangement among many of the former republics of the U.S.S.R., formed in December 1991. Includes Armenia, Azerbaijan, Byelorussia (Belarus), Kazakhstan, Kirghizia (Kyrgyzstan), Moldavia (Moldova), Russia, Tadzhikistan (Tajikistan), Turkmenistan, Ukraine, Uzbekistan, and Georgia.

Comparative advantage David Ricardo's concept that states will still benefit from free trade even if they do not have an absolute advantage in any good. Such states will still have a comparative advantage with respect to trading partners because they will still produce some goods comparatively more efficiently than others do. That comparative advantage is enough for them to benefit from trade.

Concert of Europe A system of consultation established among the European powers after the defeat of Napoleon (1815). The aim of the concert was to maintain the peace and manage the balance of power in Europe, which it did with considerable success until the outbreak of the Crimean War (1854–56).

Congress of Vienna 1814–15. Peace conference following the Napoleonic Wars at which the great powers—Austria, Russia, Prussia, Great Britain, and France—agreed on territorial and political terms of settlement.

Conscription A policy requiring all men of a certain age to serve in the military, during peace or war. Also referred to as the "draft"; conscription is very controversial in Canada and the United States but more accepted in most other countries of the world.

Constructive engagement   Trying to influence a state's domestic policies by maintaining trade and diplomatic ties, as opposed to the use of sanctions.

Containment   The United States' grand strategy during the Cold War, designed to contain the perceived military, political, and ideological threat of the U.S.S.R.

Convention on International Trade in Endangered Species of Wild Fauna and Flora (CITES) Multilateral accord (1973) that regulates export, transit, and importation of endangered animal and plant species. Meets biannually to determine species' status.

Convention on the Conservation of Antarctic Marine Living Resources (CCAMLR)   Promulgated in 1980 by consultative parties to the Antarctic Treaty System to protect the environment and resources of the Antarctic seas region.

Council of Europe   International body created in 1949 by representatives of Great Britain, France, Belgium, the Netherlands, Luxembourg, Norway, Sweden, Denmark, Ireland, and Italy; joined by Greece and Turkey in 1950; aimed toward a European federation.

Crimean War   1854–56. France, Great Britain, and Turkey allied against Russia and fought a bitter war on the Crimean peninsula.

Crimes against humanity   Genocide, enslavement, rape, deportation, imprisonment, murder, torture, or persecutions on political, racial, or religious grounds committed against any civilian population.

Crimes against peace   Generally, planning, preparing, initiating, or waging a war of aggression and participating in a common plan or conspiracy for the accomplishment of war crimes.

Cruise missile   A missile, guided remotely (from satellites in some cases), that can fly low enough to escape radar detection and can deliver conventional or nuclear warheads.

Cultural imperialism   Imposition of values on one society by another by direct administrative means (such as education) or more subtle means (such as television commercials).

Currency speculation   Purchasing of foreign currency with an aim to sell it when, and if, its value increases. Can distort government efforts to manage the economy.

Customs union   A common external tariff is applicable to all imports from outside the area; internal barriers to trade are removed. Different from a free trade area, in which internal barriers are removed but external barriers remain up to individual states.

Deficit   The amount by which a government's spending exceeds its revenues in any fiscal year.

Demographic transition theory   Argues that the decline in the industrialized states' birth rates is a direct consequence of social and economic development, and that with time other states will follow.

Dependency theory   Contends that the North has created a neocolonial relationship with the South, which is dependent on Northern capital. Originated in the work of Latin American critical theorists.

Desertification   Process in which potentially productive land is transformed into arid, desert-like territory. A severe form of land erosion.

Détente   A relaxation of tensions or a decrease in the level of hostility between the superpowers during the Cold War.

Deterrence   Persuading an opponent not to attack by making sure it is aware that a counterattack would follow. Pertains especially to the nuclear strategy of the superpowers during the Cold War.

Disinformation   Spreading of false propaganda or forged documents to confuse counterintelligence or create political confusion, unrest, and scandal. Some would argue that governments do this with their own citizens as well.

Doves   Informal term used to describe political figures or commentators who advocate less hard-line or confrontational approaches to their countries' enemies.

Dumping   The practice of exporting a good to another country and selling that good at a price below the cost of production. This will make the product attractive to purchase, thus gaining a large market share and at the same time putting competing producers out of business. The price of the product will then be raised to achieve a profit. Dumping is illegal in most international trade agreements, although accusations of dumping remain common.

Duty   Special tax applied to imported goods, based on tariff rates and schedules.

Ecocide   Deliberate destruction of the environment for military purposes. Can also refer to other forms of environmental destruction.

Economic Community of West African States (ECOWAS)   Founded in 1975 to promote cooperation in West Africa. ECOWAS currently has 15 members.

Electronic Numerical Integrator and Computer (ENIAC)   The first computer. It was so large that it filled a 9-by-17-metre room.

Embargo   The refusal of one country or a group of countries to export goods to another, for punitive reasons. One famous example is the American embargo on Cuba.

Emigration   Leaving one's home country to live in another.

Epistemic community   A global network of knowledge-based professionals in scientific and technological areas that often have an impact on policy decisions.

Ethnic cleansing   The forced removal of an ethnic group from their area of residence using tactics that include executions, the destruction of homes, and rape to instill fear in the target population. In its ultimate form, genocide.

Euro   The common currency of European Union states, introduced gradually in the late 1990s, and now in use in 12 EU states.

European Monetary System   Established in 1979 as the first major step toward the establishment of a common currency in the European Union. System collapsed in 1993, but was revived.

European Union (EU)   Previously the European Economic Community, established by the Treaty of Rome, signed on March 25, 1957, and further cemented by the Maastricht Treaty (though it was rejected by some members) of 1991. Includes Austria, Belgium, Denmark, Finland, France, Germany, Greece, Ireland, Italy, Luxembourg, the Netherlands, Portugal, Spain, Sweden, and the United Kingdom. States have coordinated policies in a number of areas, such as migration and currency, but have fallen short of a common security and foreign policy.

Exchange rate   The values of two currencies relative to each other. For example, one Canadian dollar may be worth 70 cents of an American dollar.

Exclusive economic zone   The 200-nautical-mile or 370-kilometre area in which coastal states have jurisdiction over the resources of the sea and the seabed (i.e., beyond their 12-mile or 19-kilometre territory) but not territorial rights. Accepted as customary law.

Exports   Products shipped or otherwise transferred to foreign states.

Extraterritoriality   In diplomatic practice, the tradition that visiting diplomats are exempt from local legal jurisdiction.

Fascism   An authoritarian ideology that subsumes individuals before the state; popular in Italy, Spain, and Germany in the period leading up to World War II.

Food and Agriculture Organization of the UN (FAO)   Formed in 1945 as a UN specialized agency to deal with food production; based in Rome.

Foreign direct investment (FDI)   Buying stock, real estate, or other assets in a foreign country with the aim of gaining a controlling interest (usually over 50 percent) of foreign enterprises. Differs from portfolio investment, which involves investment solely to gain capital appreciation through market fluctuations.

Fourteen Points   U.S. President Woodrow Wilson's formulation of Allied war aims and of a general peace program, delivered to Congress on January 8, 1918.

Fourth World   An expression that is usually meant to include the very least developed, or poorest, states.

La Francophonie   Group of French-speaking states that meets to coordinate development policies.

Free trade   International movement of goods unrestricted by tariffs or nontariff barriers.

Functionalism   International cooperation in largely technical areas (communications, travel, trade, environmental protection) and related theories about possibly resultant political integration.

Futurologists   People who attempt to predict the future based on present trends. (Some claim they are scientists, others do not.)

Game theory   A mathematical approach to modelling political behaviour. It is used by international relations scholars to evaluate decision-making patterns among two or more actors under certain prescribed conditions.

General Agreement on Tariffs and Trade (GATT)   Concluded in 1948, followed by successive rounds of negotiations culminating in the establishment of the World Trade Organization in 1995. General aim is to facilitate expanded international trade with the reduction of trade barriers.

General Agreement on Trade in Services (GATS)   An agreement first reached in GATT (and now is part of the WTO) that seeks trade liberalization in the service sector.

General Assembly   The democratic core of the UN, where all states are equally represented; more than 185 states are currently represented.

Generalized System of Preferences (GSP)   A system approved by GATT in 1971 that authorizes developed countries to give preferential tariff treatment to less-developed countries.

Genetic engineering   Biotechnological process by which the natural genetic code of an organism is altered, producing genetically modified organisms. A contentious ethical and trade issue today.

Genetically modified organisms (GMOs)   Plants and animals genetically altered by adding, subtracting, or changing the genetic code.

Geopolitics   A form of foreign policy analysis that emphasizes the link between geographic variables (such as location, resources, and topography) and political behaviour. Political action is seen as largely determined by geography.

Glasnost   The Soviet policy of increased openness, developed and implemented under the leadership of Mikhail Gorbachev in the late 1980s.

Global commons   Elements of the earth and atmosphere (oceans, seabed, atmosphere, outer space) that are the property of no one nation or individual but are deemed to be the property of all.

Globalization   Term used to describe the increasing interconnection between states, economies, and societies through telecommunications technology, trade, and travel such that events in one part of the world have repercussions in other parts of the world.

Golan Heights   Contested territory adjacent to Israel, which has occupied it since the 1967 war.

Good offices   Services, roles, and functions provided by a third party in an effort to resolve a dispute.

Great Depression   Severe unemployment and financial collapse of the early 1930s; international in scope.

Great powers   Term used to identify the most powerful political units in a system (usually states).

Green revolution   The increase in agricultural production in many developing countries in the 1950s and 1960s, made possible by genetically engineered grains, fertilizers, and more efficient use of land.

Gross domestic product (GDP)   A measure of national income that excludes foreign earnings.

Gross national product (GNP)   The sum of all the goods and services produced by a state's nationals, whether in that state or abroad.

Group of Eight (G-8)   The eight largest economies (the United States, Japan, Germany, France, Russia, Italy, the United Kingdom, and Canada); government representatives meet often to coordinate monetary policies.

Group of Seven (G-7)   The seven economically largest free-market states: Canada, France, United Kingdom, Italy, Japan, the United States, and Germany. Russia is now a participant in what are now referred to as G-8 conferences.

Group of 77 (G-77)   The 77 Third World states that co-sponsored the Joint Declaration of Developing Countries in 1963 calling for greater equity in North–South trade. Currently includes more than 120 members.

Groupthink   The tendency of decision makers to develop, in groups, a common perception of an issue or problem and exclude those with different opinions or ideas.

Hapsburg   Ruling house of Austria, 1282–1918; provided the emperors of the Holy Roman Empire from 1438 to 1806.

Hard power   A reference to traditional measures of power, such as economic capability, population, and especially military strength.

Hawks   An informal term for political figures or commentators who advocate more uncompromising or confrontational policies toward their country's enemies.

Head of state   An individual who represents the sovereignty of a state. In many cases, this individual is different from the head of government (e.g., the British monarch and the British prime minister; the Queen of Canada, represented by the governor general and the prime minister of Canada); in the United States, the president assumes both roles.

Hegemonic Power/Hegemon   A dominant state that uses its military and economic power to establish global rules and institutions in accord with its interests.

Hegemonic stability   Theory that a leading state can provide the public good of stability in the global political system, on the condition that it can maintain its contested hegemonic status.

Hegemony   Political dominance; either undisputed leadership in politics or dominance in the realm of ideas.

HIV   See **Acquired immune deficiency syndrome (AIDS)**

Hobson, John   1858–1940. English economist who wrote on imperialism.

Holy Roman Empire   962–1806 C.E. Western European political entity claiming to be successor to the Roman Empire (suspended in 476 C.E.); a European commonwealth; lost importance after Thirty Years' War (1618–48).

Homogenization   Any process in which different entities become increasingly similar; the diminishment of diversity.

Immigration   The arrival of foreigners in a country for the purpose of taking up residence. A vital source of economic production.

Imperialism   A policy of establishing political and economic control over foreign territories and all the intellectual accompaniments. At times used to refer to the spread of Western capitalism and the current processes of globalization.

Industrial espionage   The use of human or electronic means to covertly acquire industrial secrets.

Industrial Revolution   The mechanization of industry and associated changes in social and economic patterns in Europe (and especially Great Britain) in the late 18th and early 19th centuries.

Infanticide   The deliberate killing of children.

Intercontinental Ballistic Missile (ICBM)   A ballistic missile capable of flying from one continent to another, but especially one capable of flight between North America and Eurasia. Central to modern nuclear deterrence during the Cold War.

Intergovernmental organizations (IGOs)   International organizations created by and composed of member states.

International Atomic Energy Agency (IAEA)   A United Nations agency that inspects nuclear power plants (and carries out other periodic inspections) to ensure compliance with the Non-Proliferation Treaty; it also promotes the development of nuclear energy.

International Bank for Reconstruction and Development (IBRD)   Development-based lending agency affiliated with the UN, commonly referred to as the World Bank.

International Civil Aviation Organization (ICAO)   A specialized agency of the UN, organized in 1947; formed to expand international air trade and promote safety. Headquarters are in Montreal.

International Commission on Intervention and State Sovereignty (ICISS)   An international panel of experts convened to explore the issue of when intervention in a state was justifiable in order to protect human security. The commission's final report was titled *The Responsibility to Protect*.

International Committee of the Red Cross (ICRC)   Referred to as the International Committee of the Red Crescent in Muslim societies. A neutral humanitarian relief organization, founded in 1859, based in Switzerland. It cares for wounded during battle and observes the treatment of prisoners of war.

International Court of Justice (ICJ)   The World Court, which sits in The Hague, Netherlands, with 15 judges.

International Criminal Court (ICC)   Created in 1998 by the 120 signatories to the Rome Statute. The Rome Statute entered into force on July 1, 2002. The 18 judges of the ICC were elected in February 2003, and the ICC was formally inaugurated in March 2003.

International Development Association (IDA)   An affiliate of the World Bank (IBRD) that provides interest-free, long-term loans to developing states.

International Finance Corporation (IFC)   Created in 1956 to finance overseas investments by private companies without necessarily requiring government guarantees; borrows from the World Bank.

International Financial Institutions (IFIs)   International organizations created to manage and create rules for the conduct of international financial transactions and macro-level initiatives for development and crisis response.

International Joint Commission (IJC)   Canada–U.S. body established by the Boundary Waters Treaty of 1909 to deal mainly with transborder water resource questions. Consists of three Canadian and three American commissioners. Provides analysis and rulings related to transborder environmental issues, such as Great Lakes pollution.

International Monetary Fund (IMF)   Autonomous but affiliated with the UN since 1947; designed to facilitate international trade, reduce inequities in exchange, and stabilize currencies.

International Office of Weights and Measures   Intergovernmental organization established in 1875 to standardize weights and measures, affiliated with the UN since 1949.

International Organization for Migration (IOM)   Assists migrants as they settle in new countries; also helps with refugee assistance. Headquarters are in Geneva.

International Telecommunication Union (ITU)   Established in 1932 under the title of International Telecommunication Convention. Renamed the International Telecommunication Union in 1934. The ITU is an amalgamation of the International Telegraph Union (established 1865) and the International Radiotelegraph Union (established 1906).

Internet   An information network of computers that enables users to communicate and access information from all linked computers. Originated in a U.S. military communications project.

Intifada   A series of clashes between Palestinian youths and Israeli security forces in the occupied territories that escalated into a full-scale revolt in December 1987. The El-Aqsa Intifada began in 2000.

Iron Age   The historical epoch characterized by the widespread use of iron in tools and weapons.

Isolationism   A foreign-policy approach emphasizing self-reliance and limited economic or political interaction with the international system.

IUCN–the World Conesrvation Union (IUCN)   Promotes sustainable development and preservation of nature; involves both governments and NGOs; based in Gland, Switzerland.

Jus ad bellum   Principles used to decide whether a war is just.

Jus in bello   Principles used to decide what types of violence are permissible in war.

Kellogg–Briand Pact   Pact signed in 1928 by 44 states, renouncing war and promoting peaceful dispute settlement; named after U.S. Secretary of State Frank Kellogg and French Foreign Minister Aristide Briand.

Kennan, George   1904– . American diplomat and historian; ambassador to the U.S.S.R., 1952.

Keynesian liberalism   An approach to liberal economics that calls for higher levels of government intervention and regulation in the market than envisioned by classical liberals. Named after the influential liberal economist John Maynard Keynes.

Khmer Rouge (Red Cambodians)   Communist rulers of Kampuchea, 1975–79, under Pol Pot and Leng Saray; still a political force in the region.

Korean War   North Korea attacked South Korea in June 1950; UN forces under American command joined in late June; Chinese Communists joined North Korea in November 1950; armistice concluded in July 1953. Korea remains what many would consider to be the last Cold War front.

League of Nations   The international organization that existed, without American membership, between the end of World War I and the end of World War II.

Lenin, Vladimir I.   1870–1924. Russian revolutionist and statesman; founder of Bolshevism, the Third International, and the Soviet Union.

Less-developed countries (LDCs)   Those states in the lowest economic rankings, usually with a per capita GNP of less than U.S.$400 (1985).

Liberal institutionalism   A branch of liberal theory that emphasizes the leading role played by international organizations and regimes in world politics, especially in economic affairs.

Liberal International Economic Order (LIEO)   A term used to describe the theoretical principles and institutional structures that managed the world economy after World War II.

Lomé Convention   Agreement concluded between the EU and over 70 African, Caribbean, and Pacific (ACP) countries, allowing the latter preferential trade relations and greater economic and technical assistance. Superseded by the Cotonou Agreement of 2003.

Long cycles   The theory that hegemons rise and decline in regular patterns, which in turn influence the international economy and the outbreak of hegemonic wars.

Luxemburg, Rosa   1870–1919. German Marxist. Founded Spartacus Party during World War I; wrote on imperialism.

Maastricht Treaty   Signed by European Community on 7 February 1992, outlining steps toward further integration. See **European Union**.

Malnutrition   Results from inadequate or unbalanced diet, usually deficient in protein, vitamins, or minerals.

Marketization   Movement away from state-controlled economy toward private property rights, open competition, trade liberalization, open investment, and floating currency.

Marshall Plan   U.S. Secretary of State George Marshall's 1947 plan to aid the reconstruction of European industry after World War II.

Marx, Karl   1818–83. German economist and historian. Founder of the ideology of Communism; proponent of historical materialism.

Megacities   Generally this refers to cities (usually including their immediate municipalities) with over 10 million inhabitants.

Mercantilism   The perspective holding that international trade should be regulated by the state to maximize national income. Also known as economic nationalism and neomercantilism.

Mercosur   A trade agreement linking Argentina, Brazil, Paraguay, and Uruguay.

Middle powers   Countries that do not possess the power attributes of the great powers but that can have a significant impact on international politics in certain specific regions or in certain specific issue-areas. Canada is often described as a middle power, though some call it a satellite of the United States.

Multilateral   Involving three or more states; usually connotes cooperative action.

Multilateral Agreement on Investment (MAI)   Originally an OECD-coordinated effort to protect foreign investors from governmental intrusion; disbanded but still on the larger WTO agenda.

Multinational corporation (MNC)   A profit-seeking enterprise with operations in at least two states. Powerful actors in global politics today.

Multipolarity   A distribution of power in which there are a number of poles, or great powers, in the system. This was characteristic of the pre–World War I era, and some analysts believe it can lead to instability.

Mutual assured destruction (MAD)   The underlying nature of the nuclear stalemate between the superpowers during the Cold War. Both the United States and the Soviet Union possessed such large and capable arsenals that each side knew that if it attempted to attack the other with nuclear weapons, it would receive a devastating nuclear blow in return. As a result, both sides were deterred from using nuclear weapons against each other.

Napoleon Bonaparte (Napoleon I)   1769–1821. Emperor of France, 1804–15. Famous military general and political leader.

Napoleonic Wars   1796–1815. Waged by France under the Revolution and later under Napoleon against England, Austria, Prussia, Russia, and most of the other countries of Europe. Ended with France's defeat at Waterloo.

Nationalization   A government's assumption of the ownership of property, often previously owned by citizens from another state. Famous cases include the nationalization of the Suez Canal, and Cuban and Iranian appropriation of American commercial property.

Neo-Malthusian   Argument that resources will be outstripped by population growth in the modern era; has led to calls for strict population control.

New International Economic Order (NIEO)   Statement of priorities adopted at the Sixth Special Session of the UN General Assembly in 1974, calling for equal participation of LDCs in the North–South dialogue.

Nonaligned Movement (NAM)   An effort begun in 1955 by developing countries to cooperate on issues of joint interest, especially decolonization, neutrality in the Cold War, and a more favourable international economic environment for their products. The NAM is largely moribund today.

Nondiscrimination   A principle of free trade that requires any member of a trade organization or agreement (such as the WTO) to treat all imports entering the country in the same way. In other words, states cannot discriminate against some members of a trade agreement by imposing higher tariffs on a good coming from one country while lowering the tariff on the same good coming from another country. The tariff must be the same for both countries, provided both countries are members of the trade agreement.

Nongovernmental organizations (NGOs)   Groups that do not represent the views of governments; usually operating for the purpose of charity or value propagation. INGOs are those NGOs with operations or members in at least two states.

Non-Proliferation Treaty   Treaty signed in 1968 and in force in 1970, aimed at preventing the spread of nuclear weapons to more states.

Nontariff barriers   Erected by a government to discourage imports. Formal and voluntary quotas, prohibitions of certain imports, discriminatory restrictions, licensing requirements. Now the main way governments restrict international trade.

North American Free Trade Agreement (NAFTA)   Trilateral economic agreement reducing barriers on trade between Canada, the United States, and Mexico; contains side agreements on labour rights and environmental protection.

North Atlantic Treaty Organization (NATO)   Collective defence alliance created in 1949 to prevent the U.S.S.R. from attaining political influence or territorial conquests in Europe. Composed of 16 states in 1982 and 26 states in 2004, the alliance has restructured itself after the Cold War and admitted three new members in 1997. NATO Headquarters is in Brussels.

Northwest Atlantic Fisheries Organization (NAFO)   Multilateral body established to regulate fishing in the northwest Atlantic; includes Canada, the EU, the United States, and several Asian states, but not the United States.

Nuremberg war crimes trials   1945–49. Trials of Nazis for war crimes by an international military tribunal; several were subsequently executed. See **war crimes trials**.

Omnicide   Literally, the killing of all life, as might result from a nuclear war.

Organisation for Economic Co-operation and Development (OECD)   An organization of industrialized states.

Organization for Security and Co-operation in Europe (OSCE)   A multilateral forum for discussing a wide range of political questions in Europe; includes Canada, the United States, Russia, and all of the European states. Established in 1995 to give permanent staff and headquarters to the Council on Security and Co-operation in Europe (CSCE).

Organization of American States (OAS)   Intergovernmental organization of 35 states of North and South America etablished in 1948 as a forum for political dialogue. Canada joined in 1990.

Organization of the Petroleum Exporting Countries (OPEC)   Producers' cartel setting price floors and production ceilings of crude petroleum; its members are the Arab oil producers (Saudi Arabia, Kuwait, the United Arab Emirates, Qatar, Iran, Iraq, Algeria, and Libya), Nigeria, Venezuela, and Indonesia.

Per capita   Putting aggregate statistical information, such as GNP, into per-person form.

Perestroika   Economic reform policies instituted by Mikhail Gorbachev in the Soviet Union in the late 1980s.

Peter the Great (Peter I)   1672–1725. Czar of Russia, 1682–1725. Founder of the modern Russian state.

Polarity   The number of poles, or concentrations of power, in a region or in the international system. Systems with one dominant concentration of power are unipolar, those with two are bipolar, while those with many are called multipolar.

Politburo   The supreme decision-making body of the Soviet Union during the Cold War.

Prisoner's Dilemma   In game theory, a model that demonstrates how two actors can make self-interested decisions based on distrust and isolation from one another that leave them worse off than if they had trusted one another and cooperated instead.

Protectionism   Using tariffs and nontariff barriers to control or restrict the flow of imports into a state; usually associated with neomercantilism.

Proxy wars   Wars, usually in the South, where the great powers are indirectly involved.

Public good   Publicly funded and regulated services or infrastructure, open to use by all members of a society; in the international sense, the provision of political, military, and economic stability by a hegemon.

Quota   A quantitative limitation imposed by government, usually applied to inflows of goods or migrants.

Ratification   Official governmental acceptance of a treaty.

Rational actor model   A theory of decision making based on rational actors making decisions in a rational choice process, designed to maximize their desired outcomes.

Recession   Rise in unemployment, decline of investment and growth; usually a period of less than a year. Recessions in important markets cause international concern.

Reciprocity   The principle that a state should reciprocate when another state grants it trade concessions. This reciprocity should come in the form of trade concessions equivalent in value to the concessions granted to it by its trading partners.

Refugee   A person who has fled his or her country of origin because of fear of persecution, discrimination, or political oppression.

Regime   Rules, principles, and decision-making procedures governing international behaviour in certain issue-areas.

Relative gains   The difference between actors experiencing a different rate of increase in some measure of capacity (such as economic wealth). If one actor is gaining capacity relative to the other actors, it is experiencing a relative gain with respect to the others.

Repatriation   The resettlement by a refugee in his or her home state.

Reprisal   A hostile, illegal act that is rendered legal when carried out in response to a previous illegal act.

Resolution   Formal decision of UN body, usually either registering a widely held opinion or recommending some sort of action to a UN body or agency.

Robotics   Use of highly complex machines to perform complicated manufacturing tasks. See **automation**.

Revolution in Military Affairs (RMA)   The idea that military history has developed in a series of dramatic shifts in military capability, based on technological and social developments. The current RMA is based on computers and the information age.

Rousseau, Jean Jacques   1712–78. French philosopher, author of *The Social Contract*. Influenced the concept of popular sovereignty.

SALT   Strategic Arms Limitation Treaties between United States and U.S.S.R.; treaties signed 1972 and 1979.

Satisficing   Propensity of decision makers to select an alternative that meets minimally acceptable standards.

Schlieffen Plan   The German military strategy for the conquest of France, put into action in World War I. The plan called for German armies to sweep through neutral Belgium and envelop Paris.

Secretariat   The administrative organ of the UN, headed by the secretary-general; more generally, the administrative branch of any international organization.

Secretary-general   Chief administrative officer of the UN who also plays an important, if controversial, diplomatic role.

Security Council   Fifteen states (five permanent members) sit on this chief collective security organ of the UN.

Security dilemma   A product of international anarchy in which states seek to rely on their own means to ensure their security by developing their military forces. In doing so, they inspire fear and distrust in their neighbours, who also arm. This reaction starts an arms race in which none of the participants is any more secure (and may in fact be less secure) than it was initially.

Self-determination   The claim that people have the right to self-rule.

Severe Acute Respiratory Syndrome (SARS)   Deadly form of pneumonia, which emerged from China in November 2002 and infected many people in other countries, including Canada.

Shiite Islam   The smaller of the two major branches of Islam, often equated with Islamic fundamentalism, consisting of those who regard Ali, son-in-law of Muhammad, as the prophet's legitimate successor. The Koran is the only source of political authority.

SLBM (submarine-launched ballistic missile)   A ballistic missile launched from a nuclear-capable submarine.

Small states   Term used to identify those states that are the weakest in terms of power in a regional or global context.

Soft power   Elements of state power—such as ideological attractiveness, culture, information capacity, and education—that have traditionally been disregarded (especially by realists) in favour of military or economic strength.

Solidarity   Self-governing trade union movement in Poland that began in 1980 and eventually played a major role in changes there; led by Lech Walesa, elected president of Poland in December 1990.

Sovereignty   A government's ability to manage internal affairs and independently represent itself externally. A principle securing noninterference from other states, the keystone of the Charter of the UN.

State   A political entity possessing determined territory, permanent population, active government, and sovereign recognition by other states. Can also refer to the governing element of society with a monopoly on legitimate coercive violence; also, the instrument of the ruling economic classes.

State-sponsored terrorism   Government support for terrorist individuals or groups acting abroad.

State terrorism   The use of state power to terrorize civilians into compliance.

Strategic Arms Deduction (START)   Two treaties, START I and START II, reached between the United States and the U.S.S.R./Russia that made deep cuts in the nuclear arsenals of both countries.

Structural adjustment programs (SAPs)   Economic policies established as conditions for IMF or World Bank loans to developing countries, usually requiring such countries to limit their spending, eliminate subsidies, and promote trade liberalization.

Subsidies   Government programs that extend direct financial support, tax exemptions, or low-interest credit to certain firms engaged in the research or production of goods with considerable economic potential. Subsidies are used by governments to assist certain economic sectors to ensure their growth or survival.

Sunni Islam   The dominant branch of Islam consisting of those who regard the first four caliphs as legitimate successors of Muhammad.

Superpowers   The former U.S.S.R. and the United States during the Cold War era.

Synthesis   An idea formed by a combination of other ideas.

Tariff   A tax levied on imports. Free traders aim to eliminate them.

Thirty Years' War   1618–48. General European war fought mainly in Germany; petty German princes and foreign powers (France, Sweden, Denmark, England) against the Holy Roman Empire (Hapsburgs in Austria, Germany, Italy, the Netherlands, and Spain); also a religious war of Protestants against Catholics. Ended with the Treaty of Westphalia.

Tied aid   Foreign aid extended to recipient countries on the condition that at least part of the aid will be used to purchase goods and services from the donor country.

Torture   Deliberate inflicting of pain, physical or psychological. Often state induced.

Trade   Exchanges of products, services, or money between states.

Trade-Related Intellectual Property Rights (TRIPs)   An issue in international trade law and GATT/WTO negotiations concerning the protection of patent and copyright holders from piracy and copyright infringement.

Trilateral   An agreement or arrangement between three states or groups of states, such as NAFTA or the Trilateral Commission (United States, Western Europe, and Japan).

Truman Doctrine   Outlined to Congress by U.S. President Truman in March 1947 in support of the Greek–Turkish aid bill; calls for the containment of Communism by giving aid to like-minded governments.

UN Children's Fund (UNICEF)   Assists millions of destitute children around the globe; originally established to help war refugees in 1946.

UN Conference on Trade and Development (UNCTAD)   A coalition of Southern states that began meeting in 1964.

UN Development Programme (UNDP)   Coordinates and assists development projects related to the UN.

UN Educational, Scientific, and Cultural Organization (**UNESCO**)

UN High Commissioner for Refugees (UNHCR)

Unilateral   One-sided initiatives; the actions of a single state.

Unipolarity   A region or international system in which there is one dominant actor. Some argue that the current international system is a unipolar one, with the United States as the one remaining superpower.

Universal Postal Union (UPU)   Established in 1874 with headquarters in Bern, Switzerland; became a specialized agency of the UN in 1947.

Urbanization   The process of growth, often rapid, of cities.

USAID   American foreign-aid department.

Verification   Process of determining that all sides of an international agreement are in compliance.

Versailles Treaty   The principal treaty terminating World War I.

Veto   The right to prohibit certain actions. The permanent members of the Security Council have a veto over the Council's substantive actions.

War crimes   Includes perpetrating mass murder; ill-treatment, deportation, or forced labour of prisoners; killing hostages; plunder; and wanton destruction with no military necessity.

War crimes trials   Prosecution of war criminals by an international tribunal, following World War II at Nuremberg and Tokyo, and presently at The Hague. May also take place within domestic jurisdiction of states.

Warsaw Pact   A treaty signed by the Soviet bloc states in 1955 pledging mutual military allegiance to the Soviet Union; dissolved in 1991.

Weighted voting   A system of voting, such as that used in the IBRD, where the value of a member's vote is determined by the contribution (usually financial) the member makes.

Weimar Republic   1919–33. German state established under a democratic federal constitution passed by a constitutional assembly in the city of Weimar.

Wilson, Woodrow   1856–1924. Twenty-seventh president of the United States, 1913–21; known for his internationalism.

World Bank   Formally known as the International Bank for Reconstruction and Development, this institution, which also includes the International Development Agency, is a leading lender of money for development purposes. The World Bank Group includes the World Bank and three other agencies: the International Finance Coporation (IFC); the Multilateral Investment Guarantee Agency (MIGA); and the International Centre for Settlement of Investment Disputes (ICSID).

World Health Organization (WHO)   Specialized agency of the UN, founded in 1948; assists in health programs, including children's immunization, around the globe. Headquartered in Geneva.

World-system theory   A theoretical approach that emphasizes the global character of capitalism as the organizing principle of international politics.

World Trade Organization (WTO)   Organization that was formed in 1993 to supervise the GATT and arbitrate related trade disputes. Began operations in 1995; headquartered in Geneva.

Xenophobia   A strong dislike, fear, or suspicion of other nationalities.

Yalta Conference   A February 1945 summit meeting with Franklin Roosevelt, Josef Stalin, and Winston Churchill at which major postwar issues were discussed, such as the status of Poland and voting arrangements in the UN.

Zero-sum game   A relationship in which a gain for one actor is equal to a loss for another actor. Realists saw the Cold War as a zero-sum game.

Index